Clockwise from top left, 'Lamarque', 'La Reine Victoria', 'Maréchal Niel' and 'Mme Grégoire Staechelin'

PETER BEALES

CLASSIC ROSES

*An illustrated encyclopaedia
and grower's manual of old roses,
shrub roses and climbers*

*Expanded, revised and illustrated
with more than 600 new
full-colour photographs*

A John Macrae Book

Henry Holt and Company
New York

To my family and to all those around me who
have so often accepted second place to a rose, but
without whom I could not have grown even a briar.

Henry Holt and Company, Inc.
Publishers since 1866
115 West 18th Street
New York, New York 10011

Henry Holt ® is a registered trademark of Henry Holt and Company, Inc.

Simultaneously published in Great Britain by The Harvill Press in 1997

Published in Canada by Fitzhenry & Whiteside Ltd,
195 Allstate Parkway, Markham, Ontario L3R 4T8

Library of Congress Cataloging-in-Publication Data is available upon request

ISBN 0 8050 5584 3

Henry Holt books are available for special promotions and premiums.
For details contact: Director, Special Markets.

Revised and Enlarged Edition – 1997

Designed by Vera Brice
Typeset in Minion and Photina display at
Libanus Press, Marlborough, Wiltshire

Printed and bound in Great Britain by
Butler & Tanner Ltd, Frome, Somerset

All first editions are printed on acid-free paper ∞

1 3 5 7 9 10 8 6 4 2

Contents

Foreword to the First Edition — vii

Foreword to the Second Edition — ix

Acknowledgements — x

Preface — xi

PART I   History and Evolution of the Rose — 1

PART II   The Early Development of Modern Roses — 33

PART III   Roses in the Landscape — 49

PART IV   THE DICTIONARY — 93

The Genus *ROSA*

HULTHEMIA — 101
Hulthemia and × *Hulthemosa*, forms and hybrids

HESPERHODOS — 104
R. stellata, forms

PLATYRHODON — 106
R. roxburghii, forms

EUROSA (ROSA) — 107

BANKSIANAE — 108
R. banksiae, forms and hybrids; *R. cymosa*; *R.* × *fortuniana*

LAEVIGATAE — 111
R. laevigata, forms and hybrids

BRACTEATAE — 114
R. bracteata and hybrid

PIMPINELLIFOLIAE — 117
R. ecae, forms and hybrids; *R. foetida*, forms and hybrids; *R. hemisphaerica*; *R. hugonis*, forms and hybrids; *R.* × *involuta*; *R. koreana*; *R. pimpinellifolia* (Scotch Roses), forms and hybrids; *R.* × *hibernica*; *R. primula*; *R.* × *pteragonis*; *R.* × *reversa*; *R.* × *sabinii*; *R. sericea*, forms and hybrids; *R. xanthina*, forms and hybrid

GALLICANAE — 135
R. gallica (Gallicas), forms and hybrids; *R. centifolia* (Provence Roses, Cabbage Roses), forms and hybrids; *R. centifolia muscosa* (Mosses), forms and hybrids; *R. damascena* (Damasks), forms and hybrids; Portlands; *R. macrantha*, forms and hybrids; *R. richardii*

CANINAE 183

R. agrestis; *R. alba* (Albas), forms and hybrids; *R. biebersteinii*; *R. britzensis*; *R. canina* (Dog Rose), forms and hybrids; *R.* × *collina*; *R. corymbifera*; *R.* × *dumalis*; *R. eglanteria* (Sweet Briars), forms and hybrids; *R. glauca*, forms and hybrids; *R. inodora*; *R. jundzillii*; *R. micrantha*; *R. mollis*; *R. orientalis*; *R. pulverulenta*; *R. serafinii*; *R. sherardii*; *R. sicula*; *R. stylosa*; *R. tomentosa*; *R. villosa*; *R.* × *waitziana*

CAROLINAE 199

R. carolina, forms and hybrids; *R. foliolosa*; *R.* × *kochiana*; *R.* × *mariae-graebnerae*; *R. nitida*; *R. palustris*; *R. virginiana*, forms and hybrids

CASSIORHODON (CINNAMOMEAE) 203

R. acicularis; *R. amblyotis*; *R. arkansana*; *R. banksiopsis*; *R. beggeriana*; *R. bella*; *R. blanda*; *R. californica*; *R. caudata*; *R. coriifolia froebelii*; *R.* × *coryana*; *R. corymbulosa*; *R. davidii*; *R. davurica*; *R. elegantula-persetosa*; *R. fedtschenkoana*; *R. forrestiana*; *R. gymnocarpa*; *R. hemsleyana*; *R.* × *kamtchatica*; *R. kordesii*, form and hybrids; *R. latibracteata*; *R.* × *l'heritierana* (Boursaults), forms and hybrids; *R. macrophylla*, forms and hybrids; *R. majalis*; *R. marretii*; *R. maximowicziana*; *R. melina*; *R.* × *micrugosa*; *R. mohavensis*; *R. moyesii*, forms and hybrids; *R. fargesii*; *R. holodonta*; *R. multibracteata*, forms and hybrid; *R. murielae*; *R. nanothamnus*; *R. nutkana*, forms and hybrids; *R. paulii*; *R. pendulina*; *R. pisocarpa*; *R. prattii*; *R. pyrifera*; *R. rugosa* (Rugosas), forms and hybrids; *R. sertata*; *R. setipoda*; *R. spaldingii*; *R. suffulta*; *R. sweginzowii macrocarpa*; *R. ultramontana*; *R. wardii*; *R. webbiana*; *R. willmottiae*; *R. woodsii fendleri*; *R. yainacensis*

SYNSTYLAE 240

R. anemoneflora; *R. arvensis* (Ayrshires), forms and hybrids; *R. brunonii* and hybrid; *R. dupontii*; *R. filipes*, forms and hybrids; *R. gentiliana*; *R. helenae* and hybrid; *R. henryi*; *R. longicuspis*; *R. luciae*; *R. moschata* (Musks), forms and hybrids; *R. mulliganii*; *R. multiflora*, forms and hybrids; Hybrid Musks; Multiflora Ramblers; Modern Climbers; Modern Shrubs; Polyanthas; Floribundas (Cluster-flowered Roses); Climbing Floribundas; Miniatures and Patios (Compact Floribundas); Procumbent Shrub Roses (Ground-cover Roses); *R. phoenicia*; *R.* × *polliniana*; *R. rubus*; *R. sempervirens*, forms and hybrids; *R. setigera* and hybrids; *R. sinowilsonii* and hybrid; *R. soulieana* and hybrids; *R. wichuraiana* and hybrids

CHINENSIS 351

R. gigantea and hybrids; *R. chinensis* (Chinas), forms and hybrids; Bourbons; Climbing Bourbons; Noisettes; The Teas; Bermuda Roses; Hybrid Perpetuals; New English Roses; Hybrid Teas (Large-flowered Roses); Climbing Hybrid Teas (Large-flowered Climbers)

PART V   The Cultivation of Roses 437

Appendices
  A. World Climatic Map 467
  B. Height and Colour Charts 468
  C. Rose Societies of the World 480
  D. Rose Gardens of the World 481
  E. Rose Producers and Suppliers of the World 484

Glossary 486

Further Reading 487

General Index 490

Index of Roses 492

Foreword to the First Edition

This is a book written by an enthusiast who has devoted much of his life to old roses since he was first captivated by a 'Maiden's Blush' in the garden of his childhood home. Peter Beales' four popular little books have whetted the appetites of rose lovers for a comprehensive book on old roses from a man who has done so much, just as Graham Thomas did before him, to popularize old roses and to rediscover many which had been long forgotten or thought extinct. Often he has had to emulate Sherlock Holmes in the amount of detective work he has done to establish the identity of mystery roses from the past, cherished in some small cottage garden or revealed when a derelict garden was being restored to its earlier state.

Gradually he has built up an important collection of old roses and some favourites among more modern ones. His roses now travel across the world to give pleasure to rose lovers whose knowledge of them was often previously limited to a brief description in an old book. I expect that some roses have returned to their native countries in this way.

His history of the development of roses is based on established facts and his own research rather than on the writings of one or two earlier authors and he is prepared to challenge popular theories about the origins of some old roses.

His ideas for using shrub roses should help to make many people who have not previously appreciated the wide uses for which they are suitable to be more adventurous. He suggests roses for parks and woodlands, for landscaping, for hedges formal and informal, and for mixed shrubberies, roses to grow by water or on terraces and patios, in pots and under glass. He covers fully the very many ways in which climbing roses, old and modern, can be used to add interest to any garden, whatever its size. I hope that many readers will visit some of the many gardens in Britain and overseas with collections of old roses which he helpfully lists and appreciate their beauty, the glorious scent of so many of them and their versatility.

In the dictionary section he lists over 1,000 roses, using a combination of the old botanical classification, based on the wild or species roses from which the hybrids were derived or were thought to have come, and the modern classification which has been devised for the benefit of gardeners rather than botanists. The descriptions are based on his own knowledge and experience of each rose, and readers will find especially useful the guidance he gives about the best uses of each rose by means of symbols, for instance whether they will grow up a tall tree or thrive in partial shade.

The book is lavishly illustrated with nearly 550 colour photographs. These pictures should not only delight all who look at them, but also help readers to identify roses growing in their own gardens or give them ideas for beautifying them. The line drawings should help to simplify pruning and budding and other aspects of rose maintenance.

I hope that this book will greatly encourage all who read it to plant more of the roses Peter describes and so add greatly to the popularity of the older roses which have so much to offer in our gardens of today.

R. C. BALFOUR, MBE, DHM
Past President of the World Federation of Rose Societies and of the Royal National Rose Society, and holder of the WFRS Gold Medal and the Dean Hole Medal

Foreword to the Second Edition

I am delighted to add this postscript to my Foreword to the first edition of this important and excellent book, which has fully justified its title as a classic among the plethora of gardening books now available. There can be few rosarians round the world who have not heard of Peter Beales. Many fortunate ones will have met him and listened to his talks, others will have benefited from his great knowledge of roses and from his advice in the first edition of this book and in his two other major books, *Twentieth Century Roses* and *Roses: An Illustrated Encyclopaedia*.

In this updated and expanded edition, he has added descriptions of many more roses which he has carefully selected from recent introductions, as well as some older roses which he has rediscovered and reintroduced, treasures from the past. He has also covered the newer types of roses, such as the ground-cover or procumbent roses, and gives advice on the best ways to use them.

It is an indication of the esteem the rose world has for Peter that he has just been awarded the Dean Hole Medal, the highest personal award of the Royal National Rose Society, joining such illustrious rosarians as Her Majesty Queen Elizabeth The Queen Mother, Ralph Moore and Sam McGredy.

I hope that you will enjoy reading this new edition and sharing Peter's enthusiasm and love of the rose. Give copies to your family and friends and guide them on the way to a rosy future.

R. C. BALFOUR, MBE, DHM
*Past President of the World Federation of
Rose Societies and of the Royal National
Rose Society, Past Master of the Worshipful
Company of Gardeners, holder of the
Dean Hole Medal, the WFRS Gold Medal
and the Australian Rose Award*

Acknowledgements

Over the years countless people have made it known to me that they share my love for the genus *Rosa*, thus providing inspiration and encouragement for me both in my writing and in the building up of my rose collection. To them, and to all those who have contributed to my earlier books, thank you.

In addition I would like to acknowledge the following people for their direct and valuable input to this edition: Richard Balfour for his Foreword, William Grant for his essay on 'Rustling Roses' in the USA, Lorna Mercer for her piece 'Mystery Roses in Bermuda', Malcolm Manners for his thesis 'Rose Mosaic Virus Disease' and Mike Lowe for adding his knowledge to the Pests and Disease section. My gratitude to my wife Joan, daughter Amanda and son Richard, indeed to all my family, for their constant support. This is also an opportunity to put into print my appreciation of my sister Rosemary's and mother Evelyn May's hard work in North Norfolk, and that of all the management and staff at Peter Beales Roses Ltd – and not just for when I take extended leave to indulge myself in writing.

Not least, though, my thanks to Christopher MacLehose and his team at the Harvill Press, Katharina Bielenberg, Patty Rennie, Donna Poppy, Annie Lee, Vera Brice and to Michael Mitchell and those at the Libanus Press. The dedication shown in the making and publication of this book is immense and apparent only to the few who saw it in its raw state, as I did, six months before publication.

Preface

I was born and brought up in the countryside, and although I did not become a rose grower until the age of sixteen, I was well aware of nature's wild roses long before that age; the roses of slow meanderings through country lanes, returning from school on hot, balmy days in June. It was wartime and hedges were thriving in glorious neglect, so between daydreams I espied Dog Roses at their very best – for where hedges grow, so Dog Roses flourish. Later, when hips were ripe and orange in the autumn, I collected them at half-a-crown a stone for the war effort. I learned to notice subtle variations in the colour, shape and growth habits of those wild species and, from time to time, came upon a white one, different not only in colour of flower but in colour of stem, shape of leaf and habit of growth. Later I learned that this was the Field Rose, *Rosa arvensis*, and that the Dog Rose was *Rosa canina*. Those hedges have long since gone, but a lonely plant of *R. arvensis* and a few *R. canina* still live on in a small stretch so far saved from the plough. A simple childhood memory, but the beginning of a lifetime's fascination with roses and an on-going desire to learn all I can about them – and in the process I derive great pleasure from imparting this enchantment to others.

Since my early introduction to roses I have built up a comprehensive collection. The greater part of this is made up of the older roses – I am heavily biased towards these, since I have fallen headlong under their spell.

Throughout this book I have tried to answer the many questions I have been asked about roses over the last forty years or so, and have also tried, with my publishers, to satisfy some of the insatiable thirst that rose lovers seem to have for well-reproduced photographs. In this new edition, in fact, most of the pictures are new ones, many never before published.

The text has also been expanded, and following a brief history of the rose and its evolution are my ideas on how some of the roses of yesterday and the present can be fitted into the landscape of the modern garden, together with some practical advice, gleaned over the years, on their cultivation. This latter section has also been enlarged.

Bearing in mind the need to conserve and perpetuate many of the charming old rose cultivars, without taking the narrow view that all that is old is necessarily good, I have described in the dictionary section, with many personal opinions, a wide range of species and cultivars from both the past and the present.

In fact, as you turn the pages of this book, you will come upon many of my muddy footprints. Perhaps the odd rose petal along the way will compensate.

R. virginiana

PART I

History and Evolution
of the Rose

The First Roses

The genesis of roses and their subsequent evolution must inevitably be a matter for conjecture, but there is good reason to suppose from fossil evidence and the present-day distribution of species that the rose has flourished in some form since remote prehistoric times, long before the evolution of *Homo sapiens*. It is likely that the garden cultivation of roses began only some 5,000 years ago, probably in China. It is tempting to believe – romantic fancy though it may be – that the practical uses and attractions of the rose were recognized by early man, perhaps widely separated on different continents long before, possibly in Neolithic times.

Indeed, it seems likely that the edible properties of the rose would have been appreciated even before it became prized for its aesthetic qualities. The nutty, sweet, succulent young tips of the shoots of such species as *R. canina*, the common Dog Rose, for example, are, as I remember from childhood, quite tasty; and later in the year much nourishment and, as we now know, vitamin C supplement could have been extracted from the fleshy skin of the fruit of this and similar species. We would be arrogant indeed if we assumed that our primitive ancestors were not capable of deriving pleasure from the scent, form and colour of what, even in those far distant days, must have been an incomparably beautiful flower.

Moving forward in time, we may suppose that the earliest gardeners of history had a choice, depending on where they lived, of many of the 150 or so species of the genus *Rosa* which had then evolved and laid the foundations for the many thousands of natural mutations and man-manipulated cultivars of the present day.

Whether or not you take the view that the rose has undergone too much and too frequent manipulation by human hand and that the garden flower we know today is too far removed from that which nature intended, it is evident that our modern rose is the product of a truly multiracial plant society.

The original wild or pure roses of nature – then, of course, nameless – would have been single flowers comprising five petals, except *R. sericea* which has just four, and all would, in their natural habitat, have reproduced readily and true to type from seed when pollinated by themselves, or others of the same species. Earlier evolution would have guaranteed their survival in hostile conditions by providing thorns to deter predators, and furnishing them with scent and colour to attract insects, vital for the reproduction process.

The Distribution of Wild Roses

The species of the genus *Rosa* can be conveniently divided into four groups, each from geographically defined areas of the northern hemisphere where they are to be found growing wild. These areas are Europe, Asia, the Middle East and America. There is no evidence that any species evolved naturally south of the Equator.

European Wild Roses

The European wild roses include the Dog Rose, *R. canina*, and two similar species which are, perhaps, related to it: *R. eglanteria*, the Eglantine Rose or Sweet Briar, and *R. villosa*, the Apple Rose. All of them may be found in a variety of habitats, especially in central areas and the north of the continent. *R. arvensis*, the Field Rose, on the other hand, is a natural climber and can be found in the same latitudes but mostly in hedgerows, scrambling through and being supported by a variety of other flora. *R. pimpinellifolia*, until recently better known as *R. spinosissima* or the Scotch Rose, inhabits coastal regions and less fertile areas, especially colder areas. It is notable for its prickly nature and bushy growth.

R. canina

R. eglanteria

R. arvensis hips

R. pimpinellifolia

Further south, although less commonly now since the increase in the human population and all the problems this brings to nature, *R. gallica* can be found; its origins are perhaps more widely distributed than those of the other European species, since this rose can also be found, from time to time, growing wild further east. Another species occasionally found wild in southern regions but with a preference for the warmer climate of the Mediterranean shores is *R. moschata*. This rose, too, may well have been introduced from further east.

All of these species have, throughout the ages, played their part, to a greater or lesser extent, as studs in the development of the rose as we know it today.

The American Wild Roses

Two of the most important wild roses native to the North American continent are *R. virginiana* and *R. carolina*. Important not because they have played any part in the development of modern roses, but because, with the shorter-growing *R. nitida*, they have become valuable garden plants in their own right and, as such, useful in fulfilling a diversity of roles from hedgerow to ground-cover plants; likewise, *R. palustris*, the Swamp Rose, but to a lesser extent. *R. blanda* and *R. gymnocarpa* are perhaps the American continent's nearest equivalents to Europe's Dog Rose, at least in appearance and habit, and *R. foliolosa*, preferring the more temperate zones, is the most distinctive in that it is free of thorns and has almost grass-like foliage.

Whilst writing of American native roses it is worth mentioning at this point that several other species now grow wild all over America, having escaped from gardens at some time since their introduction during the last 200 years; and some of them enjoy their new-found habitats so much that they are seen far more commonly than their native counterparts. *R. multiflora* in particular, originally from Asia, is now considered a weed, and in the warmer areas *R. laevigata* has become so much at home as to be known as the 'Cherokee Rose'. *R. gigantea* also flourishes in the lower-rainfall areas of the south and west.

Oriental and Asian Wild Roses

The most important of the numerous species from Asia and the Orient is *R. indica*, now more correctly *R. chinensis*, which undoubtedly existed during the early Chinese dynasties although it now seems to be extinct, at least in the wild. What is certain is that it was once alive and well and this, or forms of this recurrent rose, could well have been cultivated by gardeners in China around 3000 BC. Much later, genes from this species, introduced by others by breeding, laid the foundations for our familiar modern recurrent roses. It is a sad paradox that such an important stud rose should, in its true form, have become extinct even in its native land, and its demise was probably the sin of nurserymen the whole world over, the arrogant assumption that new strains are essentially better than old.

Other fascinating species growing wild in the Far East are *R. laevigata* and *R. bracteata*, distinct but with similar characteristics. Both are climbers and have very large, single, white flowers with pronounced stamens, glossy foliage and large, cruel barbs. These roses now also grow wild in America. Quite the opposite is *R. banksiae* with its smooth, light green foliage, long, pliable, thornless shoots and large clusters of flowers.

The huge and abundant trusses of *R. multiflora* make a superb display in the wild, its generous nature now forming the basis of many modern cluster-flowered roses from Floribundas to shrub roses and ramblers. Another cluster-flowered species with climbing instincts is *R. wichuraiana*. This species, when used as a seed parent by breeders at the turn of this century, yielded some of our best-loved

R. bracteata

R. moyesii hips

R. foetida persiana

ramblers, notably 'Albéric Barbier', 'Albertine', 'Emily Gray' and 'New Dawn'. Many other less well-known, ancient species flourished in various parts of Asia and the Orient, amongst them *R. brunonii* and *R. filipes*, and in the same area can be found several of the species which bear elongated or flagon-shaped hips, such as *R. moyesii*. Southern Asia and Japan are the homes of *R. rugosa* where it grows so freely from seed. Its promiscuity has resulted in many and varied offspring since it came west, notably the hybrids 'Roseraie de l'Hay', 'Blanc Double de Coubert' and 'Fru Dagmar Hartopp'.

The Wild Roses of the Middle East

This area is best seen in our minds as covering both eastern Europe and western Asia, as well as the piece in between. It is here that we can find the only true yellow species, in the form of *R. foetida*, and nowadays yellow rose species are few and far between. Closely related are two forms, probably garden hybrids or natural mutations that occurred in the distant past – *R. foetida bicolor*, although this could have occurred anywhere at any time, and *R. foetida persiana*, the double form. The strangely shaped, very double *R. hemisphaerica* is obviously closely related to *R. foetida* but has never been seen in the wild, nor apparently has the almost extinct single form of this species. Both are rather tender in Europe so they

R. centifolia

R. phoenicia

must have come from the warmer parts of the region. *R. foetida* is, more often than not, sterile, so one wonders if this too is not a hybrid of some yellow species now extinct.

Two other roses, both hybrids, have their origins shrouded in mystery, but the probably now extinct species that sired them undoubtedly lived in this part of the world; they are *R. damascena* and *R. centifolia*, both in their forms very double and therefore incapable of perpetuating themselves except by vegetative propagation. *R. damascena*, of course, and some of its forms have been very important in parts of this region for centuries as the source of attar of roses, so it is not difficult to understand that a rose grown in such vast quantities would, from time to time, yield mutations or, indeed, chance new hybrids. However, the origins of *R. centifolia* are extremely obscure; we can surmise that it simply developed naturally from a single fertile form which once existed in the wild, but more likely it is a hybrid prized for its beauty and important as another commercial high yielder of attar, brought to Europe by traders and developed in its present-day form by the Dutch, who are said to have bred many cultivars in the seventeenth and eighteenth centuries.

The Old Garden Roses and Their Origins

Centifolias (Provence Roses)

It was in the fifteenth and sixteenth centuries that man began to interfere with the progeny of the rose to much effect. The Dutch, in particular, did pioneering work, especially in selecting improved strains of *R. centifolia* and its hybrids. Proof of this comes from the frequent appearance of these blowsy, many-petalled roses in the works of the Old Masters, captured in perpetuity, sometimes with equally well-proportioned ladies of the era.

Examination by plant cytologists in recent years of the chromosomes of *R. centifolia* proves beyond doubt that it is a complex hybrid and not, as previously thought, a true species. Apparently the Centifolias are made up of genes from *R. gallica*, *R. phoenicia*, *R. moschata*, *R. canina* and *R. damascena*. The late Dr C. V. Hurst* declared that they were one of the youngest groups, developed in Holland some 300 years ago, contradicting the belief, based on references to 'hundred-petalled roses' as early as 300 BC, that they were among the oldest. When and how such a complex line of hybridity occurred is open to speculation. If, as is said, the Dutch introduced over 200 variations of Centifolias between 1580 and 1710, this is a tremendous quantity of roses, suggesting a very fertile parent stock. One wonders how much of the work done by the Dutch was wholly original. Might they have used single or semi-double clones from warmer climates, thus building on work done by earlier civilizations? And did they perhaps witness the gradual extinction of originals in favour of over 200 novelties? There are no records to determine the origins of *R. centifolia*, which is likely to remain yet another fascinating horticultural mystery.

As garden plants, it must be said, they leave something to be desired, being awkward and ungainly in growth and rather prone to mildew. However, with support, they are easily manageable and, in good weather, rewarding, with very beautiful, superbly scented, cabbage-like flowers. Their foliage is coarse and darkish green and their shoots are very thorny.

Mosses

The first Moss rose apparently emerged as a sport from a Centifolia prior to the mid eighteenth century. In the early nineteenth century a few single-flowered forms appeared in their ranks, enabling a few hybridists to cross them with hybrids from other groups in an attempt to prolong their flowering period, but this was soon discontinued.

Rivers', Woods' and Hooker's catalogues listed some thirty between them and Paul listed thirty-two Moss roses in *The Rose Garden* (10th edn, 1903). Many of these probably came about by seedlings raised haphazardly and in large numbers, yielding a small proportion of moss-bearing offspring which, in turn, were selected for this propensity – rather than for the high quality of their flowers. Nowadays many of us still appreciate the Moss rose but we are more selective when it comes to quality.

---

* Dr Hurst's work is collated and documented in Graham Stuart Thomas's book *The Old Shrub Roses* and more recently in *The Graham Stuart Thomas Rose Book*.

'Common Moss'

'Mme Hardy'

Damasks

With the decline of the Roman Empire, roses lost much of their importance, and it was not until the Crusaders of the twelfth and thirteenth centuries brought back specimens of Damask roses from their travels to the Middle East that they once more became popular in Europe. When they proved sufficiently hardy to withstand the rigours of a more northerly latitude, they soon found their way into the gardens of noblemen and rich merchants, some of whom turned them to profit. The petals were used for making perfume and for their tenuous medical properties, exploited by the apothecaries of the day. The 'Autumn Damask' known as 'Quatre Saisons' in France would have been particularly valuable as the first rose in Europe to produce two crops of flowers every summer. There may have been more varieties in those days but there are fewer Damasks to choose from today than any other group. To the experienced eye they are distinctive in that they have grey downy soft-textured foliage and their shoots are almost always very thorny, with the flowers borne on rather short, flexible stalks.

Gallicas ('Roses of Provins')

Before the introduction of the Damasks the major source of medicine and rose oil in Europe was presumably the 'Apothecary's Rose' or 'Red Damask', *R. gallica officinalis*, later to become the emblem of the Lancastrians. This was the rose which 'sported' to produce the legendary striped rose *R. gallica versicolor*, better known perhaps as 'Rosa Mundi', named, it is said, after 'Fair Rosamund', mistress of King Henry II. If this romantic legend has any validity – and it seems plausible that such a striking sport would have created quite a sensation at that time – this would date it from the mid twelfth century; but it could well have been brought

R. gallica officinalis

back to England as a novelty by some crusading knight, implying an earlier origin. Whatever the origin of 'Rosa Mundi', I have no doubt that a striped rose of some kind existed at the time of Henry II, for the Gallicas are a very old race indeed. They also figure to some extent in the ancestry of many other roses, including some of our present-day modern hybrids. As garden plants they are most amenable, with no cultivar exceeding 4′ in height. When in flower in midsummer no other group of old roses can challenge them for quantity and, more often than not, for quality. What is more, they are easy to grow and will tolerate even the poorest soil. Their foliage is variable but, in most cultivars, it is darkish green and their shoots have few thorns of consequence.*

* Mr Peter A. Fane de Salis of Norwich recently sent me the following fascinating extract from *The Annals of Horticulture*, 1844/5 – I make no comment on the accuracy of its contents, except that it highlights the haphazard methods employed in the raising of roses in the early nineteenth century.

'Rosa Gallica, the French Rose. The Rose Nurserymen in France as well as England, are so very cunning, that they have pretended, while dividing these roses into families, to class them according to their parentage; and after raising Roses like so much small salading from hips gathered wherever they could be found, they have examined the attributes of these selected seedlings, and fastened them upon whichever they fancied they belonged to. The fine French Roses, so called, have all been derived from the original Tuscany, and others of the early Rosa Gallica, which has just as much right to the name as 'Louis-the-Sixteenth' Tulip has to be called the French Tulip. Van Eden and others, of Haerlem, raised all the early varieties in Holland; and the first man in France that succeeded in raising new varieties for them was Descemet, who resided at St Denis, and began sowing Roses when he left St Denis for Odessa. Vibert bought all his stock and continued the raising of seedlings. Rosa Gallica, therefore, is a family of which all the best and earliest were Dutch, from the old Tuscany downwards.'

Albas (White Roses)

Although normally I dislike putting roses into any sort of pecking order, since they all have their attributes, faults and appeal according to taste, the Albas occupy a high position in my league table.

They are a beautiful and intrepid group, going far back in time, and although there is some uncertainty about their origins and the early parentage of the original form, a few cultivars certainly existed in medieval times. Their foliage, fruit and stems are rather similar to *R. canina*, if more refined, supporting the belief that they are all derived from this species, the other parent being either *R. damascena* or *R. gallica*. All of the dozen or so cultivars of this group grown today are blessed with a strong constitution and start to flower in mid to late June. Few other types of rose can match their refinement of texture and quality of perfume. All are of pastel shades, from pure white through to clear deep pink.

The Flower Garden, an old gardening book of 1840, lists forty-two distinct cultivars, quite a few of whose names I have not seen recorded elsewhere and which are probably simply variations of *R. alba* 'Maxima' or 'Maiden's Blush', cultivars I frequently get asked to identify each year. These two cultivars between them have more alternative names than any others I know. 'Maiden's Blush' has been known over the years as 'La Royale', 'La Séduisante', 'La Virginale', 'Incarnata' and 'Cuisse de Nymphe', a slightly deeper form having the name 'Cuisse de Nymphe Émue'. It was this rose, growing in the garden of my birthplace in north Norfolk and affectionately known as 'Grandad's Rose', which first excited my curiosity and led to my lifelong affinity with roses. I have a vivid childhood memory of enjoying this rose, drawn to her no doubt by her 'expensive' perfume, which seemed to pervade the entire garden each June. Despite years of neglect, this old plant is still growing exactly where I remember it, and will certainly outlive me. It gives me pleasure to know that her offspring are now growing in many places around the world, since it was from this very plant that I obtained my first budding eyes of this old cultivar when starting my nursery thirty years ago.

'Maiden's Blush'

'Old Blush'

The several names for *R. alba* 'Maxima' indicate an auspicious rose, for they include 'Bonnie Prince Charlie's Rose', 'Jacobite Rose', 'Cheshire Rose' and 'White Rose of York'. The true 'White Rose of York', however, was probably a specific single form of *R. alba*, though I wonder sometimes if it might have been the white form of the common Dog Rose?

Chinas

From paintings and other artefacts depicting roses there is ample evidence that the Chinese were growing roses of considerable hybridity as early as the tenth century and probably long before. Certainly, during the sixteenth century, occasional visitors to China and other parts of the Far East reported sightings of roses which bloomed for a very long season. Later, in the eighteenth century, as travels from Europe to the East steadily increased, plant material was collected in great quantities; it is therefore not surprising that some of the old Chinese garden cultivars should find their way to Europe.

In 1781 a pink form of *R. chinensis*, now known as 'Old Blush', was planted in Holland and soon reached England. Some eight years later a red form was found growing in Calcutta and was brought to England by a captain of the British East India Company. It soon found favour and was variously named *R. semperflorens*, the 'Bengal Rose' and 'Slater's Crimson China'. This rose and 'Old Blush', then called 'Parson's Pink China', were between them responsible for the remontancy factors in most of our modern roses. Although 'Slater's Crimson China' is now

'Slater's Crimson China'

seldom seen, having been superseded by such excellent red Chinas as 'Gloire de Rosomanes' in 1825 and 'Cramoisi Supérieur' in 1832, 'Old Blush' is quite common, blessed as it is with considerable longevity and a fond liking, it seems, for neglect.

As mentioned earlier, *R. chinensis* is now thought to be extinct in the wild and I became excited in 1983 when I received a batch of cuttings and some seed from China labelled *R. chinensis*. These came at quite the wrong time of year for ideal propagation, but some of the staff of the John Innes Institute in Norwich and the late Jim Russell of Castle Howard quickly agreed to help me spread the risk and consequently, between us, we have raised several plants, both from the seeds and from some of the cuttings; although these all came from the same parent plant the number of petals (which are reddish pink) varies from five on some plants to as many as eighteen on others.

This rose and one or two other garden hybrids from China came to me via Mrs Hazel le Rougetel, who visited China in 1982. One in particular is a charming Tea with shapely flowers of sulphur-yellow flushed pinkish-red. Hazel tells me that its name translated from the Chinese is the 'Tipsy Imperial Concubine'!

Portlands

Towards the end of the eighteenth century a rose of much significance appeared in France. Its origins were obscure, as is so often the case, but its habit of flowering almost continuously throughout the season won it instant favour. It arrived there by way of England with the name *R. portlandica* but later became known as 'Duchess of Portland', after the 3rd Duchess of Portland,* who is reputed to have brought it to England from Italy. It is said to have originated from a cross between a Damask × Gallica seedling and an unknown China rose, probably 'Slater's Crimson', a mating which is thought to have established, at least in part, the invaluable remontancy habit of many of our present-day roses.

Having observed the 'Portland Rose', as it is often known, for many years, I am of the opinion that no China rose was in any way involved in this scattering of pollen, although Damask and Gallica certainly played their part: Damask in the form of *R. damascena bifera* ('Quatre Saisons'), from which it inherits its remontancy, and Gallica in the form of *R. gallica officinalis* (the 'Apothecary's Rose'), from which it inherits its tidy, compact habit. Whatever its parentage, this rose was immediately put to stud by the perceptive French hybridists, amongst whom was Comte Lelieur who was in charge of the Imperial Gardens in France at that time. It was he who raised 'Rose Lelieur', later renamed by request of Louis XVIII 'Rose du Roi'. To produce this rose it is said that Lelieur crossed the 'Portland Rose'

---

* Recent correspondence with Sally Festing, who has written a biography of the 2nd Duchess of Portland (1715–85), reveals that the rose was probably named after her and not the 3rd Duchess. The 3rd Duchess of Portland was not a keen gardener and never left England in her lifetime. Mr John C. MacGregor IV, formerly of the US Huntington Botanic Garden, brought this fact to Sally Festing's attention, pointing out that the rose was listed in an old nursery catalogue of 1782 and appeared in France three years later. This must cast doubt on Italy as its country of origin.

'Comte de Chambord'

with *R. gallica officinalis*. This is another curious fact, since such a cross brought more Gallica genes into the little dynasty of Portlands, and even more curious when one observes 'Rose du Roi' and its descendants closely. One would suspect a pollen parent or ancestor with a higher petal count. I don't doubt the use of a Gallica but why a common rose such as *R. gallica officinalis* when apparently the Empress Josephine had over 150 different Gallica cultivars in her collection at the time the cross was made?

In my small way I have dabbled with other Gallicas as both seed and pollen parents and, with few exceptions, their offspring have tended to be of shortish growth. Some years ago I crossed various named Gallicas with 'Scharlachglut', a very vigorous Gallica hybrid which seemed to contradict my theory. These yielded a number of seedlings, all of similar short to medium height; one of the taller of these has now been introduced and given the name of 'James Mason'. Judging from this and other crosses made, I cannot help feeling either that 'Scharlachglut' has somehow been wrongly classified or that its Gallica 'blood' is several times removed. Interestingly, the late Edward LeGrice used pollen from various purple Gallicas to breed his unusually coloured Floribundas. Most of these, many of which were never introduced, tended to a shortish habit with their remontancy not influenced by the introduction of Gallica genes.

Coming back to the little dynasty of Portlands raised during the nineteenth century, these are amongst the best and the most useful of all the old roses in that not only are they remontant but they are of accommodating size and ideal therefore for smaller gardens. My favourites are 'Comte de Chambord' and 'Jacques Cartier'.*

'Souvenir de la Malmaison'

Bourbon Roses

Soon after the Portlands appeared, another new race of roses came about, again by chance. It was the promiscuous old China rose 'Parson's Pink', now better known as 'Old Blush', which played its part by cohabiting, it is said, with the Damask 'Quatre Saisons' on the Ile de Bourbon, an island in the southern Indian Ocean,

---

* 'Jacques Cartier' is distributed in America as 'Marquise Boccella'.

now renamed Réunion, where roses were used as partition hedges. The results of this union were localized plants of a rose commonly called by the islanders 'Rose Édouard'. M. Bréon, director of the island's small botanic gardens, collected seeds from this rose and sent them to his friends in France among whom was M. Jacques, head gardener to the Duc d'Orléans, who recognized the resulting seedlings to be the forerunners of a new race, naming the first one 'Bourbon Rose'. Although this is generally accepted as the means by which the first Bourbon rose was born, there is reason to believe that another 'Rose Edward' had been growing in the Botanical Garden, Calcutta, for some years before M. Bréon collected his seed. Perhaps the Réunion rose had first found its way to India, maybe as seeds which could easily produce variable offspring. Since 1984 I have grown a 'Rose Edward' from Trevor Griffiths of New Zealand, originally obtained by Nancy Steen from a grower in New Delhi as the genuine Calcutta form. It is very Portland-like with high-centred flowers of reddish-pink.

Whatever its origins, several French nurserymen recognized its potential and it was used extensively for crossing and recrossing, so giving rise to a range of mostly continuously flowering shrub roses which were to adorn gardens worldwide, with very little competition, well into the nineteenth century. Some of these remain favourites to this day. Notable Bourbons which still give excellent value as shrub roses are 'Bourbon Queen', 'Souvenir de la Malmaison', 'Louise Odier', 'Mme Isaac Pereire' and, of course, the thornless 'Zéphirine Drouhin'. In the main, Bourbons are fairly vigorous shrub roses but some make excellent climbers and should be used more widely for this purpose. Bourbons fall roughly into two types: those which have inherited the flower forms of the Chinas, the best examples being 'La Reine Victoria' and its paler sport 'Mme Pierre Oger', and those that follow the form of their Damask ancestors such as 'Bourbon Queen' and 'Souvenir de la Malmaison'. Conspicuous differences also appear in their growth habits and in the form and texture of foliage and thorn patterns. This suggests that, through the years, other 'blood' has been introduced from time to time. As a rule, however, there is a correlation between flower style and growth habit which helps to iden-tify their respective ancestral types, those with few thorns and twiggy, pliable wood leaning to the Chinas and those with thorny, stiffer growth to the Damasks. Victorian writers, in particular William Paul, divided Bourbons into classes based on their predominant ancestral likenesses.

Noisettes

Another family of roses to emerge at about the same time as the Portlands and Bourbons was that of the Noisettes. These had their beginnings in America. Here again the China rose was involved, this time mating with the Musk rose, *R. moschata*.

'Parson's Pink China' or 'Old Blush' was crossed with *R. moschata* by a rice grower from Charleston, South Carolina, one John Champneys, who, in return for the original gift of 'Parson's Pink', passed on the seedlings to his friend and neighbour Philippe Noisette, a French immigrant. Philippe then made more crosses, sending both seeds and plants to his brother Louis in Paris. The latter,

'Champneys' Pink Cluster'

'Blush Noisette'

seeing them flower, and doubtless realizing the importance of his brother's gift, named the first seedling 'Rosier de Philippe Noisette', subsequently shortened to 'Noisette'. The original 'Champneys' Pink Cluster' and one of its first seedlings, 'Blush Noisette', are still widely grown today and well worth garden space.*

William Paul writes of his introduction to the Noisette group: 'The peculiar features recommended to notice were its hard nature, free growth, and a large cluster of flowers, produced very late in the year, which were indeed recommendations of no common order.'

Descendants from the first Noisette rose vary both in stature and floriferousness. Most start their flowering rather later than, for example, the Bourbons, and many repeat or flower virtually continuously throughout the summer. Later in their history they were heavily interbred with other groups, especially the Teas, and some of their distinctive Noisette characteristics were lost, not least their

---

* Interestingly, Mr Peter A. Fane de Salis of Norwich sent me the following extract from *The Annals of Horticulture*, 1846, headed 'anecdotes of Roses':

'The Noisette rose is said by Mr Rivers to have been raised from seed by Monsieur Philip Noisette in America and sent by him to his brother in Paris. Now this does not happen to be true. It was raised by a gentleman in Long Island; a plant was brought from there by Monsieur Landorms, an intimate acquaintance of the raiser, to Rouen, where it was cultivated in large quantities. Paillard, a gardener at Rouen, when Noisette of Paris received a plant from his brother in America (who, by the way, might object to inform us how he got it from Long Island) – grew it under an iron cage in one of his houses for protection, while it was being commonly sold in Rouen at a moderate rate. Prevost, the well known cultivator of roses at Rouen, can attest to these facts.'

Author's note: I take this seriously, since it was written just forty-five years after 'Champneys' Pink Cluster' was introduced. Perhaps another Noisette, now lost to time, was the first!

hardiness. Important cultivars in the group include 'Blush Noisette', 'Aimée Vibert', 'Bouquet d'Or', 'Céline Forestier' and 'Mme Alfred Carrière', to name but a few. They are still available and doing stalwart service in many gardens here in the UK today.

There is no doubt, though, that many of this group are far happier in less harsh climates than this one. During a recent trip to New Zealand I could not help feeling envious of their Noisettes. 'Lamarque' flourished, but outstanding in my memory is a superb example of 'Alister Stella Gray'. I saw it at the home of Sally and Bey Allison of Fernside, near Christchurch, but then theirs is a wonderful garden and they know just how to get the best from their roses, as indeed do most New Zealand rose lovers.

Teas

At the time the somewhat haphazard and largely undocumented scattering of pollen was taking place to bring forth the Bourbons, Noisettes, Portlands and early Hybrid Perpetuals, a few new and hitherto unknown hybrids were finding their way into the hands of rose breeders. These, like their very close relations the Chinas, had originated in the Orient and were probably the result of a much earlier programme of hybridizing by the Chinese, which started from a chance cross between *R. gigantea* and *R. chinensis*. Like the Chinas, they had the desired characteristic of remontancy. The first of these to arrive in Europe was *R. indica odorata*, soon to become known as 'Hume's Blush' after Sir Abraham Hume, to whom it was sent from the Fa Tee Nurseries of Canton in 1810. The second came

'Hume's Blush Tea-scented China'

'Parks' Yellow Tea-scented China'

in 1824, found during an expedition to China to collect plants for the Royal Horticultural Society. This was later classified as *R. odorata ochroleuca*, but its original name of 'Parks' Yellow Tea-scented China' after its collector, John Parks, has been used ever since. Yellow clouded sulphur and scented, it was this rose, in 1830, which brought forth the first of several yellow or near-yellow Noisettes, beginning with 'Lamarque' and tapering off to the last important introduction, 'William Allen Richardson', in 1878. It was Parks' rose and 'Fortune's Double Yellow', found by Robert Fortune in a Chinese mandarin's garden in 1845, which brought the valuable yellow colouring into some of the many Tea roses bred and introduced during the early twentieth century. Although the above roses were thought to be extinct for many years, I believe that I now have plants of all three, thanks to the kindness of various donors. I only hope they can endure our chilly Norfolk climate.

It seems that the early Tea roses as well as the Chinas arrived in ships of the East India Company, which were of course primarily concerned with the transporting of tea, but since a small part of their cargo yielded another new race of roses, it is possible that this, coupled with their unusual scent, led to the term 'Tea-scented rose' as a nickname coined perhaps by the sailors whose job it was to tend them. I grow several Tea cultivars and have yet to detect any real resemblance to the scent of tea in any of them.

Whatever the origins of the name, Tea roses soon became quite fashionable, especially in the warmer parts of Europe. Many were not totally hardy, but this fact, coupled with their beauty, simply made them more sought after, and the

Victorians proceeded to grow them in abundance, the hardiest outdoors, and the tender ones in conservatories and stove-houses. The blooms were borne on rather slender, weak stalks and most had high, pointed centres when in bud, which distinguished them from other roses of the day. The Victorians loved to wear roses in their buttonholes and many were grown specifically for this purpose.

The Mystery Roses of Bermuda

Members of the Bermuda Rose Society since its formation in 1954 have preserved all the many naturalized and garden roses they can find.

For those who do not know of the Bermuda mystery roses, the following account of my first visit to this lovely island will serve as an introduction.

I was attending a conference and had very little time for rose-hunting, but those I found or was shown were fascinating, and there were many I had never seen before. For a week, the island was teeming with rose people and there was much discussion. Who knows what subtle variations occur in roses that grow and flower all the year round and have never experienced frost? Can we compare such roses to those that take a rest for six months each winter in less temperate climates? Of the roses I recognized, their 'Cramoisi Supérieur', known in Bermuda as 'Agrippina', is certainly the same as the European although more vigorous. I noticed subtle differences in 'Archduke Charles', the European having fewer petals, but our 'Safrano' has more than theirs. 'Slater's Crimson', which, sadly, I have now lost, I recall having more petals than the one I saw on Bermuda. The flowers of my 'Sanguinea' are identical to those of their plant, but whereas their form grows to

The Bermuda Rose Society's Garden

more than 5′ (1.5 m) mine struggles to attain even 2′ (60 cm). Their 'Anna Olivier' is exactly the same as mine, but I believe we both have it wrongly identified. With the help of Bill and Lorna Mercer I was able to sort out a mix-up in my nursery between 'Maman Cochet' and 'White Maman Cochet'. Also, thanks to the Mercers, I came back very confused as to the true identities of 'Homère' and 'Mme de Tartas'.

By way of a positive identification of a mystery rose, the nearest I dare go is to say that the Bermudan 'Miss Atwood', although taller, closely resembles my 'Arethusa'. Interesting though a correct identification would be, I suspect that many Bermuda roses will remain mysteries, and anyone who dared name them on the evidence of roses currently available for comparison would be very brave indeed. And, until positive proof is found, they should certainly retain their charming Bermudan names – 'Smith's Parish', 'Trinity', 'St Davids' or 'Brightside Cream' – and be known under those names not just in Bermuda but throughout the world. Furthermore, any suggestion as to probable names should be based on good, sound evidence, not on tenuous descriptions from books and catalogues except where such evidence forms part of more positive proof in the form of a proven, authenticated rose.*

If I could be sure that all the names by which we now know our old roses are those designated by their raisers then I would, perhaps, take a different view. I concluded several years ago that it is impossible to be sure whether or not every rose in present-day catalogues which predates 1920 is true to the raiser's name; and this bothered me. Now I ask myself: providing it has been proved to be a garden cultivar, does the name matter? Roses are not signed like works of art, so surely what matters most is that we have the rose, by whatever name, interesting though speculation and research might be.

Naturally I am fully conscious of the importance of correct names, but for want of a name too many good roses from the past have now been lost to our gardens for ever. For the sake of our roses, let us not get bogged down by nomenclature and authenticity. I have several good but so far nameless roses sent to me over the years by keen rosarians which are probably destined never to go beyond our nursery gates. I call them 'was-not' roses – 'wait and see – name official tomorrow'.

Congratulations, Bermuda Rose Society, for naming your 'was-nots': the rose world is the richer for your doing so.

Hybrid Perpetuals

As a result of a fusion between the Bourbons and, it would seem, any other parent that came along, a race of roses appeared which, following initial confusion, became known as Hybrid Perpetuals. They were accepted as a new group some time in the 1820s and many cultivars were later to fill catalogues. Their sheer numbers and very hybridity, however, proved to be the downfall of many, and

* A special section by Lorna Mercer on the mystery roses of Bermuda can be found in the Dictionary, on page 391.

'Reine des Violettes', above, and 'Baronne Prévost'

only the best survived. Those that are still with us today are well worth a place as shrubs in the modern garden. Some, indeed, are truly beautiful, and most have a powerful scent. I like, in particular, 'Reine des Violettes', 'Baroness Rothschild', 'Baronne Prévost', 'Dupuy Jamain', 'Paul Neyron' and 'Ulrich Brunner Fils'. One of the latest to be raised and introduced, in 1901, was the indefatigable 'Frau Karl Druschki', later renamed 'Snow Queen' in the UK because it had reached the height of its popularity at about the time of the outbreak of the First World War, when anything with a Teutonic connection was frowned upon. This rose, out of character with others of its group, had no scent, but no rose has everything and 'Druschki', as it became affectionately called by nurserymen, amply makes up for this little foible in all other respects.

As stated earlier, most Hybrid Perpetuals make useful shrubs and although 'pegging-down' (see page 84) is not common practice today, some of the taller cultivars lend themselves ideally to this technique of training roses. In fact it was probably invented specifically for them by head gardeners of large estates at a time in history when labour saving was not a priority.

A few have 'sported' into climbers over the years, with 'Frau Karl Druschki' amongst them. In climbing form they are usually very vigorous and need plenty of space, but if this is a problem then several of the bush forms will grow happily as wall plants.

Pimpinellifolias (Scotch Roses)

I have already made a brief reference to the Pimpinellifolias. These charming little roses were much sought after at the beginning of the nineteenth century, declining in popularity only when superseded by longer-flowering types. Although only a few cultivars now remain, I find them delightful to grow. They are not fussy about soil and can be reproduced easily from cuttings. When grown on their own roots, they sucker freely, but in so doing never outgrow their welcome. The so-called Scotch or Burnet roses were almost as preponderant in 1824 as the Floribunda rose is today.

Although there is little doubt that the 'double' Pimpinellifolias flourished long before 1800, it is worth recalling Joseph Sabine's account of their introduction, which was published while he was Secretary of the Royal Horticultural Society in 1822. Two brothers named Brown, one of whom was a partner in a nursery trading as 'Dickson & Brown' of Perth, were apparently the first to realize the potential of these roses when one of them, Robert, found a malformed, wild 'Scotch Rose on the hill of Kinnoul' near Perth, in 1793. From this one rose, which they planted in the nursery, they collected seed. These seeds produced plants with semi-double flowers. Eventually, by continuous seed-sowing and selection, they assembled some good double forms which included a marbled pink and white cultivar. From these they increased stock and supplied nurseries on both sides of the border. In Scotland, Robert Austin of Glasgow had, by 1814, 'upwards of 100 varieties of new and undescribed sorts'. In England, William Malcolm of Kensington and Messrs Lee & Kennedy of Hammersmith had, between them, purchased most of Dickson & Brown's stock, and as a result these roses soon won

R. pimpinellifolia '**Altaica**', above, and *R.* × *harisonii*

deserved popularity in the south and subsequently spread far and wide. I have collected about ten at present but, apart from a few, I fear most, while a pleasure to grow, will be impossible to name.

The Scotch roses were formerly known as 'Spinosissimas' from *R. spinosissima*, which has recently been changed to *R. pimpinellifolia*.

In the 1830s a Mr Lee of Bedfont succeeded in crossing one of these with the 'Autumn Damask' to produce 'Stanwell Perpetual'. This rose bears a close resemblance to the Scotch roses in foliage and thorns but is taller and more straggly. Flowering almost continuously and superbly scented, it is still a favourite today.

With the notable exception of Wilhelm Kordes in Germany, who used forms of *R. pimpinellifolia* in the 1930s and 1940s to give us 'Frühlingsgold' and 'Frühlingsmorgen' among others, few other breeders have used them, at least not successfully, since their heyday, although Roy Shepherd of America produced a very worthwhile hybrid Pimpinellifolia shrub, 'Golden Wings', in 1956. Another American rose which belongs in this group is *R. × harisonii* or 'Harison's Yellow', also known as the 'Yellow Rose of Texas'. This is probably the outcome of the chance mating of *R. pimpinellifolia* and *R. foetida*. It is perhaps the most intense yellow of the group. I had always thought this rose had originated in Texas and never bothered to look deeply into its origins but, reading *Roses of America* by Stephen Scanniello and Tania Bayard recently, I discovered it was found on a farm in Manhattan in the 1830s and became so popular that it was taken west by homesteaders who planted it wherever they decided to settle.

Sweet Briars

A native of Europe, *R. eglanteria*, the wild Sweet Briar, has over a fairly long period, it would seem (since we have one, 'Manning's Blush', which dates back to 1799), produced some excellent and useful garden hybrids, all or most of which have inherited its distinctive apple-scented foliage. It is primarily this scented foliage which gives them their place in most gardens but many are worthwhile for their flowers alone. Apart from being colourful and freely produced, they usually carry the apple aroma and are followed by attractive, oval, bright orangey-red hips in late summer and autumn. Particularly interesting in this group are the Penzance Briars produced during the 1890s.

A favourite of mine is the beautiful single 'Meg Merrilies'. Until recently I had assumed that this rose carried the name of Keats' 'Old Meg' but a customer friend has now told me of a lady named Meg Merrilies who spent much of her time and money attending to 'down and outs' in the Soho district of London in the 1890s, when this rose was introduced. It is most likely therefore that it was named for her, especially as Lord Penzance, its raiser, was a judge and would have known about her good deeds.

Hybrid Musks

Strictly speaking, if age alone is the criterion for qualification, then this group should not be in this section of the book, but since I always think of them as 'classics' I cannot bring myself to place them elsewhere. They were an important development in shrub roses and emerged as a group during the first quarter or so of the twentieth century.

Tucked away in rural Essex, a clergyman, Joseph Pemberton, worked at rose-breeding and came up with a complete breakthrough. It was obvious from the start that Pemberton's roses were different, but for want of another classification they were introduced to begin with as Hybrid Teas. His first roses came on the market in 1913; they were 'Moonlight' with semi-double white flowers and 'Danaë' with smallish flowers of soft primrose-yellow. Both had flowers borne in clusters on long branches from shrubby plants. What is more, they both flowered throughout the summer and were scented. To create these and many of his subsequent introductions, Pemberton used a bushy, long-stemmed cluster rose called 'Trier', bred and introduced by Lambert of Germany in 1904. He could see at a glance that the habits of this cultivar were not too far removed from the Polyanthas, although much taller. He probably knew that 'Trier' was a seedling from a French rose called 'Aglaia', a climbing Polyantha of 1896, the parents of which were *R. multiflora* and 'Rêve d'Or', a Noisette from as far back as 1869. There is no reason to doubt this pedigree, for at certain times of the year considerable family resemblances, especially in foliage, can be seen between great-grandparent 'Rêve d'Or' and some of Pemberton's Musks. Obviously, too, it was from this lineage that his roses inherited their musk-like scent. Whoever christened Pemberton's roses could well have called them Hybrid Multifloras, but, since they and their scent can be traced directly back through the Noisettes to *R. moschata*, Hybrid Musk is quite a suitable and appropriate collective name. Most of the shrub roses to come from the Pemberton stud between 1913 and his death in 1926 still adorn our gardens unsurpassed today. In chronological order, the best are 'Pax' (1918), 'Prosperity' (1919), 'Vanity' (1920), much taller and more angular in growth than the rest, 'Francesca' (1922), 'Penelope' (1924) and the versatile 'Cornelia' (1925). Some authorities attribute 'Buff Beauty', introduced thirteen years after his death, to Pemberton. I have faded recollections of a conversation with Edward LeGrice about this rose; it took place many years ago and had I realized its importance I would have listened more closely. I feel sure it affirmed Pemberton as the raiser of 'Buff Beauty', but I cannot be certain. LeGrice, of course, would have known Pemberton well.

After Pemberton's death, one of his gardeners by the name of J. A. Bentall started growing and breeding roses on his own account, and very successfully, for in 1932 he introduced 'The Fairy' and five years later, in 1937, 'Ballerina', both invaluable and, in many ways, ahead of their time. It would seem that Joseph Pemberton had been not just an accomplished rose breeder but a first-class tutor.

As garden subjects the Hybrid Musks are invaluable today, making fine specimen plants, subjects for shrubberies and excellent ornamental informal hedges.

'Danaë', above, and 'The Fairy'

Multiflora Ramblers

R. multiflora has been mentioned several times in relation to its influence on other roses or strains of roses, but is included here for its own sake. It first came to the West from China towards the end of the nineteenth century and it did not take long after its arrival for breeders to realize its potential as a parent and put it to stud with other diverse types. It is largely this species which is responsible for almost all the cluster-flowered characteristics in modern roses; but the Multiflora ramblers were the first to emerge.

William Paul listed twenty-seven cultivars, many of which are still available today. Most of these have their place as camouflage for unsightly buildings or decrepit trees; others would be well placed both on pergolas and on walls. Most Multifloras root readily from cuttings and because of this, some cultivars were used extensively as understocks for other roses, especially during the First World War and the 1920s. A cultivar particularly favoured for this purpose was 'De la Grifferaie', a persistent rose which is often sent to me for identification, for, having shed its more delicate enforced charge of the budded rose, it seems to thrive on neglect.

R. multiflora

'De la Grifferaie'

Ayrshires

I make no apology for devoting some space to another interesting diversion from the main line of rose development, *R. arvensis*. I have always been interested in this rose and its few offspring, and since other authors have tended to neglect it, this is an opportunity to redress the balance slightly.

In its wild habitat it has great charm and is the only native climbing rose in Britain, and climb it will, to the top of the tallest thicket or hedge. No matter how coarse its competition or support, it remains graceful by cascading its long, thin,

'Splendens'

dark-coloured shoots back towards the ground. It is equally at home scrambling through undergrowth or simply creeping along the ground or banks. Of its hybrids, 'Splendens' is now the most common; and an excellent example of this, some 10′ (3 m) tall and 10′ (3 m) wide, can be seen at Castle Howard in Yorkshire, where it is grown as a specimen shrub with support. Most of the other members of this race of superb climbers, known collectively as Ayrshires, are rather overwhelmed in popularity by the Wichuraiana hybrids with their stronger colouring.

Good climbers were, of course, very scarce before the mid nineteenth century, but when they became more plentiful the Victorians used them extensively, as is evident from some of the monochrome photographs in Jekyll and Mawley's *Roses for English Gardens*, published in 1902.

Lack of authentic records prevents us from tracing the first double 'Ayrshire' back to its precise source. Various stories connect the rose with places as far apart as Germany, Canada and Yorkshire; but if not actually bred in Scotland, it certainly started its career there. I am inclined to feel, however, in spite of the work done on these roses by Mr Martin of Dundee, that had it originated there local pride would have prohibited the name 'Ayrshire', as it seems to have been called from its beginning. Of all the stories surrounding this rose, I think the following is the most plausible. It was first seen in 1776 by a Mr J. Smith of Monksgrove Nurseries, Ayrshire, growing in the garden of a Mr Dalrymple of Orangefield, near Ayr. It had been planted there by Mr John Penn, a huntsman who was a keen gardener. Penn told Smith that he had brought the rose from his native Yorkshire where he had found it growing in a garden, having supposedly been introduced there from Germany. The 'Orangefield Rose' attracted much local attention and found its way to Loudon Castle, from where it was eventually widely distributed. I believe I now have this rose, a happy rediscovery by Mrs Janet McQueen of Dunfermline, Scotland, named at her request 'Janet B. Wood' for its re-introduction in 1991.

Some of the other stories about the origin of the Ayrshires make sense only if one recognizes an understandable confusion with other climbers of this period, namely the evergreen roses.

Ayrshires are supposed to prefer a colder climate, so imagine my surprise and delight in finding an aged and struggling plant growing, tucked away from general view, I admit, in the gardens of the Getty Museum and Art Gallery, California, in 1988.

Sempervirens Roses
(the Evergreens)

The 'Evergreen Roses', as they were known by the Victorians, are hybrids of *R. sempervirens*, bred in France in the first half of the nineteenth century. They are less vigorous and have fewer thorns than the Ayrshires, although the latter are not themselves over-thorny. Furthermore, the Ayrshires produce their flowers singly, or in small clusters, while the Evergreens produce theirs in large trusses some two weeks later. Cultivars worth special mention in this group are 'Félicité Perpétue' and 'Adélaide d'Orléans'. I love these roses and am heartened by the fact that we are growing and selling more and more each year.

'Adélaide d'Orléans'

'Félicité Perpétue'

Wichuraianas

If I were just embarking upon a career of breeding roses I would pursue the development of *R. wichuraiana*, and of *R. luciae*, parents of many of our garden ramblers. Most of the impressive results achieved by Barbier (in France), by Jackson & Perkins, and by Brownell (both in the USA), came to a dead end over sixty years ago. Apart from nature herself giving us 'New Dawn', a sport from 'Dr W. Van Fleet', in 1930, the work initiated by these hybridists was, until recently, largely neglected. It is a testimony to their work that ramblers such as 'Albéric Barbier', 'Albertine', 'Sanders White' and 'Excelsa', raised in the early years of the present century, are still widely grown and still listed in most rose catalogues.

The chance birth of 'New Dawn' was indeed a happy event, for not only did it provide us with perhaps the best ever remontant climbing or rambler rose but, when used as a parent by modern hybridists, it has also given us several very good modern long-flowering climbers such as 'Bantry Bay', 'Coral Dawn', 'Pink Perpétue', 'Rosy Mantle' and 'White Cockade'. More recently *R. wichuraiana* has also become the foundation of the modern procumbent cultivars.

The Influence of Empress Josephine

By the end of the eighteenth century, the foundation for our present-day roses was well and truly established. The French, in particular, played an important role and an array of diverse cultivars emerged, inspired by the Empress Josephine, who not only filled her garden at the Château de Malmaison with a collection of her favourites, but by her patronage encouraged Pierre Joseph Redouté to make his masterly paintings of them. Redouté published his work in conjunction with Claude Antoine Thory, a botanist, who made the first serious attempt to untangle the genealogy of roses. Much of his work has been proved accurate and stands up, when tested, against the much more scientific methods employed today.

This period of rose history holds much fascination for me. To have been a French nurseryman at that time would have been fulfilling, both in job satisfaction and financial reward. How I would have survived in the Revolution I dare not speculate, but Redouté somehow managed to sit on the fence, working for both factions at various times throughout his career. I know nothing of his personality

'Château de la Malmaison'

'Empress Josephine'

but his talents somehow isolated him from the politics, intrigue and bitterness of that turbulent period of French history. Or was it his subject? Roses, at least in Europe, have somehow always emerged from troubles and strife with enhanced values, notably after the Holy Wars with the introduction of several new species to the West, the Wars of the Roses with the birth of an emblem, and the Napoleonic Wars and the French Revolution with a new-found respectability brought about by Josephine, Thory and Redouté.

Josephine's garden at Malmaison brought together the biggest collection of roses ever assembled, and it continued to expand until her death in 1814, when it quickly fell into neglect. It seems that in spite of the strife, roses still managed to pass from Britain to France, and a recently discovered irony is that one of the original designs of the rose garden at Malmaison (although I think never used) is very close to that of the Union Jack. A touch of sarcasm? A gesture of goodwill? Or patriotism from an Englishman named Kennedy employed by the Empress to help her lay out her rose garden? None of these, I suspect, merely coincidence – a rose garden can hardly be based on the design of the Tricolore.

A visit to Malmaison in 1996, a pilgrimage in fact, was a great disappointment to me. Admittedly it was autumn, the day was dull and damp and there seemed to be some sort of power cut in progress, but the interior of the Château was gloomy, a little depressing and faintly ghostly, with much about the Emperor on display and little of Josephine. The gardens are well tended, but except for an attempted re-creation of the rose garden as it was in her day, there was little to indicate that 300 years ago it had supposedly contained a very large and wonderful collection of the roses of that time. Hopefully, soon, it will become possible to restore these spacious grounds to a true celebration of Josephine's love for roses and gardening.

Rustling Roses
by William Grant

The Texans were the first to form a group called Rose Rustlers back in the 1980s. Everything in that state is done on a grand scale. So you can imagine the shock one woman had when she looked out of her farmhouse window one morning to see scores of people descending on her garden. They all had secateurs in their hands, and plastic bags. What were they doing?

Actually, she was asked first if it would be all right for some of the group to take cuttings from the roses that lined her long fence. They assured her that they would not damage the roses – they just wanted a few cuttings. She did not know the name of the rose they wanted – it had been there for ages, she said.

That is exactly why the rustlers had come to her house. Someone had admired the rose but could not find anyone who knew its name. So the cuttings were planted, rooted, and became rose bushes. Later the plant was identified as 'Grüss an Teplitz', a hardy rose created by Rudolf Geschwind, a hybridizer in the last century in central Europe.

These rustlers organized themselves, still publish a newsletter, and have uncovered just about every wild rose in Texas.

California old rose growers heard about all this and decided they would see what they could find in the rural areas of the state. Actually, nurserymen and old rose growers had been taking cuttings for ages in abandoned, pioneer and old cemeteries, especially in the Gold Country, in the foothills of the Sierra Nevada. Unlike the roses found in Texas, many of the old ones were brought to the Golden State in the second half of the nineteenth century by immigrants from England and Europe.

When the Cornish mines gave out, many of the miners heard the call of gold in 1849 and sailed to America. In their baggage they frequently brought along the plants or cuttings of roses they had grown in England. And when they died, their families would often plant a rose near the grave. I have visited these old cemeteries and read the tombstones – many record that the person who died was born in Cornwall or Devon. Recently I visited a similar cemetery in rural New South Wales and found more Cornish miners buried there. And more rose bushes.

So I think we owe the English immigrants of the last century for many of these roses we find in graveyards in New Zealand, Australia, and the United States. To say nothing of the marvellous collection of roses in Bermuda cemeteries.

The lesson all of us have learned in these rustlings is that the rose we find has probably endured drought, snow, the heat of a long summer – and survived without any human help. If a rose can do that for nearly 100 years, that is the kind we need in our own gardens, city or country. Especially in Texas and California, where water shortages are common, tough roses are ideal plants.

Most of the rustling takes place in the spring as the roses are in bloom. Without denuding the plant, a few tip cuttings are enough. We carry paper towels, a bottle of water, and scissors. Wrapping the bottom of the cuttings with wet paper, we put them into the plastic bags (or paper). They will keep this way for several days. When we get home, we plant them in pots and keep an eye on them until they are large enough to put in the garden.

Nancy Steen, the woman who won thousands to the cause of heritage roses in New Zealand and elsewhere, writes of the many graveyards and old homesteads in her country where she took cuttings, thus saving many old roses from extinction there. The main cemetery in Sydney, Australia, has more than one million graves. Heritage Roses Australia members have visited Rookwood many times to take cuttings. It is interesting to note what roses have survived well. I remember seeing many plants of 'Lady Hillingdon' there.

Rustling has bad connotations, even in Texas. I think a better word would be *adopting* something that might otherwise be lost.

PART II

The Early Development of Modern Roses

Hybrid Teas

The first Hybrid Tea was launched upon the world amid controversy. It was found by Jean-Baptiste Guillot among a patch of seedlings in his nursery at Lyons, France. Immediately he recognized it as 'something different'. Its flowers, held on a strong neck, were freely produced and rather portly in shape, at least until they were fully open; they were also high-centred in the fashion of the Teas of the day and filled out with lots of petals. Its habit of growth was upright and altogether more tidy than the rather sprawling Hybrid Perpetuals. Guillot had no idea of its true parentage but concluded that it was the result of a secret liaison between one of his 'upper class' Hybrid Perpetuals and a Tea rose with a roving eye.

Although clearly seen as 'different' by its raiser and by many of the experts in France, it took several years to convince the Rose Society there that M. Guillot had stumbled upon a rose worthy of distinction as being the first Hybrid Tea. It was named 'La France' in 1867. It took even longer to convince the British National Rose Society. It was Henry Bennett, a prominent English raiser, who forced them eventually to accept the new classification. Between 1879 and 1890, Bennett succeeded in raising several distinct cultivars from a deliberate programme of

'La France'

'Lady Mary Fitzwilliam'

crossing Teas with Hybrid Perpetuals and, in his lifetime, raised well over thirty new roses. Several, such as 'Mrs John Laing' and 'Captain Hayward', were clearly Hybrid Perpetuals but most had the characteristics of the new class. He believed and proved that all that was new and good did not necessarily have to come from France. Some of Bennett's roses won major awards; others fell by the wayside; but one in particular, 'Lady Mary Fitzwilliam', when put to stud – unlike her French counterpart, 'La France', which was virtually sterile – proved very fertile and was used extensively by both French and British breeders to produce many more good roses. Credit must go to Henry Bennett for his all-round work on the rose, but it was 'Lady Mary Fitzwilliam' above any other that established his reputation as, beyond doubt, 'Lord of the Hybrid Teas'.

I cannot exclude a personal anecdote at this juncture. It is about an illustration which appeared in a small book entitled *Late Victorian Roses*, written by myself, with photographs by Keith Money. This picture was of an unidentified cultivar discovered by Keith at Caston in 1975. We did not state dogmatically that it was 'Lady Mary Fitzwilliam', but it was hoped it might create some interest, either confirming that it was 'Lady Mary', or suggesting a suitable name. Two letters came from Australia, both expressing the opinion that the rose was indeed 'Lady Mary Fitzwilliam'. One was from Deane Ross, a professional rose grower whose father had started their business in 1906, and who, when shown the photograph, was an alert gentleman of eighty-seven years. Deane wrote: 'When I showed him your book he said, "Now that is Lady Mary Fitzwilliam."' Deane then went on to say that his father had grown this cultivar extensively in his early years as a nurseryman, and remembered it well. This does not necessarily authenticate the rose – photographs are not the easiest means of identification – but it is particularly interesting, since later I acquired a colour print of 'Lady Mary Fitzwilliam' which strengthens my belief that the rose could well have been redis-covered. It came from Mrs Margaret Meier, a niece of Henry Bennett's great-granddaughter, Mrs Ruth Burdett; and Mrs Burdett herself added support to this belief by informing me that Henry Bennett's son Charles emigrated to Australia and started commercial rose-growing there at the turn of the century, doubtless taking with him ample stocks of his father's roses.

Prior to Bennett's day, most of the best British roses had been Hybrid Perpetuals and had come from either William Paul of Cheshunt or Rivers of Sawbridgeworth. Between them, they raised some excellent roses, and although many of their cultivars appeared only fleetingly in their catalogues they must receive credit for stalwart work in helping Bennett with the initial material.

Despite Bennett, however, French breeders were still ahead of the field. In 1890 Joseph Pernet-Ducher raised what must still rank as one of the world's favourite roses, 'Mme Caroline Testout'. Today this rose is better known in its climbing form. Then, as a bush rose, it had no rivals, producing an abundance of large, blowsy, scented, satin-pink flowers on a sturdy, accommodating plant. Few gardens would have been without at least one specimen of 'Mme Caroline'. Pernet-Ducher was a discerning man and selected his introductions carefully, introducing only those which showed improvement of class or were a clear breakthrough in colour. As testimony to this he was also responsible for raising two excellent

forcing roses of the era, 'Mme Abel Chatenay' and 'Antoine Rivoire'. With 'Mme Caroline Testout' flaunting herself in gardens everywhere and his florist's roses adorning many a bridal bouquet, his Hybrid Teas had certainly made their mark. Pernet-Ducher's most important introduction, however, was 'Soleil d'Or'. It was this rose, a cross between the clear yellow *Rosa foetida persiana* and the red Hybrid Perpetual 'Antoine Ducher', which brought the first hint of yellow ever to be seen in the Hybrid Perpetuals, thus making possible the many beautiful yellow Hybrid Teas of today. Initially, 'Soleil d'Or' and its descendants were grouped together as a separate class. To honour their raiser they were called Pernetianas. Sadly, they did not make good garden plants for they were very susceptible to black spot, an affliction inherited from the yellow side of their ancestry. By the early 1930s most Pernetianas had disappeared or, for reasons of convenience in commercial catalogues, had been merged with the Hybrid Teas.

The warm and sunny climate of southern France was the main reason for the French breeders' dominance during the nineteenth century, but roses were becoming big business and the British – fed up with the many French names in their catalogues – started to raise their own new cultivars by hybridizing under glass. Henry Bennett had proved that such methods worked and they were soon adopted by others, among them the firm of Alexander Dickson of Newtownards, Northern Ireland. After several false starts, Dickson's were on the trail of some excellent Hybrid Teas and won the first ever gold medal to be given to a Hybrid Tea with a pink rose named 'Mrs W. J. Grant' (1892). One of the oldest of their cultivars still available today is the beautiful single 'Irish Elegance', raised in 1905. Since then, the Dickson family have been responsible for some very auspicious Hybrid Teas, outstanding among which are 'Dame Edith Helen', 'Betty Uprichard', 'Shot Silk', 'Hugh Dickson' and 'Grandpa Dickson'.

Soon after Dickson's began breeding, another well-established Irish nursery, Samuel McGredy of Portadown, started with their pollen brush and it was not long before they, like Dickson's, were winning high awards for beautiful roses such as 'Mrs Herbert Stevens', 'Mrs Henry Morse', 'McGredy's Yellow', 'Picture' and 'Piccadilly'. Not so famous as a garden rose but a name that will live forever is 'Margaret McGredy', raised in 1927 and pollen parent to 'Peace', the most famous rose of all. Both Pat Dickson and Sam McGredy are perpetuating the family tradition by breeding some excellent roses today, although McGredy has moved to the more reliable climate of New Zealand to pursue his quest.

Above 'Mme Abel Chatenay' and 'Hugh Dickson'

'McGredy's Yellow'

'Chinatown'

Polypompons, Polyanthas and Floribundas

It is difficult to imagine a world without roses, but even with them it would be a much duller place without Floribundas, which are now taken for granted. Imagine our parks without them. Some Hybrid Teas, I suppose, could play their part and act as bedding plants, but few could emulate the summer-long colour and floriferousness of well-grown Floribundas.

It is doubtful if the early raisers of these cluster-flowered roses had any notion of just how far-reaching and significant their haphazard experiments would prove to be. Suffice to say that however little the preconception – from the moment that genes of *R. moschata* and *R. multiflora* were linked to those of *R. chinensis* – the progress of this type of rose was assured. What has evolved, given the curiosity of rose people, was inevitable, for no raiser, however committed to the cabbage-shaped rose, could resist crossing it with a cluster-flowered rose in the hope of getting even more, if smaller, cabbage-shaped roses together on the same plant.

The early Polypompons, as they were delightfully called, were rather awkwardly grouped together, for they were a mixed bag, distinct in having clusters of blooms in one inflorescence, but diverse and varied in size, shape of bloom and habit of growth. It was, therefore, not until the early 1900s that enough uniformly distinct characteristics came forth from among them to form a splinter group, the Dwarf Polyanthas. I adore this little group of roses, or at least those still with us today. They have such cheerful dispositions, are very adaptable and are never any trouble, except for occasional bouts of mildew for which I can readily forgive them. They enjoyed deserved popularity in the period between the wars when lots and lots were introduced.

Hardiness is an attribute of the Dwarf Polyanthas which is especially useful in northern Europe and Scandinavia, where the winters are too cold for many large-flowered roses to flourish without mollycoddling. It was therefore appropriate and predictable that a Danish nurseryman should be the first to cross such roses with other types. His name was Dines Poulsen, one of a family of rose growers with a nursery at Kvistgarrd. He used as his seed parent a red Polyantha called 'Mme Norbert Levavasseur' and, for his first pollen parent, the rambler 'Dorothy Perkins'. The result was a rosy-pink which he called 'Ellen Poulsen'. This was shortish in growth after its Polyantha parent and cluster-flowered but not too different from the existing range of Polyanthas; nevertheless it was worthy of introduction and proved, as he suspected, very hardy. Dines Poulsen then produced a rose called 'Red Riding Hood' using the same seed parent but this time crossing it with the Hybrid Tea 'Richmond'. This too proved very hardy, but unlike 'Ellen Poulsen', its half-sister, its habit of growth was much less like a Polyantha.

After this foundation work, Dines' brother, Svend, took responsibility for hybridizing and soon after, using the Dwarf Polyantha 'Orléans Rose' as 'mum' and the Hybrid Tea 'Red Star' as 'dad', raised two outstanding seedlings. These were introduced in 1924; one was 'Else Poulsen', a pink semi-double, and the other was 'Kirsten Poulsen', a red single. Each had largish flowers compared to the Polyanthas and was taller in growth; the flowers, however, unlike those of their seed parent, were produced in large clusters. They also continued flowering throughout the summer, whereas most of the Hybrid Teas of the day took a rest between their first flush in June/July and their second in September. It turned out – for genetic reasons that we need not go into here – that these exciting new roses were almost sterile and not easy to breed from, but persistence paid off and more of a similar type followed from the Poulsen stable. The most famous is probably the lovely red 'Karen Poulsen' (1932). The Poulsen roses, as they became known, proved very popular and were soon widely grown throughout the world. Although not as well known as some of the others, 'Poulsen's Yellow' (1939) was of even greater significance, for it brought yellow into the colour range of the dwarf cluster-flowered roses for the first time. Talking of yellows, I rate the shrubby, well-foliated 'Chinatown' (1963) the best rose ever to come from the family Poulsen, this time from Svend's son Niels, who in the family tradition started to breed roses in the mid 1950s.

Nothing succeeds like success, and soon other breeders were following the 'Poulsen School' by working with roses of this kind. Obviously, when others started, such roses could hardly be classified as 'Poulsens'; so, after some debate, the powers-that-be grouped them together and reclassified them as Hybrid Polyanthas. They remained thus known for about two decades, but such was their advance, and for very good reasons relating to size of flower, improved colour range and growth habits, they were reclassified in the early 1950s as Floribundas. In the United States the taller Floribundas are classified as Grandiflora to separate the large-flowered, taller cluster roses from the general run of short cultivars. This classification has never been accepted in Britain because its botanical connotations are thought to be misleading.

More Recent Shrub Roses

Although differences in dimension are built into most plant families, few have such wide diversity of size as the genus *Rosa*. By providing variation within a species, nature dictates just how far man can go in capturing advantage from any given attribute. As the majority of species within the genus are tallish and shrubby and the majority of colourful hybrids are short and shrubby, there can be no more lucrative area for a hybridizer to explore in order, perhaps, to break new ground than among the middle size-ranges; that is to say shrub roses, broad or tall or both. Of course, the laws of heredity are such that dominant and recessive factors will frequently intervene, but this only adds variety and interest to the job and will keep the hybridizer's feet firmly on the greenhouse floor.

Present-day landscaping trends and those for the foreseeable future demand the use of easily maintained shrubby plants. No other group or family of plants can possibly fulfil this role more successfully than roses – more specifically, shrub roses – while, at the same time, providing a succession of flowers. Several modern rose breeders saw this trend long before me and already there is a wide range of roses for this purpose. I suspect several more exciting new ones are on the way.

As with some other groups, the early development of hybrid shrub roses was more by chance than design, so I will not dwell on those from the nineteenth century except to say that before the introduction of the Tea-scented and Chinese hybrids from the East, most of the European and Middle Eastern hybrids were, by today's criteria, shrub roses. There were one or two exceptions, such as the Dwarf Centifolias for example, but by and large the old Centifolias, Damasks and Albas were tall, lax and shrubby. The Gallicas, generally speaking, were shorter but still could only be classified as shrubs in today's sense.

How is a shrub rose defined? These days it is more a case of definition by usage rather than by description, for, of course, all roses are shrubs; some of the larger ones, admittedly, could be called trees but most of us think of trees, even small trees, as being much bigger than roses. In the past – and even now from time to time – roses were regularly referred to as trees. This is a hark back to the days when the average garden cultivar was far bigger than it is today. My own definition is very much in usage terms: bush roses are those that should not normally reach more than 4′ (1.2 m) high when fully grown and which, by their tidy habit of growth, are generally used for bedding, group planting or as border plants. Such roses invariably have a long flowering season. Shrub roses are those that are as a rule taller than 4′ (1.2 m) when mature and which can be used individually for specimen planting or grown as shrubs in a shrubbery. Shrubs can flower once, can repeat or be continuous.

Most rose breeders of this century have concentrated on working with Hybrid Teas, Floribundas and more latterly Procumbents. Although several good shrubs emerged from their work from time to time, any deliberate and planned breeding has been left to no more than a handful of dedicated men. One such man was Lord Penzance, who worked with Sweet Briars and bred no fewer than sixteen of these in the 1890s. Another was Joseph Pemberton, a clergyman turned rosarian,

'Constance Spry'

'Chianti'

who by the time he introduced his first roses in 1913 was sixty-one years of age and well respected as an authority on his subject. The work of both these breeders has already been discussed in the sections on Sweet Briars (page 24) and Hybrid Musks (page 25).

Another Briton to work primarily with shrub roses is David Austin, but his work has all been done during the last thirty-five years. Nevertheless, the first of Austin's roses has made a real impact on the rose world. It is the tall, sprawly, almost climbing rose called 'Constance Spry' (1961), the first rose raised in modern times with enough charm, personality and fragrance to compete on almost level terms with the old classic roses from the past. But Austin was not satisfied. Although 'Constance Spry' showed him and, indeed, the rest of the world that a market existed for what might loosely be called reproduction roses, it flowers for only a short season and therefore is of limited appeal. After this rose, he set about a planned programme of crossing and recrossing old roses such as Damasks and Gallicas with modern Hybrid Teas and Floribundas. Progress was slow at first, but gradually he realized that his theories were beginning to yield results. Although 'Chianti' (1967) was not remontant, most of those which have followed in steadily increasing numbers are, if not fully continuous, certainly repeat-flowering. He calls his creations as a group 'English roses' and there is little doubt that many are here to stay. Most are scented and of accommodating size, hence their popularity for smaller gardens where long flowering is an important factor.

Procumbents (Ground-cover Roses)

A most recent development, obviously through demand, has been the steady increase in the number of spreading or prostrate roses which have been bred to cover the ground. They are usually termed 'ground-cover roses', a term I dislike because I believe it exaggerates their potential and implies that all of them can be used as dense, spreading shrubs to suppress weeds or take the backache out of gardening. Only a few of them will do this. Perhaps one day many more such roses will be bred, but until then I propose to call them 'procumbents'. After all, many much older roses can be used to cover ground and only their voracious nature has prevented their widespread usage for this purpose. I am thinking, in particular, of

'Twenty-Fifth'

the Wichuraiana climbers and ramblers. Nevertheless, the recent procumbent roses are excellent garden plants, when massed in groups, not requiring too much labour to keep tidy. Several of the more recent introductions have the advantage of a much longer flowering season than those bred hitherto.

Patios

We now come to another new range of roses finding its way into most catalogues – Patio roses. 'Patio' as applied to roses is not a term that endears itself to a grower of old-fashioned roses such as myself. Its merit as a name is that it describes usage, but while a real patio may well be the thing to have in certain sections of society, such a name for a group of roses implies restrictions of use quite out of proportion to the not inconsiderable merits of these roses. I would much prefer the collective name 'Compact Floribundas'. At present 'Patio' is a term not in use in America; long may this be so.

Patios are taller than the Miniatures but not necessarily shorter than the short Floribundas; it is their denser habit and more numerous, smaller leaves that isolate them. They can be slightly spreading but not too much so, otherwise they become procumbent roses. Their flowers are always smaller than those of the shorter Floribundas; and in spite of what I have said about their group name, I can see why they are considered different from other roses and why they are here to stay. The trouble is that as they become more numerous, as they surely will to judge from the number of breeders now sending them into the marketplace, it will become more difficult to define a borderline between these and other roses.

In recent times Patios have come from all parts of the globe, but I have not seen them all. Their place in the garden and their care and cultivation are much the same as for Miniatures – in the Dictionary section of this book I have grouped the Patios and Miniatures together, selecting just a few of those I consider here to stay.

Miniatures

Throughout my horticultural career and often to my regret, I have found myself avoiding plants that appear to be at all fiddly to handle; and shying away, too, from any form of gardening that is not compatible with the wielding of a spade. Since, by definition, only roses that are smaller than others in every respect can qualify for classification as Miniatures, it would be wrong of me to pretend to know everything about this group. This is not to say that over the years I have not come to know quite a few of these little charmers, nor that these particular roses have always escaped my bedtime reading. Like all other types of small things, plants or otherwise, the more one gets to know them the more fascinating they become.

No one is quite sure from where the first true Miniature came. Several theories exist, some with credibility and considerable circumstantial evidence, but like so much of the scantily documented history of the rose one has to suspect a certain amount of factual licence. That so many hybrids, especially the early ones, have close *R. chinensis* characteristics makes the supposition that it came from China the most plausible.

R. chinensis is a far from stable species, and even within its several garden types considerable variation in growth is not uncommon. Seeds sent to me from China some years ago as the long-lost *R. chinensis* and still not authenticated, all from the same plant, have yielded offspring of considerable variation. Of course, reproduction from seed, even of a species, does not take into account the activities of some Chinese-speaking bee. It may be a whimsical thought, but could it have been an early ancestor of that self-same bee that, perchance, way back in time, pollinated *R. chinensis* to spark a fusion of genes that led to a dwarf clone of this species? A clone which was eventually to find its way, by who knows what circuitous route, into the hands of breeders to become the progenitor of the Miniatures. Even though as far as I know it does not exist today, *R. chinensis minima* would have been the obvious name and, therefore, we can accept that it came via Mauritius, having been found there by one Robert Sweet in about 1810, as was reported by the well-known and highly respected botanist Lindsey in 1920.

Little roses known as Miniatures enjoyed a longish spell of popularity as pot plants during the first part of the nineteenth century. In Victorian times other types became popular at their expense, and this, coupled with a rise in demand for other kinds of pot plants, caused Miniatures virtually to disappear from catalogues and florists. In 1918, however, so the story goes, a Swiss army officer named Roulet found in Switzerland a dwarf rose that he had never set eyes on before. A few years later, his discovery was introduced to the world as *R. rouletii*. Although designated a species it was really a hybrid, and after a short spell of popularity as a pot plant in its own right it inevitably fell into the hands of a hybridizer who put it to work as breeding stock. Others may have used it too, but the distinction of breeding the first popular hybrid Miniature goes to the Dutchman de Vink. He crossed 'Rouletii' with the Dwarf Polyantha 'Gloria Mundi' to bring forth 'Peon', a small Miniature whose red flowers each have a white eye. The polka-dot effect of each cluster was eye-catching and sales of the little rose in Holland, as a pot plant, soon proved its worth. De Vink then went on to produce a succession of other good Miniatures.

Just before the Second World War a few examples of 'Peon' found their way to North America. When it arrived a man named Robert Pyle of Pennsylvania obtained permission to change its name to 'Tom Thumb', whereupon it found a ready sale. Furthermore, no doubt to 'Tom Thumb's great delight, he was put to stud and admirably proved his worth by producing a succession of colourful progeny. After the war Miniatures, as pot plants, caught on in a big way, first in America and then throughout the world. Names were no small factor in this success story, for such roses lent themselves admirably to pretty names like de Vink's 'Cinderella' (1953) and 'Humpty Dumpty' (1952). The lovely 'Cinderella' is still popular to this day.

As garden plants Miniatures have a variety of uses, and are commanding an ever-growing slice of the overall market for roses. Their main advantage is that they provide the opportunity for gardeners with the tiniest of plots, or even just a window box, to grow roses. Furthermore, providing they can get plenty of

'Rouletii'

light, they are reasonably happy as pot plants; although, as such, they need plenty of loving care and attention. Out of doors I have seen them used for a variety of purposes from massed bedding to small group planting, and in rockeries and mixed borders.

Climbers

Although climbers have been used in our gardens ever since roses have been grown, it was not until the close of the last century and the early years of this one – when a wider colour range was introduced – that their true value was appreciated. The difference between climbers and ramblers is considerable. The obvious common factor between the two groups is, of course, their vigour. The less obvious is their ancestry. Most of our present-day garden hybrids owe their genealogy to just a handful of the many wild climbing species so far discovered growing in various parts of the world, mostly China. Just as with our bush and shrub roses, the biggest single influence on their development has been *R. chinensis*: each time a new cross is made, it is the inherent dominance of the genes of this species that dictates the result. The other wild roses to play their part are *R. moschata*, *R. multiflora*, *R. gigantea* and, to a lesser extent though no less important, *R. wichuraiana*. Here and there another gene or two, from brief encounters with other types, show their influence, but until some enlightened young hybridizer sets about exploiting the vast range of possibilities within the ranks of climbers and ramblers only those few species will dictate their future.

Once again, it was John Champneys' seedlings from his cross of 'Old Blush' with *R. moschata* that led the way. For it was the Noisettes, when fused with *R. gigantea* through the Teas, that brought forth many of the lovely old climbers of the nineteenth century. As the century progressed, more and more appeared and by 1900 the choice of cultivars was extensive. By then two clearly distinct types had evolved, one with largish flowers produced on laterals from sturdy, upright growth, known as climbers, and another with clusters of smaller flowers with a more relaxed growing behaviour, generally called ramblers.

I have already expressed the opinion that a short flowering season too often comes between a rose and success, but I fully realize that continuity of flower is of considerable importance in a small garden. There are one or two excellent cultivars from the past quite capable of flowering all summer, among them the lovely 'Zéphirine Drouhin' (1868). Others, such as 'Gloire de Dijon', produce their first flush and take a rest, giving a repeat, if slightly subdued performance in the autumn. For those with more modern tastes, however, several very good climbers have been introduced in recent years which can be relied upon to flower from June to October. To call them climbers is perhaps misleading, for they do not send up climbing shoots in the way of the once-flowering cultivars but produce flowers on the end of each vigorous shoot instead. They are best supported in some way, perhaps on walls, trellis or pillars. It is interesting that by far the majority of this type of climber raised around the world since the Second World War have come, directly or indirectly, from that superb rose for all seasons, 'New Dawn'.

R. gigantea

'Gloire de Dijon'

Other important groups of modern climbers are the Climbing Hybrid Teas and Climbing Floribundas. These have mostly come about by chance in that a bush of the same cultivar has, unprompted, turned itself into a climber.

Ramblers

Ramblers were undoubtedly the result of planned breeding by a few very worthy hybridists, most important of whom were Manda of America and Barbier of France. It was Manda, just before the turn of the century, who first crossed *R. wichuraiana*, or possibly *R. luciae* (see Graham Stuart Thomas's *Climbing Roses Old and New*), with a large-flowered hybrid to produce the first of what are now loosely termed Wichuraiana ramblers. Those were the days of Gertrude Jekyll and it was largely from her flair and imagination that gardeners of the day learned how to get the best from them. Indeed, her appreciation of the value of climbers and ramblers still has a great influence on the way we grow and use them today.

Manda's first introduction was 'May Queen' in 1898. Barbier, pursuing similar lines of breeding, gave us the lovely 'Albéric Barbier' in 1900 followed by a succession of other equally good ramblers. His last of significance was 'Albertine' in 1921. A few other breeders followed the lead given by those two men and ramblers have now become commonplace in most gardens as a result.

Another breeder to have success with ramblers was the American Van Fleet, his major contribution coming in the form of 'Dr W. Van Fleet' (1910). It was this rose that sported in 1930 to become continuous-flowering and give us the lovely 'New Dawn'.

The other types of ramblers are those that owe much of their pedigree, or at least that part which provides the cluster flowers, to *R. multiflora*. Again, breeders crossed this species with large-flowered types to good avail and several are still quite widely grown today. Although *R. multiflora* was tried as a parent as early as

'Tea Rambler'

'Rambling Rector' hips

1835 by a man named Wills to produce 'Mme d'Arblay', it was Schmitt of France who introduced the first two cultivars of significance in 'Thalia' (1895) and 'Aglaia' (1896). As already mentioned elsewhere, the latter was used to good effect by Pemberton in breeding the first of his Hybrid Musks. Numerous breeders worked with *R. multiflora* from the late nineteenth century to the 1930s, their efforts being helped considerably when 'Crimson Rambler', of unknown parentage but with obvious Multiflora leanings, arrived from Japan in 1893. This rose was also known as 'Turner's Crimson' and the 'Engineer's Rose'. The first to use it successfully was B. R. Cant of England who produced 'Blush Rambler' in 1903; Walsh of America bred 'Hiawatha' from it in 1904 and Paul of England 'Tea Rambler' in the same year; but most importantly of all Schmidt of Germany used it as a parent for the bluest of all ramblers, 'Veilchenblau', in 1909. Although almost all of the early Multiflora ramblers had quite a short flowering season, one or two eventually came along that flowered all summer through. Outstanding among these are 'Ghislaine de Féligonde', raised by Turbat of France in 1916, and 'Phyllis Bide' by Bide in 1923, both well ahead of their time and fitting comfortably into gardens today.

Scramblers

This is not a group recognized by any of the nomenclature organizations. It is a term which I consider aptly describes the most vigorous and adventurous of both climbers and ramblers, and amongst them are several hybrids from species previously not mentioned, as well as Moschatas and Multifloras.

It is from among these that we can find some of our best and most stunning tree climbers. Top of my list for this job is 'Rambling Rector'; it is far older than any of the others and its parentage is unknown, but there can be little doubt that its origins are rooted in *R. multiflora*. It is a popular rose, because of its name, and so it should be, for it is, without doubt to my eyes, the best of the middle-sized scramblers for festooning trees and covering eyesores. 'Rambling Rector's main rival for excellence as a tree climber is 'Seagull' (1907) with 'The Garland' a very close third, although, unlike the other two, the latter probably has *R. moschata* in its make-up. A very vigorous tree scrambler is the more recent 'Bobbie James' (1961), which, although again of unknown parentage, also probably owes something to *R. multiflora*. This rose is capable of reaching the top of the tallest tree.

These roses perform a valuable service in the garden landscape. The most vigorous of all is, of course, that incredible hulk 'Kiftsgate', a refined – if that is the word – form of *R. filipes* discovered at Kiftsgate Court and introduced in 1954 by the late Hilda Murrell of Shrewsbury, a dedicated rosarian.

Other scramblers from the past, but pertinent in the context of modern gardening, are numerous, and amongst these are several species such as *R. gentiliana*, *R. helenae* and *R. arvensis*, and the 'Evergreens' or hybrids of *R. sempervirens*, which, although not as vigorous as those so far mentioned, make very useful roses for smaller trees.

While writing of Evergreens, I must bring in 'Mermaid' (1918) from William Paul, a rose with vicious thorns, shiny foliage and beautiful single primrose-yellow flowers. It is not really a scrambler in this country but each time I admire a well-grown plant of this rose here in England and sing its praises to its owner I do so with tongue in cheek, for it brings back memories of a 'Mermaid' encountered in Australia in 1986. It was not only the biggest plant of this cultivar I had ever seen but probably the biggest ever rose tree. I was taken to see it by its owner, David Ruston, whose wonderful rose garden at Renmark on the Murray river 200 or

'Mermaid'

so miles north of Adelaide is one of the best in the world – Ruston is a great collector, so in addition to its loveliness there are many new and unusual cultivars to see. The gardens are surrounded by a tall, wire-mesh, kangaroo- and stock-proof fence which is festooned with climbers and ramblers, and it was among these that I found that huge plant of 'Mermaid'.

Reflections on the Future

We have now discussed the main avenues taken by the rose in its journey from prehistoric times to the twentieth century. Who knows what rose breeders will get up to next? I suspect that a writer in fifty years' time may well be using a wholly new vocabulary to discuss the results of our present endeavours. Already we talk of 'genetic engineering', 'tissue culture', 'cloning' and 'microbiology'; all this, together with the computer's capacity for detailed analysis, will certainly play its part in our future quest for 'the perfect rose'. Already, too, we see new types emerging, with breeders searching scientifically for some of the elusive qualities that will make the rose an even better garden plant.

Enlightened breeders will no doubt realize as they strive to find the 'perfect rose' that the re-awakened interest in old-fashioned roses is not just a passing fad. Although nostalgia unquestionably plays a part, their rise in popularity over these past thirty or so years could not have been sustained had it not arisen from an appreciation of their more subtle and refined attributes by a very discerning public, who are not always willing to believe that something new is necessarily something better, at least until such superiority has been proved.

PART III

Roses in the Landscape

Some Thoughts on Where, Why and How to Use Them or Not to Use Them

For several centuries roses have enjoyed the dual role of the most popular and the most versatile of all outdoor garden plants. Rose breeders over the years have successfully produced not merely pretty faces but a range of plants which, used correctly and imaginatively, can meet almost any landscaping challenge. I doubt whether so many of the now-called old-fashioned roses would have survived had they not fulfilled both roles so effectively. Yet post-war trends in landscaping seem largely to have ignored shrub and old-fashioned roses. Only since Graham Thomas revived interest in them during the late 1950s and 1960s have they become increasingly popular. To some extent this has been a cult and they have been enjoyed for their intrinsic beauty as flowers rather than for their wider value as garden plants; but the reverse is true for, in particular, the Rugosas, which are now almost 'stock in trade' for municipal landscapers, and, more imaginatively, some of the more vigorous climbers which are now enjoying a popularity they have not experienced since Gertrude Jekyll used them so cleverly in many of her gardens.

Although there is usually a rose to fit any situation, be it old or modern, this is not to advocate roses for their own sake. Good landscaping should always take all possibilities into account. The best schemes are achieved by the harmonious use of a variety of subjects in sympathy with the buildings they serve, and the wider boundaries surrounding them. The role most often given to roses in smaller and medium-sized gardens is that of 'supporting' plants, i.e. to provide background to other plants, or as individual shrubs for additional height or colour. In larger gardens, on the other hand, they usually find themselves playing the entire cast, segregated from the landscape into separate communities to form the complete rose garden. Both roles are admirable and should be encouraged, but many landscape schemes would benefit considerably if roses were given the chance to prove themselves 'good mixers'. Presumably fashion plays its part in all this, but one suspects that it goes deeper than simple vogue. Rather, it is a question of 'image'. All are inexorably linked by their given name, 'roses', and the long reign of modern Hybrid Teas and Floribundas has resulted in confusion of purpose between these and other types of roses. If we bear in mind that Hybrid Teas and Floribundas, in their widest sense, are bedding plants and old-fashioned roses are shrubs, then their virtues would not be confused merely because of a generic name. Also, many beautiful old roses would not be rejected for the sin of having a short flowering season, and would, perhaps, receive the same

R. mulliganii growing at Hatfield House, Hertfordshire

consideration as other shrubs with equally short flowering seasons, instead of living a life of inferiority simply because their shorter-growing sisters, with the same family name, can produce flowers all summer. I would never exchange one bloom of 'Mme Hardy' for an armful of 'Iceberg'. Nor would I plant a bed of 'Mme Hardy' in the middle of my lawn.

To a lesser extent, once-blooming climbing roses suffer the same fate. With few exceptions, nature has decreed that her finest blooms come in small doses; consequently, some of her most beautiful climbers are overshadowed by more flamboyant subjects whose only claim to fame is remontancy.

All roses are really equal, but some, for the wrong reasons, are more equal than others. Of course a long flowering season is important but is it as important as beauty, charm or fragrance? Some roses combine all these things but are difficult to grow. Others, with one or more of these virtues, perhaps, grow like weeds or may have other faults. It is this very unpredictability that makes them so fascinating both for their own sakes and as landscape subjects.

Another probable reason why they are used so sparsely in landscape schemes is, paradoxically, their sheer weight of numbers. With such a vast array of characteristics, the choice of roses for specific tasks is daunting both to the uninitiated and the expert alike. This is further complicated by photographs of the same cultivar which look quite different and by descriptions in catalogues and books that often contradict one another. When choosing roses, bear in mind these small discrepancies and avoid, if possible, falling into the trap of choosing from photographs alone. Read about the ones you like, preferably from more than one

'**Rambling Rector**' cascading into the moat at
Elsing Hall, Norfolk

'**Fantin-Latour**' at Elsing Hall

book, and try to see them growing either at a nursery or in one of the many
gardens that are open to the public. Advice, based on experience, from rose-
growing friends is also invaluable. Do not be afraid of making mistakes; all the
best gardens have developed by trial and error. So if a particular cultivar fails
to come up to expectation, does not suit a particular spot or, equally important,
does not fit into a preconceived colour scheme, find another home for it or just
give it away and start again with another rose.

Choosing Roses for Poorer Soils

Roses, like most plants, will flourish or struggle in direct proportion to the quality,
condition and type of soil into which they are planted and, if the soil should be
poor, according to how much is put into its preparation and how much attention
it receives after the roses are planted.

Roses have a distinct preference for clay-based, heavier soils and, in my
experience, the more hybrid the cultivar the stronger that preference. This is not
to say that there are not cultivars and types that can be grown in lighter soils.
All of the species are worth trying, as are most of the members of the following
Garden Groups – Albas, Gallicas, Damasks, Centifolias, Portlands and Mosses. The
Bourbons and Hybrid Perpetuals will find life difficult but not impossible and
the Teas, Hybrid Teas and Floribundas will really struggle without considerable

extra nourishment. The Chinas will put up with some degree of hardship, as will both the Multiflora and Wichuraiana ramblers, but Standard or Tree roses will not tolerate stress of any kind.

A point worth bearing in mind is that no rose will achieve its full potential in the more difficult, lighter soils, so allow for diminished ultimate sizes when making a selection.

The following types, over and above those already mentioned, are worth trying in poor soil conditions.

SHRUB ROSES

R. eglanteria and hybrids, *R. pimpinellifolia* and hybrids, *R. rugosa* and hybrids.

CLIMBING ROSES

'Cécile Brünner' Climbing, 'Leverkusen', 'Maigold', 'Mme Alfred Carrière', 'Parkdirektor Riggers', 'Paul's Himalayan Musk', most Wichuraianas and Multiflora ramblers, all the tree-climbing cultivars listed elsewhere.

Quite a few of the more vigorous modern procumbent cultivars are also worth trying.

Old and Shrub Roses for an Established Garden

Old roses can be mixed with most other garden subjects with comparative ease, although as a matter of personal taste, except for some of the short-growing or procumbent cultivars, I do not consider that they mix well with heathers or conifers. They can, however, cohabit happily with herbaceous plants, especially grey foliage types. I will discuss the various plants to grow with roses later, but as a general rule, when mixing old roses with herbaceous perennials, the best effect is achieved if the rose selected blends with the border in terms of both form and colour. Often this is best achieved by planting in groups of three. One group of roses, strategically placed, can add strength and maturity to flimsy areas of the border, whereas another of graceful shape will reduce the coarse lines of the more robust border plants. Try, where possible, to use upright-growing roses in the taller, upright areas of the border, and more pendulous ones in the shorter zones. These are not golden rules, but sensitivity in such matters can be most rewarding. Colour, too, is important. Soft pinks, purples and whites go very well with grey foliage plants, buffs, creams and magentas with dark green or purple foliage, and the stronger colours of red, yellow and flame with the brighter green and variegated foliage. Another important factor is the timing of flowers. Try, where possible, to achieve continuity in particular areas. Plan, too, for scent, placing a scented rose in an area where scent is absent in the other plants.

Standard roses are often difficult to position, especially in the more informal garden, but the herbaceous border is an ideal place for them, since they can provide the extra height required to give the border better contours, without seeming to intrude, as might be the case with a shrub rose. Climbing roses on

Mixed borders at Leeds Castle, Kent

Malcolm Lowe's garden in New Hampshire, USA

Climbing '**Cécile Brünner**' growing up into a laburnum tree in a London street

'**Maiden's Blush, Great**' growing with clematis

pillars are also excellent, though again care must be taken to choose colours sympathetic to the herbaceous plants.

Rustic trellis placed behind herbaceous borders to support climbers and ramblers can look effective. Remember, however, that throughout the winter most roses will lose their leaves, so care should be exercised in designing the trellis in order for it not to appear too unsightly and obtrusive when the roses are dormant.

In larger gardens very pleasant walkthroughs can be created by using a combination of old-fashioned roses, climbing roses and herbaceous plants. I am not too much in favour of walks that go nowhere; it is better if they have a purpose, such as leading to another part of the garden or to a summerhouse or some such feature. Such walks can, of course, be created from old roses alone, but they are more interesting if compatible perennials and flowering and foliage shrubs are used in moderation. The climbers can be placed on rustic trellis at the back of the border.

Smaller gardens, especially those of modern style, are often surrounded by closeboard fencing or interwoven panels. These, often by necessity, form the background to mixed or herbaceous borders, and climbing roses, with the additional help of wire, can make an ideal backdrop and camouflage for the fence.

Roses in a mixed border in the author's garden in Norfolk

Old-fashioned Roses in Mixed Shrubberies

Species, old-fashioned and shrub roses fit perfectly into mixed shrub borders and, in my opinion, are very much under-used for this purpose. I would omit a few stalwarts such as 'Canary Bird', 'Frühlingsgold', 'Nevada', *R. moyesii* and some of the Rugosas – not that these are unsuited to shrubberies, but simply because there are so many other ideal cultivars and species of diverse size and habit which are never given the chance, except occasionally by more adventurous landscape gardeners. The colour range of roses is vast when compared with that of flowering trees and shrubs. True, if left to their own devices, the more vigorous cultivars can get out of hand, and some will take over if permitted to do so. Many, however, will fit comfortably amongst shrubs and provide a variety of attributes such as scent, autumn colour and hips. In the front of the shrubbery, too, numerous short-statured shrubs, both flowering and evergreen, have grey, purple or variegated foliage, and are primarily grown for this reason; short shrub roses, planted in groups of three, can enhance such shrubs by providing a much longer flowering season.

OLDER ROSES WHICH MAKE GOOD MIXERS

Tall cultivars (5′ [1.5m] and over)
Excluding the Rugosas, Sweet Briars, Pimpinellifolias and species, all of which are good for this purpose.

Roses with grey foliage, Castle Howard, Yorkshire

'Baronne Prévost', 'Celestial', 'Celsiana', 'Georg Arends', 'Gipsy Boy', 'Honorine de Brabant', 'Maiden's Blush, Great', 'Maxima', 'Mme Hardy', 'Mme Isaac Pereire'.

Shorter cultivars (under 5′ [1.5m])
Excluding Hybrid Musks and Portlands, all of which are good for this purpose. 'Alfred de Dalmas', 'Baroness Rothschild', 'Empress Josephine', 'Grüss an Aachen', 'Ispahan', 'Marbrée', 'Paul Neyron', 'Perle d'Or', 'Prince Charles', 'Reine des Violettes'.

MODERN SHRUB ROSES WHICH MAKE GOOD MIXERS

Tall cultivars (5′ [1.5 m] and over)
'Copenhagen', 'Eddie's Jewel', 'Elmshorn', 'Erfurt', 'Fritz Nobis', 'Hamburger Phoenix', 'John Cabot', 'Nymphenburg', 'Scharlachglut', 'William Baffin'.

Shorter cultivars (under 5′ [1.5 m])
'Ballerina', 'Corylus', 'Fiona', 'Golden Wings', 'Graham Thomas', 'Kathleen Ferrier', 'La Sevillana', 'Mary Rose', 'The Fairy', 'Westerland'.
   Almost all of the procumbent cultivars and species are useful mixers.

'William Baffin'

The author's garden in Attleborough, Norfolk

Roses for Parks and Municipal Planting

A few parks departments, to their credit, already use shrubs and old-fashioned roses for municipal landscaping schemes; and more would perhaps follow suit if they could obtain them in sufficient numbers. By and large, however, with the exception of the traditional Rugosa cultivars, they tend to be neglected in favour of the modern bush roses. Admittedly, many local authorities grow their modern roses quite well, but others, where soil is less favourable, persist in growing these when common sense dictates they should be replaced with shrub and old-fashioned roses. Cost is doubtless a factor in such decisions, but surely most people would much prefer to see successful plantings of these types rather than some of the ailing apologies for rose beds so frequently encountered – probably due to an insistence on bright colour, often orange, to the exclusion of everything else. In any case, on the basis of cost per square metre, shrub roses are probably less expensive, since their planting density is lower. I suspect, however, that the biggest responsibility for lack of imagination in rose-planting schemes by local government rests with some nurserymen, who offer large numbers of modern roses at very low prices and fewer cultivars of old-fashioned roses and shrub roses.

The Rugosas, of course, have their fair share of space in parks, municipal gardens and industrial planting schemes. These are often used as 'barrier plants' between dual carriageways and also to furnish roundabouts, providing greenery and flowers without the need for expensive maintenance. Yet there are several other species roses which would serve this purpose admirably, notably *R. virginiana*, *R. woodsii fendleri*, *R. pimpinellifolia* and *R. wichuraiana* to name

Roses and water at the Brooklyn Botanic Gardens, USA

'**Cramoisi Superièure**' at Ninfa gardens, Latina, Italy

R. woodsii fendleri hips

but four. I accept that *R. rugosa* and its hybrids are excellent subjects for industrial and roadside planting, but to my mind they emit a somewhat urban aura and, perhaps because of their Japanese origin, look out of place in rural schemes where European or American species roses would be more congruous.

There are some very good modern shrub roses which are already used in high-density planting, particularly the newer prostrate cultivars, and obviously these, too, have considerable future potential. I can, nevertheless, think of several ramblers which would make admirable prostrate roses, especially for use on banks and mounds, both of which are now an almost compulsory part of the contour groundwork in modern industrial developments and roadworks. I wish, too, that climbing roses were used more freely to adorn public buildings. This is probably ruled out on grounds of cost and possibly on the basis of likely structural damage. This may have been true in the days of soft bricks and mortar, but I cannot really believe that modern building materials will come to much harm in the arms of a rose. Many new buildings cry out for greenery, if not for flowers, and it should not be too difficult to make provision for rose supports even at the design stage.

Roses for Woodland, the Wild Garden and Partial Shade

Most old roses are not too happy if planted in dense shade, but several species and cultivars will tolerate partial or dappled shade. They usually look somewhat out of place in coniferous woodland, but some species combine well with deciduous plantings or even mixed plantations where conifers are in the minority. This is not to advocate turning such areas into rose gardens, but a few groups planted here and there in glades, clearings and along paths can provide added interest to a woodland walk. Apart from the pleasure offered to the eye, they attract, in season, insects to their flowers, provide thickets for nesting birds, and, in due course, yield edible fruit for a variety of wildlife. Many species also have attractive autumn foliage.

The wild garden is sometimes an area designated as such within the garden proper, and here the single-flowered wild species can be a considerable asset by providing added interest when the wild spring flowers are over.

In more open spaces such as parkland, groups of species roses, if not overdone, can be effective. On golf courses, too, they can provide interesting hazards, grouped here and there along the edge of the fairway.

Roses in partial shade in David Ruston's garden, South Australia

A shaded shrub rose border in the author's garden in Norfolk

It is important to use group planting in all these situations. By groups I mean a minimum of five plants, but often, depending on the space, considerably more than this number would be used in one area. If a variety of groups are wanted, plant a single cultivar per group and allow ample space between each group. The density of planting within a group will depend upon the ultimate dimensions of each species, but they should be planted in such a way as to intermingle within two or three years. Soil condition is not normally a problem, but it may help to feed the soil well at the initial planting and, of course, to keep the roses free of competitors such as brambles and ivy, especially for the first year or two.

N.B. Roses suitable for woodland are marked W in the Dictionary section. Those suitable for partial shade are marked ◉.

TEN GOOD SPECIES FOR WOODLAND

R. californica plena, R. × coryana, R. × dupontii, R. eglanteria, R. gymnocarpa, R. macrantha, R. moyesii, R. nutkana, R. virginiana, R. woodsii fendleri.

SIX GOOD CLIMBING SPECIES FOR WOODLAND

'Kiftsgate', *R. arvensis, R. brunonii, R. gentiliana, R. helenae, R. mulliganii.*

TEN HYBRID SHRUB ROSES WHICH WILL TOLERATE
THE DAPPLED SHADE OF WOODLAND

'Celestial' (Alba), 'Complicata' (Gallica), 'Greenmantle' (Sweet Briar), 'Herbstfeuer' (Eglanteria), 'Karl Förster' (Hybrid Scotch), 'Lady Penzance' (Sweet Briar), 'Maiden's Blush' (Alba), 'Meg Merrilies' (Sweet Briar), 'Scharlachglut' (Hybrid Gallica), 'Semi-plena' (Alba).

Shrub Roses and Old-fashioned Roses
with Water Features

If water is present in the garden, there are usually roses that can be planted by or near to it. Roses, however, should not be planted in boggy areas, so if there is danger of frequent flooding from a natural water feature, they should be ruled out in favour of plants that enjoy higher water tables.

R. wichuraiana at Mannington Hall, Norfolk

Roses growing around David Ruston's lily pool in South Australia

It is possible to select several species to grow on the banks of natural water features such as rivers, streams, ponds and lakes. I mention species deliberately, for with few exceptions it is better to use natural plants in natural landscapes. Where water exists naturally in a garden setting, its presence should be harnessed as a natural habitat for trees and shrubs which grow in sympathy both with the water and with its surroundings. Where grassy banks or open spaces permit, a group of semi-pendulous species roses drooping towards the water can be quite enchanting when viewed from the opposite bank. Equally, if you can persuade a vigorous climber such as *R. helenae* or *R. filipes* 'Kiftsgate' to grow into overhanging trees and cascade, the effect can be very rewarding.

Man-made lakes, moats and lily ponds can all accommodate the quieter hybrids as well as species roses along their banks. Again, however, shape and ultimate dimensions of the bushes relative to other plants should provide the criteria rather than colour, important though this is. Paradoxically, the smaller the water feature, the longer the list of suitable roses. For stone or concrete ponds or small pools, perhaps with statuary, stronger colours and the more upright-growing roses may be used. In my opinion, though, any rose planted within 'reflection' distance of the water, no matter how small the pool, should at least have a semi-pendulous habit of growth; and any rose planted directly by the water's edge should be pendulous.

N.B. Roses likely to look attractive in proximity to natural water are marked with a ≋ in the Dictionary section.

'**Cerise Bouquet**' growing at Helmingham Hall, Suffolk

Roses and water in Lord Prior's garden in Suffolk

Roses and water at Plumpton Place, Sussex

TEN GOOD LANDSCAPING ROSES FOR GROWING
ADJACENT TO WATER (NOT IN BOGS)

'Abbotswood', 'Belle Amour', 'Cerise Bouquet', 'Fru Dagmar Hartopp', 'Frühlingsschnee', 'Lady Curzon', 'Pomifera Duplex', R. *elegantula-persetosa*, R. *wichuraiana*, R. *willmottiae*.

Roses for Hedges

In addition to the natural hedgerow roses, which are better grown in hedges rather than to form them, small roses for hedging fall roughly into two groups, formal and informal, the demarcation line being somewhat ill-defined, but with the majority belonging to the latter group.

Formal Hedges

When planting a formal rose hedge, consideration should be given to any upright-growing cultivar capable of reaching the desired height. Bushes should be planted either in a single row, with 18″ (45 cm) between each plant or, for a really thick hedge, a double row of staggered bushes with 12″ (30 cm) between each row and 24″ (60 cm) between each plant. It is essential to prune the bushes very hard in the first year to encourage basal growth for later years, when such hard pruning will not be possible. If formality is desired from some of the old-fashioned and species roses, traditional methods of pruning have to be abandoned in favour of shears; and since not all types take kindly to such treatment, the choice of cultivar is particularly important. Clipped hedges can look very attractive, but these must be pruned very hard in both their first and second year. Once the hedge is growing well, clipping can start, but if this is not timed correctly flowering may be affected. Clipping should be practised after flowering so that the hedge has time to make growth for the following year. Throughout the rest of the summer it should only be necessary to remove extra vigorous or 'awkward' shoots as they appear. Only the 'once-flowering' cultivars are suitable for treatment in this way. So if you require more from your hedge, such as autumn flowers and/or hips, then informality must be accepted. Planting distances for old-fashioned and species roses will depend on the cultivar but few will need to be closer than 24″ (60 cm) and most make satisfactory hedges planted 36″ (90 cm) apart.

TEN GOOD SHRUB ROSES WHICH CAN BE KEPT
TRIMMED FOR ORNAMENTAL HEDGES

'Anne of Geierstein' (Sweet Briar), 'Bourbon Queen', 'Double White', 'Magnifica' (Sweet Briar), 'Maxima' (Alba), 'Meg Merrilies' (Sweet Briar), *R.* × *dupontii*, *R. glauca*, *R.* × *hibernica*, 'Semi-plena' (Alba).

Informal Hedges

The scope of old roses available for informal hedging is vast. In fact, almost any cultivar can be used for this purpose, depending upon the degree of informality required. Some of the Hybrid Musks, for example, make quite neat plants as hedgerows, whereas the Centifolias will form wide, impenetrable, untidy jungles. The secret of good informal rose hedges, no matter what the type, is, as already stressed, hard pruning in the first year and light clipping or tidying when the hedge is matured. Feeding, too, is important to keep them at their best.

Just a note of warning. Beware of misleading claims. All rose hedges need attention, perhaps more than some traditional hedging shrubs. Low-cost rose

R. virginiana growing as a hedge in the author's garden in Norfolk

'**Buff Beauty**' growing as a hedge at Castle Howard, Yorkshire

A hedge of '**Roseraie de l'Hay**' in the author's garden in Norfolk

plants, advertised as unsurpassable, may prove a considerable disappointment. Some of those on offer are no more than simple understocks which, in spite of their apparent cheapness, are, in fact, sold at highly inflated prices.

N.B. Roses suitable for hedging are marked H in the Dictionary section.

TEN GOOD TALL, RECURRENT OLD AND SHRUB ROSES FOR USE AS INFORMAL HEDGES

'Agnes', 'Belle Poitevine', 'Blanc Double de Coubert', 'Herbstfeuer', 'Marguerite Hilling', 'Nevada', 'Pax', *R. rugosa alba*, 'Roseraie de l'Hay', 'Scabrosa'.

TEN GOOD MEDIUM GROWERS FOR INFORMAL HEDGES

'Ballerina', 'Buff Beauty', 'Commandant Beaurepaire', 'Cornelia', 'Felicia', 'Félicité Parmentier', 'Königin von Dänemark', 'Louise Odier', Pink, Red and White 'Grootendorst', 'Prosperity'.

TEN SHORTER-GROWING OLD ROSES FOR INFORMAL HEDGES

'Alfred de Dalmas', 'Comte de Chambord', 'Duchess of Portland', 'Jacques Cartier', *R. centifolia* 'Parvifolia', *R. gallica officinalis*, *R. gallica versicolor*, 'Rose de Meaux', 'Rose de Rescht', 'White Pet'.

Old Roses in Pots and Tubs for Terraces and Patios

Many gardens, especially those in towns, have paved areas suitable for pot-grown roses. Ideally, of course, roses are best grown directly in the ground, so it is a good idea, when designing such features, to make provision to accommodate the odd rose or two simply by leaving small, unpaved areas in strategic places, by surrounding a patch of soil with a low stone wall or even building double walls and filling the space between with soil. This last option will provide an admirable opportunity for growing shorter or cascading cultivars; and space can usually be left unpaved, too, at the base of these walls for growing suitably selected roses. Patios and terraces, especially those close to the house, often look incomplete simply as extensions to living-rooms. With a little care and thought they can also provide a 'lived-in' part of the garden.

Roses are far happier in pots and tubs than many gardeners realize. Their cultivation is discussed in a later chapter but the choice of suitable cultivars is almost as important as the choice of a receptacle in which they are to grow. Many garden centres offer a good choice of ornamental containers in all sizes. Rose bush

Half standard '**Ballerina**' on a patio

'**Ballerina**' growing in a pot

and container should, however, be in sympathy with each other; thus, broad, dumpy roses are best accommodated in broad, dumpy pots, whereas slender, upright pots are best for taller, erect roses, or for pendulous, cascading cultivars. Where space or walls permit, and a sufficiently large container can be provided, even climbing roses are feasible. These may never reach their full dimensions but, if properly looked after, can reach to the eaves of a two-storey house or be trained to cover adequately the side wall of an average-sized garage. Climbers, suitably staked, can also be grown in good-sized tubs as small pillar roses. Patios and terraces, especially in modern and town gardens, are often designed on fairly formal lines, as are rooftop gardens, and for these shrub roses grown as standards in square, wooden tubs are most effective.

N.B. Roses recommended for growing in pots are marked with ▽ in the Dictionary section.

TEN GOOD OLDER ROSES FOR GROWING IN POTS

'Ballerina', 'Cécile Brünner', 'Comte de Chambord', 'Grüss an Aachen', 'Jacques Cartier', 'Perle d'Or', 'Rose de Meaux', 'The Fairy', 'White Pet', 'Yvonne Rabier'.

Note: This is only a selection. Many more will do well in pots, in particular the Teas and Dwarf Polyanthas.

Climbing Roses for Pergolas, Trellis, Pillars and Arches

Read any gardening book from the Victorian or Edwardian era and it will be noticed immediately that various structures were used as props for their roses. These came in a wide range of building materials. Brick piers were highly favoured, elaborately designed wrought iron was popular for arches and railings, sophisticated timber structures were used as pergolas, gazebos and trellis. In those days, of course, labour was plentiful and materials relatively inexpensive. To indulge in such things today would be costly. Of course these are not always to our modern taste and structures of this nature are scarcely ever built today. Perhaps we have become frugal in our attitudes in this direction, open-plan gardens, lawns and the inevitable curved shrubbery being the vogue, with plants acting their part upon this stage without support or other props.

Leaving aside the capital and maintenance costs, all sorts of structures can be built quite easily with rustic poles, and provided the main posts are substantial, these can last for many years. Indeed, they can be designed and built to suit almost any type of garden. Most timber for this purpose comes from the thinning of plantations and woodlands. Spruce and larch are by far the most common. Birch can look attractive though it lasts less well than other species. Of the hardwoods, ash is particularly good. The cost of such posts and poles will depend on what is locally available, but in comparison with prepared timber, it is never expensive.

'Blush Rambler' growing on a pillar in the author's garden in Norfolk

'Seagull' growing on an arch at Nymans gardens, Sussex

It is best bought ready-treated under pressure with preservatives, thus giving it longer life.

For those seeking a more formal structure, rough-sawn timber is the least expensive of the prepared materials and should likewise be ready-treated with preservative. Upright poles or posts should be a minimum thickness of 4″ (10 cm) and should always be sunk at least 2′ (60 cm) into the ground. Rails and cross-members can be thinner than this but not less than 2″ (5 cm). Since the principal purpose of such structures is to provide support for climbing roses which will eventually cover them almost completely, the pattern created by the criss-crossing timber need not – unless so desired – be very elaborate. What is important, in order to ensure long life, is the quantity and quality of the upright poles placed in the ground. The spacing of these poles is therefore crucial. The best rustic trellis has uprights placed at about 6′ (1.8 m) intervals. Rustic arches should be well anchored in the soil at each corner.

A more simple form of support for climbers and ramblers is post and wire. Posts can be set, say, 10′ (3 m) apart, with straining wire stretched across at approximately 12″ (30 cm) vertical intervals. Remember that the roses, when fully grown, will be of considerable weight and the wire used must be of sufficient thickness to support them. All end or corner posts should have additional straining posts to enable the wire to be stretched tightly.

Although they will eventually hold one another upright, posts for pillar roses should be placed at least 2′ (60 cm) into the ground.

Tripods are an excellent means of giving support to some of the more

'Félicité Perpétue' on arches in the author's garden

awkward old shrub roses, and make it possible to use climbers and ramblers within a shrubbery to good effect. Such tripods can be of any size, and indeed can be built with specific roses in mind; three posts of rustic timber are simply placed in 'wigwam' fashion and secured at the top with wire.

The possibilities using rustic timber are unending and, with a little time and thought, structures built from it can provide the opportunity to grow a range of climbers and ramblers which, in many gardens, would otherwise be impossible.

TEN GOOD OLD-FASHIONED RAMBLERS FOR TRELLIS AND ARCH

'Albéric Barbier', 'Albertine', 'Alister Stella Gray', 'Céline Forestier', 'Chaplin's Pink', 'Emily Gray', 'Excelsa', 'Félicité Perpétue', 'New Dawn', 'Veilchenblau'.

TEN GOOD OLDER CLIMBERS FOR TRELLIS AND ARCHES

'Captain Christy' Climbing, 'Crimson Conquest', 'Desprez à Fleurs Jaunes', 'Étoile de Hollande' Climbing, 'Lady Waterlow', 'Mme Alfred Carrière', 'Mme Grégoire Staechelin', 'Mrs Sam McGredy' Climbing, 'Paul's Lemon Pillar', 'Zéphirine Drouhin'.

Assorted modern climbers at the Royal Hospital, Chelsea

Modern climbers (including 'Cadenza') at the Brooklyn Botanic Gardens

The Use of Modern Climbers

It is interesting, in view of the not inconsiderable number of modern climbers introduced over recent years, how many climbers and ramblers from earlier times are still used today. It prompts one to wonder what the great Gertrude Jekyll would have made of modern-day climbers, for she relied heavily on cascading, garlanding and festooning. Had she had the range of today's long-flowering climbers at her command, would she have ignored their existence? I doubt it. She would have realized, ahead of her time, that all that was new was not necessarily bad and would have harnessed the extensive capabilities of the modern climbing rose, painting it into her landscape just as she did delphiniums and foxgloves.

Just as I feel sure Miss Jekyll would have enjoyed our modern cultivars, I am equally sure that we should not let the utilitarian qualities of such plants dominate our thinking to the exclusion of her type of roses today. For there is a place for both in our late twentieth-century gardens. Flipping through my old copy of Jekyll and Mawley's book *Roses for English Gardens* makes me realize just how underused climbing roses now are. Why? Is it that they need attention from time to time, that they need expensive supports, that they have thorns that might grab us as we pass, that they spoil our modern sandfaced bricks or, simply, that we do not know how to use them with no modern Gertrude Jekyll to show us? It is likely a combination of all these things.

One reminder of bygone days which is certainly not out of fashion, to judge by the number sold, is the tree climber, but not many modern climbers are suitable for this. Rustic timber and iron trellis and arches can support the heaviest of climbers with ease, each eventually holding up the other. The trouble is that many modern continuous-flowering climbers are upright in stance and not flexible enough to look comfortable on an arch in the way of the older cultivars. This does not mean that modern roses fail to respond to a little persuasion. Given time and patience, 'New Dawn', for example (perhaps no longer thought of as a modern), and some of her offspring such as 'Pink Perpétue', can be bent and twisted to good effect. It is their upright stance that lends modern climbers so readily to walls and other solid structures like interwoven panels, for against such supports they need less attention than their more eager, older counterparts. Many of the modern climbing sports are also far too stiff and upright for use on anything other than a fairly strong structure; the more such roses can be bent, twisted and trained, the more productive they are.

N.B. Shrub roses suitable for use as climbing or pillar roses are marked CL in the Dictionary section; vigorous kinds suitable for growing up into trees are marked T.

TEN PROVEN MODERN CLIMBING ROSES

'Aloha', 'Bantry Bay', 'Dublin Bay', 'Handel', 'Leverkusen', 'Maigold', 'New Dawn', 'Parkdirektor Riggers', 'Pink Perpétue', 'Swan Lake'.

Roses for Walls and Fencing Panels and for Northerly Aspects

Walls and fencing come in all shapes and sizes but the one thing they have in common is the provision of an extra dimension to gardening. All the best gardens I know possess walls that are well clothed with a variety of climbing plants. Some walls may be worth admiring for their own sake, but many are not, and these could be considerably improved, even if only partially covered with plants. Builders and architects will throw up their hands in horror, but walls should be used for more purposes than that of 'retaining space'. We adorn interiors, why not exteriors? I agree that some of the most pernicious such as the more rampant species of ivy and Virginia creeper can play havoc with guttering, get under tiles and spoil the face of bricks. With few exceptions, however, no such charge can be levelled at the rose. In any case, modern building materials are far more impervious to damage from plants than were their older counterparts and few buildings less than a century old can be seriously damaged by climbing plants of any type. More care should be taken, of course, on older buildings of very soft brick, clay-lump, sandstone or timber. It boils down to common sense.

Climbing roses, if grown on walls, will need support. The commonest method is to use wire fixed to the wall by special nails with clips, or screws with eyes, which can be bought especially for this purpose. On soft walls, these are best held in with the aid of wooden plugs which, when placed into pre-drilled holes, expand when the nail or screw is driven in. Wires should be stretched parallel to the ground at 12″ (30 cm) intervals. Each wire should be held an inch or so (2.5 cm) from the wall by placing the special nails or screws approximately every 3′ (90 cm) along its length. As the climbers grow, the main shoots can be fixed to the wire, training some shoots along and others upwards; the more twists and turns the better. The shoots are usually quite pliable and a dense covering can be achieved by this means. A soft twine should be used for fixing the shoots, otherwise they can be strangled as they grow. Another method of training climbers to walls is to fix an adequately sized piece of trellis about an inch (2.5 cm) away from the wall and to train the rose as it grows, as already described. This method is probably more suitable for modern buildings since trellis can look rather out of place on an older house. Walls facing east and west, blessed with a minimum of four to six hours of sunshine daily, are probably the best for climbing roses. Roses can also be grown on south-facing walls but there temperatures can get extremely high and, unless they are well nourished and kept watered, they will have difficulty giving of their best in high summer.

The north wall is the problem wall and, I may add, not just for roses. Few worthwhile plants enjoy such a situation. Most roses will grow on such a wall but only a few will flower to their full potential. Because they show up better, Nature has decreed that the best of these will be white or cream in colour. The additional problem with a north wall and, to a lesser extent, the east wall, is hardiness. So this restricts the choice even further.

Recent years have seen the rise to prominence of the fencing panel or close-board fence, which springs up everywhere when new developments take place. Before condemning this phenomenon, it is worth asking what could be used in its place at comparable cost. Hedges, perhaps, but that is another argument. At the cost of a few strands of wire and a few nails such panels can make admirable supports for the less vigorous climbers which, when fully grown, will themselves help support the fence.

N.B. Climbing roses for colder, northerly aspects are marked with an N in the Dictionary section. Those that are tolerant of shade are marked ◐.

TEN GOOD OLDER CLIMBERS AND RAMBLERS FOR NORTH WALLS

'Aimeé Vibert', 'Albéric Barbier', 'Crimson Conquest', 'Emily Gray', 'Félicité Perpétue', 'Mermaid', 'Mme Alfred Carrière', 'Mme Grégoire Staechelin', 'Paul's Scarlet', 'Rambling Rector'.

Climbing Roses for Trees

When I was a child, our garden was relatively devoid of roses, but being fairly old, it was well populated with ancient apple trees, none of which had any real character and all of which were rather out of condition. Their names were not known, except for one which my grandfather called a 'snout', I know not why, except that when the tree deigned to produce apples, each had a nose-shaped projection at the stalk end. Year after year these trees produced varying quantities of fruit most of which was blown down by the wind to rot on the ground. Few were edible and, apart from making strong cider which I was never officially allowed to sample, they had little real use. The point of this somewhat sudden deviation is to contemplate how many such trees, of dubious purpose, exist throughout the world. All could be put to the admirable use of supporting a

'**Rambling Rector**' growing into a tree at the Royal National Rose Society gardens, St Albans, Hertfordshire

'**Complicata**' growing into a tree at Mottisfont Abbey, Hampshire

climbing rose. I am against growing roses up into trees which, in themselves, have character, but many country gardens have trees which could well be improved in partnership with a rose; and not just trees – some rather boring stretches of hedgerow, attractive only for their bird population, could well be enhanced by the addition of a few well-chosen vigorous climbing species.

Not all the vigorous climbing roses are suitable for this purpose, of course, but many are and many more could be. Nature has her own way, she does not provide for growing and flowering at the same time; thus, without exception, all the vigorous tree-climbing roses flower only once each season. Some, though, do have good autumn foliage and produce abundant hips to give colour later. As with the climbers for north walls, the most suitable, with one or two exceptions, are white, cream or yellow in colour. Size of tree should not present a problem, since some of the very vigorous climbers can reach 30′ (9 m) with ease, although it will take a number of years for these to flower very freely; probably because, until their heads appear above the branches, they are growing in relative shade.

Dead tree trunks, and trees which are past their best, can also make ideal supports for less vigorous ramblers and climbers. Even unsightly trees, perhaps awkward to remove, can become more congenial if supporting a rose.

It is best to plant these roses a little distance, about 2′ (60 cm), from the trunk on the side of the tree with most light, giving them a helping hand initially with string or wire, until they can scramble their own way up through the branches. Bear in mind that, being vigorous, they need to make big roots. If soil is poor, as so often under trees, give them a good start by adding a pocket of good soil at planting time and apply plenty of water at the height of summer.

N.B. Roses suitable for tree-climbing are marked with a T in the Dictionary section.

TEN OLDER ROSES SUITABLE FOR GROWING UP INTO TREES AND HEDGEROWS

'Bobbie James', 'Chaplin's Pink', 'Kew Rambler', 'Kiftsgate', 'La Mortola', *R. helenae*, *R. mulliganii*, 'Rambling Rector', 'Seagull', 'Wedding Day'.

'**Scharlachglut**' climbing a tree at Mannington Hall, Norfolk

‘Raubritter’ growing in the author’s garden

‘Dunwich Rose’

Procumbent and Semi-procumbent Roses

As already mentioned, I wish to avoid the term ‘ground-cover roses’. This can be misleading and wrongly equates these roses with plants better described as such. Certainly there are several shrub roses and species roses which grow broader than tall and some which prefer simply to creep along the ground, but none, to my knowledge, that do ground-cover work by excluding light and suppressing weeds in the same manner as prostrate evergreen shrubs and conifers. Nevertheless, prostrate and semi-prostrate roses will, if planted fairly close together, form impenetrable mounds over large areas of ground, so reducing maintenance to the minimum, and provide an effective display in the process. Breeders now realize the potential of such roses and are working hard to enlarge the range.

A use can be found for these roses almost anywhere where spread rather than height is an advantage – among other shrubs, to hide a manhole cover, or to camouflage, if not conceal, unsightly tree stumps. Some, if chosen with care and given space, can even be used effectively and attractively in large rockeries.

N.B. Procumbent roses suitable as ground-creepers are marked with a G in the Dictionary section.

TEN OLDER SPREADING ROSES

‘Daisy Hill’, ‘Dunwich Rose’, ‘Fru Dagmar Hartopp’, ‘Harry Maasz’, ‘Lady Curzon’, ‘Max Graf’, Paulii, Paulii Rosea, *R. wichuraiana*, ‘Raubritter’.

Old Roses for Flower Arranging

All the flower arrangers I know enjoy working with roses, though most will admit to a nervousness when using them because of their relatively short life when cut. I have never quite made up my mind whether or not I totally approve of cutting roses from the garden, a hark back, I think, to the days when it was quite in order for my grandmother to have flowers in the house, provided they came from someone else’s garden. There are no such rules in our house, however, so I suppose I belong to the cutting brigade.

Flower arranging is an art, and is all about proportion and balance. In its simplest form, one bloom placed in a vase by one person can look elegant, but by another, ridiculous. In its complex form, like painting, the same dozen roses can look either a daub or a masterpiece. At flower shows I always visit the Floral Art section but so far have seldom agreed with a judge's verdict. This makes it all the more fascinating. The ladies of flower clubs must have temperaments of steel. Some years ago, a very persuasive lady telephoned me to ask for help. 'I need a thousand blooms,' she said, 'for a festival of Rossini music and song.' Until the day I arrived in Sunderland I cursed myself for not saying No; the logistics were ridiculous – cut 1,000 blooms one day, up at the crack of dawn, travel for seven hours the next. But when I arrived at Bishopswearmouth church I knew it was all worthwhile. I was besieged, embraced and thoroughly spoilt by an army of 'Geordie' lady flower arrangers who produced some real works of art with my roses in that church. Later, when the soprano hit top C, petals fluttered to the floor to add an extra sense of unreality to my first encounter with the friendly north-east. The lady who twisted my arm to do this was Marjorie Barton, who since has become a very good friend.

Selecting roses for cutting is an acquired skill. Cut them too tight and they never open, too open and they last only fleetingly. The best stage is when the sepals have started to fold back and the furled petals are showing colour. Timing is important. Early morning or late evening is best, but at whatever time flowers are cut they should always be placed in water up to their necks and stood in a cool place for two or three hours before they are arranged. A couple of spoonfuls of sugar or even a pint of lemonade to about a gallon of water will help them to stay fresh for a few hours longer. Before placing the flowers in water it is best to remove the two bottom leaves – no more – and scrape the thorns from the bottom 3″ (7.5 cm). Some people crush the base of each stem but I usually make a cut about half an inch (1 cm) long upwards into it. This exposes a bigger area of inner tissue and enables the flower to take up more water. Cut roses will wilt in warm, dry conditions, and lightly syringing the leaves with cold water will help to revive them. I am told by the experts that plunging the bottom inch of stem into boiling water for about a minute and then placing them quickly back into cold water will sometimes revive wilting blooms.

Some people believe that harm can be done to rose bushes by the cutting of blooms, and certainly if too many are taken with long stems the plants do suffer slightly, but they should come to no real harm. Try to cut to an eye, though, so as not to leave an unsightly stump to die back on the bush.

Old-fashioned roses, in almost any context, make ideal companions in the home, the range of their colours, shapes and flower formation being adaptable to vases of all types, from the single rose on the dressing table to the large pedestal in the hall. Two or three carefully chosen bushes, growing in even the smallest garden, can usually provide enough flowers for taking indoors without any detriment to the outdoor display; and their scent will pervade the entire house, rivalling both sweet peas and ten-week stocks.

Old roses are better displayed by themselves, but this is a matter of taste. Some species and cultivars have very attractive foliage which can be used effectively with other flowers, as can their hips in the autumn.

N.B. It would be quite misleading to single out here special cultivars of old roses for cutting. Those particularly suitable are marked ✂ in the Dictionary section.

Growing Old Shrub Roses in Greenhouses

Although the very old roses such as Centifolias, Damasks and Gallicas can be grown under glass, it does not really make much sense to do this, except for exhibition purposes. In such conditions their flowering season is further shortened and their ungainly growth habit becomes difficult to tame. However, there are a number of interesting old cultivars, originating in warmer climes, notably the Teas and the Chinas, which can be very rewarding when grown in this way. No extra heat is necessary. Roses are quite happy in cold greenhouses where they will flower from early May onwards. Those with larger greenhouses or conservatories can indulge themselves by growing one or two of the more tender but very beautiful climbing Teas and Noisettes, in the way of vines on wires, about 12″ (30 cm) inside the glass. This method was often used by Victorian gardeners, for in addition to providing early flowers, the foliage provided shade for other plants growing in the conservatory in high summer.

The older Tea roses, apart from those which grow happily out of doors, actually prefer the protected environment and can give much pleasure even in the

'Niphetos'

smallest of greenhouses. They are best grown in 10″ (25 cm) pots which make them sufficiently portable to move around. In fact, they are probably better, after flowering in the spring inside, spending the summer outside.

Treatment is much the same as for outdoor roses except that the demands of early flowering will need consideration when feeding, and watering will be necessary every day as they start to grow. Pruning, too – which in the case of Teas should be sparing – is essential, otherwise, in such an environment, they will soon become 'leggy'.

N.B. Roses which grow and flower particularly well under glass are marked Gh in the Dictionary section.

TEN GOOD OLDER BUSH ROSES FOR GROWING IN GREENHOUSES

'Antoine Rivoire', 'Archiduc Joseph' ('Mons. Tillier' in America), 'Briarcliffe', 'Catherine Mermet', 'Dr Grill', 'Général Schablikine', 'Lady Hillingdon', 'Mme Bravy', 'Souvenir de la Malmaison', 'The Bride'.

TEN GOOD OLDER CLIMBERS AND CLIMBING SPECIES FOR GROWING IN GREENHOUSES IN COLDER CLIMATES

'Bouquet d'Or', 'Cloth of Gold', 'Devoniensis', 'Duchesse d'Auerstädt', 'Lamarque', 'Maréchal Niel', 'Niphetos', *R. banksiae lutea*, 'Sombreuil' Climbing, 'William Allen Richardson'.

Old Roses for Their Hips

Whatever may be said by the critics of old and shrub roses, the faculty of some to produce ornamental hips is one attribute which cannot be denied. Such is their attraction that several are well worth growing for their hips alone. In some cases the fruits far excel the flowers. Most of the species bear some form of fruit, varying in shape from plump and round to long and slender, and ranging in colour from bright orange to deep purple and black. They may be highly polished, or bristly. Some are borne erect, others pendulously; and many – presumably those that taste bitter to birds – last well into winter to brighten an otherwise dull time of year.

'Master Hugh' hips

'Eddie's Jewel'

'Scabrosa' hips

Whilst species are the main fruit bearers, some hybrids better known for their flowers also bear hips. 'Scharlachglut', for example, produces huge, urn-shaped fruit of rich scarlet and 'Mme Grégoire Staechelin', a beautiful climbing rose, will produce a good crop of large hips in a good summer.

N.B. Roses which produce a good crop of ornamental fruit are marked F in the Dictionary section.

TEN ROSES AND SPECIES WORTH GROWING FOR THE VALUE OF THEIR ORNAMENTAL HIPS

'Eddie's Jewel', 'Geranium', 'Highdownensis', 'Master Hugh', *R. altaica*, *R. davidii*, *R. rugosa* 'Alba', *R. sweginzowii macrocarpa*, *R. villosa*, 'Scabrosa'.

Roses for Their Ornamental Foliage

Although autumn coloration is not, as a rule, a major feature of shrub and old-fashioned roses, it is sufficiently important to be taken into account when planning a garden. Several species, and indeed hybrids, display richly toned foliage which will harmonize pleasingly with other trees and shrubs at the end of summer. Amongst these are most of the better known Rugosas, whose leaves change with the shortening days to mustard tints deepening to russet before

'Roseraie de l'Hay' foliage

R. × kochiana foliage

falling early in winter. 'Roseraie de l'Hay' is a particularly good example of these.

The small, almost fern-like foliage of the Burnet roses, *R. pimpinellifolia* and its hybrids, changes to russety-red which adds further to the attraction of their black hips. Outstanding, especially after a dry, hot summer with a display of rich coppery-red are the thornless Boursault climbing roses; of this group 'Morlettii' is particularly striking. As mentioned earlier, most of the American native species are conspicuous for their autumn display. *R. virginiana* is perhaps the best example, its naturally shiny leaves changing to burnished gold before the early frosts of winter persuade them, inevitably, to fall.

Autumn colour in roses is, of course, a bonus yet a wide gamut of colours can be found both in foliage and stems throughout the flowering season. Variations, though often subtle, range from the bright rich green of *R. banksiae*, the greys of *R. brunonii* 'La Mortola' and the Albas such as 'Celestial' and 'Maiden's Blush' to the rich plum colouring of *R. glauca*, better known as *R. rubrifolia*, not to mention the Moss roses with their distinctive, variably toned, mossy stems and such hybrids as the lovely 'Albertine' with its rich bronzy-red young shoots and leaflets.

Many of the species have vicious thorns, a problem when attempting to prune, but even these can be an additionally attractive ornamental feature. Such a useful species, often planted specifically for the ornamental value of its thorns, is *R. sericea pteracantha*, whose young stems, in common with others of its group, are covered with broad, wedge-shaped, cherry-red, translucent thorns which when mature become an almost impenetrable armour and give considerable character to what would otherwise be a rather dull shrub in winter. Another interesting shrub, this time for its dense population of tiny thorns, is *R. elegantula-persetosa*, the 'Threepenny Bit Rose'; after it drops its numerous small ferny leaves in winter, this semi-procumbent shrub becomes a tawny-coloured thicket of arching, hairy branches, enhanced even more by hoar frost on a winter's day.

N.B. Old-fashioned and shrub roses with colourful autumn foliage are marked with an A in the Dictionary section.

TEN SHRUB ROSES AND SPECIES WHICH GIVE GOOD AUTUMN COLOUR FROM THEIR FOLIAGE

'Corylus', *R. altaica*, *R. fedtschenkoana*, *R. glauca* (all-year colour), *R. × kochiana*, *R. × microgusa*, *R. nitida*, *R. rugosa* 'Alba', *R. virginiana*, 'Roseraie de l'Hay'.

Older Roses and Their Perfume

The principal attribute that distinguishes the old roses from their modern counterparts is their fragrance. This is not to say that modern roses are not fragrant. In fact, more perfumed roses are probably being introduced than ever before; 'Anna Pavlova', for example, a recent introduction, has a stronger perfume than any other rose I know. However, scent, being intangible, can only be evaluated subjectively, and perfume manufacturers would be out of business if this were not so. I happen to think that quality is more important than quantity, and, for sheer beauty of fragrance, the old roses still have the edge.

The variations of scent are, of course, fascinating. The heady, all-pervading, almost intoxicating perfume of the Centifolias is in no way similar to the refined elegance of that of the Albas; the spicy, somewhat lingering perfume exuded by

'Celestial'

'Louise Odier'

'Souvenir du Docteur Jamain'

the Damasks differs completely from the softer, more delicate fragrance of the Gallicas. Fragrance is not confined to flowers; foliage too can be scented. *R. primula*, for example, has leaves that smell distinctly of incense and many of the Mosses exude the strong odour of balsam from their moss, especially when touched.

High on my list of favourite perfumes from roses is that of the Sweet Briar, *R. eglanteria*. The scent comes from the foliage, especially the young foliage, after rain. Of all our senses smell is probably the most evocative. My first job as an apprentice nurseryman was to weed a large patch of Sweet Briars and a whiff of its scent even now never fails to transport me back to that time.

N.B. A fragrance rating is given to each rose in the Dictionary section.

TWENTY OLD SHRUB ROSES WITH PERFUME OF EXCEPTIONAL REFINEMENT

'Belle de Crécy', 'Celestial', 'Charles de Mills', 'Conrad Ferdinand Meyer', 'Empress Josephine', 'Fantin-Latour', 'Général Kléber', 'Gloire des Mousseux', 'Hugh Dickson', 'Kazanlik', 'Königin von Dänemark', 'Louise Odier', 'Maiden's Blush', 'Mme Hardy', 'Mme Isaac Pereire', *R. centifolia*, 'Reine des Violettes', 'Rose à Parfum de l'Hay', 'Roseraie de l'Hay', 'Souvenir de la Malmaison'.

TEN OLDER CLIMBERS WITH EXCEPTIONAL FRAGRANCE

'Étoile de Hollande' Climbing, 'Gloire de Dijon', 'Guinée', 'Mme Caroline Testout' Climbing, 'Mrs Herbert Stevens', 'Sombreuil' Climbing, 'Souvenir de la Malmaison' Climbing, 'Souvenir du Docteur Jamain', 'Surpassing Beauty', 'Zéphirine Drouhin'.

Shrub and Climbing Roses as Standards

Roses have been grown in this somewhat contrived way for many years, and it seems they have been quite popular throughout that time. I came across a delightful little snippet in *A Shilling Book of Roses* by William Paul, published in the nineteenth century:

> The late Colonel Calvert once told me that he was present at an auction sale of standard roses in London when the 'Village Maid' Rose was first introduced. Twenty plants were sold at one Guinea each. When they came to be distributed only nineteen could be found. Two purchasers seized the nineteenth plant, fought over it and paid half a Guinea each to the Auctioneer as compensation for the mischief done.

If nothing else, this should put the cost of a present-day standard rose into perspective.

Except for a few varieties of weeping standards very few old-fashioned roses are grown in this way, for although such plants are technically feasible, demand is so low as to make them uneconomical for modern nurseries. A few shrub roses, however, do make excellent standards and by searching around or ordering early, it is still possible to obtain stocks of these. Their greatest asset is that they enable other plants to be grown underneath. On my travels I have seen excellent standards, or tree roses as they are called in some parts of the world. Two, in particular, stand out in my memory, both in Australia at the Ruston rose garden; each had trunks thicker than we could ever expect in Europe and heads large

'Bonica', grown as a quarter standard

'Excelsa', grown as a weeping standard

enough to conceal their upright disposition. One was 'Buff Beauty', the other 'Veilchenblau'.

I like half standards, and it has always baffled me why these are not more popular. Their height relative to other plants makes them much less ungainly than full standards.

The cultivation and growing of weeping standard roses is discussed later in the book.

TEN SHRUB ROSES WHICH MAKE GOOD STANDARDS

'Ballerina', 'Buff Beauty', 'Canary Bird', 'Felicia', 'Marjorie Fair', 'Nozomi', 'The Fairy', 'White Pet', 'Yesterday', 'Yvonne Rabier'.

TEN RAMBLING ROSES WHICH MAKE GOOD WEEPING STANDARDS

'Albéric Barbier', 'Albertine', 'Dorothy Perkins', 'Emily Gray', 'Excelsa', 'Félicité Perpétue', 'François Juranville', 'Golden Glow', 'Minnehaha', 'Sanders White'.

Pegging Down

It is sad, though understandable, that the practice of 'pegging down' has now largely died out as a means of getting the best from roses, for it is a most effective and tidy way of persuading masses of flowers from otherwise ungainly and sometimes reluctant plants. Nowadays, however, the cost of this practice, where space might permit it, as in parks and large gardens, would be prohibitive; furthermore, with the advent of newer types of procumbent roses, such areas as lent themselves to pegged-down roses can now be furnished with relative ease. Nevertheless, there are still strong arguments for pegging, which comes into its own in herbaceous and mixed borders, especially near the front of such borders when one bush, if pegged down correctly, can cover quite a large area among other short-growing plants at very little extra cost and effort. The mechanics are quite simple. In the first year, having pruned the roses hard at planting time, the shoots should be allowed to grow up naturally. In the second year, instead of pruning, train these shoots as near to parallel to the ground as possible and also in as many directions as they will permit, holding each shoot in position some 12″ (30 cm) from the ground by wire pegs. The ends of the shoots should be pruned off to an eye. Such training will encourage each parallel shoot to send up numerous vertical shoots, most of which will flower. At the end of each season, these shoots, having flowered, can be shortened and spurred, like fruit trees. In this way – especially if new, main shoots, as they appear, are trained into position to replace less productive older ones – the plants will go on flowering quite efficiently for many years.

The main problem encountered by this method of growing roses is weed control, but if the soil is initially clean and given a generous mulching of bark chippings, any weed growth should be manageable.

Some of the Bourbons and Hybrid Perpetuals are almost custom-built for this purpose. In the past 'Frau Karl Druschki' and 'Hugh Dickson' were two great favourites for pegging down, both fairly free-flowering and with long, strong shoots.

Companion Plants for Old and Shrub Roses

Whether or not roses should be grown in association with other plants is a matter of some argument. As will by now be clear, my own opinion is that roses, admirable though they can be on their own in an enclosed area, should form part of the overall garden scheme. Sometimes roses should even play a minor role, enhancing rather than dominating the landscape. Conversely, where they are dominant, their presence can be enhanced by other plants in less commanding roles.

In the formal setting, old-fashioned roses are often grown in beds separated by paths and lined with edging plants; such edging should be quite formal in habit and not too tall. In the nineteenth century, clipped dwarf box, *Buxus sempervirens* 'Suffruticosa', was used extensively for this purpose, and this can still be effective in re-creating the atmosphere from that period, especially in conjunction with crazy-paving paths. Dwarf lavender, *Lavandula angustifolia*, especially *cv.* 'Munstead', also makes a good natural edging to borders, but careful pruning is necessary to keep it in good condition. Catmint, *Nepeta racemosa*, with its lavender-blue flowers and grey foliage, is the least expensive edging plant but looks

A mixed planting at Leeds Castle, Kent

'François Juranville' growing behind herbaceous plants at Leeds Castle, Kent

A mixed planting in the author's garden in Norfolk

bedraggled and dead in winter, unless clipped back each year. If allowed to do so, it will also over-reach into the rose bed. Other small, shrubby plants suitable for edging are some of the varieties of dwarf hebe, not all of which are fully hardy, and santolina, with grey foliage but yellow flowers, which needs careful placing. One of my particular favourites is *Berberis thunbergii* 'Atropurpurea nana', with bronzy-red foliage, which looks particularly good with roses of most shades of pink.

It is in the more informal areas that shrubby plants can be combined with shrub and old-fashioned roses with some measure of abandon. A few combinations for shrubberies, worth consideration, are as follows:

SHRUBS FOR USE WITH WHITE, PINK AND DEEP RED ROSES

Berberis thunbergii atropurpurea and its various purple forms, *Buddleja davidii* 'Royal Red', *Caryopteris* × *clandonensis*, *Ceanothus*, *Ceratostigma willmottianum*, *Cistus crispus*, *Daphne*, *Deutzia*, *Escallonia* various, fuchsias, hebes – those with grey foliage, *Hydrangea paniculata* 'Grandiflora', *Kolkwitzia*, lavender, *Olearia* × *haastii*, *Philadelphus*, *Pittosporum*, *Potentilla*, *Prunus* × *cistena*, *Romneya coulteri*, rosemary, *Viburnum* × *burkwoodii*, and *Weigela florida* 'Foliis Purpureis'.

SOME PERENNIAL PLANTS IDEAL WITH WHITE, PINK AND DEEP RED ROSES

Aquilegia, *Artemisia*, *Astilbe* – soft colours, *Campanula* – all species and cultivars,

Dianthus (pinks) – most colours, *Geranium* – cranesbill types, *Gypsophila*, *Hosta fortunei*, *Paeonia* – especially the soft-coloured species and cultivars, phlox – soft colours, *Scabiosa*, *Sedum*, *Stachys*.

SMALLER TREES SUITABLE AS A BACKGROUND FOR WHITE, PINK AND DEEP RED ROSES

Amelanchier, *Arbutus unedo*, *Betula pendula* 'Purpurea', *Cercis siliquastrum*,

Early flowering shrub roses with rhododendrons at Mannington Hall, Norfolk

Roses growing with citrus in David Ruston's gardens, South Australia

Roses with herbaceous plants at Sally Allison's garden in New Zealand

Eucalyptus gunnii, *Fagus* 'Purpurea Pendula', *Malus* (crab apple) 'Golden Hornet', 'John Downie' and *M. tschonoskii*, *Morus niger* (black mulberry), *Photinia davidiana*, *Populus alba*, *Prunus* 'Amanogawa', *Prunus* × *subhirtella* 'Pendula Rosea', *Pyrus salicifolia* 'Pendula' (willow-leaved pear), *Salix caprea* and *Salix caprea pendula* (pussy willows), *Sorbus aria* 'Lutescens' and *Sorbus aucuparia* (mountain ash).

SHRUBS FOR USE WITH BRIGHT RED, ORANGE AND YELLOW ROSES

Berberis thunbergii, *B. candidula* and *B.* × *stenophylla*, *Chimonanthus fragrans* and *C. praecox*, *Choisya ternata*, *Cornus stolonifera* 'Flaviramea', *Corylopsis pauciflora*, *Cytisus* (broom) – bright-coloured cultivars, *Euonymus* – variegated cultivars, *Genista* – most cultivars, *Hypericum* – most shrubby cultivars, *Ilex* (holly) – variegated, cultivars, *Ligustrum* (privet) – variegated cultivars, *Mahonia* – all cultivars, *Potentilla* – most shrubby cultivars, *Pyracantha*, *Sambucus nigra* 'Aurea' and *Weigela florida* 'Variegata'.

PERENNIALS FOR USE WITH BRIGHT RED, ORANGE AND YELLOW ROSES

Alchemilla mollis, *Aurinia saxatilis*, *Euphorbia* – various, *Paeonia* – brighter colours, *Rudbeckia* and *Saxifraga* (London Pride).

SMALL TREES FOR USE WITH BRIGHT RED, ORANGE AND YELLOW ROSES

Acer negundo 'Variegatum', *Acer platanoides* 'Drummondii', *Acer pseudoplatanus* 'Brilliantissimum', *Cotoneaster* 'Rothschildianus', *Cytisus battandieri*, *Liquidambar*, *Parrotia persica*, *Populus* × *candicans* 'Aurora', and *Salix alba* 'Chermesina'.

Mixed Climbing Roses

Many delightful combinations can be achieved by mixing climbing roses with other climbing plants. The scope for this is practically limitless and, provided care is taken to ensure that the marriage will work, much pleasure can be derived from experimenting with various combinations. If an interesting colour effect is desired, it is obviously important that all the plants will flower at the same time. *Clematis* (except the *montana* types, which are too vigorous) and roses flowering together are a superb combination, particularly white clematis with purple or dark red roses and vice versa. Summer jasmine also combines well with purple roses.

Roses with Bulbs, Corms, etc.

Spring-flowering bulbs can always be used with shrub and old-fashioned roses, helping to give colour to rose borders at a time of year when roses are at their least interesting. Combining and blending colours is not so important with bulbs since they come into flower well before the roses. As a matter of personal taste, I prefer to keep tulips away from the old-fashioned roses, and to plant them in beds of cluster-flowered and large-flowered cultivars; and even then I would only use the shorter-growing cultivars and some of the species. Daffodils and narcissi are quite at home among old roses, and clumps of these go well among, underneath and alongside them. However, despite their different flowering seasons, I feel that species roses are best paid the compliment of being grown with the less flamboyant bulbs.

Other bulbous plants which make good bedfellows for the older roses are alliums, camassias, chionodoxas, crocuses, galtonias, grape hyacinths, puschkinias, scillas and snowdrops. Most lilies are happy growing with roses, but I sometimes find their upright stance slightly incongruous among the taller shrub roses and therefore feel that they should be planted in fairly large groups for best effect. Most lilies also prefer to keep their heads in the sun and feet in the shade, so this is a good reason to plant them with the shorter-growing roses; and for the same reason I would exclude gladioli altogether, although the shorter-growing crocosmia can be effective. The tuberous-rooted forms of anemone are happy growing in the partial or dappled shade of shrub roses, as are hardy cyclamen. Aconites, if naturalized, give a refreshing lift to a group of rather dull, dormant shrub roses in early spring. Both the bulbous and tuberous-rooted iris flourish in most soils, and groups of these will grow harmoniously with shrub roses. All the above-mentioned flowers are, of course, suitable for growing beneath climbers and ramblers.

Annuals and Biennials with Roses

Annual bedding plants conjure up pictures of massed beds of brightly coloured salvias and French marigolds, but this need not be the case, for several of the annuals can combine well with old-fashioned roses if planted in random groups among the bushes. Petunias, clarkias, ten-week stocks and, among the taller roses, nicotiana, all blend quite well, especially if you can obtain the seed in specific colours. Old-fashioned roses grown in pots, especially those of paler shades, will not object to a few plants of lobelia and alyssum shading their roots and falling gently over the edge of their containers, nor will they object to the company of such upright plants as petunias.

Biennials, too, can look quite at home with old-fashioned roses, especially in cottage gardens where such flowers as hollyhocks, foxgloves, Brompton stocks, aubrieta, forget-me-nots, violets and pansies all help to evoke a feeling of Victoriana.

Old Roses with Herbs

Old-fashioned roses make superb companions for culinary herbs. When strategically placed in the herb garden such roses can add colour, height and scent to a visually rather drab area. Old roses have much in common with herbs,

The author's garden in Norfolk, with assorted roses and 'Shy Maiden' statue

both historically and aesthetically, and a few well-chosen cultivars will help capture an atmosphere from the past.

Conversely, herbs placed in groups among old roses can look most effective and, at the same time, keep the kitchen well supplied throughout the year.

TEN OLD ROSES WHICH FOR REASONS OF ANTIQUITY OR COMPATIBILITY MAKE GOOD COMPANIONS FOR HERBS

'Alain Blanchard', 'Chapeau de Napoléon', 'Comte de Chambord', 'Double White', 'Empress Josephine', *R. centifolia* 'Parvifolia', *R. gallica officinalis*, *R. gallica versicolor*, 'Rose de Meaux', 'Tuscany Superb'.

Fruit and Vegetables with Old Roses

To consider growing fruit and vegetables among roses may seem contrary to all the laws of gardening; but when ground space is limited, and with careful choice of subjects, there is no reason why they should not be grown together. Beetroot, for example, has lush dark red foliage, and a few plants, either in clumps or at random, cannot look out of place; nor do clumps of purple broccoli, spinach or parsley. Marrows and ridge cucumbers, provided the soil is good and fertile, will happily crawl about the shrub rose border without causing offence, least of all to the roses; and the same goes for the odd clump of rhubarb, or bush of whitecurrant, redcurrant and/or gooseberry. I would avoid blackcurrants because of their distinctive smell, but strawberries, especially the delicious alpine species, can make quite a cheerful and useful ground cover.

Wild Flowers with Old Roses

I have already mentioned the use of species roses in the wild garden; conversely, wild flowers can make a most effective ground cover through which to plant both species and many of the less hybrid cultivars of old roses. Wild flowers or even weeds, provided they are not too pernicious, would certainly be welcomed by such types of roses as the Gallicas, Centifolias and Damasks, although the more modern hybrids might well resent too many intrusions of this kind. Wild flowers can arrive naturally and be encouraged to spread by the removal only of those weeds that offend the eye, or which, at a later date, may infest other parts of the garden by their seeds or roots; in particular, couch grass, ground elder, bindweed, thistles, docks and fat hen. Alternatively, wild flowers can be introduced by the sowing of seed or, in some cases, planting; both may be obtained from specialist seedsmen or nurserymen. The list of suitable wild flowers is endless and, in any case, I do not know enough about them to be too specific. If you choose to introduce some wild flowers among your roses, do be sure to purchase your seed rather than taking seed or plants from our countryside. There are few enough left growing there now.

Roses growing amongst assorted shrubs and trees at Plumpton Place, Sussex

Roses growing with foxgloves in the wild garden at Elsing Hall, Norfolk

PART IV

The Dictionary

Introduction

SPECIES

Ever since that great Swedish botanist Carl von Linné (*Linnaeus* in the Latin) laid down the ground rules in the mid eighteenth century, plant systematics have been in a constant state of change. Despite this, however, the basic structure he, with others, devised still remains as the order of things in the plant kingdom. This structure, in simple terms, places groups of plants with common characteristics (not always apparent to the layman such as myself) into divisions. These divisions are, in turn, put into subdivisions, each of which is then split up again into classes. After classes come subclasses which are then divided into orders, the orders into families, the families into tribes and the tribes into genera.

The genus *Rosa* is part of the tribe Roseae, itself part of the family Rosaceae which as well as roses embraces plants as diverse as Potentillas and Apples. It is, however, at the genus level that enough visual characteristics and likenesses emerge within a group for easy recognition of the relationship of one plant to another; and it is at this point in the structure that species emerge: each different but obviously related one to the other and each perpetuating its kind by breeding true to type when fertilized by itself.

In the case of roses, to complicate things just a little more, the genus is split up into four subgenera, *Hulthemia*, *Hesperhodos*, *Platyrhodon* and *Eurosa* (*Rosa*). In turn *Eurosa* is further subdivided into sections according to predominant characteristics and recognizable relationships.*

Following these rules, therefore, in this dictionary I have placed each species in alphabetical order into the section to which it belongs, under its appropriate subgenus heading.

---

* Since the first edition of *Classic Roses*, 1985, my attention has been drawn to an article by Mr E. F. Allen entitled 'A Simplified Rose Classification' which appeared in the Royal National Rose Society's *Rose Annual* 1973. In this article Allen, following 'Rehder', divides the genus *Rosa* into just three subgenera and places these in natural evolutionary sequence as follows – *Hesperhodos*, *Platyrhodon* and *Eurosa* (*Rosa*). It is this sequence which BARB follows (see page 98); but with the addition of *Hulthemia* (*Simplicifolia*) as the first in line. Since in this dictionary I have included the BARB Classification System for Garden Groups, it is proper that I also follow this sequence of botanical division. Thus, the order in which the four subgenera are placed in this book is different from that of the first edition. This change in no way reflects any inaccuracy then, merely an adaptation.

HYBRIDS

Over the years, earlier by chance mutation or natural hybridity, and later by deliberate manipulation or by a combination of all these factors, hybrids occurred, or were developed, with the mixed genealogy of the various species. These lead us to what may be loosely termed the 'garden groups', *viz.* for the old roses, Albas, Gallicas, Damasks, Bourbons, Teas etc., and for the modern roses, Hybrid Teas, Floribundas etc. The garden groups are then placed in their rightful position under the species to which they most owe their lineage. Where lineage is obscure or for any reason impossible to determine, I have used either my instinct or my observations to place them under a heading that seems appropriate for a particular rose.

The Selection of the Species and Cultivars

All but the most obscure species are included, the two main criteria for selection being significance in the genealogy of a particular garden group and garden-worthiness.

In choosing which hybrids to include I analysed the most recent catalogues of the specialist rose nurseries of Britain, America, the Antipodes and the rest of the world, and my final selection consists only of cultivars that are currently available.

I confess to a degree of favouritism in my choice of several roses, but of those selected by far the majority should remain obtainable for quite a few years to come.

In addition to trade catalogues, I have relied heavily on information gleaned from the following invaluable publications: *Find That Rose*, published annually by the British Rose Growers Association; *The Rose Directory*, published periodically by the Royal National Rose Society; *The Combined Rose List* (*Roses in Commerce and Cultivation*), compiled and published annually by Beverly R. Dobson and Peter Schneider, U.S.A.; *Modern Roses 7, 8, 9* and *10*, published by the American Rose Society; Bean's *Trees and Shrubs Hardy in the British Isles* (1984); *Roses* by Gerd Krüssman; and the works of Graham Thomas, Jack Harkness, David Austin and Trevor Griffiths.

The Descriptions

Most of the roses are described from personal experience and observation. For those outside my sphere of knowledge which deserved inclusion, I have used the raiser's description or obtained the information from the most reliable source I could find.

Honours and Awards

Many roses have won awards of excellence at various trial grounds and shows throughout the world. While I acknowledge such achievements as significant and fully accept that such awards generally indicate a good cultivar, I do not believe that they necessarily reflect superiority in a worldwide context, especially where awards are made on an annual basis or after a relatively short period of, say, three years of trial. No specific honours are therefore mentioned except where appropriate in passing.

Credits

Works with more emphasis on botanic systematics and taxonomy often credit those who work or have worked in these fields by placing their names against species which they have discovered, classified, identified or named. This is a gardening book and I have not done this, largely in the interests of simplicity, and not from any lack of respect for those whose names are omitted. In the case of hybrids the raiser's name and nationality, and the hybrid's parentage and date of introduction are included where known.

Synonyms

Where a synonym is in brackets it indicates the registered name of the rose for trademark purposes. Unbracketed synonyms are the names by which they may well be otherwise known in other countries.

Dimensions

Dimensions are expressed in both imperial and metric terms and assume the cultivar to be growing in normal garden soil and pruned regularly according to need.

Presentation

Letters and symbols are used throughout to indicate the special usages, aptitudes and foibles of roses. These are intended only as a guide for those who are not familiar with a particular cultivar; they merely indicate my own experience or, in some cases, the raiser's comments. Colour and degree of fragrance are, for example, from personal observation, likewise susceptibility to disease, which can depend upon factors outside the constitution of a particular cultivar, such as weather, soil conditions or, simply, bad husbandry.

Key to Letters and Symbols

A   Good autumn foliage.

AL   Availability limited to specialist growers.

AW   Available widely.

B   Good for bedding or planting in groups.

C   More or less continuous flowering throughout summer.

CL   Suitable also for use as a climber or pillar rose.

E   Good for exhibition.

F   Worth growing for the ornamental value of their fruit.

G   Procumbent or wide-growing ground-cover cultivars.

Gh   Suitable for forcing or growing in greenhouses.

H   Suitable for hedging.

MF   Moderately fragrant.

N   Suitable for northerly aspect. (N.B.: Roses only tolerate such a situation, they don't necessarily enjoy it).

P   Tolerant of poor soils.

R   Recurrent or repeat flowering (not continuous).

S   Summer flowering only. (Seldom if ever remontant.)

SF   Slightly fragrant.

SP   Spring flowering only.

T   Suitable for growing up into trees.

VF   Very fragrant.

W   Suitable for woodland and covert planting.

BS   Susceptible to black spot.

M   Susceptible to mildew.

R   Susceptible to rust.

◎   Tolerant of shade.

☼   Prefers a sunny position to thrive.

≋   Suggested for growing adjacent to water.

WW   Hates wet weather when in flower.

✂   Good for cutting.

▽   Suitable for growing in pots.

Classification Abbreviations
(for more details see pages 97–100)

BARB = British Association Representing Breeders

MR10 = *Modern Roses 10*

WFRS = World Federation of Rose Societies

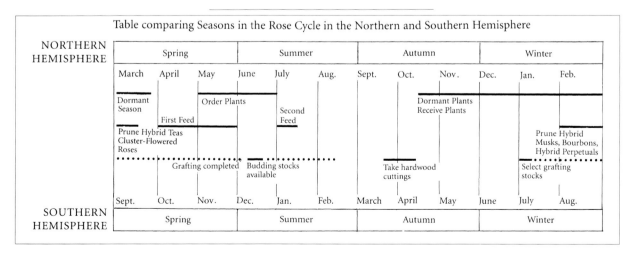

Table comparing Seasons in the Rose Cycle in the Northern and Southern Hemisphere

NORTHERN HEMISPHERE	Spring			Summer			Autumn			Winter		
	March	April	May	June	July	Aug.	Sept.	Oct.	Nov.	Dec.	Jan.	Feb.
	Dormant Season	First Feed	Order Plants		Second Feed				Dormant Plants Receive Plants			
	Prune Hybrid Teas Cluster-Flowered Roses										Prune Hybrid Musks, Bourbons, Hybrid Perpetuals	
	• • • • • Grafting completed		Budding stocks available			• • • • •	Take hardwood cuttings			Select grafting stocks		
	Sept.	Oct.	Nov.	Dec.	Jan.	Feb.	March	April	May	June	July	Aug.
SOUTHERN HEMISPHERE	Spring			Summer			Autumn			Winter		

World Classification Systems

As stated elsewhere, the genus *Rosa* is botanically very complex and its many thousands of hybrids are visually diverse. Botanical complexity, however, need not concern us here except inasmuch as it provides the ground rules for helping to segregate the vast range of hybrids into classes, with each class made up of members with sufficient common characteristics to be meaningfully different from the others.

In modern times three important organizations have concerned themselves with the formulation and the nomenclature of classes:

1. The American Rose Society through their publications *Modern Roses*, of which *Modern Roses 10* is the latest;
2. The World Federation of Rose Societies;
3. The British Association Representing Breeders.

At present, therefore, and probably for the foreseeable future, there are three different lists of classes, not one of which is universally adopted, and this is how it should be at least until there is sufficient consensus for the world to agree on one system. This state of affairs, though very interesting to the expert, is confusing to the layman, although it should not be difficult for any of us to appreciate the dilemmas and challenges these organizations have faced in arriving at their separate conclusions. There is no difficulty with species, nor is there a problem with the old garden roses; all the organizations are agreed on the classification of these since they were largely formed before the rose reached its present-day complexity and are unlikely to be added to very much in the future. It is in the moderns that their lists differ and the reasons for these differences in the end come down to:

1. Which criteria dictate the class into which a cultivar is placed? Is it botanical relationship, visual similarity, usage, habit/behaviour, flower form, flower quantity, geography, tradition, sentiment, something else, or some combination of these?
2. What name is used for a class, given that there ought to be a correlation between the class name and the criteria or criterion used in formulating the group? Or should it be some other adjectival or meaningful name?

In the end all three organizations simply use different class names for what are in fact very similarly comprised groups. The three separate lists follow overleaf.

If we briefly analyse these lists in turn, *Modern Roses 10* is seen to be the most comprehensive and, in many ways, the most accurate except that while the layman will readily understand the term 'hybrid', he or she is less likely to know the difference between one species and another. This may be good in that it stimulates interest or bad in that it can be off-putting, especially in the case of some classes.

The World Federation of Rose Societies divide their classification into three. In their modern roses they link flower form and floriferousness to the behaviour of the plant. The old roses are much the same as the others' lists although I am baffled as to why there is a class for Sweet Briars and not one for Rugosas. With their system the layman knows immediately how a particular modern rose will perform, but from a rather complex set of class names. They basically divide the species into two groups, climbing and non-climbing.

AMERICAN ROSE SOCIETY
Modern Roses 10
(Rose Classes)

1	Alba	29	Hybrid Hugonis
2	Ayrshire	30	Hybrid Laevigata
3	Bourbon	31	Hybrid Macounii
4	Boursault	32	Hybrid Macrantha
5	Centifolia	33	Hybrid Moyesii
6	China	34	Hybrid Musk
7	Climbing Bourbon	35	Hybrid Multiflora
8	Climbing China	36	Hybrid Nitida
9	Climbing Floribunda	37	Hybrid Nutkana
10	Climbing Grandiflora	38	Hybrid Perpetual
11	Climbing Hybrid Perpetual	39	Hybrid Rugosa
12	Climbing Hybrid Tea	40	Hybrid Sempervirens
		41	Hybrid Setigera
13	Climbing Moss	42	Hybrid Spinosissima
14	Climbing Miniature	43	Hybrid Suffulta
15	Climbing Polyantha	44	Hybrid Tea
16	Climbing Tea	45	Kordesii
17	Damask	46	Large-Flowered Climber
18	Eglanteria		
19	Floribunda	47	Moss
20	Gallica	48	Miniature
21	Grandiflora	49	Miscellaneous Old Garden Rose
22	Hybrid Alba		
23	Hybrid Bracteata	50	Noisette
24	Hybrid Blanda	51	Portland
25	Hybrid Bourbon	52	Polyantha
26	Hybrid Canina	53	Rambler
27	Hybrid China	54	Shrub
28	Hybrid Foetida	55	Species
		56	Tea

WORLD FEDERATION OF ROSE SOCIETIES
(Rose Classes)

Modern garden roses

1 Modern Shrub Recurrent Large-Flowered
2 Modern Shrub Recurrent Cluster-Flowered
3 Ground-Cover Recurrent
4 Large-Flowered
5 Cluster-Flowered
6 Dwarf Cluster-Flowered
7 Polyantha
8 Miniature
9 Modern Shrub Non-Recurrent Large-Flowered
10 Modern Shrub Non-Recurrent Cluster-Flowered
11 Ground-Cover Non-Recurrent
12 Rambler Recurrent
13 Large-Flowered Climber Recurrent
14 Cluster-Flowered Climber Recurrent
15 Climbing Miniature Recurrent
16 Rambler Non-Recurrent
17 Large-Flowered Climber Non-Recurrent
18 Cluster-Flowered Climber Non-Recurrent
19 Climbing Miniature Non-Recurrent

Old garden roses

20 Alba
21 Bourbon
22 Boursault
23 China
24 Damask
25 Gallica
26 Hybrid Perpetual
27 Moss
28 Portland
29 Provence (Centifolia)
30 Sweet Briar
31 Tea
32 Ayrshire
33 Climbing Bourbon
34 Climbing Boursault
35 Climbing Tea
36 Noisette
37 Sempervirens

Wild roses

38 Wild Roses Non-Climbing
39 Wild Roses Climbing

This is the system now adopted by the British Royal National Rose Society.

BRITISH ASSOCIATION REPRESENTING BREEDERS
(Rose Classes)

1	Species and Groups	16	Wichuraiana Rambler
2	China	17	Wichuraiana Carpet
3	Noisette	18	Wichuraiana Shrub
4	Tea	19	Gallica
5	Hybrid Tea	20	Damask
6	Floribunda	21	Centifolia
7	Florishrub	22	Moss
8	Miniature	23	Portland
9	Patio	24	Bourbon
10	Climbing Hybrid Tea	25	Hybrid Perpetual
11	Climbing Floribunda	26	English
12	Climbing Miniature	27	Scotch
13	Polyantha	28	Alba
14	Climbing Polyantha	29	Sweet Briar
15	Hybrid Musk	30	Rugosa

The British Association Representing Breeders, largely through the late Jack Harkness, worked out a set of classes based on a combination of simplicity and almost all the criteria mentioned earlier but with emphasis on habit and behaviour. Of the three systems theirs is the shortest list and by far the easiest to understand. Having said this, when I used their system for preparing the Dictionary for this book, I found it difficult to place several of their classes and yet still follow the ground rules of botanical accuracy, which would not have been the case, for different reasons, with either of the other lists. Notwithstanding this, I believe that with more and more diversity appearing within classes, and new types of roses emerging all the time, we have to find a system which is easy to follow, allows for expansion without having to add new classes and, above all, is based on the average person's perception of the different types of roses available to him or her; to me at least, while I do not like some of their class names, the BARB system comes closest at present to this ideal. Others will disagree, and as a lover of roses I can fully appreciate that point of view, but as a nurseryman in daily contact with the average gardener I believe the aim should be for simplicity.

At this point, I intend to indulge myself, 'tongue in cheek', by putting forward an even more simple formula. It is based on the premise that the average person grows the rose for its flower and that all other considerations are supplementary. Therefore size and quantity of flower could be the basis for classification irrespective of pedigree and since non-recurrent roses are now a thing of the past and few will be raised in the future, these could be placed into the most appropriate group of old roses which would stay classified as they are now. To achieve this the term used in America for large-flowered, taller Floribundas could be adopted, namely 'Grandiflora'. This would replace 'Hybrid Tea'. The term 'Floribunda' would stay but would embrace all cluster-flowered roses of all types. Thus, having divided all hybrid roses into two groups, the rest of classification could be based on stature as follows. Miniatures could stay as they are, and the Patios would be named 'Compact'. All roses above 1′ (33 cm) and below 3′ (100 cm) would be termed 'Bush', all those over 3′ (100 cm), 'Shrub'. A new class, 'Procumbent', could absorb the ground-coverers and wide-growing Patios. Climbers could stay as they are now. Ramblers could be placed in the old rose section. As is invariably the case in books on the subject and in nurserymen's catalogues nowadays, all other behavioural factors could be taken into account in the written descriptions of cultivars including the critical one of height, which is always stated in the descriptions of any given cultivar anyway. So my list of classifications for modern roses would be just eleven in number, as follows –

1	Grandiflora Bush	7	Floribunda Shrub
2	Grandiflora Shrub	8	Floribunda Climber
3	Grandiflora Climber	9	Floribunda Procumbent
4	Grandiflora Procumbent	10	Miniature
5	Floribunda Compact	11	Miniature Climber
6	Floribunda Bush		

Throughout the Dictionary section of this book I have indicated, usually after each group heading, the appropriate classification of that group according to each of the organizations.

R. wichuraiana

Simplicifoliae

In evolutionary terms this is the oldest of the four subgenera. It is classified outside the genus by some authorities.
Growth spreading, dense in *Hulthemia persica*, tall and dense in × *Hulthemosa hardii*. Stems angular with many thorns. Leaves entire, without stipules. Flowers produced singly. Fruit greenish, densely spiny, globose. Sepals persist.

SPECIES

Hulthemia persica
× *Hulthemosa hardii*

ORIGIN AND DISTRIBUTION

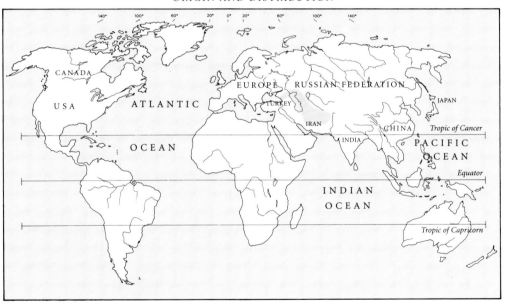

Hulthemia and × Hulthemosa

FORMS AND HYBRIDS

Although included here, strictly speaking, this subgenus may not be part of the genus *Rosa*. However, except for the foliage which is made up of simple leaves without stipules, it grows, behaves and looks just like a rose; so much so that it would be quite wrong to discriminate against it and exclude it on grounds of race. For several years the late Jack Harkness worked with this subgenus and succeeded in raising a number of seedlings, four of which have been introduced. Like their parents, these are quite fascinating and clearly different to any other group of hybrids, making useful garden plants where something out of the ordinary is fancied.

CLASSIFICATION

BARB	Species: Class 1	Hybrids: Class 1
MR10	Species: Class 55	Hybrids: Class 55
WFRS	Species: Class 38	Hybrids: Class 38

Hulthemia persica, R. persica, R. berberifolia

CENTRAL ASIA 1789

Difficult to grow but worth some perseverance. Leaves slender with no stipules. Small, single flowers of bright clear yellow with a browny-crimson splodge in the centre of each; usually borne at end of twiggy, downy, angular shoots with hooked thorns which are arranged in pairs below the leaves. Flowers produced spasmodically for a fairly long season.

S ○ ▽ AL 2′ × 2′ 60 × 60 cm

× Hulthemosa hardii, R. × hardii

Hardy FRANCE c.1830

Hulthemia persica × R. clinophylla

A medium-growing rose, very unusual with small, single, buttercup-size flowers of deep, golden yellow with a striking, bright, reddish-brown eye in the centre. Growth twiggy but dense with spiteful thorns and numerous pinnate leaves without stipules. Supposed not to be hardy.

S ○ ▽ SF AL 6′ × 4′ 1.8 × 1.2 m

'Euphrates'

'Euphrates' (HARunique)

Harkness UK 1986

H. persica seedling

Small to medium, single flowers of rosy-salmon with a pronounced brownish-scarlet blotch in the centre, borne in small clusters. Small, light green foliage similar to that of its parent in shape and produced on a low, dense plant.

S P ◉ ▽ AL 1′ 6″ × 3′ 45 × 90 cm

'Nigel Hawthorne' (HARquibbler)

Harkness U K 1989

H. persica × 'Harvest Home'
Single blooms of salmon-rose each with a pronounced red eye, produced plentifully on a dense, wiry, prickly, well foliated plant of moderately spreading habit. Named for the famous British actor.

C P G ☼ ▽ AL 3′ × 4′ 90 × 120 cm

'Tigris' (HARprier)

Harkness U K 1985

H. persica seedling
Flowers, described by its raiser as 'powder puff-like' are about 1″ (2.5 cm) across, and produced in profusion, each with attractive scarlet markings on a canary-yellow background. Growth is low, slightly spreading and dense.

C P ☼ ▽ AL 1′ 6″ × 2′ 45 × 60 cm

'Xerxes' (HARjames)

Harkness U K 1989

H. persica × 'Canary Bird'
By far the tallest of these fascinating hybrids. This rose produces considerable numbers of bright sulphur-yellow flowers each with a crimson eye. Growth upright.

S P G ☼ AL 5′ × 3′ 1.5 × 1 m

Hesperhodos

Very prickly with small leaves.

SPECIES

R. stellata

ORIGIN AND DISTRIBUTION

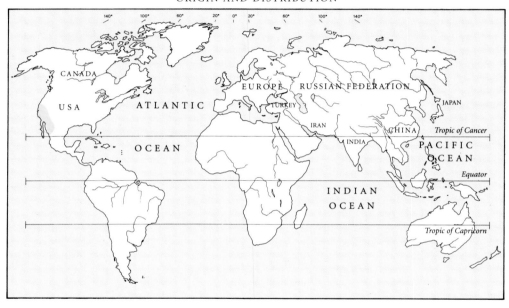

R. stellata

TWO FORMS

This species and its cultivar are both eccentrics of the rose world but this fact, in itself, makes them much more attractive. As plants, they appear and behave very much like a gooseberry bush, except not as tall. Their buds, before opening, and also their fruit, have an exaggerated gooseberry quality in that both are covered with soft spines. Their flowers are not conspicuous *en masse* but, individually, are worth closer inspection. Quite lovely.

CLASSIFICATION

BARB   Class 1
MR10   Class 55
WFRS   Class 38

'Mirifica'

'Mirifica' hips

R. stellata

S. USA 1902

An interesting species with dense, spiny wood and gooseberry-like, light green foliage. Not an easy rose to grow. Flowers rich pinkish-purple, produced solitarily among dense foliage.

S W ◉ ▽ AL 3′ × 3′ 90 × 90 cm

'Mirifica', 'Sacramento Rose'

Greene S. USA 1916

Compact plant, slightly more vigorous than the other form, with many long spines and gooseberry-like foliage. Flowers single, lilac-pink, with prominent stamens. Bush dense and reasonably compact. Easier to grow in the garden than *stellata* but quite difficult for the nurseryman to produce. Hence its rarity.

S W AL 4′ × 4′ 1.2 × 1.2 m

Platyrhodon

Flaky bark and prickly hips.
Small leaves.

SPECIES

R. roxburghii; R. roxburghii normalis; R. roxburghii plena

ORIGIN AND DISTRIBUTION

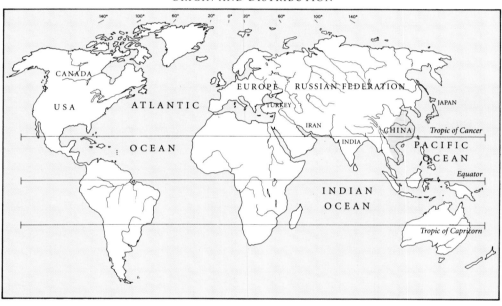

R. roxburghii

FORMS

This little group of fine shrubs deserves to be seen more often. Their weakness, I suppose, is that they are too discreet to draw attention to themselves for they never produce a large crop of flowers. Those they do bring forth are delightful in their simplicity, even the double form. Their foliage is quite refined and their general deportment places them amongst the tidier of the large shrub roses. Not to mention minor features such as peeling bark and spiny fruit which appears never to ripen.

CLASSIFICATION

BARB Class 1
MR10 Class 55
WFRS Class 38

R. roxburghii, R. microphylla, 'Burr Rose', Chestnut Rose'

CHINA 1814

Quite distinct. This medium to tall shrub has leaves composed of up to 15 small, firmly textured, light green leaflets. Stems tawny-brown and slightly angular, both in structure and direction. Bark is flaky on the older wood. Thorns stout and quite long, often arranged in pairs. Flowers single, clear shell-pink, much enjoyed by bees. Fruit spherical, orange-yellow and covered in pronounced, stiff stubble, as are the bracts.

S W P F A ◉ MF AL 8′ × 8′ 2.5 × 2.5 m

R. roxburghii normalis

CHINA 1908

A taller form with soft pink, sometimes blush-white single flowers.

S W P F A ◉ SF AL 10′ × 8′ 3 × 2.5 m

R. roxburghii plena, R. roxburghii roxburghii

1824

Less vigorous than either of the other forms. Fully double flowers, not produced very freely in my experience. A good hedge of this rose can be seen at Ninfa Gardens in Italy.

S W P F A ◉ SF AL 6′ × 5′ 1.8 × 1.5 m

R. roxburghii plena

ROSA Subgenus *Eurosa (Rosa)*

SECTION : *Banksianae*

Growth vigorous, climbing to 20′ (7 m).
Thorns few or none.
Foliage smooth – 5 to 7 leaflets.
Flowers in clusters or singly.
Hips small.
Sepals drop before ripening.

SPECIES

R. banksiae alba plena; R. banksiae lutea; R. banksiae lutescens; R. banksiae normalis; R. cymosa;
R. × fortuniana

ORIGIN AND DISTRIBUTION

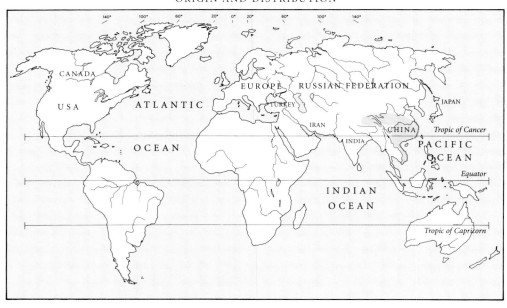

R. banksiae
FORMS AND HYBRIDS

In some parts of the world where frosty winters are not in the normal course of events, 'Banks' roses flourish and are taken for granted, almost to the point of dismissal as weeds. In colder climates, however, they are cherished as rarities and treasured for the beautiful display of scented flowers they provide each spring.

CLASSIFICATION

BARB	Species: Class 1	Hybrids: Class 1
MR10	Species: Class 55	Hybrids: Class 55
WFRS	Species: Class 39	Hybrids: Class 16

R. banksiae alba plena, R. banksiae banksiae

CHINA 1807

Small, rosette-like, double white flowers. Otherwise as *normalis*.

S ☼ Gh SF AL 20′ × 8′ 6 × 2.5 m

R. banksiae alba plena and, above right, *R. banksiae lutea*

R. banksiae lutea, 'Lady Banks Rose', 'Yellow Banksia'

CHINA *c*.1825

Needs a sheltered, sunny spot to flower but hardier than given credit for. Profuse foliage and growth produces large cascading trusses of small, pale yellow, double flowers in late spring. Slightly scented. No thorns.

S ☼ Gh SF AL 20′ × 10′ 6 × 3 m

R. banksiae lutescens

CHINA 1870

Flower diameter rather larger than that of *R. banksiae lutea*, but single and more sweetly scented. Foliage and growth habit also similar but young shoots and leaves sometimes copper-tinted. A good example can be seen on the south wall of

R. banksiae lutescens

Mannington Hall, Norfolk, home of Lord and Lady Walpole.
S ☼ Gh MF AL 20′ × 10′ 6 × 3 cm

R. banksiae normalis

CHINA 1877

Although coming to Europe rather later than its offspring, this climber is probably the true species. Flowers white and single, foliage light green and plentiful, stems free of thorns. Not fully hardy.
S ☼ Gh SF AL 20′ × 8′ 6 × 2.5 m

R. cymosa, R. microcarpa, R. sorbiflora

CHINA c.1904

A lovely but tender, vigorous climber or scrambler, amply clothed with light greyish glabrous foliage. Flowers single, white with pronounced golden-yellow stamens, produced in corymbs. Too tender for all but the warmer parts of Britain.
S ☼ Gh AL 30′ × 20′ 10 × 7 m

R. × fortuniana

CHINA 1850

Thought to be *R. banksiae* × *R. laevigata*
Not known in the wild
Large, scented, double white flowers, almost thorn-less, resembling *R. banksiae*, with slightly darker green leaves and stems. A most interesting rose but needs protection or a sheltered, warm position to flourish. From a nurseryman's viewpoint, much easier to propagate than *R. banksiae* and its other relatives. In fact in some parts of the world it is used as an understock. In its own right very beautiful.
S ☼ Gh MF AL 15′ × 8′ 4.5 × 2.5 m

R. × fortuniana

ROSA Subgenus *Eurosa (Rosa)*

SECTION : *Laevigatae*

Growth sprawling or climbing with hooked, irregular thorns.
Leaves large, mostly of 3, rarely 5, leaflets.
Almost evergreen.
Flowers produced singly.
Hips when formed have persistent sepals.

SPECIES

R. laevigata

ORIGIN AND DISTRIBUTION

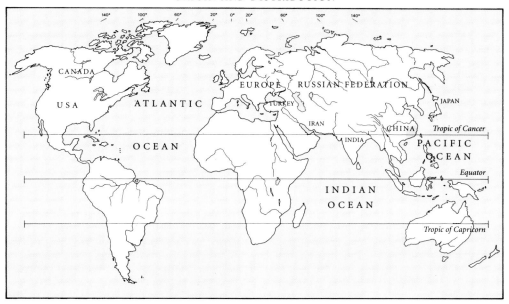

R. laevigata

FORMS AND HYBRIDS

This is another rose that is taken for granted in the more temperate parts of the world. Having struggled for years to keep mine alive and seldom having seen it flower, I recall the pleasure and excitement I felt when I first saw a plant, amongst a dozen neighbours, flowering in a roadside hedgerow in rural Texas where it was flourishing to its heart's content, quite oblivious to the fact that man had introduced it to such a friendly American habitat from its native China almost 200 years earlier.

CLASSIFICATION

BARB	Species: Class 1	Hybrids: Class 1
MR10	Species: Class 55	Hybrids: Class 30
WFRS	Species: Class 39	Hybrids: Class 16

R. laevigata, 'Cherokee Rose'

CHINA *c.*1759 Later naturalized N. AMERICA
Not hardy enough for colder climes. In southern USA, however, it grows wild, having become naturalized since arriving there from China, at the end of the 18th century. Flowers single, very large, white with superb golden-yellow stamens. Leaves crisp, polished and dark, as is the wood, which is armed with large hooked thorns. Fruit oval, with sparse bristles. I have an interesting and rare pale pink form kindly sent to me by Mr Trevor Griffiths of New Zealand, but after nearly eight years I've yet to see it flower.
SP F ☼ Gh SF AL 15′ × 15′ 4.5 × 4.5 m

'Anemone Rose', R. × anemonoides

J. C. Schmidt GERMANY 1895
R. laevigata × a Tea Rose
Large, single, papery pink flowers with a touch of

R. laevigata

'Anemone Rose'

'Cooper's Burmese', above, and 'Ramona', below

'Silver Moon'

mauve, giving this rose a vaguely oriental look. A vigorous climber with angular, branching shoots of darkish brown, liberally armed with hooked thorns. The foliage is dark green, glossy and healthy. Although it prefers a sunny position, it will tolerate sheltered shade.

R P N ○ ◉ SF AL 10′ × 8′ 3 × 2.5 m

'Cooper's Burmese', *R. cooperi*

Introduced 1927
R. laevigata hybrid
An excellent, creamy-white rose which, if carefully placed in a warm, sheltered position, can be very

rewarding. The dark, glossy foliage makes a superb foil for the large, single, scented flowers. The shoots are quite thorny, fawn-brown in colour, and produced in angular fashion. Until recently, this rose was thought to be a hybrid of *R. gigantea*.

R ○ P Gh MF AL 15′ × 15′ 4.5 × 4.5 m

'Ramona', 'Red Cherokee'

Dietrich and Turner USA 1913
'Anemone Rose' sport
This beautiful rose is of much deeper pink than its parent, almost red in fact. In other ways it is identical. It occasionally reverts back to its parent to give the two colours on the same plant.

R P N ○ ◉ MF AL 10′ × 8′ 3 × 2.5 m

'Silver Moon'

Van Fleet USA 1910
R. laevigata hybrid
An interesting rose. Large pure white, single flowers on a vigorous, well-foliated plant. Well scented. Inclined to be rather shy in flowering at times but well worth space, even for just a few of its very lovely flowers. Good in small trees or on trellis. Good examples can be seen in the Queen Mary Rose Garden, Regent's Park, London.

R T N ◉ SF AL 15′ × 8′ 4.5 × 2.5 m

ROSA Subgenus *Eurosa (Rosa)*

SECTION : *Bracteatae*

Growth climbing or angularly sprawling.
Thorns numerous, hooked and in pairs, smaller thorns scattered.
Leaves – 7 to 9 leaflets.
Hips with reflexed sepals which drop off when ripe.

SPECIES

R. bracteata

ORIGIN AND DISTRIBUTION

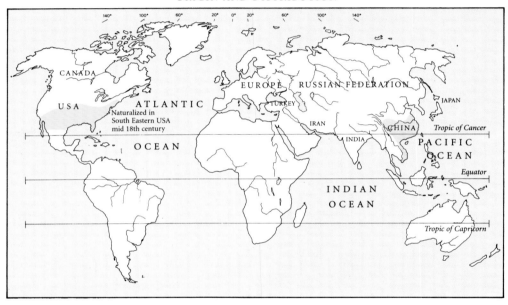

R. bracteata

AND HYBRID

In our climate these two roses can, at one and the same time, be both adorable and infuriating. For, at their best, their flowers are beautiful and, at their worst, they will get frostbite every so often and, just as they are recovering, another cold winter will set them back yet again. This is not to mention their vicious armoury of thorns which is designed to draw blood, it seems, without provocation! But do not be put off. They are both wonderful roses.

CLASSIFICATION

BARB   Class 1
MR10   Class 23
WFRS   Classes 12 and 13

R. bracteata, 'Macartney Rose'

CHINA Introduced 1793

Rather tender but, somewhat paradoxically, flowers happily when placed on a north wall. Lord Macartney brought it back from China in the late 18th century. When introduced to America in the early 19th century, it found the climate in the south and south-east much to its liking and established itself in the wild. Despite its reputation for tenderness, I would like to see this species used more nowadays, even if only as an occasional change from 'Mermaid'. Single, pure white with pronounced golden stamens, the rose has much to offer, especially as it flowers intermittently from June until the November frosts. Well armed with vicious thorns, the stems are fawny-brown and the leaves dark green and slightly downy to touch. Best grown as a climber. My stock came from 'La Landriana', a beautiful garden near Rome. Illustrated on page 4.

C N ◉ MF AL 8′ × 8′ 2.5 × 2.5 m

'Mermaid'

W. Paul UK 1917

R. bracteata × double yellow Tea Rose

Undoubtedly a most useful and beautiful climber. Almost evergreen, the foliage alone has much to commend it, being large and a rich dark green. It is vigorous and the dark brownish-maroon wood is armed with cruel thorns. The rewards from the flowers, however, give ample compensation for scratches received whilst pruning, which should be done sparingly. Each flower is single, 3″–4″ (8–10 cm) across, lemon yellow with pronounced golden brown stamens. It is also fragrant. Furthermore, the flowers are produced throughout the summer, often improving in quality as the season progresses. Slightly more hardy than its parent, *R. bracteata*, from which it inherits tolerance of shade. Quite at home on most walls, including those facing north. In very severe winters it will die back badly from frost damage. During the winters of 1981 and 1985 many well-established plants were killed in the UK.

C N ◉ MF AL 30′ × 20′ 9 × 6 m

'Happenstance', 'Baby Mermaid'

Raiser not known by author USA *c.*1950

A delightful little bush form of 'Mermaid'. Flowers similar in all respects except size, slightly smaller. I was delighted by a specimen of this rose in Kleine Lettunich's garden at Santa Cruz, California. I doubt if it would be hardy in the UK.

C G ◉ ▽ MF AL 3′ × 4′ 90 × 120 cm

'Mermaid'

SECTION : *Pimpinellifoliae*

Growth mostly upright, varying from 3′ to 12′ (1 m to 4 m).
Stems invariably very prickly with many thorns and spines.
Leaves small, some 7 to 9 leaflets, others 9 to 11.
R. sericea 13 to 17 leaflets.
Flowers mostly produced singly on short stems.
Sepals always persist on ripe hips, which are usually oval or
rounded, some smooth, others bristly. Colours varying from
bright red to black, according to species.

SPECIES

*R. × cantabrigiensis; R. dunwichensis; R. ecae; R. foetida (R. lutea); R. foetida bicolor; R. foetida persiana;
R. hemisphaerica; R. × hibernica; R. hugonis; R. × involuta (R. gracilis, R. rubella, R. wilsonii); R. koreana;
R. pimpinellifolia (R. spinosissima); R. primula; R. × pteragonis; R. × reversa; R. × sabinii; R. sericea;
R. xanthina*

GARDEN GROUPS

Austrian Briars; Scotch or Burnet Roses

ORIGIN AND DISTRIBUTION

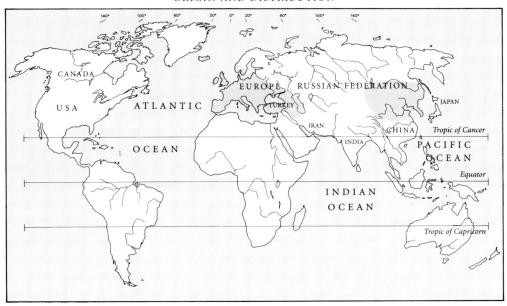

'Golden Chersonese'

'Helen Knight'

R. ecae

FORMS AND HYBRIDS

Not many hybrids have been developed from *R. ecae*, probably because this species is, perhaps, the least amenable of those in this section. However, the two I have selected are excellent and far more easy-going than the others, and can be relied upon for a veritable outburst of golden-yellow each spring.

CLASSIFICATION

	Species	Hybrids
BARB	Species: Class 1	Hybrids: Class 1
MR10	Species: Class 55	Hybrids: Class 54
WFRS	Species: Class 38	Hybrids: Class 10

R. ecae

AFGHANISTAN 1880

A small, very prickly shrub with reddish-brown twigs and small, fern-like leaves. Numerous buttercup-size flowers of deep, rich yellow with pronounced stamens. Needs extra special care, when it can be spectacular.

SP ▽ AL 4′ × 3′ 120 × 90 cm

'Golden Chersonese'

E. F. Allen UK 1963

R. ecae × 'Canary Bird'

A fine shrub with single, rich golden-yellow flowers produced profusely early in the season. Upright growth with dark brownish wood and thorns. Foliage fern-like, individually small but abundant.

SP N P ◉ AL 6′ × 4′ 1.8 × 1.2 m

'Helen Knight'

F. P. Knight UK 1966

R. ecae × *R. pimpinellifolia* 'Altaica'

A useful hybrid with large, slightly cupped, single, deep yellow flowers produced in late spring amid fern-like foliage. Vigorous shrub with darkish stems and thorns. Should be better known.

SP P ◉ AL 5′ × 4′ 1.5 × 1.2 m

R. ecae

R. foetida

FORMS AND HYBRIDS

Quite apart from its great importance as an influence for yellow in modern roses this Asian species has brought forth some interesting close relatives in the form of vigorous shrubs and accommodating climbers. Those described here are an important group in that they can provide some of the few options where a very vigorous, informal shrub of golden-yellow is called for.

CLASSIFICATION

BARB	Species: Class 1	Hybrids: Class 1
MR10	Species: Class 55	Hybrids: Class 28
WFRS	Species: Class 38	Hybrids: Class 10

R. foetida, R. lutea, 'Austrian Briar', 'Austrian Yellow'

ASIA 16th century or earlier

Large, single flowers of rich golden-yellow with prominent stamens produced in early June. Erect growth with large, blackish thorns. Wood chestnut brown. Foliage bright green and firm in texture. An important rose, being largely responsible, with its cousin *R. foetida persiana*, for the yellow colour in our modern roses. The rather unusual specific name comes from the slightly unpleasant smell of the flowers.

S ▽ BS⚘ AL 8′ × 5′ 2.5 × 1.5 m

R. foetida bicolor, R. lutea punicea, 'Austrian Copper'

ASIA 16th century or earlier

A sport from *R. foetida* which occurred at some time in the distant past. In this form the flowers are rich copper-orange, dazzling when at their best. The flower occasionally reverts to the original yellow and sometimes both colours appear on the plant simultaneously. Like its cousins, rather prone to black spot.

S P ▽ BS⚘ AL 8′ × 5′ 2.5 × 1.5 m

R. foetida persiana, 'Persian Yellow'

S.W. ASIA 1837

Very double, globular flowers of rich golden-yellow.

R. foetida, and below, *R. foetida bicolor*

Has all the attributes and faults of both previous species, except that I believe it to be slightly less vigorous. Illustrated on page 5.

S P BS⚘ AL 6′ × 4′ 1.8 × 1.2 m

'Le Rêve'

'Lawrence Johnston', 'Hidcote Yellow'

Pernet-Ducher FRANCE c.1920

Introduced 1923

'Mme Eugène Verdier' × *R. foetida persiana*

An early flowering climber, with clusters of semi-double, yellow flowers and prominent stamens. Fragrant. Very vigorous with abundant, lush, light green foliage.

R P N ◉ VF AL 20′ × 20′ 6 × 6 m

'Le Rêve'

Pernet-Ducher FRANCE c.1920

'Mme Eugène Verdier' × *R. foetida persiana*

Similar to 'Lawrence Johnston', in fact, from the same cross. Slightly less vigorous. Very fragrant. Both are excellent cultivars which should be grown more often. Both will also make good freestanding large shrubs.

R P N ◉ AL 15′ × 15′ 4.5 × 4.5 m

'Star of Persia'

Pemberton UK 1919

R. foetida × 'Trier'

An interesting hybrid from Pemberton proving that he explored other avenues of breeding while working on his Hybrid Musks. Tall, vigorous bush, or small climber. Semi-double, bright yellow flowers which, when fully open, display deep golden stamens to effect. Its parent, *R. foetida*, shows through in its growth habit and foliage. Not often seen these days.

R ☼ ▽ BS⚘ SF AL 10′ × 4′ 3 × 1.2 m

R. hemisphaerica

R. hugonis (see text opposite)

R. hemisphaerica, 'Sulphur Rose'

S.W. ASIA Pre-1625

The globular, fully double, luminous, rich sulphur-yellow flowers nod amid plentiful, greyish-light green foliage. They seldom open properly in damp weather but are well worth perseverance, since when they do open the flowers are most attractive. Prefers a warm, sheltered, sunny position to thrive. Is 'smelly' rather than scented.

S ☼ ▽ WW Gh AL 6′ × 4′ 1.8 × 1.2 m

'**Cantabrigiensis**' (see text opposite)

R. hugonis

FORMS AND HYBRIDS

The few *R. hugonis* hybrids are quite free-flowering, vigorous shrubs, noteworthy like their parent for favouring us with a profusion of fragrant, late spring flowers. They are trouble-free and will tolerate most soils.

CLASSIFICATION

BARB   Species: Class 1   Hybrids: Class 1
MR10   Species: Class 55   Hybrids: Class 29
WFRS   Species: Class 28   Hybrids: Class 10

R. hugonis, 'Golden Rose of China'

CHINA 1899

Large quantities of medium-sized, primrose-yellow flowers, when open slightly cupped, on an upright-growing bush. Densely thorny, the stems are bronzy-brown in colour. Leaves plentiful, with a fern-like quality both in appearance and to touch, turning bronzy-orange in autumn. This rose also bears small, dark red fruit in late summer.

SP P W A F ○ SF AW 8′ × 5′ 2.5 × 1.5 cm

'Cantabrigiensis', *R. × cantabrigiensis*, *R. pteragonis cantabrigiensis*

Cambridge Botanic Gardens UK c.1931
R. hugonis × R. sericea
Less upright than *R. hugonis*. The flowers are larger and slightly paler. They also withstand the weather in a more determined fashion. The shoots are graceful, arching and of a fawny-brown colour, as are the numerous thorns. Foliage is fern-like but not as colourful in autumn as its parents'.

SP P W F ○ SF AW 7′ × 5′ 2 × 1.5 m

'Earldomensis', *R. earldomensis*

Page UK 1934
R. hugonis × R. sericea
A spreading shrub, with flat reddish thorns which are translucent when young. Attractive fern-like foliage. Its flowers are rich yellow, single and produced from late May to early June. Difficult to propagate but easy to grow.

SP ○ P W A F ◉ AL 7′ × 5′ 2 × 2.5 m

'Headleyensis', *R. headleyensis*

Warburg UK c.1920
R. hugonis × unknown, possibly *R. pimpinellifolia* 'Altaica'
A handsome shrub, more compact than *R. hugonis*. Foliage is particularly good, being rich clear green and produced in profusion from thorny, brownish stems. Flowers soft primrose yellow with good perfume.

SP P W A ◉ ▽ MF AL 7′ × 4′ 2 × 1.2 m

R. × involuta, *R. gracilis*, *R. rubella*, *R. wilsonii*

N. EUROPE c.1820
Thought to be a natural hybrid between *R. pimpinellifolia* and *R. villosa*, but the pollen parent could possibly be another species of its habitat region, such as *R. tomentosa* or *R. sherardii*. Flowers of small to medium size, white on a spiny, free-suckering plant with smallish, grey-green leaves. Stems, especially the older ones, are fawnish-brown. Hips oval to round, slightly bristly. Frequently seen in the wild in parts of Scandinavia.

S W P ◉ AL 3′ × 3′ 90 × 90 cm

R. koreana

KOREA 1917
A shrubby, fairly dense, bristly plant with reddish wood. Single, white to blush-pink flowers followed by small, pendulous oval, orange hips. Leaves dark green and numerous, made up of 7 to 11 leaflets.

S W P ◉ ▽ AL 3′ × 3′ 90 × 90 cm

Pimpinellifolias (Scotch Roses)

FORMS AND HYBRIDS

A wealth of very garden-worthy shrub roses have been developed over the years by crossing all and sundry other types with the various forms of wild Scotch roses. In the last century the many and varied double forms were very popular, especially in cottage gardens. Today, they and the newer, taller shrubs developed by Kordes in the 1940s and 50s are still sought after, for they are not only trouble-free and easy to grow but early flowering; and amongst their ranks are several that provide us with the first roses of summer.

CLASSIFICATION

BARB	Species: Class 1	Hybrids: Class 27
MR10	Species: Class 55	Hybrids: Class 42
WFRS	Species: Class 28	Hybrids: Class 10

R. pimpinellifolia, R. spinosissima, 'Scotch Briar', 'Burnet Rose'

EUROPE Pre-1600

Charming, single flowers, creamy-white, sometimes with subtle hints of pink, borne freely early in the season, sometimes repeated spasmodically through to autumn. Pronounced stamens. Foliage small and coarsely fern-like. Stems very densely populated with long, needle-like prickles. Globular, almost black, shiny fruit. Suckers freely when it is grown on its own roots. Happy in most soils, particularly sandy soil. This species has given rise to many and varied hybrids over the years.
SP P W H A ◉ ▽ AW 3′ × 3′ 90 × 90 cm

R. pimpinellifolia 'Altaica', *R. spinosissima* 'Altaica'

ASIA *c.*1818

Dark brownish wood with numerous spiny thorns and soft-textured, well-serrated, greyish light green foliage. Flowers white, large and beautiful, single with pronounced golden-yellow stamens. A useful, healthy shrub with maroon-purple to black hips in the autumn.
SP H W P A F ◉ ▽ AL 5′ × 3′ 150 × 90 cm

R. pimpinellifolia hispida

N.E. ASIA, SIBERIA *c.*1781

An upright-growing shrub with slightly larger foliage than *R. pimpinellifolia* 'Altaica'. Flowers large and soft yellow to white with prominent stamens. Shoots darkish green to brown with numerous spiny thorns. Black hips. Very hardy.
SP H W P ◉ AL 6′ × 4′ 1.8 × 1.2 m

R. pimpinellifolia lutea, 'Lutea'

ASIA

Single deep yellow flowers on an upright bushy plant. Similar to *R. pimpinellifolia* 'Altaica' in growth habit but less vigorous and with smaller flowers.
SP H W P ◉ AL 4′ × 3′ 120 × 90 cm

R. pimpinellifolia 'Nana', *R. spinosissima nana*

Pre-1805

A delightful dwarf form of the Scotch rose. Semi-double to double flowers produced in great profusion in late spring to early summer on a dense mounded plant with fern-like foliage.
SP G W P H ◉ ▽ AL 12″ × 12″ 30 × 30 cm

SCOTCH OR BURNET ROSES

Many double forms of *R. pimpinellifolia* have existed over the years since the first were introduced around 1800. These came in many colours and all were named. Some of these charming little roses are still with us but their names have become lost in time.

The Royal National Rose Society has a good and varied representative collection of these which are well worth seeing in May and June, at St Albans. Only the most important are described here, otherwise the list could be endless.

'Double White', 'Double Pink', 'Double Marbled Pink', etc.

All these have cupped flowers, produced in profusion on tidy, well-foliated, thorny plants. Most produce globular, dark, almost black hips in late summer and all make useful, tidy, rounded shrubs or attractive, thick hedges.

S G F P H A ◉ ▽ SP AL 3′ × 3′ 90 × 90 cm

Double Yellow Forms

Several exist with the yellow in their make-up obviously derived from *R. foetida*. The most important are the following:

'Old Yellow Scotch'

R. × harisonii or **'Harison's Yellow'** (**Yellow Rose of Texas**) – very double USA 1846

'Williams' Double Yellow' – semi-double UK 1828

I find both of these rather coarser in growth than the other colours and prefer an old, double form which I call, simply – 'Old Yellow Scotch'. This is more compact in growth, pleasingly scented and of very ancient origin.

SP G P H ◉ ▽ AL 4′ × 3′ 120 × 90 cm

'Double White'

'Albert Edwards'

Hillier UK 1961

R. pimpinellifolia '**Altaica**' × *R. hugonis*
A free-flowering shrub. Medium-sized, single, creamy to soft yellow flowers on a tall, vigorous, well-foliated plant. One of its finest attributes is its scent. It would be a pleasure to see this rose more widely used as a specimen landscape plant.
SP H P ● MF AL 10′ × 4′ 3 × 1.2 m

'Andrewsii', *R. pimpinellifolia andrewsii*

*c.*1806

Semi-double flowers of deep pinkish-red and cream, displaying yellow stamens when fully open. A dense, well-foliated and well-prickled plant. Sometimes repeating in the autumn, an occasional trait of quite a few of the Pimpinellifolia roses.
SP G W P ● ▽ AL 4′ × 3′ 120 × 90 cm

'Dunwich Rose', *R. dunwichensis*

Discovered growing on sand dunes at Dunwich, Suffolk

UK 1956

A most useful rose, its medium-sized, soft yellow, single flowers have prominent stamens and are produced singly all along arching branches. Foliage light green and fern-like, with many spiky thorns. There is some evidence that this rose could have been growing as a garden cultivar in the late nineteenth century. Illustrated on page 75.
S P G SF ● AL 2′ × 4′ 60 × 120 cm

'Falkland'

UK

Lovely, semi-double, cupped flowers of soft lilac-pink, paling with age to blush white. Compact growth. Typical Pimpinellifolia foliage. Good-sized, deep maroon hips in late summer and autumn.
SP H W P F ● ▽ AL 3′ × 3′ 90 × 90 cm

'Frühlingsanfang'

Kordes GERMANY 1950

'Joanna Hill' × *R. pimpinellifolia* '**Altaica**'
Superb, medium-sized, single pure white flowers with prominent stamens and a strong scent. Dark green foliage on an upright yet arching, healthy plant. Large maroon hips in the autumn.
S P W H F ● VF AL 10′ × 6′ 3 × 1.8 m

'Frühlingsduft'

Kordes GERMANY 1949

'Joanna Hill' × *R. pimpinellifolia* '**Altaica**'

'Frühlingsanfang'

'Frühlingsgold', and below, 'Frühlingsschnee'

A vigorous, healthy plant with rather crinkled, dark green, glossy foliage. Flowers large, fully double, soft lemon-yellow, heavily flushed with pink and highly scented.
S P W H ◍ VF AL 10′ × 6′ 3 × 1.8 m

'Frühlingsgold'

Kordes GERMANY 1937
'Joanna Hill' × R. pimpinellifolia hybrid
Large, almost single flowers of rich golden-yellow paling to primrose. Very profuse blooms on a vigorous, upright plant with dark green foliage. Stems also darkish green and rather thorny. This

is the best known of the 'Frühlings' roses, and deservedly so, for it makes a fine flowering shrub.
SP P W H ◍ VF AW 7′ × 5′ 2 × 1.5 m

'Frühlingsmorgen'

Kordes GERMANY 1942
('E. G. Hill' × 'Cathrine Kordes') × R. pimpinellifolia 'Altaica'
Large, single flowers of cherry-pink and white with primrose centres and golden stamens. Sweetly perfumed. Starts flowering early and is occasionally recurrent. Upright. A well-foliated shrub with dark green leaves. Good maroon hips. An excellent shrub rose.
SP P W H F ◍ MF AW 6′ × 4′ 1.8 × 1.2 m

'Frühlingsschnee'

Kordes GERMANY 1954
'Golden Glow' × R. pimpinellifolia 'Altaica'
Large, single, pure white flowers opening early in the season. Upright in habit with plenty of thorns and dark green foliage.
SP P W H ◍ MF AL 6′ × 4′ 1.8 × 1.2 m

'Frühlingstag'

Kordes GERMANY 1949
'McGredy's Wonder' × 'Frühlingsgold'
Clusters of large, open, semi-double flowers of rich golden-yellow paling to soft yellow with age. Fragrant. Dark leathery foliage. Dark greenish-brown very thorny stems. Upright.
SP P W H ◍ MF AL 7′ × 4′ 2 × 1.2 m

'Frühlingszauber'

Kordes GERMANY 1942
('E. G. Hill' × 'Cathrine Kordes') × R. pimpinellifolia 'Altaica'
Large, almost double flowers of silvery-pink with abundant dark green foliage. An upright, rather thorny plant. Very healthy.
SP P W H ◍ MF AL 7′ × 5′ 2 × 1.5 m

'Glory of Edzell'

Single, clear pink with paler, almost white centres and pronounced stamens. Flowering very early each season. Foliage small but dense, growth upright, spiny.
SP P W H ◍ ▽ AL 5′ × 4′ 1.5 × 1.2 m

'Golden Wings'

Shepherd USA 1956
('Soeur Thérèse' × *R. pimpinellifolia* '**Altaica**') ×
'Ormiston Roy'
Large, clear golden-yellow flowers, almost single
with pronounced golden-brown stamens, produced
abundantly both in clusters and singly, amid rich
light green foliage. Flowers almost continuously from June to October, sweetly scented. An
accommodating shrub in all respects.
C P H ▽ MF AL 5′ × 4′ 1.5 × 1.2 m

'Karl Förster'

Kordes GERMANY 1931
'Frau Karl Druschki' × *R. pimpinellifolia* '**Altaica**'
A showy shrub. Large, almost fully double flowers
with prominent golden stamens when open. Bushy
in growth with greyish light green foliage. A most
useful, underrated rose with intermittent flowers
produced later in summer.
R P W ◕ SF AL 5′ × 4′ 1.5 × 1.2 m

'Maigold'

Kordes GERMANY 1953
'Poulsen's Pink' × 'Frühlingstag'
A superb climber. One of the first to flower each
season. Spectacular when in full flush. In a good
summer will repeat with a good crop of flowers in
the autumn. Fragrant semi-double flowers, rich
golden-yellow discreetly flushed orange. Foliage
rich green and glossy. Strong stems covered in
many reddish-brown thorns.
SP T P N ◕ MF AW 12′ × 8′ 3.5 × 2.5 m

'Mary Queen of Scots'

A beautiful rose. Single flowers with prominent
stamens. Creamy-white in the centre with lilac
and reddish brush marks which deepen towards
the edge of each petal. These are followed by
globular, blackish-maroon fruit on a tidy, twiggy,
well-foliated little plant.
SP P F ◕ ▽ SF AL 3′ × 3′ 90 × 90 cm

'Maigold', and below, '**Karl Förster**'

'Mary Queen of Scots', and below, '**Mrs Colville**'

'Mrs Colville'

Thought to be *R. pimpinellifolia* × *R. pendulina*
A fascinating little shrub with single, crimson-purple flowers, having pronounced stamens and a prominent white eye in the centre. Less thorny than most of its type, with reddish-brown wood and small but plentiful foliage.
SP H P F ◑ ▽ AL 4′ × 3′ 120 × 90 cm

'Ormiston Roy'

Doorenbos HOLLAND 1953
R. pimpinellifolia × *R. xanthina*
Single bright buttercup-yellow flowers on a thorny, dense plant with light green, fern-like leaves. Large purple to black globular hips in the autumn.
SP H P F ◑ ▽ SF AL 4′ × 3′ 120 × 90 cm

'Single Cherry'

Very bright, cherry-red, single flowers with paler, blended blotches of pink. Foliage grey-green and plentiful on a short, bushy plant. Small, rounded, blackish hips later. One of the nicest and most brightly coloured of this group.
SP H P F ◑ ▽ SF AL 3′ × 3′ 90 × 90 cm

'Stanwell Perpetual'

Lee UK 1838
R. damascena bifera × *R. pimpinellifolia*
A prickly, arching but graceful shrub with numerous greyish-green leaves, sometimes becoming mottled purple as though diseased. Though unsightly, this discoloration is not serious, nor, as far as I know, contagious, and it should not put you off this superb old cultivar. The long flowering season – rare in this group – amply compensates for a few discoloured leaves. Flowers fully-double, quartered, soft blush-pink and scented. A favourite of mine.
C H P W ◑ ▽ VF AW 5′ × 5′ 1.5 × 1.5 m

'William III'

Semi-double flowers of rich maroon paling to magenta, followed by dark chocolate-brown hips. Dense foliage on a tidy upright plant. Scented. An exquisite little rose.
S P W F ◑ ▽ MF AL 3′ × 3′ 90 × 90 cm

'Single Cherry', and below, 'Stanwell Perpetual'

R. × *hibernica*, 'Hibernica'

Templeton IRELAND 1765
R. pimpinellifolia × *R. canina*
A most interesting rose, discovered in Ireland at the end of the 18th century but now thought to be extinct there in the wild. The shrub is of medium size with leaves midway between those of *R. pimpinellifolia* and *R. canina*. A special feature of

R. × *hibernica*

this shrub is its superb hips which are coloured like those of *R. canina* and shaped like those of *R. pimpinellifolia*, retaining its sepals in the same fashion as the latter. The flowers are single, medium-sized and bright pink in colour. I have not found it remontant as is claimed for the Irish clone, but it is possible – since the two parent species are obviously compatible – that other clones exist. Professor Nelson, then of Dublin Botanic Gardens and now at Cambridge, drew my attention to the fact that a plant known to have come from Templeton's original is alive and well and growing in Belfast – I now have stock of this clone to test.

S P F W ☼ ▽ MF AL 4′ × 4′ 1.2 × 1.2 m

R. primula, 'Incense Rose'

CENTRAL ASIA, CHINA 1910

Beautiful species with strong, upright, dark brown thorny stems supporting arching laterals. The glossy fern-like foliage has a strong aroma of incense. The flowers, which appear early in the season, are single and soft buttercup-yellow with pronounced stamens; they are strongly scented. A most useful and interesting shrub which sometimes sets small reddish fruit.

SP W P A ▽ VF AL 5′ × 4′ 1.5 × 1.2 m

R. × *pteragonis*

GERMANY 1938

R. hugonis × *R. sericea*

A medium-tall shrub with broad, dark red prickles similar to those of *R. sericea* but with primrose-yellow, five-petalled flowers after those of *R. hugonis*.

SP W P ◉ AL 6′ × 4′ 1.8 × 1.2 m

R. × *reversa*

S. EUROPE 1820

R. pendulina × *R. pimpinellifolia*

Flowers variable from pink to white, mostly pink. Medium-sized oval to round, pendulous, deep red hips. Growth slightly angular with purple shoots, often quite bristly.

SP W P ◉ AL 4′ × 3′ 120 × 90 cm

R. × *sabinii*

N. EUROPE *c.*1850

Very similar to *R.* × *involuta*, differing in having longer flower stamens, large hips and paler stems. Probably a cross between *R. pimpinellifolia* and *R. mollis*.

S W P ◉ AL 3′ × 3′ 90 × 90 cm

R. sericea

FORMS AND HYBRIDS

CLASSIFICATION

BARB	Class 1
MR10	Class 55
WFRS	Class 10

R. sericea, R. omeiensis

HIMALAYAS, W. CHINA 1822

A vigorous shrub with fern-like foliage and stout branches armed with large, hooked thorns and numerous small spines. Thorns bright translucent red while young. Flowers white with pronounced, pale yellow stamens; unlike any other species of the genus, these are comprised of four petals only. Fruit bright red, almost oval but slightly pear-shaped. In some works R. omeiensis is listed as a separate species. Perhaps this is so, but they are so alike that one species is enough here.

SP P F W A AL 10′ × 6′ 3 × 1.8 m

R. sericea chrysocarpa

HIMALAYAS

The same in all aspects as R. sericea except that its fruit is bright yellow.

SP P W F A ● AL 10′ × 6′ 3 × 1.8 m

R. sericea pteracantha, R. omeiensis pteracantha

CHINA Introduced 1890

Delicate, fern-like foliage contrasting with brown stems clad with huge, wedge-shaped thorns. When young these thorns are quite spectacular, being translucent and glowing like rubies against morning and evening sun. The small – at first sight rather insignificant – flowers are quite beautiful on close inspection, being white, single and made up of four petals only. These are followed by small, oval to round, bright orange-red hips.

SP P F W A ● AW 10′ × 6′ 3 × 1.8 m

R. sericea pteracantha atrosanguinea

As above, but with slightly deeper red, translucent thorns and darker red, almost black hips.

SP P F W A ● AW 10′ × 6′ 3 × 1.8 m

Thorns and, right, the flowers of R. sericea pteracantha

'Heather Muir'

'Hidcote Gold'

'Heather Muir'

Sunningdale Nurseries UK 1957

R. sericea seedling

Pure white, single flowers produced, for such a rose, over a long season. Foliage fern-like and stems heavily covered with wedge-like thorns. Upright growth. Produces rich orange fruit.

SP W F A ● AL 8′ × 6′ 2.5 × 1.8 m

'Hidcote Gold'

Hilling and Co. UK 1948

R. sericea seedling

Bright yellow, single flowers in small clusters on a robust plant. Stems liberally covered with broad wedge-shaped thorns and ferny foliage.

SP A W ● AL 8′ × 6′ 2.5 × 1.8 m

'Red Wing'

R. sericea pteracantha × *R. hugonis*

A gracefully growing, arching plant with beautiful, red, wedge-shaped thorns. Flowers creamy-yellow, single. A lovely shrub, not difficult to grow, but difficult to produce in the nursery.

SP A W ● AL 6′ × 4′ 1.8 × 1.2 m

R. xanthina
FORMS AND HYBRID

CLASSIFICATION

BARB	Class 1
MR10	Class 54
WFRS	Class 10

R. xanthina

CHINA 1906

An angular shrub with dark stems and thorns and dark green, fern-like foliage. Flowers small, loosely and raggedly semi-double, scented, rich yellow, produced early in the season.

SP H MF AL 10′ × 6′ 3 × 1.8 m

R. xanthina lindleyii

NORTH CHINA, KOREA 1906

Medium-sized, double yellow flowers are produced from late spring to early summer. Foliage dark green and fern-like, the growth bushy.

P H VF ◉ ▽ AL 8′ × 6′ 2.5 × 1.8 m

'Canary Bird', *R. xanthina spontanea*

CHINA *c*.1908

Probably *R. hugonis* × *R. xanthina*

Tall, angular-growing shrub with dark wood and

'Canary Bird'

thorns, and dark green, fern-like foliage. Produces laterals of a graceful, pendulous habit on which the flowers are borne, making it a useful standard or tree rose in good soils. Single flowers, rich canary yellow with prominent stamens, well scented. Sometimes rather temperamental, suffering partial die-back for no apparent reason; but if the dead wood is removed, it frequently recovers. Flowers sometimes appear intermittently in the autumn.

SP H P ◉ MF AW 8′ × 6′ 2.5 × 1.8 m

R. xanthina lindleyii

'Hippolyte' (see page 143)

ROSA Subgenus *Eurosa (Rosa)*

SECTION: *Gallicanae*

Growth between 3′ to 6′ (1 m to 2 m), upright or arching.
Stems variably armed.
Foliage large, usually made up of 5 leaflets.
Flowers solitary or in threes or fours on long stems.
Sepals reflex and usually drop from hips when ripe.

SPECIES

R. centifolia; R. centifolia alba; R. centifolia muscosa; R. damascena; R. damascena bifera;
R. damascena trigintipetala; R. gallica; R. macrantha; R. richardii

GARDEN GROUPS

Gallicas (French roses); Centifolias (Provence roses); Damasks; Portlands

ORIGIN AND DISTRIBUTION

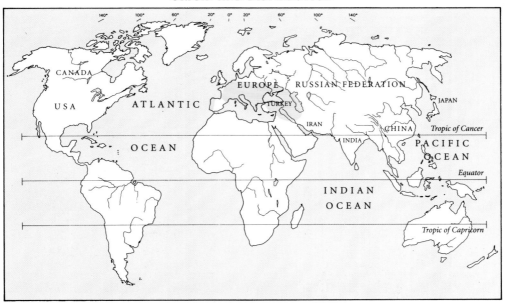

'Agatha'

Gallicas

FORMS AND HYBRIDS

This group has had a considerable influence on the evolution of modern roses. These quietly unobtrusive garden hybrids, although seldom, if ever, remontant, deserve to be far more widely used.

Note: Included in this section are the few forms of *R.* × *francofurtana* which are closely related to the Gallicas. In some works these are listed as a separate group. Likewise some cultivars listed in some works as hybrid Chinas are also included.

CLASSIFICATION

BARB   Species: Class 19   Hybrids: Class 19
MR10   Species: Class 20   Hybrids: Class 20
WFRS   Species: Class 25   Hybrids: Class 25

R. gallica, R. rubra, 'French Rose'

EUROPE, S.W. ASIA Of great antiquity

A rather insignificant rose considering that its genes permeate – to a greater or lesser extent – many modern garden hybrids. Small shrub with upright habit, bearing medium to large, single flowers with pronounced powdery-yellow stamens, petals varying from deep to soft pink. Useful for group planting, perhaps in the wild garden. Some works describe this rose as red but I believe this to be incorrect.

S W P ◍ ▽ SF AL 4′ × 3′ 120 × 90 cm

R. gallica officinalis, 'Apothecary's Rose', 'Red Rose of Lancaster', 'Rose of Provins', 'Double French Rose'

EUROPE, S.W. ASIA Of great antiquity

A showy shrub with erect yet bushy growth and slightly coarse, dark greyish-green leaves. Flowers light crimson, semi-double, quite large, highly scented and profuse in June. In the Middle Ages its scent-retaining properties were much valued by apothecaries. After a good summer, when fully ripe, the small, oval hips are attractive in the autumn.

S P F H ◍ ▽ ✂ VF AW 3′ × 3′ 90 × 90 cm

R. gallica versicolor, 'Rosa Mundi'

EUROPE, S.W. ASIA Of great antiquity

A striking rose. A sport from *R. gallica officinalis,* to which it is identical except in colour. The oldest and best known of the striped roses, it is a varied mixture of light crimson and white. The most romantic of various legends surrounding this rose is that it was named after 'Fair Rosamund', mistress of Henry II.

S F P H ◍ ▽ VF ✂ AW 3′ × 3′ 90 × 90 cm

'Agatha', *R.* × *francofurtana agatha*

EUROPE, S.W. ASIA

Possibly *R. gallica* × *R. pendulina*

Although somewhat taller, this charming rose is probably related to that lovely Gallica 'Empress Josephine'. Flowers slightly smaller and of a deeper pink shade than those of 'Josephine' and with a stronger scent. Densely arching in growth. Leaves soft to touch, yet quite crisp in texture. Few thorns of significance.

S P H ◍ ▽ VF AL 5′ × 4′ 1.5 × 1.2 m

'Agathe Incarnata'

EUROPE *c.*1800

A highly scented rose with soft pink flowers. When

R. gallica officinalis

fully open, the irregular petals create a tight, quartered effect, reminiscent of crumpled crêpe paper. Foliage is grey-green and soft to touch. Growth dense, slightly arching and somewhat thorny. My particular clone seems fairly distinct but occasionally similar cultivars crop up for identification, suggesting that others once existed as garden cultivars. Graham Stuart Thomas suggests Damask influence in the 'Agathe' type Gallicas.

S H ▽ VF P AL 4′ × 4′ 1.2 × 1.2 m

'Alain Blanchard'

Vibert FRANCE 1839

Probably *R. centifolia* × *R. gallica*
Large flowers, slightly more than single in form, crimson smudged purple with very pronounced golden stamens. Foliage dark green; growth dense and bushy. A most pleasing rose with a good scent.

S P ◉ ▽ H VF AL 4′ × 4′ 1.2 × 1.2 m

'Alexandre Laquement'

Laquement FRANCE 1906

Loosely double cupped flowers of rich crimson brushed purple, especially in the centre. Vigorous, relaxed growth. Foliage mid-green.

S P ▽ MF AL 4′ × 3′ 120 × 90 cm

'Ambroise Paré'

Vibert FRANCE 1846

Full quartered blooms on strong necks, deep crimson speckled with purple. Mid-green foliage. Floriferous and vigorous. Relatively thorn-free. Seldom seen nowadays.

S P ◉ ▽ MF AL 4′ × 3′ 120 × 90 cm

'Anaïs Ségalas'

Vibert FRANCE 1837

A shortish-growing, arching shrub, rather more Centifolia-like than Gallica. Perhaps the main feature is the superb form of the flowers, each one seemingly carefully groomed. Highly scented. Colour cerise to crimson, paling towards edges with age. Foliage small and dark green.

S P ▽ VF AL 3′ × 3′ 90 × 90 cm

'Antonia d'Ormois'

From the Roseraie de l'Hay collection FRANCE Pre-1848

Flowering slightly later than some other Gallicas. Fully double cupped flowers. The colour is of soft pink paling to almost white with age, especially at the edges. Since 1986 I have come to know this rose

'Alain Blanchard', and right, 'Assemblage des Beautés'

'Anaïs Ségalas'

well, and it gives me much pleasure each summer.
S P MF AL 5′ × 3′ 150 × 90 cm

'Assemblage des Beautés', 'Rouge Éblouissante'

Originated in Angers FRANCE c.1823
Double, bright crimson flowers changing to purple
with age. They are scented and produced in abundance on a compact, bushy shrub. Foliage rich dark
green; shoots bear few thorns. One of the nicest of
the Gallicas.
S P ◉ ▽ VF AL 4′ × 3′ 120 × 90 cm

'Beau Narcisse'

Miellez FRANCE c.1850
Smallish crimson-purple flowers, paler on the
reverse, in groups or clusters, fully double, fragrant
with green central eye. Foliage plentiful, mid-green.

Tall for a Gallica. Not common in lists these days.
S P MF AL 5′ × 4′ 1.5 × 1.2 m

'Bellard', 'Bellert'

Prior UK 1857
Medium-sized, fully double, quartered flowers with
central green button eye. Clear bright pink
with blush pink edges to the petals. Very fragrant.
Foliage plentiful, bright green. Moderately thorny
stems. Bushy.
S P VF AL 4′ × 3′ 120 × 90 cm

'Belle de Crécy'

Hardy FRANCE 1829
Fairly reliable as a grower but temperamental in
flower. At best can be one of the most beautiful in
its group; at worst, horrid. Flowers are a pleasing
mixture of pinks, greys and mauves, flat and
quartered, often with a clearly defined green eye in
the centre. Highly scented. Growth upright, foliage
grey-green. Stems almost thornless.
S P H ▽ VF MØ WW AW 4′ × 3′ 120 × 90 cm

'Belle Isis'

Parmentier BELGIUM 1845
A small to medium-growing shrub with tidy,
upright growth and grey-green foliage. The
flowers, which are fully double and open flat, are a
lovely delicate shade of pink and have a strong
perfume.
S P ⚡ VF AW 4′ × 3′ 120 × 90 cm

'Belle sans Flatterie'

Godefroy FRANCE 1820
Clusters of deepish pink, fully double, slightly
fluffy flowers with paler lilac-pink edges. Long
sepals. Foliage dark green. Growth upright.
S P MF AL 4′ × 3′ 120 × 90 cm

'Bérénice'

Vibert FRANCE 1818

A very old cultivar seldom seen these days. Crimson-purple, opening flat and quartered, with a lovely perfume. Vigorous, with mid-green, coarsish foliage.

S P VF AL 5′ × 4′ 1.5 × 1.2 m

'Boule de Nanteuil'

Roeser FRANCE 1834

A charming rose. Fully double flowers opening flattish and quartered. Colour deep pink, almost cerise with silver overtones. Like most Gallicas, it is scented. Growth robust and upright. Foliage dark green.

S P H ◍ ▽ VF AL 4′ × 3′ 120 × 90 cm

'Camaieux'

Vibert FRANCE 1830

Striking, double, pale pink blooms striped purplish-crimson, changing with age to a pleasing mixture of lavender and purple. Highly scented. These open rather loosely and are borne on arching stems amid grey-green foliage on a shortish, bushy plant.

S P H ▽ VF ✂ AW 3′ × 3′ 90 × 90 cm

'Cardinal de Richelieu'

Laffay FRANCE c.1840

Beautifully formed rich purple flowers of a delicate velvety texture borne mostly in clusters. Sweetly scented. A compact bush with thin stems which are almost free of thorns. Foliage abundant, smooth and dark green, sometimes edged with maroon.

S P H ▽ VF AW 4′ × 3′ 120 × 90 cm

'Catinat'

Robert FRANCE c.1845

Soft purple with lighter lilac spotting blooms substantially full of small petals. Flowers medium size. Growth vigorous, with mid- to dark green foliage.

S P MF WW AL 5′ × 4′ 1.5 × 1.2 m

'Charles de Mills'

From the Roseraie de l'Hay collection.
An old cultivar

A rose of uncertain origin but one of the best,

especially in good soil. Vigorous, with dark green leaves. Large flowers open to a mixture of purple and deep red. Sometimes the petals form perfect edges as if the rose were enclosed by an invisible, circular frame. When fully open, the flower is quartered and sometimes exposes a dark green eye in the centre. I have tried in vain to find the identity of the man after whom this rose is named.

S P H VF AW 4′ × 4′ 1.2 × 1.2 m

'Camaieux', and below, 'Cardinal de Richelieu'

'Charles de Mills'

'D'Aguesseau', and below, 'De la Maître d'École'

'Complicata'

Of unknown origin

An exceptional rose, good even in poor soils. Vigorous, with arching branches bearing flat, single flowers of bright pink with paler centres and gold stamens, produced freely about mid-June. Foliage matt grey-green, growth quite vigorous. This rose can range in use from a specimen shrub to an effective pillar or climbing rose, or even a tall hedge. In some works it is attributed to *R. macrantha*. Illustrated on page 73.

S P H ◉ VF AW 10′ × 6′ 3 × 1.8 m

'Conditorum'

FRANCE An ancient cultivar

A very useful rose. Rich ruby-red double flowers abundantly produced on a tidy, upright, well-foliated bush. Scented. Foliage dark green.

S H ▽ P MF AL 4′ × 3′ 120 × 90 cm

'Cosimo Ridolfi'

Vibert FRANCE 1842

Shapely cupped flowers of smoky bluish lilac, opening fully double and flat. Scented. Foliage greyish-green. Growth compact. A little-known but delightful Gallica.

S P H ▽ MF AL 3′ × 3′ 90 × 90 cm

'Cramoisi Picoté'

Vibert FRANCE 1834

An unusual rose. Compact, upright growth with thin, almost thornless shoots full of closely packed, small, dark green leaves. Flowers fully double, small and pompon-like when open. Initially crimson, later changing to deep pink with deeper flecks and markings. Sadly, little or no fragrance.

S ▽ P M◌ AL 3′ × 2′ 90 × 60 cm

'D'Aguesseau'

Vibert FRANCE 1823

Bright crimson with deeper shadings. Flowers fully double, quartered when open; each with a dark green, button eye in the centre. Bush upright and vigorous with dark foliage.

S SF AL 4′ × 3′ 120 × 90 cm

'Daphné'

Vibert FRANCE 1819

Medium-sized, rich crimson flowers changing to lilac-pink, fully double, flat and scented, produced in clusters. Vigorous. Foliage mid-green.

S P VF AL 5′ × 4′ 1.5 × 1.2 m

'De la Maître d'École'

Miellez FRANCE 1840

The large, fully double flowers, opening flat and quartered, are unusual, being predominantly pink with lilac highlights and magenta shadings. Heavy, well-spaced flowers, in trusses on an upright bush with lush green foliage and few thorns. (The rose is named after a village near Angers in France and so the name 'Rose du Maître d'École' is incorrect.)

S H P ▽ VF AL 3′ × 3′ 90 × 90 cm

'Duc de Fitzjames'

'Duc de Guiche'

'Duc de Fitzjames'

*c.*1885

For some years I have grown a beautiful, deep pink Centifolia under this name. This must now remain a mystery cultivar. The correct cultivar, which I now have, is deep maroon-purple and vigorous.
S P AL 4′ × 3′ 120 × 90 cm

'Duc de Guiche'

Prévost 1835

An outstanding Gallica. Highly scented. Double, beautifully formed, rich violet-crimson flowers opening to a charming cupped shape. When fully open it reveals a pleasing central green eye. Foliage dark green. Rather sprawly in growth.
S P ◐ VF ✂ AL 4′ × 4′ 1.2 × 1.2 m

'Duchesse d'Angoulême'

'Duchesse d'Angoulême', 'Duc d'Angoulême'

Vibert FRANCE 1835, perhaps earlier

Deep pink buds opening to fully double, small, delicate, saucer-shaped, blush-pink flowers. These appear suspended from the tops of smooth, light green shoots. Foliage crisp and bright green. Related to the Centifolias.

S P H ▽ VF ✂ WW AL 4′ × 3′ 120 × 90 cm

'Duchesse de Buccleugh'

Robert FRANCE 1860

Almost thornless with rich grey-green foliage. This vigorous shrub flowers rather later than some of its group. Well-formed flowers opening flat; their colour is rich magenta-red with pink highlights.

S P MF AL 6′ × 4′ 1.8 × 1.2 m

'Duchesse de Montebello'

Laffay FRANCE 1829

A lovely member of the Gallica family. The small, fragrant, fully double flowers of soft feminine pink are produced on a tidy, upright plant with good, dark green foliage.

S P H ◉ ▽ VF ✂ AL 4′ × 3′ 120 × 90 cm

'Empress Josephine', R. × francofurtana

Early 19th century

Thought to be R. gallica × R. pendulina

Heavily textured petals form large, loosely arranged, double, deep pink flowers with the added charm of heavy veining and lavender and paler pink highlights; scented. The bush has ample foliage, is relatively thornless and is rather sprawly, yet still remains dense. Illustrated on page 30.

S P H ◉ ▽ MF AL 5′ × 4′ 1.5 × 1.2 m

'Georges Vibert'

Robert FRANCE 1853

Colour variously described from carmine to purple but alters with the climate as do so many striped cultivars. In this rose, though, the stripes are always present amid an abundance of petals. A tidy, compact plant suitable for small gardens. Foliage dark green but rather coarse.

S P H ▽ MF AL 3′ × 3′ 90 × 90 cm

'Gloire de France'

Pre-1819

Very double, medium-sized flowers of pale pink

'Duchesse de Montebello', and below, 'Henri Foucquier'

with deeper centres, produced in great profusion, fading rapidly to soft pink, almost white in hot sunshine. Has dark, crisp foliage and is fairly low growing, almost spreading.

S G P ◉ ▽ VF AL 3′ × 4′ 90 × 120 cm

'Henri Foucquier'

Early 19th century

Fully double flowers of clear pink, reflexing when open and exposing a small, button eye. Scented. Rather sprawly, not over-tall, with dark green foliage.

S H P ▽ VF AL 4′ × 4′ 1.2 × 1.2 m

'Hippolyte'

Early 19th century

One of the nicest of the Gallicas. Flowers exquisitely formed, magenta-purple with softer highlights in the centre. Clusters of blooms on thin, almost

thornless stems, often arching downwards. Foliage plentiful, dark green and very smooth for a Gallica.
S P H ▽ VF AL 4′ × 4′ 1.2 × 1.2 m

'Ipsilanté'

Vibert FRANCE 1821
Pale lilac-pink, this lovely old rose deserves more attention. Fully double flowers, large, quartered and

scented. Foliage, on prickly stems, dark green. Growth habit perhaps rather coarse but still quite dense.
S H P ▽ VF AL 4′ × 3′ 120 × 90 cm

'James Mason'

Beales UK 1982
'Scharlachglut' × 'Tuscany Superb'
A beautiful recent introduction to the Gallica group. Flowers slightly more than single, large, up to 4″ (10 cm) across. Scented. Profuse flowering in mid-June. Flowers sometimes partially hidden amid abundant dark green foliage.
S P H ▽ VF AL 5′ × 4′ 1.5 × 1.2 m

'Jenny Duval'

Mid 18th century
Confusion reigns over this rose. In the first edition of *Classic Roses* (1985) I wrote of it as a cultivar in its own right. By the time I wrote *Roses* (1990) I had come to believe that commercial stock was synonymous with 'Président de Sèze'. Now I am not so sure. Susan Verrier in her book *Rosa Gallica* claims it to be distinct. Recently my attention was drawn to the 'Jenny Duval' in the historical collection of roses at the Winterbourne Gardens, Birmingham University, England, assembled by

'James Mason' and above, 'Ipsilanté'

'La Belle Sultane', and right, 'Marcel Bourgouin'

Professor Hawkes, which is very like 'Président de Sèze' in colour. However, neither the Winterbourne nor the Verrier descriptions conform to the old description of crimson-to-mauve. For the time being at least it remains unavailable here in the UK.

'La Belle Sultane', *R. gallica violacea*

Of considerable antiquity – pre-Redouté

Slightly more than single flowers, soft violet smudged purple with very pronounced golden-yellow stamens, produced freely on an upright shrub with rather sparse, coarse grey-green leaves.
S P H ◉ SF AL 5′ × 4′ 1.5 × 1.2 m

'La Plus Belle des Ponctuées'

Hébert FRANCE 1829

A tall, vigorous Gallica with good and ample dark green foliage. The fully double, slightly crumpled flowers are clear rich pink with smudges of softer pink throughout, giving an overall mottled effect.
S P H WW MF AL 6′ × 4′ 1.8 × 1.2 m

'Maître d'École' *see* 'De la Mâitre d'École'

'Marcel Bourgouin'

Corboeuf-Marsault FRANCE 1899

Rich, deep red to purple flowers, semi-double, sometimes showing off yellow stamens. Petals have a velvety texture. Growth upright, with smallish, dark green leaves. I was privileged to work for the late Edward LeGrice when he crossed this and 'Tuscany Superb', among others, with modern roses to breed his famous range of unusually coloured cultivars.
S H P ◉ VF AL 4′ × 3′ 120 × 90 cm

'Nanette'

Double, bright crimson flowers opening flat, with a green eye, blotched or striped with purple. A short-growing cultivar, ideal for the small garden or for growing in pots. Stems almost thornless, well-foliated with dark green leaves.
S P H ◉ ▽ VF AL 3′ × 3′ 90 × 90 cm

'Néron'

Laffay FRANCE 1841

One of the taller Gallicas if given its head. Rich red with a deeper centre, fully double and scented. Foliage mid-green and somewhat coarse in texture.
S P H ◉ SF AL 5′ × 4′ 1.5 × 1.2 m

'Nestor'

*c.*1846

A fine old cultivar. Predominantly magenta but varying with weather, and perhaps soil, from deep pink to mauve. Double, opening flat. Almost free of thorns, foliage crisp and mid-green.
S P ▽ MF ⸢⸽ AL 4′ × 3′ 120 × 90 cm

'Oeillet Flamand'

Vibert FRANCE 1845

I have grown this rose for a number of years, but am still unsure of its authenticity. Vigorous, upright in growth, large, abundant, dark green, rather coarse leaves. Flowers fully double, on erect stems, pinky-white with deeper pink, almost magenta stripes. Not my favourite, but interesting.
S H ▽ P MF AL 4′ × 3′ 120 × 90 cm

'Ohl', and below, 'Orpheline de Juillet'

'Oeillet Parfait'

Foulard FRANCE 1841

Clusters of small-to-medium, pure white flowers erratically striped with bright crimson, opening rather raggedly but fully double. Large, coarse leaves with plentiful thorns for a Gallica. Rather straggly.
S P MF AL 5′ × 4′ 1.5 × 1.2 m

'Ohl'

Vibert FRANCE 1830

A medium-sized plant but vigorous. Large, fully double flowers with deep crimson petals in the centre and violet ones around the edge. Highly scented, it should be grown more widely, for it is

a unique colour combination. Foliage dark green on stout, strong stems with few thorns.
S H ▽ P VF AL 4′ × 3′ 120 × 90 cm

'Ombrée Parfaite'

Vibert FRANCE 1823

A lesser known but good rose. Flower head comprised of several blooms of different colours from purple to pink, sometimes blush-pink, each flower fully double and scented. A short-growing plant, tidy and accommodating, with good, mid-green foliage.
S P ▽ VF AL 3′ × 2′ 90 × 60 cm

'Orpheline de Juillet'

FRANCE Before 1837

Probably related to the Damasks. Large, fully double flowers of crimson-purple turning to fiery red in the centre. Upright growth, moderately vigorous with greyish-green leaves. Similar to 'Belle de Crécy', but deeper in colour.
S H P ▽ VF AL 4′ × 3′ 120 × 90 cm

'Pompon Panachée'

Robert and Moreau FRANCE 1835

Quite old. Perhaps 18th century

A short-growing, wiry, upright plant with ample foliage. Double, shapely flowers of creamy-white to white with pronounced splashes and stripes of deep pink.
S H ▽ SF WW AL 3′ × 2′ 90 × 60 cm

'Président de Sèze', 'Mme Hébert'

Hébert FRANCE c.1836

Unique mixture of magenta and lilac with paler edges. The centre of its large flower is packed with inward-folding petals to form a neat cushion. A superb and interesting rose of manageable proportions. Leaves grey-green. Shoots more thorny than most of its group.
S P ▽ VF WW AL 4′ × 3′ 120 × 90 cm

'Rose du Maître d'École' *see* 'De la Mâitre d'École'

'Ruth'

Wright CANADA 1947

'Mary L. Evans' × 'Alika'

A modern Gallica with soft crimson semi-double to

'Scharlachglut', and below, 'Surpasse Tout'

'Sissinghurst Castle'

double clusters of flowers. Vigorous with mid-green un-Gallica-like foliage.

S P SF ◍ AL 7′ × 4′ 2.1 × 1.2 m

'Scharlachglut', 'Scarlet Fire'

Kordes GERMANY 1952
'Poinsettia' × 'Alika'
This rose is a staggering sight as a fully established shrub. The very large, single flowers are bright velvety-red with pronounced golden stamens. Foliage large, dark green tinted brownish-purple. Stems also brownish-purple and smooth, with a few vicious thorns. Fruit large, urn-shaped and bright orange when ripe. The persistent calyx, not typical of a Gallica, has prompted some to believe this rose to have *R. pimpinellifolia* in its make-up; a possibility also suggested by the shape of its thorns

'Tricolore de Flandre'

and early flowering habit. In addition to making an excellent, solid free-standing shrub, this rose is also good climbing into small trees, demonstrated admirably by a fine specimen, now well established and growing up into a white flowering cherry tree at Mannington Hall, Norfolk.

S T P W F N ◉ SF AW 10′ × 6′ 3 × 1.8 m

'Sissinghurst Castle', 'Rose des Maures'

Probably a very old cultivar, discovered at Sissinghurst and reintroduced by Vita Sackville-West in 1947. Semi-double, deep maroon petals with paler edges and lighter reverses. Prominently displayed golden anthers add to the attractions of this rose. Scented. Foliage small but abundant. Stems thin and brittle with few thorns.

S P ◉ ▽ VF AL 3′ × 3′ 90 × 90 cm

'Surpasse Tout'

Pre-1832

I have never had any great success with this rose but perhaps it is temperamental. At its best it is fully double, opening reflexed with tightly packed petals in the centre. Colour deep cerise-maroon, paling to softer shades with age. Highly scented. I find the plant rather leggy and rather short of foliage.

S P VF M◔ AL 4′ × 3′ 120 × 90 cm

'Tricolore', 'Reine Marguerite'

Lahaye Père FRANCE 1827

Deep pink to crimson flowers with petal edges tinged lilac, shapely and fully double. Scented.

Foliage dark green. Stems moderately thorny.

S H ▽ SF ✹ AL 4′ × 3′ 120 × 90 cm

'Tricolore de Flandre'

Van Houtte BELGIUM 1846

Heavily striped with purple, the pale pink flowers are shapely, almost fully double and scented. Growth upright and accommodating. Ideal for the small garden or as a single rose in pot. Foliage plentiful, smooth and dark green.

S H P ▽ MF ✹ AL 3′ × 2′ 90 × 60 cm

'Tuscany', 'Old Velvet Rose'

Beautiful rich dark red flower with pronounced stamens, seldom seen these days because it has been superseded by 'Tuscany Superb', a slightly more vigorous rose, deeper red, with equally prominent stamens and better foliage. 'Tuscany' may date back well before 1500. Certainly a rose fitting its description is to be found in *Gerards Herball*, 1596.

S P H ▽ VF AL 3′ × 3′ 90 × 90 cm

'Tuscany Superb'

W. Paul UK 1848

Probably a sport from 'Tuscany'

A superb rose. Semi-double flowers large and rich velvety dark red, displaying a golden crown of stamens when fully open. Strongly perfumed. Large, dark green leaves. Strong stems with few thorns.

S P H ▽ VF ✹ AW 4′ × 3′ 120 × 90 cm

'Velutinaeflora'

Date unknown, could be 19th century

Pointed buds with downy sepals open to fragrant, single, pinkish-purple flowers with pronounced stamens. A fascinating, short-growing shrub with dense grey-green foliage. Stems thorny by Gallica standards.

S P ◉ ▽ VF AL 3′ × 3′ 90 × 90 cm

'William Grant'

Grant USA c.1915

Chance find

Discovered in Oregon, USA, by William Grant, an eminent American rosarian, and named after him. Thought to be one of the seedlings of George Schoener, a priest who hybridized roses in California early in this century. It is very vigorous, with Gallica-like foliage. Flowers bright clear pink, semi-double with pronounced golden stamens.

S P SF AL 7′ × 4′ 2.1 × 1.2 m

Centifolias (Provence Roses, Cabbage Roses)

FORMS AND HYBRIDS

Centuries old, these 'roses of the hundred leaves' make superb shrubs. Sometimes coarse and lax in growth, they are often very prickly. The more vigorous forms usually produce large flowers of exquisite shape and intoxicating perfume, with the shorter types producing very double flowers almost invariably in perfect proportion to the size of the plant. Although their flowering season varies from cultivar to cultivar they seldom produce any more flowers after mid-summer.

CLASSIFICATION

BARB	Class 21
MR10	Class 5
WFRS	Class 29

R. centifolia, 'Cabbage Rose', 'Provence Rose'

EUROPE Pre-1600

The fully double flowers of *R. centifolia* prohibit this rose from self-perpetuation from seed. Thus, although this rose is usually listed as a species, it is probably a quite complex hybrid with a genealogy comprising *R. canina*, *R. gallica*, *R. moschata* and others. A rose similar to the present form was cultivated before 1600. A rather lax, medium-sized shrub with thick, coarse, grey-green leaves and abundant thorns. Flowers deep pink, very double, cupped or cabbage-shaped when open. Has a strong, heady perfume. Illustrated on page 6.
S P W VF WW M○ AW 6' × 5' 1.8 × 1.5 m

R. centifolia alba see 'White Provence'

R. centifolia muscosa see Mosses, page 156

'Blanchefleur'

Vibert FRANCE 1835

Flat, very double, sweetly scented flowers of white with occasional pink tints. Slightly tidier than some other Centifolias but the weight of blooms sometimes gives the plant a lax, open gait when in flower. Greyish-green foliage, soft to touch.
S P H ◉ VF AL 5' × 4' 1.5 × 1.2 m

'Bullata', 'Lettuce-leaved Rose'

Cultivated in 16th century

Very large leaves and fewer thorns distinguish this rose from others in the group. Leaves unique, being loosely crinkly both in appearance and to touch. Flowers are almost identical to those of *R. centifolia*, as is its growth habit, except that the density of foliage gives the overall appearance of a tidier plant.
S P W VF WW M○ AL 5' × 4' 1.5 × 1.2 m

'Duchesse de Rohan', 'Duc de Rohan'

c.1860

A fine rose, although in typical Centifolia mould, being rather coarse in growth. I am not sure if it is a true Centifolia, but it fits. Many-petalled flowers fade slightly with age from rich, warm pink to lavender, exuding a characteristically heady, Centifolia perfume, and occasionally repeating, which is, of course, untypical. It could be an early Hybrid Perpetual.
R W VF AL 5' × 4' 1.5 × 1.2 m

'Fantin-Latour'

A suberb mystery rose with records conspicuously absent. The soft, delicate pink flowers and their form place it here, although its foliage is smoother, darker green and more rounded than is typical. Its shoots too are less thorny. I find the all-pervading perfume rather more Alba-like than Centifolia. One theory as to its origins suggests that it was once used as an understock, but since it does not root readily from cuttings, at least for me, I think this unlikely.

S P H W VF AW 5′ × 4′ 1.5 × 1.2 m

'Juno'

1832

Not large but nevertheless an arching shrub. The globular, double flowers of pale blush-pink are produced profusely and are highly scented.

S H P ▽ VF M♂ AL 4′ × 4′ 1.2 × 1.2 m

'La Noblesse'

1856

Exceptionally tidy for a member of this group and flowering rather later in summer. Highly scented, the well-formed, fully double blooms open flat and are soft silvery-pink.

S P H VF AL 5′ × 4′ 1.5 × 1.2 m

'Fantin-Latour'

'Juno', and below, 'La Noblesse'

'Petite Lisette'

'Petite de Hollande', 'Pompon des Dames', 'Petite Junon de Hollande'

HOLLAND c.1800

An attractive and compact small shrub producing many small, double flowers about 1¹/₂″ (4 cm) across. These are cupped until fully open, and clear pink with deeper centres. Scented.

S P ▽ H VF AL 4′ × 3′ 120 × 90 cm

'Petite Lisette'

Vibert FRANCE 1817

Small pompon flowers, 1″ (2.5 cm) across, of deep rose pink, produced in considerable numbers in large, evenly spaced heads. Small, deeply serrated, greyish-green pointed foliage. Makes a useful shrub at the front of borders.

S H ◉ ▽ P VF AL 3′ × 3′ 90 × 90 cm

'Petite de Hollande' (see page 151)

'Petite Orléanaise'

*c.*1900

Another Centifolia with small, pompon-like flowers but taller than the other small-flowered cultivars. Ample foliage and a tidy disposition make this a useful shrub for growing in large tubs or pots.

S P H ▽ VF ✳ AL 4′ × 3′ 120 × 90 cm

'Pompon de Bourgogne', Burgundian Rose, 'Parvifolia', *R. burgundica*

Pre-1664

A superb little rose. Pompon flowers of rosy-claret to purple, some flecked with pink. Growth erect, with foliage packed closely along clustered, thin, stiff stems. An ideal miniature rose for terrace, patio or pot.

S H ▽ MF AL 2′ × 2′ 60 × 60 cm

'Prolifera de Redouté'

*c.*1820

Clear deep rose pink with many petals, opening cabbage-like but with a high frequency of prolifer-ation (another bud growing through the centre of the flower) which makes this a frustrating rose to enjoy. Highly scented. Growth lax, maturing to a medium-sized shrub with coarse, greyish-dark-green foliage.

S P W VF M⚘ AL 6′ × 5′ 1.8 × 1.5 m

'Reine des Centfeuilles'

BELGIUM 1824

Large, scented, double, clear pink flowers, reflexed when fully open, with spiky petals. Ample foli-age, medium to tall and, in my experience, fairly disorderly in habit.

S P MF AL 5′ × 3′ 150 × 90 cm

'Robert le Diable'

FRANCE

A very useful and interesting small shrub rose, slightly procumbent and well endowed with foliage. Colour of flowers – produced later than most – difficult to describe but on the crimson side of red, with lilac and grey highlights and dark purple shad-ings. Often exposes a small, green eye in the centre of each bloom.

S P ▽ VF M⚘ AL 3′ × 3′ 90 × 90 cm

'Robert le Diable', and below, 'Rose de Meaux'

'Rose de Meaux'

Sweet UK Pre-1789

A short, erect, well-foliated bush with massed small double pink flowers – not quite pompons, more like small Dianthus with slightly frilly petals. Scented. A superb shorter-growing rose, temperamental in some soils, but most rewarding once established in good soil. Excellent in pots.

S H ▽ MF AL 2′ × 2′ 60 × 60 cm

'Rose de Meaux White'

As 'Rose de Meaux', but white.

S H ▽ MF AL 2′ × 2′ 60 × 60 cm

'Spong', and below, Village Maid'   'White Provence'

'Rose des Peintres', *R. centifolia* 'Major', 'Centfeuille des Peintres'

A slightly more refined form of *R. centifolia*. Large flowers opening fully double with a lovely clearly defined button eye in the centre. Clear deep pink in colour, with a delicate texture to the petals. Good dark green foliage on a sprawly plant.

S P W VF ✂✕ AL 6′ × 5′ 1.8 × 1.5 m

'Spong'

Spong FRANCE 1805

An unusual name for an unusual rose. Of medium stature, rather like 'Rose de Meaux' with larger flowers and taller growth. Scented. Flowers early and needs 'dead-heading' after flowering, especially in wet weather. Good plentiful greyish-green foliage. According to Graham Stuart Thomas,

Mr Spong was a commercial gardener producing this rose in pots.

S P H ◉ ▽ VF WW AL 4′ × 3′ 120 × 90 cm

'The Bishop'

Full, rosette-shaped flowers of an unusual mixture of magenta, cerise and purple. Fragrant. Flowering rather earlier than most of this group. Upright in habit. An excellent rose although some doubt exists as to its proper classification and, indeed, its true name. In some works listed as a Gallica.

S P H ▽ MF AL 4′ × 3′ 120 × 90 cm

'Tour de Malakoff', 'Black Jack'

Soupert and Notting LUXEMBOURG 1856

A unique rose. Vivid magenta flowers flushed deep purple and fading to lilac-grey, each bloom large, double, but loosely formed. A lanky, lax plant which benefits from support.

S P CL VF ⊱ AL 8′ × 5′ 2.5 × 1.5 m

'Village Maid', 'Belle des Jardins', 'La Rubanée', *R. centifolia variegata*

Vibert FRANCE 1845

A vigorous, thorny rose with strong shoots. Rather more upright than most taller Centifolias. Soft, off-white blooms liberally streaked and striped with pink. Very floriferous when it blooms in late June. Scented. In my experience it occasionally produces the odd bloom in late summer.

S P H VF AL 5′ × 4′ 1.5 × 1.2 m

'White Provence', 'Unique Blanche', 'Vierge de Cléry', *R. centifolia alba*

Discovered in UK 1775

Probably a sport from another Centifolia
In good weather, the flowers of this rose are quite the most beautiful of all white roses. Indeed, if we only had one good summer in ten, it would be worth waiting for just one of its perfect blooms. White silk is the nearest I can come to a simile. The shrub itself is not the most elegant, but who cares, when it yields such rewards.

S P H VF WW AL 5′ × 4′ 1.5 × 1.2 m

'Wretham Rose'

'Wretham Rose'

Introduced by Beales UK 1997
Chance seedling
This rose has many Centifolia likenesses, so I place it amongst them. It is very double, glowing carmine red, almost cerise in some lights. Fragrant. Foliage is darkish green and plentiful. Growth robust. Stems stout and very thorny. Makes a good specimen shrub or even a small climber. Discovered in the gardens of Wretham Lodge by Michael Coates, Anne Hoellering's gardener, growing wild in an ancient hedgerow.

S CL H VF AL 7′ × 6′ 2.1 × 1.8 m

Mosses

FORMS AND HYBRIDS

At some point in the evolution of the Centifolias, Nature decreed that some would have whiskers. Whiskers which take a variety of forms, from multiple stiff bristles to soft, downy glands resembling moss. There are no records of exactly when the first mossy mutation occurred, but they have probably been around far longer than the 300 or so years since the first one was recorded.

Controlled breeding was made possible by the discovery of a chance, single-flowered sport at the beginning of the 19th century. Thirst for novelty then led to the breeding of an abundance of Moss roses and soon between 30 and 40 cultivars were commonly being listed in Victorian nurserymen's catalogues. Many, had they been naked, without the novelty of moss, would never have survived the competition and would quickly have faded into oblivion. They are not over-popular today but a few are underrated. The following are those still available, some of which merit wider recognition.

CLASSIFICATION

BARB	Class 22
MR10	Class 47
WFRS	Class 27

R. centifolia muscosa

17th century

Mossed form of *R. centifolia*.
Identical in all respects except for the moss, which is really closely packed reddish-brown bristles, brighter on young shoots and covering both stems and calyx. Rather prone to mildew.
S P VF MⓍ WW AL 6′ × 5′ 1.8 × 1.5 m

'Alfred de Dalmas', 'Mousseline'

Portemer FRANCE 1855

Any criticism made of Moss roses does not extend to this little charmer, which perhaps really belongs among the Portland Damasks. Blooms semi-double, creamy-pink and scented. It flowers continuously from mid-June to November. Foliage lush, growth tidy and manageable. Its moss is green, tinted pink, turning to russet on older shoots. Can fulfil a variety of roles from massed planting to an outdoor pot plant.
C P H ◍ ▽ MF AW 3′ × 2′ 90 × 60 cm

'À longues pédoncules'

Robert FRANCE 1854

Soft lilac-pink double flowers on a vigorous sprawly shrub with ample, light greyish-green leaves. Flower stalks long with profuse green mossing around globular buds.
S P ◍ W VF AL 5′ × 4′ 1.5 × 1.2 m

'Angélique Quetier'

Quetier FRANCE 1839

Related to damasks
Deep reddish-pink fully double flowers. Fragrant. Leaves crisp, small and pointed, mid-green. Growth upright. Moss greenish-brown.
S P H ◍ VF AL 5′ × 4′ 1.8 × 1.2 m

'Baron de Wassenaer'

Verdier FRANCE 1854

Vigorous, with much dark foliage and considerable moss. Flowers rich bright red to crimson, fully

'Alfred de Dalmas', and below, 'Blanche Moreau'   'Capitaine Basroger'

double, cupped, often borne in clusters on strong stems, in the way of 'William Lobb'.
S P CL VF AL 7′ × 4′ 2 × 1.2 m

'Blanche Moreau'

Moreau-Robert FRANCE 1880

'Comtesse de Murinais' × 'Quatre Saisons Blanc Mousseux'

The bristly, purple, almost black moss on this rose is too often marred by mildew for it to get much attention, although it has beautiful, fully double, pure white, perfumed flowers.
S P ▽ VF M♂ WW AL 4′ × 3′ 120 × 90 cm

'Capitaine Basroger'

Moreau-Robert FRANCE 1890

A distinct feature of this rose is its ability to produce a sparse, second flush of flowers in late summer. Double, deep crimson, scented flowers emerge from tight, globular buds, sprinkled rather than covered with moss. Vigorous, better with support.
R P VF AL 6′ × 4′ 1.8 × 1.2 m

'Capitaine John Ingram'

Laffay FRANCE 1856

Not over-tall, one of the most charming of the Moss roses, deserving more attention. Well endowed with reddish moss on stems, receptacle and calyx. Colour of the fully double flowers varies with weather from dark crimson to purple. Very strongly scented.

S P H ▽ VF AL 4′ × 3′ 120 × 90 cm

'Catherine de Würtemberg'

Robert FRANCE 1843

An upright-growing plant with sparse reddish mossing and ample small, red thorns. Flowers lilac-pink and double, with faint scent.

S P SF AL 6′ × 4′ 1.8 × 1.2 m

'Célina'

Hardy FRANCE 1855

Not exceptionally mossy. Flowers are quite distinctive, of good size, semi-double, and a mixture of cerise, pink and lavender, displaying golden anthers when open. A reasonably tidy shrub but somewhat prone to mildew later in the season.

S P H MF M⚘ AL 4′ × 3′ 120 × 90 cm

'Chapeau de Napoléon', 'Cristata', 'Crested Moss'

Vibert FRANCE 1826

Chance discovery

Fully double, highly scented, cabbage-like, silvery

'Célina', above, and 'Chapeau de Napoléon', below

deep pink flowers enhanced by a fascinating moss formation on the calyx. This is shaped like a cocked-hat, hence the name. Apart from that, it is a useful shrub of medium size, well dressed with foliage. Probably better with support.

S P H VF ✂ AW 5′ × 4′ 1.5 × 1.2 m

'Common Moss', 'Old Pink Moss', 'Communis'

FRANCE Pre-1700

Presumably so called because of its ubiquity, but I suspect it applies to a number of pink Mosses, which were, of course, very common in the 19th century. The rose I grow under this name could well be something else but I find it better than *R. centifolia muscosa* in several respects. It is softer in colour, more regular in shape and tidier in growth habit. From cuttings sent to me over the years I believe that a number of different clones exist, all derivatives of *R. centifolia muscosa*, but selected as better plants because of their more manageable dispositions. All are very well mossed and have an exceptionally strong perfume.

S P VF ✂ AW 4′ × 4′ 1.2 × 1.2 m

'Comtesse de Murinais'

Robert FRANCE 1843

A tall rose, needing support but with much to commend it. Flowers soft pink paling to creamy-white when open, fully double, opening flat, even in wet weather. Moss clear rich green and rather bristly; if touched, it exudes a powerful, lingering, balsam-like odour. Scented moss is by no means unique but in this rose it is stronger than in most others.

S VF AL 6′ × 4′ 1.8 × 1.2 m

'Crested Jewel'

R. S. Moore USA 1971

'Little Darling' × 'Chapeau de Napoléon'

A delightful, shorter-growing Moss rose from that most talented hybridizer Ralph Moore. Conspicuous crested moss formations on the sepals of high-centred, bright pink, semi-double flowers. Tough, leathery mid- to dark green foliage.

S P ▽ SF AL 3′ × 3′ 90 × 90 cm

'Crested Moss' *see* 'Chapeau de Napoléon'

'Deuil de Paul Fontaine'

'Crimson Globe'

W. Paul UK 1890

This sounds more like a vegetable than a rose and, frankly, I sometimes wonder if it is. Probably better in warmer climes.

S VF M AL 4′ × 4′ 1.2 × 1.2 m

'Cristata' *see* 'Chapeau de Napoléon'

'Deuil de Paul Fontaine'

Fontaine FRANCE 1873

Deep red to blackish-purple best describes the colour of this rose. A relatively small, very thorny plant with somewhat coarse foliage. Will repeat in most seasons.

R H ▽ MF AL 3′ × 3′ 90 × 90 cm

'Dresden Doll'

R. S. Moore USA 1975

I feel that this charming miniature Moss rose should be included although I am not sure it should be placed here. Raised recently, it is quite exquisite, with heavily mossed buds and stems and lush green foliage. The small, pointed buds open to fully double, cupped scented flowers of soft pink. Ideal for pots on patios, or even window-boxes.

C P H ▽ MF AW 9″ × 6″ 25 × 15 cm

'Duchesse de Verneuil'

Portemer FRANCE 1856

A very refined Moss rose. Medium-tall and well foliated with light green leaves and dense darker green moss. Flattish flowers composed of many folded petals, which reflex to expose pale pink beneath and brighter pink above. Foliage, moss and flowers combine to pleasing effect.

S P VF WW AL 5′ × 3′ 150 × 90 cm

'Eugénie Guinoisseau'

Guinoisseau FRANCE 1864

Scented flowers in a mixture of shades between deep pink, violet-grey and purple, substantial and more cupped in shape than most. Foliage is smooth with just a hint of gloss, moss is dark green. Bears a second crop of blooms in a good season, surprising in such a tall cultivar. Better grown with support.

S P CL MF AL 6′ × 4′ 1.8 × 1.2 m

'Eugénie Guinoisseau'

'Fairy Moss'

R. S. Moore USA 1969

('Pinocchio' × 'William Lobb') × 'New Penny'
Small mid-pink, semi-double flowers open from
well mossed, pointed buds. Foliage tough, light
green. Growth vigorous and bushy.
C P ▽ SF AL 1′ × 1′ 30 × 30 cm

'Félicité Bohain'

c.1865

A little-grown cultivar, with plentiful but small
foliage. Moss reddish, spreading to the edges of its
young leaves. Smallish flowers have a button eye,
surrounded by folded and crinkled bright pink
petals.
S H P ▽ VF AL 4′ × 3′ 120 × 90 cm

'Gabriel Noyelle'

Buatois FRANCE 1933

'Salet' × 'Souvenir de Mme Kreuger'
Shapely fully double flowers of bright salmon with
highlights of orange and yellow. Fragrant. Foliage
dark green, growth upright, bushy. Recurrent.
R H ▽ VF AL 4′ × 4′ 1.2 × 1.2 m

'Général Kléber'

Robert FRANCE 1856

An excellent cultivar both for beauty of flower and
garden value. Flowers very bright, almost shining
pink, quite large with patternless petals, rather like

'Général Kléber'

small, crumpled pink tissues. Foliage copious, large
and lush, bright green; thick stems covered in bright
lime green moss extending to the tips of the sepals.
Very few thorns.
S P H ▽ VF AL 4′ × 4′ 1.2 × 1.2 m

'Gloire des Mousseux'

Laffay FRANCE 1852

This rose probably has the largest flowers of all the
Mosses and, for once, big is beautiful. Huge, scented
blooms of clear soft pink, fully double and reflexing, produced freely on a substantial plant with light
green leaves and moss.
S P H ▽ VF WW AL 4′ × 3′ 120 × 90 cm

'Goethe'

P. Lambert GERMANY 1911

Several single Mosses existed in Victorian times but
this later cultivar is the only true single available
today. Rich magenta pink with yellow stamens.
Reddish-brown moss and dark bluish-green foliage.
When young, the shoots are pinkish-red. Very
vigorous.
S P SF MO AL 6′ × 4′ 1.8 × 1.2 m

'Gloire des Mousseux', and below, 'Henri Martin'

'Golden Moss'

Dot SPAIN 1932

'Frau Karl Druschki' × ('Souvenir de Claudius Pernet' × 'Blanche Moreau')

This relatively recent Moss rose has very little to commend it, apart from being the only yellow in its group. The flowers are pale yellow, cupped and fragrant, but it detests wet weather and can be rather shy. Perhaps I have never seen it at its best?

S H SF WW AL 5′ × 3′ 150 × 90 cm

'Henri Martin', 'Red Moss'

Laffay FRANCE 1863

Clusters of medium-sized, bright crimson, scented flowers on sparsely mossed stems. Well worth growing for the sheer quantity of flowers produced. Foliage dark green, plentiful.

S P H VF AL 5′ × 4′ 1.5 × 1.2 m

'Hunslett Moss'

Beales UK 1984

[Discovered by the late Humphrey Brooke]

Undoubtedly one of the earliest English Moss roses. Known to have been grown by Humphrey Brooke's ancestors for several generations. Large, full and heavily mossed, deep pink with a strong perfume. Foliage dark on a sturdy upright plant.

S P H ▽ VF AL 4′ × 3′ 120 × 90 cm

'James Mitchell'

Verdier FRANCE 1861

Medium-sized, double flowers of rich, bright pink, produced plentifully in early July. Scented. A healthy plant, perhaps slightly short of foliage and moss, but makes an excellent, tidy shrub.

S P H ● VF AL 5′ × 4′ 1.5 × 1.2 m

'James Veitch'

Verdier FRANCE 1865

A most interesting, short-growing Moss rose. Royal purple with slate-grey highlights. Flowers almost continuously throughout summer. But for mildew, which can be a problem, it is superb. Another Moss rose which could well be placed among the Portland Damasks.

S ▽ VF M✿ AL 3′ × 3′ 90 × 90 cm

'Japonica' see 'Mousseux du Japon'

'Jean Bodin'

Vibert FRANCE 1846

Lilac-pink flowers brushed deeper, with paler edges to the petals. Fully double with central button. Fragrant. Foliage cloudy greyish-green. Growth bushy and upright. Moss brownish and stiff to touch.

S H ▽ VF AL 3′ × 3′ 90 × 90 cm

'Jeanne de Montfort'

Robert FRANCE c.1851

One of the tallest Moss roses, needing support if placed in a shrubbery. Moss dark maroon, leaves dark green and almost glossy. Flowers clear rose pink, borne in large clusters and scented. Worth growing as a small climber or pillar rose.

S P CL VF AL 8′ × 5′ 2.5 × 1.5 m

'James Veitch', and below, 'Jeanne de Montfort'

'Laneii', 'Lane's Moss'

Laffay FRANCE 1854

Very double, crimson flowers produced freely on a sturdy plant. Scented flowers initially cupped but opening flat and reflexed, exposing a large green eye in the centre. Moss slightly darker than the deep green foliage.

S P H ▽ VF AL 4′ × 3′ 120 × 90 cm

'Little Gem'

W. Paul UK 1880

Very popular in late Victorian times, this tidy, useful little rose is very free-flowering and colourful. Flowers in clusters, evenly spaced and pompon-like, bright deep reddish-pink. Stems, which are amply clothed in moss, are provided with many small, closely packed, rich green leaves.

R H ▽ VF AL 3′ × 2′ 90 × 60 cm

'Louis Gimard'

Pernet Père FRANCE 1877

The fully double flowers open flat with rich, deep pink centres, paling towards borders to soft pink. Foliage very dark green with reddish veins and margins. Bristly moss, almost purple.

S P H MF AL 5′ × 3′ 150 × 90 cm

'Ma Ponctuée'

Guillot FRANCE 1857

A very unusual little Moss rose. Small double flowers produced intermittently throughout summer, pinkish-red with white flecks. Well mossed. It needs good soil to flourish. I suspect the cultivar has deteriorated over the years, perhaps by hosting some form of hard-to-detect growth-retarding virus.

R ▽ C SF M⬮ AL 3′ × 3′ 90 × 90 cm

'Maréchal Davoust'

Robert FRANCE 1853

An effective rose where an unusual colour is desired. Each flower's many reflexing petals combine an extraordinary mixture of purples, greys and pinks. The flower sometimes reveals a little green eye in the centre. Fairly tidy with very dark moss and grey-green foliage.

S H P ▽ VF AL 4′ × 3′ 120 × 90 cm

'Laneii', and below, 'Little Gem'

'Marie de Blois'

Robert FRANCE 1852

This free-flowering rose should be more popular. Shoots are well covered with reddish moss and bright green leaves. Flowers are made up of randomly formed clusters of bright pink petals, heavily scented and produced freely each season.

R P H MF AL 5′ × 4′ 1.5 × 1.2 m

'Mme de la Roche-Lambert'

Robert FRANCE 1851

Globular flowers which open flattish with many deep purple petals and which hold their colour even in hot sunshine. Scented. Moss is also deep purple and

'Maréchal Davoust'

'Mme Louis Lévêque'

'Mme de la Roche-Lambert'

'Mousseux du Japon'

leaves dark green. An interesting and useful medium shrub which sometimes repeats its flowers well into the autumn.

R P H ▽ VF M♂ AL 4′ × 3′ 120 × 90 cm

'Mme Louis Lévêque'

Lévêque FRANCE 1898

I first saw this rose in the late Mr Maurice Mason's famous garden at Fincham, Norfolk. Probably then at its best, it was as near perfect as any rose I have ever seen. The flowers are cup-shaped until fully open, quite large and of soft warm pink. More important than the colour is the soft, silky texture of the petals in their nest of moss. The flowers are held on an erect, mossy stem amid large, dark green foliage.

R P H ▽ VF AL 4′ × 3′ 120 × 90 cm

'Monsieur Pélisson' *see* 'Pélisson'

'Mousseline' *see* 'Alfred de Dalmas'

'Mousseux du Japon', 'Moussu du Japon', 'Japonica'

Perhaps the most heavily mossed of all roses, the moss creating an illusion that the stems are far thicker than they actually are. Flowers semi-double, soft lilac-pink with pronounced stamens. Leaves – with mossed stalks – darkish green.

R H ▽ VF AL 4′ × 3′ 120 × 90 cm

'Mrs William Paul'

W. Paul UK 1869

Short, strong stems bearing mossy buds which open to double bright pink flowers with red shadings.

Quite vigorous for such a shrubby plant. This useful rose should be better known, especially as it is spasmodically recurrent.

R H ▽ B VF AL 4′ × 3′ 120 × 90 cm

'Nuits de Young', 'Old Black'

Laffay FRANCE 1845

Compact, erect shrub with small, dark green leaves and small almost double flowers of very dark, velvety maroon-purple, emphasized by golden stamens. Although not heavily mossed, and with somewhat small foliage, this is certainly one of the

'Mrs William Paul', and above, 'Nuits de Young'

best Mosses for general effect, especially where a dark colour is needed.

S P H ▽ VF AL 4′ × 3′ 120 × 90 cm

'Old Pink Moss' *see* 'Common Moss'

'Pélisson', 'Monsieur Pélisson'

Vibert FRANCE 1848

Double flowers, opening flat, red changing to purple with age. A vigorous, upright, shortish grower. Foliage coarse dark green, deeply veined. Stems have stumpy thorns and darkish green moss.

S P ▽ VF M☿ AL 4′ × 3′ 120 × 90 cm

'Princesse Adélaide'

Laffay FRANCE 1845

Foliage dark green, often variegated. Sparsely mossed. Flowers large, shapely, double, soft pink and well scented. Sometimes classed as a Gallica.

S P H ▽ MF AL 4′ × 3′ 120 × 90 cm

'Reine Blanche'

Moreau FRANCE 1857

A lovely, short to medium Moss rose which, for some reason, is often ignored in favour of the taller 'Blanche Moreau'. 'Reine Blanche' has very good moss which is light green, as is its copious foliage. The fully double flowers, although on a weak neck, are shapely, pure white with creamy centres, each with a tight, button eye in the centre.

S P H ▽ VF AL 3′ × 3′ 90 × 90 cm

'René d'Anjou'

Robert FRANCE 1853

This rose is of the most lovely shade of pink, with quite an exquisite perfume. As a shrub, it is not too vigorous, making it ideal for the smaller garden, especially as both foliage and moss have bronze tints which are most marked when young.

S P H ▽ VF AL 4′ × 3′ 120 × 90 cm

'Robert Léopold'

Buatois FRANCE 1941

A shapely, fully double Moss rose of modern colouring, salmon with deeper pink markings on an orangey-yellow background. Sounds a gaudy combination of colour but is actually a pleasing rose. Blooms held on sturdy, stout, well mossed

'Robert Léopold', and below, 'Salet'

stems. Moss brownish. Growth upright. Foliage dark green but rather coarse.

R P ▽ MF AL 4′ × 3′ 120 × 90 cm

'Salet'

Lacharme FRANCE 1854

A rose with considerable character, especially useful for the smaller garden. Flowers clear rose pink, deeper in the autumn, double and somewhat muddled when fully open. Not very mossy, but the leaves are bright green especially when young.

R P H ▽ VF AL 4′ × 3′ 120 × 90 cm

'Shailer's White Moss'

Shailer UK *c.*1788

Supposed to be the white form of *R. centifolia muscosa* but, unless I have a different rose, I find it less sprawly and with darker green foliage. Well mossed, highly scented; full, flat and quartered flowers with the outer layer of petals rather spiky, mostly white but with occasional hints of pink. Very free-flowering.

S P ◉ VF MǑ AL 5′ × 4′ 1.5 × 1.2 m

'Soupert et Notting'

Pernet Père FRANCE 1874

A useful, short-growing, dense bush with well mossed stems and buds. Flowers deep pinkish-red, fully double and quartered when fully open. Sadly, mildew needs to be controlled to get the best from the autumn blooms.

R H ▽ VF MǑ AL 3′ × 2′ 90 × 60 cm

'Souvenir de Pierre Vibert'

Moreau-Robert FRANCE 1867

The fully double flowers are a mixture of red, deep pink and violet, and are produced throughout summer. The shrub is somewhat lax for such a short plant but effective if placed correctly. Ample moss and foliage.

R H ▽ VF AL 4′ × 3′ 120 × 90 cm

'Striped Moss'

Not, I find, the most shapely of roses. The small flowers are various shades of pink with random red markings. Its small upright stature makes it an ideal pot plant.

S P H ▽ MF AL 3′ × 2′ 90 × 60 cm

'White Bath', 'White Moss', 'Clifton Moss'

Salter UK c.1817

Said to be sport of 'Common Moss'

Large fully double pure white flowers. Heavily scented. Foliage, stems and buds well mossed. Of medium vigour.

S P H ◉ ▽ VF MǑ AL 4′ × 3′ 120 × 90 cm

'William Lobb', 'Duchesse d'Istrie', 'Old Velvet Moss'

Laffay FRANCE 1855

Very vigorous, often producing long stems each with large clusters of flowers, so heavy as to bend almost to the ground. Best with support, perhaps of another rose, say a climber of similar colour such as 'Veilchenblau' or a vigorous creamy-white rambler. Well mossed, with ample, large leaves. Flowers large,

'Striped Moss', and below, 'White Bath'

semi-double, a mixture of purple, grey, magenta and pink, slightly paler on the reverse.

S P CL VF AL 8′ × 5′ 2.5 × 1.5 m

'Zenobia'

W. Paul UK 1892

A tall-growing, rather lanky rose with well mossed buds and stems and thick, leathery foliage. Flowers fragrant, globular, reminiscent of an old Hybrid Perpetual in shape, even when fully open. Colour on the cerise side of pink.

S P VF AL 6′ × 4′ 1.8 × 1.2 m

'William Lobb'

'Zoé'

Vibert FRANCE 1830

A free-flowering Moss rose with medium-sized, bright pink, fully double flowers opening flat and made up of many narrow, fluted petals. Scented. Well endowed with brownish red moss. Foliage mid-green. An excellent example of this rose can be seen at Castle Howard, Yorkshire.

S P H ▽ VF AL 4′ × 3′ 120 × 90 cm

Damasks

FORMS AND HYBRIDS

There is little doubt that the Damasks have a close affinity to the Gallicas; the more I delve into the complex lineage of roses, the more confused I become about them. As a mere grower of roses I can only follow, or attempt to follow, the rules laid down by others.

CLASSIFICATION

BARB   Class 20
MR10   Class 17
WFRS   Class 24

R. damascena bifera see '**Quatre Saisons**'

R. damascena trigintipetala see '**Kazanlik**'

R. damascena versicolor see '**York and Lancaster**'

'**Autumn Damask**' *see* '**Quatre Saisons**'

'Belle Amour'

Discovered by Nancy Lindsay 1950
Rich yellow stamens framed by layers of crinkled, salmony-pink petals. Possibly related to the Albas but its foliage and growth, respectively greeny-grey and thorny, places it here among the Damasks.
S P H W MF AL 5′ × 3′ 150 × 90 cm

'Blush Damask', and below, 'Botzaris'

'Blush Damask'

A vigorous, dense but sprawly shrub, very floriferous when in bloom but with fleeting effect. The double medium-sized flowers are rich pink, paling to soft pink at the edges. Needs dead-heading, as the decayed flowers are very reluctant to fall. Probably of ancient origin.
S P H W VF M♂ WW AL 4′ × 3′ 120 × 90 cm

'Botzaris'

1856

Flattish, fully double flowers of creamy-white, often quartered when fully open. Another Damask with an affinity to the Albas, hence its quality perfume. Wood thorny, foliage rich light green. A superb rose which will never outgrow its welcome, even if left unpruned.

S P W H VF AL 4′ × 3′ 120 × 90 cm

'Celsiana'

Pre-1750

An attractive shrub in full bloom, its downy, light grey-green foliage and reasonably contained habit help make it quite unobtrusive whilst 'resting' in late summer. Flowers highly scented, borne in nodding clusters, semi-double, displaying yellow anthers to effect. Clear pink fading to pinkish-white in hot sun.

S P H W VF AW 5′ × 4′ 1.5 × 1.2 m

'Coralie'

c.1860

A rather thorny shrub of medium stature with small greyish-green leaves. Soft pink flowers open flat, rather more than semi-double, petals inclined to fold backwards when fully open. Still attractive when faded to blush-white in hot sun.

S P H W ▽ VF AL 4′ × 3′ 120 × 90 cm

'Gloire de Guilan'

MIDDLE EAST
Introduced by Nancy Lindsay 1949
The flowers, which are very double, and flat when open, are often beautifully quartered, clear pink in colour and richly fragrant. Flowering early summer, inclined to sprawl without support. Foliage light green, wood densely populated with small thorns. Probably of some antiquity.
S P W VF AL 6′ × 4′ 1.8 × 1.2 m

'Hebe's Lip', 'Rubrotincta', 'Reine Blanche'

W. Paul UK Introduced 1912
Thought to be *R. damascena* × *R. eglanteria*
Of unknown but probably very ancient origin. Slightly scented foliage. Flowers almost single, white, tinged with red at the petal edges. Thorny with coarse foliage. Open habit of growth. In the first edition of this book I put this in under the Sweet Briar heading – I now believe it is more correct as a Damask.
S P H W ◍ ▽ VF AL 4′ × 4′ 1.2 × 1.2 m

'Ispahan', 'Rose d'Isfahan'

MIDDLE EAST Pre-1832
Flowering for a long season compared with others of this group, the shapely double, light pink flowers hold both their shape and colour well. Very fragrant. It has attractive foliage and its stems are not over-thorny.
S P H ▽ VF AL 4′ × 3′ 120 × 90 cm

opposite, 'Belle Amour'
'Ispahan', below, and right, 'Gloire de Guilan'

'Kazanlik', *R. damascena trigintipetala*, 'Trigintipetala'

MIDDLE EAST Very ancient

A vigorous rose originating in the rose fields of Bulgaria as one of the cultivars used in the manufacture of 'attar of roses'. Ideal for making potpourri. The soft-textured petals are warm pink and very fragrant. Flower opens to a somewhat shaggy semi-double bloom. Foliage dark green; although it makes a good shrub, it is better with support.

S P W ◒ VF AL 5′ × 4′ 1.5 × 1.2 m

'La Ville de Bruxelles'

Vibert FRANCE 1849

Large, full, pure pink blooms with quartered and incurving centres. Highly scented. A strong, vigorous and upright shrub, which is good for specimen planting.

S P W VF M♔ AL 5′ × 3′ 150 × 90 cm

'Leda', 'Painted Damask'

Probably early 19th century

Double flowers, blush-pink to white, with interesting crimson markings on the margins of each petal. Scented. Tidy and compact, foliage downy grey-green.

S P H ▽ VF AL 3′ × 3′ 90 × 90 cm

'Léon Lecomte'

Origin obscure

Bright glowing pink double flowers, fading to softer shades. Foliage greyish-green. Growth vigorous, tall and upright.

S H P VF AL 5′ × 4′ 1.5 × 1.2 m

'Marie Louise'

*c.*1813

Glowing pink double flowers, full and flat when fully open, well perfumed. Shrub compact, bushy with good foliage, fairly free of at least any vicious thorns.

S P H ▽ VF AL 4′ × 3′ 120 × 90 cm

'Kazanlik', and above, 'Leda'

'Mme Hardy'

'Mme Hardy'

Hardy FRANCE 1832

An elegant and sumptuous rose which can hold its own against any in the shrubbery. Flowers pure white, fully double and quite large considering the number it produces. Centre petals are folded inwards, exposing a rich green eye. Strongly scented. Growth, although strong and vigorous, is accommodating. Foliage bright, almost lime-green, especially when young. An outstanding old cultivar.
S P H ◐ VF AW 5′ × 5′ 1.5 × 1.5 m

'Mme Zöetmans'

Marest FRANCE 1830

Deserving more attention. Soft pink, double, sometimes quartered flowers, paling to blush-white, each with a prominent green eye. A tidy compact shrub for a Damask, with darkish green foliage.
S P H ▽ VF AL 4′ × 3′ 120 × 90 cm

'Omar Khayyam', and right, 'Quatre Saisons'

'Omar Khayyam'

1893

Undoubtedly of some antiquity. Propagated from a plant growing on Edward Fitzgerald's grave in Suffolk, planted there in 1893 from seed gathered from plants on Omar Khayyam's tomb in Nashipur. Medium-sized light pink flowers, double and scented. Shrub shortish, foliage grey-green and downy.
S H ▽ VF AL 3′ × 3′ 90 × 90 cm

'Pink Leda'

Probably GERMANY Pre-1844

Bright clear pink. Identical in all other respects to 'Leda' including the red markings on the outer edge of its petals. Perhaps 'Leda' is a sport from this cultivar.
S P H ▽ MF AL 3′ × 3′ 90 × 90 cm

'Quatre Saisons', *R. damascena bifera*, 'Autumn Damask'

MIDDLE EAST Extremely ancient
Thought to be *R. gallica* × *R. moschata*
A very old rose, loosely double with large, sometimes rather crumpled petals. Colour clear but silky

pink, highly scented. Shrub rather sprawly, foliage greyish and downy. Remontant, it tolerates pruning better than most others in this group. Good for making pot-pourri.

R P W H VF MⒻ AL 4′ × 3′ 120 × 90 cm

'Quatre Saisons Blanc Mousseux'

Laffay FRANCE

'Quatre Saisons' sport

This is a name sometimes applied to other remontant Moss roses. This cultivar is well endowed with brownish-green moss on both stems and buds. Otherwise, except for its white colour, the same as 'Quatre Saisons'. An ancient rose.

R P ◉ VF MⒻ AL 4′ × 3′ 120 × 90 cm

'Rose d'Hivers'

An odd little rose, placed here for want of another home. Rather un-Damask-like, with small, grey foliage and twiggy, yellowish-green shoots. Its flowers are small, though quite shapely; they pale towards the margins from clear pink to white. I have somehow managed to lose this rose from stock.

R P H W ◉ ▽ SF AL 3′ × 3′ 90 × 90 cm

'St Nicholas'

James UK 1950

Possibly a chance seedling of an unknown Damask × *R. gallica* An odd rose but none the less attractive for that. Short-growing, the shrub has downy grey leaves and vicious thorns. Flowers are almost single, pink with rich golden anthers. A charmer when seen

'St Nicholas'

in early evening sunlight. If not dead-headed, produces good, attractive hips.

R H ▽ VF MⒻ AL 3′ × 3′ 90 × 90 cm

'Trigintipetala' *see* 'Kazanlik'

'York and Lancaster', *R. damascena versicolor*

Pre-1551

Inconsistent blush-pink and white flowers. Sometimes mottled, sometimes with two colours on different flowers on the same head, semi-double and scented. Inclined to be rather untidy. Foliage grey, thorns numerous. More a collector's rose than of real garden merit, in my opinion at least.

S P H W ◉ VF AW 5′ × 4′ 1.5 × 1.2 m

Portlands

Although in some works this group is classified as a sub-group of the Damasks, it is now generally accepted that they have enough unique common characteristics to be grouped together as a separate class. It is true that *R. damascena* and perhaps some of its hybrids played an important part in its early development but, as this class has evolved, its genealogy has become mixed and other influences dominate it, not least that of the Gallicas, from where, I believe, several of its subjects have acquired their short, tidy growth habit.

Amongst the ranks of the Portlands are some of the most useful of the old garden roses, for with their accommodating nature and willingness to flower throughout the summer they make ideal subjects for the smaller garden and for growing in containers.

CLASSIFICATION

BARB	Class 23
MR10	Class 51
WFRS	Class 28

'Arthur de Sansal'

'Arthur de Sansal'

Cartier FRANCE 1855

A short-growing rose, well-foliated and very free-flowering, sadly marred by a strong desire to mildew. Flowers very double, rosette-form, dark crimson-purple and scented.

R H ▽ VF M⚬ AL 3′ × 2′ 90 × 60 cm

'Blanc de Vibert'

Vibert FRANCE 1847

White, double flowers with a touch of pale lemon in the base and a strong scent. Bush upright, well clothed with Gallica-like foliage. Very useful but quite rare these days. Flowers sometimes fail to develop properly in wet weather or poor soil.

R B ▽ VF AL 3′ × 3′ 90 × 90 cm

'Comte de Chambord'

Moreau-Robert FRANCE 1863

'Baronne Prévost' × 'Portland Rose'

An outstanding member of this group, with plentiful, large, grey-green foliage which sometimes hides the buds, at least until the flowers are fully open. Flowers are large – for such a small plant – with many petals of rich warm pink, exuding a strong, heady perfume.

C P H B VF ✂ AW 3′ × 2′ 90 × 60 cm

'Comte de Chambord', and below, 'Jacques Cartier'

'Delambre'

Moreau-Robert FRANCE 1863

Fully double, deep reddish-pink flowers freely borne on a compact plant. Dark green, healthy foliage.

P H B ◉ ▽ VF AL 3′ × 2′ 90 × 60 cm

'Duchess of Portland', 'Portland Rose'

ITALY c.1790

Parentage obscure, said to be 'Quatre Saisons' × 'Slater's Crimson China'

A very useful rose, of ancient origin, important as the progenitor of its race. Single to semi-double flowers freely borne on a short, well-foliated plant, cerise-red with pronounced golden stamens. Scented. Useful for group planting but needs dead-heading for best effect.

R P H B ▽ SF AL 3′ × 2′ 90 × 60 cm

'Indigo'

Laffay FRANCE c.1830

Freely produced, fully double, glowing deep purple flowers with an occasional thin white stripe on some of the petals. A few stamens show through when fully open. Scented. Foliage plentiful, rich green. Growth upright. A most useful and lovely cultivar.

R P H B VF AL 3′ × 2′ 90 × 60 cm

'Duchess of Portland'

'Jacques Cartier'

Moreau-Robert FRANCE 1868

Very much like 'Comte de Chambord', especially in growth habit. Flowers, however, less cupped and much flatter in appearance, both when in bud and fully open; shortish petals give it an attractive, ragged look. The colour is deep pink fading towards the edges to soft pink. It is blessed with a good perfume. Strong, leathery dark green foliage. *Note:* 'Jacques Cartier' is grown and sold as 'Marquise Boccella' in the USA but I have yet to be convinced that the European cultivar is incorrect.

C P H B ◍ ▽ VF ⊰ AL 3′ × 2′ 90 × 60 cm

'Marbrée'

Robert and Moreau FRANCE 1858

An interesting cultivar. Slightly taller than most of this group, with ample, dark green foliage. Double flowers opening flat, deep pinkish purple, with paler mottling. Sadly, only slightly fragrant.

R H P B ▽ SF AL 4′ × 3′ 120 × 90 cm

'Mme Knorr'

Verdier FRANCE 1855

Similar in stature to 'Comte de Chambord', with slightly fewer leaves. Semi-double flowers of bright pink. Has a good strong fragrance.

R H P ▽ VF AL 3′ × 3′ 90 × 90 cm

'Panachée de Lyon'

Dubreuil FRANCE 1895

Sport from 'Rose du Roi'

Many-petalled flowers, a mixture of purple and crimson. Upright growth with mid-green foliage

R P VF ▽ AL 3′ × 2′ 90 × 60 cm

'Pergolèse'

Moreau FRANCE 1860

A very good rose. Small to medium-sized, fully double, scented flowers, of rich purple-crimson sometimes paling to soft lilac-mauve, produced in small spaced clusters on a plant which is well endowed with darkish green foliage. If pruned regularly, will repeat in most seasons. Shows considerable Gallica influence, in my opinion.

R P H ▽ VF AL 3′ × 3′ 90 × 90 cm

'Rose de Rescht', and below, 'Rose du Roi'

'Rembrandt'

Moreau-Robert FRANCE 1883
Small, double, loosely petalled pinkish-crimson flowers blotched purple. Growth dense and upright. Foliage smallish, dark green.
C P H VF ▽ AL 3′ × 3′ 90 × 90 cm

'Rose de Rescht'

Discovered by Nancy Lindsay
This is a fascinating little rose. Very Gallica-like in foliage, the only concession to Damask being a short flower stalk. Highly scented. The flowers, which are rich fuchsia-red in colour with strong purple tints changing with age to magenta-pink, are tightly formed rosette shaped, almost pompon, and produced in small, upright clusters amid lots of foliage. Well worth a place in any garden. Very remontant, especially when young: needs hard pruning to remain so when over five years old.
R H P B ◐ ▽ VF AL 3′ × 2′ 90 × 60 cm

'Rose du Roi', 'Lee's Crimson Perpetual'

Lelieur FRANCE 1815
'Portland Rose' × *R. gallica officinalis*?
An important rose. See page 12. Sometimes classi-fied a Hybrid Perpetual, but I prefer to place it here. Flowers are double, red mottled purple, loosely formed when open and highly scented. Short growing but slightly straggly. Foliage small, rather pointed and dark green.
R P H ▽ VF AL 3′ × 3′ 90 × 90 cm

'Rose du Roi à Fleurs Pourpres', 'Roi des Pourpres', 'Mogador'

1819
Said to be a sport of 'Rose du Roi'
An interesting rose, the red-violet-purple flowers are similar to those of 'Rose du Roi' and freely produced throughout the season. Plant short, bushy and slightly straggly.
C P H ▽ VF AL 3′ × 3′ 90 × 90 cm

'Rose du Roi à Fleurs Pourpres'

R. macrantha

R. macrantha

FORMS AND HYBRIDS

This species, if indeed it is a true wild rose, has many similarities to *R. gallica*, an exception being its very vigorous, speading habit, probably derived from *R. arvensis*. From it have come a number of very useful, delightfully pretty hybrids, all of which have inherited the wide-growing characteristic of their parent. They are all easy to grow but some, sadly, have a proneness to mildew. They are best used for partial ground cover or as specimen shrubs in their own right.

CLASSIFICATION

BARB	Species: Class 1	Hybrids: Class 1
MR10	Species: Class 55	Hybrids: Class 32
WFRS	Species: Class 38	Hybrids: Class 10

R. macrantha

*c.*1880

Possibly of Gallica origin

A vigorous spreading and arching shrub bearing many attractive single flowers of clear pink, fading to white, with prominent stamens and a good fragrance. Plentiful dark, veined foliage. Globular red hips in autumn.

S W F P G AL 4′ × 6′ 1.2 × 1.8 m

'Chianti'

Austin UK 1967

R. macrantha × 'Vanity'

Semi-double blooms of rich purple-maroon with pronounced golden anthers when fully open, these are produced in clusters on a well-foliated plant. Foliage matt, dark green. Scented. Illustrated on page 39.

S P H W MF ✂ AL 5′ × 4′ 1.5 × 1.2 m

'Daisy Hill'

Kordes GERMANY 1906

Large, slightly more than single, rich pink flowers, well perfumed. Vigorous, rather wider than high in habit. Abundant dark foliage and globular red hips.

S W F G MF ≋ AL 5′ × 8′ 1.5 × 2.5 m

'Harry Maasz'

Kordes GERMANY 1939

'Barcelona' × 'Daisy Hill'

A good but little known spreading rose with dark, greeny-grey foliage. Very vigorous. Single flowers large and cherry-red, paling to pink towards centre, each with a prominent arrangement of stamens. Scented.

S P G ◉ W MF ≋ AL 5′ × 8′ 1.5 × 2.5 m

'Raubritter', 'Macrantha Raubritter'

Kordes GERMANY 1967

'Daisy Hill' × 'Solarium'

A trailing shrub of great charm. Excellent for banks and similar features. Trusses of clear, silvery-pink, semi-double blooms of cupped, Bourbon form. Flowers borne all along rather thorny branches amid dark, greyish-green, matt foliage. Inclined to suffer badly from mildew, but this can be excused as it usually occurs well after flowering is finished in late summer.

S P G ◉ MF ≋ M♂ AL 3′ × 6′ 90 × 180 cm

'Scintillation'

Austin UK 1967

R. macrantha × 'Vanity'

Clusters of blush-pink, semi-double flowers on a

sprawly, useful-sized plant. Foliage grey-green and plentiful.

S P G W ◍ SF ≋ AW 4′ × 8′ 1.2 × 2.5 m

R. richardii, R. sancta, '**Holy Rose**'

ABYSSINIA 1897

Probably a Gallica hybrid of considerable antiquity A low-growing, slightly sprawly plant with dark green, matt-finished leaves. Flowers single, beautifully formed, soft rose pink.

S P G W ◍ ▽ ≋ MF AL 3′ × 4′ 90 × 120 cm

'**Raubritter**', and below, *R. richardii*, the '**Holy Rose**'

ROSA Subgenus *Eurosa (Rosa)*

SECTION : *Caninae*

Growth upright and arching. Thorns usually hooked and numerous.
Foliage medium-sized, mostly greyish-green, 7 to 9 leaflets.
Flowers usually in small clusters.
Hips generally oval to round.
Sepals no consistent pattern.

SPECIES

R. agrestis; R. alba; R. biebersteinii; R. britzensis; R. canina; R. × collina; R. corymbifera; R. × dumalis;
R. eglanteria; R. glauca; R. inodora; R. jundzillii; R. micrantha; R. mollis; R. orientalis; R. pulverulenta;
R. serafinii; R. sherardii; R. sicula; R. stylosa; R. tomentosa; R. villosa; R. villosa duplex; R. × waitziana

GARDEN GROUPS

Albas; Dog Roses; Sweet Briars

CLASSIFICATION

BARB   Species: Class 1   MR10   Species: Class 55   WFRS   Species: Classes 38 and some 39
For classification of hybrids in this section see under garden group headings.

ORIGIN AND DISTRIBUTION

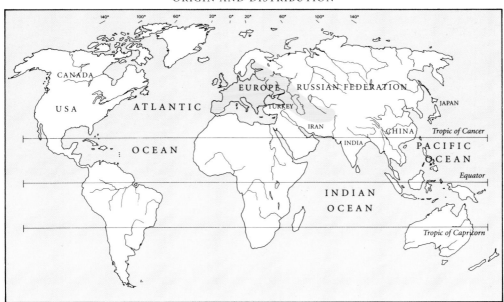

'Maxima' (see page 187)

R. agrestis

S. EUROPE 1878

A tall shrub related to the better known *R. eglanteria*, to which it is similar in many respects except that the foliage is without scent until the leaves are crushed.

S W P ◉ AL 10′ × 8′ 3 × 2.5 m

Albas

FORMS AND HYBRIDS

As a garden group the Albas are exceptionally healthy and comprise some of the most beautiful roses from the past. They are mostly of pastel shades and, without exception, are superbly scented. Notes on their history can be found on pages 10–11. Of all the older roses they are perhaps the easiest to grow. They make agreeable specimen shrubs and the quiet charm of their flowers coupled with their greyish-green foliage makes them very compatible with other plants in shrubberies and herbaceous borders, some make good climbers.

CLASSIFICATION

BARB	Class 28
MR10	Class 1
WFRS	Class 20

R. alba, 'White Rose of York'

EUROPE Pre-16th century

A lovely shrub, closely related to the Dog Rose. Single flowers, pure white and sweetly scented. Foliage matt-grey and smooth. Stems light green with an average population of stout thorns. Seldom seen in gardens today. Sometimes in hedgerows growing wild, clearly different from the Dog Rose in habit.

S P W H VF ≋ AL 6′ × 4′ 1.8 × 1.2 m

'À Feuilles de Chanvre', *R. cannobina*, *R. alba cimbaefolia*

Ancient cultivar

Semi-double smallish flowers of pure white, *canina*-like. Foliage grey-green. Growth bushy, relatively thornless. I have never seen this rose.

S VF AL 3′ × 3′ 90 × 90 cm

'Amelia'

Vibert FRANCE 1823

One of the less vigorous Albas with possibly some Damask influence. Large, semi-double, pink flowers up to 3″ (8 cm) with pronounced golden anthers. Superb scent. Grey-green foliage. Often confused with and grown as the Damask 'Celsiana'.

S P W H VF AL 4′ × 3′ 120 × 90 cm

'Blanche de Belgique', 'Blanche Superbe'

Vibert FRANCE 1817

Pure white flowers of good size and shape with a superb perfume. Foliage grey-green and healthy. Growth vigorous, bushy and upright.

S P H W ◉ VF AL 6′ × 4′ 1.8 × 1.2 m

'Blush Hip'

*c.*1840 – according to Graham Stuart Thomas
Similar to 'Maiden's Blush' but taller. I have never
seen this rose.
S VF AL 10′ × 6′ 3.1 × 1.8 m

'Celestial', 'Celeste'

Very ancient
Beautiful, semi-double, soft pink flowers combining well with leaden grey foliage. A healthy, robust
yet charming rose with a superb, 'expensive'
perfume. Illustrated on page 81.
S W P H ◉ VF AL 6′ × 4′ 1.8 × 1.2 m

'Chloris', 'Rosée du Matin'

Very ancient
Not seen as often as some other Albas, it has dark
green leaves, and is comparatively thornless.
Flowers double, with incurving petals curling into
a tight central button. Colour soft satiny-pink.
Scented.
S W P H ◉ VF AL 5′ × 4′ 1.5 × 1.2 m

'Cuisse de Nymphe' *see* 'Maiden's Blush, Great'

'Cuisse de Nymphe Émue'

The name given in France to a slightly deeper pink
form of 'Maiden's Blush'.

'Félicité Parmentier'

Pre-1828
A tidy shrub bearing an abundance of flat, reflexing
flowers similar in colour to pink coconut ice. Good
healthy dark greyish-green foliage.
S W P H ◉ VF ✂ AL 4′ × 3′ 120 × 90 cm

'Jeanne d'Arc'

Vibert FRANCE 1818
Rather sprawly but nevertheless a very useful shrub.
Darkish foliage shows off to advantage the creamy
rather muddled flowers, fading to white in hot sun.
S P W H ◉ VF AL 6′ × 5′ 1.8 × 1.5 m

'Königin von Dänemark', 'Queen of Denmark'

1826
The individual flowers of this rose are slightly
smaller than most other Albas and its colour a
deeper pink. The shoots are somewhat more than
typically thorny and the foliage, although greyish-

'Félicité Parmentier', and above,'Königin von
Dänemark'

green, is more coarse. Superbly scented, this rose is an excellent ambassador for the Albas as a whole.
S P H W ▽ ◐ VF ✄ AL 5′ × 4′ 1.5 × 1.2 m

'Maiden's Blush, Great', 'Cuisse de Nymphe', 'Incarnata', 'La Virginale', 'La Séduisante'

EUROPE 15th century or earlier

In France this rose is known by the very seductive name 'Cuisse de Nymphe', but in England, Victorian prudery caused it to be known by the more refined but equally suggestive name 'Maiden's Blush'. This most lovely of roses combines all the best Alba attributes. Blush-pink, it has a refined perfume and is amply clothed with blue-grey leaves. 'Cuisse de Nymphe Émue' (thigh of the passionate nymph) is the name applied to more richly coloured clones of this cultivar. Illustrated on pages 10 and 54.
S P H W CL ◐ VF ✄ AW 6′ × 5′ 1.8 × 1.5 m

'Maiden's Blush, Small'

Kew Gardens UK 1797

Parentage unknown, probably sport of 'Maiden's Blush, Great'
Similar in all respects to its sister but slightly smaller, both in stature and size of flower.
S P H W ▽ ◐ VF ✄ AL 4′ × 3′ 120 × 90 cm

'Maxima', 'Jacobite Rose', 'Bonnie Prince Charlie's Rose', 'White Rose of York', 'Great Double White', 'Cheshire Rose'

EUROPE 15th century or earlier

Possibly *R. canina* × *R. gallica*
Pure white, sometimes creamy-white with a very slight blush, very double flowers in an upright cluster of 6 to 8 blooms. Healthy, grey-green foliage. Sometimes with good narrowly oval-shaped autumn fruit.
S P W H VF AL 6′ × 4′ 1.8 × 1.2 m

'Mme Legras de St Germain'

Early 19th century

A relatively thornless rose. Medium-sized, very double creamy-white flowers produced in large clusters, highly scented, standing up well to inclement weather. Light grey-green foliage, soft and downy to touch. Equally good as shrub or climber, when with support it will attain at least double its usual height.
S P W CL ◐ N VF ✄ ≋ AL 7′ × 6′ 2 × 1.8 m

'Mme Legras de St Germain', and below, 'Mme Plantier'

'Mme Plantier'

Plantier 1835

An interesting rose, best classified as an Alba. Probably an Alba/Moschata cross. Capable of climbing, when it will reach perhaps 20′ (6 m) into small open trees, but good as a lax shrub or pillar rose. Flattish flowers, made up of many convoluted petals, pale cream, changing to pure white, borne in very large clusters on long, sometimes arching stems. Foliage and stems light greyish-green. Few thorns.
S T P ◐ N CL VF ✄ ≋ AL 12′ × 8′ 3.5 × 2.5 m

'Morning Mist'

Austin UK 1996

Related to the Albas. A pure single described by the raiser as coppery-red. Very free-flowering, with disease-resistant mid-green foliage. Growth bushy and dense.
C P ▽ SF AL 5′ × 4′ 1.5 × 1.2 m

'Pompon Blanc Parfait'

c.1876

An upright-growing cultivar not altogether typical of an Alba in growth habit, being rather stubby, apart from the occasional longer shoot. Smooth foliage and short leaf stalks. Scented, pure white flowers produced very freely in small clusters.

S P W H ▽ ◉ N VF AL 4′ × 3′ 120 × 90 cm

'Princesse de Lamballe'

An Alba seen mentioned from time to time but with which I am not familiar. Others, too, have become lost in the ravages of time. In fact, in one of my favourite old books, *The Flower Garden*, 1843, some 50 or so Albas are mentioned.

'Semi-plena', *R. alba suaveolens, R. alba nivea*

EUROPE 16th century or earlier

Semi-double, sweetly scented, pure white flowers with pronounced anthers borne on an upright but graceful bush with matt, grey-green leaves. Good autumn fruit. An underrated form of *R. alba*, deserving more attention, especially as an informal hedge or lax shrub in the wilder garden.

S P W H CL N ◉ VF AW 8′ × 5′ 2.5 × 1.5 m

'The Alexander Rose'

Austin UK 1992

Related to the Albas. Pretty single flowers of coppery-pink similar to those of the Dog Rose, *R. canina*, with conspicuous stamens. Foliage greyish-green.Growth vigorous and bushy.

C P H SF ▽ AL 5′ × 4′ 1.5 × 1.2 m

OTHER ALBAS

A number of modern hybrid Albas were raised and released by German breeder Rolf Sievers of Kiel in 1988. These are beginning to catch on around the world. I have not grown them, but those I have seen have looked impressive and beautiful. They are said to be very hardy.

These are as follows:

'Crimson Blush' (SIEson) Crimson, fully double and fragrant.

S 6′ × 6′ 1.8 × 1.8 m

'Lemon Blush' (SIElemon) Soft yellow, double, fragrant.

S 6′ × 6′ 1.8 × 1.8 m

'Morning Blush' (SIEmorn) Pure white, semi-double, fragrant.

S 6′ × 7′ 1.8 × 2.1 m

'Royal Blush' (SIEroyal) Soft blush pink, fully double, fragrant.

S 6′ × 6′ 1.8 × 1.8 m

'Summer Blush' (SIEsummer) Bright red, fully double, slight fragrance.

S 6′ × 4′ 1.8 × 1.2 m

'White Blush' (SIEwhite) Pure white, fully double, fragrant.

S 7′ × 7′ 2.1 × 2.1 m

R. biebersteinii

R. biebersteinii, R. horrida

EUROPE AND W. ASIA 1796

A curious, almost gooseberry-like bush with small, white flowers followed by globular red hips.

S P F W ▽ AL 2′ × 2′ 60 × 60 cm

R. britzensis

MIDDLE EAST 1901

A tallish upright shrub with bluish-green, relatively thornless branches and greyish-green leaves. Flowers large, up to 3″ (8 cm) across, blush-white and scented. Hips biggish, oval and dark red with sparse bristles.

S F W P ◉ AL 8′ × 6′ 2.5 × 1.8 m

R. canina

FORMS AND HYBRIDS

The Dog Rose, *R. canina*, is one of our prettiest native hedgerow plants and I often think it surprising that more hybrids have not been developed from this species. Of those that have come forth, I mention just four here, although scattered throughout the book are a number of other roses with lesser amounts of *R. canina* in their make-up. These three are best allowed to have their heads in a woodland or wild garden setting.

CLASSIFICATION

BARB   Class 1
MR10   Class 26
WFRS   Class 10

R. canina, 'Dog Rose'

EUROPE Ancient species

The most common wild rose native to Britain and Europe, also occasionally found naturalized in other temperate areas such as North America. Although a coarse, somewhat awkward shrub, its individual flowers are quite beautiful. Usually pale or blush pink, they sometimes vary from district to district. I have recently found one of pure white. They also have a sweet scent. A distinctive feature is the abundance of orange-red hips produced in autumn. These are rich in vitamin C and used in rose hip syrup; they also make a good wine. Until superseded by 'Laxa', the common Dog Rose was the most widely used understock in Europe for the production of modern roses. *R. canina inermis* is a fairly thornless form now sometimes used as an understock.

S F P N ◉ W MF ≋ AW Up to 10′ × 6′ 3 × 1.8 m

R. canina hips

'Abbotswood', 'Canina Abbotswood'

Hilling UK 1954

R. canina × unknown garden cultivar
A chance hybrid with scented, double, pink flowers, most useful where a well-armed, dense shrub is needed for a specific purpose.

S P N ◉ W VF ≋ AL 10′ × 6′ 3 × 1.8 m

'Andersonii'

Hillier UK 1935

Chance hybrid of *R. canina* × possibly *R. arvensis* or *R. gallica*
A deep pink, larger-flowered form of *R. canina* with fewer thorns and, in my experience, tidier habit.

S F P N ◉ W VF ≋ AL 8′ × 6′ 2.5 × 1.8 m

'Andersonii', and below, 'Kiese' hips

'Kiese'

Kiese GERMANY 1910
'Général Jacqueminot' × R. canina
Almost single bright orange-red flowers in trusses
on a vigorous shrub with dark green glossy foliage.
Good autumn hips.
S P ◐ H F W SF AL 8′ × 6′ 2.5 × 1.5 m

'Pfander', R. canina 'Pfander', 'Pfander's Canina'

Pfander GERMANY 1954
Not important as a garden plant, although it
produces an abundance of pale rosy-pink, single
flowers and a good crop of bright red, sizeable oval
hips. Its main use has been as an understock in the
commercial production of roses.
S P W H ◐ SF F AL 10′ × 6′ 3 × 1.8 m

R. × collina

CENTRAL EUROPE 1779
R. corymbifera × R. gallica
A medium-growing shrub with sparse, reddish
thorns and pale, greyish-green leaves. Flowers mid-
to pale pink followed by oval, bright red hips.
S F W P ◐ SF ≋ AW 6′ × 4′ 1.8 × 1.2 m

R. corymbifera

E. EUROPE AND ASIA 1838
Obviously related to R. canina, which it resembles
both in size of plant and in foliage. Flowers are
slightly larger in size, creamy white with hints of
blush pink. Good orange-red hips, again similar to
those of R. canina.
S P W F ◐ SF AL 10′ × 6′ 3 × 1.8 m

R. × dumalis

E. EUROPE, MIDDLE EAST 1872
A medium shrub related to, and similar to, R.
canina, found mostly in mountainous regions in
southern Europe. Flowers large, 2¹/₂″ (7 cm), clear
rose pink, scented. Large oval to round red fruit.
S F W P ◐ SF AL 6′ × 5′ 1.8 × 1.5 m

Sweet Briars

FORMS AND HYBRIDS

Very closely related to the Dog Rose, *R. eglanteria* is better known for the distinctive apple perfume of its foliage than for its flowers; and, while some of its less vigorous hybrids make extremely useful and easy-going garden shrubs, the majority are best let loose to grow naturally. Failing that, they make very good impenetrable hedges, quite formal if pruned or clipped regularly, and a large plus in their favour is a regular crop of bright orangey-red hips each autumn.

CLASSIFICATION

BARB	Class 29
MR10	Class 18
WFRS	Class 30

R. eglanteria, R. rubiginosa, 'Sweet Briar', 'Eglantine Rose'

EUROPE

Similar to *R. canina*, distinguished by its perfumed foliage and higher density of prickles. Flowers single, smallish and blush-pink. Fruits freely, the hips staying on the bush well into winter. Given its head it will reach 6′ or 7′ (1.8–2 m) in the open and twice this height if grown as a hedgerow plant, which it prefers. In the garden, it is best clipped each year to encourage young growth, for it is the young tips which exude the strongest scent. *R. eglanteria* is a native of Europe and has probably been appreciated for its perfumed leaves since civilization began. Many cultivars are listed in 19th-century catalogues, but most of these seem to have disappeared now.

S P F H W ◍ ▽ VF AW 12′ × 8′ 3.5 × 2.5 m

'Amy Robsart'

Penzance UK *c.*1894

Dull for most of the year but spectacular in full bloom; a mass of scented, deep pink, almost single blooms in June on a vigorous bush. The hips, which do not always set, can compensate in late summer. Foliage only slightly scented.

S P F H W ◍ VF ≋ AL 10′ × 8′ 3 × 2.5 m

'Anne of Geierstein'

Penzance UK *c.*1894

This is a very vigorous member of its group, with

'Amy Robsart'

sweetly scented foliage and single, gold-centred crimson flowers, followed by oval scarlet hips in autumn.

S P F H W ◍ VF ≋ AL 10′ × 8′ 3 × 2.5 m

'Catherine Seyton'

Penzance UK 1894

Lovely soft pink, single flowers with pronounced golden-yellow stamens. Rich green foliage on a vigorous shrub. Both flowers and foliage are scented. Orange-red hips in autumn.

S P W F H ◉ VF AL 8′ × 5′ 2.5 × 1.5 m

'Edith Bellenden'

Penzance UK 1895

A good but little-known Sweet Briar with well-scented foliage. Its scented flowers are single, pale rosy-pink, produced very freely in season and followed by good, oval, red hips.

S P W H F ◉ VF AL 8′ × 6′ 2.5 × 1.8 m

'Flora McIvor'

Penzance UK c.1894

A medium-tall vigorous shrub bearing single, deep pink flowers with white centres, followed by oval orange-red hips in late summer. Foliage scented, but leaves need to be rubbed between the fingers for this to be noticeable.

S P F H W ◉ VF AL 8′ × 6′ 2.5 × 1.8 m

'Goldbusch'

Kordes GERMANY 1954

A most useful shrub and should be grown more widely. Large, semi-double flowers produced freely in clusters amid an abundance of lush, light green, healthy, scented foliage. Flowers also well scented.

S P H W ◉ CL VF BS⚥ AL 8′ × 5′ 2.5 × 1.5 m

'Greenmantle'

Penzance UK 1894

Single rose-red with golden stamens. Fragrant foliage. A lesser known Sweet Briar which should be more popular.

S P H W ◉ VF AL 8′ × 5′ 2.5 × 1.5 m

'Herbstfeuer', 'Autumn Fire'

Kordes GERMANY 1961

Clusters of large, semi-double, dark red, fragrant flowers which are occasionally repeated in the autumn; these are produced on a vigorous bush with dark green foliage. Very large, elongated-pear-shaped, bright orange-red fruit. I have never understood why this rose is not better known. Foliage not scented.

R P W H F ◉ A VF AL 6′ × 4′ 1.8 × 1.2 m

'Janet's Pride', 'Clementine'

W. Paul UK Introduced 1892

Semi-double flowers, white with bright pink

'Anne of Geierstein'

'Goldbusch', and below, 'Herbstfeuer'

markings at petal edges. Scented. Not as vigorous as some of this group. Coarse foliage not unattractive. Interesting and unique.

S H P W ◐ VF AL 5′ × 4′ 1.5 × 1.2 m

'Julia Mannering'

Penzance UK c.1895

Bright, clear pink, heavily veined single flowers. Good, dark foliage, well scented, as are the flowers.

S H P W ◐ VF AL 6′ × 4′ 1.8 × 1.2 m

'La Belle Distinguée', 'Scarlet Sweetbriar', 'La Petite Duchesse'

Probably a very old cultivar. A most interesting rose,

not very tall and of an upright, bushy habit with numerous, small, slightly aromatic leaves. At first sight, the young bush is reminiscent of the Centifolia 'Rose de Meaux'. Flowers almost scarlet, fully double and produced freely.

S P H ▽ MF AL 5′ × 4′ 1.5 × 1.2 m

'Lady Penzance'

Penzance UK c.1894

R. eglanteria × R. foetida bicolor

A dense, vigorous shrub, probably the best known of the Sweet Briars, with by far the strongest-scented foliage. Flowers single, coppery-salmon and pink with pronounced yellow stamens, followed by bright red hips.

S F P W H ● VF BS♂ AW 7′ × 6′ 2 × 1.8 m

'Lord Penzance'

Penzance UK c.1890

R. eglanteria × R. × harisonii

A vigorous, dense shrub with sweetly scented foliage. Flowers single, buff-yellow tinged pink, followed by bright red hips.

S F P W H VF BS♂ AL 7′ × 6′ 2 × 1.8 m

'La Belle Distinguée'

'Lady Penzance'

'Lucy Ashton'

Penzance UK 1894

Lovely, single, pure white flowers with the edges of each petal touched with pastel pink. Scented foliage. Makes a good vigorous shrub.

S P H W F VF AL 6′ × 5′ 1.8 × 1.5 m

'Magnifica'

Hesse GERMANY 1916

'Lucy Ashton' seedling

A splendid shrub rose which should be more widely grown. Semi-double flowers purplish-red, of good size and quality. Foliage only slightly scented but dense and dark green. Makes a very good hedge.

S P H W ◉ VF AL 6′ × 5′ 1.8 × 1.5 m

'Manning's Blush'

c.1800

A very good shrub rose. Flowers large, white flushed pink, fully double, opening flat, and fragrant. Foliage scented, small and plentiful, suggesting *R. pimpinellifolia* influence. The shrub is bushy and dense and, although it is not generally recurrent, I have seen the odd flower in early autumn.

S P W H ◉ ▽ VF AL 5′ × 4′ 1.5 × 1.2 m

'Mechtilde von Neuerburg'

Boden GERMANY 1920

Semi-double flowers of an attractive pinkish-red. Foliage slightly aromatic, dark and plentiful. Has a vague Gallica look, belied by its size.

S P W F CL ◉ VF ≋ AL 10′ × 8′ 3 × 2.5 m

'Meg Merrilies'

Penzance UK c.1894

An extremely vigorous and prickly shrub rose. Bright crimson semi-double flowers followed by an abundance of good red hips. One of the best of its group, with scented flowers and foliage.

S P W H F VF ✂ AL 8′ × 7′ 2.5 × 2 m

'Rose Bradwardine'

Penzance UK 1894

Clusters of single, clear rose-pink flowers on a vigorous, well-proportioned plant with good, dark green, aromatic leaves, good hips.

S P H W F ◉ VF AL 6′ × 5′ 1.8 × 1.5 m

Top left, 'Magnifica', right, 'Manning's Blush', and bottom, 'Meg Merrilies'

R. glauca (R. rubrifolia)

FORMS AND HYBRIDS

CLASSIFICATION

BARB	Class 1
MR10	Class 54
WFRS	Class 10

R. glauca, R. rubrifolia

EUROPE 1830

A very useful, ornamental shrub with glaucous-purple stems and foliage. Clusters of small, rather inconspicuous, yet quite beautiful flowers of soft mauve-pink. Oval reddish-purple hips in autumn. Useful for flower arranging, as one or two plants will give an almost unending supply of foliage for this purpose. For many years better known as *R. rubrifolia*. This is botanically erroneous, *R. glauca* now accepted as its true name.

S F N H W P A ● SF AW 6′ × 5′ 1.8 × 1.5 m

R. glauca

'Carmenetta'

Central Experimental Farm CANADA 1923

R. glauca × R. rugosa

Slightly more vigorous and consequently less graceful than its seed parent. Foliage and stems glaucous purple with numerous small thorns. Hips of similar size and colour, and flowers slightly larger than those of *R. glauca*.

S F N H W P A SF ∾ AL 7′ × 7′ 2 × 2 m

'Sir Cedric Morris'

Sir Cedric Morris, introduced by Beales UK 1979

R. glauca × R. mulliganii

The identity of the male or pollen parent is an assumption by the late Sir Cedric. It was a foundling, growing among other *R. glauca* seedlings at his home, Benton End, Hadleigh, Suffolk, and introduced by me in 1979. A specimen of *R. mulliganii*, or what we know as such, was growing close by, flowering at the same time as *R. glauca*. I was staggered by my first sight of this rose. The glaucous purple (not as purple as *R. glauca*) foliage is abundant and large. Stems are thick, also glaucous and very thorny. Flowers are evenly spaced in huge clusters and, when established, grow in massed profusion. These are single, pure white and display prominent golden anthers. The scent is strong, sweet and pervading. It bears a lavish crop of small, orange hips in autumn.

S F T P W A N VF ∾ AL 30′ × 20′ 9 × 6 m

R. inodora, R. graveolens, R. obtusifolia

S. EUROPE 1905

A coarse, vigorous, thorny shrub with scented (Sweet Briar) foliage, ideal for naturalizing or

'Sir Cedric Morris'

growing into hedgerows, almost a less refined form of *R. eglanteria*. Flowers single, soft pink to blush-white. Oval, bright red hips.
S F W P ◉ SF AL 8′ × 5′ 2.5 × 1.5 m

R. jundzillii, R. marginata

E. EUROPE 1870

A handsome rose. Flowers single, quite large, bright pink, produced freely on a medium-sized, moderately prickly plant bearing ample darkish green, serrated leaves. Smooth bright red round to oval hips in autumn.
S P F ◉ SF AL 5′ × 4′ 1.5 × 1.2 m

R. micrantha

E. EUROPE 1900

Similar to *R. eglanteria* but slightly less vigorous, with smaller flowers and only slightly scented foliage.
S F W P ◉ SF AL 6′ × 4′ 1.8 × 1.2 m

R. mollis

N EUROPE 1818

A small, shrubby plant with greyish to red stems and grey, downy foliage. Flowers mid-pink, borne mostly in small clusters of three or four fragrant blooms in mid-summer. Bristly, occasionally smooth, globular hips.
S F W P ◉ SF AL 3′ × 3′ 90 × 90 cm

R. orientalis

S. EUROPE/MIDDLE EAST 1905

A shrubby, short-growing plant with slender, hairy branches. Leaves made up of five, seldom seven, small, oval leaflets of bright green. Papery flowers of soft pink. Hips small, narrow, oblong and bright red.
S W P F SF AL 2′ × 2′ 60 × 60 cm

R. pulverulenta, R. glutinosa

MEDITERRANEAN REGIONS Introduced 1821

Short growing and prickly, with small pinkish-white single flowers followed by small globular hips. Foliage smells of pine.
S P F ◉ ▽ SF AL 3′ × 3′ 90 × 90 cm

R. serafinii

EASTERN MEDITERRANEAN 1914

Small single pink flowers on a short-growing, thorny, rather sprawly plant. Rounded, bright orange-red fruit. Foliage serrated and glossy.
S P W F ◉ SF AL 2′ × 2′ 60 × 60 cm

R. sherardii, R. omissa

N. CENTRAL EUROPE 1933

Medium-sized shrub with angular, sometimes zig-zag, branches and bluish-green foliage. Deep pink flowers usually in small clusters followed by smallish, almost urn-shaped hips.
S W P F ◉ MF AL 6′ × 4′ 1.8 × 1.2 m

R. sicula

S. EUROPE AND N. AFRICA *c.*1894

A short, free-suckering shrub similar to *R. serafinii*, with reddish wood when young. Foliage is greyish-green and slightly scented, as are the flowers which are soft pink in colour. Hips round to oval.

S H P F ◉ SF AL 3′ × 2′ 90 × 60 cm

R. villosa hips, and below, *R. villosa duplex*

R. stylosa

EUROPE 1838

An arching shrub with small, narrow, oval, mid-green leaves. Its flowers are produced in small clusters, and individually are of medium size (1¹/₂″, 5 cm). They are blush-pinkish-white followed by smooth, oval red hips.

S F W P ◉ SF AL 10′ × 8′ 3 × 2.5 m

R. tomentosa

EUROPE Ancient species

Tall shrub rose, similar in many respects to *R. canina*. Medium-sized, clear, soft pink flowers with a good display of soft, creamy-yellow stamens. Scented. Foliage matt grey-green, softer in both appearance and touch than that of the Dog Rose. Bright red, oval fruit. Grows wild in many parts of mainland Europe and the British Isles. I have come upon one or two in Norfolk hedgerows.

S F P W ◉ ≈ VF AL 10′ × 8′ 3 × 2.5 m

shorter in growth. Flowers semi-double and clear pink. Sets hips only rarely but repeats flowers intermittently when growing in good situations, suggesting hybrid origin.

S P F W N ◉ AL 5′ × 4′ 1.5 × 1.2 m

R. villosa, R. pomifera, 'Apple Rose'

EUROPE/ASIA 1761

Medium-sized shrub with greyish, downy leaves, which are fragrant though this is barely perceptible in my plant. Flowers scented, clear pink and single. Fruit large, orange, apple-shaped and well covered with bristles.

S P F E N ◉ VF ≈ AL 6′ × 5′ 1.8 × 1.5 m

R . villosa duplex, R. pomifera duplex, 'Wolly Dodd's Rose'

Discovered in the garden of the Rev. Wolly-Dodd, Cheshire, *c.*1900
Similar in most respects to *R. villosa* but slightly

R. × waitziana

EUROPE 1874

R. canina × *R. gallica*
A medium to tall shrub with stems and armature similar to those of *R. canina*. Medium-sized, deep pink flowers. Fruit seldom sets fully in the cultivated form.

S W P ◉ AL 6′ × 4′ 1.8 × 1.2 m

SECTION : *Carolinae*

Growth shortish, upright. Thorns short, usually in pairs, hooked.
Leaves composed of 7 to 9 leaflets – usually good in autumn.
Flowers mostly singly on short stalks.
Hips mostly roundish. Sepals drop when ripe.

SPECIES

R. carolina; R. carolina alba; R. carolina plena; R. foliolosa; R. × kochiana; R. × mariae-graebnerae;
R. nitida; R. palustris; R. virginiana

CLASSIFICATION

BARB   Species: Class 1   Hybrids: Class 1   MR10   Species: Class 55   Hybrids: Class 54
WFRS   Species: Class 38   Hybrids: Classes 9 and 10

ORIGIN AND DISTRIBUTION

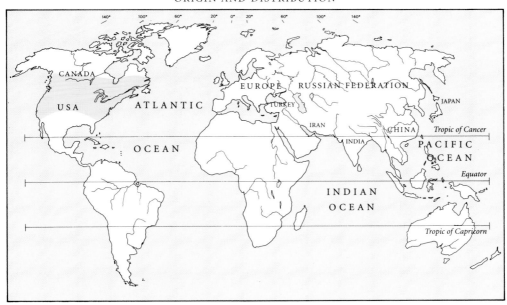

R. carolina

FORMS AND HYBRIDS

CLASSIFICATION – see section heading

R. carolina

N. AMERICA *c.*1826

A useful, free-suckering rose – when on its own roots – with thin, relatively thornless shoots and completely thornless lateral branches. Ample, slightly glossy foliage. Flowers clear, soft pink, borne solitarily, followed by roundish, red hips.
S F A P ▽ SF AL 3′ × 3′ 90 × 90 cm

R. carolina alba, R. virginiana alba

Garden discovery USA 1867

But for its single, white flowers, it is similar in most respects to *R. carolina*. Slight differences in foliage suggest the influence of genes from another species or cultivar. This difference is most marked on the underside of leaves, with more numerous tiny hairs, making them appear greyer than those of the pink form.
S F A P W ◍ ▽ AL 3′ × 2′ 90 × 60 cm

R. carolina plena, 'Double Pennsylvanian Rose'

USA *c.*1790 (Lynes rediscovery 1955)

Charming, small, double flowers of clear pink paling to almost white at the edges. Foliage smooth and dark green. Makes a tidy, short-growing, free-suckering plant when on its own roots, which is perhaps the best way it can be reproduced and grown. For more details of the rose and its rediscovery, see Graham Thomas's book *Shrub Roses for Today*.
S P ▽ ◍ AL 2′ × 2′ 60 × 60 cm

R. foliolosa, and opposite, *R. × kochiana* and *R. nitida* below

R. foliolosa

N. AMERICA 1880

Bright pink, solitary, slightly ragged flowers amid strange, narrow, elongated foliage. Free suckering when on its own roots. No thorns. Short-growing and tolerant of the wettest soils. Fruits small, spherical and bright red.

S P A F SF AL 3′ × 3′ 90 × 90 cm

R. × kochiana

N. AMERICA 1869

Probably *R. palustris* × *R. pimpinellifolia*
I have become very fond of this little shrub. The pleasing, bright lime-green foliage remains healthy all summer and changes to a rich, russet-red in autumn. Few but strong thorns on stiff, thin, angular shoots. Flowers solitary and deep rose pink, reminiscent of those of the shrub *Cistus crispus*.

S P W ▽ A AL 3′ × 2′ 90 × 60 cm

R. × mariae-graebnerae

H. Dabel GERMANY 1900

R. palustris × *R. virginiana*
A most useful, rare but striking little shrub. Bright rose pink flowers, produced at first in profusion and then intermittently throughout the summer. Sparsely thorned shoots with semi-glossy foliage. Small, round hips and good autumn colour.

R F A W P G ◉ AL 3′ × 2′ 90 × 60 cm

R. nitida

N. AMERICA 1807

A free-suckering, short shrub with thin, prickly stems and small, dainty, fern-like foliage which turns to rich crimson in the autumn. Flowers small, single, numerous and deep rose pink. A useful shrub. Hips small, oval and slightly bristly.

S G F A ◉ ▽ AL 3′ × 3′ 90 × 90 cm

R. palustris, 'Swamp Rose'

N. AMERICA 1726

A vigorous rose with abundant, mid- to dark-green foliage, reddish stems and an upright habit. Single, deep pink flowers produced intermittently over a long season, followed by oval hips in the autumn. Will tolerate wet, boggy conditions.

S A P F W ▽ AL 4′ × 3′ 120 × 90 cm

R. virginiana

FORMS AND HYBRIDS

CLASSIFICATION – see section heading

R. virginiana

N. AMERICA c.1807

At home in most soils, this very useful shrub does particularly well in light, sandy conditions. Well-foliated with light green glossy leaves, very colourful in autumn. Upright and bushy in growth. Blooms single, rich clear pink with yellow stamens and a good scent. Flowers appear later than in some species, followed by orange, plump, round hips which remain on the plant well into winter.

S H P W A F ◉ MF AL 5′ × 3′ 150 × 90 cm

R. virginiana, and below, 'Rose d'Amour'

'Rose d'Amour', 'St Mark's Rose', *R. virginiana plena*

Pre-1870

Taller than *R. virginiana* but the plant has many characteristics in common with the species. Flowers beautiful, quite small, high-centred and fully double, with petals scrolled as they open, pastel pink deepening towards the centre of each bloom. An excellent example can be seen at the Royal Horticultural Society's Gardens at Wisley, Surrey, where it has grown quite tall as a wall plant.

R P A ◉ MF WW AL 7′ × 5′ 2 × 1.5 m

'Rose d'Orsay'

Flowers, foliage and colour of wood are almost identical to those of 'Rose d'Amour', but its habit of growth and freedom of flower is quite different, being shorter, more branchy and untidy, and flowering for a much longer season. A superb rose, one fault being a reluctance to shed its dead petals, thus dead-heading is important for the best results.

C P A ◉ MF WW AL 4′ × 4′ 1.2 × 1.2 m

NOTE

For a number of years I have grown seedlings of *R. virginiana* from imported seed. When young, the plants look identical but in their second year become more varied, some almost thornless, some densely thorny, others growing much taller, with variation in colour and size of hips. The only constant and typical feature is their leaves. At least one of these seedlings – mistakenly sent to an anonymous buyer and presumably lost for ever – had a few more than the expected number of petals. One day, perhaps, I will track down the source of this seed. I suspect it comes from somewhere near the eastern Mediterranean. Graham Thomas explained the difference between 'Rose d'Amour' and 'Rose d'Orsay', and the part he played in their respective identifications, in an article in the Royal National Rose Society's *Rose Annual*, 1977.

SECTION : *Cassiorhodon (Cinnamomeae)*

Growth mostly shrubby and upright. Variable from 3′ to 12′ (1 m to 4 m).
Thorns often large and in pairs. Leaves with 5 to 9, sometimes 11, leaflets.
Flowers mostly in groups, colours usually red or pink except in *R. wardii* and *R. rugosa*.
Hips are usually a special feature, large, variously shaped – sepals held erect when ripe.

SPECIES

*R. acicularis; R. acicularis nipponensis; R. amblyotis; R. arkansana; R. banksiopsis; R. beggeriana; R. bella;
R. blanda; R. californica; R. californica plena; R. caudata; R. coriifolia froebelii; R. × coryana; R. corymbulosa;
R. davidii; R. davurica; R. elegantula-persetosa; R. fargesii; R. fedtschenkoana; R. forrestiana; R. gymnocarpa;
R. hemsleyana; R. holodonta; R. × kamtchatica; R. kordesii; R. latibracteata; R. × l'heritierana;
R. macrophylla; R. majalis; R. marretii; R. maximowicziana; R. melina; R. × micrugosa; R. × micrugosa alba;
R. mohavensis; R. moyesii; R. multibracteata; R. murielae; R. nanothamnus; R. nutkana; R. paulii;
R. paulii rosea; R. pendulina; R. pisocarpa; R. prattii; R. pyrifera; R. rugosa; R. rugosa alba; R. rugosa rubra;
R. rugosa typica; R. sertata; R. setipoda; R. spaldingii; R. suffulta; R. sweginzowii macrocarpa;
R. ultramontana; R. wardii; R. webbiana; R. willmottiae; R. woodsii; R. woodsii fendleri; R. yainacensis*

GARDEN GROUPS

Boursaults; Kordesii; Rugosas;

CLASSIFICATION

BARB   Species: Class 1   MR10   Species: Class 54   WFRS   Species: Class 38
For classification of hybrids in this section, see under garden groups.

ORIGIN AND DISTRIBUTION

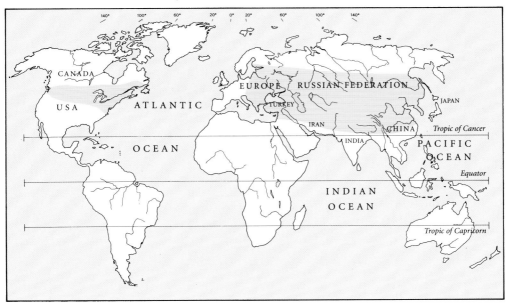

R. acicularis

N.E. ASIA, N. AMERICA AND N. EUROPE
1805
Rich pink solitary flowers, 1¹/₂″ (4 cm) in diameter, occasionally in twos or threes. Bright red, plump, smooth, pear-shaped hips of approximately 1″ (2.5 cm) in length. Foliage mid-green to grey on a lax plant with thin shoots, an abundant amount of variably sized bristles and few real thorns.
S P W H F MF AL 6′ × 5′ 1.8 × 1.5 m

R. acicularis nipponensis

JAPAN 1894
Solitary flowers of 1¹/₂″ to 2″ (4–5 cm), deep pink, almost red, followed by plump, small, pear-shaped hips. Greenish-grey foliage. Flower stalks and hips bristly. Stems with few real thorns.
S P W H F MF AL 5′ × 4′ 1.5 × 1.2 m

R. amblyotis

N.E. ASIA 1917
An upright, medium-sized shrub similar to R. majalis, to which it is obviously related. Medium-sized red flowers followed by medium-sized globular to pear-shaped red hips.
S F W P ◉ MF AL 6′ × 4′ 1.8 × 1.2 m

R. arkansana

USA 1917
A prickly, short-growing dense shrub with a fairly long flowering season in mid-summer. Foliage almost glossy and heavily veined. Flowers 1³/₄″ (5 cm), bright red with yellow stamens, usually in clusters. Small, round, reddish hips.
S P G ◉ MF AL 2′ × 2′ 60 × 60 cm

R. banksiopsis

CHINA 1907
I lost my only plant of this in the severe winter of 1981 and never saw it flower. It is described in Hillier's *Manual of Trees and Shrubs* as being a medium-sized shrub with small, rose-red flowers followed by flask-shaped hips.
S P F W SF AL 5′ × 4′ 1.5 × 1.2 m

R. acicularis nipponensis

R. beggeriana

CENTRAL ASIA 1869
Not the most auspicious of species but it has a long flowering season from mid-summer onwards when the early flowers, small and white, are followed by small round orange hips. Stems covered with light-ish coloured hooked thorns. Greyish-green foliage.
S P F W ◉ A MF AL 8′ × 7′ 2.5 × 2 m

R. bella

CHINA 1910
An upright-growing, rather prickly shrub with many of the characteristics of R. moyesii. Flowers single, bright pink. Medium-sized flask-shaped orange fruit.
S W P F S MF AL 8′ × 6′ 2.5 × 1.8 m

R. blanda, 'Smooth Rose', 'Meadow Rose', 'Hudson Bay Rose', 'Labrador Rose'

N. AMERICA 1773
Subtly similar to R. canina except for fewer thorns and deeper pink flowers. Also less vigorous. Hips

R. blanda, and below, *R. californica plena*

rather more pear-shaped than oval. A few other strains exist but none of great interest to the gardener.

S P W F ◉ MF AL 5′ × 3′ 150 × 90 cm

R. californica

N.W. AMERICA 1878

Uncommon in UK. Described in McFarland's *Modern Roses* as up to 8′ (2.5 m) with corymbs of single pink flowers 1½″ (4 cm) across. A large specimen is growing at the John Innes Institute near Norwich, but I have not seen it flowering.

S P SF AL 8′ × 4′ 2.5 × 1.2 m

R. californica plena

Date attributed 1894

An excellent garden shrub with lilac-pink flowers,

shaped rather like the individual blooms of a small semi-double hollyhock. The shrub is healthy, upright in habit and amply foliated with grey-green leaves. The wood is dark and has few thorns. Hips small, rounded, orange-red.

S P W F ◉ MF AL 8′ × 5′ 2.5 × 1.5 m

R. caudata

CHINA 1907

Very similar to the better known *R. setipoda*, to which it could well be related. However, since it is usually listed as a separate species, I have followed that rule. It forms a dense shrub with thick, well armed branches. Flowers, produced in large clusters, are pale pink, followed by flagon-shaped, bristly hips.

S P W F ◉ SF AL 7′ × 5′ 2 × 1.5 m

R. coriifolia froebelii,
R. dumetorum laxa, 'Laxa'

EUROPE 1890

A dense shrubby rose, with greyish-green wood and foliage. Moderately thorny, flowers white, hips plump but oval. Of little use ornamentally but invaluable and widely used, especially in Europe, as an understock under the name 'Laxa'. Produces fewer suckers than most other understocks.

S W 5′ × 4′ 1.5 × 1.2 m

R. × coryana

Cambridge Botanical Gardens UK 1926
R. macrophylla × *R. roxburghii*

A medium-sized shrub with leanings towards *R. roxburghii* in appearance, and an ideal woodland subject. Large, single, deep pink flowers produced in early summer. Interesting but not significant.

S P W SF AL 6′ × 4′ 1.8 × 1.2 m

R. corymbulosa

CHINA 1908

A medium, rather lax, almost thornless, thin-stemmed shrub; small leaves, with slightly hairy undersides, changing from green to deep purple in autumn. Flowers single, deep pinkish-red, with a white eye. Hips medium-sized, rounded and red.

S P W F AL 5′ × 4′ 1.5 × 1.2 m

R. davidii

CHINA 1908

A useful, later (mid June) flowering species with soft pink flowers borne, sometimes in clusters, along the length of each stem, sometimes singly. Upright and vigorous, with heavily veined, light green foliage and orange-red flagon-shaped hips in autumn.

S P F W ◍ MF AL 10′ × 5′ 3 × 1.5 m

R. davurica

N. CHINA AND ASIA 1910

A shortish, averagely thorned shrub with small leaves and medium-sized pink flowers followed by small oval hips.

S F W P ◍ AL 3′ × 3′ 90 × 90 cm

R. elegantula-persetosa, R. farreri persetosa, 'Threepenny Bit Rose'

CHINA 1914

A charming, sprawly shrub with fine, fern-like leaves which turn purple and crimson in the autumn. Hips, produced in profusion, are bright orange-red. These features, together with its habit of growth, are perhaps more important than its small lilac-pink flowers. Shoots biscuit brown, densely covered in minute but fairly harmless thorns, giving an almost mossed effect. Rather enjoys partial shade. Better known by its older name, R. farreri persetosa.

S F G W P A ◍ AW 5′ × 5′ 1.5 × 1.5 m

R. fedtschenkoana

S.E. EUROPE/ASIA 1880

A most useful shrub with single white, papery flowers, produced at first in profusion then intermittently throughout summer. Foliage light grey-green and feathery. Small, sparsely bristled oval-to-pear-shaped hips, setting only occasionally. Slowly becoming better known and more widely grown – as indeed it should be.

R P H W A MF AW 5′ × 4′ 1.5 × 1.2 m

R. forrestiana

W. CHINA 1918

Pinkish-crimson flowers with lots of creamy-buff anthers freely produced in small clusters, followed by small bottle-shaped red hips. Ample, purplish-green foliage. Growth also purplish-green, arching, dense and vigorous. Long, thin, sharp prickles

S P F G W SF AW 7′ × 7′ 2 × 2 m

R. gymnocarpa

N. AMERICA 1893

Graceful, vigorous shrub with moderately thorny, wiry shoots and numerous small roundish leaves. Flowers small, single, pale pink. Small, red, pear-shaped, smooth hips in autumn. My stock came direct from seed collected by a friend in Nova Scotia, where it grows in the wild.

S F P W ◍ MF AL 8′ × 10′ 2.5 × 3 m

R. hemsleyana

CHINA 1904

Vigorous shrub similar to R. setipoda. Medium-sized pink single flowers borne in clusters, followed by bottle-shaped, bristly, orange-red hips.

S F P W ◍ ▽ AL 5′ × 4′ 1.5 × 1.2 m

R. × kamtchatica, R. ventenatiana

Kamtchatka c.1770

R. rugosa × R. amblyotis?

Often seen listed as a form of R. rugosa, but despite an obvious affinity to that species, I place it here. Flowers smallish, single, pink touching cerise. Slightly scented. Mid-green foliage; stems well armed but less so than R. rugosa. Hips small to medium, round and bright red.

C W F P H A ◍ MF AL 7′ × 6′ 2 × 1.8 m

R. kordesii

FORM AND HYBRIDS

Most of these hybrids make excellent short climbers or specimen shrubs. If they have a fault it is a distinct dislike of orderliness, but this is easily overlooked when one considers that they will stand even the coldest climate and will flower on and on throughout every summer.

CLASSIFICATION

BARB   Species and hybrids: Class 1
MR10   Species and hybrids: Class 45
WFRS   Species and hybrids: Classes 2 and 14

R. kordesii

Kordes GERMANY 1950
'Max Graf' seedling
This rose was never officially introduced by Herr Kordes but he used it extensively in the breeding of some very important hybrids. Offspring from this rose are particularly disease-resistant. Flowers double, pinkish-red, in small clusters. Foliage dark green, growth spreading.
R ◍ P AL 5′ × 5′ 1.5 × 1.5 m

R. kordesii, and opposite, *R. fedtschenkoana*

'Champlain'

Department of Agriculture CANADA 1982
R. kordesii × seedling × ('Red Dawn' × 'Suzanne')
Large, double, dark red flowers with a moderate fragrance. Foliage light green, small. Bushy growth. Amply armed with soft yellow thorns. Very hardy.
R ◍ ▽ H MF G AL 4′ × 4′ 1.2 × 1.2 m

'Dortmund'

Kordes GERMANY 1955
Seedling × *R. kordesii*
Large, single, crimson flowers with a pale, almost white, central eye. Produced in large clusters on a vigorous, thorny plant with dark green foliage.
R P N ◍ CL SF AW 8′ × 6′ 2.5 × 1.8 m

'Hamburger Phoenix'

Kordes GERMANY 1954
R. kordesii × seedling
Clusters of large, semi-double, rich crimson flowers on a spreading, vigorous shrub or short climber with dark green foliage. Hips good in autumn.
C P F N CL ◍ MF AL 8′ × 5′ 2.5 × 1.5 m

'Henry Kelsey'

Department of Agriculture CANADA 1984
R. kordesii × seedling
Double, mid-red fragrant flowers in clusters on a

'Dortmund', and below, 'Hamburger Phoenix', left, and 'Henry Kelsey', right

wide-growing shrub with dark green, glossy foliage. Very hardy.

R ◉ ▽ G MF AL 4′ × 5′ 1.2 × 1.5 m

'John Cabot'

Department of Agriculture CANADA 1978
R. kordesii × seedling
Clusters of large, fully double, soft red, fragrant

'John Cabot', and below, 'Karlsruhe'

blooms amid abundant light green foliage. Growth vigorous and upright. Extremely hardy. A useful rose.

R ◉ ▽ H MF G AL 5′ × 4′ 1.5 × 1.2 m

'Karlsruhe'

Kordes GERMANY 1950
R. kordesii seedling
Large clusters of slightly fragrant, deep rosy-pink, fully double flowers cupped until fully open and then flat; these repeat regularly each summer. Foliage plentiful, mid-green, glossy. Growth vigorous, sprawling. An excellent, little-known rose.

R G CL T N ◉ SF AL 8′ × 6′ 2.5 × 1.8 m

'Laura Louise'

Riches UK 1995 Introduced Beales UK 1995
'Leverkusen' sport
A super replica of its parent 'Leverkusen' except for its colour, which is bright mid-pink-to-salmon. Named in memory of its discoverer's mother and mother-in-law.

C P N CL ◉ MF AL 10′ × 8′ 3 × 2.5 m

'Laura Louise'

'Leverkusen', and below, 'Parkdirektor Riggers'

'Leverkusen'

Kordes GERMANY 1954

R. kordesii × 'Golden Glow'

Semi-double, lemon-yellow flowers which, when open, have attractively ragged edges. Sweetly scented, continues blooming all summer. Attractive, glossy, light green, deeply serrated foliage. As so often with Kordes roses, rudely healthy.

C P N CL ◉ MF AW 10′ × 8′ 3 × 2.5 m

'Parkdirektor Riggers'

Kordes GERMANY 1957

R. kordesii × 'Our Princess'

A very good climbing rose. Large clusters of deep red to crimson, almost single, firm-textured flowers. Plant upright and vigorous. Foliage healthy, dark green and glossy.

C P N ◉ CF SF AL 10′ × 6′ 3 × 1.8 m

'Raymond Chenault'

Kordes GERMANY 1960

R. kordesii × 'Montezuma'

Large, semi-double blooms of bright red borne in clusters. Fragrant. Foliage dark green and glossy. Growth very vigorous, spreading and bushy.

R ◉ N G CL MF ≋ AL 10′ × 8′ 3 × 2.5 m

'William Baffin'

Department of Agriculture CANADA 1983

R. kordesii seedling

Clusters of large, semi-double to double deep clear pink blooms on a vigorous, wide-growing shrub with abundant, glossy, mid- to dark green foliage. A marvellous sight when, as a mature plant, it is seen in full flush. Very hardy. Can also be used as a climber. Illustrated on page 115.

R ◉ N AL 8′ × 6′ 2.5 × 1.8 m

R. latibracteata

CHINA 1936

Similar in most respects to *R. webbiana*, which is better known, but the lilac-pink flowers are borne in small corymbs rather than solitarily. Grey-blue foliage as in *R. webbiana* but slightly larger. Growth habit arching, making a broad, solid plant. Hips broadly bottle-shaped.

S P H W ◉ ▽ AL 7′ × 7′ 2 × 2 m

Boursaults

FORMS AND HYBRIDS

The Boursaults are but few and until recently it was assumed that *R. × l'heritierana,* from which they descend, had occurred from a cross between *R. pendulina* and *R. chinensis.* Certainly their smooth stems, dark wood and leaf shape point in that direction. However, authoritative opinion varies, and chromosome counts seem to prove conclusively an error in this assumption. Thus I have placed them here.

CLASSIFICATION

BARB   Species and hybrids: Class 1
MR10   Species and hybrids: Class 4
WFRS   Species: Class 39   Hybrids: Class 22

R. × l'heritierana

Probably EUROPE Pre-1820

Unarmed cane-like stems, variable from green to reddish-brown. Foliage dark green, rather blackberry-like, but smooth. Flowers double, opening flat, deep pinkish-red to blush-white. Smooth round hips, when and if they set.

S W P A AL 10′ × 8′ 3 × 2.5 m

R × l'heritierana

'Amadis', 'Crimson Boursault'

Laffay FRANCE 1829

A climbing thornless rose with long, arching shoots changing from green when young to almost chocolate-purple when mature. Smooth dark green foliage. Flowers semi-double, deep reddish-purple, rather ragged when open, produced both singly and in small clusters. Said to repeat but my plant has not done so to date.

S P A SF AL 10′ × 6′ 3 × 1.8 m

'Blush Boursault', 'Calypso', 'Rose de l'Isle'

Probably FRANCE 1848

Flowers fully double, opening flat, with slightly ragged petals of pale blush-pink. Long, arching, thornless branches less purple than 'Amadis' but reddening with age. Foliage, dark green and plentiful, gives good display of autumn colour.

S P A SF AL 15′ × 10′ 4.5 × 3 m

'Mme de Sancy de Parabère'

Bonnet FRANCE c.1874

A beautiful rose of rich pink. Fully double, opening flat with the elongated outer layer of petals giving the effect almost of a ragged rose within a rose. Foliage handsome, darkish green. Thornless stems deepening from green to soft greeny-brown as they mature.

S P A ◉ MF AL 15′ × 10′ 4.5 × 3 m

'Morlettii', *R. inermis morlettii*, *R. pendulina plena*

Morlet FRANCE 1883

Slightly less vigorous than other Boursaults although foliage and stems similar. Foliage particularly colourful in autumn. Flowers deep pinkish-magenta, almost double, rather ragged when fully open.

S P A SF AL 8′ × 6′ 2.5 × 1.8 m

'Mme de Sancy de Parabère', and above, 'Morlettii'

'Amadis'

R. macrophylla
FORMS AND HYBRIDS

The few hybrids which have come forth from this Himalayan species are all robust and vigorous. With the odd exception, these are perhaps better grown for the size and quality of their hips rather than for any intrinsic beauty of their flowers.

CLASSIFICATION

BARB	Species and hybrids: Class 1	
MR10	Species: Class 55	Hybrids: Classes 46 and 54
WFRS	Species: Class 38	Hybrids: Classes 10 and 17

R. macrophylla

HIMALAYAS 1818

Medium-tall shrub with bright, cerise-pink flowers amid large, purplish-green leaves. Wood purple and smooth. Large orange fruits hang conspicuously, rather like small, slim, bristly pears.
S P F W SF AL 10′ × 4′ 3 × 1.2 m

'Arthur Hillier'

Hillier UK 1938

R. macrophylla × R. moyesii
An erect-growing rose of considerable vigour. Masses of small clusters of large, single, rosy-crimson flowers with prominent yellow stamens heavily laden with pollen. These start in mid June and last well into July. Each flower is slightly concave. A special feature in autumn is the fiery-red hips which are in drooping clusters and flask-shaped. Foliage dark green with a dull gloss.
S P W F ◍ SF AL 10′ × 6′ 3 × 1.8 m

'Auguste Roussel'

Barbier FRANCE 1913

R. macrophylla × 'Papa Gontier'
A vigorous climber or large arching shrub with large, semi-double, bright pink flowers. Apart from its flowers, which are beautiful, this shrub lacks the character of others in its group, especially in fruit.
S P F ◍ MF AL 15′ × 8′ 4.5 × 2.5 m

R. macrophylla hips

'Doncasterii', *R. doncasterii*

E. Doncaster UK 1930

R. macrophylla seedling
A good rose, more arching than others of its type

'Auguste Roussel', and below, 'Doncasterii'

'Master Hugh'

and less tall. Inherits dark, plum-coloured wood and purplish-green leaves from *R. macrophylla*, together with large, pear-shaped hips. Flowers pink verging on red.

S P F W ◐ AL 6′ × 4′ 1.8 × 1.2 m

'Master Hugh'

L. M. Mason UK 1966

R. macrophylla seedling

This rose provides us with some of the largest hips of all. They are orange-red in colour and flagon-shaped. The shrub is similar in other respects to its parent, except that its leaves are larger and it grows more vigorously.

S P F ◐ W AL 15′ × 8′ 4.5 × 2.5 m

'Rubricaulis', *R. macrophylla rubricaulis*

HIMALAYAS Introduced by Hillier

Similar to the species but wood darker and often covered in a greyish bloom. Said to be less hardy but I have no experience to prove this.

S F W ◐ AL 8′ × 4′ 2.5 × 1.2 m

R. majalis, R. cinnamomea, 'Cinnamon Rose'

N.E. EUROPE 17th century or earlier

An upright-growing, yet branching rose with slightly downy greyish-green foliage and mauvish-purple stems. The flowers, which are variable from pale to mid-pink, occur quite early in summer or, in good seasons, late spring. Medium-sized round fruit.

SP F W SF AL 6′ × 4′ 1.8 × 1.2 m

R. majalis plena, R. cinnamomea plena, 'Rose du Saint Sacrement', 'Whitsuntide Rose'

N. AND W. ASIA Cultivated pre-1600

This is the double form of *R. majalis* and is the same in all respects except for its flowers, which are rather lovely for a short time in late spring to early summer. More commonly known as *R. cinnamomea plena*.

SP F W AL 6′ × 4′ 1.8 × 1.2 m

R. marretii

MIDDLE EAST 1908

An upright-growing shrub with purple wood and medium-sized, mid-green foliage. Flowers mid- to pale pink, usually in small clusters. Hips red, round and of medium size.

S F W P ◐ SF AL 6′ × 4′ 1.8 × 1.2 m

R. maximowicziana

N.E. ASIA 1905

Single white flowers in small spaced clusters, sometimes hidden among soft-textured, serrated foliage. Not tall. Mine, after three years, admittedly in a shady position, has reached 5′ (1.5 m), bushy with thin, sparsely spiny stems with many lateral branches on which flowers are produced. Perhaps a rogue hybrid, as none of its characteristics fits any other description I have found. Similar is *R. fedtschenkoana.*

S P W ◍ AL 6′ × 4′ 1.8 × 1.2 m

R. melina

N. AMERICA 1930

A short-growing, dense shrub with large, soft rose pink flowers. I have not met this rose as a mature shrub. As a maiden, it has greyish-green foliage.

S P W ◍ AL 3′ × 3′ 90 × 90 cm

R. melina hips, and below, *R. × micrugosa alba*

R. × micrugosa

Foundling at Strasbourg Botanical Institute *c.*1905

R. roxburghii × R. rugosa

A dense, medium-sized shrub with rugose foliage. Large, delicate, single, pale pink flowers, produced throughout the summer; stubbly, round, orange-red hips.

R H W F P A MF ◍ ▽ AL 5′ × 4′ 1.5 × 1.2 m

R. × micrugosa alba

Dr Hurst UK 1910

Very beautiful white flowers with pronounced stamens. Continuity of bloom should encourage its wider use. More upright in habit than its parent *R. × micrugosa*, but otherwise similar in growth.

R H W F P A ◍ ▽ MF AL 5′ × 4′ 1.5 × 1.2 m

R. mohavensis

S. USA *c.*1930

A short-growing, dense shrub with numerous slender stems and an average population of thorns. Small, mid-green leaves. Flowers small, mid- to soft pink. Rounded red hips. Enjoys moisture.

S F W P ◍ ≋ AL 3′ × 3′ 90 × 90 cm

R. moyesii

FORMS AND HYBRIDS

It is not surprising that breeders, from time to time, have experimented with this rose as a parent; for as a species it is one of the best and most garden-worthy of all the wonderful wild roses to have come to us from the wilds of China. I have selected here about a dozen, representing perhaps the best of its several hybrids. Every garden should have at least one, for not only do they produce a good crop of flowers but, with one or two notable exceptions, where fruit is not important anyway, they all bear a heavy crop of very attractive hips each autumn.

CLASSIFICATION

BARB   Species and hybrids: Class 1
MR10   Species: Class 55   Hybrids: Class 33
WFRS   Species: Class 38   Hybrids: Class 10

R. moyesii

W. CHINA Discovery 1890, introduction 1894

Despite the very attractive deep crimson flowers and distinctive dark green foliage, it is undoubtedly the fruit that makes this rose and its hybrids so popular. Although the hips are not as large as in some other species, the plant can usually be relied upon to yield a large crop each year. Produced pendulously, they are orange-red and flagon-shaped, with a five-pointed crown of sepals. As a shrub it is vigorous and solid but if allowed to grow for too long without pruning it gets gaunt and coarse at the base. I have seen this rose making a splendid, if unusual, wall plant. Beware of growing this rose from seed or purchasing plants grown by this means, as many are sterile and never produce hips. Illustrated on page 5.

S P W F ◍ ≋ AL 10′ × 6′ 3 × 1.8 m

R. moyesii 'Pink Form'

CHINA

Similar in most respects to R. moyesii except for the colour of the flower which is, of course, pink. Several variable forms seem to have been distributed, presumably from seedlings of R. moyesii or its forms, raised deliberately or by chance.

S P W F ◍ AL 10′ × 6′ 3 × 1.8 m

'Eddie's Jewel'

'Eddie's Crimson'

Eddie CANADA 1956

'Donald Prior' × *R. moyesii* hybrid

A double deep blood-red with Moyesii-like foliage. In full flush it makes an impressive shrub. Upright in growth. Fruit not so obviously Moyesii, spherical in shape and deep red in colour.

S P W F CL ◉ SF AL 10′ × 6′ 3 × 1.8 m

'Eddie's Jewel'

Eddie CANADA 1962

'Donald Prior' × *R. moyesii* hybrid

Significant, in that I can vouch for this rose repeating in good seasons. Each double flower bright brick-red. Shoots dark browny-red. Foliage in Moyesii mould. Achieved from same cross as 'Eddie's Crimson'. In the first edition of *Classic Roses* I indicated that I had not seen fruit set on this cultivar. I now correct this: my plant has now produced a good crop of plump orange-red hips in each of the last three years.

R P W F CL ◉ SF AL 8′ × 6′ 2.5 × 1.8 m

'Eos'

Ruys USA 1950

R. moyesii × 'Magnifica'

An attractive shrub rose, very profuse in bloom, with medium-sized, almost single flowers of bright pinkish-red with white centres, produced all along rather stiff but arching stems. Scented. Sometimes fails to set fruit.

S F P W CL ◉ ≋ MF AL 8′ × 5′ 2.5 × 1.5 m

'Eos', left, and 'Geranium' below
opposite 'Highdownensis' and far right, 'Hillieri'

'Fred Streeter'

Jackman UK 1951

R. moyesii seedling

A denser shrub than any other Moyesii hybrid, with arching, spindly growth, bearing bright pink, single flowers along its length, followed by pendulous, large red hips.

S P W F CL ◉ SF AL 8′ × 6′ 2.5 × 1.8 m

'Geranium'

Royal Horticultural Society UK 1938

R. moyesii seedling

The most widely grown and best known of the Moyesii hybrids. Its single flowers are a beautiful, bright orange-red with a waxy texture. Its creamy anthers often powder the petals with pollen. Less vigorous than its parent and more angular in growth, with lighter green leaves, paler stems, and larger, equally shapely but less deep red fruits.

S F P W CL ◉ AL 8′ × 5′ 2.5 × 1.5 m

'Highdownensis'

Hillier UK 1928

R. moyesii seedling

Arching branches of single, light crimson flowers on a bushy, dense, tall shrub with ample foliage. Fruit large, reddish-plum-coloured and flagon-shaped.

S F P W CL ◉ ⧼ AL 8′ × 6′ 2.5 × 1.8 m

'Hillieri', *R. × pruhoniciana hillieri*

Hillier UK 1920

R. moyesii × R. multibracteata

Very dark red flowers, single with prominent anthers. Fewer thorns than others of this group, with smaller and perhaps fewer leaves. Growth angular but stiff. Vigorously graceful. Not all the

flowers set their fruit, which is large, orange and flagon-shaped.

S P W F ◉ ⧼ AL 8′ × 6′ 2.5 × 1.8 m

'Marguerite Hilling'

Hilling UK 1959

'Nevada' sport

This is a splendid, pink sport of the well-known 'Nevada', which it fully resembles except for its soft rose-pink colour. In first flush this rose is very showy and, like its parent, very floriferous from late May to mid-June, with intermittent flowers throughout the remainder of summer, and well into autumn.

R P W H CL ⧼ MF AL 8′ × 7′ 2.5 × 2 m

'Nevada'

Dot SPAIN 1927

R. moyesii hybrid?

A superb shrub. Large, single, slightly blowsy flowers produced in profusion on a vigorous, dense but tidy shrub in late May and early June. Plentiful light green foliage. Dark chocolate-brown stems with sparse thorns. Usually flowers on intermittently throughout the summer, and often gives a good display in the autumn. Opinions vary as to its proper parentage. It has some affinity in looks with *R. moyesii* and is usually placed here – a course that I follow despite tending to agree with the late Jack Harkness, who suggests it might be better placed among the *R. pimpinellifolia* hybrids. I have also received corespondence from John Clifton of Stafford, England, drawing my attention to Roy Genders' 1965 book *A Complete Handbook*

'Marguerite Hilling', and below, 'Nevada'

of *Roses* which also suggests *R. pimpinellifolia* parentage.

R P W H CL ≋ MF AL 8′ × 7′ 2.5 × 2 m

'Sealing Wax'

Royal Horticultural Society UK 1938

R. moyesii hybrid

A fine hybrid, very similar in habit and foliage to 'Geranium' except for its bright pink flowers. Fruit bright red, in the expected flagon shape.

S P W F CL ◉ AL 8′ × 5′ 2.5 × 1.5 m

'Wintoniensis'

Hillier UK 1928

R. moyesii × *R. setipoda*

Of interesting parentage, giving rise to a vigorous shrub which romps away, both in height and girth. Its light grey foliage is slightly scented. Its flowers are single, deep pink and its fruits are large and very hairy.

S F P W CL ◉ SF AL 12′ × 10′ 3.5 × 3 m

R. fargesii

Veitch UK 1913

Very similar in stature to *R. moyesii* but slightly less vigorous. Flowers more pink than red and foliage

smaller. Hips are of the same shape but usually larger and perhaps fewer.

S F P W CL ◉ ≋ AL 8′ × 5′ 2.5 × 1.5 m

R. holodonta

CHINA 1908

Glowing pink flowers in small clusters on an upright-growing, well-armed plant. Hips pendulous and flagon-shaped. This name is sometimes attributed to all pink forms of *R. moyesii*. It is now accepted that *R. holodonta* is distinct and more akin to *R. davidii* than to *R. moyesii*. See Bean, *Trees and Shrubs Hardy in the British Isles*, Vol. IV, 8th edition, 1981.

S P W F ≋ AL 10′ × 6′ 3 × 1.8 m

R. multibracteata
FORMS AND HYBRID

CLASSIFICATION

BARB	Species: Class 1	Hybrid: Class 1
MR10	Species: Class 55	Hybrid: Class 54
WFRS	Species: Class 38	Hybrid: Class 10

R. multibracteata

CHINA 1908

An elegant shrub with fern-like leaves from thick stems with numerous, spiky thorns, usually in pairs. Single flowers are produced in bunched clusters, often at the ends of arching shoots; these are lilac-pink and produced on thin petioles which have alternating bracts along their length. Has a long flowering season although it is never very floriferous. The small hips, which retain their sepals, are rounded, bright red and sparsely bristly.
R F P W ◉ AL 6′ × 5′ 1.8 × 1.5 m

'Cerise Bouquet'

Kordes GERMANY 1958

R. multibracteata × 'Crimson Glory'
As so often with roses, one takes them for granted until a specimen is seen at its very best. At Helmingham Hall, Suffolk, Lord and Lady Tollemache have one shrub of this cultivar at least 12′ (3.5 m) high and 12′ (3.5 m) wide, standing alone in an open part of their garden and quite spectacular in full flush. Double bright cerise flowers are produced in profusion on long, arching branches amid dense greyish-green foliage.
S P W CL ◉ ≋ SF AL 12′ × 12′ 3.5 × 3.5 m

'Cerise Bouquet'

R. nanothamnus

CHINA, CENTRAL ASIA 1936

A close relative of the better-known *R. webbiana* and similar to this species in all respects except for its slightly smaller flowers and foliage.
S P H W ◉ ▽ AL 6′ × 6′ 1.8 × 1.8 m

R. murielae

W. CHINA 1904

A rare, medium-growing, widish shrub with thin stems of reddish brown and mid-green to greyish foliage. White flowers in small corymbs. Hips small, flagon-shaped and a bright orange red.
S F W P ◉ AL 8′ × 6′ 2.5 × 1.8 m

R. nutkana

FORMS AND HYBRIDS

The two hybrids of this American species described here are seldom seen outside botanical gardens and rose collections. This is a pity, for both are easy-going and garden-worthy, and will do well in almost any garden.

CLASSIFICATION

BARB   Species: Class 1
MR10   Species: Class 37
WFRS   Species: Class 10

R. nutkana

N. AMERICA 1876

A strong-growing shrub liberally endowed with dark greyish-green foliage and strong, relatively thornless, nut-brown stems. The single flowers are clear lilac-pink; these are followed by smooth, rounded fruit left untouched by birds until well into winter. One of my favourite species.

S P W F ◑ ▽ SF AL 6′ × 4′ 1.8 × 1.2 m

'Cantab'

Hurst UK 1939

R. nutkana × 'Red Letter Day'

A lovely rose which should be more widely used where a medium-sized shrub is required. The flowers, which appear in July, are large, single and deep pinkish-lilac with pronounced creamy-yellow stamens. These are followed by plumply oval hips of clear deep red when ripe, which remain on the plant

R. nutkana

well into winter. The dark stems are moderately armed and the foliage greyish-green.

S P W F ◐ AL 8′ × 5′ 2.5 × 1.5 m

'Schoener's Nutkana'

Schoener USA 1930

R. nutkana × 'Paul Neyron'

A vigorous shrub with large, single, clear rose-pink flowers. Quite fragrant. Growth arching but dense, with few thorns on darkish wood with grey-green foliage. American rosarian Bill Grant sent me the following facts about George Schoener, who bred this rose, amongst others. He went to live in California from Germany as a child and grew up there to become a Catholic priest. His interest in roses spanned a lifetime, and he specialized in trying to breed disease-free cultivars. He certainly succeeded with this one.

S P H W F ◐ AL 5′ × 4′ 1.5 × 1.2 m

R. paulii, R. rugosa repens alba see '**Paulii**', page 326

R. paulii rosea see '**Paulii Rosea**', page 326

R. pendulina, R. alpina, '**Alpine Rose**'

EUROPE *c*.1700

Arching, reddish-purple stems form a short, slightly spreading, almost thornless bush. Foliage dark green. Flowers single deep pink with pronounced yellow stamens, followed by handsome, elongated but plumpish hips.

S A P F W ◐ AL 4′ × 4′ 1.2 × 1.2 m

R. pendulina

R. pisocarpa

N. AMERICA 1882

A medium-sized shrub with a dense, slightly procumbent habit; plentiful smallish leaves and shoots covered in spines. Flowers in little clusters, single and lilac-pink. Fruit small, round, sometimes slightly elongated, bright red.

S A W F ◐ ▽ AL 3′ × 3′ 90 × 90 cm

R. prattii

W. CHINA 1908

An almost thornless, short to medium shrub with purple stems. Thorns that exist are yellow. Foliage greyish-green. Flowers pink, in small corymbs, followed by small, oval, whiskery fruit.

S W P ◐ ▽ AL 4′ × 3′ 120 × 90 cm

R. pyrifera

W. USA *c*.1931

A short to medium, quite dense shrub. In many ways very similar to the better-known *R. woodsii*. Flowers white, usually in corymbs. Hips smallish, deep red and almost pear-shaped.

S F W P ◐ ▽ AL 3′ × 3′ 90 × 90 cm

Rugosas

FORMS AND HYBRIDS

The many attributes of the Rugosa hybrids make them a race apart. They are invariably healthy, will grow almost anywhere without mollycoddling, and provide flowers throughout most of the summer. They are becoming increasingly popular as subjects for massed planting in parks, as barriers for motorways and as trouble-free screens for factories. Yet in gardens, too, their versatility can be harnessed to great and varied effect.

CLASSIFICATION

BARB   Species and hybrids: Class 30
MR10   Species: Class 55   Hybrids: Class 39
WFRS   Species: Class 38   Hybrids: Class 2

R. rugosa

JAPAN/PARTS OF W. ASIA 1796

A vigorous, thorny shrub freely sending up long canes. Over the years various forms of this species have been used to produce standard roses. It is these which appear, almost from nowhere, in derelict gardens as the result of having reproduced themselves from the original root of a standard rose,

R. rugosa

having long ago cast off its enforced, more delicate charge. Its willingness, too, to chance-hybridize with other roses and produce seedlings with minor variations has led to uncertainty as to which form is the true species. All the semi-wild forms have lightish to mid-green, sometimes wrinkled but always rough-textured foliage. The scented flowers are single and in most clones have prominent, soft yellow stamens, their colours ranging from clear deep pink to deep cerise red. The hips are globular, usually rich red, and variable in size according to clone.

C W F P H A ◉ VF AW 7′ × 6′ 2 × 1.8 m

R. rugosa alba

*c.*1870

This is one of the best forms of *R. rugosa*, making a most useful garden plant. The flowers are large, pure white and scented. It is a vigorous, bushy plant with fine, deeply veined, coarse textured but slightly glossy leaves. The stems are thick, buff-greyish and densely populated with small thorns of similar colouring. The fruit is large and tomato red in colour.

C W F P H A ◉ VF AW 7′ × 6′ 2 × 1.8 m

R. rugosa rubra, R. rugosa atropurpurea

JAPAN

Large deep crimson-purple flowers with creamy-yellow stamens. Habit of growth and foliage not unlike that of *R. rugosa typica*, though slightly more vigorous.

C W F P H A ◉ VF AW 6′ × 5′ 1.8 × 1.5 m

R. rugosa typica, R. rugosa rugosa

JAPAN *c.*1796

Makes a dense, rounded shrub and probably nearest to the true wild species. Single, scented flowers, deep reddish-carmine, followed by bright red, globular hips. This form makes a useful hedge and is frequently used in municipal planting schemes.

C W F P H A ◉ VF AW 5′ × 5′ 1.5 × 1.5 m

'Agnes'

Saunders Central Experimental Farm
CANADA 1922
R. rugosa × *R. foetida persiana*
A bushy, dense rose with dark green, rather crinkled foliage on thorny stems, one of the few yellows of this group. Flowers fully-double and highly

R. rugosa alba

'Agnes', and below, 'Belle Poitevine'

scented, amber yellow fading to white, repeated intermittently throughout season after a good first flush in June.

R P H ◉ ▽ VF AL 6′ × 5′ 1.8 × 1.5 m

'Belle Poitevine'

Bruant FRANCE 1894

Long pointed buds opening to large, almost double flowers of rich magenta pink. Foliage lush, heavily veined and dark green Slightly angular in growth but bushy. Occasionally sets large dark red fruit.

R A P H F ◉ ▽ VF AL 6′ × 5′ 1.8 × 1.5 m

'Blanc Double de Coubert'

Cochet-Cochet FRANCE 1892

R. rugosa × 'Sombreuil'

One of the outstanding Rugosa hybrids. Pure white, almost fully double flowers, exuding a superb perfume. Foliage rich dark green, plant dense and bushy. Fruit, sometimes quite large, only sets intermittently. Good autumn colour.

R F A P H ◉ ▽ VF AL 5′ × 4′ 1.5 × 1.2 m

'Blanc Double de Coubert', and right, 'Dr Eckener'

'Conrad Ferdinand Meyer'

'Calocarpa', 'André', *R.* × *calocarpa*

Pre-1891

R. rugosa × *R. chinensis*
Single rosy-pink flowers with pronounced stamens on a vigorous, sturdy plant with ample, deepish-green foliage. Sets abundant, sizeable, shapely hips.
R P H A F ◉ VF AL 6′ × 5′ 1.8 × 1.5 m

'Carmen'

Lambert GERMANY 1907

R. rugosa × 'Princesse de Béarn'
Single blooms with prominent stamens; deep, velvety crimson. Dark foliage on a bushy plant. A useful and under-used rose.
R A P H ◉ ▽ VF AL 4′ × 4′ 1.2 × 1.2 m

'Conrad Ferdinand Meyer'

F. Müller GERMANY 1899

R. rugosa hybrid × 'Gloire de Dijon'
A very strong, robust rose with stout stems and large thorns. Foliage rather coarse, dark green. Flowers large and full, unchanging silver-pink. Very highly scented. Unfortunately rather prone to rust, which can invade very early in the season.
R P W H VF R⚲ AW 10′ × 8′ 3 × 2.5 m

'Corylus'

Hazel le Rougetel UK 1988

R. rugosa × *R. nitida*
More akin to *R. nitida* in appearance than *R. rugosa*. The beautiful, mid-silver-pink and sizeable flowers are scented and have pronounced stamens. They are freely produced among dense, feathery, light green foliage. Bright orange-red hips follow on. The foliage turns a rich tawny-yellow in the autumn. An upright and dense rose, free-suckering making it good for mass planting.
C P SF ◉ ▽ AL 3′ × 3′ 90 × 90 cm

'Culverbrae'

Gobbee UK 1973

'Scabrosa' × 'Francine'
Very full, crimson-purple flowers on a well-foliated, bushy plant. Well-scented. Size makes it a useful cultivar. Slightly prone to mildew late in the season.
R W H VF M⚲ AL 5′ × 4′ 1.5 × 1.2 m

'Delicata'

Sizeable, delicate-textured, bright rosy-to-mid-pink flowers in clusters, displaying creamy-yellow stamens to effect when fully open. Sweetly scented. Growth short by Rugosa standards but making a

'**Corylus**' (photo Hazel le Rougetel)

'Fimbriata', and right, 'Fru Dagmar Hartopp'

tidy, densish bush. Foliage quite rugose, mid-green. Sets fruit intermittently.

R H ◐ ▽ VF AL 3′ × 3′ 90 × 90 cm

'Dr Eckener'

Berger GERMANY 1930

'Golden Emblem' × *R. rugosa* hybrid

Huge, scented, semi-double flowers of pale yellow and coppery-bronze changing with age to a slightly muddy pink; pronounced stamens when fully open. Well-scented. Foliage rather coarse, growth vigorous and also rather coarse. With spiteful thorns.

R W P H ◐ VF AL 10′ × 8′ 3 × 2.5 m

'Fimbriata', 'Phoebe's Frilled Pink', 'Dianthiflora'

Morlet FRANCE 1891

R. rugosa × 'Mme Alfred Carrière'

Not a typical Rugosa hybrid. Small semi-double

'F. J. Grootendorst'

frilly petalled flowers reminding one of Dianthus, white with pale pink blushes. Bushy, upright shrub with numerous light green leaves.

R P H W A ◐ ▽ VF AL 4′ × 4′ 1.2 × 1.2 m

'F. J. Grootendorst'

de Goey HOLLAND 1918

R. rugosa rubra × 'Nobert Levavasseur'

Clusters of small, crimson double flowers with frilly petals. Copious and somewhat coarse dark green foliage on a vigorous bushy plant. Continuously in flower throughout the summer.

C H P W ◐ ▽ VF AL 4′ × 3′ 120 × 90 cm

'Fru Dagmar Hartopp', 'Fru Dagmar Hastrup', 'Frau Dagmar Hartopp'

Hastrup GERMANY 1914

Beautiful, clear, silver-pink flowers with pronounced stamens especially good in autumn. Scented. Foliage dark green. Plant bushy, growing wider than tall. Excellent tomato-like hips. Sold under all these names by various nurseries around the world but its correct name is 'Fru Dagmar Hartopp'.

C P F W A ◐ G ▽ MF AW 3′ × 4′ 90 × 120 cm

'George Will'

Skinner USA 1939

(*R. rugosa* × *R. acicularis*) × unknown

This is a very good, interesting rose. Deep pink,

fully double flowers in tight clusters with a scent of cloves. Foliage follows its Rugosa parent. Growth twiggy but dense.

C P H ◐ ▽ VF AL 4′ × 3′ 120 × 90 cm

'Grootendorst Supreme'

Sport from 'F. J. Grootendorst' with deeper red flowers.

C H P W ◐ ▽ VF AL 4′ × 3′ 120 × 90 cm

'Hansa'

Schaum and Van Tol HOLLAND 1905

Very free-flowering. Double, highly scented, reddish-purple flowers. Vigorous, medium-sized plant with dark green foliage. Excellent red fruit. This is one of the best all-round Rugosas.

C H P F W ◐ ▽ VF AL 4′ × 3′ 120 × 90 cm

'Hunter', and above, 'Hansa' hip and flower

'Hunter'

Mattock UK 1961

R. rugosa rubra × 'Independence'
Scented, fully double, bright crimson flowers on a rugged, medium-sized, bushy plant with dark green foliage. A useful rose.
C P W ◉ ▽ VF AL 4′ × 3′ 120 × 90 cm

'Jens Munk'

Department of Agriculture CANADA 1974

'Schneezwerg' × 'Fru Dagmar Hartopp'
This is a delightful rose in all respects. Deliciously fragrant flowers of soft lilac-pink, semi-double when fully open with pronounced primrose-yellow stamens, followed by smallish round-to-oval hips. Foliage dark green and plentiful. Dense, bushy growth. Hardy.
C P H F A ▽ VF AL 4′ × 3′ 120 × 90 cm

'Lady Curzon'

Turner UK 1901

R. macrantha × *R. rugosa rubra*
An arching shrub with very thorny wood and dark green foliage. Lovely large, single, pale rose-pink, fragrant flowers. A vigorous, procumbent cultivar, favouring its pollen parent in most characteristics except habit, which is why I place it here rather than with *R. macrantha* hybrids.
R P G W ◉ ▽ MF AL 3′ × 6′ 90 × 180 cm

'Marie Bugnet'

Bugnet USA 1963

('Thérèse Bugnet' × seedling) × 'F. J. Grootendorst'
Pure white, very fragrant double flowers of a tousled form in small clusters amid plentiful, light green, crinkled foliage. Compact, bushy growth. Hardy. A lovely rose.
C ▽ H P VF AL 4′ × 3′ 120 × 90 cm

'Martin Frobisher'

Department of Agriculture CANADA 1968

'Schneezwerg' seedling
Well-scented, shapely, double, soft pink flowers. Foliage dark green, growth upright and very prickly. Not often seen but should be more widely grown.
R H P W ◉ ▽ SF AL 4′ × 4′ 1.2 × 1.2 m

'Jens Munk', and below, 'Martin Frobisher'

'Mary Manners'

Leicester Rose Company UK 1970

Probably sport of 'Sarah Van Fleet'
Pure white, semi-double flowers in profusion on an upright, thorny bush with ample dark green foliage. Highly scented. A useful rose, if a little prone to rust.
C H P W ◉ ▽ VF R◌ AL 4′ × 3′ 120 × 90 cm

'Max Graf'

Bowditch USA 1919

R. rugosa × *R. wichuraiana*
A trailing rose, ideal for banks, etc. Single, deep silvery-pink flowers paling slightly towards the centre with pronounced stamens. Shoots heavily dressed with large, dark, slightly glossy leaves. Seldom sets any fruit.
S F P G ◉ MF AW 2′ × 8′ 60 × 250 cm

'Mme Georges Bruant', and below, 'Nova Zembla'

'Nyveldt's White'

'Mrs Anthony Waterer'

Waterer UK 1898

R. rugosa × 'Général Jacqueminot'
Semi-double, shapely, rich deep crimson flowers, freely produced on a vigorous, broad, thorny bush with dark green foliage. Well-scented.
C W P H ◉ VF M♂ AL 4′ × 5′ 1.2 × 1.5 m

'Mrs Doreen Pike' (AUSdor)

Austin UK 1993

'Martin Frobisher' × 'Roseraie de l'Hay'
Large, warm pink, fully double fragrant flowers. Bushy compact growth with lots of light green foliage.
C P W H VF ◉ AL 4′ × 4′ 1.2 × 1.2 m

'Mme Georges Bruant'

Bruant FRANCE 1887

R. rugosa × 'Sombreuil'
Loosely formed, semi-double, creamy-white, scented flowers. Ample, rather coarse, dark green foliage on a vigorous, very thorny bush. Makes an impenetrable hedge.
C W P H ◉ VF AL 5′ × 4′ 1.5 × 1.2 m

'Nova Zembla'

Mees UK 1907

Pure white sport of 'Conrad Ferdinand Meyer' with all the same characteristics except colour of flower.
R P W H VF R♂ AL 4′ × 5′ 1.2 × 1.5 m

'Moje Hammarberg'

Hammarberg SWEDEN 1931

Very fragrant, large, nodding, deep purplish-red, fully double blooms followed by large, red, globular hips; together giving a striking effect in late summer. Growth vigorous, with good, tough, darkish green foliage. Extremely hardy.
R P H A F ◉ VF AL 6′ × 5′ 1.8 × 1.5 m

'Nyveldt's White'

Nyveldt HOLLAND 1955

(*R. rugosa rubra* × *R. majalis*) × *R. nitida*
Large, pure white, single flowers on a vigorous, dense, thorny bush. Dark green stems and foliage. Produces an excellent crop of round, bright red hips unfailingly each autumn.
C F P W H A ◉ VF AL 5′ × 4′ 1.5 × 1.2 m

'Pink Grootendorst', and below, 'Rose à Parfum de l'Hay'

'Pink Grootendorst'

Grootendorst HOLLAND 1923

'F. J. Grootendorst' sport
This rose is soft pink, otherwise the same in all respects as its parent. Tends to revert to red, sometimes giving both colours on the same head of blooms.
C H P W ◍ ▽ VF AL 4′ × 3′ 120 × 90 cm

'Robusta'

Kordes GERMANY 1979

R. rugosa × seedling
Large, single, rich scarlet-red flowers on a strong, robust, dense, thorny plant with good, dark if somewhat coarse foliage. Scented. Makes a very good, impenetrable hedge.
C P H ◍ VF AL 5′ × 4′ 1.5 × 1.2 m

'Rose à Parfum de l'Hay', 'Parfum de l'Hay'

Gravereaux FRANCE 1901

(*R. damascena* × 'Général Jacqueminot') × *R. rugosa*
Large, globular buds opening flat to rich, bright red flowers which turn deeper in hot sun. It is fragrant and, at its best, very beautiful. The foliage is dark green on a bushy plant with ample thorns. It has a tendency to mildew later in the season. Difficult to classify but best here on account of several *R. rugosa* characteristics.
C W ◍ ▽ VF M♂ AL 4′ × 3′ 120 × 90 cm

'Roseraie de l'Hay'

Cochet-Cochet FRANCE 1901

Sport from unknown hybrid of *R. rugosa*
One of the best loved of all the Rugosa hybrids. Splendid, semi-double flowers of crimson-purple, large and opening loosely flat. Strongly scented of cloves. Makes a dense, vigorous, bushy shrub, and is almost constantly in flower. Foliage dark green. Sadly, only occasionally sets fruit, but compensates with very good autumn foliage.
C P W H A ◍ VF AW 6′ × 5′ 1.8 × 1.5 m

'Ruskin'

Van Fleet USA 1928

'Souvenir de Pierre Leperdrieux' × 'Victor Hugo'
A bushy, well-foliated, recurrent rose which deserves more attention. Flowers large, fully double, crimson and highly scented.
R P H ◍ ▽ VF AL 4′ × 3′ 120 × 90 cm

'Sarah Van Fleet'

Van Fleet USA 1926

R. rugosa × 'My Maryland'
Semi-double, silky-pink blooms produced in profusion on a well-foliated but viciously thorny bush. Growth upright but bushy. Foliage dark green. Seldom sets fruit. Rather inclined to rust, especially after its first flush of flowers.
C P W H ◍ ▽ VF R♂ AW 4′ × 3′ 120 × 90 cm

'Roseraie de l'Hay', and below, 'Sarah Van Fleet

opposite: 'Ruskin', and 'Scabrosa', below

'Scabrosa'

Harkness UK Introduced 1960

As often happens, this foundling turned out well. The late Jack Harkness tells the story of this rose in his excellent book *Roses*. Sufficient to say here that it came on the scene through good observation. One of my favourite Rugosas. Large, single, rich silvery-cerise flowers with prominent anthers, often accompanied by large, tomato-shaped hips which are produced as abundantly as its flowers. Foliage dark, of thick texture, heavily veined and almost glossy green. Makes a dense, upright shrub. Particularly good for hedging. Very sweetly scented.

C F H P W A ◉ VF AL 6′ × 4′ 1.8 × 1.2 m

'Schneelicht'

Geschwind HUNGARY 1894

R. rugosa × *R. phoenicia*
Clusters of large, pure white, single flowers on a strong, impenetrable shrub with dark, viciously armed stems. Dark green foliage. Excellent as a dense hedge.

R P W H ◉ VF AL 6′ × 4′ 1.8 × 1.2 m

'Schneezwerg', 'Snow Dwarf'

P. Lambert GERMANY 1912

R. rugosa × a Polyantha rose
An interesting, slightly smaller member of the Rugosas. Pure white, semi-double, well-formed flowers with pronounced yellow stamens when fully open. Plentiful greyish dark green foliage. Rich red medium-sized hips set intermittently, often appearing together with the flowers later in the season.

C F P W H A ◉ ▽ VF AL 5′ × 4′ 1.5 × 1.2 m

'Sir Thomas Lipton'

Van Fleet USA 1990

R. rugosa alba × 'Clotilde Soupert'
Not unlike 'Blanc Double de Coubert' in many ways, including colour, but with a few more petals in its flowers. Fragrant. Growth vigorous and bushy with dark green, leathery foliage.

C P H A ◉ ▽ VF AL 5′ × 4′ 1.5 × 1.2 m

'Snowdon'

Austin UK 1989

Fully double, shapely, fragrant blooms in pure white old-fashioned style. Good healthy mid-green foliage. Vigorous growth.

C P W H ◉ MF AL 6′ × 6′ 1.8 × 1.8 m

'Souvenir de Philémon Cochet'

Cochet-Cochet FRANCE 1899

'Blanc Double de Coubert' sport
Like its parent in all but colour. Soft blush-pink with deeper tones in the centre.

C P H W ◉ VF AL 5′ × 4′ 1.5 × 1.2 m

'Thérèse Bugnet'

Bugnet CANADA 1950

(*R. acicularis* × *R.* × *kamtchatica*) × (*R. amblyotis* × *R. rugosa plena*) × 'Betty Bland'
A very hardy rose. Large, double flowers, clear red

'Schneelicht', and below, 'Schneezwerg'

'Thérèse Bugnet'

'Will Alderman'

Skinner USA 1954

(*R. rugosa* × *R. acicularis*) × unknown Hybrid Tea
Large, shapely, fully double, clear pink flowers.
Highly scented. Growth upright but bushy. Foliage
mid-green. Hardy.
R P H ◉ ▽ A VF AL 4′ × 3′ 120 × 90 cm

'Yellow Dagmar Hastrup', 'Rustica '91', 'Topaz Jewel' (MORyelrug)

Moore USA 1987

'Golden Angel' × 'Belle Poitevine'
Sizeable semi-double primrose-yellow flowers with
prominent deep yellow stamens. Growth spreading. Foliage rugose and coarse to touch. Stems very
thorny. Branching, with spreading habit of growth.
C P G ◉ ▽ VF AL 3′ × 3′ 90 × 90 cm

paling to pink. Fragrant. Good foliage. *R. rugosa*
influence not immediately recognizable.
C P H ◉ VF AL 6′ × 6′ 1.8 × 1.8 m

'Vanguard'

Stevens USA 1932

(*R. wichuraiana* × *R. rugosa alba*) × 'Eldorado'
A vigorous shrub, rather untypically Rugosa,
bearing semi-double flowers of salmon burnished
bronze. Very fragrant. Upright growth, well-foliated
with glossy, bronzy-green leaves.
R P W H F ◉ VF ⚏ AL 8′ × 6′ 2.5 × 1.8 m

'White Grootendorst'

Eddy USA 1962

'Pink Grootendorst' sport
Identical to other 'Grootendorsts', but with white
flowers and lighter green foliage.
C P W H ◉ ▽ VF AL 4′ × 3′ 120 × 90 cm

'Yellow Dagmar Hastrup'

R. sertata

W. CHINA 1904

A loose shrub with thinnish, arching, brownish branches with few thorns and greyish-green leaves. Deep pink flowers in small clusters followed by small, narrowly oval, dark red hips.

S F W P ◉ AL 4′ × 3′ 120 × 90 cm

R. setipoda hips

R. setipoda

CENTRAL CHINA 1895

A medium-sized, shrubby rose with thick stems and well-spaced strong thorns. Scented foliage, noticeable only when leaves are crushed. Exquisite flowers, produced in large clusters, clear, pale pink, single and quite big, with yellow stamens. Flower stalks strangely purple. Finishes the season with large, pendulous, plump, flagon-shaped, bristly deep red hips.

S P W F ◉ SF AL 8′ × 5′ 2.5 × 1.5 m

R. spaldingii

N. AMERICA 1915

Medium shrub with yellowish-green stems and soft greyish-green foliage. Flowers pink and slightly crinkled when fully open, flowering rather shyly and intermittently for a long season. I have the white form, which is rather charming. Small, round, red fruit in autumn.

S P F W A ◉ ▽ SF AL 4′ × 3′ 120 × 90 cm

R. spaldingii white, and below, *R. suffulta* hips

R. suffulta

Greene N. AMERICA 1880

Clusters of single, pink flowers followed by small orange hips. A short dense plant with soft grey foliage and thin, spiny stems.

S W F ◉ SF AL 4′ × 3′ 120 × 90 cm

R. sweginzowii macrocarpa hip

R. sweginzowii macrocarpa

This garden form from GERMANY

Original from N.W. CHINA

The thick, smooth, light brown stems viciously armed with thorns belie the beauty of this rose. Flowers numerous, single and bright pink, followed by large, shiny, plump, flagon-shaped hips of rich bright red. Well-foliated and rather angular in growth.

S P F W A ◍ SF AL 10′ × 8′ 3 × 2.5 m

R. ultramontana

USA 1888

A short to medium shrub with few or no thorns of consequence. Small to medium-sized clusters of pink flowers in mid-summer. Small, smooth, rounded, red hips.

S W F P ◍ ▽ AL 3′ × 3′ 90 × 90 cm

R. wardii

TIBET *c*.1924

A medium-growing, lax shrub which now appears to be extinct in its native form. *R. wardii* 'Culta' was raised at Wisley from seed, from the original form, and introduced in this name. Flowers single and white, rather like those of *R. moyesii*, with distinct brownish stigmas and yellow stamens. Shoots brownish, thorns sparse but sharp. Foliage bright green.

S F W ◍ ▽ AL 6′ × 5′ 1.8 × 1.5 m

R. webbiana

HIMALAYAS, E. ASIA 1879

A good and interesting shrub with long, arching,

R. webbiana hips, and below, *R. woodsii fendleri*

almost trailing, pliable shoots, densely clothed with small grey-blue foliage and fairly harmless thorns – at least until they become old and more stubborn. Small, numerous, scented soft pink flowers, followed by small orange-red bottle-shaped hips in the autumn.

P F W ◍ ▽ MF AL 7′ × 7′ 2 × 2 m

R. willmottiae

R. willmottiae

W. CHINA 1904

A superb shrub with arching stems of a darkish plum colour with a grey bloom. Grey-green, fern-like foliage, slightly scented when crushed. The plant, of arching angular habit, bears small, single, deep lilac-pink flowers with creamy-yellow anthers, followed by small, elongated, vaguely pear-shaped orangey-red hips.

S F W P ◉ ▽ SF AL 6′ × 6′ 1.8 × 1.8 m

R. woodsii, R. macounii

N. AMERICA 1820

Pink medium-sized single flowers in small clusters, followed by sizeable, globose bright red hips. Foliage mid-green and healthy, colourful in the autumn. Growth bushy, dense.

S P A F ◉ H W AL 3′ × 3′ 90 × 90 cm

R. woodsii fendleri

N. AMERICA 1888

Makes a superb shrub of upright habit with numerous thin spiky thorns on greyish wood. The flowers, plentifully produced on a well-foliated plant, are single, bright lilac-pink and followed by a crop of deep, waxy-red, globular hips which persist well into winter.

S H W P F ◉ SF AL 5′ × 5′ 1.5 × 1.5 m

R. yainacensis, R. myriadenia

N. AMERICA c.1912

Closely resembling *R. nutkana*, to which it is obviously related. Smallish but numerous deep lilac-pink flowers followed by small, rounded, bright red hips. Growth strong with darkish-brown stems. Foliage grey-green.

S P W F ◉ AL 5′ × 4′ 1.5 × 1.2 m

SECTION : *Synstylae*

Growth vigorous, climbing and flexible, 6′ to 30′ (2 m to 10 m).
Thorns variously sized, curved, some species sparse, others none.
Leaves mostly 5 to 7, sometimes 9, leaflets.
Flowers mostly in corymbs or clusters.
Hips mostly small, oval or round.
Sepals drop when hips are ripe.

SPECIES

*R. anemoneflora; R. arvensis; R. brunonii; R. dupontii; R filipes; R. gentiliana; R. helenae; R. henryi;
R. longicuspis; R. luciae; R. moschata; R. moschata nastarana; R. mulliganii; R. multiflora;
R. multiflora carnea; R. multiflora cathayensis; R. multiflora platyphylla; R. multiflora watsoniana;
R. multiflora wilsonii; R. phoenicia; R. × polliniana; R. rubus; R. sempervirens; R. setigera; R. sinowilsonii;
R soulieana; R. wichuraiana*

GARDEN GROUPS

Ayrshires; Floribundas; Hybrid Musks; Miniatures and Patios; Modern Climbers; Modern Shrubs;
Multiflora Ramblers; Polyanthas; Procumbent Shrub Roses

CLASSIFICATION

BARB Species: Class 1   MR10 Species: Class 55   WFRS Species: Classes 38 and 39
For classification of hybrids in this section, see under garden group headings.

ORIGIN AND DISTRIBUTION

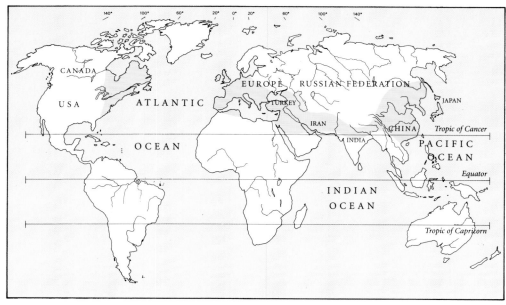

R. anemoneflora, R. triphylla

E. CHINA 1844

A climbing rose, the garden form of which has small clusters of double white flowers (in the wild, single). These are made up of large outer petals and many smaller ones in the centre. Quite interesting and unique. Growth is vigorous with few or no thorns. Needs mollycoddling for best results in colder climates.

S ○ T AL 12′ × 8′ 3.5 × 2.5 m

Ayrshires

FORMS AND HYBRIDS

This interesting group of medium-sized ramblers and scramblers is useful for a variety of purposes, from tree climbing to ground covering. When compared to some other groups of ramblers they may appear rather dull, since their colour range is restricted to white and shades of pink, but to my mind their flowers, without exception, have a simple refinement unsurpassed by those of any other equivalent group. At the same time, since they are derived from our native 'field rose', they are all very hardy and robust.

CLASSIFICATION

BARB   Class 1
MR10   Class 2
WFRS   Class 16

R. arvensis, 'Field Rose'

EUROPE

A beautiful, pure white single rose with medium-sized flowers and showy golden anthers. A ground-creeper or rambler with thin dark wood and foliage and well-spaced thorns. Frequently seen in hedgerows, especially in southern England.

S P G ◉ F W P ≈ AL 20′ × 10′ 6 × 3 m

'Ayrshire Queen'

1835

Sadly, another rose which seems to have become extinct. Descriptions suggest it was creamy-white with a purple throat.

'Bennett's Seedling', 'Thoresbyana'

Bennett UK 1840

Another double white which I have never seen. Said to be fragrant and very free-flowering.

S P G W ◉ ≈ MF AL 20′ × 10′ 6 × 3 m

'Dundee Rambler'

Martin SCOTLAND c.1850

A double white with flowers rather smaller than *R. arvensis* and growth more dense.

S P G W ◉ ≈ MF AL 20′ × 10′ 6 × 3 m

R. arvensis

'Queen of the Belgians'

'Düsterlohe'

Kordes GERMANY 1931

'Venusta Pendula' × 'Miss C. E. Van Rossen'
Large, semi-double flowers of rich pink, paling towards the centre. Foliage dark green and plentiful. Rather untidy but spreading to a dense wide shrub. Orange-red, plumpish, oval hips.
S F P G MF AL 5′ × 8′ 1.5 × 2.8 m

'Janet B. Wood'

Discovered by Mrs McQueen SCOTLAND 1984
Introduced by Beales UK 1989
R. arvensis hybrid
A delightful rediscovery to add to the important group of Ayrshire ramblers. The small, semi-double, pure white flowers are mostly produced in small clusters, but sometimes singly, having a slight scent. Foliage is ample and dark green, stems wiry, reddish and thorny. Since it is distinct from any other Ayrshire I know, I believe this to be an important rediscovery in that it complies in all respects with descriptions (admittedly somewhat scant) of the original Double Ayrshire of 1768. See page 28.
S P T N ◉ SF AL 15′ × 10′ 4.5 × 3 m

'Queen of the Belgians'

Pre-1948

Small pure white double flowers opening to show off golden stamens produced in tidy clusters. Foliage mid-green. Growth flexible and vigorous.
S P T N ◉ SF AL 15′ × 10′ 4.5 × 3 m

'Ruga', *R. × ruga*

ITALY Pre-1830

R. arvensis × R. chinensis
Semi-double flowers in large, loose clusters. Pale pink and well scented. Darkish-green wood, well foliated with mid-green leaves. Very vigorous.
S W P N T ◉ ≋ MF AL 30′ × 20′ 9 × 6 m

'Splendens', 'Myrrh-scented Rose'

Pre-1937

A good semi-double rose. Shapely buds opening to cupped flowers, white with hints of pink at the edges of each petal. Has an unusual perfume, and is sometimes called the 'myrrh-scented' rose. Stems dark purplish-green, foliage dark green. Illustrated on page 28.
S P G W ◉ ≋ VF AL 20′ × 10′ 6 × 3 m

'Venusta Pendula'

An ancient cultivar
Reintroduced Kordes GERMANY 1928

Clusters of cascading, small, white flushed pink, fully double flowers on spindly, dark plum-red shoots with dark, dull-green foliage. Moderately thorny, little or no scent.
S P G W ◉ ≋ AL 18′ × 10′ 5.5 × 3 m

R. brunonii

AND HYBRID

CLASSIFICATION

BARB	Class 1
MR9	Classes 53 and 55
WFRS	Classes 39 and 14 or 16

R. brunonii, R. moschata nepalensis

HIMALAYAS c.1823

A densely foliated, vigorous climber. Leaves large, downy in texture and drooping, light grey-green. Shoots grey-green, with young wood a tarnished, pinkish brown. Extremely vigorous and armed with hooked thorns. Flowers are single, tissuey in texture, creamy white, produced in clusters in July. Until recently this species was thought to belong under R. moschata but it is now accepted as distinct.

S N P T W ◖ VF AL 25′ × 15′ 7.5 × 4.5 m

R. dupontii, 'Dupontii'

EUROPE Pre-1817

Possibly R. gallica × R. moschata
Beautifully shaped pure white flowers with pronounced golden-brown stamens. Sweetly scented. Flowering rather later than many species, linking it perhaps with R. moschata. Also it has an occasional flower later in the summer. Growth is strong, with light green wood and ample greyish-green foliage. Fruit, when set, ripens very late in autumn.

S P H W MF AW 7′ × 4′ 2 × 1.2 m

R. brunonii

R. dupontii

'La Mortola'

La Mortola Gardens ITALY c.1936

Introduced to UK by Sunningdale Nurseries, 1959
Probably sport from R. brunonii
A more refined or less refined form, depending on your viewpoint, of R. brunonii. Foliage of the same texture but larger and more obviously grey. Flowers slightly larger and perhaps more numerous. Seems quite hardy here in Norfolk.

S N P T W ◖ VF AL 20′ × 12′ 6 × 3.5 m

'La Mortola' (see page 243)

R. filipes

FORMS AND HYBRIDS

R. filipes is best known for its prowess as a climber and its few direct descendants have, without exception, inherited that trait. They are not candidates for the smaller garden, being capable of climbing the tallest tree and completely smothering an average-sized house. However, they have their place and no garden that can accommodate them should be without at least one, preferably all.

CLASSIFICATION

BARB   Class 1
MR10   Classes 53 and 55
WFRS   Class 16 or 18

R. filipes

CHINA 1908

A vigorous species capable of growing 30′ (9 m) or more especially with the support of trees, and producing large panicles of single, creamy-white scented flowers each with golden stamens. Lush, light green foliage, numerous hips in autumn. Now more commonly seen in the better garden form, 'Kiftsgate'.

S N P F G T A ◉ ≋ MF AL 30′ × 20′ 9 × 6 m

'Kiftsgate'

'Brenda Colvin'

Colvin UK 1970

Probably 'Kiftsgate' seedling

Medium flowers of soft blush-pink to white, single, in clusters. Strongly perfumed. Very vigorous and healthy. Foliage dark green and glossy.

S P T ◉ ≋ VF AL 30′ × 20′ 9 × 6 m

'Kiftsgate'

Murrell UK 1954

Sport or form of *R. filipes*, found at Kiftsgate Court, Gloucestershire, England

A strong, vigorous climber capable of climbing to considerable heights. The fragrant, creamy-white flowers with golden stamens are borne in huge cascading trusses in mid-summer, followed by thousands of small, red hips in the autumn. The foliage is large, profuse and glossy, green tinted copper when young. It also changes to rich russet in autumn. It tolerates considerable shade and consequently it is an ideal subject for climbing into trees. Also an effective ground cover but only where its enthusiasm can be left unchecked.

S N P F G T A ◉ ≋ MF W 30′ × 20′ 9 × 6 m

'Treasure Trove'

Treasure UK 1979

'Kiftsgate' × Hybrid Tea

A superb seedling from 'Kiftsgate' with all the vigour and performance of its parent. Large trusses of semi-double creamy-apricot flowers changing with age to blush pink. Quite outstanding, with a strong scent. Foliage changes from pinkish-red through to mid-green as it ages.

S N P F G T A ◉ ≋ VF AL 30′ × 20′ 9 × 6 m

R. gentiliana, R. polyantha grandiflora

CHINA 1907

Single to semi-double, creamy-white flowers produced in dense, cascading clusters from an exceptionally vigorous climbing plant, followed by small orange hips in autumn. Very large, glossy foliage of light green with coppery overtones. Its stems, which are similar in colour to its leaves, are also shiny with a sparse mixture of broad, hooked thorns, and smaller, more numerous, bristles.

S P F T A ◉ ≋ AL 20′ × 10′ 6 × 3 m

'Treasure Trove'

R. gentiliana

R. helenae

AND HYBRID

CLASSIFICATION

BARB   Class 1
MR10   Classes 53 and 55
WFRS   Class 16 or 18

R. helenae

CHINA 1907

A vigorous rose well worth its popularity as a climber into small trees. Foliage large, plentiful and grey-green. Stems thick, sometimes mottled brown. Single flowers, scented, creamy-white and borne in dense corymbs during mid to late June, followed by small, oval, red hips in early autumn, which alone can be quite spectacular.

S F P W T ◉ ≋ AL 20′ × 15′ 6 × 4.5 m

'Lykkefund'

Olsen DENMARK 1930

R. helenae × seedling

Huge trusses of single, scented, creamy-yellow flowers tinted pink. Foliage lush, light green tinted bronze. Shoots quite thornless and vigorous. Ideal for growing up into trees and sturdy enough to make a large specimen shrub.

S P T W ◉ MF AL 18′ × 15′ 5.5 × 4.5 m

R. henryi

CHINA 1907

A vigorous shrub or small climber with ample almost glossy foliage and large, hooked thorns. Dense corymbs of white flowers from early to mid-summer followed by masses of small, round, dark red hips.

S P F T ◉ AL 15′ × 10′ 4.5 × 3 m

R. longicuspis

F. Kingdom Ward W. CHINA c.1915

Almost evergreen, this rose is very vigorous with profuse, long, leathery, serrated, dark green foliage, reddish-pink when young. Very floriferous; huge, cascading panicles of bunched, medium-sized, single, white flowers each with pronounced yellow stamens. The growth is as tall but not as coarse as, for example, 'Kiftsgate'. The strong, wiry stems are excellent in assisting it to achieve great heights into trees. The flowers have little or no scent and are followed by small, oval, orange-red hips. Not totally hardy but well worth trying in the south. The species grown and sold as this cultivar in most modern-day catalogues is actually R. mulliganii.

S G P T F N SF AL 30′ × 15′ 9 × 4.5 m

R. luciae

E. ASIA c.1880

Very similar to the better-known and more widely grown R. wichuraiana. A dense, spreading shrub with plentiful, almost glossy, dark green leaves. Clusters of medium-sized white flowers are produced in late spring/early summer. Scented. It is now thought that this species was used to produce many of the hybrid Wichuraiana ramblers of late Victorian and Edwardian times.

S W T ◉ ≋ MF AL 10′ × 8′ 3 × 2.5 m

R. helenae (see page 247)

Musks

FORMS AND HYBRIDS

R. moschata has a number of direct descendants, and currently growing in our gardens are many more a few generations removed, for genes from this species inhabit the chromosomes of many of our modern roses.

The following are those directly related; there were once others. William Paul listed nine, excluding 'noisettes', in the tenth edition of *The Rose Garden*. I will describe only those hybrids known to be available today and which are probably true to name.

CLASSIFICATION

BARB   Class 1
MR10   Class 34
WFRS   Classes 12 and 18

R. moschata, '**Musk Rose**'

S. EUROPE/MIDDLE EAST

An ancient cultivar probably introduced during the reign of Henry VIII

Medium to short-growing climber or shrub rose with grey-green, slightly drooping foliage. Stems also grey-green, sparsely populated with hooked thorns. Flowers, produced in large spaced clusters, are cream until fully open, when they change to white. Starts flowering in July and continues until well into September. Hips, when produced, are small and oval.

S P W T N ◉ AL 8′ × 6′ 2.5 × 1.8 m

R. moschata floribunda

A very vigorous, spreading, dense, relatively thorn-less climber with large, long, lightish-green leaves and thick, green, slightly downy stems. The large, tightly packed clusters of single white flowers are produced rather earlier in the season than other Moschata hybrids. Each flower has an attractive ring of yellow stamens and emits a pleasant musk scent; they are followed by oval to round, orange hips. This is a pleasing and under-used cultivar.

S P T F N ◉ MF AL 20′ × 15′ 6 × 4.5 m

R. moschata grandiflora

Bernaix FRANCE 1866

An extremely vigorous climbing rose with typical Moschata-type foliage and extremely large clusters of single, white flowers, each with golden stamens. Fragrant. Round orange hips in autumn.

S P T F N ◉ MF AL 30′ × 20′ 9 × 6 m

R. moschata nastarana, '**Persian Musk Rose**'

ASIA MINOR 1879

Possibly hybrid between *R. moschata* and *R. chinensis*

Similar in many respects to *R. moschata* but more vigorous in growth and with more numerous, smaller leaves. Flowers, although similar in form to those of the species, are semi-double and touched with pale lilac-pink; they can also be fractionally larger in some ideal situations. Flowers are provided well into autumn.

S P W N T ◉ VF AL 15′ × 10′ 4.5 × 3 m

'**Autumnalis**', *R. moschata* '**Autumnalis**'

Probably *R. moschata* × *R. chinensis*

An interesting rose. The rose I describe is the cultivar I have grown under this name for many years but I have never been quite sure if it is correct. It is a small climber similar to 'Princess of Nassau'

R. moschata, and below, *R. moschata nastarana*, and '**Narrow Water**', right

except more vigorous. Large clusters of semi-double, cupped flowers of creamy-white to pure white, produced, it seems, with some reluctance from August through to early winter. Slightly scented. Foliage light green. Stems, almost thornless, also light green. Probably better in warmer climates than Norfolk.

C T N ◉ SF AL 10′ × 6′ 3 × 1.8 m

'Narrow Water'

Daisy Hill Nurseries IRELAND C.1883

Not much is known about this rose, but it probably belongs in this section. A tallish shrub or small climber with dark foliage and large clusters of semi-double, lilac-pink flowers with a good scent. Particularly useful in that it flowers late into autumn. I have become very fond of it.

R P ◍ VF AL 8′ × 6′ 2.5 × 1.8 m

'Paul's Himalayan Musk'

W. Paul UK Probably late 19th century

Perhaps nearer to *R. multiflora* or even *R. sempervirens* than its name suggests. Its drooping leaves (a clue to Moschata) are slightly glossy and darkish green, with hints of copper when young. Broad, hooked thorns on long, pliable wood. Very profuse when blooming in July. Flowers small, double, pinkish-lavender, produced in drooping clusters. Quite hardy, an outstandingly useful climbing rose.

S P T ◍ ≋ SF AL 20′ × 12′ 6 × 3.5 m

'Paul's Perpetual White', 'Paul's Single White'

W. Paul UK 1882

The flowers, large and single, and the way they are displayed, solitarily or in small clusters, suggest a liaison with *R. laevigata*. The foliage and habit of growth, however, belie this. It is light green and well spaced on relatively thornless, almost lime-green

shoots. Moderately vigorous. From the first flush which occurs in July, flowers continue to appear throughout the season until well into autumn. Not easy to grow.

R P ◍ SF AL 10′ × 8′ 3 × 2.5 m

'Princess of Nassau'

Probably early 19th century

A recent rediscovery, I believe by Graham Thomas, who sent me budwood in 1982. These flowered as maiden plants, coinciding with *R. moschata*, and going on well into autumn, fitting Paul's descriptions almost perfectly: 'Flowers, yellowish-straw,

'Princess of Nassau', and above, 'Paul's Perpetual White'

form cupped, very sweet.' I add to this, light green foliage. I can now vouch for its hardiness since it survived the severe winter of 1984/5, and again in 1995, with only moderate frost damage. Quite vigorous.

R P ◕ MF AL 10′ × 8′ 3 × 2.5 m

'The Garland'

Wills UK 1835

R. moschata × *R. multiflora*

Vigorous, spreading climber flowering in early July in great profusion. Masses of small, semi-double, daisy-like flowers, creamy-white, sometimes tinged pink. Very fragrant. Foliage mid- to dark green and not as large as in most other Moschata hybrids. Stems are well armed with stout, hooked thorns. An excellent rose.

S P N T ◕ ≋ VF AL 15′ × 10′ 4.5 × 3 m

'The Garland', and below, *R. mulliganii*

R. mulliganii

Forrest S. CHINA 1917

A medium vigorous species with broad, sharp, hooked thorns. Similar in many respects to *R. rubus*. Young shoots and foliage purplish-green; greyish-green when older. Flowers single in small spaced clusters, pure white and scented. Fruit small, red, round and conspicuous. Many of the plants grown and sold as *R. longicuspis* over recent years are actually this species and I confess myself in common with others to this error in identity.

S G P T F N ◕ ≋ MF AL 15′ × 10′ 4.5 × 3 m

R. multiflora

FORMS AND HYBRIDS

R. multiflora has had great influence in the development of the modern rose and I could almost fill two books of this size with hybrids which have *R. multiflora* somewhere in their lineage. I will place a number of important groups under this heading, since this is where in my opinion they are best placed in the family tree of roses.

I will first deal with the Multiflora species, and will then subdivide the hybrids of this lineage into their garden groups, each with a brief note of introduction as follows: Hybrid Musks, Multiflora Ramblers, Modern Climbers, Modern Shrubs, Polyanthas, Floribundas and Climbing Floribundas. Most of these groups, especially the Modern Shrubs, Floribundas and Modern Climbers, owe almost as much in lineage to section *Chinensis* as *Synstylae* but their cluster inflorescences place them here.

CLASSIFICATION

BARB   Species: Class 1
MR10   Species: Class 35
WFRS   Species: Class 16

R. multiflora

E. ASIA Late 18th, early 19th century

Very floriferous, at least during its relatively short flowering season. Flowers small, single, creamy-white, growing in large clusters on wood produced in the previous season. When in full flush, they almost obscure the leaves which are smooth and lightish green. Stems also smooth and fairly free of thorns. Fruit is small, round to oval, smooth and red in colour. Until recently it was popular as an understock both from seed and – as it roots easily – from cuttings. Illustrated on page 27.

S F P T N ◍ ⁂ SF AL 15′ × 10′ 4.5 × 3 m

R. multiflora carnea

CHINA 1804

A fully double form of *R. multiflora* with stronger shoots and larger leaves. Flowers globular, white faintly tinted pink.

S P W F T N ◍ ⁂ MF AL 18′ × 10′ 5.5 × 3 m

R. multiflora cathayensis

CHINA 1907

Pink form of *R. multiflora* with larger flowers and lighter-coloured foliage.

S F P T N ◍ ⁂ MF AL 15′ × 10′ 4.5 × 3 m

R. multiflora platyphylla, *R. multiflora grevillei*, 'Seven Sisters Rose'

CHINA 1816

A vigorous climbing rose with large, dark green, rather coarse foliage and stiff, dark green stems. Flowers are double, quite large, and borne in very big trusses; they vary from deep to soft pink with sometimes lilac and even deep red blooms all produced together in the same truss. Scented. Common in Victorian times, when it was called 'Seven Sisters', derived from the seven different colours to be seen in each truss of flowers, another rose bearing this nickname being 'Félicité Perpétue', which is actually a *R. sempervirens* hybrid.

S P T N ◍ ⁂ VF AL 12′ × 10′ 3.5 × 3 m

R. multiflora platyphylla

R. multiflora watsoniana

JAPAN 1870

This unusual form of *R. multiflora* is probably an old garden hybrid. Slim, trailing stems with small, hooked thorns and small, narrow, light green leaves marbled grey, often wavy at the edges. Large panicles of small, closely packed, single flowers of off-white to pale pink. Masses of small, globular, red hips in autumn and early winter. More of a novelty than a useful garden plant. Not fully hardy.

S F ☼ SF AL 5′ × 4′ 1.5 × 1.2 m

R. multiflora wilsonii

1915

Rounded trusses of medium-sized single white flowers, produced very freely on a vigorous, moderately thorny plant bearing shiny foliage. Fruit orange, smooth, rounded but quite small.

S W P T N F ◉ AL 15′ × 10′ 4.5 × 3 m

Hybrid Musks

These are among the most useful of shrubs, having, by and large, long flowering seasons and agreeable habits of growth. For details on their history see page 25. Some of these make excellent small climbers for walls.

CLASSIFICATION

BARB   Class 15
MR10   Class 34
WFRS   Class 2

'Aurora'

Pemberton UK 1928
'Danaë' × 'Miriam'
Large clusters of almost single flowers of rich yellow, fading (like so many yellow Hybrid Musks) to creamy-white. Foliage mid-green, semi-glossy. Growth shortish and a little awkward in habit.
C P H SF ◉ AL 3′ × 3′ 90 × 90 cm

'Autumn Delight'

Bentall UK 1933
Soft, buff-yellow from shapely, deeper-coloured buds. The semi-double flowers are produced in large trusses on an almost thornless, upright but bushy shrub with dark green, leathery foliage.
C P H SF AL 4′ × 4′ 1.2 × 1.2 m

'Ballerina'

Bentall UK 1937
An outstanding rose with many uses from bedding to growing in pots. Huge sprays of small, single, pink flowers, each with a white centre. These are delightfully and daintily displayed throughout the summer on a bushy, upright, dense shrub with plentiful, mid-green foliage. Illustrated on page 66.
C B P H ◉ ▽ SF AW 4′ × 3′ 120 × 90 cm

'Autumn Delight', and right, 'Belinda'

'Belinda'

Bentall UK 1936

Huge trusses of semi-double flowers of mid-pink. Very vigorous and strong, with plenty of darkish green foliage. Fragrant. One of the less well-known Hybrid Musks but well worth consideration where a long-flowering shrub or ornamental hedge is required.

C P H ◉ ▽ MF AL 5′ × 4′ 1.5 × 1.2 m

'Bishop Darlington'

Thomas USA 1926

'Aviateur Blériot' × 'Moonlight'

Large flowers, semi-double, creamy-white to pink with a yellow base to each petal and a strong scent. Bush vigorous, with mid to dark green foliage.

R P H SF AL 5′ × 5′ 1.5 × 1.5 m

'Bloomfield Dainty'

Thomas USA 1924

'Danaë' × 'Mme Edouard Herriot'

Long, pointed, orange buds open to single blooms of soft clear yellow. Quite fragrant. Foliage glossy mid-green on a vigorous, upright-growing plant.

R P CL N ◉ MF AL 8′ × 4′ 2.5 × 1.2 m

'Buff Beauty'

Bentall UK 1939

'William Allen Richardson' × unknown

One of the best of its group. A vigorous shrub with

'Bloomfield Dainty', and below, 'Buff Beauty'

spreading growth and dark green foliage. Flowers fully double, opening flat from tight, cupped buds and produced in large trusses. Colour varies with weather and, I suspect, the soil in which they are growing, from buff-yellow to almost apricot, at times paling to primrose. Strongly scented.

C P H CL ◉ ▽ VF AW 5′ × 5′ 1.5 × 1.5 m

'Bishop Darlington'

'Callisto'

Pemberton UK 1920

'William Allen Richardson' × 'William Allen Richardson'

Sizeable clusters of small, shapely, semi-double to

'Cornelia'

double flowers of rich yellow, paling to soft yellow with age. Quite vigorous in that its flowers are carried on long, sometimes arching stems, giving the effect of a rather open plant. Medium-sized foliage of lightish green. Few thorns.
C P H ◉ ▽ AL 5′ × 4′ 1.5 × 1.2 m

'Clytemnestra'

Pemberton UK 1915
'Trier' × 'Liberty'
Large clusters of soft lemony-beige flowers gently suffused salmon with pronounced anthers of golden yellow. Fragrant. Individually an untidy flower but very effective *en masse*. Foliage dark green and leathery on a wide, vigorous shrub. This rose should be far better known.
C P H B ◉ ▽ MF AL 4′ × 4′ 1.2 × 1.2 m

'Cornelia'

Pemberton UK 1925
Conspicuous bronzy foliage produced on long, dark brownish shoots. The small, fully double flowers, which are produced in large clusters, blend superbly with the foliage, being apricot-pink flushed deep pink with paler highlights. Particularly good in the autumn.
C P H CL ◉ ▽ MF AW 5′ × 5′ 1.5 × 1.5 m

'Danaë'

Pemberton UK 1913
'Trier' × 'Gloire de Chédane-Guinoisseau'
Clusters of semi-double, bright yellow flowers changing to buff and then to cream with age. A healthy, vigorous plant with dark foliage. A most useful lesser-known Hybrid Musk, well worth growing, where a shrub of this colour is sought. Illustrated on page 26.
C P CL H ◉ MF AL 5′ × 4′ 1.5 × 1.2 m

'Daphne'

Pemberton UK 1912
One of the first Pemberton Musks and one of the least known. Clusters of soft pink to blush, semi-double flowers with a good perfume. Growth moderately vigorous. Foliage mid-green, semi-glossy.
C P H ▽ ◉ MF AL 4′ × 4′ 1.2 × 1.2 m

'Daybreak'

Pemberton UK 1918
'Trier' × 'Liberty'
Rather less than double flowers, lemon-yellow paling to primrose, produced on strong stems in medium-sized, well-spaced clusters. Foliage coppery, especially when young. Seldom gets very tall and never outgrows its welcome in any garden.
C P B H ▽ MF AL 4′ × 3′ 120 × 90 cm

'Eva'

Kordes GERMANY 1938
'Robin Hood' × 'J. C. Thornton'
Trusses of good-sized, almost single bright carmine to red flowers which pale towards the centre to white. This lesser-known cultivar is well scented. Dark green foliage on a fairly tall-growing plant.
C P H MF AL 6′ × 4′ 1.8 × 1.2 m

'Felicia'

Pemberton UK 1928
'Trier' × 'Ophelia'
This rose is among the best of its group. The fully

'Felicia'

double flowers open from a rather muddled bud to shapely blooms of quite a charming mixture of rich pink with salmon shadings; they pale slightly with age but I find this an added attraction. Foliage crisp, slightly crinkled at the edges and dark green. The bush retains its shape well with judicious pruning, making it ideal for specimen planting.

C P H ▽ MF AW 4′ × 4′ 1.2 × 1.2 m

'Francesca'

Pemberton U K 1928

'Danaë' × 'Sunburst'

Large sprays of semi-double, apricot-yellow flowers on strong, dark stems with glossy dark green foliage.

Useful, since its strong yellow colour is rare amongst shrub roses generally.

C P H CL ◑ ▽ SF AL 4′ × 4′ 1.2 × 1.2 m

'Kathleen'

Pemberton U K 1922

'Daphne' × 'Perle des Jeannes'

Very vigorous rose. Dark green foliage rather sparse for my taste. Stems greyish-green. Flowers almost single, medium-sized, best described as clear pink with deeper shadings.

R P MF AL 8′ × 4′ 2.5 × 1.2 m

'Lavender Lassie'

Kordes G E R M A N Y 1960

Large trusses of beautiful, double, lavender-pink flowers, opening flat, produced throughout the summer on a healthy bush with dark green foliage. An ideal rose which can fulfil a variety of roles in the modern garden.

C P H CL ◑ MF AL 5′ × 4′ 1.5 × 1.2 m

'Moonlight'

Pemberton U K 1913

'Trier' × 'Sulphurea'

Long, well-foliated stems with clusters of creamy-

'Kathleen', and above, 'Francesca'

'Lavender Lassie', and below, 'Moonlight'

'Nur Mahal'

produced freely in massive clusters. Foliage mid-green on a dense and bushy plant.
C P B H ▽ AL 4′ × 3′ 120 × 90 cm

'Nur Mahal'

Pemberton UK 1923
'Château de Clos Vougeot' × Hybrid Musk seedling
Large clusters of bright crimson, semi-double flowers well perfumed. An interesting rose with much to commend it, not least its healthy dark foliage.
C P CL H ◉ MF AL 5′ × 4′ 1.5 × 1.2 m

'Pax'

Pemberton UK 1918
'Trier' × 'Sunburst'
Very large semi-double flowers, creamy-white to pure white, with obvious golden stamens. Blooms produced in large, well-spaced clusters which are held on long, arching stems. Foliage crisp and very dark green. A superb rose.
C P H ◉ CL MF AW 6′ × 5′ 1.8 × 1.5 m

'Penelope'

Pemberton UK 1924
'Ophelia' × 'Trier'
A favourite amongst the Hybrid Musks. This very pretty rose has large, semi-double flowers which, when open, show off to advantage the slightly frilled petal edges; creamy-pink with deeper shadings, especially on frilled edges. Scented. Foliage dark green with plum-red shadings, likewise the stems. A little prone to mildew.
C P H ◉ ▽ M♂ SF AW 5′ × 4′ 1.5 × 1.2 m

'Pink Prosperity'

Bentall UK 1931
Large trusses of small, clear pink, fully double

white almost single flowers with pronounced stamens. Scented. Vigorous and healthy.
C P H ◉ MF AL 5′ × 4′ 1.5 × 1.2 m

'Mozart'

Lambert GERMANY 1937
'Robin Hood' × 'Rote Pharisäer'
Small single carmine flowers with white centres are

'Penelope', and below, 'Prosperity', and 'Robin Hood', right

blooms with deeper shadings on an upright bush with dark green foliage. Scented.
C P B H ▽ SF AL 4′ × 4′ 1.2 × 1.2 m

'Prosperity'

Pemberton UK 1919
'Marie-Jeanne' × 'Perle des Jardins'
Large, double, creamy-white flowers produced in large even clusters on strong arching shoots with dark green foliage. The arching effect, caused largely by bending from the weight of flowers, rather than any tendency to sprawl, adds to its attraction. Well worth growing.
C P CL H ◍ MF AW 5′ × 4′ 1.5 × 1.2 m

'Robin Hood'

Pemberton UK 1927
Seedling × 'Miss Edith Cavell'
Large clusters of medium-sized flowers, rather more than single, bright scarlet ageing to crimson. Good, dark green foliage with a bushy, tidy growth habit.
C H ▽ SF AL 4′ × 3′ 120 × 90 cm

'Sadler's Wells'

Beales UK 1983
'Penelope' × 'Rose Gaujard'
The newest member of this group. Makes a fine

'Sadler's Wells'

continuous-flowering shrub. Semi-double slightly scented flowers produced in large, well-spaced clusters on a vigorous but tidy bush. The background colour is silvery-pink, with each petal laced with cherry red, especially at the edges. The autumn flowers are particularly good, when the enriched colouring seems almost impervious to inclement weather. When cut, the sprays last very well in water. Foliage is dark green and glossy. Named for the English Ballet Company.

C P H ◉ ⚡ SF AL 4′ × 3′ 120 × 90 cm

'Thisbe'

Pemberton UK 1918
'Daphne' sport
Sulphur-straw coloured, the flowers are semi-double rosettes borne in large clusters on a bushy upright shrub with glossy, mid-green foliage.

C P H ▽ MF AL 4′ × 4′ 1.2 × 1.2 m

'Vanity', and right, **Will Scarlet**'

'Vanity'

Pemberton UK 1920
'Château de Clos Vougeot' × seedling
Large sprays of fragrant, rose-pink, almost single flowers of considerable size, produced freely on a vigorous, bushy but somewhat angular shrub. Rather short on foliage for my taste, but brightness and density of flowers probably make up for this minor fault.

C P CL MF AL 6′ × 5′ 1.8 × 1.5 m

'Wilhelm', 'Skyrocket'

Kordes GERMANY 1944
'Robin Hood' × 'J. C. Thornton'
Clusters of crimson, almost single flowers on stout, strong stems. A very useful rose, since good red cultivars are scarce among the Hybrid Musks. Foliage is dark green and healthy. Gives a good display of hips if not dead-headed.

C H F P CL ◉ AL 5′ × 4′ 1.5 × 1.2 m

'Will Scarlet'

Hilling UK 1947
'Wilhelm' sport
Almost identical to 'Wilhelm', except being brighter red.

C F H P CL ◉ AL 5′ × 4′ 1.5 × 1.2 m

'Astra Desmond'

Multiflora Ramblers

The Multiflora Ramblers were developed towards the end of the Victorian era and were very popular, alongside the Wichuraianas, for the first quarter of this century. As a group, they span a wide colour range and all are very floriferous for about four weeks in early summer. Generally speaking they are robust, healthy and easy to grow, and an advantage in the eyes of many gardeners is that, relatively speaking, they have few thorns. Although their popularity has declined since the advent of modern remontant climbers, they are far from out of place in the modern garden.

CLASSIFICATION

BARB	Class 15
MR10	Class 35
WFRS	Class 16

'Aglaia', 'Yellow Rambler'

Schmitt FRANCE 1896

R. multiflora × 'Rêve d'Or'

Small, semi-double flowers of pale primrose yellow. Growth upright, stems almost thornless. Foliage bright light green with bronzy tints, especially when young. Important as one of the roses used initially by Pemberton in breeding his race of Hybrid Musks.

S P ◉ N SF AL 8′ × 6′ 2.5 × 1.8 m

'Apple Blossom'

Burbank USA 1932

'Dawson' × *R. multiflora*

Huge trusses of apple-blossom-like pink flowers with crinkled petals. Foliage rich green with copper overtones. Wood is similar in colour to its foliage, with few or no thorns.

S P ◉ SF AW 10′ × 6′ 3 × 1.8 m

'Astra Desmond'

This rose has to be included in any serious book of roses for it is one of the loveliest of the Multiflora Ramblers. Its flowers are small and semi-double, off-white to cream, and they are produced very freely in huge trusses from mid-June to mid-July. Fragrant. The foliage is light green and crisp. Growth is very vigorous. In the first edition of *Classic Roses* it was described under the name of 'White Flight'. I have since found out its origin from Mrs Neame of Bedford (granddaughter of Sir Thomas Neame of Farnham, Kent, who was married to the opera singer Astra Desmond) and it was he, realizing its value and being a keen rosarian, who passed it to Hilliers of Winchester, Hampshire, for introduction in the 1960s.

S T ◉ N MF AL 20′ × 10′ 6 × 3 m

'Bleu Magenta'

*c.*1900

One of the daintiest of flowers. Rich deep purple with yellow stamens peeping from beneath folded, centre petals. Sweetly scented. Foliage dark and free of thorns. Although not recurrent, flowers later in summer than most Multiflora hybrids.

S P N ◉ MF AL 12′ × 10′ 3.5 × 3 m

'Blush Rambler'

B. R. Cant UK 1903

'Crimson Rambler' × 'The Garland'

A vigorous, almost thornless rose, popular as a cottage rambler in Edwardian days. Fragrant flowers blush-pink in colour, borne in cascading clusters. Foliage plentiful and light green.

S P SF AL 12′ × 10′ 3.5 × 3 m

'Bleu Magenta', and below, 'Blush Rambler'

'Bobbie James'

'Bobbie James'

Sunningdale Nurseries UK 1961

Capable of considerable climbing feats, especially into trees and hedges. I rate this rose as one of the best for this purpose. The individual white flowers are of cupped shape and quite large, rather more than single, highly scented, and displayed in large, drooping clusters. The foliage is rich coppery green and polished. Stems are strong and well equipped with sharp, hooked thorns.

S A P T N ◉ VF AW 30′ × 20′ 9 × 6 m

'Crimson Rambler', 'Turner's Crimson', 'Engineer's Rose'

JAPAN 1893

More important as a stud rose in the development of ramblers than as a garden plant. Semi-double crimson flowers produced in clusters. Foliage light green. Rather disease-prone, which is the main reason for its virtual disappearance from modern gardens.

S SF M◔ AL 12′ × 10′ 3.5 × 3 m

'De la Grifferaie'

Vibert FRANCE 1845

A vigorous, dark-wooded, rather coarse-foliaged plant, extensively used in the past as an understock and hence frequently found in old gardens. Trusses of spaced, fully double flowers of magenta fading to cloudy white. Well scented, not of great garden value. Illustrated on page 27.

S P N ◉ VF AL 8′ × 4′ 2.5 × 1.2 m

'Euphrosine'

Schmitt FRANCE 1895

R. multiflora × 'Mignonette'

Small clear pink double flowers in clusters. Fragrant. Plentiful mid-green foliage. Vigorous.

S P T ◉ MF AL 15′ × 10′ 4.5 × 3 m

'Francis E. Lester'

Lester Rose Gardens USA 1946

'Kathleen' × unnamed seedling

Very large trusses of well-spaced, medium-sized, single flowers, white with splashes of pink on the edges of each petal. A special feature is its strong perfume. The shrub is vigorous but not

'Ghislaine de Féligonde', and below, 'Hiawatha'

'Francis E. Lester', and below right, 'Goldfinch'

over-powering, with lush, coppery-tinted, glossy foliage. Small red hips in autumn.
S T F P N ◉ MF AL 15′ × 10′ 4.5 × 3 m

'Ghislaine de Féligonde'

Turbat FRANCE 1916
'Goldfinch' × unknown
A small climber or, if space permits, can be grown as a large shrub. Fully double, orange-yellow flowers in very large clusters. Healthy, large, glossy foliage. Almost thornless. I can't think of a good reason why this rose has not gained the popularity it deserves.
R P N ◉ MF AL 8′ × 8′ 2.5 × 2.5 m

'Goldfinch'

W. Paul UK 1907
'Hélène' × unknown
Less vigorous than some, but very useful where a small rambler or climber is required. Small cupped flowers a mixture of golden-yellow and primrose with pronounced golden-brown anthers, still charming even when fading to cream in hot sun. Almost thornless greenish-brown stems and glossy foliage.
S P N ◉ MF AL 8′ × 5′ 2.5 × 1.5 m

'Hiawatha'

Walsh USA 1904
'Crimson Rambler' × 'Paul's Carmine Pillar'
Single, deepish pink to crimson flowers with paler, almost white centres. These are borne in clusters on a vigorous, free-growing plant with lightish green leaves. Another rose awkward to classify, but

'Madeleine Selzer', and below, 'Mrs F.W. Flight'

probably best here because of obvious Multiflora influence.

S P ◐ T AL 15′ × 12′ 4.5 × 3.5 m

'Lauré Davoust', 'Marjorie W. Lester'

Laffay FRANCE 1934

Flowers which are small, cupped and double change with age from bright pink through to soft pink and then white. Foliage mid-green. Growth fairly upright and healthy. A useful, lesser known small rambler or tall shrub.

S P ◐ MF AL 10′ × 8′ 3 × 2.5 m

'Leuchtstern'

J. C. Schmidt GERMANY 1899

'Daniel Lacombe' × 'Crimson Rambler'

Clusters of medium-sized, single deep pink flowers with centres paling to white. Good, mid-green foliage. Not often seen but a good, shorter rambler.

S P N ◐ AL 10′ × 8′ 3 × 2.5 m

'Madeleine Selzer', 'Yellow Tausendschön'

Walter FRANCE 1926

'Tausendschön' × 'Mrs Aaron Ward'

Attractive, almost thornless rose with bronzy-green foliage, bearing trusses of fully double, scented, lemon to white flowers. Quite a spectacle when in full flush. An excellent medium-growing rambler.

S P SF AL 10′ × 6′ 3 × 1.8 m

'Mme d'Arblay'

Wills UK 1835

R. multiflora × *R. moschata*

Drooping clusters of small, flattish-topped yet slightly cupped flowers comprised of randomly arranged, shortish petals, fragrant, blush-pink paling to white. A very vigorous climber with darkish green foliage. Now quite rare.

S P T N ◐ VF AL 20′ × 20′ 6 × 6 m

'Mrs F. W. Flight'

Cutbush UK 1905

'Crimson Rambler' × unknown

Small, semi-double, rose-pink flowers in large clusters, on a short to medium-growing plant with large, soft mid-green foliage. An excellent, very free-flowering cultivar.

S SF AL 8′ × 6′ 2.5 × 1.8 m

'Paul's Scarlet'

W. Paul UK 1916

'Paul's Carmine Pillar' × 'Rêve d'Or'

Double, bright scarlet flowers in small spaced clusters. One of the brightest and most popular ramblers of its day, and still worth a place in today's gardens. Foliage dark green, as are its relatively thornless stems. I am not sure it should be in this group, but where else to place it?

S P N ◐ AL 10′ × 8′ 3 × 2.5 m

'Phyllis Bide'

Bide UK 1923

'Perle d'Or' × 'Gloire de Dijon'

Small, slightly ragged, large pyramidal clusters of flowers of mixed colouring including yellow, cream and pink, sometimes deepening with age and becoming mottled. Foliage plentiful but each leaf quite small. Growth vigorous and relatively thorn-free. A superb and important rose flowering continuously throughout the season, perhaps nearer to the section *Chinensis* than to *Synstylae*.

R P N ◐ SF AL 10′ × 6′ 3 × 1.8 m

'Paul's Scarlet', and below, 'Rambling Rector'
opposite, 'Thalia'

'Rambling Rector'

Very old cultivar

Large clusters of fragrant, semi-double flowers, creamy to begin with, then opening white to display rich yellow stamens. These are produced in abundance on a vigorous, healthy, scrambling shrub. Plentiful foliage, small, grey-green and downy. Superb as a tree or hedgerow climber. Produces a good display of small hips in the autumn. Many an old corrugated iron shed would become less of an eyesore if supporting 'Rambling Rector'.

S P W F T N ⬤ VF AL 20′ × 15′ 6 × 4.5 m

'Rose Marie Viaud'

Igoult FRANCE 1924

'Veilchenblau' seedling

Smallish very double flowers of rich purple, produced in small trusses on a vigorous rambler with light green foliage and relatively thornless, light green shoots.

S P ⬤ M☾ AL 15′ × 6′ 4.5 × 1.8 m

'Russelliana', 'Old Spanish Rose', 'Russell's Cottage Rose', 'Scarlet Grevillei'

Probably SPAIN 1840

Probably a cross between *R. multiflora* and *R. setigera*

A rose of some antiquity with very double, medium-sized flowers borne in clusters. Its colour is a mixture of crimson and mild purple, giving an overall red appearance. Well worthy of garden space. Foliage dark green and stems rather thorny, belying its Multiflora ancestry. Good specimens can be seen at both Cranborne House, Dorset, and Mottisfont Abbey, Hants, England.
S P N T ◉ VF AL 10′ × 10′ 3 × 3 m

'Seagull'

Pritchard UK 1907
R. multiflora × 'Général Jacqueminot'
Bright yellow stamens surrounded by a single layer of white petals. Scented flowers borne in large clusters on a vigorous, well-foliated plant which has grey-green leaves. An established plant in full flush of flower is a sight to remember. Illustrated on page 68.
S P N T ◉ MF AL 25′ × 15′ 7.5 × 4.5 m

'Tausendschön', 'Thousand Beauties'

J. C. Schmidt GERMANY 1906
'Daniel Lacombe' × 'Weisser Herumstreicher'
An interesting rose. The flowers, which are large, double and borne in loose clusters, are pink with white towards their centre. Growth is strong, with thornless shoots, amply clothed with mid-green foliage.
S P SF AL 10′ × 8′ 3 × 2.5 m

'Tea Rambler'

W. Paul UK 1904
'Crimson Rambler' × a Tea rose
Fragrant, double, soft pink flowers with brighter highlights on a vigorous plant with mid-green foliage. Illustrated on page 46.
S P T ◉ SF AL 15′ × 8′ 4.5 × 2.5 m

'Thalia', 'White Rambler'

Schmitt FRANCE Introduced by P. Lambert GERMANY 1895
Quite a good rose, not often seen today. Flowers white, smallish, semi-double and highly scented, produced profusely in large clusters. Growth vigorous and only moderately thorny. Foliage mid-green and mildly glossy.
S P T N ◉ VF AL 12′ × 8′ 3.5 × 2.5 m

'Toby Tristram'

Hilliers UK *c.*1970
Multiflora seedling?
Very floriferous when in flower in early summer. Huge trusses of creamy-white single flowers, spasmodically repeating, produced on a very vigorous plant with soft mid-green foliage, followed by orange hips. I can find very little in my library about the origins of this rose but it should be more widely grown.
S T ≋ ◉ N F MF AL 30′ × 20′ 10 × 6 m

'Trier'

P. Lambert GERMANY 1904
'Aglaia' × unknown
An upright-growing climber or, if preferred, tall shrub with small, creamy-yellow, single or near-single flowers in clusters. Foliage small, almost daintily so. Used much by breeders earlier this century, especially in development of Hybrid Musks.
R P ◉ SF AL 8′ × 6′ 2.5 × 1.8 m

'Turner's Crimson' *see* 'Crimson Rambler'

'Toby Tristram', and below, 'Violette'

'Veilchenblau'

J. C. Schmidt GERMANY 1909

'Crimson Rambler' × unknown seedling

A vigorous rambler sometimes called the 'Blue Rose'. Large trusses of small, semi-double flowers of lavender-purple occasionally flecked with white, especially in their centres. They mature to bluish-lilac and fade to lilac-grey. Scented. An ideal companion for cream and white ramblers, when their respective flowers can merge to good effect.
S P T N ◉ MF AL 15′ × 12′ 4.5 × 3.5 m

'Violette'

Turbat FRANCE 1921

Very double, cupped, rosette flowers of rich violet-purple with hints of yellow in their base. Flowers in clusters, scented. Foliage rich dark green. Growth is vigorous and shoots have few thorns.
S P T ◉ MF AL 15′ × 10′ 4.5 × 3 m

'Wind Chimes'

Lester USA Pre-1946

Clusters of small, double, rosy-pink blooms on a very vigorous shrub or small climber with good clear mid-green foliage.
C P W ◉ VF AL 12′ × 8′ 3.5 × 2.5 m

'Veilchenblau'

'Altissimo'

Modern Climbers

In recent years a most useful trend has occurred in modern roses: the development of a number of continuously flowering climbers. To be more accurate, they are really large shrubs which, if placed by a wall or given support, will behave rather like climbers. They do not send up long climbing shoots as do, for example, climbing Hybrid Teas (which are placed elsewhere despite the BARB classification that puts many of them into that group). They usually flower on wood produced in the same season. As for classification, they are a mixed bunch and now very hybrid indeed. But much of their vigour and floriferousness must be derived from *R. multiflora*, which enables me to place them here.

Most have been raised as seedlings and are not climbing sports. More and more are coming in each year and it is difficult to keep up to date, but those chosen for inclusion are all well-tried cultivars.

CLASSIFICATION

BARB   Classes 10, 11 and 12. Some 7
MR10   Class 46
WFRS   Classes 13 and 17

'Agatha Christie', 'Ramira' (KORmeita)

Kordes GERMANY 1990
Large, classical, clear pink blooms freely produced throughout the summer, set off by striking, dark green glossy foliage.
C P SF ✃ AL 8′ × 4′ 2.5 × 1.2 m

'Alchymist'

Kordes GERMANY 1956
'Golden Glow' × *R. eglanteria* hybrid
An unusual but beautiful medium-growing, climbing rose with rich green foliage and thorny wood. The very double flowers, mostly opening quartered, are a rich mixture of yellow and yolky-orange with a strong scent. These are produced quite early in the season; some of the first flowers are much paler than the later ones. Black spot can be troublesome.
S P ◍ VF BS○ AL 12′ × 8′ 3.5 × 2.5 m

'Aloha'

Boerner USA 1949
'Mercedes Gallart' × 'New Dawn'
A sumptuous and most attractive rose comprising 60 or more rose-pink petals, each with a deeper reverse and shadings of magenta, strongly fragrant. Healthy, dark bronze foliage. Has an upright habit and is seldom not in flower throughout the summer. In all respects a first-class rose.
C P ✃ VF AW 10′ × 6′ 3 × 1.8 m

'Altissimo'

Delbard-Chabert FRANCE 1967
'Ténor' × unknown
Large, bright red, single flowers borne in small-spaced clusters, sometimes singly amid dark green foliage. A superb rose for pillar work or trellis. Does not do well as a wall plant, at least for me.
C P SF AL 10′ × 6′ 3 × 1.8 m

'America'

Warriner USA 1976
'Fragrant Cloud' × 'Tradition'
Fully double flowers of rich salmon with lighter reverses. Very fragrant. Foliage mid-green. Growth vigorous.
R P VF AW 15′ × 10′ 4.5 × 3 m

'Alchymist', and below, 'Aloha'

'Antique', 'Antike '89' (KORdalen)

Kordes GERMANY 1989

Large, fully double, Centifolia-like flowers of rose pink, paler in the centres. Foliage lush. Growth vigorous.

C P SF AL 8′×4′ 2.5×1.2 m

'Ash Wednesday', 'Aschermittwoch'

Kordes GERMANY 1955

Said to be *R. eglanteria* hybrid

Although of Eglanteria descent, this rose is probably better placed here among modern climbers since I can detect no perfume from its foliage. Trusses of ashen-white to soft lilac, double blooms on a vigorous, thorny, well-foliated plant.

S P N ◉ SF AL 10′×6′ 3×1.8 m

'Autumn Sunlight'

Gregory UK 1965

'Danse de Feu' × 'Goldilocks'

Large clusters of fully double, orange-vermilion flowers. Foliage rich mid-green. Growth upright and tall.

C P SF AL 12′×8′ 3.5×2.5 m

'Bantry Bay'

McGredy UK 1967

'New Dawn' × 'Korona'

Large, scented, semi-double flowers opening rather blowsily, deep pink with quieter reflections. Foliage lush and dark green. One of the best and most free-flowering of its type.

P C MF AW 12′×8′ 3.5×2.5 m

'Breath of Life'

Harkness UK 1981

'Red Dandy' × 'Alexander'

Rich but not dazzlingly so. Apricot flowers are shapely, Hybrid Tea-like, and scented. Foliage dark green. A good and apparently reliable rose for those who like the orange shades, which are never the easiest of roses to grow.

C ⊱ MF AL 10′×6′ 3×1.8 m

'Butterscotch' (JACtan)

Warriner USA 1986

('Buccaneer' × 'Zorina') × 'Royal Sunset'

Double, shapely, tan-to-orangey-yellow flowers

'Ash Wednesday', and below, 'Bantry Bay'

opening cupped, produced in clusters on a vigorous, dense plant with mid-green, semi-glossy foliage.

C P ○ SF AL 10′×6′ 3×1.8 m

'Casino'

McGredy UK 1963

'Coral Dawn' × 'Buccaneer'

Clusters of large, full, globular, clear yellow scented blooms on strong, dark stems with contrasting light green, glossy foliage. Can be relied upon as a good pillar rose.

R VF AL 10′×8′ 3×2.5 m

'**Breath of Life**', and below, '**Casino**' and '**City of York**', right

'Château de La Juvenie'

FRANCE *c*.1901 Raiser not known by author
R. roxburghii hybrid
Large double shapely flowers in shades of pink.
Foliage matt dark green. Growth dense and spreading. I first saw this rose in the garden of William
Christie, the American composer, in the south-west
of France, and was most taken by it. Sometimes

remontant. Available only from André Eve, France,
at this time.
S ◉ MF AL 10′ × 8′ 3.3 × 2.6 m

'City Girl' (HARzorba)

Harkness UK 1994
'Armada' × 'Compassion'
Large clusters of medium-sized bright coral pink

scented flowers produced on a vigorous shrubby plant with glossy mid-green foliage.
C MF ❀ AL 8′ × 6′ 2.5 × 1.8 m

'City of York', 'Direktor Benschop'

Tantau GERMANY 1960
'Prof Gnau' × 'Dorothy Perkins'
A good vigorous climber with ample glossy foliage. Flowers creamy-white with lemon centres, semi-double and cupped. Individually beautiful and produced very freely to give a superb overall effect. Scented.
S P W N T ◉ MF AL 15′ × 10′ 4.5 × 3 m

'Clair Matin'

Meilland FRANCE 1960
('Fashion' × 'Independence') × unnamed Multiflora seedling
Free-branching, with large trusses of clear pink blooms, each with cream highlights. Almost but not quite single. A free-flowering habit makes this rose outstanding. Foliage dark green and stems chocolate-purple. Also makes a good free-standing shrub or tall hedge.
C P N ◉ SF AL 8′ × 4′ 2.5 × 1.2 m

'Colcestria'

B. R. Cant UK 1916
A beautiful, large, full flower of silvery-pink with reflexing petals opening flat. Very fragrant. Foliage light green. Growth – a little reluctant but well worth the effort.
R ▽ Gh ☼ VF ❀ AL 8′ × 5′ 2.5 × 1.5 m

'Compassion'

Harkness UK 1974
'White Cockade' × 'Prima Ballerina'
Dark green, glossy foliage on dark wood bearing shapely blooms of apricot and copper with yellow highlights. Scented.
R ❀ VF BS◯ AW 10′ × 6′ 3 × 1.8 m

'Constance Spry'

Austin UK 1960
'Belle Isis' × 'Dainty Maid'
A beautiful rose in the old-fashioned style. Large, clear, bright pink, very full with a myrrh-like perfume. Copious grey-green foliage on a vigorous,

'Compassion', and below, 'Constance Spry'

quite thorny plant. Ideal for most situations. Particularly good on a tripod.
S P H ◉ VF M◯ AL 20′ × 10′ 6 × 3 m

'Coral Creeper'

Brownell USA 1938
('Dr Van Fleet' × 'Emily Gray') × 'Jacotte'
Coral-pink semi-double fragrant flowers, very freely produced in clusters on a vigorous plant. Foliage semi-glossy, leathery. Upright dense growth.
S P ◉ H MF AL 12′ × 8′ 3.5 × 2.5 m

'Danse des Sylphes', and below, 'Dixieland Linda'

'Coral Dawn'

Boerner USA 1952
'New Dawn' × unnamed yellow Hybrid Tea
Large, full, rather plump, coral-pink blooms amid
ample dark green, healthy foliage. Scented. A first-
class free-flowering rose.
R N ◉ SF AL 12′ × 8′ 3.5 × 2.5 m

'Danse de Feu', 'Spectacular'

Mallerin FRANCE 1953
'Paul's Scarlet' × unnamed Multiflora seedling
So bright, this rose almost screams, which makes it
difficult to place with other climbers. Nevertheless,
an excellent, free-flowering rose with shapely buds
opening flat and fully double. Colour bright brick-
red. Copious foliage but I find this cultivar rather
prone to black spot.
C ◉ BS♂ AW 12′ × 8′ 3.5 × 2.5 m

'Danse des Sylphes'

Mallerin FRANCE 1959
'Danse de Feu' × ('Peace' × 'Independence')
Rich bright red, a seedling from 'Danse de Feu'.
Almost as bright but far more refined.
C ◉ SF AL 12′ × 8′ 3.5 × 2.5 m

'Della Balfour' (HARblend)

Harkness UK 1994
Rich orange-salmon fully double high-centred
flowers, freely produced, with a lemon fragrance.
Foliage leathery dark green. Growth sturdy and
upright.
C P VF ⇒< AL 8′ × 6′ 2.5 × 1.8 m

'Dixieland Linda'

Beales UK 1996
'Aloha' sport
A bright orange sport bringing forward all the
many attributes of its parent 'Aloha'. Named to
commemorate the joint fiftieth birthdays of Linda
and Gordon Bonneyman. Found in Peter Beales'
rosefields by a member of staff, Simon White.
C P VF ⇒< AW 10′ × 6′ 3 × 1.8 m

'Don Juan', 'Malandrone'

Jackson and Perkins USA 1958
'New Dawn' seedling × 'New Yorker'
Fully double, cupped flowers of velvety dark red,
very fragrant and borne in clusters. Foliage glossy,
dark green and leathery. Growth upright but
branching.
R P VF AW ⇒< 10′ × 6′ 3 × 1.8 m

'Dreaming Spires'

Mattock UK 1977
'Buccaneer' × 'Arthur Bell'
Shapely, high-centred, deep yellow flowers with

discreet touches of orange, fading to primrose with age. Fine, dark foliage on a vigorous plant.
C P SF AL 12′ × 8′ 3.5 × 2.5 m

'Dublin Bay'

McGredy UK 1976
'Bantry Bay' × 'Altissimo'
A very good pillar rose with large, glossy leaves. Clusters of medium-sized, rich blood-red flowers. Almost constantly in flower throughout the summer. Can also be grown successfully as a large shrub.
C P SF AL 7′ × 5′ 2 × 1.5 m

'Eden Rose '88', 'Pierre de Ronsard' (MEIviolin)

Meilland FRANCE 1987
Its fully double flowers are in the old-fashioned style; their colour is creamy-white shaded with lavender-pink at the base of the petals. Foliage dark

'Eden Rose '88'

'Dublin Bay', and below, 'Etendard'

green and glossy. Growth upright and bushy. An exceptionally fine rose.

C SF AL 8′ × 6′ 2.5 × 1.8 m

'Étendard', 'New Dawn Rouge', Red New Dawn'

Robichon FRANCE 1956

'New Dawn' × seedling

Double bright red 'New Dawn' sized flowers in clusters. Fragrant. Glossy dark green foliage. Growth vigorous.

C P SF AL 10′ × 6′ 3 × 1.5 m

'Étude'

Gregory UK 1965

'Danse de Feu' × 'New Dawn'

Clusters of semi-double, deep rose-pink blooms with a good fragrance. Glossy, light green foliage on a vigorous, upright-growing plant.

C P N ◉ ❀< ⬭ MF AL 10′ × 8′ 3 × 2.5 m

'Fugue' (MEItam)

Meilland FRANCE 1958

'Alain' × 'Guinée'

A very good but little known cultivar with fully

double flowers of rich, deep red. Dark glossy foliage and vigorous growth. A useful pillar rose.

C P SF AL 10′ × 6′ 3 × 1.8 m

'Galway Bay'

McGredy UK 1966

'Heidelberg' × 'Queen Elizabeth'

Large, double, shapely flowers, of salmon-pink. Scented. Foliage profuse and glossy dark green. The plant is vigorous and has a tidy growth habit.

C P ◉ SF AL 12′ × 8′ 3.5 × 2.5 m

'Golden Showers'

Lammerts USA 1956

'Charlotte Armstrong' × 'Captain Thomas'

Large, loosely and, rather raggedly formed flowers, of deep golden-yellow fading quickly to cream. Flowers continuously from June to October. Foliage rich dark green and glossy. Also capable of making a good free-standing shrub.

C P ◉ SF AW 10′ × 6′ 3 × 1.8 m

'Grand Hotel' (MACtel)

McGredy UK 1972

'Brilliant' × 'Heidelberg'

Semi-double, sizeable flowers of rich scarlet borne

'Golden Showers'

in clusters. Foliage dark green and semi-glossy. Growth upright and bushy.

C P SF AL 8′ × 4′ 2.5 × 1.2 m

'Handel'

McGredy UK 1956

'Columbine' × 'Heidelberg'

A good cultivar with dark stems and glossy, dark green, almost purple leaves. Large, semi-double flowers, cupped until fully open, silver-white with pink to red markings especially on the petal edges. These markings intensify with age. An excellent rose, but somewhat 'pretty' for my taste.

C P SF AW 12′ × 8′ 3.5 × 2.5 m

'Highfield'

Harkness UK 1982

A paler sport of 'Compassion', preferred by some because it is less severe in colour.

C ✂ VF AL 8′ × 6′ 2.5 × 1.8 m

'Ilse Krohn Superior'

Kordes GERMANY 1957

'Golden Glow' × *R. kordesii*

Fully double, pure white flowers from shapely, pointed buds. Slightly scented. Foliage rich green and glossy. Growth vigorous.

S T N P ◍ SF AW 12′ × 10′ 3.5 × 3 m

'Intervilles'

Robichon FRANCE 1968

'Étendard' seedling

Semi-double to double bright red flowers, produced amid good healthy dark green foliage on a vigorous, slightly spreading plant. Good examples may be seen at Roseraie de l'Hay, Paris.

C ◍ SF AL 10′ × 3′ 3.3 × 2.2 m

'John Grooms'

Beales UK 1993

'Fritz Nobis' × 'Compassion'

Beautifully formed flowers of rich bright salmon flushed with softer shades of pink, with soft prim-rose tones at the base of the petals. Very fragrant. Free-blooming in early summer with intermittent blooms later. Foliage dark green, matt. Stems plum-coloured, with few thorns. Also good as a free-standing shrub. Named for the John Grooms Association for disabled people.

R P ◍ VF ✂ AL 10′ × 8′ 3 × 2.2 m

'Handel', and below, 'Intervilles'

'Köln am Rhein'

Kordes GERMANY 1956

Fragrant, double, deep salmon-pink flowers produced in clusters on a healthy robust plant. Foliage rich dark green and glossy. Not often seen, but well worth garden space.

R P N ◍ AL 15′ × 10′ 4.5 × 3 m

'Laura Ford' (CHEwarvel)

Warner UK 1989

Although 'climbing miniature' is in some ways a contradiction in terms, this one is delightful, with small flowers and small leaves, as one would expect in a miniature. Strong yellow with amber shades – especially in the autumn. Constantly in flower, it makes a good pillar rose.

C ▽ AL 8′ × 3′ 250 × 90 cm

'Lavinia', 'Lawinia' (TANklewi)
Tantau GERMANY 1980
Large, fragrant, cupped, double flowers of mid-pink borne amid large, mid-green, semi-glossy foliage on a vigorous, wide-growing plant.
R T VF ✁ AW 12′ × 8′ 3.5 × 2.5 m

'Leaping Salmon' (PEAmight)
Pearce UK 1986
('Vesper' × 'Aloha') × ('Paddy McGredy' × 'Maigold') × 'Prima Ballerina'
Large salmon-pink, fragrant, almost double flowers produced freely on a bushy, upright plant amid plentiful, mid-green, glossy foliage.
R P SF ✁ AL 10′ × 6′ 3 × 1.8 m

'Malaga'
McGredy UK 1971
('Hamburger Phoenix' × 'Danse de Feu') × 'Copenhagen'
Large, deep rose-pink flowers in good clusters on a medium but vigorous plant with dark green foliage. A special feature is the distinctive Sweet Briar fragrance.
R P ✁ VF AL 8′ × 4′ 2.4 × 1.2 m

'Morning Jewel'
Cocker UK 1968
'New Dawn' × 'Red Dandy'
Large, semi-double flowers, fragrant, rich pink. Very free-flowering with glossy, clear green foliage.
R P MF AL 10′ × 8′ 3 × 2.5 m

'Malaga', and below, 'John Grooms'

'Night Light' (POUllight)

Poulsen DENMARK 1982
'Westerland' × 'Pastorale'
Sizeable sprays of large, double, deep yellow flowers. Foliage dark green and glossy. Growth upright.
C SF AL 10′ × 8′ 3 × 2.5 m

'Norwich Gold'

Kordes GERMANY 1962
Fragrant flowers of yellow shaded orange, very full, opening flat. Foliage rather dull green.
R P MF AL 10′ × 8′ 3 × 2.5 m

'Norwich Pink'

Kordes GERMANY 1962
Semi-double, bright cerise flowers with a strong fragrance. Foliage dark and glossy.
R P VF AL 10′ × 8′ 3 × 2.5 m

'Norwich Salmon'

Kordes GERMANY 1962
Fully double, soft salmon-pink flowers produced in large clusters on a vigorous, bushy plant. Foliage dark green and glossy.
R SF AL 10′ × 8′ 3 × 2.4 m

'Parade'

'Parade'

Boerner USA 1953
'New Dawn' seedling × 'World's Fair'
Cerise-red to crimson flowers, fully double and scented. Foliage glossy, profuse and healthy. Excellent both as a pillar rose and a free-standing shrub.
C P ◉ ⤜ SF AL 10′ × 8′ 3 × 2.5 m

'Pierre de Ronsard' *see* 'Eden Rose '88'

'Pinata'

Susuki JAPAN 1978
Fully double, high-centred flowers of clear yellow overlaid vermilion. Slightly fragrant. Foliage large, light to mid-green. Growth vigorous, dense.
C P ◉ SF AL 10′ × 6′ 3 × 1.8 m

'Pinkie' Climbing

Bush form Swim USA 1947
Sport from bush form Dering, Armstrong Nurseries USA 1952
'China Doll' × seedling
This is an outstandingly free-flowering climber. When in full flush its mass of semi-double, bright pink flowers is a sight to behold. The foliage, soft to touch, is a glossy light green. Growth wiry and dense. More often seen in America and the Antipodes. I recall seeing a particularly good plant at the Antique Rose Emporium, Brenham, Texas.
R P ▽ ⊙ MF AL 10′ × 8′ 3 × 2.5 m

'Pink Perpétue'

Gregory UK 1965
'Danse de Feu' × 'New Dawn'
One of the outstanding modern climbers. Its colour is perhaps rather hard for some tastes, but it can be relied upon to produce masses of deep pink, rather cupped, semi-double to double flowers throughout the summer. Its very dark green foliage has glossy purple overtones, making an excellent foil for the flowers.
C P N ◉ MF AL 12′ × 8′ 3.5 × 2.5 m

'Rhonda'

Lissmore USA 1968
'New Dawn' × 'Spartan'
Large, fully double flowers in clusters, deep

'Pink Perpétue'

carmine-rose. Fragrant. Foliage mid-green, semi-glossy. Growth vigorous and upright.
R P SF AW 10′ × 6′ 3 × 1.8 m

'Ritter von Barmstede'

Kordes GERMANY 1959
Deep pink, double flowers in large clusters. Somewhat untidy in growth but has excellent, glossy dark green foliage.
R P ⬤ AL 10′ × 10′ 3 × 3 m

'Rosy Mantle'

Cocker UK 1968
'New Dawn' × 'Prima Ballerina'
Silver-pink, fully double flowers with a strong perfume. Rather sprawly if not tethered, but very showy when in full flush. Good, glossy dark green foliage.
C N ⬤ ⬅ VF AL 8′ × 8′ 2.5 × 2.5 m

'Royal Gold'

Morey USA 1957
'Goldilocks' × 'Lydia'
Not the most free-flowering of climbers, but its flowers are usually of good quality, golden-yellow, almost non-fading, of classic Hybrid Tea shape, opening loosely formed and quite large. Foliage glossy, mid- to dark green. Needs a warm sheltered position to insure against a slight tenderness.
C ⦾ ⬅ VF AL 8′ × 8′ 2.5 × 2.5 m

'Schoolgirl'

McGredy UK 1964
'Coral Dawn' × 'Belle Blonde'
Rich, coppery-orange flowers, Hybrid Tea-shaped in bud, opening loosely flat and semi-double. Highly scented. A little short on foliage and, in my opinion, rather overrated.
C ⬅ VF AW 10′ × 8′ 3 × 2.5 m

'Soldier Boy'

LeGrice UK 1953
Unnamed seedling × 'Guinée'
A rose of considerable beauty. Flowers are single, rich scarlet with pronounced golden anthers. Foliage profuse and matt dark green. Repeats intermittently throughout summer.
R P N ⬤ VF AL 10′ × 8′ 3 × 2.5 m

'Rosy Mantle', below, 'Royal Gold', right 'Schoolgirl'

'Sparkling Scarlet', 'Iskra' (MEIhaiti)

Meilland FRANCE 1970
'Danse des Sylphes' × 'Zambra'
Clusters of semi-double, very bright scarlet flowers, with large, mid-green, semi-glossy foliage on an upright, branching plant.
C P VF AL 10′ × 8′ 3 × 2.5 m

'Spectacular' *see* 'Danse de Feu'

'Sourire d'Orchidée'

Croix FRANCE 1985
Large semi-double flowers of soft pink with deeper shadings, in clusters. An outstandingly good rose with good mid-green, semi-glossy foliage and vigorous bushy growth.
C ◉ MF AL 10′ × 8′ 3.3 × 2.6 m

'Sourire d'Orchidée'

'Summer Wine' (KORizont)

Kordes GERMANY 1985

Its large, semi-double, deep pink flowers have red stamens and come in clusters. Foliage mid-green and semi-glossy. Growth upright and bushy.

C P MF AL 10′ × 6′ 3 × 1.8 m

'Swan Lake'

McGredy UK 1968

'Memorium' × 'Heidelberg'

A beautiful rose, shapely in bud, opening large and fully double, white with a pale pink flush in the centre, and produced freely all summer. Rounded, dark green foliage, liberally produced on an upright, tidy plant.

C P ⊱ SF AW 8′ × 6′ 2.5 × 1.8 m

'Sympathie'

Kordes GERMANY 1964

Fragrant, dark red, fully double and shapely blooms produced freely and continuously throughout summer. Foliage dark green and glossy.

C P MF AL 10′ × 8′ 3 × 2.5 m

'Tempo'

Warriner USA 1975

'Climbing Ena Harkness' × unknown

Fully double, shapely, fragrant, deep red flowers in profusion. Growth vigorous. Foliage dark green, glossy.

R P VF AW 15′ × 10′ 4.5 × 3 m

'Warm Welcome' (CHEwizz)

Warner UK 1990

Another good miniature-flowered climber from the raiser who brought out 'Laura Ford'. This one is very bright indeed and described by Warner as 'lively orange-vermilion'. Good leathery foliage.

C ▽ AL 8′ × 3′ 250 × 90 cm

'Swan Lake', and below, 'White Cockade'

'White Cockade'

Cocker UK 1969

'New Dawn' × 'Circus'

A thorny, upright climber with small but ample, dark, glossy foliage, combining well with fully double, pure white flowers which open into rather triangular shapes, hence its name. One of the best white climbers, but not the most vigorous; good grown as a pillar rose.

C ⊱ SF AL 8′ × 6′ 2.5 × 1.8 m

Modern Shrubs

An increasing demand for shrub roses has prompted breeders to produce and introduce many and varied tall cultivars, all with long flowering seasons. These, as with modern climbers, are of very mixed progeny; and many, in addition to making excellent shrubs, may also be adapted to make admirable small climbers or pillar roses. Some also make very good hedges, both informal and formal.

CLASSIFICATION

BARB   Class 7
MR10   Class 54
WFRS   Classes 1 and 2

'Alexander'

Harkness U K 1972
'Super Star' × ('Ann Elizabeth' × 'Allgold')
Shapely pointed buds opening to large, slightly ragged flowers of a very bright luminous vermilion, displaying creamy yellow stamens to good effect. Foliage rich green and healthy. Growth upright, with strong thorny stems.
C P H CL ◑ ✂ SF AW   6′ × 4′   1.8 × 1.2 m

'Angelina'

Cocker U K 1976
('Super Star' × 'Carina') × ('Cläre Grammerstorf' × 'Frühlingsmorgen')
An extremely free-flowering, shortish shrub rose. The fragrant flowers are large, slightly fuller than single, and bright rose-pink. These are produced in large clusters on upright stems with dark green foliage.
C H P ▽ MF AL   4′ × 3′   120 × 90 cm

'Alexander', and below, 'Anna Zinkeisen'

'Anna Zinkeisen'

Harkness U K 1983
A shrubby rose with good mid-green foliage. Fully double flowers, ivory-white with golden-yellow tones in the base, borne in clusters. Has a distinctive perfume.
C G P ◑ ▽ VF AL   4′ × 3′   120 × 90 cm

'Applejack'

Buck USA 1973

'Goldbusch' × ('Josef Rothmund' × *R. laxa retzius*)
Small, pointed buds open to loose, semi-double
flowers of deepish rose-pink discreetly dappled red,
very fragrant, very free-flowering. Foliage profuse,
mid-green, leathery. Growth vigorous and widely
bushy. A delightful all-rounder. Hardy.
P CL H ▽ VF ✁ AL 8′ × 7′ 2.5 × 2.1 m

'Armada' (HARuseful)

Harkness UK 1988

'New Dawn' × 'Silver Jubilee'
The rich clear pink blooms hold their colour well.
They are semi-double and come in large clusters,
leaving handsome hips in the autumn. Foliage
bright green and glossy. Upright, bushy growth.
C H F CL ▽ AL 5′ × 3′ 150 × 90 cm

'Autumn Bouquet'

Jacobus USA 1948

'New Dawn' × 'Crimson Glory'
Long, pointed buds open to large and fully double,
carmine to silvery-deep-pink flowers. Foliage
leathery and dark green. Growth upright and bushy.
C P VF H ▽ ◉ ✁ AL 4′ × 3′ 120 × 90 cm

'Autumn Sunset'

Lowe USA 1987

Sport from 'Westerland'
The medium-sized flowers, fully double, cupped
and loosely formed, are apricot with touches of
orange and deep yellow. Glossy, mid-green foliage.
Growth tall and bushy.
C CL P MF H ◉ ✁ AL 6′ × 4′ 1.8 × 1.2 m

'Ballerina' *see* **Hybrid Musks**, page 255

'Berlin'

Kordes GERMANY 1949

'Eva' × 'Peace'
Large single flowers, bright, rich red, paling towards
the centre to white. Pronounced yellow stamens.
Upright but not tall. Foliage dark and crisp. The
young wood especially is dark, with lots of thorns.
C CL P H AL 5′ × 3′ 150 × 90 cm

'Angelina', and below, 'Autumn Sunset'

'Biddulph Grange' (FRYdarkeye)

Fryer UK 1988

An unusually coloured rose, velvety bright red,
deeper in the centre of each petal and deepening
with age. The base and reverse of each petal is
white. Borne in large clusters on a shrubby small
plant with good healthy foliage.
C ▽ H G AL 4′ × 3′ 120 × 90 cm

'Bonica '82' (MEIdomonac)

Meilland FRANCE 1982

The double flowers are made up of rather frilled
petals of delicate pink with deeper centres; these are

produced along strong arching stems throughout the summer. Foliage coppery light green and glossy. This is an outstanding cultivar. Not to be confused with another rose of this name raised by Meilland in 1953.

C P G H ▽ AW 3′ × 6′ 90 × 180 cm

'Bonn'

Kordes GERMANY 1950

'Hamburg' × 'Independence'

Freely produced semi-double flowers of bright orange-red fading rather with age, though not offending the eye in so doing. A vigorous upright bush, with rich dark green foliage.

C P CL H SF AL 6′ × 4′ 1.8 × 1.2 m

'Butterfly Wings'

Gobbee UK 1976

'Dainty Maid' × 'Peace'

A beautiful rose. Large, refined, single flowers of blush-white with touches of red around their edges. Ample, dark green foliage. Not over-tall.

C ▽ ○ AL 4′ × 3′ 120 × 90 cm

'Canterbury'

Austin UK 1969

('Monique' × 'Constance Spry') × seedling

Large, silky, fragrant, almost single flowers of pure rose-pink with well-displayed golden stamens in their centres. Foliage mid-green, plentiful. Growth, bushy.

R ▽ H MF AL 3′ × 3′ 1 × 1 m

'Cardinal Hume', and right, 'Bonica '82'

'Cardinal Hume' (HARregale)

Harkness UK 1984

[('Lilac Charm' × 'Sterling Silver') × ('Orangeade' × 'Lilac Charm')] × [('Orange Sensation' × 'Allgold') × *R. californica*] × 'Frank Naylor'

A most unusual rose. The rich tyrian purple flowers are double, made up of a multitude of many narrow petals, and borne in clusters which remain close to the plant, almost amongst the plentiful dark green foliage. Slightly wider than tall, but not wide enough to qualify as procumbent.

R G P ◉ BS♂ VF AL 3′ × 4′ 90 × 120 cm

'City of London' (HARukfore)

Harkness UK 1987

'New Dawn' × 'Radox Bouquet'

Large, shaggy, blush-pink blooms with a heady perfume are produced in clusters. Large, bright green leaves on an upright and bushy plant.

C P H VF CL AL 5′ × 3′ 150 × 90 cm

'Cocktail'

Meilland FRANCE 1959

('Independence' × 'Orange Triumph') × 'Phyllis Bide'

A bright rose with clusters of burnished red, single flowers each with yellow centres; the red intensifies with age. Upright, thorny growth with numerous, deep green, deeply serrated leaves.

C CL P H ◉ ▽ SF AL 6′ × 4′ 1.8 × 1.2 m

'Copenhagen'

Poulsen DENMARK 1964

Seedling × 'Ena Harkness'

Double, scarlet flowers in clusters on an upright plant with good, bronzy foliage. Can also make a good, short-growing climber.

C P CL AL 8′ × 4′ 2.5 × 1.2 m

'Country Dancer'

Buck USA 1973

'Prairie Princess' × 'Johannes Boettner'

Large, fully double flowers of rosy-red. Fragrant. Borne on a bushy, upright-growing plant with abundant, glossy dark green foliage.

R ▽ H ◉ VF AL 3′ × 3′ 90 × 90 cm

'Cocktail'

'Country Music'

Buck; Iowa State University USA 1972

('Paddy McGredy' × 'Worlds Fair') × ('Floradora' × 'Applejack')

Clusters of double cupped flowers of soft pink, darker on reverse. Fragrant. Good leathery healthy mid-green foliage. Upright bushy growth.

R P ◉ H MF AL ✄ 3′ × 3′ 90 × 90 cm

'Cuthbert Grant'

Canada Department of Agriculture CANADA 1967

('Crimson Glory' × 'Assiniboine') × 'Assiniboine'

Sizeable, almost double deep red flowers with a hint of purple, cupped and fragrant. Foliage glossy. Bushy vigorous growth.

R P ◉ H W MF AL 4′ × 3′ 1.2 m × 90 cm

'Cymbeline' (AUSteen)

Austin UK 1983

Seedling × 'Lilian Austin'

Greyish-pink, loosely double, myrrh-scented flowers are borne in clusters on a spreading but

'Cuthbert Grant'

'Elmshorn'

bushy plant with abundant mid-green, semi-glossy foliage.
R G P VF AL 5′ × 5′ 1.5 × 1.5 m

'Dapple Dawn'

Austin UK 1983
Sport from 'Red Coat'
Large, single, slightly scented, delicate pink flowers in clusters on a vigorous, upright-growing plant. Thorny with dark green foliage.
R H CL P ◉ SF AL 5′ × 4′ 1.5 × 1.2 m

'Dentelle de Malines', 'Lens Pink'

Lens BELGIUM 1983
A tallish spreader. Trusses of blush-pink to white cupped flowers on an arching shrub with plentiful, mid-green foliage. A lovely rose with much to commend it.
R ▽ ◉ SF W G H ≈ AL 4′ × 5′ 1.2 × 1.5 m

'Dorothy Wheatcroft'

Tantau GERMANY 1960
Large, semi-double, bright red flowers, made up of petals that are slightly crimped on their outer edges. These are borne in large clusters on a vigorous, well-foliated, thorny shrub.
C P H AL 5′ × 4′ 1.5 × 1.2 m

'Dr Jackson'

Austin UK 1987
Sprays of single, brilliant scarlet-crimson flowers on a strong-growing, widely bushy plant with darkish green foliage.
S H B P ◉ SF AL 3′ 6″ × 3′ 110 × 90 cm

'Elmshorn'

Kordes GERMANY 1951
'Hamburg' × 'Verdun'
Large clusters of smallish, vivid pink, double flowers on a vigorous bush, carrying abundant, slightly crinkled, dark greyish-green foliage. A very good, free-flowering shrub rose, deservedly popular.
C P H CL ◉ ▽ AL 5′ × 4′ 1.5 × 1.2 m

'Erfurt'

Kordes GERMANY 1939
'Eva' × 'Réveil Dijonnais'
Single flowers of rich, cerise pink, paling towards the centre to almost white; prominent brown anthers. The rather beautiful flowers are enhanced by healthy, plentiful coppery-green foliage. Stems are coppery-brown with numerous hooked thorns. An outstanding shrub rose.
C P H ◉ SF AL 5′ × 4′ 1.5 × 1.2 m

'Fountain'

Tantau GERMANY 1972
Sizeable, blood-red flowers in clusters on a medium-growing shrub with thick, dark green foliage. A good, healthy cultivar.
C P H CL ▽ ⤰ SF AW 7′ × 4′ 2 × 1.2 m

'Frank Naylor'

Harkness UK 1978
[('Orange Sensation' × 'Allgold') × ('Little Lady' × 'Lilac Charm')] × [('Blue Moon' × 'Magenta') × ('Cläre Grammerstorf' × 'Frühlingsmorgen')]
Clusters of single red flowers with yellow centres. Good, healthy dense growth. Foliage long and reddish-green. A very good shorter-growing shrub

'Erfurt', and below, 'Fountain'

rose where a bright colour is needed. Good hips later.

P H F CL ▽ SF AL 6′ × 3′ 180 × 90 cm

'Freckles'

Buck; Iowa State University USA 1976
Light red flowers flushed yellow, freckled with

deeper red. Foliage leathery dark green. Growth upright, bushy, very healthy.

C P ▽ H MF AL 3′ × 4′ 90 × 90 cm

'Fred Loads'

Holmes UK 1968
'Dorothy Wheatcroft' × 'Orange Sensation'
Large, almost single blooms in impressive-sized trusses, rich, bright salmon-pink. A vigorous and upright rose with large, leathery leaves.

C P H CL AW 5′ × 4′ 1.5 × 1.2 m

'Fritz Nobis'

Kordes GERMANY 1940
'Joanna Hill' × 'Magnifica'
A beautiful rose, flowering only once each season, but nonetheless useful. A dense shrub, extremely healthy, with small but numerous grey-green leaves. Flowers are soft blush-pink to quiet salmon, fully double and produced in great abundance; followed in autumn by an impressive crop of small but colourful orange hips.

S P H F CL ◉ AW 5′ × 4′ 1.5 × 1.2 m

'Fred Loads', and below, 'Horatio Nelson'

'Grandmaster'

Kordes GERMANY 1954
'Sangerhausen' × 'Sunmist'
Pointed buds opening to large, semi-double flowers of apricot-pink with lemon shadings. Scented. Foliage light green on a bushy plant.
C P SF AL 5′ × 4′ 1.5 × 1.2 m

'Hawkeye Belle'

Buck; Iowa State University USA
('Queen Elizabeth' × 'Pizzicato') × 'Prairie Prince'
Double white flowers with blush centres. Fragrant. Foliage dark green, leathery. Bushy upright growth. Very hardy.
C P ▽ H VF AL ✂ 4′ × 3′ 120 × 90 cm

'Heidelberg'

Kordes GERMANY 1958
'World's Fair' × 'Floradora'
Very bright rose, crimson-scarlet splashed deep orange, fully double, produced in large trusses. Foliage dark green and tough-looking.
C P CL AL 6′ × 5′ 1.8 × 1.5 m

'Hon. Lady Lindsay'

N. J. Hanson USA 1938
'New Dawn' × 'Rev. F. Page Roberts'
Double flowers of clear pink with deeper pink reverses. Foliage dark green on a widely bushy plant. Enjoys a good hot summer or warmer climates.
C H P ☼ Gh ▽ SF AL 3′ × 3′ 90 × 90 cm

'Horatio Nelson'

Beales UK 1997
'Aloha' × 'Centenaire de Lourdes'
A delightful medium-short shrub rose. Freely produced fully double shapely flowers in the

old-fashioned style when fully open, of many shades of pink. Very fragrant. Foliage dark green. Growth dense and wide.

C P ▽ VF AL 4′ × 4′ 1.2 × 1.2 m

'Jacqueline du Pré' (HARwanna)

Harkness UK 1989

'Radox Bouquet' × 'Maigold'

A delightful large, ivory-white, almost single rose with prominent golden-red stamens and a good scent (musk). Flowers are freely produced on a strong-growing shrub which bears abundant darkish green foliage.

R P H ▽ VF AL 4′ × 5′ 1.2 × 1.5 m

'Jayne Austin' (AUSbreak)

Austin UK 1990

Noisette-related

Flowers beautifully shaped rosette form with a button eye, produced in clusters. Soft apricot-yellow in colour. Very fragrant. Foliage plentiful light green. Widely bushy. Vigorous.

R H G ✂ ▽ VF AL 4′ × 3′ 120 × 90 cm

'John Franklin'

Department of Agriculture CANADA 1980

'Lilli Marlene' × unnamed seedling

Sizeable, double (25 petals), fragrant red flowers borne in small clusters. Rounded leaves of mid- to dark green on an upright, bushy plant amply endowed with yellowish-cream thorns.

R N ◉ ▽ H CL MF AL 5′ × 4′ 1.5 × 1.2 m

'Joseph's Coat'

Armstrong & Swim USA 1964

'Buccaneer' × 'Circus'

Often listed as a climber, but I feel it is better as a free-standing shrub or, at most, a pillar rose. Loosely formed multicoloured flowers from shapely buds, borne in large trusses on a thorny, upright plant with light green, glossy foliage.

C P H CL MF AW 7′ × 4′ 2 × 1.2 m

'Kassel'

Kordes GERMANY 1957

'Obergärtner Wiebicke' × 'Independence'

Trusses of closely spaced, double flowers on strong stems; orange-scarlet deepening with age to bright

'Jacqueline du Pré'

'Kassel'

'Kathleen Ferrier', and below, 'Lafter'

red. Foliage leathery, slightly glossy. Upright bushy growth. Stems brownish-red.

C P H ▽ AL 5′ × 4′ 1.5 × 1.2 m

'Kathleen Ferrier'

Buisman HOLLAND 1952

'Gartenstolz' × 'Shot Silk'
Small clusters of semi-double, rich salmon-pink flowers. Vigorous and upright growth with dark green, glossy foliage. A first-class rose.

C H CL SF AL 5′ × 4′ 1.5 × 1.2 m

'Lady Sonia'

Mattock UK 1961

'Grandmaster' × 'Doreen'
A free-flowering, semi-double rose of deep golden-yellow. Shapely in bud and well formed when open. Foliage dark and leathery. Growth upright and free-branching.

C P ✂ AL 5′ × 4′ 1.5 × 1.2 m

'Lafter'

Brownell USA 1948

['V for Victory' × ('Général Jacqueminot' × 'Dr Van Fleet')] × 'Pink Princess'
A most useful shrub. Clusters of semi-double, rather loosely formed flowers of salmon-pink and apricot, with hints of yellow. Foliage dark green, slightly glossy but leathery. Upright but bushy growth.

C P CL H SF AL 5′ × 4′ 1.5 × 1.2 m

'La Sevillana' (MEIgekanu)

Meilland FRANCE 1982

Very healthy, abundant rich red, semi-double flowers which hold their colour well, even in hot sun. Rich dark green foliage. Dense, bushy but spreading growth.

C H P G AW 4′ × 5′ 1.2 × 1.5 m

'Lichtkönigin Lucia' (KORlilub)

Kordes GERMANY 1966

'Zitronenfalter' × Cläre Grammerstorf'
Clusters of closely arranged, canary-yellow, semi-double flowers with a good fragrance. Foliage mid- to light green, glossy. Medium-tall, bushy growth. A useful yellow shrub rose.

C ▽ H P MF ✂ AL 4′ × 3′ 120 × 90 cm

'L'Oréal Trophy' (HARlexis)

Harkness UK 1982

Sport from 'Alexander'

Softer in colour than its parent, otherwise identical.

C P H SF ▽ ⤫ AL 6′ × 4′ 1.8 × 1.2 m

'Lyda Rose' (LETlyda)

Lettunich USA 1994

Seedling of 'Francis E. Lester'

Large clusters of single blush-white flowers, edged pink. Fragrant and continuously produced. Foliage plentiful rich green. Like its parent, very disease-resistant. Growth dense and wide. Named after the raiser's daughter.

C H ▽ ◉ MF AL 4′ × 4′ 1.2 × 1.2 m

'Lichtkönigin Lucia'

'Magenta'

Kordes GERMANY 1954

Yellow Floribunda seedling × 'Lavender Pinocchio'

A moderately vigorous shrub bearing double flowers of unusual shades, fawn and purple with pink and lilac highlights, opening flat in the old-fashioned style and produced in large clusters. Foliage dark green and growth openly bushy. This rose can be frustratingly temperamental.

C H ▽ VF AL 4′ × 4′ 1.2 × 1.2 m

'Malcolm Sargent' (HARwharry)

Harkness UK 1988

'Herbstfeuer' × 'Trumpeter'

Hybrid Tea-shaped flowers of shining crimson-scarlet, with rich green sparkling foliage on a bushy, upright plant.

C H ▽ ⤫ AL 4′ × 3′ 120 × 90 cm

'Many Happy Returns' (HARwanted)

Harkness UK 1991

Large clusters of soft-blush, semi-double flowers produced throughout the summer and autumn on a healthy, bushy plant with greyish-green semi-glossy foliage.

C P ▽ SF AL 3′ × 3′ 90 × 90 cm

'Magenta', and right, 'Many Happy Returns'

'Märchenland', 'Exception'

Tantau GERMANY 1951

'Swantje' × 'Hamburg'

Very large trusses of well-spaced, almost single flowers, bright pink with deeper shadings. Very free-flowering. Foliage dark green, slightly glossy and plentiful. Upright bushy growth. This is a most underrated shrub rose.

C P ▽ AL 5′ × 4′ 1.5 × 1.2 m

'Marjorie Fair'

Harkness UK 1978

'Ballerina' × 'Baby Faurax'

A good shorter shrub rose bred from 'Ballerina', and which could well be included among the Hybrid Musks. The flowers, which are produced in large trusses, are small, single and red with a pinkish-white eye. Foliage plentiful and mid-green. Growth bushy and tidy.

C H P ▽ ◉ AW 4′ × 3′ 120 × 90 cm

'Mary Hayley Bell', 'Abunancia' (KORparau)

Kordes GERMANY 1989

Clusters of pretty, soft pink, semi-double blooms amid good mid-green foliage. Growth bushy.

C ▽ H P SF AL 5′ × 4′ 1.5 × 1.2 m

'Mountbatten'

Harkness UK 1952

('Anne Cocker' × 'Arthur Bell') × 'Southampton'

Huge clusters of clear yellow, fully double flowers on an upright but thorny plant with good, clean, light green foliage. Makes an excellent hedging rose.

C H P ☼ ▽ ✂ MF AW 5′ × 3′ 150 × 90 cm

'Nymphenburg'

Kordes GERMANY 1954

'Sangerhausen' × 'Sunmist'

A vigorous upright shrub or pillar rose. Semi-double flowers, salmon-pink with lemon and deeper pink highlights. Very free-flowering. Foliage dark green and glossy.

C P H MF CH AW 6′ × 4′ 1.8 × 1.2 m

'Parkjuwel', 'Parkjewel'

Kordes GERMANY 1956

'Independence' × a red Moss rose

A vigorous shrubby plant with wrinkled, rather leathery foliage and good well-mossed buds.

'Mountbatten', and below, 'Nymphenburg'

Flowers large, very double, globular, light soft pink. Loses nothing by not repeating.

S P H CL ◉ ▽ SF AL 6′ × 4′ 1.8 × 1.2 m

'Peach Blossom' (AUSblossom)

Austin UK 1990

Large yet delicate semi-double, rose-pink flowers in clusters, produced very freely throughout the summer, with a slight fragrance. These are followed by a good crop of hips in the autumn. Foliage mid-green, plentiful. Growth shrubby and wide.

R F ▽ H ◉ SF AL 4′ × 3′ 120 × 90 cm

'Pike's Peak'

Gunter USA 1940

R. acicularis × 'Hollywood'

Light red with a yellow centre paling with age, semi-double, borne in clusters. Light green, wrinkled foliage. Bushy, vigorous growth.

S H P AL 5′ × 3′ 150 × 90 cm

'Pink La Sevillana', 'Rosy La Sevillana' (MEIgeroka)

Meilland FRANCE 1983

Sport from 'La Sevillana'

A pink sport from 'La Sevillana' with all its parent's characteristics except colour.

C P H SF AL 4′ × 4′ 1.2 × 1.2 m

'Pleine de Grâce' (LENgra)

Lens BELGIUM 1983

'Ballerina' × *R. filipes*

An outstanding shrub or climber. Large trusses of single, creamy-white flowers, fragrant, borne on arching branches well covered with light green foliage.

S T N ◉ CL W ▨ VF AL 10′ × 13′ 3 × 4 m

'Poulsen's Park Rose'

Poulsen DENMARK

'Great Western' × 'Karen Poulsen'

An outstanding shrub, vigorous, dense and broad in habit with trusses of large, shapely, silvery pink flowers and good clean dark green foliage.

R P ◉ CL VF AL 6′ × 6′ 1.8 × 1.8 m

'Prairie Breeze'

Buck; Iowa State University USA 1975

'Dornröschen' × ('Josef Rothmund' × *R. laxa*)

Clusters of double, fragrant, mauve-pink flowers. Small but plentiful dark green foliage. Growth spreading and vigorous with large thorns. Good hips.

C P F ◉ H VF AL 4′ × 3′ 120 × 90 cm

'Prairie Flower'

Buck; Iowa State University USA 1975

('Rose of Tralee' × 'Queen Elizabeth') × ('Morning Stars' × 'Suzanne')

Bright carmine single fragrant blooms with white centres, very freely borne on a vigorous shrub of upright growth.

C P CL ◉ H MF AL 6′ × 4′ 1.5 × 1.2 m

'Prairie Lass'

Buck; Iowa State University 1979

('Hawkeye Belle' × 'Vera Dalton') × ('Dornröschen') × ('World's Fair' × 'Applejack')

Clusters of double carmine blooms dappled red, spicy scent. Abundant large leathery foliage on an upright bushy plant. Very hardy.

C P ◉ H MF AL ⚔ 4′ × 3′ 120 × 90 cm

'Prairie Princess'

Buck USA 1972

'Carrousel' × ('Morning Stars' × 'Suzanne')

Large, semi-double, soft coral-pink flowers in profusion amid abundant large, dark green leaves. Growth upright and bushy.

C H ▽ SF AL 5′ × 4′ 1.5 × 1.2 m

'Prestige'

Kordes GERMANY 1957

'Rudolph Timm' × 'Fanal'

Large, semi-double, light crimson flowers are carried in clusters with plentiful, dark green, matt foliage on a bushy plant.

C P H SF AL 4′ × 3′ 120 × 90 cm

'Rachel Bowes Lyon'

Harkness UK 1981

'Kim' × ('Orange Sensation' × 'Allgold') × *R. californica*

Semi-double, peachy-pink flowers of medium size in large clusters on a medium-tall but bushy, well-foliated plant.

C P H AL 5′ × 4′ 1.5 × 1.2 m

'Radway Sunrise'

Waterhouse Nurseries UK 1962

'Masquerade' seedling

A striking, moderately vigorous shrub bearing clusters of single flowers; these are a mixture of flame, cerise-pink and yellow. The colours are suffused to give the general effect of glowing warmth, eye-catching but not gaudy. Foliage dark green and glossy.

C P H ▽ SF AL 4′ × 3′ 120 × 90 cm

'Roundelay', and right, 'Sally Holmes'

'Red Coat'

Austin UK 1973

Seedling × 'Golden Showers'

Large, single, slightly scented, rich crimson flowers produced in clusters and in great profusion throughout summer. Foliage dark green. Growth upright and thorny.

R H W CL P SF AL 5′ × 4′ 1.5 × 1.2 m

'Roundelay'

Swim USA 1953

'Charlotte Armstrong' × 'Floradora'

An upright, free-flowering shrub with large trusses of cardinal-red flowers, fully double, opening flat. Has a good perfume. Healthy dark green foliage. Deserves more attention.

C P H VF AL 4′ × 3′ 120 × 90 cm

'Sally Holmes'

Holmes UK 1976

'Ivory Fashion' × 'Ballerina'

A short-growing, almost Floribunda-type rose with an upright habit and good foliage. Trusses of single flowers of soft, pale pink to white.

C H ▽ ◉ AL 4′ × 3′ 120 × 90 cm

'Shropshire Lass'

Austin UK 1968

'Mme Butterfly' × 'Mme Legras de St Germain'

Large, flat, almost single flowers of delicate flesh-pink fading to white with age, prominent stamens. Fragrant. Foliage plentiful mid-green. Growth robust, bushy.

S H W P CL SF AL 6′ × 4′ 1.8 × 1.2 m

'Sparrieshoop'

Kordes GERMANY 1953

('Baby Château' × 'Else Poulsen') × 'Magnifica'

An interesting shrub with pointed buds opening to large, pale pink flowers, borne in trusses but sometimes singly. Upright bushy growth and healthy foliage.

R P ◉ SF AL 5′ × 4′ 1.5 × 1.2 m

'Summer Wind'

Buck USA 1975

('Fandango' × 'Florence Mary Morse') × 'Applejack'

Large, fragrant (clove), not quite single flowers of orangey-red. Leathery, dark green foliage. Growth upright and bushy.

R H ◉ MF AL 4′ × 3′ 120 × 90 cm

'Till Uhlenspiegel'

Kordes GERMANY 1950

'Holstein' × 'Magnifica'

An arching tall shrub with large, almost burnished, glossy green leaves. Large single flowers of glowing dark red with white centres. Scented.

S P ◉ CL MF AL 10′ × 8′ 3 × 2.5 m

'Uetersen', and below, 'Uncle Walter'

'Uetersen', 'Zenith', 'Rosarium Uetersen'

Tantau GERMANY 1939
'K of K' × 'Stämmler'
Large, semi-double flowers of glowing pinkish-red in clusters. Slightly fragrant. Foliage dark green, glossy. Growth bushy and vigorous. A useful, underrated and little seen shrub rose.
R CL H T ◉ SF AL 8′ × 6′ 2.5 × 1.8 m

'Uncle Walter'

McGredy UK 1963
'Detroiter' × 'Heidelberg'
Hybrid Tea-shaped flowers borne in clusters and opening to an attractively muddled shape; bright red, good for cutting. Foliage is dark green and plentiful. Often listed as a Hybrid Tea, but is much too vigorous and is better placed amongst shrub roses.
C P H ✂ AW 5′ × 4′ 1.5 × 1.2 m

'Yesterday'

'White Spray', and below, 'William and Mary'

lemon-yellow set off by attractive stamens and dark green foliage. Growth compact, dense and branching.

C B H ▽ MF AL 2′ × 2′ 60 × 60 cm

'William and Mary'

Beales UK 1988

Seedling × 'Constance Spry'
Large, fully double, blowsy blooms in the old-fashioned style. Deep silvery-pink with crimson and carmine highlights, produced singly and in clusters. Foliage greyish-green and matt. Growth bushy and upright.

S P H VF CL ✂ M AL 6′ × 4′ 1.8 × 1.2 m

'Windrush' (AUSrush)

Austin UK 1984

Seedling × ('Canterbury' × 'Golden Wings')
Clusters of semi-double, soft medium-yellow flowers with pronounced stamens. Very fragrant. Foliage sizeable, light green. Growth bushy, branching but fairly dense.

C H VF AL 4′ × 4′ 1.2 × 1.2 m

'White Spray'

LeGrice UK 1974

Seedling × 'Iceberg'
A superb white cultivar deserving of more attention. An accommodating-sized shrub with good, mid-green foliage. Flowers white to cream, fully double, shapely and produced in large clusters on a bushy plant.

C P H ▽ ● AL 4′ × 4′ 1.2 × 1.2 m

'Wild Flower' (AUSwing)

Austin UK 1986

'Canterbury' × Seedling
Fragrant, medium to small, single flowers of

'Yesterday'

Harkness UK 1974

('Phyllis Bide' × 'Shepherd's Delight') × 'Ballerina'
An aptly named cultivar. Masses of small, almost single, rich pinky-purple, slightly scented flowers in large trusses on a sturdy, rather spreading bush.

C P G H ▽ ● SF AW 4′ × 4′ 1.2 × 1.2 m

Polyanthas

From the beginning of this century until the early 1940s, Dwarf Polyanthas reigned supreme as bedding roses and many new cultivars were introduced. Ironically, they only lost their supremacy when they were put to stud with the Hybrid Teas and became parents to the larger-flowered Hybrid Polyanthas. As their popularity has declined their numbers have inevitably dwindled and several good cultivars are now lost for ever. Those that remain are fairly widely available and I have briefly described most of them here. Several are sports from others, mainly 'Orléans Rose'. Their colours are, in fact, rather unstable, and variations can occur within a flower cluster from time to time.

These little roses are very easy to grow and have numerous uses, from massed display to hedging and edging. In groups they look most effective among herbaceous plants and are quite at home providing prolonged colour at the front of shrubberies. They also make useful, decorative plants in tubs, urns and other containers, and they are not at all out of place in modern settings; in fact, when planted closely, they readily take on the role of a 'Patio' rose (a term for the 'Compact Floribundas' described on page 317). They also last quite well in water when they are cut and taken indoors.

CLASSIFICATION

BARB	Class 13
MR10	Class 52
WFRS	Classes 5 and 6

'Anna-Maria de Montravel'

Rambaud FRANCE 1880
A Polyantha × 'Mme de Tartas'
Small semi-double white flowers in large clusters. Slightly fragrant. Foliage plentiful, mid-green. Growth twiggy, bushy and compact.
C ◐ ▽ B SF AL 2′ × 2′ 60 × 60 cm

'Baby Faurax'

Lille FRANCE 1924
Large clusters of double, violet-coloured, fragrant, small blooms on a short, bushy plant with small, mid-green foliage.
C ◐ G H ▽ B AW 1′ × 1′ 30 × 30 cm

'Cameo'

de Ruiter HOLLAND 1932
'Orléans Rose' sport
Dense clusters of small, semi-double, cupped flowers of soft salmon-pink, deepening with age; these are produced on stocky, bushy plants which have strong shoots, these bearing a few large, cruel thorns and many smaller, kinder ones. Foliage plentiful and light greyish-green.
C P G H ◐ ▽ AL 2′ × 2′ 60 × 60 cm

'Clotilde Soupert'

Soupert and Notting LUXEMBOURG 1890
'Mignonette' × 'Mme Damaizin'
Large clusters of very double, small, soft, creamy-white blooms with soft pink centres. Fragrant. Foliage rich light green. Growth bushy.
C ◐ G H ▽ B MF AL 1′ 6″ × 1′ 6″ 45 × 45 cm

'Cameo'

'Gloria Mundi'

'Dick Koster'

Koster HOLLAND 1931

Sport of 'Anneke Koster'

Large, tidy clusters of globular, deep orange-pink flowers on a compact, short shrubby little plant with good mid-green foliage.

C ◉ G H ▽ B AL 1′ × 1′ 30 × 30 cm

'Gloria Mundi'

de Ruiter HOLLAND 1929

'Superb' sport

Similar to 'Cameo' in flower shape and form, except with slightly fewer petals. Rich, scarlet-red with occasional flecks of white on the inner petals. Upright growth. Foliage dark green.

C P G H ◉ ▽ AL 2′ × 2′ 60 × 60 cm

'Golden Salmon Superior'

de Ruiter HOLLAND 1926

'Superb' sport

Of similar flower formation and growth habit to 'Gloria Mundi' and 'Cameo' but with a strong, orange-salmon colouring. One of the best for a massed, bright effect.

C P G H ◉ ▽ AL 2′ × 2′ 60 × 60 cm

'Jean Mermoz'

Chenault FRANCE 1937

R. wichuraiana × a Hybrid Tea

Fully double, reddish-pink, small blooms in dense

corymbs. Slightly fragrant. Foliage rather small, glossy and dark green. Vigorous and bushy.

C ◉ G ▽ B SF AL 2′ × 1′ 6″ 60 × 45 cm

'Katharina Zeimet', 'White Baby Rambler'

P. Lambert GERMANY 1901

'Etoile de Mai' × 'Marie Parvie'

Rather different from others in that the flowers, although in large clusters, are more widely spaced. Growth too is more angular, the foliage darker and perhaps less dense.

C P G H AL 2′ × 2′ 60 × 60 cm

'Margo Koster'

Koster HOLLAND 1931

Sport of 'Dick Koster'

Large, tidy clusters of globular, salmon flowers on a compact, short, shrubby little plant with good mid-green foliage.

C ◉ G H ▽ B AL 1′ × 1′ 30 × 30 cm

'Mignonette'

Guillot Fils FRANCE 1880

R. chinensis × *R. multiflora*

Small globular, double, blush-pink to white flowers, borne in large clusters. Plant dwarf and compact. Probably the earliest bred Polyantha still available.

C G P AL 1′ × 1′ 30 × 30 cm

'Miss Edith Cavell'

'Miss Edith Cavell'

de Ruiter HOLLAND 1917

'Orléans Rose' sport

Rich red to scarlet sometimes overlaid crimson. Flowers in clusters, globular in bud, opening semi-double and flattish. Foliage dark green, stems slightly lighter. Like others of its race, has little or no scent.

1985 was the 70th anniversary of the execution of Nurse Edith Cavell. For a time we lived near her birthplace, the village of Swardeston near Norwich. As part of the planned commemorative events, the vicar of Swardeston, the Rev. Philip McFadyen, asked me if I could obtain some plants of the 'Cavell' rose for him to plant in the village. After an initial search and inquiries in the rose trade, I was forced to conclude that the rose had become extinct.

Philip set about proving me wrong by writing to the *Eastern Daily Press*, while I sped all over Norfolk looking at potential resurrections, none of them this elusive rose. Finally I called on a charming and spritely octogenarian, Mrs Doris Levine, at Brundall, a village adjacent to the Norfolk Broads. She and her late husband George had been given half a dozen plants of 'Miss Edith Cavell' soon after they were married in 1934. Fifty years on, only one rather gnarled bush remained alive; from this I was able to propagate some ten plants and the life of another, almost extinct rose was rekindled, together with a little bit of Norfolk heritage.

C P G H AL 2′ × 2′ 60 × 60 cm

'Pinkie'

Swim USA 1947

'China Doll' × unknown

Large trusses of cupped, semi-double flowers of bright rosy-pink very freely produced. Very fragrant. The foliage is bright green and glossy, soft to touch. Growth vigorous and bushy.

C ▽ G H B VF AL 2′ × 1′ 6″ 60 × 45 cm

'The Fairy'

Bentall UK 1932

'Paul Crampel' × 'Lady Gay' (not a 'Lady Godiva' sport, as often stated)

After a spell in obscurity, this rose is currently enjoying a new lease of life, and deservedly so. The small, globular, pink flowers are produced in profusion all over a dense, spreading bush with attractive foliage. It is procumbent enough to be used for partial ground cover as well as for group planting and patio work. Illustrated on page 26.

C P G H ◉ ▽ AW 2′ × 4′ 60 × 120 cm

Floribundas
(Cluster-flowered Roses)

The classification 'Floribunda' covers all bush cluster-flowered roses other than Miniature Polyanthas and the groups known in the BARB classification as 'Patio' roses.

Many hundreds and probably thousands have been raised and introduced worldwide during the last fifty or so years and it would be impossible to include them all. I have selected only 32 which I believe to be a fair representation of modern cultivars today, together with a few classics from the past, and if the latter are not readily available, they are included as being important and outstanding examples that should be in a book of this type.

Floribundas have many uses, the most common of which is for bedding. Many make excellent hedging plants and most can be used for group planting in herbaceous borders or among other shrubs. More than a few, especially the shorter ones, make very good pot plants for urns, tubs and the like. Others, especially the taller ones, make ideal cut flowers.

CLASSIFICATION

BARB	Class 6
MR10	Class 19
WFRS	Class 5

'Allgold'

LeGrice UK 1956
'Goldilocks' × 'Ellinor LeGrice'
An outstanding old cultivar, with loosely arranged clusters of clear golden-yellow, semi-double flowers. Its foliage is small, mid-green and glossy. Growth upright.
C P SF B ▽ ⊱ AW 2′ × 2′ 60 × 60 cm

'Amber Queen' (HARroony)

Harkness UK 1984
'Southampton' × 'Typhoon'
Large, well-packed clusters of fully double blooms of amber-yellow. The foliage is large, maroonish, almost glossy. Growth bushy.
C MF B Gh ▽ ⊱ AW 2′ × 2′ 60 × 60 cm

'August Seebauer', 'Queen Mother'

Kordes GERMANY 1944
'Break o' Day' × 'Else Poulsen'
Large, double, clear pink and high-centred blooms are carried in sizeable clusters. Foliage small but plentiful, mid-green and semi-glossy. Growth bushy and vigorous.
C P SF B H ▽ AL 2′ 6″ × 2′ 75 × 60 cm

'Centenaire de Lourdes', 'Mrs Jones', 'Delge'

Delbard-Chabert FRANCE 1958
('Frau Karl Druschki' × seedling) × seedling
Huge clusters of well-spaced flowers, each shapely both in bud and when fully open, of bright shrimp-pink. Foliage large, dark green and shiny. Growth bushy and upright. A little tender for cold districts, but a superb cultivar.
C P SF B H AL 3′ × 2′ 90 × 60 cm

'Chanelle'

McGredy UK 1959
'Ma Perkins' × ('Fashion' × 'Mrs William Sprott')
Large clusters of semi-double, creamy apricot flowers are carried on a vigorous plant with good, dark green, glossy foliage. Growth bushy.
C MF B H AW 2′ 6″ × 2′ 75 × 60 cm

'**Amber Queen**', and '**August Seebauer**', below, '**Chanelle**', right

could well be used as a free-standing shrub rose. Illustrated on page 36.

C P VF B H AW 4′ × 3′ 120 × 90 cm

'Chinatown' (Ville de Chine)

Poulsen DENMARK 1963

'Columbine' × 'Cläre Grammerstorf'

The very large, fully double flowers of clear yellow are often flushed pink. These are displayed in medium-sized clusters amid lush, light green foliage. Growth upright and vigorous. This cultivar

'Dainty Maid'

LeGrice UK 1940

'D. T. Poulsen' × unknown

The beautiful, large, single flowers of silvery-pink have a deeper reverse and pronounced yellow stamens, and are carried in large clusters. Foliage dark green and leathery. Growth upright.

C P B H AL 3′ × 2′ 90 × 60 cm

'Centenaire de Lourdes'

'Dusky Maiden'

LeGrice UK 1947

('Daily Mail Scented Rose' × 'Étoile de Hollande') × 'Else Poulsen'

Large, single, deep velvety-red blooms are borne in clusters on an upright, sturdy plant with dark green foliage. A superb old cultivar.

C P B H VF ▽ ✂ AL 2′ × 2′ 60 × 60 cm

'Elizabeth of Glamis', 'Irish Beauty' (MACel)

McGredy UK 1964

'Spartan' × 'Highlight'

The superbly formed, well-scented double flowers of rich salmon-pink are produced in large clusters. Foliage dark green, matt. Growth upright. Needs protection in cold districts.

C B H VF ▽ BS⊘ M⊘ ✂ AW 2′ 6″ × 2′ 75 × 60 cm

'Escapade' (HARpade)

Harkness UK 1967

'Pink Parfait' × 'Baby Faurax'

Scented, semi-double blooms of rosy-violet with hints of lavender are borne in large clusters. Foliage light green and semi-glossy, on an upright and branching bush.

C P B H MF ▽ ✂ AW 3′ × 2′ 90 × 60 cm

'Dusky Maiden', left, and 'Escapade' above

'Frensham'

Norman UK 1946
Floribunda seedling × 'Crimson Glory'
Shapely, pure crimson flowers are borne in clusters on a vigorous, angular plant with bright green foliage and vicious thorns.
C P B H M⚭ AL 4 × 2′ 6″ 120 × 75 cm

'Grüss an Aachen'

Geduldig GERMANY 1909
'Frau Karl Druschki' × 'Franz Deegen'
A charmer from the past, its fully double, creamy-white flowers have soft pink and peachy highlights and are very freely produced in smallish clusters. Foliage matt dark green. Growth bushy, upright.
C B H Gh SF ▽ AL 1′ 6″ × 1′ 6″ 45 × 45 cm

'Horstmann's Rosenresli'

Kordes GERMANY 1955
'Rudolph Timm' × 'Lavender Pinocchio'
Pure white, fully double flowers in large clusters. Foliage mid-green, semi-glossy on a plant of bushy and upright growth. An excellent cultivar.
C P B H SF ▽ AL 2′ 6″ × 2′ 75 × 60 cm

'Iceberg', 'Schneewittchen', 'Fée des Neiges' (KORbin)

Kordes GERMANY 1958
'Robin Hood' × 'Virgo'
One of the best Floribundas ever raised, its shapely little buds open to loosely formed flowers of pure white which are carried in large trusses. Foliage light green and glossy, the stems also light green. Growth upright and bushy.
C P B H Gh MF ▽ ⤙ AW 3′ × 2′ 90 × 60 cm

'Irene of Denmark', 'Irene von Dänemark'

Poulsen DENMARK 1948
'Orléans Rose' × ('Mme Plantier' × 'Edina')
Very double, shapely flowers of pure white with a creamy base which are cupped until fully open, then flat and well formed. Foliage mid-green and glossy. Growth upright and bushy.
C P B H MF ▽ ⤙ ◉ AL 2′ 6″ × 2′ 75 × 60 cm

'Irène Watts'

Guillot FRANCE 1896
Although it was raised in 1896, I could not resist including this charming little rose, for it is well placed even ninety years on and has superbly shaped, scented blooms of ivory with pinkish-orange shadings, especially deep in the centre. Foliage dark green, matt. Growth bushy and short.
C B H MF Gh ▽ AL 1′ 6″ × 1′ 6″ 45 × 45 cm

'Grüss an Aachen', and below, 'Horstmann's Rosenresli'

'Irène Watts', and below, 'Jiminy Cricket'

'Jiminy Cricket'

Boerner USA 1954
'Goldilocks' × 'Geranium Red'
Shapely buds open to loosely formed blooms of pinkish-coral-orange in medium-sized clusters on a twiggy but dense plant with good, dark, glossy foliage.
C B H ▽ AL 2′ 6″ × 2′ 75 × 60 cm

'Korresia', 'Fresia', 'Friesia', 'Sunsprite'

Kordes GERMANY 1977
'Friedrich Wörlein' × 'Spanish Sun'
Rounded buds, arranged in large flat clusters, open to fully double bright yellow flowers on a sturdy, bushy plant. Foliage lightish green.
C P B H VF ▽ AL 2′ × 2′ 60 × 60 cm

'Léonie Lamesch'

P. Lambert GERMANY 1899
'Aglaia' × 'Kleiner Alfred'
One of the first Polyanthas. Placed here because it was ahead of its time when introduced. A short cultivar with rather stubby growth but ample, leathery, dark green foliage. Flowers are small, full double, borne in clusters and an odd mixture of yellow, orange and red.
P ▽ C AL 2′ × 2′ 60 × 60 cm

'Lilac Charm'

LeGrice UK 1952
Bred from a *R. californica* seedling
A beautiful rose, with large clusters of single, or almost single, soft pastel-mauve flowers which have

'Lilac Charm', and below, 'Margaret Merril'

pronounced gold and red stamens. Foliage dark matt green. Growth sturdy and bushy.
C P B H MF ▽ AL 2′ × 2′ 60 × 60 cm

'Margaret Merril' (HARkuly)

Harkness UK 1977
('Rudolph Timm' x 'Dedication') × 'Pascali'
A superb cultivar, the flowers are white with blushes of soft pink and have pronounced golden stamens when fully open. They are highly scented and are carried in small clusters. Foliage dark green, matt. Growth sturdy and upright.
C P B H Gh VF ▽ ✂ AW 2′ 6″ × 2′ 75 × 60 cm

'Marie-Jeanne'

Turbat FRANCE 1913
Clusters of fully double, rosette-shaped flowers of soft pink to almost white with deeper-coloured centres. Slightly scented. Foliage glossy light green tinted bronze, especially when young. Vigorous. Can be left unpruned to produce an excellent, shortish shrub.
C H P ▽ ◉ AL 3′ × 3′ 90 × 90 cm

'Masquerade'

Boerner USA 1949
'Goldilocks' × 'Holiday'
The forerunner of many brightly coloured Floribundas. Semi-double flowers of bright yellow changing through pink and orange to deep red

with age are produced in very large clusters. Foliage small, dark and leathery. Growth upright. The hips set easily and therefore must be dead-headed in order to encourage the autumn flowers.

C P B H ▽ AW 2′ 6″ × 2′ 75 × 60 cm

'Nathalie Nypels', 'Mevrouw Nathalie Nypels'

Leenders HOLLAND 1919

'Orléans Rose' × ('Comtesse du Cayla' ×
R. foetida bicolor)

One of the best and most reliable of the cluster-flowered roses from the past. Large clusters of double, silky-textured, deep pink to salmon flowers are borne on strong stems from a bushy and branching plant with good, dark green foliage.

C P B H ▽ AL 2′ 6″ × 2′ 75 × 60 cm

'Norwich Castle'

Beales UK 1979

('Whisky Mac' × 'Arthur Bell') × seedling

Closely packed clusters of Hybrid Tea-shaped flowers, flat when fully open, of deep coppery-orange paling to soft apricot. Very free-flowering, with light green, shiny foliage and of upright growth.

C P B H Gh ▽ ⊰ AL 2′ 6″ × 2′ 75 × 60 cm

'Norwich Union'

Beales UK 1975

'Arthur Bell' × (seedling × 'Allgold')

Large, fully double, cupped flowers of deep clear yellow paling to lemon with age, but losing nothing in doing so, are produced in small, upstanding clusters. Foliage bright green and glossy. Growth stocky and upright.

C B H Gh VF ◉ ▽ ⊰ AL 1′ 6″ × 1′ 6″ 45 × 45 cm

'Norwich Castle', and above, 'Nathalie Nypels'

'Pink Parfait', and right, 'Rosemary Rose'

'Plentiful'

'Picasso' (MACpic)

McGredy UK 1971
'Marlena' × ['Evelyn Fison' × ('Frühlingsmorgen' × 'Orange Sweetheart')]
Semi-double flowers are produced in clusters, their petals deep rose-pink, the edges and reverse silvery. The foliage is small and dark green on a bushy plant. This was the first of several 'hand-painted' roses, as their raiser calls them.
C P H ⬓ BS♂ AL 2′ 6″ × 2′ 75 × 60 cm

'Pink Parfait'

Swim USA 1960
'First Love' × 'Pinocchio'
Attractive buds open to large, semi-double blooms made up of several shades of pink which are produced in large numbers in clusters of variable size. The foliage is semi-glossy and leathery, the growth upright and bushy. Without any doubt, this is an outstanding rose.
C P B H SF Gh ⬓ ✂ AL 3′ × 2′ 90 × 60 cm

'Plentiful'

LeGrice UK 1961
Large, deep pink and scented flowers packed with petals of different lengths to create a very old-fashioned, quartered effect when fully open. Foliage dark green, leathery and veined. Growth angular, with many thorns.
C P B MF ⬓ ✂ AL 2′ 6″ × 2′ 6″ 75 × 75 cm

'Queen Elizabeth', 'Queen Elizabeth Rose'

Lammerts USA 1954
'Charlotte Armstrong' × 'Floradora'
This outstanding rose has deserved all the attention it has ever received. Long, high-centred buds open to large blooms of clear pink, produced in clusters. The foliage is large, dark green, leathery and glossy on a very vigorous, upright plant.
C P H Gh SF ⬓ ✂ AW 5′ × 2′ 6″ 150 × 75 cm

'White Pet'

'Rosemary Rose'

de Ruiter HOLLAND 1954

'Grüss an Teplitz' × a Floribunda seedling

The fully double, flattish carmine-red flowers are crammed, it seems, with petals in *R. centifolia* style, and likewise are occasionally quartered. They are carried in large, heavy clusters. Foliage darkish green to maroon, the stems plum-red. Growth, though bushy, is often bent by the sheer weight of flowers.

C B H ▽ ⇜ M◔ AL 2′ 6″ × 2′ 75 × 60 cm

'White Pet', 'Little White Pet'

P. Henderson USA 1879

'Félicité Perpétue' sport

Large clusters of small white fully double rosette flowers on a bushy plant which is abundantly clothed in dark green foliage. A useful and superb little rose for any garden. Should strictly be under forms of *R. sempervirens*, but as the only dwarf in that section is better placed here.

C P G ◉ ▽ AW 2′ × 2′ 60 × 60 cm

'Yvonne Rabier'

Turbat FRANCE 1910

R. wichuraiana × a Polyantha rose

Often listed amongst Polyanthas but its flowers are larger and the plant taller. Its true place would be among Wichuraiana hybrids, but in garden terms it is too short for this. Semi-double, pure white blooms in clusters on a healthy, well-foliated plant. Leaves light rich green; the stems, also light green, are almost free of thorns.

C P G ◉ ▽ AL 3′ × 2′ 90 × 60 cm

Climbing Floribundas

Floribunda roses occasionally produce climbing sports. For some reason these are not nearly as numerous as climbing Hybrid Teas, but since Floribunda numbers are fewer, I suspect they occur in roughly the same ratio. I describe seven, not necessarily as my favourites, but as a representative selection of those which should be available commercially and which will perform well in any situation. They provide a profusion of flowers on vigorous plants, and therefore have wider applications than some of the more modern, long-flowering climbers, which sometimes lack climbing ability.

CLASSIFICATION

BARB   Class 11
MR10   Class 9
WFRS   Class 18

'Allgold' Climbing

Bush form LeGrice UK 1958

'Goldilocks' × 'Ellinor LeGrice'

This form Gandy UK 1961

An excellent climber and, since good yellow climbers are scarce, well worth consideration where such colour is needed. Clear yellow, almost unfading flowers open to semi-double blooms produced in upright clusters on strong stems. Slightly scented. Leaves small but numerous, rich dark green.
S P SF AW 15′ × 10′ 4.5 × 3 m

'Allgold' Climbing

'Arthur Bell' Climbing

Bush form McGredy UK 1965

'Cläre Grammerstorf' × 'Piccadilly'

This form Pearce UK 1979

Clusters of deep yellow, double flowers paling to soft yellow with age on a tall, upright plant with exceptionally glossy, deep green foliage.
S P VF ✁ AL 12′ × 8′ 3.5 × 2.5 m

'Fashion' Climbing

Bush form Boerner USA 1949

'Pinocchio' × 'Crimson Glory'

This form Boerner USA 1951

Another identical climbing form introduced by Mattock UK in 1955

This rose has fallen from favour as a bush because of its proneness to rust, but this does not seem to be a problem for the climbing form, probably because of its extra vigour. Clusters of double, bright coral-salmon flowers in profusion on a fairly thornless plant with coppery-green shoots and foliage.
S P ☼ MF AL 15′ × 10′ 4.5 × 3 m

'Iceberg'

'Iceberg' Climbing, 'Schneewittchen'

Bush form Kordes GERMANY 1958

'Robin Hood' × 'Virgo'

This form Cants UK 1968

A shortage of good white climbers justifies the inclusion of this rose, which retains all the good qualities of the bush with the added dimensions of a climber. Freely produced, large trusses of almost double, pure white flowers. Climbing shoots almost thornless with crisp, shiny, pale green leaves.

S P N ◉ SF AL 18′ × 10′ 5.5 × 3 m

'Korona' Climbing

Bush form Kordes GERMANY 1955

'Obergärtner Wiebicke' × 'Independence'

This form Kordes GERMANY 1957

Clusters of semi-double, bright orange-scarlet flowers on a vigorous, fairly thorny plant with dark green foliage. Rather bright for my taste but included for its remarkable resistance to rain and inclement weather.

S P N ◉ AL 15′ × 10′ 4.5 × 3 m

'Masquerade' Climbing

Bush form Boerner USA 1949

'Goldilocks' × 'Holiday'

This form Gregory UK 1958

Clusters of semi-double flowers opening soft yellow, changing to soft pink and then to almost crimson as they age. Vigorous, moderately thorny stems. Dark green foliage.

S P SF AL 18′ × 10′ 5.5 × 3 m

'Queen Elizabeth' Climbing

Bush form Lammerts USA 1954

'Charlotte Armstrong' × 'Floradora'

This form Wheatcroft UK 1960

A very vigorous climber, almost too vigorous since its flowers are often borne too high up in the branches to be enjoyed. Flowers rich, clear silvery-pink, produced in large clusters. Foliage large, healthy and dark green.

S P AW 20′ × 10′ 6 × 3 m

Miniatures and Patios (Compact Floribundas)

Miniature roses enjoyed a brief spell of popularity during the early years of the nineteenth century, but the colour range of the first cultivars was limited and they soon fell from favour and disappeared from cultivation until rediscovery in 1918 (*see* 'Rouletii'). Since then they have established themselves as popular little roses and many hundreds have been raised and introduced. Because I feel they should be represented in this book I have selected just 19, including some of the more recent 'Patio' cultivars. The Patios are slightly more bushy and taller than the Miniatures but shorter and of smaller proportions than the dwarf Floribundas.

Both Miniatures and Patios grow well on their own roots and, with the advent of micropropagation, more and more are being produced in this way. Own-root Miniatures are usually smaller than those produced by other methods of propagation such as grafting or budding, so it is wise to inquire how they have been grown before purchase. In the garden their uses are several, from close-density bedding and edging to group-planting among other subjects. They also make useful pot plants and will do well in window boxes. They never enjoy growing indoors as house plants.

CLASSIFICATION

BARB	Classes 8 and 9
MR10	Class 48
WFRS	Class 8

'Baby Darling' [Miniature]

Moore USA 1964
'Little Darling' × 'Magic Wand'
Apricot-orange flowers, quite large and double, borne in medium-sized clusters, with mid-green foliage. Growth upright and bushy. Quite nice when cut for miniature flower arrangements.
C B SF ▽ ✃ AW 1′ 30 cm

'Baby Masquerade', 'Baby Carnaval', 'Tanbakede' (TANba) [Miniature]

Tantau GERMANY 1956
'Peon' × 'Masquerade'
The almost double blooms, in sizeable clusters, are yellow with red, the red deepening with age. Foliage

'Baby Masquerade'

'Harvest Fayre', and below, 'Little Flirt'

dark green, almost glossy, and leathery. Growth upright and bushy.
C P B SF ✄ AW 1′ 6″ 45 cm

'Cinderella' [Miniature]

De Vink HOLLAND 1953
'Cécile Brünner' × 'Peon'
Very double, slightly fluffy blooms of white tinged pink. Foliage light green. Growth dense, upright and almost thornless.
C P SF ▽ ✄ AW 1′ 30cm

'Harvest Fayre' (DICnorth) [Patio]

Dickson UK 1990
Large clusters of semi-double, apricot-orange flowers on a healthy, strong, bushy plant with glossy mid-green foliage. Starts flowering rather later than most Floribundas but more than makes up for this by improving steadily later in the year when its colour is enhanced by autumn light. British 'Rose of the Year' 1990.
C ▽ B H ✄ SF AL 3′ × 2′ 6″ 90 × 75 cm

'Little Buckaroo' [Miniature]

Moore USA 1956
(*R. wichuraiana* × 'Floradora') × ('Oakington Ruby' × 'Floradora')
Double, loosely formed, bright red flowers with white centres are borne in clusters. Foliage bronzy and glossy. Growth upright and tallish.
C B ▽ ✄ AW 15″ 38 cm

'Little Flirt' [Miniature]

Moore USA 1961
(*R. wichuraiana* × 'Floradora') × ('Golden Glow' × 'Zee')
Fully double, shapely flowers of rich orange-yellow, with clear yellow on the reverse, their pointed petals giving a star-like appearance. Foliage light green on a bushy plant.
C B ▽ BS♂ AW 15″ 38 cm

'Mr Bluebird' [Miniature]

Moore USA 1960
'Old Blush' × 'Old Blush'
Small, rounded buds in clusters produce semi-double, lavender-blue flowers in profusion. Foliage dark and matt-finished. Growth upright and bushy.
C ▽ AW 1′ 30 cm

'Orange Sunblaze', 'Orange Meillandina' (MEIjikatar) [Patio]

Meilland FRANCE 1982
'Parador' × ('Baby Bettina' × 'Duchess of Windsor')
Bright orange-red, double, cupped flowers are borne

'Mr Bluebird', and right, 'Regensberg'

in profusion in small clusters. Foliage plentiful, light-green and matt. Growth bushy and dense.
C P B SF G ▽ AW 15″ 38 cm

'Peon', 'Tom Thumb' [Miniature]

de Vink NETHERLANDS 1936
'Rouletii' × 'Gloria Mundi'
Its small, semi-double flowers are deep red with a white centre. Foliage light green and leathery on a bushy, compact plant. A rose with a place in the pedigree of many Miniatures.
C ▽ AL 9″ 23 cm

'Perla de Montserrat' [Miniature]

Dot SPAIN 1945
'Cécile Brünner' × 'Rouletii'
Very shapely blooms borne in upright sprays reminiscent of its parent, 'Cécile Brünner'. They are of soft pink deepening towards the centre. Foliage darkish green and matt. Growth upright and bushy.
C ▽ ✄ AW 9″ 23 cm

'Pour Toi', 'For You', 'Para Ti', 'Wendy' [Miniature]

Dot SPAIN 1946
'Eduardo Toda' × 'Pompon de Paris'
Semi-double flowers, white with yellow deep in the centre, produced in small clusters. Foliage mid-green and glossy. Growth short and bushy.
C ▽ AW 9″ 23 cm

'Red Ace', 'Amruda', 'Amanda' [Miniature]

de Ruiter HOLLAND 1977
'Scarletta' × seedling
Shapely, double, deep red flowers are carried in small clusters. Foliage mid-green and semi-glossy. Growth compact and bushy.
C SF ▽ AW 1′ 30 cm

'Regensberg', 'Young Mistress', 'Buffalo Bill' (MACyoumis) [Patio]

McGredy NEW ZEALAND 1979
'Geoff Boycott' × 'Old Master'
Its double flowers of soft pink with their petals edged white have prominent yellow stamens. Foliage plentiful and mid-green. Growth compact, spreading and bushy.
C B H VF G ▽ AL 1′ 6″ 45 cm

'Robin Redbreast' (INTerrob) [Patio]

Ilsink HOLLAND 1984
Seedling × 'Eyepaint'
Small, single blooms of dark red with creamy-yellow centres and silvery reverses are produced in profusion. Mid-green, glossy foliage, the stems thorny. Growth bushy and spreading.
C B H G ▽ AL 1′ 6″ 45 cm

'Rouletii', *R. rouletii* [Miniature]

Correvon SWITZERLAND 1922
Cultivar of *R. chinensis minima*
The first of the modern Miniatures, discovered growing in pots on a window ledge in Switzerland by Major Roulet in 1918. Double flowers of deep rose-pink produced singly or in small clusters. Foliage dark green and matt. Growth bushy and compact. Illustrated on page 43.
R ▽ AL 9″ 23 cm

'Robin Redbreast'

'Snowball', 'Angelita' (MACangel) [Miniature]

McGredy NEW ZEALAND 1982
'Moana' × 'Snow Carpet'
Fully double, white, globular blooms are produced in clusters. Foliage light green and dense. Growth bushy.
C ▽ AW 1′ 30 cm

'Sweet Dream' (FRYerminicot) [Patio]

Fryer UK 1987
Masses of double, peachy-apricot blooms in clusters. Foliage plentiful and mid-green. Growth wide and bushy.
C B H ▽ AL 1′ 6″ 45 cm

'Twenty-Fifth' (BEAtwe) [Patio]

Beales UK 1996
'Robin Redbreast' × 'Horstman's Rosenresli'
Rich ruby-red semi-double flowers displaying rich golden stamens to effect. Plentiful dark green semi-glossy foliage. Growth compact, bushy. Raised by Amanda Beales. Illustrated on page 40.
C G ▽ B SF AL 1′ 6″ × 2′ 45 × 60 cm

'Yellow Doll' [Miniature]

Moore USA 1962
'Golden Glow' × 'Zee'
Its shapely, fully double flowers of creamy-yellow are not unlike miniature Hybrid Teas. Foliage mid-green and glossy. Growth vigorous and bushy.
C Gh SF ▽ ✂ AW 1′ 30 cm

Procumbent Shrub Roses
(Ground-cover Roses)

Roses have been planted for ground cover since the nineteenth century. In those days, however, the main sources of material were the relaxed ramblers such as the Ayrshires and the Evergreens (the Sempervirens). Later, mostly during the first two decades of this century, the introduction of the flexible Wichuraiana hybrids provided a greater range of colour. The weakness of most ramblers is, of course, their relatively short flowering season, which means that although they are ideal for covering banks and mounds, they are seldom used for this purpose today; more's the pity.

Since the Second World War, and with landscape gardeners demanding cost-effective plants, ground-cover roses have been in great demand and breeders have not been slow to react, developing a steadily increasing number of both once-flowering and remontant cultivars.

Personally, I have never been happy with the term 'ground cover' for roses of any kind. Although I accept that some are suitable for the purpose, only a very few that I know of are sufficiently dense to suppress weeds in the same way as more traditional ground-cover plants such as *Hypericum calycinum* and *Vinca major*. In fact, spreading roses can make weed-infested ground more rather than less difficult to cultivate, and so may create a problem rather than solve one. I prefer the term 'procumbent' which adequately describes their habit with no misleading connotations.

Procumbent roses can be used in a variety of ways. They are most commonly planted for massed displays to give colour to municipal and industrial landscapes. In the garden they can serve useful purposes on banks or in beds where too much height is undesirable. They also look good planted in groups to provide colour lower down in shrubberies and many are excellent grown in tubs, pots or urns, or cascading down from short walls or troughs. One or two smaller cultivars make fine rockery subjects.

One clear advantage of this type of rose is that many flourish on their own roots, thus eliminating any difficulties in removing suckers.

Most modern catalogues and, indeed, most good garden suppliers now offer a considerable range of these roses; it has not been an easy task to choose those for inclusion. Those selected, however, are a fair cross-section of old and new, and most can be obtained without difficulty both in the UK and abroad.

There are quite a number of roses other than those described in this section which fall into the procumbent category, but for reasons of heredity I have placed them under their rightful family group headings.

CLASSIFICATION

BARB	Class 17
MR10	No specific class; best covered by Class 54
WFRS	Classes 3 and 11

'Alba Meidiland' (MEIflopan)

Meilland FRANCE 1987

Tight, heavy clusters of pure white and fully double flowers, which are good for cutting. Foliage mid-green. Growth dense and spreading.

C G H SF ◉ ▽ ✂ AL 3′ × 4′ 90 × 120 cm

'Avon', 'Fairy Lights', 'Sunnyside' (POUlmulti)

Poulsen DENMARK 1992

Pearly-white with blush overlay semi-double flowers in clusters. Foliage dark green. Growth dense and spreading.

C ▽ G ◉ SF AL 1′ × 3′ 30 × 90 cm

'Berkshire', 'Pink Sensation', 'Sommermärchen' (KORpinka)

Kordes GERMANY 1991

Bright pinkish-red scented flowers with conspicuous stamens produced in clusters. Foliage dark green, glossy. Growth bushy and wide.

C G ▽ MF AW 2′ × 4′ 60 × 120 cm

'Bonica '82' (MEIdomonac) see Modern Shrubs, page 288

'Broadlands', 'Sonnenschirm' (TANmirsch)

Tantau GERMANY 1993

Soft yellow, cupped, fragrant, fully double flowers in clusters. Soft light green foliage. Growth vigorous and spreading.

C G ◉ MF AW 3′ × 5′ 90 × 150 cm

'Cambridgeshire' (KORhaugen)

Kordes GERMANY 1994

Flowers cupped, semi-double, a mixture of gold, light red and pink produced in clusters. Dark green glossy foliage. Growth shortish, dense and spreading.

C G ◉ ▽ AW 1′ 6″ × 3′ 50 × 90 cm

'Candy Rose' (MEIranovi)

Meilland FRANCE 1980

(*R. sempervirens* × 'Mlle Marthe Carron') × [('Lilli Marlene' × 'Evelyn Fison') × ('Orange Sweetheart' × 'Frühlingsmorgen')]
Semi-double flowers of deep pink with a reddish reverse. Foliage small, light green and glossy. Growth bushy and spreading.

C G P ▽ AL 4′ × 6′ 1.2 × 1.8 m

'Cardinal Hume' (HARregale) see Modern Shrubs, page 290

'Carefree Beauty' (BUCbi)

Buck USA 1977

Seedling × 'Prairie Princess'
Semi-double, fragrant, creamy-buffy-pink flowers produced in large quantities throughout the summer. Foliage plentiful, deep green, semi-glossy. Growth bushy and wide. A good rose in all respects.

C ▽ P H G MF AW 5′ × 4′ 1.5 × 1.2 m

'Caterpillar' see 'Pink Drift'

'Chatsworth', 'Mirato' (TANotax)

Tantau GERMANY 1990

Semi-double, fragrant, mid- to deep pink blooms opening flat. Foliage glossy dark green. Growth dense and spreading. Named for the famous historic house, the seat of the Duke of Devonshire.

C G ▽ ◉ MF AW 2′ × 3′ 60 × 90 cm

'Chilterns', 'Fiery Sunsation' (KORtemma)

Kordes GERMANY 1990

Clusters of semi-double deep crimson flowers showing off golden stamens to effect. Small shiny mid-green foliage. Growth vigorous and spreading.

C G ▽ ◉ SF AW 2′ × 7′ 60 × 210 cm

'Daisy Hill' see Forms and Hybrids of *R. macrantha*, page 181

'Dunwich Rose' *see* Forms and Hybrids of
R. pimpinellifolia, page 126

'Essex' (POUlnoz)

Poulsen DENMARK 1987
Small, deep pink, single blooms in profusion. After
the habit of 'Nozomi'. Very free-flowering.
C ▽ G ◎ AW 2′ × 5′ 60 × 180 cm

'Eyeopener' (INTerop)

Ilsink HOLLAND 1987
(Seedling × 'Eyepaint') × (Seedling × 'Dortmund')
Its bright flowers have white centres. Foliage dense
and mid-green on a vigorous, spreading bush.
C P G ◎ AL 1′ × 3′ 30 × 90 cm

'Fairy Changeling' (HARnumerous)

Harkness UK 1981
'The Fairy' × 'Yesterday'
Plump little buds open to small, cupped, fully
double flowers of soft clear pink in large trusses.
Foliage small, dark green and semi-glossy. Growth
bushy and spreading.
C P G SF ▽ AL 1′ 6″ × 2′ 45 × 60 cm

'Fairy Damsel' (HARneatly)

Harkness UK 1981
'The Fairy' × 'Yesterday'
Dark red, small, double flowers, cupped at first

'Fairyland', and left, 'Fairy Damsel'

then flattish in small trusses. Foliage dark green and
glossy. Growth bushy and spreading.
C P G SF ▽ AL 2′ × 5′ 60 × 150 cm

'Fairyland' (HARlayalong)

Harkness UK 1980
'The Fairy' × 'Yesterday'
Soft pink, cupped, small, fully double flowers are
borne in large trusses. Foliage mid-green and glossy.
Growth bushy and spreading.
C P G SF ▽ AL 2′ × 5′ 60 × 150 cm

'Ferdy' (KEItoli)

Suzuki JAPAN 1984
Climbing seedling × 'Petite Folie' seedling
Has deep salmon-pink flowers, small and fully
double. Foliage small, plentiful and light green.
Growth bushy, spreading and dense.
C P G ▽ AW 2′ × 3′ 60 × 90 cm

'Fiona' (MEIbeluexen)

Meilland FRANCE 1982
'Sea Foam' × 'Picasso'
Large clusters of dark red flowers, slightly paler in

'Grouse'

the centre. Smallish, dark green and glossy foliage. Growth bushy and spreading.

C P G MF H ▽ AW 3′ × 4′ 90 × 120 cm

'Flamingo Meidiland' (MEIsolroz)

Meilland FRANCE 1990

Attractive, clear pink flowers produced in profusion throughout summer followed by bright red-orange hips. Good foliage on a dense, wide-growing but bushy plant. Could also make a useful specimen shrub or dense hedge. A good landscape rose.

C H ▽ F G ◉ AW 3′ × 4′ 90 × 120 cm

'Flower Carpet' (NOAtraum)

Noack GERMANY 1990

Huge trusses of sizeable, double, deep pink flowers produced in abundance throughout the summer. Foliage glossy light green. Growth dense and wide. Has won several awards for excellence.

C ▽ G AW 1′ 6″ × 4′ 45 × 120 cm

'Francine Austin' (AUSram)

Austin UK 1988

Sprays of small, pompon-like, fully double flowers

of pure glistening white. Foliage light green and plentiful. Growth vigorous, bushy and wide.

R ▽ G P ◉ AL 3′ × 4′ 90 × 120 cm

'Grouse', 'Immensee' (KORimro)

Kordes GERMANY 1982

'The Fairy' × R. wichuraiana seedling

Clusters of small, single, white flowers with pink blushes and prominent stamens. Foliage mid-green and glossy on a prostrate, spreading plant.

R P G MF ◉ AW 2′ × 10′ 60 × 300 cm

'Gwent', 'Aspen', 'Gold Magic Carpet', 'Suncover' (POUlurt)

Poulsen DENMARK 1992

Deep golden-yellow semi-double cupped flowers. Dark green glossy foliage. Growth compact, spreading.

C G ▽ SF AW 1′6″ × 3′ 45 × 90 cm

'Hampshire' (KORhamp)

Poulsen DENMARK 1989

A ground-hugging shrub. Small, single flowers of bright scarlet. Good foliage.

R ▽ G ◉ AL 2′ × 4′ 60 × 120 cm

'Harry Maasz' see Forms and Hybrids of R. macrantha, page 181

'Heidekönigin' see 'Pheasant'

'Hertfordshire' (KORtenay)

Kordes GERMANY 1991

Single, carmine blooms borne in great profusion on a low, spreading plant liberally endowed with good, healthy foliage.

R ▽ G AL 1′ 6″ x 3′ 45 × 100 cm

'Immensee' see 'Grouse'

'Kent', 'White Cover' (POUlcov)

Poulsen DENMARK 1987

Trusses of semi-double, white flowers produced in great quantities. Impervious to weather, it is said. Compact and wide.

R ▽ ◉ G AL 1′ 6′ x 3′ 45 × 100 cm

'Norfolk'

'Lady Curzon' *see* Forms and Hybrids of Rugosas, page 231

'Laura Ashley' (CHEwharla)

Warner UK 1990
Pretty lilac-pink flowers in clusters. Sweetly scented. Very free-flowering. Foliage mid-green. Growth dense and wide.
C ▽ G MF AL 2′ × 3′ 60 × 90 cm

'Magic Carpet' (JAClover)

Jackson Perkins USA 1994
'Grouse' × 'Class Act'
Pink flowers with a hint of lavender showing through, semi-double with spicy perfume. Foliage dark green, very glossy and healthy. Growth bushy but spreading.
C G ▽ VF AW 2′ × 5′ 60 cm × 1.5 m

'Max Graf' *see* Forms and Hybrids of Rugosas, page 231

'Norfolk' (POUlfolk)

Poulsen DENMARK 1989
One of the very few procumbents with any yellow in their make-up. This one has clusters of small, double, bright yellow flowers amid good foliage.
R ▽ ◍ G AL 1′ 6″ x 2′ 45 × 60 cm

'Northamptonshire' (MATtdor)

Mattock UK 1990
Shapely, small flowers (similar to 'Cécile Brünner') of soft pink borne amid fresh green foliage on a dense, ground-hugging plant.
R ▽ ◍ G AL 1′ 6″ × 3′ 45 × 100 cm

'Nozomi'

Onodera JAPAN 1968
'Fairy Princess' × 'Sweet Fairy'
Small, single, star-like flowers of pearly-pink in small trusses. The foliage is very small, plentiful, dark green and glossy, with arching plum-coloured young stems, the older wood dark green. Growth very dense and spreading.
S G P H ◍ ▽ AW 3′ × 6′ 90 × 180 cm

'Nozomi', and opposite **'Pearl Drift'**

'Partridge', **'Weisse Immensee'** (KORweirim)

Kordes GERMANY 1984
'The Fairy' × *R. wichuraiana* seedling
Small, single, white flowers develop from pink buds in clusters. Foliage small, dark green and glossy, though bronzy when young. Growth prostrate and spreading.
R P G MF ◍ AL 2′ × 10′ 60 × 300 cm

'Paulii', *R. paulii*

Paul UK c.1903
R. arvensis × *R. rugosa*
The large, single, white flowers have 5 spaced petals and prominent yellow stamens. Foliage slender, rugose, light to mid-green, the young wood pinkish, and with many thorns. Growth prostrate.
S G SF ◍ M♂ AL 3′ × 10′ 90 × 300 cm

'Paulii Rosea', *R. paulii rosea*

c.1912
A possible sport from 'Paulii' but there are many differences
The large, single, soft rose-pink flowers, their petals less spread than 'Paulii', have pronounced yellow stamens. Foliage mid-green and rugose, the stems

thorny. Young wood is lime-green. Its growth is prostrate but denser than 'Paulii'.
S G SF MÖ AL 3′ × 10′ 90 × 300 cm

'Pearl Drift' (LEGgab)

LeGrice UK 1980
'Mermaid' × 'New Dawn'
Sizeable, semi-double, white flowers flushed pink borne in large trusses. Foliage dark green and semi-glossy. Growth dense, bushy and spreading.
C P G MF ◍ ▽ AW 3′ × 4′ 90 × 120 cm

'Pearl Meidiland' (MEIplatin)

Meilland FRANCE 1989
The raiser describes this rose as pale ochre, flowers produced in clusters on a dense, spreading plant with glossy foliage.
R ▽ G ◍ AW 2′ × 4′ 60 × 120 cm

'Pheasant', 'Heidekönigin' (KORdapt)

Kordes GERMANY 1986
'Zwergkönig '78' × R. wichuraiana seedling
Modest clusters of small, deep rose-pink, double flowers, with mid-green glossy foliage on a plant of prostrate, spreading growth.
R P G MF ◍ AL 2′ × 10′ 60 × 300 cm

'Pink Bells' (POUlbells)

Poulsen DENMARK 1983
'Mini-Poul' × 'Temple Bells'
Small, fully double, bright pink flowers borne in profusion. Foliage mid-green, semi-glossy, small but plentiful. Growth dense and spreading.
S P G SF ◍ ▽ AW 2′ × 4′ 60 × 120 cm

'Pink Chimo' (INTerchimp)

Ilsink HOLLAND 1990
Attractively formed deep pink flowers on a dense, wide-growing plant with good leathery foliage.
C ▽ ◍ G AL 2′ × 3′ 60 × 90 cm

'Pink Drift', 'Kiki Rose', 'Caterpillar' (POUlcat)

Poulsen DENMARK 1984
'Temple Bells' × seedling
Large trusses of small, semi-double, light pink blooms are freely produced. Foliage plentiful, small, dark green and glossy. Growth bushy and spreading.
C P G MF ◍ ▽ AL 2′ × 3′ 60 × 90 cm

'Pink Bells'. Opposite,'Red Blanket' and 'Red Max Graf', below

'Pink Meidiland', 'Schloss Heidegg' (MEIpoque)

Meilland FRANCE 1983
'Anne de Bretagne' × 'Nirvana'
The single flowers of deep pink have a white eye. Foliage smallish, mid-green and semi-glossy. Bushy, spreading habit of growth.
C G H SF ◍ ▽ AW 2′ × 2′ 60 × 90 cm

'Pink Wave' (MATtgro)

Mattock UK 1983
'Moon Maiden' × 'Eyepaint'
Soft pink, semi-double flowers are borne in clusters. Foliage mid-green and semi-glossy. Growth bushy and spreading.
C P G MF ◍ ▽ AL 2′ × 3′ 60 × 90 cm

'Queen Mother' (KORquemu)

Kordes GERMANY 1991
Pure soft pink semi-double flowers produced in great profusion and set off by plentiful glossy foliage. Growth rounded, bushy and slightly spreading.
C ▽ B SF G AW 1′ × 1′ 6″ 30 × 45 cm

'Raubritter', 'Macrantha Raubritter' *see* Forms and Hybrids of *R. macrantha*, page 181

'Red Bells' (POUlred)

Poulsen DENMARK 1983
'Mini-Poul' × 'Temple Bells'
Small, fully double, red flowers are produced in great abundance. Foliage mid-green, semi-glossy, small and plentiful. Growth dense and spreading.
S P G SF ◍ ▽ AL 2′ × 4′ 60 × 120 cm

'Red Blanket' (INTercell)

Ilsink HOLLAND 1979
'Yesterday' × unnamed seedling
The flowers, semi-double and medium-sized, are borne in small clusters and are deep pink to almost red. Foliage dark green and glossy. Growth dense and spreading.
C P G SF ◍ ▽ BS☼ AW 3′ × 4′ 90 × 120 cm

'Red Max Graf', 'Rote Max Graf' (KORmax)

Kordes GERMANY 1980
R. kordesii × seedling
Bright red, medium-sized, single flowers are borne

in large clusters. The abundant foliage is matt, dark green and leathery on a coarsely spreading plant.
C P G SF ◉ AW 3′ × 6′ 90 × 180 cm

'Red Trail' (INTerim)

Ilsink HOLLAND 1991
Large quantities of bright red flowers on a vigorous, wide-growing, ground-covering plant with ample foliage.
R G ◉ AL 3′ × 5′ 90 × 150 cm

'Repens Meidiland' (MEIlontig)

Meilland FRANCE 1987
Small, single, white flowers in profusion. Foliage small, mid-green and glossy. Growth very prostrate and vigorous.
S P G ◉ AL 6″ × 10′ 15 × 300 cm

'Rosy Carpet' (INTercarp)

Ilsink HOLLAND 1983
'Yesterday' × seedling
Light pink, single blooms are very freely produced in large clusters. Foliage dark green and glossy. Growth prickly, dense and spreading.
R P G MF ◉ ▽ AL 2′ × 4′ 60 × 120 cm

'Rosy Cushion' (INTerall)

Ilsink HOLLAND 1979
'Yesterday' × seedling
Soft pink, almost single blooms are borne in large clusters. Foliage dark green and glossy. Growth dense, bushy and spreading.
R P G SF ◉ ▽ AW 3′ × 4′ 90 × 120 cm

'Rutland' (POUlshine)

Poulsen DENMARK 1988
Masses of small, single, pink blooms on a compact cushion-like plant. Foliage ample, deep green and glossy.
R ▽ ◉ G AL 1′ × 1′ 30 × 30 cm

'Simon Robinson', and below, 'Suffolk'

'Scarlet Meidiland' (MEIkrotal)

Meilland FRANCE 1987
Heavy clusters of bright cherry-red flowers, with dark green, glossy foliage on a dense and spreading bush. Particularly good in the autumn.
C G H SF ⬤ ▽ ✂ AL 3′ × 4′ 90 × 120 cm

'Scintillation' see Forms and Hybrids of R. macrantha, page 181

'Sea Foam'

E. W. Schwartz USA 1964
('White Dawn' × 'Pinocchio') × ('White Dawn' × 'Pinocchio') × ('White Dawn' × 'Pinocchio')
Double whitish-cream flowers in sizeable clusters. Slightly fragrant. Foliage glossy. Growth very vigorous and spreading.
R SF G AL 4′ × 6′ 1.2 × 1.8 m

'Simon Robinson' (TRObwich)

Robinson UK 1982
R. wichuraiana × 'New Penny'
Medium to small, single, mid-pink flowers are borne in clusters. Foliage dark green and glossy. Growth bushy and spreading.
C P G SF ⬤ ▽ AL 2′ 6″ × 4′ 75 × 120 cm

'Smarty' (INTersmart)

Ilsink HOLLAND 1979
'Yesterday' × seedling
Large clusters of almost single, smallish blooms of light pink. Foliage bright green and matt-finished. Growth quite thorny, bushy and spreading.
R P G SF ⬤ ▽ AL 3′ × 4′ 90 × 120 cm

'Snow Carpet' (MACcarpe)

McGredy NEW ZEALAND 1980
'New Penny' × 'Temple Bells'
Small, very double, pure white flowers are produced in small clusters. Foliage small, light green and semi-glossy. Growth prostrate and spreading.
R MF G ⬤ AW 1′ × 3′ 30 × 90 cm

'Suffolk', 'Bassimo' (KORmixal)

Kordes GERMANY 1988
Scarlet, single blooms on a wide, creeping plant with ample light green foliage.
R ▽ ⬤ B AW 2′ × 4′ 60 × 120 cm

'Suma' (HARsuma)

Onodera JAPAN 1989
Parentage includes 'Nozomi'
Fully double flowers of ruby-red open to display golden stamens creating a most colourful effect. Foliage plentiful, small and glossy dark green. Growth dense, wide and trailing. A first-class cultivar.
R ▽ ⬤ G AW 1′ × 3′ 30 × 90 cm

'Summer Sunrise'

Beales UK 1994
'Bonica '82' × 'New Dawn'
Masses of candy-pink semi-double flowers with creamy stamens, opening flat in large clusters. Foliage glossy mid-green. Growth bushy, spreading and very healthy. The first rose to be raised by the author's daughter Amanda.
C G ▽ ⬤ SF AL 1′6″ × 3′ 45 × 90 cm

'Summer Sunrise', and 'Summer Sunset'

'Summer Sunset'

Beales UK 1994

'Bonica '82' × 'Robin Redbreast'
Abundantly produced semi-double deep pink flowers streaked with white, displaying gold stamens when fully open. Foliage darkish green. Growth dense and wide. Raised by the author's daughter Amanda.
C G ▽ ◉ SF AL 1′6″ × 3′ 45 × 90 cm

'Surrey', 'Summerwind' (KORlanum)

Kordes GERMANY 1987

Clusters of soft pink, double blooms produced in profusion on a wide-growing plant.
R ◉ ▽ G AL 2′ × 4′ 60 × 120 cm

'Sussex' (POUlave)

Poulsen DENMARK 1991

Double flowers of apricot to pink and buff, produced in large clusters. Foliage plentiful, mid-green. Growth dense and spreading.
R ▽ G AL 2′ × 3′ 60 × 90 cm

'Swany' (MEIburenac)

Meilland FRANCE 1978

R. sempervirens × 'Mlle Marthe Carron'
Yields large clusters of very double, cupped flowers of pure white. Foliage dark green and glossy with bronze overtones. Growth vigorous, bushy and spreading.
C P G ◉ ▽ AW 3′ × 5′ 90 × 150 cm

'Tall Story' (DICkooky)

Dickson UK 1984

'Sunsprite' × 'Yesterday'
Medium-sized, soft yellow, semi-double flowers in clusters along arching branches. Foliage light green and semi-glossy on an arching and spreading plant.
C P G VF ◉ ▽ AL 2′ × 4′ 60 × 120 cm

'Temple Bells'

Morey USA 1971

R. wichuraiana × 'Blushing Jewel'
Small, single, white flowers open in profusion at first, then spasmodically. Foliage small and light green. Its hugging, prostrate growth makes this rose well suited to rockeries.
R G ◉ ▽ AW 2′ × 4′ 60 × 120 cm

'Surrey'

'The Fairy' *see* Polyanthas, page 304

'Warwickshire' (KORkandel)

Kordes GERMANY 1991

Freely produced single blooms of deep rosy-red each with a prominent white eye. Foliage dark green, glossy. Growth dense and spreading.
C ▽ G SF AL 1′6″ × 3′ 45 × 100 cm

'Weisse Immensee' *see* **'Partridge'**

'White Bells' (POUlwhite)

Poulsen DENMARK 1983

'Mini-Poul' × 'Temple Bells'
The white, fully double flowers have hints of soft yellow. Foliage small, mid-green and semi-glossy. Growth dense, bushy and spreading.
S P G SF ◉ ▽ AW 2′ × 4′ 60 × 120 cm

'White Max Graf', 'Weisse Max Graf' (KORgram)

Kordes GERMANY 1983

Seedling × R. wichuraiana seedling
Pure white, single flowers, slightly cupped, in clusters. Foliage light green and semi-glossy. Growth vigorous and spreading.
C G H SF ◉ ▽ AW 3′ × 6′ 90 × 180 cm

'White Meidiland' (MEIcoublan)

Meilland FRANCE 1986

Bears pure white flowers in clusters on a bushy, spreading plant with plentiful, smallish, mid-green and semi-glossy foliage.
C G H SF ◉ ▽ AW 2′ × 4′ 60 × 120 cm

'Swany'

'Wiltshire' (KORmuse)

Kordes GERMANY 1993
Double, initially cupped, reddish-pink flowers in clusters. Glossy light green foliage. Growth bushy and spreading.
C G ▽ SF B AW 2' × 4' 60 × 120 cm

R. × *polliniana*

CENTRAL EUROPE *c*.1880
Single, blush-pink flowers on a sprawly plant with dark green stems and foliage. The stems are moderately thorny – not a contender for space in today's gardens, but could be useful in woodland.
S W P ◍ AL 15' × 10' 4.5 × 3 m

R. phoenicia

MIDDLE EAST 1885
A very vigorous, slender growing climber with few thorns. Ample greyish-green leaves. White flowers in large corymbs. Hips small, round and dark red. Not easy to grow but interesting enough to warrant the effort. Has a particular liking for dry, sandy soils. An important if seldom seen species that is now recognized as part of the complex genealogy of *R. centifolia.*
S MF AL 20' × 10' 6 × 3 m

R. rubus, 'Blackberry Rose'

MIDDLE EAST 1907
A vigorous climber with numerous thorns, greenish-purple stems and glossy, dark green foliage. Young shoots are a clear purplish-red. Fragrant white flowers in large clusters, similar to those of the wild blackberry from which it gets its name. Small, round, red hips in profusion in autumn.
S P F T ◌ AL 20' × 15' 6 × 4.5 m

R. sempervirens

FORMS AND HYBRIDS

These were known as evergreen roses in Victorian days and, indeed, it is true that they retain their lush foliage in most winters. I suspect that, like *R. arvensis*, this species has had more influence on our modern climbers than has ever been acknowledged. Most of the hybrids described here have been with us for many years; in fact few have been introduced since early Victorian times. They make useful dense ramblers and scramblers and ideal subjects for arches, pergolas and trellis as well as for walls. They are healthy and easy to grow and to live with.

CLASSIFICATION

BARB   Class 1
MR10   Class 40
WFRS   Class 37

R. sempervirens

S. EUROPE 17th century
White, fragrant, single flowers produced in small clusters on a semi-vigorous plant. Foliage mid- to dark green, as near evergreen as a rose can be. Small orange-red fruit in late autumn.
C P W F T ◉ ≋ SF AL 20′ × 8′ 6 × 2.5 m

'Adélaide d'Orléans'

Jacques FRANCE 1826
R. sempervirens hybrid
Clusters of small, shapely, semi-double, powder-pink to white flowers cascading in profusion from a well-foliated, evergreen climber. Vigorous in a rather refined way. Illustrated on page 29.
S P T H ◉ MF AL 15′ × 10′ 4.5 × 3 m

'Belvedere' *see* 'Princesse Marie'

'Félicité Perpétue'

Jacques FRANCE 1827
Vigorous climber bearing clusters of small, creamy-white, fully double, cupped, rosette-shaped flowers often with a hint of pink. Well-scented. Makes an admirable climber, with dark green, glossy leaves offsetting the flowers to good effect. Relatively thornless. Often thought of, mistakenly, as the 'Seven Sisters Rose'. The dwarf form of this rose, 'White Pet', is described among the Floribunda roses. The name of this rose has recently been changed from 'Félicité et Perpétue', which was incorrect. Illustrated on page 29.
P T N ◉ ≋ S MF AL 15′ × 10′ 4.5 × 3 m

'Flora'

Jacques FRANCE 1829
Good, medium-sized climber with dark green foliage and growth. The flowers, produced in clusters, are cupped, open flat and are full of small, folded petals. Colour lilac and soft whitish-pink. Has a refined perfume.
S P T N ◉ VF AL 12′ × 8′ 3.5 × 2.5 m

'Princesse Louise'

Jacques FRANCE 1829
Double, cupped flowers of creamy-white with lilac-pink shadings. A beautiful rose produced in cascading clusters on a healthy, almost evergreen plant.
S P T N ◉ MF AL 15′ × 8′ 4.5 × 2.5 m

'Princesse Marie'

'Princesse Marie'

Jacques FRANCE 1929

Large cascading clusters of cupped flowers filled
with numerous shortish petals, which open flattish
but fully double and charmingly ragged. Colour
bright pinkish-lilac on an off-white ground. Foliage
dark green on long pliable stems with few thorns.
Note: This rose is now widely distributed under the
name 'Belvedere'. I am not comfortable with this
(although I realize how it came about), since I have
in my collection the rose which fits old descriptions
perfectly. I, therefore, will continue to list it as
'Princesse Marie'. To go on – Peter Beales Roses
have listed and sold a rose under the name of 'Ethel'
(a name I have never been happy with) for a
number of years. This rose seems to me more likely
to be that now renamed 'Belvedere'. I am now
growing all three candidates together to try to sort
them out.

S P T N ◉ MF AL 15′ × 10′ 4.5 × 3 m

'Spectabilis'

c.1850

A useful, shorter-growing, climbing rose with small,
cupped, double flowers, creamy-lilac to white,
produced in clusters, sometimes giving a surprise
repeat performance later in the summer. Dark,
almost evergreen foliage.

R P N ◉ MF AL 10′ × 6′ 3 × 1.8 m

R. setigera

AND HYBRIDS

From this species has come a most useful group of ramblers which for some reason, probably availability, since they seem to be quite hardy, are far more popular on the other side of the Atlantic than they are here. 'Baltimore Belle', probably the best known, seems to crop up everywhere one goes in America, and a great deal of pleasure it gives. My favourite, though, is the lesser-known, pure white, double cultivar 'Long John Silver'.

Following the character of their parent, the hybrids are all well endowed with healthy foliage and they almost all flower rather later in the season and, in some cases, for longer than most of their better-known counterparts.

CLASSIFICATION

BARB	Class 1
MR10	Class 41
WFRS	Class 18

R. setigera, **'Prairie Rose'**

N. AMERICA 1810

A trailing but shrubby species with lightish green foliage and long, arching branches. The flowers, which are produced in clusters, are single, deep pink paling to soft pinkish-white, followed by small, globular, red hips.

S W F P G A ◉ ≋ SF AL 5′ × 6′ 1.5 × 1.8 m

R. setigera

'Baltimore Belle'

Feast USA 1843

R. setigera × *R. gallica* hybrid
A healthy, climbing rose bearing smallish clusters of very double pale pink flowers in profusion. Foliage mid-green. Flowering somewhat later than most climbers and remaining in flower for rather longer.

S P T N ◉ MF AL 15′ × 8′ 4.5 × 2.5 m

'Doubloons'

Howard USA 1934

R. setigera hybrid × *R. foetida bicolor* hybrid
Double, cupped flowers of deep rich yellow borne in clusters on strong, stout stems. Fragrant. Foliage plentiful and glossy mid-green. Sometimes repeats its flowers in the autumn.

R P T N ◉ VF AL 15′ × 8′ 4.5 × 2.5 m

'Erinnerung an Brod', 'Souvenir de Brod'

Geschwind HUNGARY 1886

R. setigera hybrid
My plant has now passed away, so I have not, so far, met this cultivar as a mature plant. I include it because it crops up from time to time as a parent

'Baltimore Belle', and right, 'Long John Silver'

to other roses. Flowers double, deep pink to magenta-purple.
S P T N ◑ SF AL 12′ × 8′ 3.5 × 2.5 m

'Jean Lafitte'

Horvath USA 1934

R. setigera seedling × 'Willowmere'

Rich green leathery foliage and strong stems among which are produced many rich pink, cupped, double flowers, each with a good perfume.
R P T N ◑ VF AL 12′ × 8′ 3.5 × 2.5 m

'Long John Silver'

Horvath USA 1934

R. setigera seedling × 'Sunburst'

This rose deserves more attention, being seldom seen, at least in Britain. Flowers large, double, and cupped rather like a small, silky-white water-lily, produced freely on strong stems amid large, leathery leaves. Very vigorous and slightly scented.
S P T N ◑ ⁙ SF AL 15′ × 10′ 4.5 × 3 m

'Queen of the Prairies', 'Beauty of the Prairies', 'Prairie Belle'

Feast USA 1843

R. setigera × *R. gallica*

Clusters of large, fully double, plumpish blooms of bright pink, most but not all having a few distinctive white flecks or stripes. Very fragrant. It is vigorous and very hardy with ample mid- to dark green foliage. I find it interesting that such a cross should produce such offspring.
S W P T N ◑ VF AL 15′ × 8′ 4.5 × 2.5 m

R. sinowilsonii

AND HYBRID

R. sinowilsonii

CHINA 1904

A large, climbing rose with superb, glossy, heavily veined foliage. Flowers white, large, single and produced in flat trusses followed by small, red fruit. Said not to be hardy but seems to survive our Norfolk winters, even that of 1983 when temperatures dropped to 15°F (−9°C).

S A F ● ▒ AL 12′ × 8′ 3.5 × 2.5 m

'Wedding Day' (Climbing)

Stern UK 1950

R. sinowilsonii × unknown

An outstanding rose with bright green, glossy foliage and clear green, relatively thornless wood. Flowers large, compared with other such roses. These are single, creamy-white, with prominent yellow stamens and are produced in large trusses. Growth is rampant, capable of considerable climbing feats when festooning trees, seeming not to mind the shade.

S P N T ● ▒ VF AL 30′ × 15′ 9 × 4.5 m

Hips on **'Wedding Day'**, grown as a standard at Roseraie de l'Hay, Paris

R. soulieana

AND HYBRIDS

R. soulieana

CHINA 1896

A vigorous, dense shrub with thin, arching branches bearing grey, rather fluffy foliage and numerous small yellowish spines. Single white flowers, produced in trusses, followed by bunches of oval, orange-red hips.

S P F W ◑ ≋ AL 10′ × 6′ 3 × 1.8 m

'Chevy Chase'

N.J. Hansen USA 1939

R. soulieana × 'Éblouissant'

A spectacular rose which, in full flush, has large clusters of small, very double, fragrant blooms of rich deep crimson produced in great profusion in early summer. Abundant, light green, crinkled foliage on a dense, vigorous plant. Until now this rose has not been seen in the UK but it is widely grown in America.

S P W N ◑ MF AL 15′ × 10′ 4.5 × 3 m

'Chevy Chase'

'Kew Rambler'

Royal Botanic Gardens, Kew UK 1912

R. soulieana × 'Hiawatha'

An interesting, vigorous rambler showing the influence of its seed parent *R. soulieana* in the small, plentiful greyish-green foliage, and of its pollen parent 'Hiawatha' in the shape and colour of its

R. soulieana, and right, **'Kew Rambler'**

'Wickwar'

flowers, which are individually single, small, pink with a central white eye, and produced in packed clusters. Stems thorny and stiffish but still pliable. Good orange hips in the autumn.

S W F T N ◉ ≋ MF AL 18′ × 12′ 5.5 × 3.5 m

'Ohio'

Shepherd USA 1949

R. soulieana × 'Grüss an Teplitz' seedling
Interesting, recurrent rose, bushy but vigorous with semi-double, bright red flowers. Very hardy.

R H P ▽ SF AL 4′ × 3′ 120 × 90 cm

'Wickwar'

Steadman UK 1960

Seedling of *R. soulieana*
An unusual and pleasing rose which should perhaps have received more attention in the 25 or so years since its introduction. A short to medium, dense-growing climber with small, greyish-green foliage. Medium-sized, single, creamy-white flowers. Very fragrant.

S P N ◉ ≋ VF AL 12′ × 5′ 3.5 × 1.5 m

R. wichuraiana
AND HYBRIDS

R wichuraiana has contributed much to modern roses, being directly or indirectly responsible for many ramblers and climbers, especially those with glossy foliage.* A number of breeders used them with much success around the turn of the century, and many a rusty iron arch remains standing, supported by such a rose planted fifty or more years ago. Apart from a proneness to mildew in a few cultivars, these are among our healthiest roses. They are easy to grow and amongst their ranks can be found a colour to suit every taste. For the best results prune them immediately after flowering.

* Graham Stuart Thomas now believes that *R. luciae* was the parent of some of these hybrids and he puts forward some good and interesting reasons for this being so.

It could be that both *R. wichuraiana* and *R. luciae* were involved, with breeders in America and Europe separately using these two very similar species.

CLASSIFICATION

BARB	Class 16
MR10	Class 53
WFRS	Class 16

R. wichuraiana

CHINA 1860

An almost evergreen species, making a dense, procumbent shrub or short climber. Foliage dark green and glossy. Shoots dark and pliable. Flowers single, white, profusely if briefly produced in mid-July. The small oval dark red hips are much enjoyed by birds. Ideal as a ground-cover plant. Illustrated on page 100.

S P G W ◉ ≋ SF AW 6′ × 20′ 1.8 × 6 m

'Albéric Barbier'

Barbier FRANCE 1900

R. wichuraiana × 'Shirley Hibbard'
Superb glossy foliage produced on long, pliable stems. Flowers shapely, slightly scrolled in bud, opening to double, creamy-white flushed lemon-yellow. Healthy. One of the best ramblers.

S P T N ◉ SF AW 15′ × 10′ 4.5 × 3 m

'Albertine'

Barbier FRANCE 1921

R. wichuraiana × 'Mrs Arthur Robert Waddell'
A famous old rambler with glossy leaves, heavily burnished with coppery-red, especially when young. Shoots vigorous, equipped with large, spiteful, hooked thorns. Very floriferous in full flush. Flowers open from shapely buds to rather muddled, full blooms of lobster pink each with a golden base, and paling to blush-pink with age. Highly scented. Rather prone to mildew, but usually only after flowering.

S P T VF M◔ AW 15′ × 10′ 4.5 × 3 m

'Alexander Girault'

Barbier FRANCE 1909

R. wichuraiana × 'Papa Gontier'
Vigorous with dark green, glossy foliage on pliable shoots. Very prostrate if not trained as a rambler. Flowers are double, opening flat with muddled centres. These are borne in clusters, and are a mixture of deep rose-pink and copper with hints of yellow. Has a strong, fruity scent.

S G P ◉ VF AL 12′ × 12′ 3.5 × 3.5 m

'Albéric Barbier', and below, 'Alida Lovett'

'Alida Lovett'

Van Fleet USA 1905
'Souvenir de Président Carnot' × *R. wichuraiana*
Fragrant, large, double flowers of soft shell-pink with a yellow base; opening flat, and borne in clusters on a vigorous, relatively thornless plant with dark green, glossy foliage.
S P T MF AL 12′ × 10′ 3.5 × 3 m

'American Pillar'

Van Fleet USA 1909
(*R. wichuraiana* × *R. setigera*) × 'Red Letter Day'
A vigorous, almost coarse rose with strong, thorny, green stems and large, glossy leaves. Single flowers, at first reddish-pink, paling to deep pink with off-white centres, usually in large trusses.
S P T ◉ SF AW 15′ × 10′ 4.5 × 3 m

'Améthyste'

Nonin FRANCE 1911
'Non Plus Ultra' sport
Trusses of tightly packed, double, violet to crimson flowers, produced on long, firm but arching shoots. Foliage glossy.
S P T N ◉ SF AL 12′ × 10′ 3.5 × 3 m

'Auguste Gervais'

Barbier FRANCE 1918
R. wichuraiana × 'Le Progrès'
Very vigorous, with smallish, plentiful shiny dark green leaves. Flowers large by the standards of its type, semi-double, coppery-yellow suffused salmon, paling quickly to creamy-white. Very fragrant.
S N P T VF AL 12′ × 8′ 3.5 × 2.5 m

'Aviateur Blériot'

Fauque FRANCE 1910

R. wichuraiana × 'William Allen Richardson'
Vigorous but more upright than most of its kind
and rather less thorny. Large trusses of scented,
double, orange-yellow flowers, fading to creamy-
yellow with age. Foliage dark green, burnished
bronze, healthy.
S P MF AL 12' × 6' 3.5 × 1.8 m

'Awakening', 'Probuzini'

Blatna Nurseries CZECHOSLOVAKIA 1935

Reintroduced Beales UK 1990

Sport of 'New Dawn'
A form of 'New Dawn' with all its parent's attributes
except that each bloom is made up of twice the
number of petals, creating a sumptuous, old-
fashioned, muddled effect. An outstanding rose in
all respects. Brought back from Czechoslovakia by
Richard Balfour in 1988.
C P N ◉ ▽ VF ✄ AL 10' × 8' 3 × 2.5 m

'Blaze'

Kallay USA 1932

'Paul's Scarlet' × 'Grüss an Teplitz'
Similar to 'Paul's Scarlet' in both colour and form
but with the considerable advantage of repeat
flowering. Cupped, double flowers of bright scarlet
in clusters. Scented. Foliage leathery dark green.
Growth upright and vigorous.
R P N T ◉ MF ✄ AL 10' × 8' 3 × 2.5 m

'Breeze Hill', and left, 'Awakening'

'Breeze Hill'

Van Fleet USA 1926

R. wichuraiana × 'Beauté de Lyon'
Very double, cupped flowers, clear pink flushed
tawny-orange, produced in clusters on a vigorous
plant with glossy, dark green foliage. Not too
well known but worth growing, especially as a
tree climber. An excellent specimen festoons an
apple tree at Sheldon Manor, near Chippenham,
Wiltshire.
S P N T ◉ ⊰⊱ MF AL 18' × 12' 5.5 × 3.5 m

'Cadenza'

Armstrong USA 1967

'New Dawn' × climbing 'Embers'
Double, dark red flowers of some size and substance
produced freely in clusters. Fragrant. Abundant,
glossy, dark green foliage on a medium-sized plant
which can be used as either a small climber or a
large shrub.
R P ▽ MF AL 10' × 6' 3 × 1.8 m

'Chaplin's Pink', 'Chaplin's Pink Climber'

Chaplin Bros UK 1928

'Paul's Scarlet' × 'American Pillar'
This rose of mixed pedigree might have been
better placed among the Multiflora Ramblers but
its main characteristics are derived from *R.
wichuraiana*. Glossy, mid-green foliage and pliable
growth. Flowers semi-double, bright, startling pink,

'Cadenza', and right, 'Dorothy Perkins'

accentuated by yellow stamens. Very free-flowering; not for those who like a quiet life.
S P N T ◉ MF AL 15′ × 10′ 4.5 × 3 m

'Chaplin's Pink Companion'

Chaplin & Sons UK 1961

'Chaplin's Pink' × 'Opera'
Semi-double flowers of bright silvery-pink. Less 'noisy' than 'Chaplin's Pink' but still brightly coloured. Foliage glossy dark green. Vigorous growth.
S P N T ◉ MF AL 15′ × 10′ 4.5 × 3 m

'Crimson Showers'

Norman UK 1951

'Excelsa' seedling
Crimson, pompon-like blooms, slightly scented, in large, pendulous clusters on a wiry, vigorous plant. Foliage mid-green and glossy.
S P T G ◉ SF AL 15′ × 8′ 4.5 × 2.5 m

'Debutante'

Walsh USA 1902

R. wichuraiana × 'Baroness Rothschild'
Clusters of small, fragrant, fully double blooms of soft rose-pink, borne amid dark green, glossy foliage to good effect. Vigorous, healthy and of slightly spreading habit.
S P G T ◉ SF AL 12′ × 10′ 3.5 × 3 m

'Dorothy Perkins'

Jackson & Perkins USA 1902

R. wichuraiana × 'Gabriel Luizet'
A very famous rose known, by name at least, to most gardeners. Colourful cascades of clear pink flowers with the occasional almost white bloom among the cluster. Foliage, when free of mildew early in the season, is bright, glossy dark green. Growth is pliable and semi-vigorous. Well-scented.
S P G VF M♂ AL 10′ × 8′ 3 × 2.5 m

'Dr Huey', 'Shafter'

Thomas USA 1920

'Ethel' × 'Grüss an Teplitz'
Showy, sizeable, semi-double blooms of crimson-maroon with prominent yellow anthers. Slightly fragrant. Borne in clusters on a vigorous upright plant with rich green, semi-glossy foliage. Used extensively as an understock under the name 'Shafter', especially in the USA and Australia. Consequently it crops up frequently as a garden plant in its own right, and so it should.
S P ▽ SF ◉ N AW 12′ × 8′ 3.5 × 2.5 m

'Dr W. Van Fleet'

Van Fleet USA 1910

R. wichuraiana × 'Safrano'
A vigorous, well-foliated plant with rather thorny stems and dark green glossy leaves. Flowers are shapely in bud and open to semi-double, soft blush-pink. Perfumed.
S P T N ◉ MF AL 15′ × 10′ 4.5 × 3 m

'Easlea's Golden Rambler'

Easlea UK 1932

Placed here because of its rich glossy foliage. Could well have been included among the Climbing

'Easlea's Golden Rambler', and below, 'Emily Gray'

Hybrid Teas. An aristocrat of yellow climbers, with shapely, rich golden-yellow flowers on long, strong stems. Growth vigorous and extremely healthy, with plenty of reddish thorns.
S P T ◐ MF AL 20′ × 15′ 6 × 4.5 m

'Elegance'

Brownell USA 1937
'Glenn Dale' × ('Mary Wallace' ×
'Miss Lolita Armour')
Large, shapely, fully double, clear yellow flowers, losing none of their charm as they pale with age to lemon. Good, healthy, dark green foliage. Sometimes gives a subdued repeat performance in autumn.
R P SF AL 10′ × 8′ 3 × 2.5 m

'Emily Gray'

A. H. Williams UK 1918
'Jersey Beauty' × 'Comtesse du Cayla'
An outstanding rose with shapely buds opening to almost double yellow flowers, which pale with age to lemon. Fragrant. Very floriferous on a vigorous plant with rich green, highly polished foliage.
S P T N ◐ MF AW 15′ × 10′ 4.5 × 3 m

'Ethel' ('Belvedere' ?)

Turner UK 1912

'Dorothy Perkins' seedling

Large, cascading clusters of mauve-pink, double flowers on a vigorous, scrambling-type plant with glossy foliage and ample thorns. A most useful rose, much healthier than its parent.

NOTE: This rose fits the description of the rose marketed by some nurseries as 'Belvedere'; see note under 'Princesse Marie', page 335.

S P T N ◉ VF AL 20′ × 15′ 6 × 4.5 m

'Evangeline'

Walsh USA 1906

R. wichuraiana × 'Crimson Rambler'

Healthy, leathery foliage providing an ideal foil for the clusters of single, soft pinkish-white flowers. These are produced advantageously rather later in the season than those of most others of its type.

S P T N ◉ SF AL 15′ × 12′ 4.5 × 3.5 m

'Excelsa', 'Red Dorothy Perkins'

Walsh USA 1909

Large trusses of small, crimson flowers, densely produced on strong, pliable shoots. Foliage exceptionally dark green. Rather inclined to mildew after flowering, especially around the soft, immature thorns. A most useful rambler or prostrate rose, flowering well into August.

S T P G N ◉ ≋ SF M♡ AL 15′ × 12′ 4.5 × 3.5 m

'François Juranville'

Barbier FRANCE 1906

R. wichuraiana × 'Mme Laurette Messimy'

A tangle of petals creates an unusual individual bloom. Spectacular in full flush, this rose, clear pink with deeper shadings, is a rather refined 'Albertine', with which it is sometimes confused. Foliage dark green, burnished bronze. Growth pliable and dense, with few thorns of consequence. Illustrated on pages 69 and 86.

S T P G N ◉ SF AL 15′ × 10′ 4.5 × 3 m

'Fräulein Octavia Hesse'

Hesse GERMANY 1909

R. wichuraiana × 'Kaiserin Auguste Viktoria'

Creamy-white, semi-double flowers with a fruity scent, produced in small clusters on vigorous, wiry growth with dark green foliage.

S P G MF AL 12′ × 10′ 3.5 × 3 m

'Gardenia'

Manda USA 1899

R. wichuraiana × 'Perle des Jardins'

Shapely, fully double flowers of creamy-white. These open from pointed buds to give a lovely muddled effect with deeper creamy-yellow centre petals. They are produced in small clusters on short, lateral stems along strong but pliable branches of the previous year's growth. Pleasing fragrance reminiscent of apples. Foliage dark green and glossy, growth very vigorous. Quite rare these days.

S P T ◉ ≋ MF AL 20′ × 15′ 6 × 4.5 m

'Gerbe Rose'

Fauque FRANCE 1904

R. wichuraiana × 'Baroness Rothschild'

A vigorous, healthy climber with abundant, green foliage. The large, double flowers, opening flat, are soft rosy-pink with a faint but sweet fragrance.

S T N ◉ MF AL 10′ × 8′ 3 × 2.5 m

'Golden Glow'

Brownell USA 1937

'Glenn Dale' × ('Mary Wallace' × a Hybrid Tea)

Shapely, cupped, almost double flowers of golden-yellow, retaining their colour fairly well as they age. Foliage crisp, dark green and plentiful. Growth strong with an average number of thorns.

S P N ◉ AL 10′ × 8′ 3 × 2.5 m

'Jersey Beauty'

Manda USA 1899

R. wichuraiana × 'Perle des Jardins'

Clusters of good-sized, single, whitish to creamy yellow, sweetly scented flowers with deep golden stamens. Flowers show up well against lush, dark green, glossy foliage. Interesting single with the same parents as 'Gardenia', which is fully double.

S P T N ◉ ≋ SF AL 15′ × 10′ 4.5 × 3 m

'Léontine Gervais'

Barbier FRANCE 1903

R. wichuraiana × 'Souvenir de Claudius Denoyel'

Clusters of medium-sized, fully double, flat flowers opening rather muddled, deep salmon with yellow, red and orange highlights. A semi-vigorous, pliable plant with ample, dark green, glossy foliage.

S P T N ◉ ≋ SF AL 15′ × 10′ 4.5 × 3 m

'Excelsa'

'Minnehaha', and left, 'Gardenia'

'Mary Wallace'

Van Fleet USA 1924

R. wichuraiana × a pink Hybrid Tea
Warm pink almost double flowers, with a good perfume, produced freely on a vigorous, relatively upright plant amid dark, shiny but not glossy foliage. Leaves spaced rather wider apart than others of this family.
S P N ◉ MF AL 10′ × 8′ 3 × 2.5 m

'May Queen'

Manda USA 1898

R. wichuraiana × 'Champion of the World'
Free-flowering. The semi-double, lilac-pink flowers are well scented. They appear in clusters on a vigorous, densely growing climber with darkish thorns and dark green foliage.
S G N T ◉ VF AL 15′ × 8′ 4.5 × 2.5 m

'Minnehaha'

Walsh USA 1905

R. wichuraiana × 'Paul Neyron'
Large clusters of cascading, pink flowers which pale almost to white with age. The plant is well endowed with small, dark green, glossy leaves.
S P N T G ◉ ≋ MF AL 15′ × 8′ 4.5 × 2.5 m

'Mme Alice Garnier'

Fauque FRANCE 1906

R. wichuraiana × 'Mme Charles Small'
Slender branches carrying small but numerous glossy, dark green leaves. Medium-sized clusters of scented, double flowers, bright orange-pink with yellow centres. Vigorous and, when required, procumbent.
S P N G ◉ SF AL 10′ × 8′ 3 × 2.5 m

'New Dawn'

Somerset Rose Company USA 1930

'Dr Van Fleet' sport
An outstanding rose, one of the most useful sports ever discovered. Well-scented flowers identical to those of 'Dr Van Fleet', with slightly tubby buds opening to semi-double flowers of soft blush-pink. Foliage dark green and glossy. Its greatest advantage over all others of this group is its remontancy. Flowers freely from June to October. In fact, the ideal smaller rambling rose.
C P N ◉ VF AW 10′ × 8′ 3 × 2.5 m

Paul Transon'

Barbier FRANCE 1900

R. wichuraiana × 'l'Idéal'
Medium-sized fully double flowers opening flat, rich salmon with coppery overtones and a creamy-yellow base to each petal. Foliage shiny, coppery

'New Dawn'

tinted, light green, combining beautifully with the flowers to give a pleasing overall effect. Sometimes repeats in autumn, especially if placed in a warm position.

R ○ P ◐ MF AL 10′ × 8′ 3 × 2.5 m

'Primevère', 'Primrose'

Barbier FRANCE 1929

R. wichuraiana × 'Constance'

Sizeable double flowers of primrose-yellow in small clusters produced in profusion, on longish stems for this type of rose. Foliage abundant, glossy, bright green. Growth very vigorous. A superb example can be seen at La Bonne Maison, Lyons – the gardens of Odile and Georges Masquelier.

S P T G ◐ SF AL 20′ × 15′ 6 × 4.5 m

'Purity'

Hoopes Bros & Thomas USA 1917

Unnamed seedling × 'Mme Caroline Testout'

Large pure white shapely flowers, opening semi-double and perfumed. Foliage light green and glossy on a vigorous, somewhat thorny plant.

S P ◐ MF AL 12′ × 8′ 3.5 × 2.5 m

'Sanders White'

'Windermere'

'René André'

Barbier FRANCE 1901

R. wichuraiana × 'L'Idéal'

The semi-double flowers, which open flat, are a mixture of coppery-pink and yellow, changing with age to carmine and soft pink. Growth is very vigorous, with ample, dark green, slightly glossy leaves. The flowers occasionally repeat.

R G N ◉ AL 15′ × 8′ 4.5 × 2.5 m

'Sanders White', 'Sanders White Rambler'

Sanders & Sons UK 1912

One of the best white ramblers. Abundant, almost rosette-shaped pure white flowers in cascading clusters, sometimes singly. Foliage is dark green and growth pliable with ample, stubby thorns.

S P T G N ◉ ≋ SF AL 12′ × 8′ 3.5 × 2.5 m

'Snowdrift'

Walsh USA 1913

Small pure white fully double flowers in large clusters, produced in great profusion on a medium-sized yet vigorous plant with large, light green foliage. A useful rose which is not widely enough known.

S P N T ◉ AL 12′ × 8′ 3.5 × 2.5 m

'Thelma'

Easlea UK 1927

R. wichuraiana × 'Paul's Scarlet'

A pleasing mixture of coral-pink and deeper pink with a hint of lemon faintly visible in the centre. Semi-double and quite large when open. Foliage rather coarse, deep green and glossy. Growth robust with few but large thorns.

S P T ◉ SF AL 12′ × 8′ 3.5 × 2.5 m

'Wickmoss'

Barbier FRANCE 1911

R. wichuraiana × 'Salet'

Sizeable clusters of shapely, well-mossed buds open to small, soft, creamy-white flushed pink semi-double flowers with a good fragrance. An unusual rambler with ample dark green, leathery foliage.

S P T MF M♂ AL 10′ × 8′ 3 × 2.5 m

'Windermere'

Chaplin Bros UK 1932

Clusters of sizeable, almost double, rich carmine flowers bordering on purple-red. Foliage dark green, glossy. Growth vigorous and dense. An underused rose.

S P T N ◉ MF AL 15′ × 10′ 4.5 × 3 m

ROSA Subgenus *Rosa* (Eurosa)

SECTION : *Chinensis*

Growth very variable, usually upright from 3′ to 10′ (1 m to 7 m).
Thorns sparse or relatively so, usually hooked.
Leaves 5 to 7 leaflets.
Flowers in small clusters.
Hips mostly roundish.
Sepals dropping when hips ripe.

SPECIES

R. × borboniana; R. chinensis (R. indica, R. sinica); R. gigantea; R. × odorata;

GARDEN GROUPS

Bermuda Roses; Bourbons; Chinas; Climbing Bourbons; Climbing Hybrid Teas; Hybrid Perpetuals;
Hybrid Teas; New English Roses; Noisettes; The Teas;

CLASSIFICATION
BARB   Species: Class 1   MR10   Species: Class 55   WFRS   Species: Class 39
For classification of hybrids in this section, see under garden group headings.

ORIGIN AND DISTRIBUTION

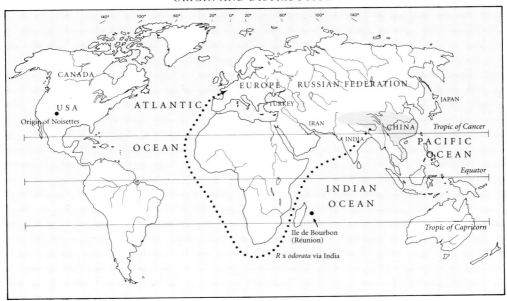

R. gigantea

AND HYBRIDS

This species is very important both historically and genetically, in that it gave rise to the old Tea-scented roses cultivated in China long before they found their way to the West. Sadly, it is not hardy enough to perform well in the UK except perhaps in the south-west. A few interesting hybrids have been raised direct from this species over the years and these are described here. Some, like their parent, are a little tender but all are well worth growing.

R. gigantea

HIMALAYAS 1889

In specific form this rose has little garden value in cold districts of the world, but it is excellent and quite beautiful in warm temperate zones. Flowers large, white and single, produced somewhat reluctantly on a vigorous, thorny, climbing shrub with crisp, dark foliage. I believe a less vigorous clone exists, since I have seen an obviously aged plant no more than 5′ (1.5 m) tall and 6′ (1.8 m) wide at the Huntington Botanic Gardens, California.

S P T ◉ VF AL 40′ × 10′ 12 × 3 m

'Belle Portugaise', 'Belle of Portugal'

Cayeux PORTUGAL c.1900

R. gigantea × 'Reine Marie Henriette'?
Flowers semi-double, made up of loosely arranged petals of pale pink with deeper shadings. Makes a good climbing rose, flowering profusely and growing vigorously. Needs a warm sheltered position to give of its best. Foliage dark green and slightly crumpled.

S T ◉ MF AL 15′ × 10′ 4.5 × 3 m

'Lorraine Lee'

Clarke AUSTRALIA 1924

'Jessie Clarke' × 'Capitaine Millet'
Falls into this group as a second-generation bybrid, 'Jessie Clarke' being a R. gigantea seedling which is now seemingly extinct in Europe. Double, fragrant rich pinkish apricot flowers, with lush green, very glossy foliage. Not hardy enough for northern Europe. Excellent in Australia.

S Gh VF AL 10′ × 6′ 3 × 1.8 m

'Sénateur Amic'

'Sénateur Amic'

P. Nabonnand FRANCE 1924

R. gigantea × 'General MacArthur'
Much hardier than given credit for. I know an old, established plant growing as a dense pillar rose in south Norfolk, which must have survived many a biting north-easterly. Quite beautiful, the flowers are semi-double, large, loosely formed when open, rich pink with hints of yellow at the base and prominent stamens. Superb scent. Growth not as thorny as one would expect. Foliage dark with a dull gloss.

R VF AL 10′ × 8′ 3 × 2.5 m

'Sénateur La Follette', 'La Follette'

Busby FRANCE c.1900

R. gigantea × unknown
A very attractive rose, sadly not hardy enough for British gardens. Makes a good climber for growing under glass or in warmer climates, with large, fragrant, deep pink flowers and dark, abundant foliage. This rose has been distributed throughout the world, erroneously, as simply 'La Follette'. I know not why.

R Gh VF AL 20′ × 15′ 6 × 4.5 m

Chinas

FORMS AND HYBRIDS

These roses were, initially, the group that brought the valuable remontancy factor into modern cultivars.

As garden plants they have a wide range of uses, from group planting and bedding in some cases, to specimen and shrubbery planting in others. In northern European climates, however, the majority are best used as conservatory subjects, when they come into their own, especially when grown in tubs, pots or urns. I have learned to appreciate their quiet charm and relaxed behaviour far more since I have seen them growing in warmer parts of the world than East Anglia. Having said this, all those who love and enjoy their roses, no matter where in the world, will derive a great deal of pleasure from the little extra care they will need to take in growing these.

Note: Amongst the roses described in this group are a few cultivars which, in appearance at least, have an obvious affinity to other types, in particular, the Gallicas. In the United States and, to a lesser extent, other parts of the world, the 'less obvious' Chinas have become known by a separate collective name, 'Hybrid Chinas'. There is probably a good case to be made for this term, although I, personally, find it confusing since, broadly speaking, almost any modern rose is a 'Hybrid China'. However, where such a classification is thought appropriate, I have indicated it.

CLASSIFICATION

BARB   Class 2
MR10   Class 6
WFRS   Class 23

R. chinensis, '**China Rose**', '**Bengal Rose**', *R. indica, R. sinica, R. nankiniensis*

It is not known whether the originally discovered species still exists, but this is the name given to the species thought to have been the parent of wide and varied Chinese hybrids which reached us, by way of India, in the early 18th century. The last recorded sighting in China itself is reported to have been made around 1885, but this remains speculative. This rose is described as single, red to white, of variable height from 4′ to 20′ (1.2 to 6 m). Hardly the description of a species, although such erratic heights and colour variations are characteristic of several China hybrids; so possibly it does have chameleon-like qualities.

Note: Since publication of the first edition of *Classic Roses,* Roy Lancaster has brought back a rose from China which is almost certainly *R. chinensis spontanea.*
C ▽ ○ Ch H AL 6′ × 4′ 1.8 × 1.2 m

'Archduke Charles', 'Archiduc Charles'

Laffay FRANCE *c.*1825
Freely produced, shapely, rounded buds open to almost double flowers of claret with paler reverses, sometimes marbled. Growth branching, perhaps awkward. Temperamental, does better in warmer climates but quite hardy.
C ▽ ○ Gh H AL 4′ × 3′ 120 × 90 cm

'Arethusa', and below, 'Beauty of Rosemawr'

'Arethusa'

W. Paul UK 1903

The double flowers, which are a mixture of sulphur-yellow, lemon and apricot, are made up of a host of rather ragged petals and are produced in clusters. Foliage shiny but somewhat sparse.

C P ▽ SF AL 3′ × 3′ 90 × 90 cm

'Beauty of Rosemawr'

Van Fleet USA 1904

A twiggy but dense, upright-growing cultivar producing loosely formed, sweetly scented flowers of soft carmine with softer veining. Rather short of foliage for my taste.

C Gh P ▽ ○ AL 4′ × 2′ 120 × 60 cm

'Bloomfield Abundance', 'Spray Cécile Brünner'

Thomas USA 1920

Said to be 'Sylvia' × 'Dorothy Page-Roberts'

One of the tallest bush Chinas. The small compact blooms of shell-pink are exquisite and are produced freely throughout summer in huge, well-spaced clusters, each on a lengthy stalk – ideal for button-holes. Wood smooth, brownish-purple, sometimes spindly, with few thorns. Foliage dark green and also smooth. The individual blooms are very similar to and sometimes confused with 'Cécile Brünner', which is a much shorter grower. The most marked difference, however, is seen in the sepals – on 'Bloomfield Abundance' long and extending well beyond the petals, and visible, even when the flower is fully open; on 'Cécile Brünner' shorter, sometimes but not always folding back towards the receptacle. Nurserymen have for many years added to a confusion between these two roses. 'Bloomfield Abundance' is unquestionably easier to produce, yet 'Cécile Brünner' sells better, leading one to wonder sadly, how many mistakes have been deliberate?

Note: Over recent years there has been, and still is, some controversy about 'Bloomfield Abundance'. In America it is now sometimes listed as 'Spray Cécile Brünner'. This name has not been adopted elsewhere in the world so far. Climate, without doubt, influences the China roses more than most and the present rose may not be the one originally given this name by its raiser. In my opinion, however, it is not a sport from 'Cécile Brünner', a conclusion reached after observing the behaviour and habits of both cultivars in my nursery over several years. It is easy to become dogmatic in matters such as this and I must keep an open mind, but unless the true 'Bloomfield Abundance' is found alive and well I can see no reason to change the name of the one we have now, at least here in the UK, especially so since I recall growing 'Bloomfield Abundance' in the 1950s and early 60s, the very same rose which had been growing under that name in England since the 30s, well before 'Spray Cécile Brünner' was introduced in America in 1940.

C H P ▽ SF AW 6′ × 4′ 1.8 × 1.2 m

'Brennus' [Hybrid China]

1830

Probably a China × Gallica cross

Bears little resemblance at first sight to a typical China, being more upright and less branchy, with larger, more plentiful and less shiny foliage. Flowers cupped, full, rich reddish-carmine.

R P SF AL 5′ × 4′ 1.5 × 1.2 m

'Camellia Rose'

Prévost FRANCE pre-1830

Clusters of rounded buds on rather weak necks open to fully double, ragged, camellia-shaped blooms of lilac-pink, sometimes flecked deeper, with an occasional whitish streak in some petals. This description perhaps sounds off-putting but, in fact, the overall effect is quite delightful. Foliage semi-glossy, mid-green and plentiful. Growth vigorous with many thinnish, upright shoots, making a dense plant.

C ▽ H Gh ◐ AL 5′ × 3′ 150 × 90 cm

'Brennus', and below, 'Cécile Brünner'

'Cécile Brünner', 'Sweetheart Rose', 'Mignon', 'Maltese Rose'

Pernet-Ducher FRANCE 1881

A Polyantha rose × 'Mme de Tartas'

Without doubt, one of the most charming of roses, sometimes temperamental, but capable of giving a lifetime of pleasure. Colour and shape of flowers already discussed under 'Bloomfield Abundance'. Although the plant is short, spindly and rather lacking in foliage, this is fairly typical of the Chinas and should not put you off this superb little rose. Flowers faintly but distinctively scented.

C Gh ▽ MF AW 4′ × 2′ 120 × 60 cm

'Cécile Brünner' Climbing

Hosp USA 1904

'Cécile Brünner' sport

Contradicts its parent by growing into a very vigorous climber indeed. Well-endowed with dark green foliage and tolerant of most soils. Flowers, identical to those of the bush form, freely produced but sometimes hidden by dense foliage. Ideal for growing into trees or over unsightly buildings. Illustrated on page 54.

S P B N T Gh ◉ MF AL 25′ × 20′ 7.5 × 6 m

'Cécile Brünner' White

Fauque FRANCE 1909

'Cécile Brünner' sport

White with a hint of yellow and peach. Quite rare now. In all other respects the same as its parent.

C Gh B ▽ MF AL 4′ × 2′ 120 × 60 cm

'Comtesse du Cayla'

Guillot FRANCE 1902

A most useful, brightly coloured cultivar. Almost single flowers of orange and pink with red highlights. Angular growth and vigorous, its lack of foliage amply compensated for by its free-flowering habit. One of the most highly scented China roses.

C Gh P ▽ VF AL 3′ × 3′ 90 × 90 cm

'Cramoisi Supérieur', 'Agrippina'

Coquereau FRANCE 1832

An outstanding China rose forming a compact, tidy bush. The flowers, which are produced in large clusters, are semi-double and cupped, especially when in bud. Their colour is clear unfading red with paler centres and with the odd petal sometimes faintly streaked with white. Has little or no perfume.

C P B ▽ AL 3′ × 2′ 90 × 60 cm

'Cramoisi Supérieur' Climbing

Couturier FRANCE 1885

'Cramoisi Supérieur' sport

This sport from the bush form makes an extremely good, healthy climber and is well worth a prominent position, since few red climbers retain their colour so well, even in hot sun.

S P ▽ AL 12′ × 8′ 3.5 × 2.5 m

'Comtesse du Cayla'

'Cramoisi Supérieur'

'Duke of York'

1894
The double flowers are variably mixed rosy-pink and white and produced freely on a bushy, branching shrub, with dark shiny foliage.
C Gh ▽ SF AL 3′ × 2′ 90 × 60 cm

'Fabvier'

Laffay FRANCE 1832
A very showy rose, tidy in habit and ideal for massed bedding where an older cultivar is needed. Bright crimson flowers, semi-double, and produced in large clusters. Foliage is very dark, glossy and tinted purple.
C P B ▽ AW 3′ × 2′ 90 × 60 cm

'Fellemberg', 'La Belle Marseillaise'

Fellemberg GERMANY 1857
Cupped, fully double cerise to crimson flowers, borne in trusses on a vigorous plant. Attractive cascading habit if grown free of support. Makes a useful pillar rose. Foliage mid-green and generously produced. Stems more thorny than most other Chinas. Some authorities list it as a Noisette.
C P AW 7′ × 4′ 2 × 1.2 m

'Fellemberg'

'Gloire des Rosomanes', 'Ragged Robin', 'Red Robin'

Vibert FRANCE 1825

A vigorous hybrid China, semi-double flowers of bright crimson-cerise, very floriferous. Once used extensively as an understock, especially in the USA. Was important in the early breeding of the Bourbons.

C P N ▽ ◉ SF AL 4′ × 4′ 1.2 × 1.2 m

'Grüss an Teplitz' Hybrid China

Geschwind HUNGARY 1897

('Sir Joseph Paxton' × 'Fellemberg') × ('Papa Gontier' × 'Gloire de Rosomanes')
Rather difficult to classify but has enough China characteristics to be placed here. Shapely crimson flowers deepening with age, borne in loose clusters but sometimes individually. Good light green foliage but rather inclined to mildew if not in good soil. Sometimes used successfully as a small climber. Makes a good hedge. Occasionally listed as a Bourbon.

C H SF M◌ AL 6′ × 4′ 1.8 × 1.2 m

'Hermosa', 'Armosa', 'Mélanie Lemaire', 'Mme Neumann'

Marcheseau FRANCE 1840

Definitely a good rose for the front of a border or for the smaller garden, where it is best grown in groups of three. Full, globular buds opening to cup-shaped flowers of delicate bright mid-pink. Leaves greyish-green, rather small but numerous.

C ◉ ▽ SF AL 3′ × 2′ 90 × 60 cm

'Le Vésuve'

Laffay FRANCE 1825

Very free-flowering, this rose has shapely, pointed buds which open to loosely formed, sometimes quartered flowers of silvery-pink with carmine highlights. Needs mollycoddling to give of its best. Good under glass.

C ◌ Gh ▽ SF AL 3′ × 3′ 90 × 90 cm

'L'Ouche' Hybrid China

Buatois FRANCE 1901

Large, full, pointed buds open to fully double, cupped blooms of flesh pink lightly flecked with buff-yellow. Scented. Not entirely typical of a

'Hermosa'

China, being rather upright in growth with fairly dark, thick foliage.

C MF AL 4′ × 3′ 120 × 90 cm

'Louis Philippe'

Guérin FRANCE 1834

(Another rose of this name was introduced by Hardy (France) in 1824)

Deep crimson to purple with some petals white at the margins, as though the dye has been removed. Flowers loosely double, retaining their cupped shape throughout. An interesting rose, which prefers good soil. Foliage moderately sparse, growth angular and twiggy.

C ○ Gh ▽ SF AL 2′ × 2′ 60 × 60 cm

'Louis XIV', top, and 'Mme Laurette Messimy' below

'Louis XIV'

Guillot Fils FRANCE 1859

Well scented, rich deep crimson, semi-double to double flowers displaying golden stamens when fully open, and produced on a rather angular plant amid glossy but somewhat sparse foliage. Relatively thornless.

C ○ Gh ▽ AL 2′ × 2′ 60 × 60 cm

'Mateo's Silk Butterflies' (LETsat)

Lettunich USA 1994

Seedling of 'Mutabilis'

Very freely produced silky-pink flowers in the style of 'Mutabilis'. Typical China rose foliage. Growth dense and bushy. A very beautiful rose.

C ○ ▽ MF AL 5′ × 4′ 90 × 120 cm

'Minima', *R. chinensis minima*, 'Miss Lawrance's Rose', 'Fairy Rose'

CHINA 1815

Not so important as a garden rose as for its role in the lineage of modern miniature roses. Single flowers, soft creamy-pink with rather pointed, well-spaced petals, tips slightly deeper coloured. Dwarf spreading habit with ample small leaves and few thorns.

C ○ Gh ▽ AL 1′ × 2′ 30 × 60 cm

'Mme Laurette Messimy'

Guillot FRANCE 1887

'Rival de Paestum' × 'Mme Falcot'

One of the best hybrid Chinas. A healthy rose with multitudes of semi-double flowers of bright pink bordering on salmon, each petal suffused yellow at its base. The shrub, fairly tall for a China, is bushy but upright in growth with ample glossy leaves of greyish-green. Good for bedding.

C Gh B ▽ ◉ SF AL 2′ × 2′ 60 × 60 cm

'Mutabilis', 'Tipo Ideale', *R. turkistanica*

CHINA 1932

Although thought by some to be a species, this rose is probably an old Chinese garden hybrid with characteristically mysterious origins. An interesting and useful garden shrub which, I am convinced, has a well developed sense of humour. Capable of reaching a height of 6′ (1.8 m) but more likely to stay relatively dwarf, continuously producing single flowers of honey-yellow, orange and red.

'Papillon', and left, 'Mutabilis'

'Perle d'Or'

Sometimes when fully open, the petal formation is rather like a butterfly. Extremely healthy and very much older than the given date. About two acres devoted to over 300 'Mutabilis' can be seen in the gardens at La Landriana, created by the Marchesa Lavinia Taverna over the last thirty years close to the site of the Second World War battle fields at Anzio, near Rome.

C P H CL ▽ N ◉ SF AL 3′ × 2′ 90 × 60 cm

'Old Blush', 'Parson's Pink', 'Monthly Rose', 'Pallida', 'Common Monthly'

Parson CHINA 1789
Introduced to Europe 1789
An important rose. This is one of the most garden-worthy of the old Chinas, silvery-pink with a deeper flush. Highly scented. The bush is practically thorn-less, upright in stature and, if grown as a small climber, will attain 6′–8′ (1.8–2.5 m) in height. Has probably been cultivated in China for many centuries. I have seen a climbing form listed in some catalogues but have never seen it myself. Illustrated on page 10.

C P N CL ◉ VF AL 6′ × 4′ 1.8 × 1.2 m

'Papa Hémeray'

Hémeray-Aubert FRANCE 1912
A very good China rose. Clusters of small bright pink to rosy-red flowers, single, with a pronounced white central eye. Growth bushy but upright, foliage dark green. Stems have few thorns.

C P ▽ ☼ AL 2′ × 2′ 60 × 60 cm

'Papillon'

Probably FRANCE 1900
A vigorous, angular shrub. This rose is well named. The roughly triangular petals which form the semi-double flowers often stand up charmingly like butterfly wings. Colour predominantly shrimp-pink, with copper and yellow reflections from a deeper base. Foliage deep green and coppery.

C ☼ Gh ▽ SF AL 4′ × 3′ 120 × 90 cm

'Perle d'Or', 'Yellow Cécile Brünner'

Dubreuil FRANCE 1884

R. multiflora seedling × 'Mme Falcot'

Clusters of spaced, small, exquisitely shaped, creamy-buff yellow flowers with hints of pink. Slightly perfumed. Ample rich dark green foliage with twiggy, almost thornless stems. Quite vigorous and dense in growth. Can be temperamental. In good situations will attain a height of over 6′ (1.8 m) but normally only 4′ (1.2 m). Remarkably similar to 'Cécile Brünner' in many respects, save in colour, casting doubt on its recorded parentage.

C Gh SF AW 4′ × 2′ 120 × 60 cm

'Pompon de Paris' Climbing

Bush form 1839

A fascinating climber, dainty in growth but vigorous with small, greyish-green foliage and twiggy growth. Flowers small and button-like, produced profusely in small clusters. An excellent plant can be seen at the Royal Horticultural Society's Gardens, Wisley, Surrey. Also good when grown as a prostrate shrub rose.

S G Gh ▽ AL 12′ × 6′ 3.5 × 1.8 m

'Pumila'

Colville UK *c.*1806

Small, double, almost star-like flowers, usually borne singly on a short, slightly spreading, miniature plant with long (for size of plant) thin mid-green leaves.

R ☼ Gh ▽ R AL 1′ × 1′ 30 × 30 cm

'Queen Mab'

W. Paul UK 1896

Fully double flowers; an interesting mixture of soft apricot and pink with deeper shadings, paler on the reverse with hints of purple. Foliage dark green. Growth bushy.

C ▽ ☼ AL 4′ × 3′ 120 × 90 cm

'Rouletii' *see* Miniatures and Patios, page 319

'Saint Prist de Breuze'

Desprez FRANCE 1838

Globular flowers fully double and muddled when open. Rich dark red with centre petals paler and sometimes discreetly streaked white. Bush twiggy

'Sanguinea'

in growth, upright with ample foliage, similar to 'Louis Philippe'.

C ▽ Gh ☼ AL 4′ × 3′ 120 × 90 cm

'Sanguinea', 'Miss Lowe's Rose'

Probably CHINA Discovered in 1887

Seedling of 'Slater's Crimson'

Single Titian-red, colour deepening with age. Angular growth. Interesting more for its historic and genetic associations than for its garden value.

C ☼ ▽ AL 3′ × 2′ 90 × 60 cm

'Slater's Crimson China', 'Semperflorens', 'Old Crimson China'

Discovered in CHINA Introduced to UK by Slater 1792

A medium to short, branching bush with darkish green foliage and sparse, broad, flattish thorns. Semi-double flowers of crimson to red with the centre petals sometimes slightly streaked with white. Good as a small wall plant. Illustrated on page 16

C ☼ ▽ AL 3′ × 3′ 90 × 90 cm

'Sophie's Perpetual', and below, 'Viridiflora'

'Sophie's Perpetual'

UK An old cultivar reintroduced 1960 Discovered by the late Mr Humphrey Brooke

A superb shrub or small climber. Globular flowers, pale blush-pink heavily overlaid with deep pink and cerise-red. Ample healthy, dark green foliage. Almost thornless stems.

C P VF AL 8' × 4' 2.5 × 1.2 m

'Tipo Ideale' *see* 'Mutabilis'

'Triomphe de Laffay'

Laffay FRANCE *c.*1930

Double flowers of considerable size for a China, off-white heavily flushed pink. Growth medium short. Foliage small, dark green.

C ▽ Gh ☼ AL 3' × 3' 90 × 90 cm

'Viridiflora', 'Green Rose', *R. viridiflora*

*c.*1833

A strange and novel rose, very easy to grow and quite without any disease problems. Flowers formed by a multitude of green and brown bracts with no petals in the accepted sense. These are produced quite freely, making this rose useful for the flower arranger's collection, especially as they change to purplish-brown with age.

C P ▽ ◉ AL 3' × 3' 90 × 90 cm

Bourbons

The origin of the Bourbons is discussed in an earlier chapter but, briefly, they arose from a cross between *R. chinensis* or one of its hybrids and *R. damascena bifera*, the 'Autumn Damask', on the Isle de Bourbon in 1817. They reigned supreme during the mid nineteenth century. Making excellent shrubs and being relatively easy to grow in most climates, a Bourbon can usually be found to fulfil any role asked of it in the modern garden. Amongst their ranks are some of the most beautiful and well loved of the old 'Classics'.

CLASSIFICATION

BARB	Class 24
MR10	Class 3
WFRS	Class 21

R. × *borboniana*, '**Bourbon Rose**'

FRANCE 1817
Thought to be 'Old Blush' × 'Quatre Saisons'
This, the first Bourbon, is either now extinct or synonymous with 'Rose Edward' – no one can be sure. The flowers are said to be deep red, repeating in the autumn; the plant, vigorous.
R 4′ × 3′ 120 × 90 cm

'**Adam Messerich**'

P. Lambert GERMANY 1920
'Frau Oberhofgärtner Singer' × ('Louise Odier' seedling × 'Louis Philippe')
Semi-double, bright rosy-red flowers produced in clusters abundantly throughout the season. The shrub is upright and well foliated. Flowers fade to a soft but still pleasing pink in very hot weather and have a good scent.
C P ✄ MF AL 5′ × 4′ 1.5 × 1.2 m

'**Blairii No. 1**' *see* Climbing Bourbons, page 371

'**Blairii No. 2**' *see* Climbing Bourbons, page 371

'Adam Messerich'

'**Boule de Neige**'

Lacharme FRANCE 1867
'Blanche Lafitte' × 'Sappho'
A fine shrub, upright in growth, with dark green almost glossy foliage and few thorns. Flowers fully double, globular, sometimes tinged reddish-purple on the petal edges while in bud, but opening to pure white with a strong fragrance.
R H ▽ VF AL 4′ × 3′ 120 × 90 cm

'Bourbon Queen', 'Queen of Bourbons', 'Reine des Iles Bourbon', 'Souvenir de la Princesse de Lamballe'

Mauget FRANCE 1834

A sturdy shrub with thick branches and copious foliage. Semi-double, rose-pink flowers large and cupped when fully open. Highly scented but, sadly, seldom repeats in the autumn. I recall finding a very old plant of this growing wild on the south-east side of the mound of Pembroke Castle, where it was competing admirably with brambles and had been doing so for many years, proving a very strong constitution.

S P H ◉ VF AL 6′ × 4′ 1.8 × 1.2 m

'Charles Lawson'

Lawson UK 1853

Not often seen today, probably because of its relatively short flowering season and rather ungainly habit. With support, however, this rose, soft pink with deeper shadings, is a useful shrub.

S ◉ CL MF AL 6′ × 4′ 1.8 × 1.2 m

'Commandant Beaurepaire'

Moreau-Robert FRANCE 1874

A strong, dense bush with plentiful fresh green leaves. Large double crimson flowers streaked pink and purple and marbled white. An interesting rose worthy of a place in any shrubbery.

R P H ◉ MF AL 5′ × 5′ 1.5 × 1.5 m

'Coquette des Blanches'

Lacharme FRANCE 1867

'Blanche Lafitte' × 'Sappho'

Fully double, fragrant flowers, at first cupped but opening flat, white brushed delicately with soft pink. Foliage mid-green, plentiful. Growth vigorous.

R P H ▽ MF ✂ AL 5′ × 4′ 1.5 × 1.2 m

'Coupe d'Hébé'

Laffay FRANCE 1840

Bourbon hybrid × China hybrid

Tall shrub bearing attractive, light green foliage, which can be marred later in the season by mildew if precautions are not taken in time. Very free-flowering, especially in first flush. The globular, pale pink, fully double flowers have a good scent.

R P CL MF M✍ AL 7′ × 5′ 2 × 1.5 m

'Fulgens'

'Eugène E. Marlitt', 'Mme Eugène Marlitt'

Geschwind HUNGARY 1900

Fully double flowers of bright carmine splashed scarlet. Good mid-green foliage. Growth vigorous, with few thorns of consequence. A bright sensation in its heyday, now very rare.

R P H ⬱ MF AL 4′ × 3′ 120 × 90 cm

'Fulgens', 'Malton'

Guérin FRANCE 1830

This rose is thought to have been one parent in the early development of the Hybrid Perpetuals. Bright cerise-crimson semi-double flowers. Although the plant is somewhat sprawly, it nevertheless makes a useful shrub.

R MF AL 5′ × 4′ 1.5 × 1.2 m

'Gipsy Boy', 'Zigeunerknabe'

P. Lambert GERMANY 1909

'Russelliana' seedling

Where space permits this rose is probably best grown as a shrub, but it can also be happy as a small climber. Coarse, rather Centifolia-like foliage should not put you off this lovely rose. Double flowers of deep crimson to almost purple-black with primrose-yellow anthers.

Note: Bill Grant of California, who has spent many years researching the work of Hungarian breeder Geschwind, attributes this rose to him, not Lambert.

S P ◉ CL VF AW 6′ × 4′ 1.8 × 1.2 m

'Gipsy Boy'

'Giuletta'

Laurentius FRANCE 1859

Delightful, fully double, quartered, initially cupped then flattish flowers of soft blush-pink with a lovely fragrance. Greyish-green foliage on a bushy, upright growing plant.

R P ⬱ MO͡ VF AL 3′ × 3′ 90 × 90 cm

'Great Western'

Laffay FRANCE 1838

Once flowering, this rose has large, full, quartered flowers of maroon-purple. Its foliage is dark green and its shoots well endowed with thorns.

S P ◉ VF AL 5′ × 4′ 1.5 × 1.2 m

'Gros Choux d'Hollande'

Obviously an old cultivar with full, cupped, very double, soft pink blooms. Very fragrant and very vigorous.

R P CL VF AL 7′ × 5′ 2 × 1.5 m

'Honorine de Brabant'

One of the most acceptable striped roses. Delicate shades of lilac with purple markings on a large, cupped flower, which is sometimes hidden by lush foliage. Vigorous, with few thorns. I have also seen this rose grown successfully as a climber.

C P ◉ CL VF AL 6′ × 5′ 1.8 × 1.5 m

'Kathleen Harrop' *see* Climbing Bourbons, page 371

'Kronprinzessin Viktoria'

1888

'Souvenir de la Malmaison' sport

Has the beautiful petal formation of its parent, together with its superb perfume and grace. Creamy-white with lemon shadings. Very free-flowering and ideal for small gardens, but dislikes wet weather.

C ⬱ WW ○ MO͡ MF AL 4′ × 3′ 120 × 90 cm

'La Reine Victoria'

Schwartz FRANCE 1872

A slender, erect bush bearing soft green leaves and beautiful, rich lilac-pink, cupped blooms with silky textured petals. The overall picture is sometimes spoilt by a proneness to black spot and a dislike of all but the best soils.

C ⬱ ✂ BSO͡ VF AL 4′ × 3′ 120 × 90 cm

'La Reine Victoria', and below, 'Louise Odier

'Lewison Gower', 'Malmaison Rouge'

Béluze FRANCE 1846

'Souvenir de la Malmaison' sport

A bright pink to red cultivar with all the virtues and faults of its parent, though with its harder colouring it loses some of Malmaison's sophistication. One of Mr Arthur Wyatt's rediscoveries.

Note: Mr Wyatt did much to rekindle interest in the old roses in the 1950s and 1960s and led a successful search for many old cultivars that were then in danger of extinction.

C ▽ WW ○ M♂ VF AL 4′ × 3′ 120 × 90 cm

'Louise Odier'

Margottin FRANCE 1851

Very double, almost camellia-like bright rose-pink flowers on a vigorous bush. Flowers are produced in dense clusters which sometimes weigh down the slender branches to give an arching effect. Superbly perfumed.

C H ◉ ✂ MF AL 5′ × 4′ 1.5 × 1.2 m

'Malton' *see* 'Fulgens'

'Martha' *see* Climbing Bourbons, page 372

'Michel Bonnet', 'Catherine Guillot'

Guillot FRANCE 1861

'Louise Odier' × unknown

Large, fully double, quartered, deep cerise-crimson flowers. Well scented. Foliage purplish when young,

maturing to deep mid-green. Growth vigorous and arching. Also makes a useful small climber.
R ▽ VF CL AL 7′ × 5′ 2 × 1.5 m

'Mme Dubost'

Pernet Père FRANCE 1890
Shapely, fully double flowers of soft pink with deeper shading in the centres. Fragrant. Foliage crisp, mid-green. Growth bushy.
R ▽ MF AL 4′ × 3′ 120 × 90 cm

'Mme Ernst Calvat'

Schwartz FRANCE 1888
'Mme Isaac Pereire' sport
Large, shaggy, pale rose-pink blooms with a strong perfume. Slightly less vigorous than its famous parent, otherwise the same in all but colour.
C P ◉ VF AL 5′ × 4′ 1.5 × 1.2 m

'Mme Isaac Pereire'

Garçon FRANCE 1881
Huge, shaggy, purplish deep-pink blooms exuding a heady perfume and carried on a large, strong bush. Has its critics, but few other Bourbons can rival its bold character. Early blooms can sometimes suffer from malformation but this should not put you off. Equally good as a small climber.
C P CL ◉ VF AL 7′ × 5′ 2 × 1.5 m

'Mme Lauriol de Barny'

Trouillard FRANCE 1868
The flat, quartered, fully double blooms of deep silver-pink are blessed with an unusual but pleasant,

'Mrs Paul', and below, 'Mme Pierre Oger'

fruity perfume. The plant is vigorous and healthy. A very worthwhile cultivar, especially good if 'pegged down' in the old style of training.
R P ◉ VF AL 5′ × 4′ 1.5 × 1.2 m

'Mme Pierre Oger'

Verdier FRANCE 1878
'La Reine Victoria' sport
Very pale silvery-pink, translucent, cupped flowers with the form of small water-lilies, sweetly scented. The flowers are borne on a bush of medium vigour, sadly marred by the same disease problems as its parent, 'La Reine Victoria', but what are a few 'black spots' between friends?
C ▽ ✂ BS♂ VF AL 4′ × 4′ 1.2 × 1.2 m

'Mrs Paul'

W. Paul UK 1891
Large, soft pale pink to white, fully double though somewhat blowsy flowers borne amid plentiful if rather coarse foliage. Vigorous.
R VF AL 5′ × 3′ 150 × 90 cm

'Parkzierde'

P. Lambert GERMANY 1909
Very floriferous for a short period in early summer. Scarlet-crimson flowers on long stems, useful for cutting. Foliage dark green.
S ◉ P S ✂ VF AL 5′ × 4′ 1.5 × 1.2 m

'Paul Verdier'

Verdier FRANCE 1866
A very good rose which deserves more attention, useful as shrub or climber. Fully double, slightly frilly flowers of deep rose pink, opening flat from globular bud, produced along the length of arching, rather thorny canes amid dark green foliage.
R P VF AL 5′ × 4′ 1.5 × 1.2 m

'Prince Charles'

Pre-1918

A medium-tall if somewhat lax bush bearing heavily veined crimson to maroon flowers of considerable size when fully open, tending to fade slightly but enhanced by golden yellow anthers. The bush has large, thick leaves with a heavy texture. Its origin is a mystery and the exact date unknown to me.

S H P ◉ VF AL 5′ × 4′ 1.5 × 1.2 m

'Queen of Bedders'

Noble UK 1871

Seedling from 'Sir Joseph Paxton'

A compact-growing Bourbon. Out of date now for bedding but very useful as a shorter growing cultivar for the front of shrubberies, herbaceous borders or for growing in pots. Shapely, double flowers of deep carmine softening to deep pink with age.

R ▽ B VF AL 3′ × 2′ 90 × 60 cm

'Queen of Bourbons' *see* 'Bourbon Queen'

'Reverend H. d'Ombrain'

Not well known, this rose has flattish, double flowers of clear rose-pink with a quiet, refined perfume. Matt green foliage rather prone to mildew but the bush is of quite tidy habit.

R VF M♂ AL 5′ × 4′ 1.5 × 1.2 m

'Rivers George IV', 'George IV'

Rivers UK 1820

R. damascena × a China Rose

Loose, double cupped flowers of deep red to maroon-crimson. Foliage and growth rather China-like. Not the most distinguished Bourbon but one of the very first introductions.

S ▽ VF AL 4′ × 4′ 1.2 × 1.2 m

'Robusta'

Soupert and Notting LUXEMBOURG 1877

Well-scented flowers opening from tight, rounded buds to shapely rosettes, flat and quartered, rich crimson dusted purple borne in small, tightly packed clusters on long, thin, arching branches. Foliage plentiful. Growth upright, openly bushy. Not to be confused with the modern Rugosa of this name.

R ▽ VF AL 6′ × 5′ 1.8 × 1.5 m

'Rose Édouard', 'Rose Edward'

Bréon, ILE DE RÉUNION *c*.1818

'Old Blush' × 'Quatre Saisons'?

Two roses of this name existed in the early days of the Bourbons. Which one I have I do not know. Richly perfumed, it forms a low bush with fragrant reddish-scarlet double flowers. Trevor Griffiths of New Zealand sent me the budwood, having received it from his friend, the late Nancy Steen, who in turn had obtained it from India.

R P ◉ M♂ VF AL 3′ × 3′ 90 × 90 cm

'Sir Joseph Paxton'

Laffay FRANCE 1852

Shapely, fully double flowers of deep carmine to red tinted violet. Fragrant. Foliage greyish-green on a moderately vigorous shrub.

R ▽ MF M♂ AL 4′ × 3′ 120 × 90 cm

'Souvenir de la Malmaison', 'Queen of Beauty and Fragrance'

Beluze FRANCE 1843

'Mme Desprez' × a Tea Rose

This rose, at its best, is the most beautiful of all Bourbons, but at its worst can be horrid. It hates wet weather and in such conditions seldom opens properly without help. Flowers blush-white with face-powder-pink shadings, each bloom beautifully proportioned and opening to a flat, quartered shape. The finest example I ever knew was at Lime Kiln, Claydon, Suffolk, the home of the late Mr Humphrey Brooke, who did so much to promote 'old roses'. It was a plant of huge proportions, an unforgettable sight in full flush. This plant, however, was not typical and no others I know have reached this size. Lime Kiln is not open to the public at present, but is being restored and will be open again in the future.

C ▽ WW MÖ VF AL 6' × 6' 1.8 × 1.8 m

'Souvenir de la Malmaison' Climbing Form
see Climbing Bourbons, page 372

'Souvenir de la Malmaison', and below, 'Souvenir de Mme Auguste Charles'
opposite, top 'Parkzierde' and 'Prince Charles' below

'Souvenir de St Anne's'

'Souvenir de Mme Auguste Charles'

Moreau-Robert FRANCE 1866

Fully double, slightly fimbriated large blooms opening flat and quartered, flesh pink to soft rosy-pink, fragrant. Foliage mid-greyish-green, almost rugose. Growth wide but bushy.

R ▽ MF AL 4′ × 4′ 1.2 × 1.2 m

'Souvenir de St Anne's'

Hilling UK 1950

Sport of 'Souvenir de la Malmaison'

A semi-double form of 'Souvenir de la Malmaison'. Its fewer petals enable it to open better in wet weather. Like its parent, very free-flowering and although not quite as refined, it is none the less attractive. Deliciously scented.

C ▽ H VF AL 5′ × 4′ 1.5 × 1.2 m

'Variegata di Bologna'

Bonfiglioli ITALY 1909

Double cupped flowers with pronounced, irregular stripes of purple on a creamy-white background, reminding me of the semolina and blackcurrant jam of school dinner days. A tall, rather lax bush with somewhat sparse and rather coarse foliage.

R P M♂ VF AL 6′ × 5′ 1.8 × 1.5 m

'Vivid'

W. Paul UK 1853

A very brightly coloured rose of vivid magenta-pink to red. Vigorous, upright and rather prickly. Occasionally repeating.

R P VF AL 5′ × 4′ 1.5 × 1.2 m

'Zéphirine Drouhin' *see* Climbing Bourbons, page 372

'Zigeunerknabe' *see* 'Gipsy Boy'

Climbing Bourbons

'Blairii No. 1'

Blair UK 1845

Similar in most respects to the better known and more widely grown 'Blairii No. 2' but more clearly and consistently soft pink. Has a few more petals and is quite beautiful at its best, but rather shy.
R M VF AL 12′ × 6′ 3.5 × 1.8 m

'Blairii No. 2'

Blair UK 1845

This rose can be excused a slight proneness to mildew late in the season, for it is very beautiful. Large, flattish blooms, pale pink with deeper shadings towards the centre. Growth and foliage is somewhat coarse but this is not a problem. The overall effect of an established climber in full flush is staggering. Particularly good when grown on a tripod or similar supporting structure.
R VF M AL 12′ × 6′ 3.5 × 1.8 m

'Kathleen Harrop'

Dickson UK 1919
'Zéphirine Drouhin' sport
Oblivious to weather, this rose flowers on from mid-June well into winter. Flowers semi-double, shell-pink and fragrant. Can be grown in children's

'Blairii No. 2'

'Kathleen Harrop'

'Zéphirine Drouhin'

play areas or by the front door since, like its parent 'Zéphirine Drouhin', it is completely thornless.

C N P ◉ VF AL 10′ × 6′ 3 × 1.8 m

'Martha'

Zeiner FRANCE 1912

'Zéphirine Drouhin' sport

Thornless and very long-flowering. The colour is a slightly paler pink than 'Zéphirine', with a creamy touch to the centre of each flower.

C N P ◉ VF AL 9′ × 6′ 2.8 × 1.8 m

'Souvenir de la Malmaison' Climbing

Bush form Beluze 1843

This form Bennett UK 1893

Unlike the bush form, this rose repeats only in good years, but flowers generously in late June, so is well worth growing where space permits. Best on a south wall where it is less likely to encounter too much rain, which, like its parent, its flowers hate.

R WW MÖ VF AL 12′ × 8′ 3.5 × 2.5 m

'Zéphirine Drouhin'

Bizot FRANCE 1868

Lovely though the flowers are, this legendary rose would hardly have gained such popularity had it not been for its long flowering season and its thornless shoots. Flowers semi-double, cerise-pink and distinctly fragrant. Young shoots and leaves are bronzy-red in the first stages of growth, changing to dull greyish-green when mature. In spite of my earlier comments, a fine rose.

C N P ◉ VF MÖ BSÖ AL 10′ × 6′ 3 × 1.8 m

Noisettes

The development and popularity of the Noisettes ran roughly parallel to that of the Bourbons and Teas. Most significantly, they added a new range of colours, especially yellow, to the rather dull climbing and rambler roses of those early days. Many of the Noisettes are still with us, and deservedly so, adding much charm to the modern garden.

It is worth remembering that the Noisettes have a certain reputation for tenderness. My experience of growing them in chilly Norfolk leads me to believe that they can stand more frost than they are ever given credit for. In the winters of 1981, 1987 and 1996 – our coldest recently – one or two were badly frosted, but most came through with no more than a little damage, from which they quickly recovered. Apart from this and a slight propensity to mildew these most beautiful of roses are quite easy to grow.

CLASSIFICATION

BARB   Class 3
MR10   Class 50
WFRS   Class 36

'Aimée Vibert', 'Bouquet de la Mariée', 'Nivea'

Vibert FRANCE 1828
'Champney's Pink Cluster' × *R. sempervirens* hybrid
Small clusters of scented double pure white flowers on a vigorous, almost thornless plant with lush healthy, light green leaves. As with several Noisettes, this rose comes into flower a week or two later than, say, the Bourbon climbers, and repeats its flowers in a good season.
R P ◉ VF AL 12′ × 10′ 3.5 × 3 m

'Alister Stella Gray', 'Golden Rambler'

A. H. Gray UK 1894
Clusters of double, shapely flowers in cascading clusters. Yellow with 'eggy' centres paling to cream and, eventually, white at the edges. Perfumed – of tea, it is said. Shrub vigorous, producing long, slightly spindly branches ideal for arches and trellis. Fairly free of thorns with ample, darkish green foliage. Repeats intermittently.
R ○ T ◉ MF AL 15′ × 10′ 4.5 × 3 m

'Belle Vichysoise'

Lévêque FRANCE 1897
Large clusters of small pinkish-white flowers on a vigorously growing plant with darkish green foliage.
R ○ P MF AL 15′ × 8′ 4.5 × 2.5 m

'Blanc Pur'

Mauget FRANCE 1827
A vigorous yet shorter growing Noisette, at least with me. Flowers full and large, opened quartered, produced sometimes singly, sometimes in small clusters. Pure white and scented. Foliage large and mid- to dark green. More thorny than most of its group. Probably closer to a Tea than a Noisette.
R ▽ ○ CL MF AL 8′ × 6′ 2.5 × 1.8 m

'Blush Noisette'

Noisette USA 1825
Seedling from 'Champney's Pink Cluster'
An attractive rose of gentle growth, producing large clusters of semi-double flowers of blush-lilac-pink with pronounced stamens. Can, given time, make a useful short climber or pillar rose but also makes a good, free-standing shrub. Few thorns and dark green foliage. One of the first Noisettes introduced. Illustrated on page 16.
C P N ◉ MF AL 7′ × 4′ 2 × 1.2 m

'Aimée Vibert', and below, 'Alister Stella Gray'

'Céline Forestier', and bottom left, 'Bouquet d'Or'

'Bouquet d'Or'

Ducher FRANCE 1872
'Gloire de Dijon' × unknown seedling
A vigorous rose with fully double, quartered or muddled, coppery salmon and yellow flowers, slightly scented. Growth vigorous, foliage dark green and semi-glossy.
R ☼ Gh SF AL 10′ × 6′ 3 × 1.8 m

'Céline Forestier'

Trouillard FRANCE 1842
Large flowers opening attractively to flat blooms with muddled centre petals, primrose-yellow with deeper shadings, sometimes tinged pink, scented. Makes an excellent free-flowering small climber. Seldom without a flower throughout the summer. Growth vigorous, not in any way coarse, with profuse, light green, healthy foliage.
C P Gh ▽ MF AL 8′ × 4′ 2.5 × 1.2 m

'Champney's Pink Cluster'

Champneys USA 1802
R. chinensis × *R. moschata*
If not the first, then one of the first Noisettes. Long clusters of semi-double to double flowers of blush-pink, flushed deep pink, highly scented. Growth vigorous, extremely healthy with mid- to dark green foliage. Illustrated on page 16.
S P T VF AL 15′ × 8′ 4.5 × 2.5 m

'Claire Jacquier'

Bernaix FRANCE 1888
Possibly *R. multiflora* × a Tea Rose
A very useful rose with considerable prowess as

a climber. Flowers shapely, double, not large, rich egg-yolk-yellow, paling to cream with age and produced in large clusters, pleasingly perfumed. Foliage rich, lightish green. Repeats in most seasons.
R N T ◉ MF AL 15′ × 8′ 4.5 × 2.5 m

'Cloth of Gold', 'Chromatella'

Coquereau FRANCE 1843

'Lamarque' seedling

Fully double flowers, of soft sulphur-yellow with deeper centres, fragrant, borne on long stems. Copious light green foliage. Quite vigorous, needs mollycoddling in cold districts. Excellent under glass.
R ○ Gh ▽ VF AL 12′ × 8′ 3.5 × 2.5 m

'Crépuscule'

Dubreuil FRANCE 1904

Double if rather muddled flowers of rich apricot. An excellent cultivar but somewhat tender. Foliage light green with darker shoots with few thorns.
R ○ Gh MF AL 12′ × 5′ 3.5 × 1.5 m

'Deschamps'

Deschamps FRANCE 1877

Cupped flowers of bright cerise to cherry red,

'Deschamps'

'Desprez à Fleurs Jaunes', and left, 'Crépuscule'

opening full, almost blowsy. Very free-flowering. Foliage large and darkish mid-green. Vigorous, with few thorns.
R P Gh ◉ MF AL 15′ × 10′ 4.5 × 3 m

'Desprez à Fleurs Jaunes', 'Jaune Desprez'

Desprez FRANCE 1835

'Blush Noisette' × 'Parks' Yellow China'

A beautiful, double, quartered rose in the style of the Tea Rose 'Gloire de Dijon'. Flowers are a mixture of yellow, orange and buff, with a fruity scent, borne in clusters, often at the end of long shoots. Growth is vigorous and the foliage light green. A particular feature of this cultivar is a dark mottling on the stems, which is particularly prominent in winter and should not cause any concern.
R P Gh T ◉ MF AL 20′ × 10′ 6 × 3 m

'Duchesse d'Auerstädt'

'Lamarque', and opposite, 'Mme Alfred Carrière'

'Duchesse d'Auerstädt'

Bernaix FRANCE 1888

'Rêve d'Or' sport

A little-known cultivar which deserves more attention. The scented flowers are fully double, opening quartered but rather muddled, with an intense colouring of buff, apricot and gold. Growth is vigorous and foliage dark.

R Gh ○ VF AL 10′ × 8′ 3 × 2.5 m

'L'Abundance'

Moreau-Robert FRANCE 1887

A small climber of distinction, although little-known. Flowers are flesh-pink and double, in well-spaced clusters. Growth moderately vigorous and foliage mid-green. Repeats only in the best seasons.

S P MF AL 10′ × 6′ 3 × 1.8 m

'Lady Emily Peel'

Lacharme FRANCE 1862

'Blanche Lafitte' × 'Sappho'

White double flowers with blush to carmine high-lights. Fragrant. Tall and vigorous with ample

mid-green foliage. Needs that little extra care to give of its best. Better in warmer climates than in my part of the world – Norfolk, a cold area of the UK.

R ○ T Gh MF AL 15′ × 10′ 4.5 × 3 m

'Lamarque'

Maréchal FRANCE 1830

'Blush Noisette' × 'Parks' Yellow China'

This very beautiful rose will thrive if given a warm, sheltered position but needs cold greenhouse protection in colder areas. Fragrant, pure white blooms borne on long stems amid copious mid- to light green foliage under glass, darker outdoors. Stems have few thorns.

R Gh ○ ⤙ VF AL 15′ × 8′ 4.5 × 2.5 m

'Leys Perpetual', 'Lais'

Damaizin FRANCE 1867

This may well be the climbing form of an original bush Tea rose, for it behaves in every way as one would expect of a climbing sport. It is a rose that gives me much pleasure. Fully double shapely flowers open flat and quartered in a muddled sort of way. Lemon-yellow and deliciously fragrant. Good foliage of darkish-green.

R ○ ▽ Gh VF AL 12′ × 8′ 3.5 × 2.5 m

'Louise d'Arzens'

Lacharme FRANCE 1860

Pinkish buds open to fully double flowers of creamy-white. Foliage mid-green and glossy. Growth moderately vigorous. Rare and unusual but well worth growing, especially in warmer climates, although it seems to be quite hardy.

R ▽ ○ Gh SF AL 10′ × 6′ 3 × 1.8 m

'Manettii', *R. noisettiana manettii*

Botanic Gardens, Milan ITALY 1837

Not an important garden rose. Once used extensively as a rootstock, especially in the USA. A dense shrub with pale pink semi-double flowers. Wood reddish when young, streaked or mottled when older. Well endowed with dark thorns.

S P H W ◉ ▽ SF AL 6′ × 4′ 1.8 × 1.2 m

'Maréchal Niel'

Pradel FRANCE 1864

Seedling from 'Cloth of Gold'

Huge, golden-yellow, double flowers emerging from shapely, pointed buds. Very fragrant. Needs a warm, sheltered position or greenhouse to survive in colder climates. Growth vigorous, with large, dark, coppery-green foliage.

R ○ Gh ⊰ ▽ VF AL 15′ × 8′ 4.5 × 2.5 m

'Mme Alfred Carrière'

J. Schwartz FRANCE 1879

A superior rose. The lovely, rather loosely formed flowers are large and white with occasional hints of soft pink, highly scented. Growth is vigorous, with sparse thorns. Leaves large, plentiful and light green. This rose flowers almost continuously throughout the season and is quite tolerant of a north wall situation.

C Gh P ◉ T ⊰ VF AL 15′ × 10′ 4.5 × 3 m

'Mme Driout'

Thiriat FRANCE 1902

Sport of 'Reine Marie Henriette'

Shapely buds opening flat and quartered. Deep reddish-pink with flecks of white. Foliage quite large, dark green. Growth moderately vigorous. Needs extra attention to behave at its best.

R ○ ▽ MF ⊰ AL 10′ × 8′ 3 × 2.5 m

'Reine Olga de Wurtemberg'

G. Nabonnand FRANCE 1881

Rich red, fully double blooms of medium size, initially high-centred, opening flat. Fragrant. A vigorous climber with good mid- to dark green foliage.

R P ○ T MF AL 15′ × 8′ 4.5 × 2.5 m

'Maréchal Niel'

'Rêve d'Or'

Ducher FRANCE 1869

'Mme Schultz' seedling

This is a very good rose. Shapely, fully double blooms in the mould of 'Gloire de Dijon'. Buff to yellow with sometimes a hint of pink. Fragrant. Growth is strong and the foliage dark green. Rather tender.

R ○ Gh ▽ ✂ VF AL 12′ × 8′ 3.5 × 2.5 m

'William Allen Richardson'

Ducher FRANCE 1878

'Rêve d'Or' sport

Medium-sized, fully double buff to apricot flowers, very free-flowering. This climber needs a warm, sheltered spot to flourish. Stems are dark, with dark green, copper-tinted foliage.

R Gh ▽ ○ ✂ VF AL 15′ × 8′ 4.5 × 2.5 m

'Rêve d'Or', and below, 'William Allen Richardson'

The Teas

Teas were very popular garden roses in Europe during the latter half of the nineteenth century. Sadly many have now become extinct, but some of the best have survived and a few still have sufficient stamina – with our help – to go on for a long time yet. Gardeners in colder zones, concerned with overall effect, should avoid growing these roses. However, they make excellent subjects under glass and for growing in tubs and urns. They are best just lightly pruned, reacting against hard pruning with a reduced yield of flowers. The climbing forms are, unless absolutely necessary, best left unpruned. In warmer climates they are undoubtedly excellent garden subjects, and readers should bear in mind that the dimensions indicated in these descriptions are those for the UK, and that they could well attain double these sizes where winters are not as cold.

CLASSIFICATION

BARB	Class 4
MR10	Class 56
WFRS	Class 31

'Adam', 'The President'

Adam UK 1833

A large, fully double rose of buff, amber and apricot, with tints of pink deep in the centre. The fully open flowers are often quartered. Said to be the first of the Tea roses. Probably a vigorous bush but better as a climber on a short wall, where it can enjoy protection from the severest weather of winter. Well-foliated with large dark green leaves.

R ○ Gh ▽ VF AL 7′ × 5′ 2 × 1.5 m

'Alexander Hill Gray', 'Yellow Maman Cochet', 'Yellow Cochet'

Dickson UK 1911

Large full flowers of bright yellow, deepening with age to tawny-yellow. Fragrant. Foliage mid-green, semi-glossy. Growth vigorous and angular. Bushy.

C ○ Gh ▽ VF ✄ AL 4′ × 3′ 120 × 90 cm

'Amazone'

Ducher FRANCE 1872

'Safrano' × unknown

Soft yellow with soft rosy-pink markings on reverse of petals, shapely, high-centred, double. Foliage dark green, semi-glossy, bronzy-red when young. Growth vigorous and angular.

C ○ Gh ▽ SF ✄ AL 4′ × 3′ 120 × 90 cm

'Anna Olivier'

Ducher FRANCE 1872

A mixture of flesh-pink and deep rose. Fragrant. Shapely, high-centred blooms on a vigorous, branching bush with good mid-green foliage.

Note: A soft primrose-yellow mystery Tea rose is sometimes grown and sold erroneously as this cultivar. I think it could be an old cultivar called 'Leda'.

C ○ Gh ▽ ✄ MF AL 3′ × 3′ 90 × 90 cm

'Archiduc Joseph'

G. Nabonnand FRANCE 1872

Seedling from 'Mme Lombard'

One of the outstanding Tea roses. Flowers, opening flat, are made up of many petals, the whole a pleasing mixture of pink, purple, orange and russet with tints of gold and yellow in the centre. The foliage is dark, glossy and abundant. The stems have

'Adam', and below, 'Anna Olivier'

'Archiduc Joseph', and below, 'Baronne Henriette de Snoy'

few thorns. Apparently quite hardy. Can be used both as a shrub and small climber.
Note: The rose described here and grown under the name 'Archiduc Joseph' in the UK is known and sold as 'Mons. Tillier' in the USA.
C P Gh ▽ ○ MF AL 5′ × 3′ 150 × 90 cm

'Baronne Henriette de Snoy'

Bernaix FRANCE 1897
'Gloire de Dijon' × 'Mme Lombard'
The scented flowers are flesh-pink with a deeper reverse, and open double from fairly high-centred

buds. The bush is angular and the leaves large and mid-green.
C ○ Gh ▽ VF AL 4′ × 3′ 120 × 90 cm

'Belle Lyonnaise'

Levet FRANCE 1870
A climbing Tea rose which is not often seen but is worthy of any warm, sheltered garden or cold greenhouse. Not over-vigorous but quite generous with its flowers which are large, scented, full, flat, quartered and soft yellow fading to creamy-white with age.
R ○ Gh ▽ VF AL 10′ × 6′ 3 × 1.8 m

'Bon Silène'

Hardy FRANCE 1839
Fragrant, fully double, deep rosy-red flowers produced in profusion on a compact, vigorous

plant. Foliage mid-green and stems moderately thorny.

C ☼ Gh ▽ VF AL 4′×3′ 120×90 cm

'Catherine Mermet'

Guillot Fils FRANCE 1869

Shapely, high-centred buds opening to semi-double lilac-pink flowers, held on longish stems. Well-foliated and bushy, with healthy, mid-green, coppery-tinged leaves. An excellent greenhouse cultivar but equally at home in an open, sunny, warm position.

C ☼ Gh ▽ ✂ MF AL 4′×3′ 120×90 cm

'Clementina Carbonieri'

Bonfiglioli ITALY 1913

An outstanding Tea rose. Fully double flowers opening flat and quartered, their colour a grand mixture of orange, pink and salmon, all on a bright mustard-yellow background. They are freely produced and scented. Foliage dark green on an angular but dense plant with an average number of thorns.

C ☼ GH ▽ MF AL 3′×2′ 90×60 cm

'Dean Hole'

A. Dickson UK 1904

Large by Tea rose standards. The flowers are an interesting combination of silvery-pink, flushed apricot and gold. Growth is vigorous and thorny, with darkish green foliage.

S ☼ Gh ▽ VF AL 3′×2′ 90×60 cm

'Devoniensis', 'Magnolia Rose'

Foster UK 1838

Very large flowers, creamy-white with an occasional blush of pink. A refined rose which needs planting in a warm, sheltered position or under glass to be appreciated fully. Ample, light to mid-green foliage and few thorns. Foliage darker outdoors.

R ☼ Gh ▽ AL 12′×7′ 3.5×2 m

'Dr Grill'

Bonnaire FRANCE 1886

'Ophirie' × 'Souvenir de Victor Hugo'

A branching, angular plant which would be better with more foliage. Flowers exquisite, pink overlaid with copper. High-centred in bud but opening flat and full, sometimes quartered. Fragrant.

C ☼ Gh ▽ VF AL 3′×2′ 90×60 cm

'Clementina Carbonieri', and below, 'Dr Grill'

'Duchesse de Brabant', 'Comtesse de Labarthe', 'Comtesse Ouwaroff'

Bernède FRANCE 1857

Very double flowers, clear pink to rose, shapely, cupped and free-flowering. The bush has a spreading habit and is well foliated for a Tea. Beautiful. This cultivar is known as 'Shell' in Bermuda.

C ☼ Gh ▽ VF AL 3′×3′ 90×90 cm

'Enchantress'

W. Paul UK 1896

Deep rose-pink changing to deeper pink, almost

crimson with age. Very double when fully open, showing a kind of orangey-yellow deep down. Fragrant. Foliage round, deep green. Upright for a Tea.

C ☼ Gh ▽ VF ✂ AL 4′ × 3′ 120 × 90 cm

'Étoile de Lyon'

Guillot FRANCE 1881

Rich golden-yellow flowers held on flimsy flower stalks on a twiggy, angular bush with sparse foliage. Its main attributes are a strong colour and a strong scent.

R Gh ☼ ▽ VF AL 2′ × 2′ 60 × 60 cm

'Fortune's Double Yellow', 'Beauty of Glazenwood', 'San Rafael Rose'

Fortune Discovered in CHINA 1845

An old Chinese garden rose brought back to Europe by Robert Fortune. Slightly tender. The plant is best grown with support. Loosely formed double flowers of buff-yellow with faint tints of orange. Scented. Foliage dark green and glossy, few thorns.

R ☼ Gh CL VF AL 8′ × 4′ 2.5 × 1.2 m

'Francis Dubreuil'

Dubreuil FRANCE 1894

Long pointed buds opening to large high-centred flowers, blowsy when fully open, dark crimson red paling slightly with age. Foliage somewhat sparse, glossy, dark green. Stems moderately thorny.

R ☼ Gh ▽ MF AL 3′ × 2′ 90 × 60 cm

'Freiherr von Marschall'

P. Lambert GERMANY 1903

'Princess Alice de Monaco' × 'Rose d'Evian'
Pointed buds opening to flattish flowers of rich carmine and red. Foliage particularly good, being plentiful, dark green and heavily tinted with red.

C ☼ Gh ▽ VF AL 3′ × 2′ 90 × 60 cm

'Général Galliéni'

G. Nabonnand FRANCE 1899

'Souvenir de Thérèse Levet' × 'Reine Emma des Pays-Bas'
One of the most popular roses of its day. Main colour buff, but heavily overlaid with red and pink with hints of yellow in the base. Vigorous and relatively free of thorns, with good, mid-green foliage.

R ☼ Gh ▽ VF AL 4′ × 3′ 120 × 90 cm

'Fortune's Double Yellow', and below, 'Francis Dubreuil'

'Général Schablikine'

G. Nabonnand FRANCE 1878

A useful rose. Very double flowers opening flat, combining copper-red and cherry to good effect. A compact and well-foliated plant. The gardens at Ninfa, Latina, Italy, have many good examples of this fine rose.

C ☼ Gh ▽ MF AL 3′ × 2′ 90 × 60 cm

'Gloire de Dijon'

Jacotot FRANCE 1853

Unknown Tea rose × 'Souvenir de la Malmaison'
This is a deservedly well-loved old cultivar, made

'Général Schablikine', and below, 'Gloire de Dijon', left and 'Homère', right

famous by the writings of the Rev. Dean Reynolds-Hole, first president of the National Rose Society. It was his favourite rose. Large, perfumed flowers, full, opening flat and quartered, of buff-apricot to orange, often giving a second flush in the autumn. Foliage dark green but slightly prone to black spot, especially after the first flush. Flowers dislike wet weather. With all her faults, well worth living with.

R ☼ Gh BS☙ WW VF AL 12′ × 8′ 3.5 × 2.5 m

'Grüss an Coburg'

Felberg-Leclerc GERMANY 1927

'Alice Kaempff' × 'Souvenir de Claudius Pernet'

Shapely, globular flowers of yellow flushed orange-apricot with a tawny-pink reverse. Very fragrant. Foliage bronzy deep green. Growth angular. Vigorous. Perhaps a Hybrid Tea?

C ☼ ▽ Gh VF AL 4′ × 3′ 120 × 90 cm

'Homère'

Robert and Moreau FRANCE 1858

If some of the other Teas are not fully hardy, 'Homère' definitely is. Shapely, cupped flowers are a pleasing mixture of soft blush-pink and pure white, sometimes with the margins of petals blushed red. A relatively thornless bush with a twiggy growth habit and dark foliage.

C Gh ▽ AL 4′ × 2′ 120 × 60 cm

'Hume's Blush Tea-scented China', 'Odorata', *R. × odorata*

Fa Tee Nurseries, Canton CHINA 1810

Thought to be *R. chinensis × R. gigantea*

Found cultivated in China, this, the first Tea rose from that country, is probably the result of a spontaneous cross but could have been deliberate hybridization by an early Chinese gardener. Flowers vary from off-white – sometimes with hint of lemon – to blush-pink, sometimes almost brownish-pink, semi-double to almost single. Growth vigorous but erratic. Foliage slightly glossy, mid-green. My stock arrived by a circuitous route from Sangerhausen, East Germany, and I believe it to be correct. Illustrated on page 17.

R ☼ Gh VF AL variable from 4′ × 4′ to 15′ × 10′ 1.2 × 1.2 m to 4.5 × 3 m

'Isabella Sprunt'

Sprunt USA 1855

Sport from 'Safrano'

Semi-double to double flowers of rich sulphur-yellow. Shapely buds open to attractively ragged, full blooms. Foliage plentiful, mid-green. Bush open and branching.

C ▽ Gh ☼ SF ✂ AL 4′ × 3′ 120 × 90 cm

'Jean Ducher'

Ducher FRANCE 1873

Peachy-pink overlaid salmon-orange, full and rounded blooms on a fairly vigorous, relatively hardy plant with good foliage.

C ▽ Gh ☼ MF AL 4′ × 3′ 120 × 90 cm

'Lady Hillingdon'

Lowe and Shawyer UK 1910

'Papa Gontier' × 'Mme Hoste'

An outstandingly good rose, deservedly popular since its introduction. The long, pointed buds are rich yolky-yellow, opening to large, blowsy, semi-double flowers with a lovely perfume. Leaves glossy, dark purplish-green, combining superbly with relatively thornless, plum-coloured shoots.

C Gh ▽ ✂ VF AL 3′ × 2′ 90 × 60 cm

'Lady Hillingdon' Climbing

Hicks UK 1917

Undoubtedly outstanding as a climber. Its plum-coloured wood and dark foliage are great assets. Needs careful placing but its reputation for tenderness is somewhat exaggerated; although sometimes forcibly pruned by frost, it will survive most winters.

R ☼ P ✂ VF AL 15′ × 8′ 4.5 × 2.5 m

'Lady Hillingdon'

'Lady Plymouth'

A. Dickson UK 1914

A lovely old cultivar. Flowers ivory-white to flushed cream and blush-pink, well-formed and evenly spaced. Slightly scented. Bush dense and thorny, although it would be better with more of its darkish green foliage.

C ☼ Gh ▽ MF AL 3′ × 3′ 90 × 90 cm

'Lady Roberts'

F. Cant UK 1902

Sport of 'Anna Olivier'
A brightly coloured Tea rose, apricot with deeper base heavily burnished with reddish-orange. Fully double, shapely. Good scent. Foliage dark green. Growth bushy.

C ▽ Gh ☼ VF AL 4′ × 3′ 120 × 90 cm

'Maman Cochet'

Cochet FRANCE 1893

'Marie Van Houtte' × 'Mme Lombard'
A very free-flowering rose, initially globular, opening blowsy, pale pink flushed deeper pink with a lemon centre. The bush is vigorous with few thorns, carrying dark green foliage of a leathery texture.
Note: A white form of this rose exists and in some districts the two have become confused. I confess my own guilt at being caught up in this in the past.

C ☼ Gh ▽ ✂ MF AL 3′ × 2′ 90 × 60 cm

'Marie Lambert' *see* 'Snowflake'

'Marie van Houtte'

Ducher FRANCE 1871

'Mme de Tartas' × 'Mme Falcot'
Bright pink tinged with orange and suffused cream. Fragrant and very free-flowering. Rich green foliage on a vigorous but sprawly plant.

C ☼ Gh ▽ VF AL 3′ × 2′ 90 × 60 cm

'Mlle Franziska Krüger', 'Grand Duc Héritier de Luxembourg'

G. Nabonnand FRANCE 1880

'Catherine Mermet' × 'Général Schablikine'
Sizeable very double flowers of deep coppery-yellow overlaid pink sometimes, greeny-looking especially in the centre. Blooms hang down from a weak neck.

C ☼ Gh ▽ MF ✂ AL 3′ × 2′ 90 × 60 cm

'Mme Antoine Mari'

Mari FRANCE 1901

Fragrant with shapely flowers, especially in the late bud stage. Pink in bud, opening to soft flesh pink with lavender-lilac highlights. Foliage light to mid-green on an angular but tidy plant.

R ☼ Gh ▽ MF AL 3′ × 3′ 90 × 90 cm

'Mme Bérard'

Levet FRANCE 1879

'Mme Falcot' × 'Gloire de Dijon'
Fully double cupped largish flowers of a pleasing mixture of bright pink and yellow. Good mid- to dark green foliage. Growth generous for a climbing Tea. Given to me by Hazel le Rougetel.

C ☼ ▽ Gh SF AL 10′ × 8′ 3 × 2.5 m

'Mme Berkeley'

Bernaix FRANCE 1899

A mixture of salmon, pink, cerise and gold. Flowers initially high-centred, opening somewhat muddled, but attractively so. Extremely free-flowering on a vigorous plant.

C ☼ Gh ▽ MF AL 3′ × 2′ 90 × 60 cm

'Mme Bravy', 'Adèle Pradel', 'Mme de Sertot'

Guillot Père FRANCE 1846

One of the early Teas. Large, double, creamy-white flowers with pink shadings. Very free-flowering and with a strong, supposedly 'tea' fragrance. Plant dense and bushy.

C ☼ Gh B ▽ ✂ MF AL 3′ × 2′ 90 × 60 cm

'Mme Jules Gravereaux'

'Mme Wagram', and right, 'Mlle Franziska Krüger'

'Mme de Tartas'

Bernède FRANCE 1859

An important rose, used extensively at stud in Victorian times. Flowers large, full and cupped, blush-pink, scented. Bush vigorous, rather sprawly in habit but none the less charming. Foliage dark green and leathery. Quite hardy, probably one of the few Teas better outdoors than in.
C ☼ P ▽ MF AL 3′ × 3′ 90 × 90 cm

'Mme de Watteville'

Guillot Fils FRANCE 1883

A dense medium-growing plant with small but plentiful dark green foliage and several thorns. Flowers shapely, fully double, soft yellow with pinkish tinges to the petal edges, scented.
C ☼ ▽ SF AL 3′ × 3′ 90 × 90 cm

'Mme Joseph Schwartz'

J. Schwartz FRANCE 1880

A white sport from 'Duchesse de Brabant', with all the lovely attributes of its parent.
C ☼ Gh ▽ VF ✂ AL 3′ × 3′ 90 × 90 cm

'Mme Jules Gravereaux'

Soupert and Notting LUXEMBOURG 1901

I am very fond of this accommodating climbing rose and can only assume that its suspect hardiness has prevented more widespread distribution. Shapely, fully double, sometimes quartered blooms of yellowish-buff, shaded peach with hints of pink as undertones. It is scented. Foliage lush, dark green and the wood also dark. The best plant I know is at Mottisfont Abbey, Hants.
R ☼ Gh ✂ VF AL 8′ × 6′ 2.5 × 1.8 m

'Mme Lombard'

Lacharme FRANCE 1878
'Mme de Tartas' seedling

Flowers full, very double, salmon with deeper centres, scented. Bush vigorous, with dark green foliage. Similar, save in colour, to Mme de Tartas.
C ☼ ▽ MF AL 3′ × 3′ 90 × 90 cm

'Mme Wagram', 'Comtesse de Turin'

Bernaix FRANCE 1895

Large rosy-red petals with yellow bases make up fully double, globular flowers, borne freely on a healthy bush with dark green foliage.
C Gh ▽ SF AL 3′ × 3′ 90 × 90 cm

'Mons. Tillier'

Bernaix FRANCE 1891

A good but little known rose better endowed than most Teas with foliage. Large loosely double flowers, blood-red with violet smudges, freely produced on a vigorous bush. Growth quite tall and lax. The rose sold under this name in the USA is the one sold in the UK as 'Archiduc Joseph'.
C Gh ▽ SF AL 4′ × 3′ 120 × 90 cm

'Maman Cochet', and below, 'Papa Gontier'

'Mrs B. R. Cant'

B. R. Cant UK 1901
Soft rose-pink, deeper base with buffish under-
tones. Petals deeper on the reverse. Well scented.
Cupped until fully open. Foliage mid- to dark green,
leathery. Growth vigorous, branching and bushy.
C ▽ Gh ○ MF ⊰ AL 4′ × 3′ 120 × 90 cm

'Mrs Campbell Hall'

Hall, introduced by Dickson UK 1914
Creamy-white-edged salmon flowers with deeper
salmon centres, quite large and high-centred in bud,
opening full and somewhat blowsy. Dark, leathery
foliage on a vigorous bush.
C ○ Gh ▽ SF AL 4′ × 3′ 120 × 90 cm

'Mrs Dudley Cross'

W. Paul UK 1907
Fully double blooms of soft yellow deepening
with age, especially in full sun, to become flushed
with pink at first and then crimson. Slight
fragrance. Foliage darkish green on almost thornless stems. Growth vigorous, open and bushy. Seems
quite hardy.
C ▽ ○ Gh SF AL 4′ × 3′ 120 × 90 cm

'Mrs Foley Hobbs'

Dickson UK 1910
Beautifully textured creamy-white fully double
flowers with edges of petals tinged soft pink. Foliage
mid- to dark green. Young growth reddish. Growth
vigorous. Upright. Bushy.
C ○ Gh ▽ MF ⊰ AL 4′ × 3′ 120 × 90 cm

'Niphetos'

Bush form Bougère FRANCE 1843
Climbing form Keynes, Williams and Co. UK 1889
Used extensively as a florist's rose during late
Victorian and Edwardian times. Lovely, creamy
buds open to pure white, with pointed petals
creating a muddled, star-like shape. Foliage light
green under glass, darker outdoors. Makes a
vigorous climber but needs placing under glass for
the best blooms. Illustrated on page 70.
R ○ Gh ▽ VF AL
Bush form 4′ × 3′ 120 × 90 cm
Climbing form 10′ × 6′ 3 × 1.8 m

'Noella Nabonnand' Climbing

G. Nabonnand FRANCE 1901
'Reine Marie Henriette' × 'Bardou Job'
Not often seen, perhaps because it seldom repeats
and because of its reputation for tenderness.
Nevertheless, a fine cultivar. Globular yet pointed
buds open to a large, blowsy, rose of velvety
crimson. Foliage mid-green and quite healthy.
S Gh P VF AL 10′ × 6′ 3 × 1.8 m

'Papa Gontier'

G. Nabonnand FRANCE 1883
Used extensively as a forcing rose in its early career.
Flowers rich pink, almost red, sometimes slightly
mottled and with a deeper reverse, semi-double
and slightly scented. Growth habit rather twiggy;
I would prefer to see more of its dark green glossy
foliage.
C ○ Gh ▽ ⊰ SF AL 3′ × 2′ 90 × 60 cm

'Parks' Yellow Tea-scented China',
R. × odorata ochroleuca

CHINA 1824
Said to be the original Tea rose. I believe I have this
rose, but sadly have no recollection or record of
whence or from whom it came. Perhaps a reader
will remember and remind me to acknowledge. It
is an angular-growing climber with fairly large,

'Perle des Jardins', and right, 'Safrano'

'Rosette Delizy'

double, cupped flowers of soft, sulphur-yellow, unusually perfumed, although I fail to detect any resemblance to tea. The foliage, although large, is none the less typical of a China or Tea. It has but few thorns. Illustrated on page 18.

R ☼ Gh ▽ MF AL 6' × 4' 1.8 × 1.2 m

'Perle des Jardins'

F. Levet FRANCE 1874
'Mme Falcot' seedling
A fragrant, many-petalled rose, often opening quartered. Sulphur-yellow to buff on a sturdy compact plant. Apparently quite hardy out of doors but probably better under glass in cold or wet districts, since it fails to open properly in such conditions.

C Gh ▽ ☼ VF AL 3' × 2' 90 × 60 cm

'Rival de Paestum'

W. Paul UK 1848
Fully double flowers, ivory-white tinged pink, more so in the bud stage. Scented. Bush well-foliated with dark green leaves. Twiggy in habit.

C Gh ▽ MF AL 3' × 2' 90 × 60 cm

'Rosette Delizy'

P. Nabonnand FRANCE 1922
'Général Galliéni' × 'Comtesse Bardi'
Pleasing combination of rose-pink, buff and apricot with deeper colouring on the outside of each petal. Bush branchy but nevertheless refined in habit with good foliage.

C ☼ Gh ▽ ⊱ SF AL 3' × 2' 90 × 60 cm

'Rubens'

Robert and Moreau FRANCE 1859
Freely produced large, blowsy flowers, full of petals, a mixture of pinks with hints of yellow deep down. Foliage mid-green, semi-glossy. Growth bushy.

C ☼ Gh ▽ SF ⊱ AL 3' × 3' 90 × 90 cm

'Safrano'

Beauregard FRANCE 1839
This rose, one of the oldest of the Teas, is still worthy of consideration, especially if planted in groups or in pots. Will not enjoy an exposed position. Very floriferous, each flower fully double, opening flat from a high-centred bud, buff and pinkish-apricot with a sulphur-yellow base. Foliage mid-green and plentiful.

C ☼ Gh ▽ MF AL 3' × 2' 90 × 60 cm

'Snowflake', 'Marie Lambert', 'White Hermosa'

E. Lambert FRANCE 1866
Sport of 'Mme Bravy'
Pure white, unblemished in good weather. Large and fully double. Exceptionally free-flowering with a good fragrance. Growth dense and bushy. Foliage mid-green and plentiful.

C ☼ Gh ▽ VF ⊱ AL 3' × 2' 90 × 60 cm

'Sombreuil' Climbing

'Solfaterre', 'Solfatare'

Boyau FRANCE 1843

Seedling from 'Lamarque'

A beautiful, large, double, pale sulphur-yellow rose, which needs extra loving care and a warm, sheltered site or greenhouse to flourish, when it can be most rewarding.

R ☼ ▽ MF AL 10′ × 8′ 3 × 2.5 m

'Sombreuil' Climbing

Robert FRANCE 1850

A fully double, flattish flower, pure white with hints of cream in the base, sweetly scented. A beautiful rose which, with loving care, is most rewarding. With its ample, lush green foliage it makes a dense shrub or small climber.

R Gh ⅊< VF AL 8′ × 5′ 2.5 × 1.5 m

'Souvenir d'Elise Vardon'

Marest FRANCE 1855

A shapely, fragrant rose of cream overlaid coppery-yellow. Foliage leathery and glossy. Rather tender.

C ☼ Gh ▽ SF AL 3′ × 2′ 90 × 60 cm

'Souvenir de Mme Léonie Viennot' Climbing

Bernaix FRANCE 1897

Fragrant, shapely flowers. A mixture of primrose-yellow with variable coppery-orange overtones, sometimes veined pink. A very good climbing rose. My stock came from Keith Money, whose mother sent it to him from New Zealand, wrapped in polythene, in a pencil case.

R ☼ Gh ◉ VF AL 12′ × 8′ 3.5 × 2.5 m

'Souvenir d'un Ami'

Bélot-Defougère FRANCE 1846

Fully double flowers of rose-pink tinted deeper pink to salmon. Highly scented. Foliage rich green on a vigorous plant.

R P Gh VF AL 8′ × 4′ 2.5 × 1.2 m

'The Bride'

May USA 1885

'Catherine Mermet' sport

Pure white with a mere hint of pink on each petal edge. William Paul said of it 'in all respects a first class rose'. Quite vigorous. Good foliage.

C Gh ▽ ⅊< VF AL 4′ × 3′ 120 × 90 cm

'The Bride'

'Triomphe de Luxembourg', and below, 'William R. Smith'

'Tipsy Imperial Concubine'

'Tipsy Imperial Concubine'

Introduced Beales UK 1982

Large double flowers of soft pink, subtly overlaid with tones of yellow and red. Very free-flowering. Came from China and is believed to be an old Chinese garden cultivar. It was discovered by Hazel le Rougetel.

C ☼ Gh ▽ SF AL 2′ × 2′ 60 × 60 cm

'Triomphe de Luxembourg'

Hardy FRANCE 1839

Fully double flowers; salmon-pink to pinkish-buff. Foliage dark green. I dated this rose from an old catalogue of 1839, when it was priced at 7s 6d (37.5 pence) each – a week's wages for a gardener in those days.

C Gh ▽ MF AL 3′ × 2′ 90 × 60 cm

'William R. Smith', 'Charles Dingee', 'Blush Maman Cochet', 'President William Smith', 'Jeanette Heller'

Bagg USA 1909

Flowers creamy-white flushed pink with buff and gold at the base, blowsy when fully open but produced on a tidy plant.

C Gh ▽ ⊰ MF AL 3′ × 2′ 90 × 60 cm

Bermuda Roses

As mentioned in an earlier chapter (pages 19–20), the Bermuda Rose Society, since its formation in 1954, has rescued and gathered together these roses, many of them very old. Most were probably taken there by settlers or imported by the keen gardeners of the island during the nineteenth century. They are an important little group and appear to be unique to Bermuda. Some are, undoubtedly, roses now extinct in the rest of the world, which, in the course of time, have lost their true identity. Others may simply be climatically induced variations of cultivars we already know, but sufficiently different to defy identification. A clue to their age is that most are akin to the Teas and Chinas. In truth they would struggle to survive in the colder climates but, in their new-found identities, they fully deserve to be reintroduced to the rest of the world. Anyway they are safe in Bermuda, for not only are they now grown extensively in private gardens there but the full collection, along with the other named roses which have been rescued, has been planted in a newly created public rose garden in the grounds of what was once the Premier's residence, the historic Camden House.

Although I have now come to know some of these fascinating roses, it would be presumptuous of me to attempt to describe them and so I am delighted that Lorna Mercer, a past President of the Bermuda Rose Society, has agreed to do so for me. The photographs in this section are by the late Bill Mercer.

MYSTERY ROSES IN BERMUDA
By Lorna Mercer

The mystery roses in Bermuda are those whose original name or provenance is unknown, but which have grown here for many years. Most of these roses have been given the name of the area where they were found, or sometimes the name of the owner of the garden. The mystery roses, which are all old garden roses, have now been included in the Bench Competitions of the Bermuda Rose Society and at the annual Agricultural Exhibition. A trophy was given in 1987 by Peter Beales to the Bermuda Rose Society and this is awarded annually for Mystery Roses.

NOT CLASSIFIED

'Brightside Cream', and right, 'Miss Atwood'

'Brightside Cream'

Probably a Noisette. Large vigorous climber with clusters of double cream flowers. Flowers about 3″ (8 cm) across. Strong scent. Foliage mid-green. Blooms all year round. Called 'Brightside' after the home of a past president of the Bermuda Rose Society.

C Gh VF ○ AL 12′ × 8′ 3.5 × 2.5 m

'Carnation'

Deep pink double flowers with a mauve tinge. Petals have frilly edges. Very like a carnation! This rose is inclined to hang its head. Bush has dark green foliage.

C Gh ▽ ○ AL 3′ × 3′ 90 × 90 cm

'Maitland White'

Large double white rose with a pink blush near the centre. Tall stick-like bush with mid-green foliage. Good fragrance. Found a few years ago in the garden of a Mr Maitland.

C Gh ▽ ○ VF AL 6′ × 4′ 1.8 × 1.2 m

'Miss Atwood'

This large bush has double apricot-coloured flowers. Rather untidy when fully open but with a lovely fragrance. Mid-green foliage and large hips. This rose was found in the garden of a very old house belonging to Miss Atwood, which has since been demolished.

C Gh ▽ VF AL 6′ × 4′ 1.8 × 1.2 m

'Pacific'

Some say this is a Hybrid Perpetual. According to Bermuda legend this rose was brought to the island about 100 years ago by a Captain Nelmes, who while sailing in the Pacific Ocean gave water to a French ship and was given this rose as a thank-you. Deep pink or red, very double flower. Has mid-green foliage. A thin spindly bush which never grows very tall. Captain Nelmes was the great-grandfather of the founding President of the Bermuda Rose Society.

C Gh ▽ ○ AL 3′ × 3′ 90 × 90 cm

'Smith's Parish'

Large bush with very light green foliage. The flowers are semi-double – sometimes all white, sometimes with one or more red stripes. Sometimes the bush will have an all red flower. Very pale yellow stamens. Originally found in Smith's Parish, hence the name.

C Gh ▽ AL 6′ × 5′ 1.8 × 1.5 m

'Spice'

Pale pink rose, semi-double with loose petals in the centre. Small mid-green foliage on a small bush – it grows to no more than 4′ (1.2 m). This rose has been named 'Spice' because of its strong spice scent. It has been in Bermuda a very long time and it is suspected that it might be 'Hume's Blush Tea-scented China'.

C Gh ▽ VF ○ ⅙ AL 4′ × 3′ 120 × 90 cm

'Trinity'

Pure white semi-double rose, buds touched with pink. Dark green shiny foliage. Bush grows to about 5′ (1.5 m). This mystery rose was found in the graveyard of Holy Trinity Church.

C Gh ▽ ☼ AL 5′ × 4′ 1.5 × 1.2 m

'Vincent Godsiff'

A deep pink single rose. Dark green foliage. A small spindly bush. Possibly a seedling.

C Gh ▽ ☼ AL 3′ × 3′ 90 × 90 cm

There are also a great many Teas which do very well in the Bermuda climate and have grown large and strong over the years. Some of these are as follows – 'Duchesse de Brabant', 'Mme Lombard', 'Dr Grill', 'Maman Cochet' and 'White Maman Cochet', 'Niles Cochet', 'Papa Gontier', 'Rosette Delizy', 'Mme Berkeley', 'Général Schablikine', 'William R. Smith', 'Baronne Henriette de Snoy' and 'Homère'.

'Smith's Parish'

Hybrid Perpetuals

The Hybrid Perpetuals emerged in the 1830s and were born from a varied and complex union, in which the Chinas, Portlands, Bourbons, Noisettes and, later, the Teas all played their part.

Few were completely perpetual, but most were remontant to some degree. After a few years of uncertain popularity in competition with the Bourbons, they became one of the major groups of roses.

Throughout Queen Victoria's reign they led the field as exhibition roses, and as flower shows became fashionable, breeders felt impelled to seek ever larger, more shapely blooms. Despite this quest for size of flower, many very useful garden shrubs emerged and, as such, many have come down to us today, as true aristocrats from an important era in rose development.

CLASSIFICATION

BARB	Class 25
MR10	Class 38
WFRS	Class 4

'Alfred Colomb'

Lacharme FRANCE 1865
'Général Jacqueminot' × unknown
A large, full rose, rounded in late bud and high-centred, brickish-red with flecks of deep pink and carmine. Slightly vulgar but nevertheless appealing. Growth tidy and foliage abundant.
R P ▽ ⊰ SF AL 4′ × 3′ 120 × 90 cm

'American Beauty', 'Mme Ferdinand Jamin'

Lédéchaux FRANCE 1875
First introduced as a forcing cultivar, its longish, strong stems making it ideal for bouquets. Also a useful garden plant. Crimson high-centred flowers, rather modern in appearance. The bush was perhaps rather ahead of its time in being very Hybrid Tea-like in stature.
R Gh ▽ ⊰ MF AL 3′ × 3′ 90 × 90 cm

'Anna de Diesbach', 'Gloire de Paris'

Lacharme FRANCE 1858
'La Reine' × seedling
A tall rose with many fragrant flowers of rich, deep rose-pink with deeper shadings, initially quite large

and cupped, later opening rather flat. Bush tall, a little ungainly, but well-foliated.
R ▽ MF AL 4′ × 3′ 120 × 90 cm

'Archiduchesse Elizabeth d'Autriche'

Moreau-Robert FRANCE 1881
Soft rose-pink flowers, fully double, opening flat. I find the plant rather inclined to sprawl, but effective if pruned hard each season. Obviously enjoys full sun.
R ☼ SF AL 5′ × 4′ 1.5 × 1.2 m

'Ardoisée de Lyon'

Damaizin FRANCE 1858
Superb, fully double, quartered flowers of rich cerise with violet and purple shadings, held on a strong neck and exuding a rich perfume. Ample greyish-green foliage on a compact, tidy plant with numerous thorns. Little known but a splendid rose.
R P ▽ VF AL 4′ × 3′ 120 × 90 cm

'Ards Rover'

Dickson UK 1898
Excellent old pillar rose. Shapely, crimson flowers

'Baroness Rothschild', and left, 'Alfred Colomb'

opening blowsily, with a strong scent. Definitely has a place in the modern garden, especially since good, deep red climbers are so few. Of medium stature, it can fulfil the role of either wall climber or pillar rose to considerable effect, especially as it is sometimes, in good seasons, recurrent. Foliage quite lush and dark green. Needs attention for mildew early each season for it to give of its very best.

R ✂ VF M⚬ AL 10′ × 6′ 3 × 1.8 m

'Arrillaga'

Schoener USA 1929

(*R. centifolia* × 'Mrs John Laing') × 'Frau Karl Druschki'
Freely produced flowers of very bright pink with hints of gold in the base, large and full and held on strong stems. Good mid-green foliage.

R P H ▽ VF ✂ AL 5′ × 4′ 1.5 × 1.2 m

'Baron de Bonstetten'

Liabaud FRANCE 1871

'Général Jacqueminot' × 'Géant des Batailles'
Very double, very dark red and very fragrant. Upright and vigorous in growth and rather thorny with mid- to dark green foliage.

R ▽ VF AL 4′ × 3′ 120 × 90 cm

'Baroness Rothschild', 'Baronne Adolphe de Rothschild'

Pernet Père FRANCE 1868

'Souvenir de la Reine d'Angleterre' sport
A superior member of its group. Large, full flowers remain slightly cupped when fully open, held erect on strong, stout stems. Petals are of a soft to clear rose-pink colour and have a soft silky texture. Bush well covered with large grey-green foliage.

Note: I was wrong in the first edition of this book to describe this rose as 'highly scented' – although some noses can detect no fragrance, mine does – another case of 'roses for noses and noses for roses'.

R P H B ▽ ✂ SF AL 4′ × 3′ 120 × 90 cm

'Baron Girod de l'Ain'

Reverchon FRANCE 1897

'Eugène Fürst' sport
A popular novelty since its introduction, this unusual rose is well worth garden space. Its very double flowers are bright crimson, and they open cup-shaped, with the petal edges rather ragged-looking, an illusion enhanced by the fringe of white edging the margins. As a shrub it is rather straggly but quite dense with firm, stout thorns and leathery dark green leaves.

R P MF M⚬ AL 4′ × 3′ 120 × 90 cm

'Baronne Prévost'

Desprez FRANCE 1842

Deep rose-pink scented flowers opening flat and double from globular buds. A reliable rose of considerable longevity, with many bushes still growing in cottage gardens, having survived from its heyday. Somewhat coarse in growth and rather thorny, it still makes a most useful shrub.

R P VF AL 5′ × 4′ 1.5 × 1.2 m

'Black Prince'

W. Paul UK 1866

Vigorous cultivar with good foliage, if rather prone to mildew. Flowers large and cupped, opening from shapely buds of rich dark crimson to almost black. Scented.

R VF MⒸ AL 5′ × 3′ 150 × 90 cm

'Candeur Lyonnaise'

Croibier FRANCE 1914

'Frau Karl Druschki' seedling

Large, fully double flowers open from shapely, pointed buds. Soft yellow to pure white. Vigorous, with sizeable mid-green leaves.

R P H ▽ AL 5′ × 4′ 1.5 × 1.2 m

'Captain Hayward' Climbing

Bush form Bennett UK 1893

'Triomphe de l'Expédition' seedling

This form W. Paul 1906

A tall rose, needing support as a shrub. Ideal as a pillar rose, when its healthy disposition can be fully appreciated. Pinkish-crimson flowers, large and cupped until fully open, when they then become rather blowsy. Does not always repeat. Hips large and quite attractive, so dead-heading best avoided.

R P F VF AL 8′ × 4′ 2.5 × 1.2 m

'Champion of the World', 'Mrs de Graw'

Woodhouse UK 1894

'Hermosa' × 'Magna Charta'

A presumptuous name, probably describing the size of its deep rosy-pink flowers. A bush of medium stature, rather sprawly, leaves dark green.

R P ▽ MF AL 4′ × 3′ 120 × 90 cm

'Charles Lefèbvre', and left, 'Baronne Prévost'

'Charles Gater'

W. Paul UK 1893

An upright-growing plant which can be slotted into the smallest space. Flowers clear bright red and globular throughout their life. Scented. Good strong foliage. Stems rather thorny. Inclined to mildew after the first flush.

R ▽ MⒸ VF AL 4′ × 2′ 120 × 60 cm

'Charles Lefèbvre'

Lacharme FRANCE 1861

'Général Jacqueminot' × 'Victor Verdier'

Very large, many-petalled flowers of rich crimson shaded maroon, high-centred, opening cupped, held on a strong, firm neck. Foliage dark green and sufficient.

R ▽ ⤞ VF AL 4′ × 3′ 120 × 90 cm

'Clio'

W. Paul UK 1894

Clusters of fully double, initially cupped, fragrant, soft silvery-pink flowers on strong, almost arching stems. Rich leathery foliage on a vigorous, if somewhat sprawly plant, with ample thorns.

R VF AL 4′ × 4′ 1.2 × 1.2 m

'Comtesse Cécile de Chabrillant'

Marest FRANCE 1858

The clear mid-pink flowers are shapely, full and globular, and strongly perfumed. They are supported on strong flower stalks. Growth is upright,

and the rose is very free-flowering which qualifies this excellent cultivar for general use.
R ▽ VF AL 4′ × 4′ 1.2 × 1.2 m

'Countess of Oxford', 'Comtesse d'Oxford'

Guillot Père FRANCE 1869
William Paul spoke highly of this rose. Double globular flowers opening cupped, of rich carmine-red and scented. A vigorous, tidy plant with ample healthy foliage.
R P ▽ VF AL 4′ × 3′ 120 × 90 cm

'Crown Prince'

W. Paul UK 1880
A free-flowering fully double rose of purple and red. Tidy and compact in growth, with dark green foliage.
R ▽ MF AL 3′ × 3′ 90 × 90 cm

'Dembrowski'

Vibert FRANCE 1849
Very shapely, fully double, reddish-purple flowers on a strong but medium-growing plant with mid-green foliage.
C MF AL 4′ × 3′ 120 × 90 cm

'Dr Andry'

E. Verdier FRANCE 1864
Very bright red with deeper shadings towards the centre of each fully double flower. Only a slight scent. Vigorous growth with dark green foliage.
R ▽ SF AL 4′ × 3′ 120 × 90 cm

'Duke of Edinburgh'

Paul UK 1868
'Général Jacqueminot' × unknown
Not easy to grow except in the very best soils, where it can be rewarding. Shortish in stature and slightly spreading in habit, it produces semi-double flowers of bright scarlet to crimson, sweetly scented.
R ▽ VF AL 2′ × 2′ 60 × 60 cm

'Duke of Wellington'

Granger FRANCE 1874
A surprising name for a French rose? Large, shapely, high-centred flowers of deep crimson; these tend to dislike hot sun, which turns their outer petals somewhat blackish. Upright in growth, the blooms are

'Dr Andry'

'Duke of Edinburgh', and below, 'Dupuy Jamain'

produced on thick, stout, thorny stems with dark foliage.
R ▽ VF AL 4′ × 3′ 120 × 90 cm

'Dupuy Jamain'

Jamain FRANCE 1868
I place this rose high on my list of favourite Hybrid

Perpetuals. Large, full, cerise-red flowers held on strong necks, with a good, strong perfume. The shrub is healthy, with an abundance of lush, grey-green leaves. Relatively free of thorns, upright growth.

R P ▽ ⊰ MF AL 4′ × 3′ 120 × 90 cm

'Éclair'

Lacharme FRANCE 1833

'Général Jacqueminot' × unknown

Well-scented, very dark red, almost black flowers, opening flat in rosette shape. Not the easiest of roses to grow but well worth some extra loving care. Upright in growth. Can perhaps be faulted by its rather sparse foliage. Almost fits the Portlands in type. Sent to me by Margaret Wray of Langport, near Taunton. A valuable rediscovery.

R ▽ ⊰ VF AL 4′ × 3′ 120 × 90 cm

'Elisa Boelle'

Guillot Père FRANCE 1869

A vigorous rose having shapely, cupped, whitish-pink, scented flowers, with incurving centre petals. Ample foliage on a tidy, well-groomed plant.

R ▽ MF AL 4′ × 3′ 120 × 90 cm

'Empereur du Maroc', 'Emperor of Morocco'

Guinoisseau FRANCE 1858

'Géant des Batailles' seedling

Very double flowers, opening flat; deep crimson tinged maroon. A superb rose when weather permits. Flowers borne in large clusters which are sometimes too heavy for the thorny branches to support, but hard pruning helps correct this fault over the years. Needs precautions against both black spot and mildew.

R VF BS⚬ M⚬ AL 4′ × 3′ 120 × 90 cm

'Enfant de France'

'Enfant de France'

Lartay FRANCE 1860

For a number of years I have grown the rose here described under this name uncertain as to whether it is correct, but it fits the descriptions I have read in old books and catalogues. Whatever its name, such a good rose should not be omitted. The fully double flowers, which are sometimes quartered, are silky pink and beautifully perfumed. Growth is upright and foliage plentiful. Rather in the Portland mould.

R Gh P ▽ VF AL 3′ × 2′ 90 × 60 cm

'Eugène Fürst'

Soupert and Notting LUXEMBOURG 1875

'Baron de Bonstetten' × unknown

Ragged-edged, crimson-purple cupped flowers of considerable size, highly scented. The bush is upright in growth and the flowers are borne on strong necks amid good, dark green foliage.

R ▽ M⚬ VF AL 4′ × 3′ 120 × 90 cm

'Everest'

Easlea UK 1927

'Candeur Lyonnaise' × 'Mme Caristie Martel'

One of the last Hybrid Perpetuals introduced, and one of the most beautiful. Substantially sized, high-centred flowers of creamy-white. Foliage light green. Growth low, making a wide, bushy plant.

R P H ▽ ⊰ VF AL 3′ × 3′ 90 × 90 cm

'Ferdinand de Lesseps'

Verdier FRANCE 1869

An interesting rose bearing shapely flowers of lavender, shaded purple and magenta, opening flat, with many petals in the Centifolia form. Bush shrubby and vigorous.

R VF AL 4′ × 3′ 120 × 90 cm

'Ferdinand Pichard'

Tanne FRANCE 1921

Flowers of rich, carmine red, heavily laced and striped with white, opening large and cup-shaped with a distinct scent; these combine well with rich green foliage and are produced on a vigorous, healthy shrub. One of the best of the striped roses available today.

R P H VF AL 5′ × 4′ 1.5 × 1.2 m

'Fisher Holmes', 'Fisher and Holmes

Verdier FRANCE 1865
'Maurice Bernardin' seedling
Well-formed, double flowers from shapely, pointed buds. Shades of scarlet and crimson. Scented. Bush of medium height and moderately vigorous with good foliage. Rather prone to disease, the result perhaps of over-propagation, for it was very popular in Victorian times.
C ▽ VF M⚭ R⚭ AL 3′ × 3′ 90 × 90 cm

'Frau Karl Druschki', 'Snow Queen', 'Reine des Neiges', 'White American Beauty'

P. Lambert GERMANY 1901
'Merveille de Lyon' × 'Mme Caroline Testout'
For many years the most popular white rose, and deservedly so, its only significant faults being a lack of scent and a dislike of wet weather. Pure white blooms large and globular, with high centres in bud. Shrub vigorous and strong, with plenty of leathery, lightish green leaves.
R P AL 5′ × 3′ 150 × 90 cm

'Frau Karl Druschki' Climbing

Lawrenson UK 1906
As bush form, except that it makes a vigorous and useful climber.
S P AL 15′ × 8′ 4.5 × 2.5 m

'Général Jacqueminot', 'General Jack', 'Jack Rose'

Roussel FRANCE 1853
'Gloire des Rosomanes' seedling
Clear red, shapely, pointed buds opening to well-formed, perfumed flowers, produced on fairly long stems. A vigorous shrub with rich green foliage. Rather prone to rust from mid-summer onwards.
R VF R⚭ AL 5′ × 4′ 1.5 × 1.2 m

'Georg Arends', and left, 'Ferdinand Pichard'

'Georg Arends', 'Fortuné Besson'

W. Hinner GERMANY 1910
'Frau Karl Druschki' × 'La France'
A first-class rose. Large, initially high-centred but blowsy blooms of clear rose-pink paling to soft pink. Free-flowering, fragrant and, as a shrub, vigorous with plenty of large, grey-green leaves.
C H P ✁ MF AL 5′ × 4′ 1.5 × 1.2 m

'Gloire de Bruxelles', 'Gloire de l'Exposition'

Soupert and Notting LUXEMBOURG 1889
'Souvenir de William Wood' × 'Lord Macaulay'
Sixty or more velvety petals make up a flower which opens flat in large rosette form, dark red to crimson-purple and scented. The shrub is loose and untidy despite small stature but well worth the effort of support.
R VF M⚭ AL 4′ × 4′ 1.2 × 1.2 m

'Gloire de Chédane-Guinoisseau'

Chédane-Pajotin FRANCE 1907
'Gloire de Ducher' × unknown
Shapely cupped flowers produced in considerable numbers, bright rich pinkish-red, scented. Foliage dark green and abundant on a vigorous, quite healthy plant.
R P ▽ VF AL 4′ × 3′ 120 × 90 cm

'Gloire de Ducher'

Ducher FRANCE 1865
More credit is due to this rose than it has ever

'Gloire de Ducher', and below, 'Gloire Lyonnaise' opposite, 'Heinrich Schultheis'

received. Huge, fully double blooms of deep purplish-red, somewhat blowsy in structure, produced freely along long, arching branches amid dark grey-green leaves. Well scented.

R P VF M♂ AL 6′ × 4′ 1.8 × 1.2 m

'Gloire de l'Exposition' *see* 'Gloire de Bruxelles'

'Gloire de Paris' *see* 'Anna de Diesbach'

'Gloire d'un Enfant d'Hiram'

Vilin FRANCE 1899

Large, bright pink, scented, cupped flowers on a strong, sturdy, upright-growing plant with few thorns and good, greyish-green leathery foliage.

R P ▽ MF AL 4′ × 3′ 120 × 90 cm

'Gloire Lyonnaise'

Guillot Fils FRANCE 1885

'Baroness Rothschild' × 'Mme Falcot'

A favourite of mine, this creamy-white rose has semi-double flowers that open flat with a good perfume. The shrub is upright in growth, with strong stems supporting the flowers without

arching. Few thorns, foliage dark green and healthy. Should be more widely grown.
C P H B ▽ VF AL 4′ × 2′ 120 × 60 cm

'Hans Mackart'

E. Verdier Fils FRANCE 1885
Double flowers of bright but deep pink, opening flat from cupped buds, inclined to sprawl. Ample lightish-green foliage with but few thorns.
R P VF AL 5′ × 3′ 150 × 90 cm

'Heinrich Münch'

W. Hinner GERMANY 1911
'Frau Karl Druschki' × ('Mme Caroline Testout' × 'Mrs W. J. Grant')
Fully double, large, soft blush-pink blooms with a good fragrance, produced on a strong, branching shrub with good, mid- to dark green foliage. A good rose for the 'pegging down' system of training.
R P VF ✂ AL 6′ × 4′ 1.8 × 1.2 m

'Heinrich Schultheis'

Bennett UK 1882
'Mabel Morrison' × 'E. Y. Teas'
A Victorian exhibition rose which probably won many prizes for size alone. Flowers high-centred until fully open, then cupped, flat-topped and slightly ragged, rich pink with hints of a deeper shade in the base, scented. Vigorous, well-foliated and upright. Worth growing.
C ▽ ✂ VF AL 4′ × 3′ 120 × 90 cm

'Henry Nevard'

Cants UK 1924
Fragrant bright crimson cupped flowers of considerable size. Bushy growth with dark green, leathery leaves.
R MF AL 4′ × 3′ 120 × 90 cm

'Her Majesty'

Bennett UK 1885
'Mabel Morrison' × 'Canary'
Huge, fully double blooms of clear pink. Another Victorian exhibition rose well worth growing today. Foliage large and grey, but inclined to mildew. Shrub vigorous but less tall than most of its type.
R ▽ VF M♂ AL 3′ × 2′ 90 × 60 cm

'Horace Vernet'

Guillot Fils FRANCE 1866
'Général Jacqueminot' × unknown
A high-centred rose of rich crimson, fragrant, retaining its shape well into maturity. The shrub is upright, tidy in habit, with abundant dark foliage.
R ▽ MF AL 4′ × 3′ 120 × 90 cm

'Hugh Dickson'

Dickson UK 1905
'Lord Bacon' × 'Grüss an Teplitz'
A tall lanky rose from the latter end of the Hybrid Perpetual cycle. Rich dark red, powerfully perfumed flowers borne on long, arching stems, making it an ideal rose for 'pegging down' or for pillars. Can be grown as a shrub but needs support. Foliage rich, dark green with hints of maroon. Illustrated on page 35.
R P ✂ VF AL 8′ × 5′ 2.5 × 1.5 m

'James Bourgault'

Renault FRANCE 1987
Shapely soft pink to white blooms, fully double and fragrant. A little known Hybrid Perpetual with much to commend it. Foliage ample, dark green. Growth vigorous and upright.
R P H ▽ MF ✂ AL 4′ × 3′ 120 × 90 cm

'Jean Rosenkrantz'

Portemer FRANCE 1864
Big flowers of neatly formed, deep pinkish-red petals with perfume. The shrub is well-foliated, vigorous and upright.
R ▽ MF AL 4′ × 3′ 120 × 90 cm

'James Bourgault', and below, 'John Hopper'

'John Hopper'

Ward UK 1862

'Jules Margottin' × 'Mme Vidot'
The large fragrant flowers are a pleasing combination of bright pink and lilac, with deeper centres produced on an upright vigorous plant which remains tidy and seems to enjoy most soils. A first-class rose.
R H P ▽ VF AL 4′ × 3′ 120 × 90 cm

'Jules Margottin'

Margottin FRANCE 1853

'La Reine' seedling
This rose has lots of thick, dark green foliage on strong, thorny stems. From these emerge equally strong, pointed buds opening into large, flattish flowers of deep carmine, each with a strong scent.
R VF AL 4′ × 3′ 120 × 90 cm

'Juliet'

W. Paul UK 1910

'Captain Hayward' × 'Soleil d'Or'
A multi-coloured rose. Flowers open from shapely, golden-yellow buds to a rich pink to a deep rosy-red

on the inside of each petal with clear tawny-gold on the outside. Fragrant. Plentiful wrinkled dark green foliage. Quite vigorous and bushy.
R Gh VF ▽ ✂ AL 4′ × 3′ 120 × 90 cm

'Kaiserin Auguste Viktoria'

P. Lambert GERMANY 1891

'Coquette de Lyon' × 'Lady Mary Fitzwilliam'
Shapely, very double flowers open flattish from high-centred buds. Pure white with lemon centres and a delicious perfume. Mid-green foliage on a vigorous if somewhat twiggy, bushy plant.
R P ▽ Gh VF ✂ AL 3′ × 3′ 90 × 90 cm

'La Reine', 'Reine des Français'

Laffay FRANCE 1842

Large, globular almost portly blooms, high-centred as buds but opening to cupped blooms with flattish tops, the numerous petals giving an almost serrated effect. Colour silvery rose-pink with an undertone of lilac. The shrub is upright, well-foliated but not too tall. One of the first Hybrid Perpetuals, its influence can still be seen in roses to this day.
C ▽ VF AL 3′ × 2′ 90 × 60 cm

'Le Havre'

Eudes FRANCE 1871

Scented, very double, almost vermilion-red flowers on a healthy, strong plant with dark green, leathery foliage.
R ▽ VF AL 4′ × 3′ 120 × 90 cm

'Mabel Morrison'

Broughton UK 1878

'Baroness Rothschild' sport
A white sport of the excellent 'Baroness Rothschild', inheriting most of her attributes except height, as this rose – for me at least – is somewhat shorter. Flowers pure white with flecks of pink in hot weather.
R P H B ▽ VF AL 4′ × 3′ 120 × 90 cm

'Magna Charta'

W. Paul UK 1876

Bright pink flowers with deeper carmine shadings, fully double and cupped when fully open. Scented. Dark green, leathery foliage. Bushy, tidy growth.
P R ▽ VF AL 3′ × 3′ 90 × 90 cm

'Mabel Morrison', and below, 'Magna Charta'

'Marchioness of Londonderry'

Dickson UK 1893

Fragrant white blooms tinted soft pink, large and full. Good mid-green foliage. Very vigorous.

R P VF ✄ AL 6' × 4' 1.8 × 1.2 m

'Marguerite Guillard'

Chambard FRANCE 1915

'Frau Karl Druschki' sport

Has fewer petals than its parent, enabling it to open in wet weather. Otherwise similar in both colour and habit.

R AL 5' × 3' 150 × 90 cm

'Merveille de Lyon'

Pernet Père FRANCE 1882

Sport of 'Baroness Rothschild'

Large, full flowers, cupped when fully open and held on strong, stout stems. Pure white flushed soft pink, especially at the petal edges. Scented. Very free-flowering. Foliage large, greyish dark green. Growth sturdy and upright. A little prone to mildew but well worth living with.

R P H ▽ Gh VF ✄ AW 4' × 3' 120 × 90 cm

'Mme Bruel', 'Mme François Bruel'

Levet FRANCE 1882

'Victor Verdier' × 'Countess of Oxford'

Sizeable rich carmine-pink double flowers on a relatively thorn-free, shrubby plant. Foliage soft mid-green.

C H ▽ VF ✄ AL 4' × 3' 120 × 90 cm

'Mme Ferdinand Jamin' *see* 'American Beauty'

'Mme Gabriel Luizet'

Liabaud FRANCE 1877

Large, often quartered, fully double flowers of deep glowing pink with paler petal edges when fully open. Very vigorous, with good foliage and stout strong stems. Seldom remontant, although the occasional autumn bloom can be rewarding.

S P VF AL 6′ × 4′ 1.8 × 1.2 m

'Mme Scipion Cochet'

S. Cochet FRANCE 1873

Attractively wrinkled cup-shaped flowers, deep purplish-pink paling to softer shades at the edges, good, dark green foliage and vigorous, bushy growth.

R VF AL 4′ × 3′ 120 × 90 cm

'Mme Victor Verdier'

E. Verdier FRANCE 1863

'Sénateur Vaisse' × unknown
Huge buds open to shaggy but attractive double, light crimson to carmine flowers with slightly weak necks. Plenty of good, dark green foliage. Shrub vigorous and healthy.

R P H VF AL 5′ × 4′ 1.5 × 1.2 m

'Mrs John Laing'

Bennett UK 1887

'François Michelon' seedling
Undoubtedly one of the superior Hybrid Perpetuals and one of the best from Henry Bennett's stable in late Victorian times. Upright in growth, with large, grey-green leaves. A healthy plant producing an abundance of scented, shapely, silver-pink flowers, which would have been used extensively for exhibition by Victorian and Edwardian gardeners. Today it makes an excellent bushy shrub.

R Gh P H ▽ VF AL 4′ × 3′ 120 × 90 cm

'Paul Neyron'

Levet FRANCE 1869

'Victor Verdier' × 'Anna de Diesbach'
This sturdy, healthy cultivar should be grown more extensively. Very large unfading, rich, warm pink flowers with a pleasing, muddled appearance when fully open. Scented. Growth strong and upright, with large, matt, dark green leaves.

R Gh P H B ▽ VF AL 3′ × 2′ 90 × 60 cm

'Marguerite Guillard'

'Mrs John Laing', and below, 'Paul Neyron'

'Prince Camille de Rohan'

'Paul Ricault'

Portemer FRANCE 1845
A rose with large, almost Centifolia-like, fully
double flowers opening flat and quartered, borne
along long, arching stems on a vigorous, thorny,
well-foliated shrub.
R P VF AL 5′ × 4′ 1.5 × 1.2 m

'Paul's Early Blush', 'Mrs Harkness'

W. Paul UK 1893
'Heinrich Schultheis' sport
Blush-pink flowers which, as the name suggests,
appear a few days earlier than most, large, very
double and scented, produced on a strong, thorny
bush, with thickish branches. Foliage dark green.
R P ▽ VF M○ AL 4′ × 3′ 120 × 90 cm

'Pierre Notting'

Portemer FRANCE 1863
'Alfred Colomb' seedling
An upright grower with deep crimson, globular
flowers. Highly scented. One of many such types
from the middle of the 19th century, presumably
owing their survival to a strong constitution, which
this rose certainly has.
R P VF AL 4′ × 3′ 120 × 90 cm

'Prince Camille de Rohan', 'La Rosière'

E. Verdier FRANCE 1861
'Général Jacqueminot' × 'Géant des Batailles'
Can be faulted by its very weak neck, otherwise
a fascinating rose. Deep blackish-red blooms of
colossal size, opening flat and deepening with age.
The shrub is rather sprawly and until mature has
difficulty in carrying the weight of the blooms on
its thinnish stems. Foliage dark green.
R ▽ VF BS○ M○ AL 4′ × 3′ 120 × 90 cm

'Reine des Violettes', 'Queen of the Violets'

Millet-Malet FRANCE 1860
'Pius IX' seedling
If I had to choose just one Hybrid Perpetual, it
would have to be this one. An upright-growing and
almost thornless shrub with stout, erect branches.
Foliage grey-green and soft to touch. Flowers, sometimes charmingly hidden among the foliage, with
which they blend so well, are soft, velvety violet,
opening flat and quartered. To cap all this, it has
a lovely perfume. Flowers shatter very quickly after
reaching perfection, but this small fault helps me
appreciate it even more. Illustrated on page 21.
C P H ▽ VF AL 5′ × 3′ 150 × 90 cm

'Reynolds Hole'

W. Paul UK 1874
'Duke of Edinburgh' cross
Large, medium full, deep reddish-pink flowers on
long stems. Fragrant. Vicious plentiful thorns.
Foliage deep greyish-green. This variety, believed to
be true to name, was sent to me by Mr James Naylor,
President of the Royal National Rose Society
1995–6, he having found it in the garden of a house
where the Rev. Dean Hole, first President of the
Royal National Rose Society, lived as a young man.
R MF AL 4′ × 3′ 120 × 90 cm

'Roger Lambelin'

Schwartz FRANCE 1890
'Fisher Holmes' sport
A strange rose, whose addiction to mildew and
other diseases renders it no more than a novelty.
Flowers double and crimson-maroon with white
streaks and stripes, especially on the edges of the
petals.
R ▽ M○ R○ VF AL 4′ × 3′ 120 × 90 cm

'Roger Lambelin', and below, 'Souvenir d'Alphonse Lavallée'

'Ruhm von Steinfurth', 'Red Druschki'

Weigand GERMANY 1920
'Frau Karl Druschki' × 'Ulrich Brunner Fils'
An old exhibition cultivar. Plump, double, high-centred flowers of ruby red fading to cerise, cupped when open. Scented. Bush upright and sturdy with leathery, dark green foliage. A Hybrid Tea in all but pedigree.
R P ▽ VF AL 3′ × 2′ 90 × 60 cm

'Sidonie'

Vibert FRANCE 1847
Almost a Portland. Scented, slightly fimbriated, fully double flowers of medium size and of clear glowing pink, usually in well-spaced clusters. Has a short tidy habit but is vigorous with good if some-what coarse foliage and an unfortunate addiction to black spot.
C P ▽ BS⚵ VF AL 3′ × 2′ 90 × 60 cm

'Snow Queen' *see* 'Frau Karl Druschki'

'Souvenir d'Alphonse Lavallée'

Verdier FRANCE 1884
For years there has been some confusion between

this rose and another Hybrid Perpetual, 'Souvenir du Docteur Jamain'. 'Lavallée' is a lovely full, scented rose, combining several shades of crimson and purple. Inclined to wander if grown as a shrub unless tethered to a stake or a tripod. Best grown as a small climber. More thorny than 'Jamain'.
R P VF AL 8′ × 6′ 2.5 × 1.8 m

'Souvenir de Jeanne Balandreau'

Robichon FRANCE 1899

The large, double, cupped flowers, of deep cerise with pink stripes and vermilion highlights, are shapely and held erect on strong necks amid good dark grey-green foliage on an upright, tidy shrub.
R P H ▽ VF AL 4′ × 3′ 120 × 90 cm

'Souvenir du Docteur Jamain'

Lacharme FRANCE 1865

'Charles Lefèbvre' seedling

A superb rose if kept away from scorching sun, which it hates. Flowers are rich ruby-red and, although semi-double, open to a cupped shape, sometimes showing off their anthers to good effect. Foliage is dark green and the stems relatively thornless. Scented. At its best it is of rare beauty and even at its worst can still be enjoyed.
R N P ◉ VF AL 10′ × 7′ 3 × 2 m

'Spencer'

W. Paul UK 1892

'Merveille de Lyon' sport

Fully double flowers opening flat from globular buds, soft satin-pink, with paler, almost white reverse. Growth vigorous but tidy, with good dark foliage.
R ▽ VF AL 4′ × 3′ 120 × 90 cm

'Star of Waltham'

W. Paul UK 1875

Flowers rich carmine-red opening shapely, slightly cupped to flat, with tidily arranged petals. Fragrant and held on a strong neck. Foliage large, darkish green. Stems fairly free of prickles. Growth upright and bushy.
R H ▽ Gh VF Mᶜ AL 3′ × 3′ 90 × 90 cm

'Surpassing Beauty', 'Woolverstone Church Rose'

Rediscovered by the late Mr Humphrey Brooke

Reintroduced Beales UK 1980

An old climbing rose discovered growing at Woolverstone Church, Suffolk. Flowers deep red to crimson, blowsy when open and very strongly fragrant, appearing particularly early each season. Well worth its reintroduction. Growth relaxed and vigorous.
R P VF Mᶜ AL 8′ × 6′ 2.5 × 1.8 m

'Souvenir du Docteur Jamain', and below, 'Spencer'

'Ulrich Brunner Fils', 'Ulrich Brunner'

A. Levet FRANCE 1882

Confused parentage – probably 'Paul Neyron' sport Large, plump, initially high-centred blooms opening rather loosely but attractively; rosy-carmine fading to pink with age. Sweetly scented. The bush is upright and well endowed with dark green foliage. Stems have few thorns.
R H P ▽ VF AL 4′ × 3′ 120 × 90 cm

'Vick's Caprice'

Vick USA 1891

'Archiduchesse Elizabeth d'Autriche' sport Large, double, cupped flowers with high centres.

'Vick's Caprice', and below, 'Xavier Olibo'

'Yolande d'Aragon'

An unusual colour combination of pale pink and lilac with white flecks and stripes of deeper pink. Foliage large, attractively light green, taking an upright stance on relatively thornless shoots.
C H ▽ P MF AL 4′×3′ 120×90 cm

'Victor Hugo'

J. Schwartz FRANCE 1884
('Charles Lefèbvre' × unknown) × unknown
Fragrant, large flowers of deep rosy-red shaded purple, fully double and cupped. Foliage leathery, dark green. Growth vigorous and bushy.
R ▽ Gh VF AL 4′×3′ 120×90 cm

'Victor Verdier'

Lacharme FRANCE 1859
'Jules Margottin' × 'Safrano'
Large, fully double, clear bright rose-pink flowers held on a firm neck, with a good perfume. Stems strong and thorny with good dark green foliage. Upright in growth. An important stud rose.
R P ▽ VF AL 4′×3′ 120×90 cm

'Xavier Olibo'

Lacharme FRANCE 1865
'Général Jacqueminot' sport
This rose has all the attributes and faults of 'Général Jacqueminot', but its colour is a much darker red.
R VF R AL 5′×4′ 1.5×1.2 m

'Yolande d'Aragon'

Vibert FRANCE 1843
Flat, fully double flowers of considerable size, bright purplish to rich pink, scented. A good, healthy shrub with strong upright growth and light green foliage.
R P ▽ VF AL 4′×3′ 120×90 cm

New English Roses

Over the past thirty or so years, a range of very interesting roses has been developed which, because of its obvious differences from the general run of modern roses, has emerged as a new group in its own right. These differences are most obvious in the shape and structure of the flowers, which are seldom high-centred but are either cupped or flat or both, and are invariably made up of many more smaller petals than, say, the average Hybrid Tea.

Further differences also show up in many cultivars in both foliage and thorn patterns and, sometimes, in the general demeanour of the plant. They are almost all fragrant to some degree.

With one or two exceptions all have been developed by the English rose producer and hybridizer David Austin: prompted, no doubt, by his own taste in roses and by the realization that a certain section of the public prefers the charm of the 'old' to what they consider the brashness of the 'new'. David, to his eternal credit, set about capturing the best of both worlds and, slowly at first, but of late rapidly, this is exactly what he has done, creating remontant cultivars in the style of the old Gallicas, Centifolias, Damasks and Bourbons, some with the growth habit of the modern Shrub Roses, Floribundas and Hybrid Teas.

Austin has called this new group 'New English Roses' and, wherever I have been in the world, I have come upon them growing in some very prominent places; furthermore, whatever he prefers to call them himself, they are generally known as 'Austin' roses, a testimony indeed to him and his work.

Having said all this, Austin, I feel, would be the first to admit that some of the roses in this group need a little extra loving care to give of their best and a small minority are martyrs to mildew and black spot, especially the early ones, but then so are many modern roses, so this criticism should be seen in that context only and should not put anyone off growing any of these charming, excellent cultivars.

I am not sure if I have placed these rightfully in the correct order of things in this book but, since their remontancy no doubt owes its allegiance to the Chinas, the section *Chinensis* would seem to be correct.

CLASSIFICATION

BARB   Class 26
MR10   Class 54
WFRS   Classes 1 and 2

'Abraham Darby' (AUScot)

Austin UK 1985

'Aloha' × 'Yellow Cushion'

Full, large, cupped blooms in shades of apricot and yellow with a fruity fragrance. Strong, arching growth habit, quite thorny with dark green, leathery foliage.

R ▽ P VF ✂ AW 5′ × 4′ 1.5 × 1.2 m

'Admired Miranda' (AUSmira)

Austin UK 1983

'The Friar' × 'The Friar'

Large, fully double, light pink blooms opening flat and reflexing. Foliage mid-green and semi-glossy. Growth upright.

C VF ▽ AL 3′ × 2′ 90 × 60 cm

'Ambridge Rose' (AUSwonder)

Austin UK 1990

'Charles Austin' × seedling

Medium-sized flowers at first cupped, later loosely rosette-shaped. Deep apricot-pink paling towards the edges. Foliage mid-green. Growth bushy.

C ▽ B H SF AL 2′ 6″ × 2′ 75 × 60 cm

'Belle Story' (AUSelle)

Austin UK 1984

('Chaucer' × 'Parade') × ('The Princess' × 'Iceberg')

Freely produced pale pink flowers of an unusual formation, described by its raiser as 'wide but incurving with a pronounced boss of stamens at the centre'. These are produced on an open shrub with few thorns and mid-green, glossy foliage.

R ▽ H VF ✂ AL 4′ × 4′ 1.2 × 1.2 m

'Bibi Maizoon' (AUSdimindo)

Austin UK 1989

Very full flowers, deeply cupped and fragrant, of pure clear rich pink, outer petals paler. Growth slightly arching but bushy. Foliage mid-green and plentiful.

R ▽ H VF ✂ AW 3′ 6″ x 3′ 6″ 1.1 × 1.1 m

'Bredon' (AUSbred)

Austin UK 1984

'Wife of Bath' × 'Lilian Austin'

Medium to small-sized, fragrant, fully double,

'Abraham Darby'

neatly formed flowers of buff-yellow. Foliage light green, matt. Growth upright, bushy.

C ▽ P H VF AL 3′ × 2′ 90 × 60 cm

'Brother Cadfael' (AUSglobe)

Austin UK 1990

Richly fragrant, huge, fully double, globular peony-like flowers of soft pink. Foliage large, mid-green. Growth stout, bushy.

R ▽ H VF ✂ AL 3′ 6″ × 3′ 110 × 90 cm

'Charles Austin'

Austin UK 1973

'Chaucer' × 'Aloha'

Large, cupped, full blooms of apricot-yellow paling slightly with age. Very fragrant. Foliage mid-green, plentiful. Growth arching.

R H P CL VF ✂ AL 5′ × 5′ 1.5 × 1.5 m

'Charles Rennie Mackintosh' (AUSren)

Austin UK 1988

Seedling × 'Mary Rose'

Fully double flowers, cupped with muddled petals when fully open. Lilac-pink with a very strong

perfume. Foliage plentiful, mid-green, on a rugged, thorny, bushy shrub.
C ▽ B H CL VF ✂ AL 3′ 6″ × 3′ 110 × 90 cm

'Charmain' (AUSmain)

Austin U K 1982
Seedling × 'Lilian Austin'
Clusters of fully double, rich deep pink flowers opening flat with reflexing outer petals. Fragrant. Foliage semi-glossy, mid-green. Growth spreading and bushy.
C ▽ B H P VF AL 3′ 6″ × 3′ 6″ 1.1 × 1.1 m

'Chaucer'

Austin U K 1970
Seedling × 'Constance Spry'
Mid-pink blooms open cupped and quartered with a strong scent, produced in small clusters. Foliage mid-green. Growth vigorous but bushy, with a multitude of pink, viciously hooked thorns.
R ▽ B H VF M♂ AL 3′ 6″ × 3′ 110 × 90 cm

'Claire Rose' (AUSlight)

Austin U K 1986
'Charles Austin' × (seedling × 'Iceberg')
Fragrant, initially cupped flowers opening to many-petalled, flat, large, rosette shapes, clear blush-pink in colour fading to almost white when fully open. Foliage large, light green. Growth upright, vigorous.
R H P WW MF M♂ AL 4′ × 3′ 120 × 90 cm

'Cottage Rose' (AUSglisten)

Austin U K 1991
'Mary Rose' × 'Wife of Bath'
Medium-sized, fully double cupped blooms of warm pink produced throughout the summer. Fragrant. Foliage plentiful. Growth free-branching, bushy.
C ▽ H MF AL 3′ 6″ × 3′ 110 × 90 cm

'Country Living' (AUScountry)

Austin U K 1991
'Wife of Bath' × 'Graham Thomas'
Delicate pink flowers fading to almost white, cupped and made up of a multitude of short petals to form a perfect rosette. Foliage plentiful, small. Growth twiggy and bushy.
C ▽ SF AL 4′ × 3′ 120 × 90 cm

'Cressida' (AUScress)

Austin U K 1983
Beautiful, large, apricot-pink flowers open full, flat with somewhat muddled petals adding to its attractiveness and exuding a distinct myrrh-like fragrance. Foliage coarse, darkish-green. Growth vigorous, upright and thorny.
R H CL P MF M♂ AL 5′ × 4′ 1.5 × 1.2 m

'Dark Lady' (AUSbloom)

Austin U K 1991
'Mary Rose' × 'Prospero'
Large peony-like, fully double, loosely arranged flowers of deep rosy-red, strongly fragrant. Foliage dark green. Wider than tall.
R ▽ G H VF AL 3′ × 3′ 6″ 90 × 110 cm

'Dove' (AUSdove)

Austin U K 1984
'Wife of Bath' × 'Iceberg' seedling
Fully double, Hybrid Tea-like flowers at first, opening to loose, rosette form. Colour soft blush-pink to white and produced in small clusters. Slightly fragrant. Growth wide, bushy. Foliage mid- to dark green, semi-glossy.
C B P ✂ SF AL 3′ 6″ × 4′ 1.1 × 1.2 m

'Ellen' (AUScup)

Austin U K 1984
Flowers fully double, cupped, rich apricot in colour, deepening towards the centre. Very fragrant. Foliage large, mid-green. Growth dense, wide and bushy.
C H B ✂ VF M♂ AL 4′ × 4′ 1.2 × 1.2 m

'Emanuel' (AUSuel)

Austin U K 1985
('Chaucer' × 'Parade') × (seedling × 'Iceberg')
Freely produced large, rosette-shaped blooms of delicate blush pink with hints of gold deep in the centre of each bloom. Very fragrant. Foliage mid-green. Growth bushy, upright.
C ▽ H B ✂ VF AL 4′ × 3′ 120 × 90 cm

'English Elegance'

Austin U K 1986
Large, fully double blooms, blush pink at the edges with tints of bright pink, salmon and orange in the

'Fisherman's Friend', and left, 'English Garden'

centres. Foliage mid-green, growth arching, bushy and vigorous.

C ▽ H P ⊱< SF M⊙ AL 4′ × 3′ 6″ 1.2 × 1.1 m

'English Garden' (AUSbuff)

Austin UK 1987

'Lilian Austin' × (seedling × 'Iceberg')

The flat, rosette-like flowers, sizeable and with many petals, are pale yellow deepening towards the centre. Foliage mid-green. Growth compact and upright.

C H VF ▽ AL 4′ × 3′ 120 × 90 cm

'Evelyn' (AUSsaucer)

Austin UK 1991

'Graham Thomas' × 'Tamora'

Shallow, cup-shaped, fully double flowers of bright orange-apricot. Richly fragrant. Foliage plentiful, mid-green. Growth vigorous, bushy.

R ▽ H ⊱< VF AL 4′ × 3′ 120 × 90 cm

'Fair Bianca' (AUSca)

Austin UK 1982

Very double flowers opening flat and quartered, soft yellow and white in colour with reflexed edges. Fragrant. Foliage semi-glossy, mid- to light green. Growth short, upright and bushy.

C ▽ B H ⊱< MF M⊙ AL 3′ × 2′ 90 × 60 cm

'Financial Times Centenary' (AUSfin)

Austin UK 1988

Seedling × seedling

Highly fragrant, deep clear pink, globular flowers opening flat but blowsy. Foliage rich dark green. Growth strong and upright.

C ▽ B H ⊱< VF AL 3′ 6″ × 3′ 110 × 90 cm

'Gertrude Jekyll'

'Fisherman's Friend' (AUSchild)

Austin UK 1987

'Lilian Austin' × 'The Squire'

Rich crimson flowers, very large and full in the old style. Mid-green foliage on a robust plant.

C H VF ▽ AL 4′ × 3′ 120 × 90 cm

'Gertrude Jekyll' (AUSbord)

Austin UK 1987

'Wife of Bath' × 'Comte de Chambord'

Its deep pink, fully double flowers are in the old style, and are very fragrant. Greyish-green foliage comes on an upright, bushy plant.

C H VF AL 4′ × 3′ 120 × 90 cm

'Glamis Castle' (AUSlevel)

Austin UK 1992

'Graham Thomas' × 'Mary Rose'

Fully double cupped pure white flowers, produced very freely, with a fragrance of myrrh. Foliage mid-green. Growth compact and bushy.

C VF ▽ AW ✂ 3′ × 2′ 90 × 60 cm

'Graham Thomas' (AUSmas)

Austin UK 1983

Seedling × ('Charles Austin' × 'Iceberg' seedling)

A very good cultivar. The large, fully double, many-petalled flowers are in the old-fashioned style but with the modern colour of rich yellow with a deeper centre. Fragrant. Foliage dark green and glossy on a bushy plant.

C P H VF ▽ AW 4′ × 3′ 120 × 90 cm

'Heritage' (AUSblush)

Austin UK 1984

Seedling × 'Iceberg' seedling

Cupped, fully double flowers of light pink with deeper centres. Foliage smallish and dark green with a slight gloss. Growth bushy.

C H P VF ▽ AL 4′ × 4′ 1.2 × 1.2 m

'Hero' (AUShero)

Austin UK 1983

'The Prioress' × seedling

The eye-catching mid-pink blooms are cupped and moderately full. Foliage mid-green and semi-glossy. Growth upright and bushy.

C H VF ▽ AL 4′ × 4′ 1.2 × 1.2 m

'Hilda Murrell' (AUSmurr)

Austin UK 1984

Seedling × ('Parade' × 'Chaucer')

Shapely, fully double flowers opening flat and quartered, of a rich clear pink colouring and with a pure fragrance. Foliage mid-green, matt. Growth upright, bushy, a little shy in autumn.

R ▽ H P VF ✂ AW 4′ × 4′ 1.2 × 1.2 m

'Kathryn Morley' (AUSvariety)

Austin UK 1990

Clear soft pink, cup-shaped flowers with a delicious perfume, produced very freely on a broad, bushy,

'Graham Thomas', and below, 'Heritage'

low-growing plant amid plentiful, light green foliage.

C ▽ B H ✂ VF AL 3′ × 3′ 90 × 90 cm

'L. D. Braithwaite' (AUScrim)

Austin UK 1988

'The Squire' × 'Mary Rose'

Richly fragrant, fully double, heavy flattish blooms of rich glowing crimson with a hint of cerise. Very freely produced on a vigorous, wide-growing, bushy plant amid good greyish-green foliage.

R ▽ G ✂ VF AL 3′ × 4′ 90 × 120 cm

'Leander' (AUSlea)

Austin UK 1982

'Charles Austin' × seedling

Fragrant shapely flowers are made up of a multitude of deep apricot petals, to give a finished bloom in the style of the Gallica 'Charles de Mills'. Foliage glossy, dark green. Growth, tall, bushy and wide.

R ▽ G B Gh VF M⟳ AL 6′ × 5′ 1.8 × 1.5 m

'Lilian Austin'

Austin UK 1973

'Aloha' × 'The Yeoman'

The semi-double flowers of salmon-pink tinged apricot, deepening towards the centre, open flat and are produced in clusters. Foliage mid-green and glossy. Growth bushy and arching.

C SF AL 4′ × 4′ 1.2 × 1.2 m

'Lucetta' (AUSsemi)

Austin UK 1983

Clusters of very large, semi-double, scented flowers of soft blush-pink paling with age to white. Foliage mid-green. Growth wide and spreading.

R ▽ H G ◉ VF AL 4′ × 4′ 1.2 × 1.2 m

'Mary Rose' (AUSmary)

Austin UK 1983

Seedling × 'The Friar'

Very double flowers in the old-fashioned form, warm mid-pink with a deeper centre and cupped. Foliage glossy and mid-green. Upright and bushy growth.

C B VF ▽ AW 4′ × 3′ 120 × 90 cm

'Mary Rose', and above, 'Othello'

'Othello' (AUSlo)

Austin U K 1983

'Lilian Austin' × 'The Squire'

Rich dusky-crimson flowers, large, fully double and cupped changing to purple with age. Good perfume. Foliage dark green. Growth dense, bushy and upright bearing numerous vicious thorns.

C ▽ B H ⊰ VF M♂ AL 3′ 6″ × 2′ 6″ 110 × 75 cm

'Pat Austin' (AUSmum)

Austin U K 1995

Very bright copper, paler on reverse, semi-double to double, cupped. Very fragrant. A bright new colour to the Austin range. Foliage crisp, darkish-green. Growth vigorous, tall and bushy.

C H VF ⊰ AL 5′ × 4′ 1.5 × 1.2 m

'Perdita' (AUSperd)

Austin U K 1983

'The Friar' × (seedling × 'Iceberg')

Very fragrant, apricot-blush coloured, fully double, flat, quartered flowers borne amid dark green foliage on a dense, bushy plant.

C ▽ B H ⊰ SF AL 3′ 6″ × 2′ 6″ 110 × 75 cm

'Potter & Moore'

Austin U K 1988

'Wife of Bath' seedling

Large, rose pink flowers of many petals in the cupped style of the old Bourbons. Scented and very freely produced on a short, bushy plant with plenty of mid-green foliage.

C ▽ B H ⊰ VF AL 3′ × 3′ 90 × 90 cm

'Pretty Jessica' (AUSjess)

Austin U K 1983

'Wife of Bath' × seedling

Shapely, cupped blooms, fully double, of rich warm pink with a lovely perfume, produced in abundance on a bushy, tidy plant with ample mid-green foliage.

C ▽ B H ⊰ VF AL 2′ 6″ × 3′ 75 × 90 cm

'Prospero' (AUSpero)

Austin U K 1983

'The Knight' × unnamed seedling

Very dark red, fully double, very well-formed flowers in the style of the old double Gallicas,

ageing to purple. Very fragrant. Foliage matt, dark green. Growth spreading. Needs extra special care to thrive.

C ▽ B Gh ⊰ VF M♂ BS♂ AL 2′ × 3′ 60 × 90 cm

'Queen Nefertiti' (AUSap)

Austin U K 1988

Rosette blooms of good size, soft yellow brushed apricot. Fragrant. Foliage plentiful, mid-green. Growth bushy, branching freely.

C ▽ B H ⊰ VF AL 3′ × 2′ 6″ 90 × 75 cm

'Radio Times' (AUSsal)

Austin U K 1994

Rich pink fully double flowers of rosette shape. Very fragrant. Foliage mid-green. Growth short and bushy.

C ▽ B ⊰ VF AL 3′ × 2′ 90 × 60 cm

'Scepter'd Isle' (AUSland)

Austin U K 1996

Cupped flowers almost fully double, clear pink, opening to show off yellow stamens with a fragrance of myrrh. Foliage dark green. Growth upright, with flowers held on long stems.

C ▽ B ⊰ VF AL 3′ × 2′ 90 × 60 cm

'Sharifa Asma' (AUSreef)

Austin U K 1987

'Mary Rose × 'Admired Miranda'

Fragrant, cupped flowers open reflexed to form a very double rosette of delicate blush-pink, fading with age to almost pure white on the outer petals. Foliage mid-green. Growth arching and bushy.

C ▽ B H ⊰ VF AL 3′ × 2′ 6″ 90 × 75 cm

'Sir Walter Raleigh'

'Sir Edward Elgar' (AUSprima)

Austin UK 1992

Deep cerise to crimson cupped rosette-shaped double flowers, changing to purple with age. Foliage dark green. Growth upright and bushy.
C ▽ B SF AL 3′ × 3′ 90 × 90 cm

'Sir Walter Raleigh' (AUSspry)

Austin UK 1985

'Lilian Austin' × 'Chaucer'
Its peony-like flowers, cupped with open centres displaying golden stamens, are clear warm pink. Foliage large and mid-green. Growth bushy.
C H VF ▽ AL 4′ × 4′ 1.2 × 1.2 m

'Swan' (AUSwhite)

Austin UK 1987

'Charles Austin' × (seedling × 'Iceberg')
Huge, pure white, fully double, flat, rosette-shaped flowers with hints of buff as they open. Fragrant. Foliage soft mid-green. Growth vigorous, upright and shrubby.
R H W ⚬< VF AL 4′ × 3′ 6″ 1.2 × 1.1 m

'Sweet Juliet' (AUSleap)

Austin UK 1989

'Graham Thomas' × 'Admired Miranda'
Shallow, cupped, fragrant, apricot-yellow flowers produced in profusion on a bushy plant with plentiful, mid-green foliage.
C B H ⚬< VF AL 3′ 6″ × 3′ 110 × 90 cm

'Symphony' (AUSlett)

Austin UK 1986

'The Friar' × 'Yellow Cushion'
Soft yellow rosette-shaped flowers freely produced

'Symphony', and left, 'Sweet Juliet'

on a bushy, upright plant with an abundance of light green foliage. A delightful rose.
C ▽ B H ⚬< VF AL 3′ 6″ × 3′ 110 × 90 cm

'The Countryman' (AUSman)

Austin UK 1987

Seedling × 'Comte de Chambord'
Flat, many-petalled, rosette-shaped, old-fashioned style, fragrant flowers of bright rose pink. Foliage is abundant dark greyish-green. Growth dense and arching.
R ▽ B H ⚬< VF AW 3′ × 3′ 6″ 90 × 110 cm

'The Miller'

Austin UK 1970

'Baroness Rothschild' × 'Chaucer'
Rounded buds open to fully double, rosette-shaped blooms of mid-pink produced in small, evenly spaced clusters. Foliage mid-green, matt. Growth vigorous, upright, bushy and well armed with reddish thorns.
R H P ⚬< VF AL 6′ × 5′ 1.8 × 1.5 m

'The Nun'

Austin UK 1987

Sprays of deeply cupped (tulip-shaped) semi-double flowers of pure white, the deep-down stamens displayed to advantage. Foliage mid-green. Growth twiggy and upright.
C ▽ H B ⚬< SF AL 4′ × 3′ 120 × 90 cm

'The Pilgrim'

Austin UK 1991

Delicate, pure yellow, fully double flowers opening flat and evenly shaped. A special feature is its pleasing softness of texture. Very fragrant. Foliage healthy mid-green. Growth strong and bushy.
C H ✄ VF AL 3′6″ × 3′6″ 1.1 × 1.1 m

'The Prince' (AUSvelvet)

Austin UK 1990

Initially cupped, the flowers open to full rosette form, starting off as rich crimson and changing to royal purple as they develop. Very fragrant. Foliage is dark dusky green. Growth is low and bushy.
C ▽ B H ✄ VF AL 2′ × 2′ 60 × 60 cm

'The Prioress'

Austin UK 1969

'La Reine Victoria' × seedling
Semi-double, chalice-shaped flowers of blush-white displaying stamens to advantage when fully open. Fragrant. Foliage mid-green. Growth vigorously upright.
R ▽ H ✄ MF BS⚘ AL 4′ × 3′ 120 × 90 cm

'The Reeve'

Austin UK 1979

'Lilian Austin' × 'Chaucer'
Its deep pink, very double flowers are in the old-fashioned style and are produced in clusters. Reddish-green foliage. Growth bushy, spreading.
R H VF ▽ ✄ AL 4′ × 4′ 1.2 × 1.2 m

'The Squire'

Austin UK 1977

'The Knight' × 'Château de Clos Vougeot'
Very full, deeply cupped flowers of dark crimson. Fragrant. Foliage coarse dark green. Growth sparsely bushy, thorny.
R ▽ G MF M⚘ AL 3′ × 3′6″ 90 × 110 cm

'The Yeoman'

Austin UK 1969

'Ivory Fashion' × ('Constance Spry' × 'Monique')
The very full flattish flowers are salmon-pink and apricot. Mid-green foliage on a compact bush.
C H VF B ▽ ✄ AL 3′ × 2′ 90 × 60 cm

'Warwick Castle'

'Tradescant' (AUSdir)

Austin UK 1993

'Prospero' seedling
Deep glowing crimson fully double flowers, produced in clusters. Arching spreading growth with dark green foliage.
C B ▽ VF AL 2′ × 2′ 60 × 60 cm

'Trevor Griffiths' (AUSold)

Austin UK 1994

Flowers open flat and double, dusky deep pink in colour. Foliage darkish green. Growth angular, branching and spreading. Named for the celebrated New Zealand rose grower and author.
C B ▽ MF AL 3′ × 4′ 90 × 120 cm

'Troilus' (AUSoil)

Austin UK 1983

'Duchesse de Montebello' × 'Chaucer'
Deeply cupped, fully double flowers of honey-buff. Fragrant. Foliage mid-green. Growth sturdy and upright.
R H ✄ VF M⚘ AL 4′ × 4′ 1.2 × 1.2 m

'William Shakespeare'

'Warwick Castle' (AUSlian)

Austin UK 1986
'The Reeve' × 'Lilian Austin'
Shapely blooms of glowing pink packed with a multitude of small petals to form flat rosettes, produced in small, well-spaced clusters. Fragrant. Foliage greyish dark green. Growth spreading and bushy.
C ▽ B ✂ MF BS◌ AL 2′ × 2′ 6″ 60 × 75 cm

'Wenlock' (AUSwen)

Austin UK 1984
'The Knight' × 'Glastonbury'
Large, cupped, medium-full, fragrant blooms of mid-crimson, freely produced amid plentiful, dark green, semi-glossy foliage on a bushy, vigorous plant.
C H ✂ VF AL 4′ × 3′ 120 × 90 cm

'Wife of Bath'

Austin UK 1969
'Mme Caroline Testout' × ('Ma Perkins' × 'Constance Spry')
Flowers deep rose-pink with a paler reverse, semi-double and cupped. Foliage small and mid-green. Growth compact and bushy.
C H VF B ▽ ✂ AW 3′ × 2′ 90 × 60 cm

'William Shakespeare' (AUSroyal)

Austin UK 1987
'The Squire' × 'Mary Rose'
Fully double flowers in the old-fashioned style, of rich crimson turning to purple with age. Foliage dark green. Growth bushy.
C H VF B ▽ ✂ AL 4′ × 3′ 120 × 90 cm

'Winchester Cathedral' (AUScat)

Austin UK 1988
Sport from 'Mary Rose'
All the characteristics of its parent 'Mary Rose' except colour, which is white brushed buff in the centres.
C ▽ B H VF AW 4′ × 3′ 120 × 90 cm

'Wise Portia' (AUSport)

Austin UK 1982
'The Knight' × seedling
Very fragrant, mauve to purple, fully double flowers in profusion on a bushy plant with dark green, semi-glossy foliage.
C ▽ B H ✂ VF M◌ AL 2′ 6″ × 2′ 6″ 75 × 75 cm

'Yellow Button'

Austin UK 1975
'Wife of Bath' × 'Chinatown'
Soft yellow, full, button-like rosettes with deeper centres, produced freely on a wide-growing, compact bush well endowed with dark green foliage.
C ▽ B H G ✂ SF AL 3′ × 3′ 90 × 90 cm

'Yellow Charles Austin'

Austin UK 1981
Sport from 'Charles Austin'
All the characteristics of its parent 'Charles Austin' except colour, which is lemon-yellow.
R H P CL VF ✂ AL 5′ × 5′ 1.5 × 1.5 m

Hybrid Teas
(Large-flowered Roses)

The classification 'Hybrid Tea' covers all 'Hybrids of the Teas' but whilst a high-centred shape of flower is their main recognition feature, many modern cultivars now have a far more complex genealogy than the earlier ones.

Thousands have been raised and introduced since the first was named 'La France' in 1867 and many, probably deservedly, have quickly fallen by the wayside. Here are 40, comprising the best of the up-to-date cultivars and several of my special favourites; above all, I have tried to present a fair representation of the history of this much loved and auspicious group of roses.

Their uses are numerous. Many of the modern cultivars are almost as floriferous as Floribundas and lend themselves readily to bedding and massed display. Many will grow happily among other plants; in a herbaceous border, for example, they can be very effective. Only a few are good as hedging plants, but most, if not all, will make themselves at home growing in urns or tubs. Almost without exception they are good for providing flowers for cutting and taking indoors. Some, in the right hands, will win prizes at shows; and quite a few more will be quite happy grown under glass.

CLASSIFICATION

BARB	Class 5
MR10	Class 44
WFRS	Class 4

'Angèle Pernet'

Pernet-Ducher FRANCE 1924
'Bénédicte Sequin' × a Hybrid Tea
A beautiful rose of exquisite form and one of the most lovely to have come from the auspicious stable of Pernet-Ducher. Not an easy rose to grow and not the most free with its flowers, which are coppery-orange with no trace of garishness. Rich, dark, glossy foliage.
C MF ▽ AL 2′ × 2′ 60 × 60 cm

'Anna Pavlova'

Beales UK 1981
A beautiful, full, many-petalled cultivar with a strong scent, each flower of blush-pink with deeper shadings held on a very strong neck. When fully open, some petals are fimbriated. Foliage large,

'Anna Pavlova'

rounded and rich dark green. In poorer soils this rose is best left unpruned.

C VF E Gh WW ☼ ▽ ✄ AL 4′ × 3′ 120 × 90 cm

'Blessings'

Gregory UK 1967
'Queen Elizabeth' × seedling
A very free-flowering, shapely rose of soft salmon,

'Dainty Bess', and below, 'Dame Edith Helen'

producing ample foliage on dark stems. Its growth is fairly dense but upright. A good rose for massing in beds.

C MF B P ✄ AW 2′ 6″ × 2′ 75 × 60 cm

'Chrysler Imperial'

Lammerts GERMANY 1952
'Charlotte Armstrong' × 'Mirandy'
Pointed buds open to large, full, somewhat muddled, deep velvety-red flowers. Its foliage is dark green, its growth bushy and vigorous. This rose has a fair scent.

C SF B E AL 2′ 6″ × 2′ 75 × 60 cm

'Comtesse Vandal'

Leenders HOLLAND 1932
('Ophelia' × 'Mrs Aaron Ward') ×
'Souvenir de Claudius Pernet'
A very beautiful rose, especially to those who like their roses classically high-centred. Pointed, orange-toned buds open to pinky-apricot with deepening tones in the centre. A superb old cultivar, vigorous, bushy and well-foliated.

C MF Gh B E ▽ ✄ AL 2′ 6″ × 2′ 75 × 60 cm

'Crimson Glory'

Kordes GERMANY 1935
'Cathrine Kordes' seedling × 'W. E. Chaplin'
A fine old rose from the past, its large, globular, deep velvety-red blooms are superbly scented. They are, however, carried on a rather weak neck. Its foliage is dark green and a little sparse, with thorny stems on a bushy, angular plant.

C Gh B WW MF AL 2′ × 2′ 60 × 60 cm

'Dainty Bess'

Archer UK 1925
'Ophelia' × 'K of K'
A superb, single, Hybrid Tea whose large, silvery-rose-pink flowers are produced in well-spaced clusters. The effect is considerably enhanced by rich, golden-brown stamens. Sweetly scented, with large, healthy foliage.

C P H MF ▽ AL 3′ × 2′ 90 × 60 cm

'Dame Edith Helen'

Dickson UK 1926
Very large, many-petalled, cupped flowers, some-times opening quartered in the old-fashioned style,

of rich, deep, silvery-pink. The blooms are held on a strong neck. Glossy, mid-green foliage and of upright but bushy growth.

R VF ▽ WW AL 3′ × 2′ 90 × 60 cm

'Diamond Jubilee'

Boerner UK 1947
'Maréchal Niel' × 'Feu Pernet-Ducher'
One of the classic Hybrid Teas. Shapely, buff-apricot blooms are produced freely on a strong, healthy plant with leathery, dark green foliage.

C P E B ▽ Gh ✂ AL 3′ × 2′ 90 × 60 cm

'Double Delight' (ANDeli)

Swim & Ellis USA 1977
'Granada' × 'Garden Party'
Blooms large and reasonably full, creamy-white with pinkish-red brush strokes on the edge of the petals. A superb rose at its best but not easy to grow.

C Gh VF ▽ ○ WW AW 3′ × 2′ 90 × 60 cm

'Ellen Willmott'

Archer UK 1936
'Dainty Bess' × 'Lady Hillingdon'
A charming, single cultivar. Pronounced golden anthers framed by wavy petals of cream and pink. Growth vigorous and bushy with dark green foliage.

C ▽ B SF AL 4′ × 3′ 120 × 90 cm

'Éna Harkness'

Norman UK 1946
'Crimson Glory' × 'Southport'
Bright velvety-crimson blooms, very shapely and free-flowering though held on a weak neck. The foliage is a little sparse with thorny stems.

C P Gh MF B WW AL 2′ × 2′ 60 × 60 cm

'Étoile de Hollande'

Verschuren NETHERLANDS 1919
'General MacArthur' × 'Hadley'
'Étoile de Hollande' is seldom seen today except as a climber, but merits inclusion as an important rose from the past. Very fragrant, cloudy red blooms with dark green foliage, soft to the touch, on a plant of bushy, angular growth. A good forcer in its day.

C VF Gh M○ ✂ AL 2′ × 2′ 60 × 60 cm

'Diamond Jubilee', and below, 'Golden Melody'

'Golden Melody', 'Irene Churruca'

La Florida USA 1934
'Mme Butterfly' × ('Lady Hillingdon' × 'Souvenir de Claudius Pernet')
A beautiful rose, one of the best from the 1930s, with large, shapely, high-centred, moderately full blooms of soft yellowish-buff flushed pink with deeper centres. It has dark green foliage, with darker, almost maroon, stems and large, sparse thorns. A plant of angular growth.

C VF B E ▽ ✂ AL 2′ 6″ × 2′ 75 × 60 cm

'Helen Traubel'

'Grace Darling'

Bennett UK 1884

A very useful, older Hybrid Tea; indeed, one of the first to be introduced. Globular flowers of creamy-white with petal edges touched pink, scented and produced freely on rather angular but sturdy plants with dark, neat, grey-green foliage.

B R ☼ ▽ SF AL 3′ × 2′ 90 × 60 cm

'Grandpa Dickson', 'Irish Gold'

Dickson UK 1966

('Perfecta' × 'Governador Braga da Cruz') × 'Piccadilly'
Very large, graceful, shapely lemon-yellow blooms, sometimes faintly brushed pink. Fully open, they are often splashed pink. Strong and upright growth with ample, mid-green foliage, and very thorny.

C SF ▽ B E ✂ AW 2′ 6″ × 2′ 75 × 60 cm

'Helen Traubel'

Swim USA 1951

'Charlotte Armstrong' × 'Glowing Sunset'
A beautiful rose with long, pointed buds opening to pinkish-apricot. Rather a weak neck but many good points to make amends for this. Tall and upright, with large and darkish green foliage.

C H MF B WW AL 3′ 6″ × 2′ 105 × 60 cm

'Joanna Hill'

Hill USA 1928

'Mme Butterfly' × 'Miss Amelia Gude'
Long, pointed buds open to high-centred, full flowers of creamy-yellow flushed orange in the base. Like its famous parent, 'Mme Butterfly', expensively perfumed and classy. Foliage dark and leathery. Growth bushy. At times, temperamental.

C ▽ B Gh ✂ VF AL 2′ × 2′ 60 × 60 cm

'Just Joey'

Cant UK 1972

'Fragrant Cloud' × 'Dr A. J. Verhage'
A superb rose, its large, ragged-edged flowers are coppery-orange with soft pink paling at the edges when the flowers open. The foliage is dark green, leathery and semi-glossy on a rather angular plant.

C MF B ▽ ✂ AW 2′ × 2′ 60 × 60 cm

'Lady Mary Fitzwilliam'

Bennett UK 1882

'Devoniensis' × 'Victor Verdier'
Large, freely produced, soft pink flowers, flushed deeper pink. Shapely, high-centred and scented. Not over-vigorous but quite bushy. Ample, good, dark green foliage. This is a famous old rose, parent to many of the early British Hybrid Teas. A re-discovery at Caston, Norfolk, by Keith Money in 1975. Illustrated on page 33.

C MF B ▽ AL 2′ × 2′ 60 × 60 cm

'La France'

Guillot Fils FRANCE 1865

Probably 'Mme Falcot' seedling
Said to be the first Hybrid Tea ever introduced. High-centred flowers of silvery-pink borne in small clusters and scented, opening to show rather muddled centres. Bush upright and foliage mid-green. A beautiful if somewhat inconspicuous rose to carry the mantle of being the first of its race. Illustrated on page 33.

R Gh B ▽ VF AW 4′ × 3′ 120 × 90 cm

'Marchioness of Salisbury'

Pernet FRANCE 1890

Scented, very large, globular yet high-centred flowers of rich deep red, held erect by short, very stout stems. Foliage abundant with dark green leaves very closely packed on stems. Growth bushy and upright. One of the first deep red Hybrid Teas introduced.

R ▽ B Gh ✂ VF AL 2′ × 2′ 60 × 60 cm

'Michèle Meilland'

Meilland FRANCE 1945

'Joanna Hill' × 'Peace'
A classic from the past, with exquisitely formed creamy-buff blooms, shaded pink and salmon. Free-flowering on a bushy, upright plant with dark foliage and stems.

C MF B Gh ▽ ✂ ☼ AL 2′ × 2′ 60 × 60 cm

'Mme Louis Laperrière'

'Mme Louis Laperrière'

Laperrière FRANCE 1951

'Crimson Glory' × seedling

Rich deep crimson flowers are produced in profusion on an upright yet bushy plant with dark green, matt foliage. A very good cultivar, especially for bedding.

C P VF B ▽ AL 2′ × 2′ 60 × 60 cm

'Monique'

Paolino FRANCE 1949

'Lady Sylvia' × seedling

Shapely buds open to lovely, large, but well-proportioned flowers, cup-shaped with flattish tops, their colour an exquisite mixture of pinks. Matt, mid-green foliage and of upright and tidy growth.

C VF B ▽ ✂ AL 2′ 6″ × 2′ 75 × 60 cm

'Mrs Oakley Fisher'

Cant UK 1921

Large clusters of evenly spaced, deep buff-yellow, single flowers with pronounced amber stamens, and dark green, bronzy and semi-glossy foliage. The stems are plum-coloured and thorny. An eye-catcher from the past.

C P MF B ▽ AL 2′ × 2′ 60 × 60 cm

'Mrs Sam McGredy'

McGredy UK 1929

('Donald Macdonald' × 'Golden Emblem') × (seedling × 'Queen Alexandra Rose')

Large, slightly shaggy blooms of burnt-salmon-orange with their reverses flushed red and their centres yellow, and bronzy and glossy foliage, the stems dark. Awkward, angular growth.

R P MF B ▽ AL 3′ × 2′ 90 × 60 cm

'Mrs Oakley Fisher'

'Ophelia'

'Ophelia'

W. Paul UK 1912

Probably a seedling from 'Antoine Rivoire'

A classic. The superbly shaped soft pink blooms have a soft yellow base. Beautiful in bud and when fully open, displaying golden stamens to advantage. Dark green foliage on a plant of upright growth. The progenitor of several sports of equal stature, in particular 'Mme Butterfly' and 'Lady Sylvia'.

C P VF B Gh ▽ ✂ AL 2′ × 2′ 60 × 60 cm

'Peace', and right, 'Pinta', with 'Silver Jubilee' below

'Papa Meilland' (MEIsar)

Meilland FRANCE 1963

'Chrysler Imperial' × 'Charles Mallerin'
Superb, deep velvety-crimson blooms with obvious veining. Mid- to dark green, semi-glossy foliage on an upright plant with large thorns. Not an easy rose to grow but well worth the effort.
R VF M♂ BS♂ AW 3′ × 2′ 90 × 60 cm

'Peace', 'Gloria Dei', 'Mme A. Meilland', 'Gioia'

F. Meilland FRANCE 1945

('George Dickson' × 'Souvenir de Claudius Pernet') × ('Joanna Hill' × 'Chas. P. Kilham') × 'Margaret McGredy'
Perhaps the best known and one of the best loved roses of all time. Large, high-centred, opening cupped, sometimes delightfully ragged. Tending to vary in colour from soil to soil and even from day to day in the same garden. Most often creamy-yellow (sometimes almost golden-yellow in cooler weather), with a pinkish edging to each petal intensifying almost to red as the flower ages. Can be rather shy at times. Subtly perfumed. Beautiful deep green, glossy foliage plus a strong constitution makes this a superb rose for any garden. Unpruned, in good soil, much taller than the height stated.
C P H E ✂ SF AW 4′ × 3′ 120 × 90 cm

'Pinta'

Beales UK 1973

'Ena Harkness' × 'Pascali'
Very free-flowering, with clusters of shapely, creamy-white flowers on a robust, slightly angular plant with dark green stems and mid-green, matt-finished foliage. A special feature is the distinct fragrance of eglantine.
C P H VF E R W ▽ AW 3′ 6″ × 2′ 6″ 105 × 75 cm

'Royal William', 'Duftzauber '84' (KORzaun)

Kordes GERMANY 1984

'Feuerzauber' × seedling
High-centred, deep red and shapely blooms are freely produced on an upright plant with dark green, semi-glossy foliage.
C B MF ▽ ✂ AW 2′ 6″ × 2′ 75 × 60 cm

'Shot Silk'

Dickson UK 1924

'Hugh Dickson' seedling × 'Sunstar'

Without doubt one of the best of the Dickson roses from before the Second World War. Globular, full, high-centred flowers of near salmon with a yellow base and a silky sheen. Luxuriant foliage, plentiful and glossy. Growth bushy, upright and shortish.

C H Gh B MF ▽ ✄ AL 1′ 6″ × 1′ 6″ 45 × 45 cm

'Silver Jubilee'

Cocker UK 1978

[('Highlight' × 'Colour Wonder') ×
('Parkdirektor Riggers' × 'Piccadilly')] × 'Mischief'

A shapely, very free-flowering rose of silvery-pink and apricot with a deeper reverse. The flowers are produced in clusters; disbudded, they become huge. Foliage glossy. Growth very bushy but upright, the stems amply endowed with thorns. One of the best roses ever raised.

C P MF H Gh B E ▽ ✄ AW 3′ 6″ × 2′ 105 × 60 cm

'Sir Frederick Ashton'

Beales UK 1985

Sport from 'Anna Pavlova'

Very highly scented, large, full blooms of pure white with creamy centres. Foliage large, rounded and dark matt green. Stems strong, from upright growth.

C VF E Gh WW ☼ AL 4′ × 3′ 120 × 90 cm

'Soleil d'Or'

Pernet-Ducher FRANCE 1900

'Antoine Ducher' × *R. foetida persiana*

An important rose, being with 'Rayon d'Or' one of

'Violinista Costa', and above, 'Sir Frederick Ashton'

'White Wings'

the 'Pernettiana' roses, significant as the source of most of the yellow and bright colours in today's roses. This classification has since been dropped and such roses are now included in Hybrid Teas. 'Soleil d'Or' is very large and double, opening to a cupped, flattish flower with a muddled centre, fragrant, deep orange-yellow to tawny-gold shaded red. Foliage rich green on a thorny plant.
R Gh P ▽ WW VF AL 3′ × 3′ 90 × 90 cm

'Sutter's Gold'

Swim USA 1950
'Charlotte Armstrong' × 'Signora'
Very free-flowering, the slim buds held on long, strong necks open to loosely formed, attractive flowers of deep yellow brushed and shaded with orange and pink. Foliage mid-green and semi-glossy. Growth upright but bushy.
C P MF B Gh ▽ ⤚ AW 3′ × 2′ 90 × 60 cm

'The Doctor'

Howard USA 1936
'Mrs J. D. Eisele' × 'Los Angeles'
A famous cultivar which, despite a martyrdom to

black spot, should not be allowed to vanish into oblivion. It has large flowers of rich silver-pink with a satin sheen, shapely and high-centred at the mid-open stage. Foliage matt grey-green. Growth vigorous and upright.
C VF B E ▽ BS◯ WW ⤚ AL 2′ 6″ × 2′ 75 × 60 cm

'Violinista Costa'

Camprubi SPAIN 1936
'Sensation' × 'Shot Silk'
Shapely flowers, freely produced, of deep orange-pink with deeper undertones and a yellow base, at times almost red. Foliage mid-green, glossy, the stems well armed with thorns. Growth angular.
C P H B SF ▽ AL 2′ 6″ × 2′ 75 × 60 cm

'White Wings'

Krebs USA 1947
'Dainty Bess' × seedling
Long, pointed buds open to large, single, pure white flowers with pronounced chocolate-brown stamens. A beautiful rose when the right situation is found. Foliage mid-green and matt. Growth bushy.
C MF ▽ ◌ AL 3′ 6″ × 3′ 6″ 110 × 75 cm

Climbing Hybrid Teas
(Large-flowered Climbers)

From time to time during their lifetimes, some cultivars of Hybrid Teas (as with Floribundas, see page 305) have spontaneously produced a climbing shoot from an otherwise non-climbing plant. The reason is genetic and the survival of the new form depends upon the nurseryman reproducing the shoot by budding and grafting. Many Hybrid Teas make very worthy climbers, the best of which are described here. They make good wall subjects, but because of their vigour and lanky growth need training to give of their best.

CLASSIFICATION

BARB   Class 10
MR10   Class 12
WFRS   Class 17

'Allen Chandler'

Chandler USA 1923

'Hugh Dickson' × seedling

A sturdy, healthy rose of brilliant red. Large, semi-double flowers displaying golden stamens to advantage. A good, repeat-flowering cultivar with dark green foliage.

R P SF AL 12′ × 8′ 3.5 × 2.5 m

'Bettina' Climbing

Bush form Meilland FRANCE 1953

'Peace' × ('Mme Joseph Perraud' × 'Demain')

This form Meilland FRANCE 1958

Shapely, cupped flowers opening flat; orange suffused with salmon. Foliage very dark green on relatively thornless stems. Needs a sheltered, warm situation to thrive.

S ☼ ✂ VF AL 15′ × 8′ 4.5 × 2.5 m

'Blessings' Climbing

Bush form Gregory UK 1967

'Queen Elizabeth' × seedling

This form Gregory UK 1968

A shapely rose of soft salmon, highly scented. Growth vigorous, with ample mid-green foliage.

S P MF ✂ AL 15′ × 8′ 4.5 × 2.5 m

'Captain Christy' Climbing

Bush form Lacharme FRANCE 1873

'Victor Verdier' × 'Safrano'

This form Ducher FRANCE 1881

Semi-double soft pink with deeper pink centres, cupped until fully open. Flowers generously produced and fragrant, occasionally repeated in the autumn. Growth upright and vigorous with mid-green foliage.

R P VF AL 15′ × 8′ 4.5 × 2.5 m

'Allen Chandler'

'Captain Christy' Climbing

'Columbia Climber'

'Château de Clos Vougeot' Climbing

Bush form Pernet-Ducher FRANCE 1908

This form Morse UK 1920

Flowers of a superb, deep velvety red, highly scented. An awkward rose, however, with angular growth and sprawly habit. Shoots relatively thornless. Foliage dark green but rather sparse.

S VF AL 15′ × 8′ 4.5 × 2.5 m

'Christine' Climbing

Bush form McGredy UK 1918

This form Willink IRELAND 1936

Shapely flowers of rich golden yellow, semi-double and unusually well-scented for a yellow. Growth upright and foliage medium-sized, mid- to light green.

S P VF AL 12′ × 8′ 3.5 × 2.5 m

'Columbia Climber'

Bush form Hill & Co USA 1916

'Opelia' × 'Mrs George Sawyer'

This form Lens BELGIUM 1929

I have only recently discovered the true name of this rose. The blooms are large, full, highly scented and rosy-pink in colour. They are produced amid good mid-green foliage on a medium-vigorous plant. My thanks to Vivian Russell for introducing me to this seductive cultivar.

R ▽ Gh ☼ VF ✂ AL 8′ × 5′ 2.5 × 1.5 m

'Comtesse Vandal' Climbing

Bush form Leenders HOLLAND 1932

('Ophelia' × 'Mrs Aaron Ward') × 'Souvenir de Claudius Pernet'

This form Jackson & Perkins USA 1936

A very beautiful, rather elegant rose with long pointed buds opening to loosely formed flowers of silvery-buff pink with orange shadings and deeper reverse. Slightly scented. Growth vigorous and upright. Foliage large and dark green.

S P ✂ SF AL 12′ × 8′ 3.5 × 2.5 m

'Crimson Conquest'

Chaplin Bros UK 1931

'Red Letter Day' sport
Medium-sized, semi-double, rich crimson flowers on a healthy plant with dark green, glossy foliage. An excellent, underrated climbing rose, perpetuating a famous old bush Hybrid Tea now extinct.

S N P ● SF AL 15′ × 8′ 4.5 × 2.5 m

'Crimson Glory' Climbing

Bush form Kordes GERMANY 1935

'Cathrine Kordes' seedling × 'W. E. Chaplin'

This form Jackson & Perkins USA 1946

The climbing form of this famous Hybrid Tea makes an excellent specimen. The colour speaks for itself. Blooms velvety and very full of petals. Its notoriously weak neck is an advantage since, as it climbs higher, the flowers can hang down to effect. Has a strong, heady perfume. Wood reddish-brown and foliage dark green.

S P ✂ VF AL 15′ × 8′ 4.5 × 2.5 m

'Cupid'

B. R. Cant UK 1915

A lovely single cultivar. Superbly formed, large, peachy-pink flowers with a yellow base and pronounced golden anthers. Sometimes rather shy but worth growing even for one perfect bloom each year; however, it occasionally repeats in autumn. A specimen I saw in New Zealand belies its reputation for shyness.

S P N ● SF AL 10′ × 6′ 3 × 1.8 m

'Cupid'

'Eden Rose' Climbing

Bush form F. Meilland FRANCE 1953

'Peace' × 'Signora'

This form F. Meilland FRANCE 1962

The shapely, large, high-centred bud opens to a blowsy, fully double bloom of bright pink with silvery highlights. Very fragrant. Foliage large, crisp and glossy, produced on thick, strong stems. Very vigorous.
S P N ◍ VF AL 15′ × 10′ 4.5 × 3 m

'Ena Harkness' Climbing

Bush form Norman 1946

'Crimson Glory' × 'Southport'

This form Murrell UK 1954

Flowers shapely in the Hybrid Tea style, with pointed buds of rich velvety crimson, highly scented. The weak neck inherited from its parent 'Crimson Glory' can be an advantage in the climber. Wood dark and thorny with plentiful dark, matt-green foliage.
S P ✄ VF AL 15′ × 8′ 4.5 × 2.5 m

'Étoile de Hollande' Climbing

Bush form Verschuren HOLLAND 1919

'General MacArthur' × 'Hadley'

This form Leenders HOLLAND 1931

A red rose, very famous and popular between the wars. Superbly fragrant. Rich velvety red with shapely flowers – turning purple with age – its only fault. Shoots plum-coloured and foliage dull dark green.
S M♂ VF AL 12′ × 8′ 3.5 × 2.5 m

'Fragrant Cloud' Climbing

Bush form Tantau GERMANY 1963

This form Collin UK 1973

Seedling × 'Prima Ballerina'
Its shapely blooms are coral-red, though variable. Foliage dark reddish-green. Growth upright, sturdy.
S VF ✄ BS♂ AL 12′ × 8′ 3.5 × 2.5 m

'General MacArthur' Climbing

Bush form E. G. Hill & Co. USA 1905

This form Dickson UK 1923

Large, deep, rosy-red, highly scented, loosely formed blooms emerge from pointed buds. Free-flowering and very vigorous. Wood maroon with large dark green leaves.
S P VF AL 18′ × 10′ 5.5 × 3 m

'Golden Dawn' Climbing

Bush form Grant AUSTRALIA 1929

'Elegante' × 'Ethel Somerset'

This form LeGrice UK 1947

Its name is rather misleading in that its colour is yellow with hints of pink. Flowers large and globular, with a strong, sweet perfume. Foliage quite

'Étoile de Hollande'

striking, dark green overlaid with copper. Vigorous and healthy.

S N P ◉ VF AL 12′ × 8′ 3.5 × 2.5 m

'Grandmère Jenny' Climbing

Bush form Meilland FRANCE 1950

'Peace' × ('Julien Potin' × 'Sensation')

This form Meilland FRANCE 1958

The long pointed buds produce flowers of considerable size. Their colour is primrose overlaid with copper and pink. Sounds vulgar but the effect is quite refined. Growth is vigorous, foliage large and very dark green.

S P ✂ MF AL 18′ × 10′ 5.5 × 3 m

'Guinée'

Mallerin FRANCE 1938

'Souvenir de Claudius Denoyel' × 'Ami Quinard'

Very dark crimson, the double flowers emerge from rather tubby buds to open flat and display golden-brown anthers, surrounded by velvety-textured petals. Fragrant. A superb cultivar with dark wood and dark green foliage. Sometimes produces a second flush in the autumn.

R P VF AL 15′ × 8′ 4.5 × 2.5 m

'Home Sweet Home' Climbing

Bush form Wood & Ingram UK

This form origin unknown

Large, globular flowers of pure rose-pink with a large number of velvety-textured petals and considerable scent. Thick, very vigorous stems. Well endowed with large, dark foliage.

S P VF AL 15′ × 8′ 4.5 × 2.5 m

'Irish Fireflame' Climbing

Bush form Dickson UK 1914

This form Dickson UK 1916

Large, single flowers with pronounced anthers, a mixture of quiet orange, yellow and peach, the name belying its refinement. A healthy shrub, which is not too tall. Ideal for pillar work, especially as it often repeats in the autumn. Foliage dark green.

R AL 10′ × 6′ 3 × 1.8 m

'Josephine Bruce' Climbing

Bush form Bees UK 1949

'Crimson Glory' × 'Madge Whipp'

'Guinée', and below, 'Lady Sylvia' Climbing

This form Bees UK 1954

Fully double flowers of deep velvety red, at times quite blackish. Highly scented. As a climber, it is superior to the bush form. Foliage is plentiful, dull, dark green, and borne on vigorous thorny stems.

S P VF AL 15′ × 10′ 4.5 × 3 m

'Lady Sylvia' Climbing

Bush form Stevens UK 1926

'Mme Butterfly' sport

This form Stevens UK 1933

One of the most popular roses of the 1930s. Shapely buds, opening to full flowers of flesh-pink with deeper undertones, and a fine perfume. Makes an outstanding climber with an upright habit and grey-green foliage. Good for cutting.

S Gh P ✂ VF AL 15′ × 10′ 4.5 × 3 m

'Lady Waterlow'

G. Nabonnand FRANCE 1903

'La France de '89' × 'Mme Marie Lavalley'

Semi-double flowers of soft pink with deeper undertones and veining, particularly at the edges of

the petals. A healthy, robust climber, amply foliated and upright in growth. Scented.
S P N ◉ MF AL 15′ × 8′ 4.5 × 2.5 m

'Meg'

Gosset UK 1954

Thought to be 'Paul's Lemon Pillar' × 'Mme Butterfly'

An outstandingly beautiful climber. The large, almost single flowers are scented, and have pronounced russet-red stamens and petals of buff-yellow, flushed apricot and peach. The foliage is dark green, glossy and healthy.
R P MF AL 8′ × 4′ 2.5 × 1.2 m

'Mme Abel Chatenay' Climbing

Bush form Pernet-Ducher FRANCE 1895

'Dr Grill' × 'Victor Verdier'

This form Page UK 1917

One of the early climbing Hybrid Teas and still worth garden space even at the exclusion of others. Flowers globular but pointed, scented, soft silky-pink with a deeper centre when open. I suspect that over the years this rose may have lost some vigour. Foliage small but dense and dark green. Growth rather angular and thorny. Illustrated on page 35.
R VF AL 10′ × 8′ 3 × 2.5 m

'Mme Butterfly' Climbing

Bush form Hill & Co. USA 1918

'Ophelia' sport

This form E. P. Smith UK 1926

Shapely scrolled buds open to full, pale soft pink flowers with a fine perfume, strong-necked, good for cutting. Grey-green foliage on an upright vigorous plant.
S Gh P ✂< VF AL 15′ × 10′ 4.5 × 3 m

'Mme Caroline Testout' Climbing

Bush form Pernet-Ducher FRANCE 1890

'Mme de Tartas' × 'Lady Mary Fitzwilliam'

This form Chauvry FRANCE 1901

A very vigorous climber with lush grey-green foliage and thick, upright, thorny shoots. Flowers large, cabbage-like, deep silvery-pink, with a strong perfume. Sometimes remontant.
R P N ◉ VF AL 15′ × 8′ 4.5 × 2.5 m

'Mme Édouard Herriot' Climbing, 'Daily Mail Rose' Climbing

Bush form Pernet-Ducher FRANCE 1913

'Mme Caroline Testout' × a Hybrid Tea

This form Ketten Bros LUXEMBOURG 1921

A vigorous climbing rose, coral with a faint yellow base. Pointed buds open loosely to semi-double, flattish flowers. Growth upright and thorny with brownish flecks on the bark. Foliage light green.
S MF AL 12′ × 8′ 3.5 × 2.5 m

'Mme Grégoire Staechelin', 'Spanish Beauty'

Dot SPAIN 1927

'Frau Karl Druschki' × 'Château de Clos Vougeot'
A climbing rose of exceptional vigour. The large pale-pink flowers have a deeper pink reverse and are heavily veined at the edges. Early-flowering and very free-blooming. Growth vigorous and foliage dark green. If it is not dead-headed it produces superb, large, orange-red hips in the autumn. An excellent cultivar.
R F P N ◉ VF AL 15′ × 10′ 4.5 × 3 m

'Mme Henri Guillot' Climbing

Bush form Mallerin FRANCE 1938

'Rochefort' × R. foetida bicolor seedling

This form Meilland FRANCE 1942

Large, rather loose semi-double flowers of deep, burnt orange. Not much scent. A vigorous grower with plentiful dark green leaves.
S P N ◉ SF AL 15′ × 10′ 4.5 × 3 m

'Mme Grégoire Staechelin', and below, 'Meg'
opposite, 'Mme Caroline Testout' Climbing

'Mrs Aaron Ward' Climbing

Bush form Pernet-Ducher FRANCE 1907

This form Dickson UK 1922

High-centred buds opening to shapely flowers of
creamy yellow flushed pink, occasionally deeper in
dull weather, free-flowering, scented. Strong growth
with plenty of dark green foliage.

S P MF AL 15′ × 8′ 4.5 × 2.5 m

'Mrs G. A. van Rossem' Climbing

Bush form Van Rossem HOLLAND 1929

'Souvenir de Claudius Pernet' × 'Gorgeous'

This form Gaujard FRANCE 1937

Large globular buds opening to flowers of orange
and apricot on a yellow backcloth with a much
deeper reverse. Growth strong and upright. Foliage
highly glossed; rich dark green shoots have only
a few thorns.

S P SF AL 12′ × 10′ 3.5 × 3 m

'Mrs Herbert Stevens' Climbing

Bush form McGredy UK 1910

'Frau Karl Druschki' × 'Niphetos'

This form Pernet-Ducher FRANCE 1922

One of the best white climbers. Shapely flowers produced in quantity, superbly scented. Foliage dark, on vigorous shoots. An old favourite, frequently found in older gardens and often sent to me for identification. Quite happy in difficult situations.
R P N ◐ ⚔ VF AW 12′ × 8′ 3.5 × 2.5 m

'Mrs Sam McGredy' Climbing

Bush form McGredy IRELAND 1929

('Donald Macdonald' × 'Golden Emblem') × (seedling × 'Queen Alexandra Rose')

This form Buisman HOLLAND 1937

Very vigorous rose with coppery-red foliage and orange-red young shoots. Flowers shaggy when fully open, fiery copper-orange and scented. Needs plenty of space to develop fully.
R P N ◐ ⚔ MF AL 20′ × 15′ 6 × 4.5 m

'Ophelia' Climbing

Bush form W. Paul UK 1912

This form Dickson IRELAND 1920

Shapely buds opening soft flesh-pink with deeper shadings and light yellow tints in the centre. Has a strong fragrance. Upright in growth with plenty of foliage.
R P ⚔ VF AL 15′ × 10′ 4.5 × 3 m

'Paul Lédé' Climbing, 'Mons. Paul Lédé'

Bush form Pernet-Ducher FRANCE 1902

This form Lowe UK 1913

Large, shapely flowers of soft pink with peachy shadings in the base, sweetly scented and free-flowering. Foliage plentiful and mid-green. Seldom seen but a sight to remember in full flush.
R P VF AL 12′ × 8′ 3.5 × 2.5 m

'Paul's Lemon Pillar'

Paul UK 1915

'Frau Karl Druschki' × 'Maréchal Niel'
Massive blooms of creamy-white suffused with lemon; of unusually high quality in most weathers. Scented. A vigorous climber with very thick branches and large, dark green leaves. A deservedly popular old cultivar.
S P N ◐ ⚔ VF AL 15′ × 10′ 4.5 × 3 m

'Paul Lédé' Climbing, and below, 'Paul's Lemon Pillar'

'Picture' Climbing

Bush form McGredy UK 1932

This form Swim USA 1942

Flowers not large but shapely, rich clear pink, suffused with many other shades of pink. Scented. An upright grower with plenty of prickles and ample, if somewhat small foliage.
S P ⚔ VF AL 15′ × 8′ 4.5 × 2.5 m

'Reine Marie Henriette'

F. Levet FRANCE 1878

'Mme Bérard' × 'Général Jacqueminot'
Large, loosely double flowers, deep cherry-red, very

'Réveil Dijonnais'

free-flowering and scented. Foliage large, leathery and dark green. Stems maroon, with few thorns. Vigorous.

R VF AL 12′ × 8′ 3.5 × 2.5 m

'Réveil Dijonnais'

Buatois FRANCE 1931

'Eugène Fürst' × 'Constance'

A striking rose. Loosely formed, semi-double flowers of vivid orange, red and yellow, slightly fragrant. Prolific light green leaves and very thorny stems.

R P N ◉ SF AL 10′ × 6′ 3 × 1.8 m

'Richmond' Climbing

Bush form E. G. Hill & Co. USA 1905

'Lady Battersea' × 'Liberty'

This form Dickson UK 1912

Variable, from light carmine to scarlet, semi-double, scented blooms cupped initially, opening flattish, freely produced. Foliage dark green with upright growth.

S N P SF AL 10′ × 6′ 3 × 1.8 m

'Roundelay'

Bush form Swim USA 1954

'Charlotte Armstrong' × 'Floradora'

This form Langbecker AUSTRALIA 1970

Large trusses of cardinal-red flowers, fully double, opening flat, with a good fragrance. Foliage dark green. Stems dark, with large angular thorns. In all respects a good rose. Summer flowering, with a few more in autumn.

R P ◉ VF AL 10′ × 8′ 3 × 2.5 m

'Shot Silk' Climbing

Bush form Dickson UK 1924

'Hugh Dickson' seedling × 'Sunstar'

This form C. Knight AUSTRALIA 1931

A popular cultivar, one of the nicest and most reliable. Fully double, cupped flowers, soft cherry-cerise with golden-yellow and lemon base, fragrant, freely produced. Petal texture silky, but stands up to weather very well. Foliage lush dark green and plentiful.

R P N ◉ ✁ VF AW 18′ × 10′ 5.5 × 3 m

'Souvenir de Claudius Denoyel'

Chambard FRANCE 1920

'Château de Clos Vougeot' × 'Commandeur Jules Gravereaux'

Shapely, double, cupped flowers of rich red to scarlet, produced in loose clusters. Fragrant. Foliage large and darkish green. Growth vigorous and rather angular. Not the easiest to grow.

R VF AL 12′ × 8′ 3.5 × 2.5 m

'Spek's Yellow' Climbing, 'Golden Sceptre'

Bush form Verschuren-Pechtold HOLLAND 1950

'Golden Rapture' × unnamed seedling

This form Walters USA 1956

Double, rich golden-yellow flowers from pointed, shapely buds with long stems, ideal for cutting. Foliage particularly good, light green and glossy. Growth upright and vigorous.

S N P Gh ◉ ✁ MF AL 15′ × 10′ 4.5 × 3 m

'Sutter's Gold' Climbing

Bush form Swim USA 1950

This form Weeks USA 1950

'Charlotte Armstrong' × 'Signora'

Slim buds held on long stems open loosely to deep yellow flowers brushed orange and pink. Foliage mid-green and semi-glossy. Growth upright.

S P VF AW 12′ × 8′ 3.5 × 2.5 m

'Vicomtesse Pierre du Fou'

'Talisman' Climbing

Bush form Montgomery & Co. USA 1929

'Ophelia' × 'Souvenir de Claudius Pernet'

This form Western Rose Co. USA 1930
Fully double flowers, golden-yellow with orange and copper highlights. Foliage tough and leathery on vigorous, upright, thorny shoots.
S P ✂ SF AL 12′ × 8′ 3.5 × 2.5 m

'Vicomtesse Pierre du Fou'

Sauvageot FRANCE 1923
'L'Idéal' × 'Joseph Hill'
The luxuriant, glossy foliage of copper-dark green makes an ideal foil for the fragrant, double, loosely quartered flowers, which are coppery-pink when fully open. Vigorous and branching in habit.
R P N ◉ MF AL 15′ × 10′ 4.5 × 3 m

'Whisky Mac' Climbing (ANDmac)

Bush form Tantau GERMANY 1967

This form Anderson UK 1985
Shapely blooms of rich golden-amber, with dark green, semi-glossy foliage on an upright plant. Needs placing in a sheltered, warm position to thrive in colder districts.
S VF ✂ AL 12′ × 8′ 3.5 × 2.5 m

PART V

The Cultivation of Roses

Choosing and Buying Roses

Unless you have a good all-round knowledge of roses to the point where you know the foibles and limitations of those you wish to grow, choosing roses is not a straightforward exercise. It is not like buying a manufactured commodity. A spade is a spade and, as a general rule, will be as good as the price you wish to pay. While the adage 'you get what you pay for' can be applied to roses in the commodity sense, often depending on where you buy them, it does not necessarily follow that a more expensive cultivar in any one catalogue will be any better than a less expensive one of the same colour. It could be worse, in fact, for the pricing of different cultivars is not determined by their size or quality. It is usually calculated by balancing the following factors: the degree of difficulty in producing the rose, the length of time it has been on the market, the royalty the nurseryman has to pay to its raiser, its rarity and the likely demand in comparison to other cultivars.

Roses can be purchased in three different ways. By far the most common way and undoubtedly the best is direct from the nursery which has produced them, usually by mail order. Most such roses are termed 'bare root' or 'open ground' plants. In Britain the rose industry is well served by the BRGA (British Rose Growers' Association), an organization which is run by its members and is consumer-orientated, setting standards of quality and service to the public besides attending to the needs of its membership. There is no price fixing within the industry, so prices vary from nursery to nursery and region to region, but by and large a rose purchased from a member of the Association should be at least up to the standard recommended as first-class quality by the British Standards Institute. Other countries have similar guidelines for growers. This does not mean that there are no good growers outside the BRGA, of course, but beware of cheap roses, for inferior stock sometimes finds its way on to the market through dealers who have never grown a rose themselves. Such roses may be sub-standard, wrongly labelled or both – you may be lucky but not often.

The second way to purchase roses is in containers. These are usually obtained from garden centres, although many specialist growers offer a selection. They are seldom, if ever, sent by mail order. Those bought from garden centres will have been acquired for resale from a wholesale grower. Containerized roses are becoming very popular – though the range of cultivars on offer is often limited – because they have the one clear advantage that you can see what you are buying. They are usually sold in spring and summer when it is impossible to plant bare-root specimens. It is also possible to buy root-wrapped plants from garden centres, usually in the spring. These are bare-root plants placed in a polythene bag with damp peat to keep them fresh.

The third method of purchase is through a shop or store. Roses sold through these outlets are usually packaged in polythene, often with an exaggerated colour picture of their contents displayed on the bag. If you intend to buy such roses, examine them carefully; and if they are at all dry or have less than two strong shoots at a minimum – think twice.

It is important to buy roses only of the highest quality, for if you start with good plants they give far better value for money over the years. There is no doubt, however, that roses are best bought freshly dug from a nurseryman who has grown them himself. He is usually confident of his product and will seldom decline to replace any that fail to grow during the first few weeks of the growing season after purchase.

As for selecting cultivars, again there is no better place than a nursery to see roses growing, either in the fields or in a display garden. Some roses are more photogenic than others and printing processes vary too, so although most catalogues are written in a helpful way, try not to make your choice from pictures alone. Decide on your needs from written descriptions and speak to someone who knows. Most specialist rose growers are too concerned with their reputation to sell you something you don't want or a cultivar that is not up to your needs.

Flower shows provide good opportunities to see roses, but sometimes those on display have been produced under glass, especially for spring shows, so do not order without first speaking to the grower. Once you have made your choice, order early. Bare-root roses can be safely planted at any time during the dormant season, but if you wish to plant them in November you will need to order by midsummer at the latest. As most nurseries dig up and dispatch their orders in rotation as received (and most good growers deal with thousands of orders in the lifting season), it is, therefore, impossible to send them all out at the same time. Another good reason for not ordering late is that if a cultivar is in short supply or in demand, you will be disappointed and it may well be too late to place an order elsewhere. This applies particularly to rare and unusual cultivars and to those newly on offer. If you do have to place an order late in the season, prepare a small piece of ground by covering it with frost-proof material in readiness for your roses so that they can be heeled-in whatever the weather. Most nurseries will try to avoid sending roses during severe, frosty spells but sometimes, when the weather changes suddenly after dispatch, they are caught out. If the ground is too hard for heeling-in when the roses arrive, plunge their roots (still in their bundle) into a bucket or box of soil or sand and leave them in the garage or a shed until the weather improves. Those that look a little dry on arrival should be completely buried for a couple of weeks; no harm will come to them and they will be as good as new when dug up.

N.B. An availability rating is given to each rose in the Dictionary section.

BUYING CONTAINERIZED ROSES

Roses can be bought, already flowering, in containers. They are naturally more expensive than bare-root stock because of the extra work and material needed to produce them. Many garden

A container rose

centres offer a range of both modern and old-fashioned roses in this form. Some people prefer not to buy such roses and whereas I agree there is no substitute for traditional winter planting, containerized roses are certainly here to stay and will become available in increasing numbers. Provided we learn to adapt to the new techniques of planting and aftercare, buying roses in full flower can be a worthwhile and pleasant experience.

SUCKERS AND UNDERSTOCKS

A rose planted from the nursery actually comprises two different roses, the roots being one species, i.e. the stock, and the shoots another, i.e. the cultivar chosen. When it is planted the root sometimes decides to become independent and send up a shoot of its own; this is called suckering. Since the roots of the stock are usually more vigorous than their enforced guest, the shoot or shoots, if allowed to grow, will eventually take over and smother the cultivar. Suckers, when they appear, should be removed before they have a chance to grow to any size. Experience will enable a gardener to recognize them as slightly different from the young shoots which sprout on the stems above the ground, for suckers always appear from below ground level and

Examples of a good-quality and a poor-quality plant

A badly planted rose with suckers

often some little distance from the plant. It used to be said that shoots from the rootstock had leaves comprised of seven leaflets and that the leaves of the proper rose were made up of five. This has never been a very reliable guide to the recognition of suckers even on modern hybrid roses and should be treated almost as an old wives' tale. It is even less true in the case of the species, old-fashioned shrub roses, climbers and ramblers, since many of them have the same number of leaflets per leaf as those of the rootstock. If doubtful, scrape a little soil away from the rose bush and try to find the original union of stock and scion. If the shoot is coming from below the graft union, then it is a sucker. Remove it at the point where it joins the root; if it is cut higher up, even more suckers will be created in gratitude for pruning. Pulling suckers from the root is more effective than cutting them, especially when they are young. In days now gone, gardeners and rose-growers used a special tool called a 'spud' for removing suckers. Shaped like a miniature blunt spade, it could be pushed into the soil close to the rose bush in a downward tearing motion, thus eliminating any possibility of secondary growth. Apart from removing suckers as and when they

appear, the best remedy for their prevention is to ensure that the roses are planted sufficiently deep to cover the complete rootstock. Suckers are sometimes encouraged to grow from wounded roots, so avoid inflicting damage when hoeing or digging around roses.

The understocks used in modern rose production are chosen according to the soil and to the experience of the nurseryman. A selected form of *R. coriifolia froebelii*, commonly known as 'Laxa', a strong-rooted species which produces few suckers, is by far the most widely used in Europe today. In America, Australia and New Zealand *R. multiflora* and 'Dr Huey' are in most widespread use. The common Dog Rose, *R. canina*, has now largely disappeared as an understock; a blessing both to nurserymen and to gardeners, for it was very prone to suckering. Standard roses are usually grown on *R. rugosa* stems, largely because they are the easiest type to grow straight and firm. These can send up both root and stem suckers especially in their early years after transplanting, and a wary eye should be kept open for these as the plants grow. In other countries, where such roses are generally known as 'Tree roses', *R. multiflora* is usually used for this purpose. Until recently, 'Rugosa' stems were grown from cuttings and took three years to develop. Over the last few years, however, stems have been successfully produced in two years by budding specially selected forms of *R. rugosa* on to 'Laxa' stocks. The two cultivars currently available in Britain are 'Rocket', developed by Harkness, and 'Chesham's Choice', developed by Paul Chesham.

Planting

HEELING-IN

The term 'heeling-in' simply means the digging of a trench large enough to accommodate the roots of roses so as to hold them temporarily in good condition until they can be planted in their permanent position.

Place the bushes in the trench about 3–6″ (7.5–15 cm) apart and at an angle of 45° to prevent them being blown about in strong wind. Then replace the soil so that it covers the roots, firming with the heel. It is important to ensure that the union, or junction of roots and shoots, is about 2″ (5 cm) below ground level to protect the union from frost. They will keep this way for weeks, even months, until the weather is right for planting.

Roses are very hardy plants and usually quite difficult to kill unless maltreated. The two best ways of killing them before planting are to allow the roots to become frosted while they are out of the ground, or to expose them to drying winds with their roots unprotected.

WINTER PROTECTION

In extreme climates, such as North America and Canada, only the hardiest roses will survive outside during the winter months and it may be necessary to protect them by earthing them up, or insulating the roots.

Malcolm Lowe advises: Use an insulation that doesn't take on moisture – rigid foams for example. Rose cones are also effective; wrapping plants provides more protection than layering – if layering is indicated, pine needles are better than salt marsh hay (the latter retains moisture, thereby attracting field mice that eat the canes). A winter's blanket of snow will protect roses but as a result of the global warming of the past decade, snow is less frequent and melts quickly. A wind-break will also provide protection.

SOILS AND SOIL PREPARATION

Roses prefer soil with a pH of about 6.5, in other words slightly acid or neutral, although they are not too fussy about alkalinity and many will tolerate up to pH 7.5. Should you suspect that the pH of your soil is lower or higher than these tolerance levels, then either have your soil tested or do so yourself with one of the inexpensive soil-testing kits available from most good garden centres.

Good preparation of soils before planting is always rewarded by more contented roses. It is advisable, therefore, to dig over the soil well in advance of planting, incorporating some form of organic material. Well-rotted farmyard manure is undoubtedly the best, but failing this, a mixture of coarse, damp peat* and bonemeal can be used or, better still, well-rotted compost from a compost heap. If the soil is very poor, a balanced fertilizer with added trace elements can be broadcast over

* Peat is a finite resource, and whilst about 8 per cent of the earth's land surface is peatland, it is without doubt ecologically harmful to peat bogs for us to continue to use it in the quantities we demand today. So, as and when alternatives to peat become available, these should be used instead. One possible alternative at present is pulverized tree bark. Another, becoming available in increasing quantities, is coconut fibre.

the soil ahead of planting. Special rose fertilizer can be bought from most garden centres – a worthwhile investment when you consider that the roses being planted are to last for many years; the same type of fertilizer can be used as top-dressing after the roses are established, preferably before the start of the growing season, usually at the time of pruning. This gives the nutrients the chance of penetrating the soil, prior to the beginning of maximum root activity. On good soils, one top-dressing should be enough to sustain the rose throughout the summer, and no further feeding should be necessary until the following spring. For impoverished soils, however, a second dressing should be applied in early summer, by which time the rose will be seeking further nourishment to provide a second flush of flowers or secondary growth, depending on its habit.

The proprietary brands of fertilizer are specially prepared for roses and will usually contain the proper mix of nutrients in the most beneficial proportions. Should any other type of balanced fertilizer be used – and there is no reason why it should not – it should be low in nitrogen and high in potash, with a good mix of the major trace elements. Iron is particularly important, especially if your soil is alkaline; so is magnesium, which is frequently deficient in many soils. Those who practise organic gardening can supply nutrition by means of liquid seaweed, spent hops, farmyard manure, fish meal, etc., but the levels of potash must be kept up by the use of soot or wood ashes. All soils, of course, are improved by the incorporation of organic materials, but I do not greatly favour constant mulching of rose beds with farmyard manure. This practice, apart from looking unsightly for much of the year, tends to harbour the spores of diseases by giving them a perfect environment from which to launch themselves at the rose each spring. Mulching, if considered necessary, should be to suppress weeds rather than as a source of nutrition. Bark chippings are ideal, especially if applied to the depth of about 1″ (2.5 cm), to fairly clean ground. Nor do I consider the use of lawn trimmings a good practice; in any event, they should only be applied in moderation. They are best composted and spread at a later date; again, this should be done sparingly, for the high nitrogen content of such compost can lead to abundant growth, fewer flowers and less immunity to disease.

The nutritional requirements of roses growing in containers are the same as for those growing in open ground; remember, however, that nutrients leach from potted soil far more quickly than they do from natural soil, so more frequent applications of fertilizer are necessary. Liquid fertilizer can be applied when watering. Roses also respond to foliar feeding, but this should not be done in hot sunshine.

To sum up, if you love roses, it is worth growing them whatever your soil, provided you do not expect rewards out of proportion to the loving care you give them.

SPECIFIC REPLANT DISEASE

Roses should not be planted in soil where other roses have been grown. This is because of a soil condition known as 'rose sickness'. Soil becomes contaminated by secretions from rose roots, which newly planted bushes find offensive. Such a condition is called 'specific replant disease' and manifests itself in stunted, rather reluctant bushes which never develop satisfactorily, no matter how well they are tended. It is for this reason that commercial rose producers never grow successive crops of roses on the same land without at least a two-year break between each crop. If waiting two years is impossible, the soil should be changed. This is very important and should not present too much of a problem. It is simply a matter of juxtaposing two lots of soil, one, say, from the vegetable garden or from any spot where the soil is good and has not previously grown roses, and the other from the site where the new rose is to be planted. There are no short cuts; soil must be changed even if you are replacing a young bush. If this is not possible, old bushes should be removed and the soil in which they were growing rested for a period of at least two years before new bushes are planted. The vacant plot can, of course, be used for another catch* crop, such as vegetables or bedding plants, whilst resting from roses.

PLANTING BUSH, SHRUB AND OLD-FASHIONED ROSES

Holes should be large enough to take the root of each plant without cramping; about one spade's depth is usually enough. When the hole is dug throw in a handful of bonemeal, then with the spade mix this thoroughly with the soil in the bottom. Scatter another handful of bonemeal on the heap of soil which is to go back into the hole.

* A Norfolk term for a quick-growing interim crop.

A newly planted rose

The rose should then be stood in the centre, ensuring that the roots are well spread out; enough soil is then placed around the roots to hold it in an upright position, thus enabling more soil to be added using both hands on the spade. When half the soil has been replaced, the bush should be given a little shake to ensure that soil falls between the roots, then tread the soil with the feet, firmly enough to hold the rose tight but not so firm as to compact the soil. The lighter the soil the more heavily it will need to be pressed or trodden. With the rose standing upright in the hole, replace the rest of the soil, leaving the last half-spadeful for a tilth around the rose after treading. Having made sure that the label is firmly attached, tidy up any footprints and leave the rose to settle in. If it has been planted in the autumn or winter, it may need a light retreading a few weeks later or in the spring before it starts to grow.

PLANTING CONTAINERIZED ROSES

More often than not containerized roses are purchased during the summer months, but it is quite in order to plant them at any time of the year.

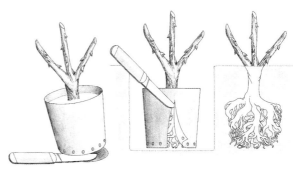

Remove bottom of polythene pot

Place in hole and slit side of pot – remove polythene

Planted rose showing depth of planting

When removing the pot, the soil packed around the roots must not be disturbed. Once the plant with its undisturbed ball of soil is in position, refill the hole with care. Since most composts used for container roses are peat-based, which is difficult to moisten, plunge the rose for half an hour or so into a bucket of water before planting out. As with bare-root roses, make sure that the union is 1″ (2.5 cm) below soil level; this is very important as it reduces the possibility of suckers and stabilizes the bush against wind damage.

Standard or tree roses, either bare-root or containerized, require a good stake to support them. This should always be in position before the tree is planted and should be driven at least 18″ (45 cm) into the soil to give adequate support, even deeper if the soil is sandy. Note: Most roses purchased in containers have not been grown in the pot. They are simply open-ground plants containerized a few months earlier. This is because they are not as amenable to being container-grown as some other plants.

PLANTING SPECIMEN ROSES IN LAWNS

When planting specimen roses in lawns or shrub roses in rough grass, it is important to leave an ample circle of soil around the bush. Roses do not like the competition of tall uncut grass, especially in their early years; and, apart from looking untidy, it is difficult to remove it from around an established plant and it also makes mowing difficult.

PLANTING CLIMBING ROSES

Adopt the same method for planting climbing roses as with bush roses, but when they are to grow on walls, remember that the soil is often poorer near the house or building and that a little extra organic material will be needed at planting time. Newly planted climbing roses are often the first to suffer from drought, since they have extra foliage to support. Frequently, too, they miss out on some of the rain, especially those on south-facing walls or fences. If planning to plant on pillars or tripods, the structure should be erected in advance of planting.

PLANTING AND STAKING STANDARD ROSES

For standard shrub roses and weepers, stout, tall stakes should be positioned in advance of planting and inserted at intervals of 18″ (45 cm) into the ground. At least two rose tree ties will be needed to fix the stem to the stake. For weeping standards, which are sometimes 5′ (1.5 m) tall, three ties may be necessary. Stakes usually have a shorter life than the rose itself, so at some point it will need restaking. Provision for this can be made at planting time by placing a metal or plastic tube, of sufficient size to take the stake, vertically into the ground to the correct depth and placing the stake into this before planting the rose. This will enable the replacement of stakes to take place later without too much disturbance to the soil surrounding the roots.

Should a dry or hot spell of weather arrive during the first season, or indeed in succeeding seasons, the rose will need water. The fact that it is deep-rooted and does not show obvious signs of suffering is no reason for neglecting its thirst.

PLANTING ROSES INTO POTS

In an earlier chapter I discussed the growing of roses in pots, tubs and urns, so it is worth describing how these should be planted. Whatever the type of rose, a good, large container is important. Free drainage is essential, so in addition to providing drainage holes, shingle or broken bricks should be placed in the bottom of the container. A thin layer of organic substance should be placed over the drainage material, followed by John Innes Potting Compost No. 3. If this is dry, dampen it slightly before use, since once *in situ* it is much more difficult to moisten thoroughly. The container should be filled to about 2″ (5 cm) from the top to allow watering without spilling both water and soil over the edge. The rose should be planted deep enough for the shoots to come from below the soil surface. If a wooden container is used, its life can be prolonged by lining the inside with thick polythene before filling with soil, remembering to allow sufficient drainage holes in the bottom. If the roses are already in containers or pots, these should be removed before planting, taking care not to disturb the ball of soil around the roots. For several weeks after planting they will sustain themselves from the ball of soil in which they have been growing and, until they start making additional roots, will need liberal and frequent watering. Like all pot plants, roses grown in containers will need repotting from time to time. This should be done only in the dormant season, and some of the existing soil should be retained around the roots, especially in the case of older plants.

Pruning

How and when to prune roses usually provokes friendly disagreement among rosarians, and in my experience almost all the arguments in favour of this method or that have some weight to them. In fact, pruning is far less complicated than many books and articles on the subject may suggest. The most important 'tools' a pruner needs are, first, common sense; secondly and most important, a feeling for the plant; thirdly, a strong pair of gloves to give confidence; and fourthly, good, sharp secateurs. Modern secateurs are well-made, precision instruments and it is important to choose only the

Pruning a newly planted rose

best. These should have a good, clean cutting edge and a design that provides maximum cutting action with a minimum of effort. For older, more mature shrub roses and climbers, a pair of long-handled pruners, suitable for operating with both hands, will also be needed.

There is one golden rule which applies to all roses, both ancient and modern, be they climbers or shrubs: that no matter what size plants are received from the nursery, they should always be pruned very hard after planting.

The reason for such treatment is to encourage all new shoots to grow from the base, or near to the base of the young bushes. If left unpruned or pruned lightly, the first season's growth will start from the top end of the plant and it will be difficult to induce basal growth in succeeding years.

PRUNING ONCE-FLOWERING ROSES

Pruning can undoubtedly benefit some shrub roses but it must be stressed that others are best left unpruned, except on a general maintenance basis. It is often far more difficult to decide whether or not to prune than how to prune. When in doubt, the best policy to adopt for the vast majority of old-fashioned and shrub roses is to do nothing. I believe that many of the older roses, such as Albas,

Pruning a three-year-old bush; *left*, before, and *right*, after pruning

---

NORTH AMERICAN PLANTING AND PRUNING SEASONS

The USA is divided into nine climatic zones for pruning and planting (see below). As a general rule 'prune when the forsythia blooms'– a rule which applies wherever forsythia grows.*

ZONE	PLANT	PRUNE
Northeast	March–May, October–November	March–April
Eastern Seaboard	March–May, October–November	March
North Central	April–May, October–November	March
Subtropical	December–January	December–January
Mid-South	February–March and November	December–February
South-Central	December–February	January
Southwest	December–January	December–January
Pacific Seaboard	January–February	December
Pacific Northwest	January–April	January

*Except for climbers and ramblers, which are discussed below

Centifolias, Damasks and Gallicas, are best pruned in summer after flowering. This enables them to refurbish themselves with flowering wood and give a better display the following year. To prune these roses, remove any dead or diseased wood and any weak shoots that look incapable of supporting flowers the following season. Remove, too, any shoots that are chafing and rubbing against one another, and thin out overcrowded areas likely to give the plant a leggy appearance. Care should be taken, however, not to destroy the general character of the shrubs. Furthermore, try not to overdo the summer pruning, since this will result in much loss of sap, and the plants will not recover in time to make growth for the following year. If severe treatment is necessary, this should be done in the dormant season.

Species roses, Scotch Roses and Sweet Briars are, by and large, best left to develop their own personalities until they risk getting out of hand, when it does no harm to prune them fairly hard to keep them within bounds.

PRUNING REPEAT-FLOWERING SHRUB ROSES

The Portlands are usually repeat or continuous flowering, an attribute which in my opinion is positively encouraged if they are pruned whilst dormant each season and dead-headed in summer when necessary.

Except in the largest gardens where they can be given their heads, Hybrid Musks, Bourbons and Hybrid Perpetuals are best pruned every winter. If done sensibly, this will keep them replenished with young shoots and stop them becoming leggy and unkempt. I also believe that intelligent, moderate pruning will help prolong their life. Prune them in February by removing all superfluous shoots, i.e. those too thin to support many flowers. Remove, too, any wood that is overcrowding the shrub, usually from the centre of the bush; and reduce the length of some of the main shoots by one-third, so as to encourage early flowers. The remaining shoots can be reduced by up to two-thirds or more; these will not only produce flowers but usually provide the foundation for strong growth and replacement wood for future seasons.

Whether grown as a hedge or as individual specimens, Rugosa roses should only be pruned lightly to keep the hedge or shrub in shape. For the first year, of course, they need to be pruned hard. But should they get out of hand in later years they will tolerate harsh pruning and easily recover. The Chinas and older Hybrid Teas should be pruned in the same way as modern roses by removing twiggy, thin or dead wood, and cutting back the stronger shoots to about one-third of their length each year, aiming if possible to encourage basal growth. Tea roses prefer to be treated more sparingly; they need to be pruned, of course, in order to keep them in shape, and to prevent them developing too much old unproductive wood, but not pruned for pruning's sake.

PRUNING CLIMBING ROSES AND RAMBLERS

Climbing roses fall roughly into two categories, those that flower on wood produced in the same year and those that flower on wood produced in the previous year. In the first category are the Noisettes (especially the larger flowering cultivars), the Hybrid Teas, the Climbing Teas and the Hybrid Perpetuals; these flower on lateral growths and at the same time send up long, strong shoots. They need help and support to be effective as wall plants, especially in their early years. The dual object, therefore, in pruning these types of climbing roses is to encourage ample climbing shoots and to persuade those shoots to produce as many flowers as possible by the development of laterals from the stems. Thus, the method of pruning climbers alters somewhat as the plant ages and settles into its chosen position. Over the first few years, the strong climbing shoots should be trained in as many directions as possible without giving the plant too much of a contrived look. Shoots can be twisted, turned and bent into position by securing them to trellis or wires fixed to the wall. The lateral growths produced by these shoots can then be cut back each year to about one-third of their length. These 'spurs' will then each produce several flowering shoots which, when similarly pruned in their turn the following year, will produce more, and so on. The same treatment applies to climbing roses growing on pillars, pergolas and arches. Species such as *R. bracteata* and *R. laevigata* and their hybrids are likewise best pruned by this method.

In the second category are the ramblers or scramblers, which mostly flower on wood produced the previous season. They can be distinguished from the climbers by their habit of growth, in that they produce shoots which are thinner and more pliable. The types that fall into this bracket are the hybrids of *R. arvensis*, *R. wichuraiana*, *R. sempervirens*, *R. multiflora* and *R. setigera*. To get the best from these roses (unless they are growing up into trees), they should be given their heads for the first few years, with the shoots trained in as many directions as possible until they have formed a dense covering over their supports. Where pruning is necessary, it should be done after they have flowered in early summer. Winter pruning is only practical when severe treatment is needed, such as the removal of old wood. Generally speaking, these types of roses are difficult to kill, and if drastic measures are employed, they will usually recover, given time.

Roses of these types that are growing up into trees, covering large buildings or being used as free-growing prostrate plants on banks or in woodlands, are a law unto themselves and best left unpruned, except in necessity. The same advice applies to the specialist tree climbers such as *R. filipes*,

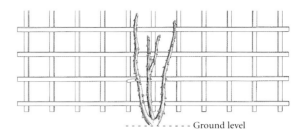

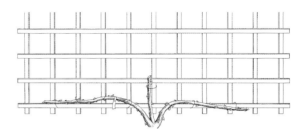

First-year climber or rambler before *(above)* and after *(below)* pruning and training to trellis

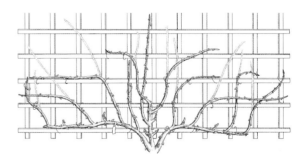

Pruning and training a second-year climber or rambler

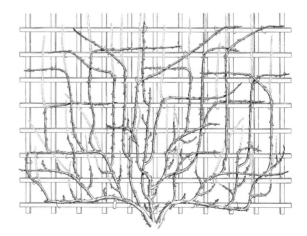

Pruning and training a third-year climber or rambler

Pruning climbing or rambler roses

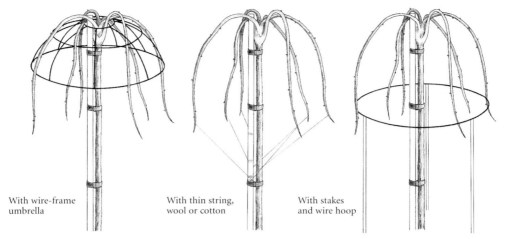

With wire-frame umbrella

With thin string, wool or cotton

With stakes and wire hoop

Three ways of training weeping standard roses

R. moschata and *R. helenae*. When grown on a sheltered wall *R. banksiae* delights in finding its way into nooks and crannies and twining itself behind guttering; it will even blot out windows if so allowed. To get the best results, let it grow freely without pruning until it becomes a nuisance, then restrain it by pruning in early summer, after it has flowered, removing only the older wood.

PRUNING WEEPING STANDARDS

Weeping standards are cultivars of rambling roses, budded by nurserymen on to straight stems. The best weepers are those from the Multiflora and Wichuraiana groups with pliable shoots and a natural tendency to grow towards the ground. These require a combination of winter pruning and summer trimming, by removing any untoward shoots as and when they appear and keeping the dense growth at the top thinned out as necessary.

Reluctant weepers can be trained to 'weep' by three methods. The first is to purchase or make an umbrella-shaped wire frame which can be fixed at the top of the stake supporting the rose, thus enabling the shoots to be trained downward as they grow. The trouble with this method is that the frames are unsightly and will often spoil the appearance of the garden. Far better is the method of attaching nylon fishing-line to the ends of the branches which are not naturally weeping and either pegging these to the ground, thus pulling the shoots downward, or attaching a heavy stone to the nylon line to keep the shoots angled downwards. The third method is to attach a hoop on to three equally spaced stakes around the stems. The hoop should be about 3′ (90 cm) above the ground. The shoots are then tied to the hoop, thus training them downwards to give a good weeping effect.

Old-fashioned roses, species roses or shrub roses growing as standards need the same treatment as afforded to their shrub counterparts, but they will need tidying more frequently to keep them in shape.

DEAD-HEADING

Dead-heading is in many ways far more important to some cultivars than pruning, although this can be rather a nuisance where large numbers of old roses are concerned. It is less of a drudge, however, if the habit of carrying secateurs at all times is adopted whilst walking round the garden, and snip-

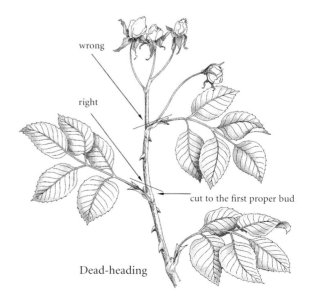

wrong

right

cut to the first proper bud

Dead-heading

ping off any unsightly dead heads as and when they occur. It is best to make the cut at the first proper bud below the flower stalk. Only dead-head those cultivars which retain their dead petals and become unsightly. Many others will eventually produce hips – pleasing, not least to the birds.

PRUNING NEGLECTED ROSES

Old, neglected rose specimens pose yet another difficult pruning problem. Breathing new life into old shrub roses and climbers, however, is often impracticable, so it would be misleading to suggest ways of attempting this. Roses do not live for ever and their longevity is often related to the treatment they receive throughout their lives. Broadly speaking, the nearer a rose to a true species, the longer its life. It follows, therefore, that it is easier to rejuvenate an old-fashioned rose than a modern hybrid. Sentiment plays an important part in these decisions but where a rose is obviously approaching its twilight years, it is better to replace it with another. As mentioned earlier, the soil will need changing but provided the cultivar can still be obtained, this is the most economical procedure. If its name is unknown and identification has proved impossible, some specialist nurseries will produce new plants from stock taken from the old plant. By this means direct offspring can be replanted and an old cultivar may possibly be saved from extinction.

PRUNING MODERN ROSES

As mentioned in connection with the older roses, the chief and only golden rule that I apply to pruning is the vital one of pruning hard in the first year after planting. Without fail, all newly planted roses should be pruned to approximately 3″ (7.5 cm) or 3–4 eyes from the bottom of each stem; this applies not only to bush roses but also to climbers, shrub roses and standards. The reason is to encourage all new growth to sprout from as near the base of the plant as possible and so to lay the foundation for well-balanced, sturdy growth in the future. There can be no doubt that timid pruning at this early stage leads to more disappointment with new roses than any other single malpractice. In the interest of satisfied customers, I would dearly love to send out all our modern roses ready pruned, but when we tried this some years ago, even with a note of explanation, we received too many complaints about quality and size to warrant perseverance.

In subsequent years pruning need not be so severe. It then becomes a question of judgement as to how many shoots to remove and by how much to reduce the length of the remaining ones. Remember, rose bushes will quickly become leggy and bare-bottomed if given half a chance. As a general guide, shoots of Hybrid Teas and Floribundas thinner than a pencil are unlikely to produce flowers of any decent size, so they should be cut back harder than thicker shoots. Bear in mind that all things are comparative, so the thickness of wood will depend upon the overall size of the plant. All dead wood should be removed and the aim should be to keep the centre of the plant as open as possible. I do not place as much importance on a slanting cut as some people do, but where possible the cut should be made just above a bud, preferably a healthy bud, facing outwards from the plant. As time goes on you will learn by your mistakes – but if in doubt, hard pruning is better than no pruning at all. As for timing, there are advocates of autumn pruning, winter pruning and spring pruning, and to some extent the choice is governed by location and the severity of cold weather. Here in Norfolk, late February to early March is about the right time but a few weeks either side might be more appropriate in other temperate climates. Whatever time is chosen for the main pruning, always tidy up the plant by removing a few inches of shoots in late autumn. This will improve the appearance of the garden and help to reduce wind-rock during the winter.

Weed Control

Gardeners fall into two categories where weeds are concerned: those who tolerate weeds and are prepared to live happily with them, and those who insist upon their removal from every nook and cranny. Both schools tend to frown at each other's philosophy. From a nurseryman's point of view, wild flowers or wild plants growing rampant among roses are a problem, and they have to be kept under control. However, as I said earlier, I favour leaving weeds until they become a nuisance and start to hamper the performance of the roses.

The most troublesome weeds are the perennial and deep-rooted types, especially couch grass and thistles, which have a habit of taking refuge among the bushes themselves and growing up through the lower branches. If this is permitted the rose definitely suffers and the weeds become almost impossible to eradicate. It is therefore important for roses to start in soil which is as free as possible from perennial weed infestation. Thus, in the initial preparation of the ground, make sure that such weeds are dealt with severely. This can be done very successfully with hormone-based herbicides, applied several months in advance of planting and while the weeds are still growing. For those who prefer not to use chemicals, it is a case of backache and blisters, forking out all the roots and rhizomes from the soil all around the area to be planted. Any small pieces of root left in the ground will rapidly take hold and reinfest the soil with renewed vigour.

Annual weeds, which usually invade in large armies, are not quite such a problem since, apart from reinfestation by seed, they succumb to the hoe pretty quickly on a hot day. There are chemicals that will deal with these both at the pre-emergent stage and whilst they are growing. Such chemicals must be used with great care, not only for the well-being of the roses but, more importantly, for the good of the soil, the animal and bird population, and not least ourselves. This is no place to discuss the rights and wrongs of their usage; but before any chemicals are used, read the specific instructions carefully and carry them out to the letter. There are a number of herbicides available, and advice can best be obtained from those experts who supply them.

Another far less obnoxious method of suppressing weeds is to spread a mulch of sterile material to a depth of 2–3″ (5–7.5 cm) over the soil. Bark chippings make by far the best and are obtainable either from garden centres or direct from sawmills, if you are lucky enough to live near to a forest. Sawdust, too, can be used but it will be toxic unless it is from mature wood and, being light, may also blow about in dry weather. No matter what is used as a mulch, it is advantageous to both the roses and the soil to till the ground beneath at least once a year, perhaps at pruning time. One of the disadvantages of chemicals and, to a lesser extent, of mulches is that they prohibit or restrict underplanting of rose beds with companion plants, which is yet another way of hampering weeds, particularly under old-fashioned roses and shrub roses. This subject has been dealt with earlier in the book.

Propagation of Roses

Vegetative propagation as a means of reproducing plants has probably been practised since civilization began. If man had not learned to work with nature and use such means of reproduction, many of our oldest cultivars, incapable of self-perpetuation, would have been lost.

Species, of course, can reproduce themselves from seed. So from the beginning they have been relatively independent, needing man's assistance only to develop their hybrids and to help them multiply by producing them from cuttings or by grafting or budding. Although a form of grafting is still practised in the commercial production of roses, this is now done on a limited scale, usually in the form of bench-grafting to propagate difficult subjects such as 'Mermaid', *R. banksiae lutea* and a few others which do not lend themselves readily to the technique of budding.

GRAFTING

Bench-grafting is a fairly sophisticated means of propagation and its success depends mainly on the skill and experience of the nurseryman. Grafting involves placing a branch or shoot from a pre-selected cultivar on to the root or shoot of another, thus creating a union between the two and the eventual growth of a complete plant in its own right. The host plant providing the root is termed the 'stock', and its enforced guest which supplies the branches is called the 'scion'. By careful selection of compatible species and cultivars, each will influence the other and so enable hybrids to perpetuate in their exact form. The choice of stocks with specific attributes enables them to influence the scion and, to some extent, vice versa. These reciprocal influences are not so pronounced in roses as they are, for example, in apples, where the ultimate size of the tree is controlled by the stock on which the cultivar is grafted. Stocks are usually grown from seed by specialist growers. In recent years, as mentioned earlier, the most commonly used stock has been 'Laxa'.

For bench-grafting roses, suitable stocks are selected each year in early January and plunged, in bundles of fifty or so, into damp sterile peat, under glass. These are forced into early growth for about two to three weeks until root activity is well under way. Scions are then taken from dormant plants of the cultivar to be propagated, and grafted on to each active stock, the top of the stock having first been removed at a point a few inches above the roots. The scion selected is usually of one-year wood, 3–4″ (6.5–10 cm) long, with three or four buds. The top end of the scion is usually cut slightly slanted, immediately above a growing point or bud. The bottom is cut into a half-wedge shape and an inverted cut made upwards into the wedge on the exposed-tissue side of the cut. A similar cut

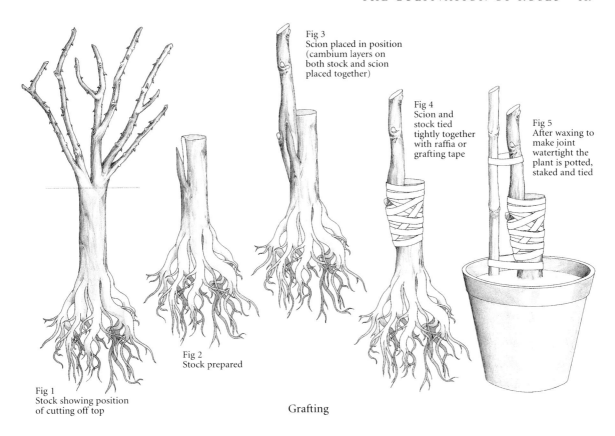

Fig 3
Scion placed in position
(cambium layers on
both stock and scion
placed together)

Fig 4
Scion and
stock tied
tightly together
with raffia or
grafting tape

Fig 5
After waxing to
make joint
watertight the
plant is potted,
staked and tied

Fig 2
Stock prepared

Fig 1
Stock showing position
of cutting off top

Grafting

is made to match the slant of the scion on one side of the stock, and a reverse cut made, so the two can be joined together in a neat and tidy fashion. Care is taken to ensure that the two cambium layers, which are situated under the bark, are placed together. This done, the joint is bandaged with grafting tape or raffia and waxed watertight, either with grafting wax or petroleum jelly. The top of the scion is also sealed to reduce dehydration.

The stock with scion attached is then potted with enough nutrients in the compost to see it through one season. It is then placed in a heated greenhouse. Within a few weeks the two will fuse together and the scion will begin to grow. Fairly soon, after it becomes obvious that the graft has taken, a 2–3′ (60–90 cm) cane should be placed in the pot with the plant. This should be fixed firmly to both stock and scion by raffia to provide a splint for support during the crucial few weeks whilst complete fusion takes place. By early summer the join should be secure enough to release the grafting-tape or raffia from the union, thus avoiding strangulation as both stock and scion swell with growth. This method of grafting is known as 'whip and tongue', but there are a number of variations on this, such as 'wedge-grafting', 'saddle-grafting', 'chip-grafting' and so on.

All rely on the compatibility of stock and scion and the alignment of their respective cambium layers. The result should be a sizeable plant by the end of the first growing season.

BUDDING

Budding is by far the most widely used method of producing roses. Success with budding, even on the smallest scale, gives one a very satisfying feeling of achievement and there is no reason why the amateur should not try to produce a few rose bushes by this means. All that is needed is a budding knife with specially shaped blade and handle, available, in various designs, from good gardening shops and ironmongers. Most rose nurserymen will sell a few stocks, knowing that, however successful, no threat is posed to their business.

Budding is an acquired technique, and nurseries employ skilled propagators who are capable of working very rapidly, handling up to 400 bushes an hour. Speed is essential since budding is usually done at the peak growing season with both stock and scion in active growth. Stocks for this purpose are normally planted as one-year seedlings in rows

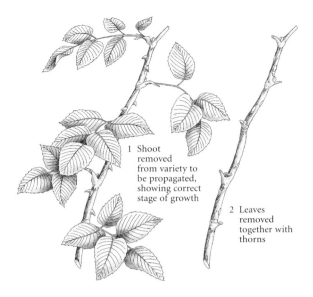

1 Shoot removed from variety to be propagated, showing correct stage of growth

2 Leaves removed together with thorns

Preparation of wood for budding

root protruding above ground level. The scions or buds are selected by taking a ripe flowering shoot from a ready-made rose bush. The shoot is usually ripe when the flower has started to open. The flower and the top 2″ (5 cm) of the stem are removed together with the leaves, to facilitate handling. It is a good idea to leave about $1/3″$ (1 cm) of leaf stalk attached to the stem, depending upon the cultivar. Most rose 'sticks' will have between four and eight buds. At no time must the stick be allowed to become dry. It can be kept fresh for several days if necessary by placing it in damp newspaper and polythene.

To perform the budding operation, first make sure that the stock is clean and free of soil at ground level. Open the bark of the stock with the knife to form a T-shaped cut, taking care not to damage or scrape the tissue inside the bark. A vertical cut about 1″ (2.5 cm) long is enough to tease back the bark at the top of the 'T'. The stock prepared, the scion is then placed in the free hand and held by the index finger and the thumb, palm uppermost, with the thin end or top of the scion pointing towards the wrist. The index finger should be placed directly under the first or top bud on the stick to give support. The first bud is then cut from the stick with one cutting motion of the knife. With

during the preceding winter. By mid-June these are ready for budding and will remain in this state of readiness for about two months. The stocks are planted in such a way as to leave 1–2″ (2.5–5 cm) of

Above left, removing bud from 'stick', and *right*, bud ready for placing in stock
Below left, bud attached to stock, and *right*, latex tie being applied

the thumb of the knife hand, press the 'sliver' that is being removed firmly on to the knife blade. Having made a clean cut to about $^1/_3''$ (1 cm) above the bud, the bark can then be torn back to remove it completely from the stick, still holding it between knife blade and thumb. Experts retain the stick in their hand as they complete each budding operation but at this point the novice is best advised to place the stick aside and retain only the bud between finger and thumb. The wood from the bud is then separated from the bark, usually in two stages. Holding the blunt end between thumb and finger, with the thumbnail for support, remove half the wood from the top downwards and the other half from the bottom upwards, exposing a plump little bud on the inside of the bark. If there is a hole instead, throw it away and start again.

The next stage calls for dexterity. Hold the top end of the bud with one hand, and use the other to hold open the bark of the stock with the handle of the budding knife; then carefully slide the bud into position under the bark of the stock, finally cutting off any spare bark from the bud at the top of the 'T'. Lastly, the wound has to be bandaged, both to

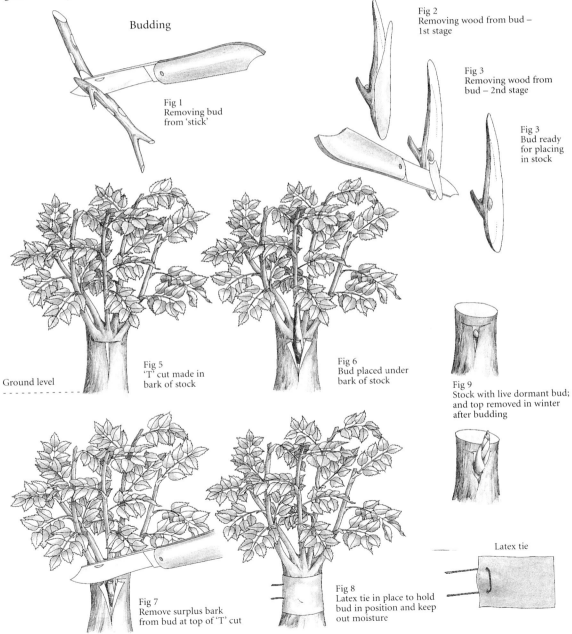

Budding

Fig 1
Removing bud
from 'stick'

Fig 2
Removing wood from bud –
1st stage

Fig 3
Removing wood from
bud – 2nd stage

Fig 3
Bud ready
for placing
in stock

Ground level

Fig 5
'T' cut made in
bark of stock

Fig 6
Bud placed under
bark of stock

Fig 9
Stock with live dormant bud;
and top removed in winter
after budding

Fig 7
Remove surplus bark
from bud at top of 'T' cut

Fig 8
Latex tie in place to hold
bud in position and keep
out moisture

Latex tie

hold it together and to prevent moisture getting in. Nurserymen use special, inexpensive latex patches for this, but if these cannot be obtained, use some thin raffia, winding it around the cut: beneath the bud three times and above the bud four times, and knotting it carefully at the top. After three or four weeks the 'bandage' can be removed; success or failure will be immediately obvious. If the bud has failed to take and there is still time, another attempt can be made on the other side of the stock. If it has taken it should be left untouched until mid-winter, when the complete top of the stock should be removed at about $1/3''$ (1 cm) above the bud. The following summer, lo and behold, a rose! This can either be left where it is for life or transplanted to another position in the following dormant season.

ROSES FROM CUTTINGS

Many gardeners, having had success at rooting roses from cuttings, are mystified by the fact that this is not done commercially, enabling them to purchase roses which will be free of troublesome suckers. A few types of roses lend themselves readily to this method of propagation, notably *R. rugosa* and its hybrids, and these are sometimes offered commercially on their own roots, as are some of the species and unusual hybrids which have proved resistant to budding or grafting techniques. But most attempts at commercial production over the years have failed. Nowadays, with sophisticated hormone rooting powders and mist units, getting them to root is not a problem; in fact, many cultivars root readily without such aids. The difficulty is growing enough stock plants to provide the cuttings. With the budding method, six buds are the equivalent of only one cutting, so a nurseryman would need six times as many stock plants to produce plants for sale. Although recent developments in tissue culture might provide the answer, I can see no way around the difficulties which arise later when the bush has to be transplanted. Except for some species, the root systems are small when compared with budded roses, and they do not take readily to transplanting. Thus there is a high failure rate for open-ground, bare-root plants produced from cuttings. To counteract this, they have to be grown in pots from an early age, so enabling them to be transplanted complete with soil. This is fine where plants can be sold locally and in garden centres, but it presents a problem for dispatch by mail order. Another difficulty is to produce bushes large enough to satisfy the long-established pattern of quality demanded by the public. An own-root

rose needs to be at least one year older than its budded counterpart to get anywhere near an equivalent size. I recall vividly an occasion several years ago when a customer asked me to produce for her thirty different roses on their own roots. I explained all the pros and cons and she said that she was prepared to wait. In order to be sure of enough plants I produced six of each, which took two years of patient work. When she received them, she promptly returned the lot, saying they were too small! The only consolation, apart from not seeing that lady again, was a lot more experience at growing roses from cuttings.

Despite all this, Malcolm Lowe of Nashua, New Hampshire, USA, has established a system of 'own-root roses' whereby plants are produced to order. He roots his cuttings under glass in early autumn and plants the rooted plants straight into the ground the following spring. His success rate is apparently high, but I think the climate of New Hampshire is more conducive to such a method of rose production than ours in the UK. Mike and Jean Shoup of the Antique Rose Emporium, Brenham, Texas, have also evolved methods of successfully producing roses commercially from softwood cuttings. They are particularly efficient with the Old Teas.

The best time to take hardwood cuttings is when the leaves begin to fall and the wood has had all the summer to ripen. For cuttings of this type, select mature, one-year wood, preferably the thickness of a pencil or more, though this will depend somewhat on the cultivar. The ideal cutting should be about $6''$ (15 cm) long and cut to a growth bud at both the top and bottom. For heel cuttings, the bottom should have a small slice of two-year wood still attached. Leaves, where present, should be removed before placing the cutting straight into the ground to a depth of half its length, preferably in a sheltered, warm part of the garden. If the soil is heavy, a little sand placed in the bottom of the trench before planting will help rooting, having first dipped the bottom $1/3''$ (1 cm) or so of the cutting into rooting hormone. Alternatively, the cuttings can be placed directly into a pot containing equal parts of sand and soil, and placed in a cold frame or cold greenhouse.

By early spring these cuttings should start to root and will grow into reasonable small bushes by the following autumn, when they can be transplanted into permanent positions.

If preferred, cuttings can be taken from late June onwards, but these need slightly more coddling. Shoots of the current year's wood should be cut from the bush and cuttings made to a length of

Cuttings growing at Mike Shoup's nursery, Texas

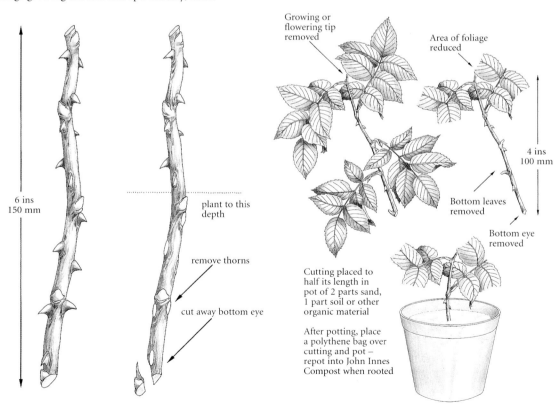

6 ins
150 mm

plant to this
depth

remove thorns

cut away bottom eye

Hardwood cuttings taken in autumn

Growing or
flowering tip
removed

Area of foliage
reduced

4 ins
100 mm

Bottom leaves
removed

Bottom eye
removed

Cutting placed to
half its length in
pot of 2 parts sand,
1 part soil or other
organic material

After potting, place
a polythene bag over
cutting and pot –
repot into John Innes
Compost when rooted

Softwood cutting taken in summer

about 4″ (10 cm), again cutting to an eye, top and bottom. Remove all leaves except for the top two, which, if need be, should be reduced to just two leaflets to reduce transpiration. The prepared cuttings should then be placed in pots in a mixture of soil and sand, watered, and covered with a polythene bag, held in position with a piece of cane acting as a tent peg and a rubber band to anchor the bag around the top edge of the pot. By this system, cuttings should root quite quickly, especially if the pots are kept in a warm place such as a greenhouse or on a windowsill. During this period very little watering is necessary since moisture builds up within the sealed environment. Placing the pot in a saucer of shingle, into which water can be poured periodically, will ensure that the cutting never dries out before it makes roots. When the cuttings have made some small amount of growth, the polythene can be removed and the plant slowly hardened-off before winter. During the winter, the plant can be repotted into better nourished soil and eventually planted into a permanent situation.

These are just two of the ways of producing roses from cuttings. Remember, however, that not all roses will root successfully and that others will not make such large plants or grow as quickly as those produced from budding.

MICROPROPAGATION

Amateurs are unlikely to practise this form of propagation, but since more and more of the roses bought in the future will be produced by this means, a few words should be included to give a brief outline of the process. Micropropagation of plants is a form of vegetative propagation carried out in sterile growing rooms or laboratories. Roses produced in this way are grown on their own roots, like cuttings. Before the technique was discovered, biologists and botanists believed that roots and shoots could be formed only from the actual growing parts of plants. Micropropagation is a type of tissue culture and involves the taking of a small piece of tissue, or even a single cell, from a growth point or axillary bud and stimulating this to produce more growth points which, in turn, produce more and so on. At first the shoots are without roots, so these are induced by adding naturally occurring, root-stimulating hormones to the medium in which they are grown. Once roots have formed, the tiny plants are grown on for a time and then carefully weaned into ordinary compost to take their place in the outside world.

There is still some way to go before this form of propagation becomes common practice in the commercial production of roses. The most difficult stage is the weaning of plants into ordinary soil, but research work is going on all the time and there is no doubt that ways and means will be found to make this easier.

Not all types of roses take readily to micropropagation. Hybrid Teas and Floribundas, by and large, do not grow as well on their own roots as they do when budded, and some shrub roses are even more reluctant. Many of the Miniatures and Procumbents seem to thrive, however, and it is these that are mostly produced by micropropagation at present. This is probably because plants formed in this way sprout many more shoots from the base in the first year than those produced by budding or from cuttings. One significant advantage of micropropagation is the speed of rooting; another is the large number of plants produced from just one small piece of tissue. By harnessing this technique, breeders can build up numbers and launch new cultivars far more quickly than by conventional means, but this practice is by no means widespread.

LAYERING

Layering is not often practised with roses but, depending upon the cultivar, it is quite a feasible method of propagation. Although it is not possible with sturdy, upright growers, since they will refuse to bend to the ground, it is, however, a fairly efficient way of propagating the more flexible old-fashioned roses, climbers and ramblers.

Simply arch a one-year shoot to the ground and place the point of contact – about 12″ (30 cm) from the tip – into a shallow trench, tethering it with a wire pin or similar aid. A knife wound in that part of the bark which is placed underground will sometimes aid rooting; then cover with soil. This can be done at almost any time of the year but rooting is naturally quicker in spring, just before seasonal growth begins.

Layering

Once rooting has occurred, the protruding tip will start to grow and the parent shoot can be cut away. The new rose can then be transplanted into a permanent position at any time during the dormant season.

DIVISION

Division as a means of propagation is common practice with many plants, though this is not normally associated with roses; nevertheless, there are some species and cultivars where such a method can be adopted quite successfully. The only necessary condition is that candidates for such treatment should actually be growing on their own roots and not grafted or budded on to an understock.

Several species of roses and their hybrids are naturally free-suckering plants; if these suckers are removed from the bush with a section of root attached they become new plants in their own right. The Scotch Roses are perhaps the best subjects for this form of propagation; indeed it may be their propensity for free-suckering that accounts for their longevity. One frequently comes upon such roses in old gardens, having way outlived their companions from an earlier age and multiplied themselves by suckers several times over and retaining none of their original root systems; in fact, they were probably planted as suckers in the first place. Other types of roses which can be multiplied in this way are *R. wichuraiana*, *R. palustris*, *R. nitida*, *R. virginiana*, *R. eglanteria* and, of course, the ubiquitous *R. rugosa*. Most forms and hybrids of all these species lend themselves to division, provided, as already said, that they are growing on their own roots.

ROSES FROM SEED

All true species will of course grow from seed, but to be sure of identical offspring, parent seed plants need to be grown in isolation in order to avoid becoming 'chance hybridized' with other compatible species or hybrids. Such chance hybrids occur sometimes with only minor differences from their parents, having been fertilized by bees or by some other natural pollen-carrying agent.

Hybrids sometimes pop up in gardens from seeds which have either simply dropped off the plant or have been distributed by birds, *R. glauca* and *R. filipes* being just two species which have produced foundlings in this way. Some hybrids, too, in particular the Rugosas, if growing close to other roses, will sometimes produce interesting if not startling variations from their self-sown seeds.

All rootstocks used in modern rose production in the UK are grown from seed. Parent plants of suitable species such as 'Laxa' and forms of *R. multiflora* are grown in relative isolation, usually in the warmer parts of the eastern Mediterranean. The seed is collected from parent plants and sold to specialist rose stock growers in Europe, in particular Holland and Germany but lately in the UK as well. Seeds are sown in very early spring and the seedlings are produced, all in one growing season, by the tens of millions. These are then sold to rose nurserymen who produce saleable bushes two growing seasons later by budding. Thus the roots of bought roses are well-travelled; excluding the age of the seed, they are three years old by the time they are planted in the garden.

Economics is not the only reason why rose stocks are grown from seed. Viruses are less likely to be transmitted by this means than by vegetative propagation. Seeds gathered from garden hybrids, even those which have been self-pollinated, yield rather different results from those collected from species, in that none will come true and each seedling produced will differ from its parents, only one of which, of course, will always be known. Seed pods from most garden hybrids need a long summer to ripen. Only those from hips provided by the earliest flowers of summer are usually viable in the UK and similar latitudes; this is why hybridizing, north of about latitude 45°, is carried out in greenhouses.

Growing seed from garden hybrids can be interesting, if not particularly fruitful. An unsophisticated method is to collect ripe hips in early winter and to place them in flower pots full of sharp sand, keeping these outdoors where the greatest fluctuations in temperature can be obtained until about February. Choose a position which can be protected from mice, for these little creatures seem to enjoy the flavour of rose seeds.

The number of seeds in each hip will vary from one or two to as many as fifty in some roses. Seeds should be taken from the hips in early February, by which time the fleshy part of the pods will have rotted away. They should then be washed and sown about $1/4''$ (0.5 cm) deep in good compost in a seed tray or flower pot; then placed in a warm greenhouse with bottom heat to warm the soil to a temperature of about 45°F (about 6°C). Haphazard germination will start a few weeks later as the days lengthen and may continue spasmodically until early summer. Transplant any seedlings into a good potting compost in $3''$ (7.5 cm) pots soon after germination and keep them in the greenhouse. Shade them for a few days until they take root. They should flower within a few weeks, depending on the type of rose. Climbers etc. may not flower until the following summer. If budding is not possible, repot them into larger pots and await a second flowering the following year. There is little point in planting them into the garden until they have proved worthwhile. All this has little to do with rose growing, but it is enjoyable, and no matter how poor the seedlings, at least they will be unique, which may give encouragement to progress to a little real hybridizing.

Pests and Diseases

The belief that shrub and old-fashioned roses are less troubled by pests and diseases than some of their modern cousins may not bear close analysis. The fact that this often appears to be the case is probably due more to their vigour and ability to overcome affliction than to any inherent resistance to contracting disease. This is further borne out by the fact that many have come down to us from the distant past. Frequently, too, the once-flowering cultivars and species will have finished their main flush of flowers before diseases or pests have a chance to affect them seriously, whereas in modern roses, if left unchecked, such afflictions as black spot and rust can cause havoc in late summer and autumn. There is undoubtedly a correlation between the vigour of a rose and its resistance to disease; some of the larger shrub roses, and in particular the vigorous climbers, are usually more healthy than their shorter counterparts.

Good cultivation, adequate feeding and, especially, good drainage and irrigation are the best methods of avoiding problems from diseases. Contented bushes will always give better rewards. Black spot and rust, probably the two worst diseases, have both been given a new lease of life since the late 1950s in the UK when Clean Air legislation was passed – hence less healthy roses – a small price to pay, admittedly, for the improvement to our own health. Most other countries have similar legislation and their rose growers similar problems. Our best hope in the control of rose diseases comes from the breeders who are becoming ever more conscious of the need to raise healthier stocks. To achieve this they will have to search back among old-fashioned roses and species to find the elusive, disease-resistant genes.

Pests

APHIDS

When conditions are right, aphids of many types attack roses but by far the most common are greenflies and a severe infestation can be very troublesome. Aphids have a number of natural predators, in particular the delightful and harmless ladybird, although it is unlikely that she alone will provide any measure of control. Ants, too, are often seen in company with aphids, but these are attracted to the sticky deposits left behind rather than to the pests themselves. Aphids multiply rapidly if left unchecked. In days gone by gardeners used soapy water to control these pests, and they also sprayed tobacco water on infested shoots. Some even purchased special aphid brushes to remove them, cleverly designed to avoid any damage to the roses. Nowadays we use insecticides, some so sophisticated that they are harmless to birds and predatory insects. The most effective of these are 'systemic', which work from within the plant, thus preventing infestation before it occurs. Such sprays need applying at about 10– to 14–day intervals. Contact insecticides actually kill aphids after infestation, and such sprays need repeating as and when aphids are seen to be present.

CAPSID BUGS

These are less common than aphids and can be quite elusive little pests, quickly moving on from one bush to another. They damage succulent growing tips, leaving them stunted, withered and peppered with tiny holes. Systemic insecticides are the best preventative measures, although the capsids will often cause some damage before succumbing to their effects.

CATERPILLARS

Various caterpillars occasionally attack the leaves of roses. Evidence of their presence is usually the disappearance of whole sections of leaf or the growing tips of young tender shoots. A search through the foliage usually finds them, for removal and instant disposal.

Caterpillars are the larvae of moths which themselves do not feed on roses, so chemical control is more difficult. Specific chemicals for caterpillar control are nevertheless available. Advice on these should be sought from experts if the infestation is troublesome.

Pests and diseases

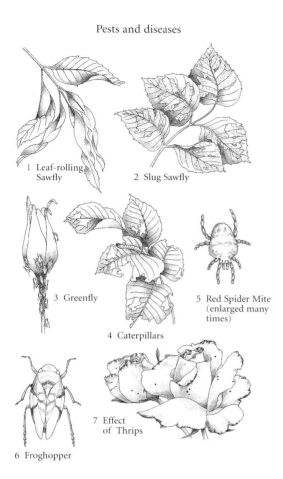

1 Leaf-rolling Sawfly

2 Slug Sawfly

3 Greenfly

5 Red Spider Mite (enlarged many times)

4 Caterpillars

7 Effect of Thrips

6 Froghopper

CUCKOOSPIT

The unsightly appearance of this pest is probably more offensive than the pest itself, at least on roses. It is more common on roses with heavy weed infestation or those growing in herbaceous borders than on those in the open. The spittle-like substance surrounding the froghopper nymph can usually be washed away by an extra strong jet from the sprayer, whilst spraying against other pests or diseases.

LEAF-ROLLING SAWFLY

Damage caused by this insect usually manifests itself too late for any remedy. The only answer – and this is rather hit-and-miss – is to start spraying with contact insecticides very early in the year to try to catch adult flies whilst they seek out suitable young leaves to infest with their eggs. Not all damaged leaves will have fertile eggs; most, it would seem, are injected by the sawfly with a chemical which causes the leaf to curl, thus protecting the larvae when they hatch. Heavy infestation can be

very unsightly in early summer, but the bush, although suffering slightly from the interruption to its natural process, soon recovers. No real harm is done, except perhaps to render it more prone to diseases such as mildew. Spraying with the same chemical as that used for caterpillars will give some measure of control over the developing larvae, but the curled leaves make this extremely difficult.

Another species of sawfly following the same life cycle is known as the slug sawfly. This is less common but can be devastating if an infestation occurs. The larvae feed on the surface tissue of the leaf, leaving just a skeleton structure behind. Control of this is the same as that for the leaf-rolling sawfly.

RED SPIDER

This very difficult little curse is more troublesome on roses under glass than on those outdoors. The mites are almost invisible to the naked eye and live on the undersides of the leaves. They multiply very quickly and often have a severe hold over the roses before an infestation can be diagnosed, causing leaves to lose colour, become limp and eventually fall to the ground; the eggs then lie in the soil throughout the winter. Control is difficult and more effective before severe infestation occurs. Pirimiphos-methyl seems, at present, to be the most effective chemical if applied whilst the mites are active in summer. If the presence of this pest is suspected without actual evidence, give the ground around the bushes a good winter-wash with old-fashioned tar oil while the roses are dormant. This will destroy any eggs before they hatch.

THRIPS

This pest is more troublesome on modern roses than on old-fashioned roses, preferring the tighter buds of the large-flowered roses. It usually occurs in hot, thundery weather and is seldom nuisance enough to warrant spraying, except perhaps on some of the climbing Hybrid Teas and the more doubled Bourbons, Noisettes and Teas. Again prevention is better than cure, and spraying with a systemic or contact insecticide just before the flower buds begin to open will usually stop the tiny little flies from nibbling at the edges of the petals and disfiguring the flowers.

RABBITS AND DEER

Rabbits can be quite a serious pest to roses in country gardens, especially in winter, and particularly in those situated near golf courses and heathland, and open acres of farmland, where rabbits are more numerous. Their activities are unpredictable. In spring baby rabbits, in particular, find the young, succulent tips of roses most acceptable; and in winter rabbits of all ages indulge in what appears to be malicious vandalism, stripping the bark completely off shoots of any age, to tiptoe height. If planting roses in a country garden, take the precaution of fencing them off against rabbit invasion; failing this, encircle each bush, at least during its first years, with small-mesh wire. There are chemicals, offensive to rabbits, which are supposed to keep them off, but these, in my experience, provide only flimsy defence.

Deer, too, enjoy a good meal of roses, especially when hungry in deep mid-winter. They can be a particular problem in the USA; but in Britain, where they are still shy creatures, they should only present a threat to roses growing near woodlands or on parkland. Roses are sometimes grown around paddock fences and the like, and it should be remembered that most grazing animals will sample the taste of any roses they can reach. The most positive precaution here is to plant only the most thorny cultivars and species.

Three Persistent North American Pests
By Malcolm Lowe

CANE BORERS

Cane borers are the larvae of wasps and sawflies which lay their eggs in the ends of freshly cut stems in early summer. Their presence is indicated by sawdust extruding from holes in the stems. Their presence causes canes to die back, often to the bud union. Serious infestations may be fatal. To prevent cane borer damage, seal all cuts in canes larger in diameter than a pencil with household glue. It is advisable to add a few drops of food colouring to the glue so that the treated canes may be identified.

JAPANESE BEETLES

This half-inch-long metallic green scourge of the American rose-grower emerges from mid-May in the South to early July in New England, after spending ten months underground as a grub. Their period of greatest activity lasts from four to six weeks. Japanese beetles fly only during the day and are most active on sunny days. They congregate and feed on leaves and flowers, eating away large areas of foliage and entire blossoms. Female beetles burrow into turf to lay their eggs, after which they return to the plants to feed again. The most effective controls are those insecticides used for turf and golf courses – 1-Methylethyl-2 (Oftanol) will kill the grubs; carbaryl is good against adult beetles. To be really effective, control procedures should be carried out with near neighbours.

MIDGE

These minute yellow-brown flies lay eggs on leaf and flower buds. The larvae hatch and feed on the leaves causing them to dry up and die, at which time the larvae fall to the ground where they develop into adults. The whole life cycle takes only two weeks. Insecticides sprayed on the foliage and ground in two thorough applications ten days apart will give some control. At one time it was thought that midge had been eradicated by DDT, but it is reappearing exponentially.

Diseases

BLACK SPOT

Of all the diseases to affect roses, with the possible exception of rust, black spot is the most pernicious. Persistent attack on some cultivars can leave the shrubs somewhat jaded each year and ultimately reduce them to a fraction of their true selves.

The disease attacks the leaves, usually from mid-summer onwards, often resulting in complete defoliation. Even a partial or mild attack will render bushes unsightly. It can be recognized easily by the black or dark brown patches which spread rapidly over leaves and often extend to the young stems, causing them initially to become mottled and later to die. Each leaf that falls carries with it millions of spores which overwinter in the soil, ready for an attack the following season.

The removal and burning of infected leaves, both from the bush and from the surrounding ground, will therefore help prevent the disease spreading to less susceptible cultivars. Black spot is a fact of life in roses and little can be done remedially once the disease has taken hold. A number of chemicals are available which, if sprayed in advance of the infection, will keep the disease at bay, at least until the first flush of the flowers is over. Manu-

Black spot

CROWN GALL

This bacterial disease, prevalent throughout the USA and Canada, causes rough irregular galls on stems near the bud union. The only known control is to remove the galls and paint the wounds with a dilute solution of a suitable bleach (take advice at your local garden centre). If this is not effective the bush and the surrounding soil should be dug out, as the bacteria can live in the soil for up to two years after the infected plant is removed.

POWDERY MILDEW

facturers' claims as to the degree of control can only be justified if their instructions are strictly followed and accompanied by good husbandry and cleanliness.

Experience has convinced me that regular overhead irrigation will control black spot, provided it is carried out overnight to avoid scorching the foliage. This should be done, at minimum intervals of ten days, for about five hours on each occasion. From the point of view of cleanliness, a winter wash both of the plant and the surrounding ground with a solution of Jeyes Fluid helps to kill off any spores lurking on decaying leaves or in the soil and helps delay infection from the disease in early summer.

Powdery mildew attacks roses from early summer onwards and, if allowed to flourish, can be quite a serious problem on some cultivars. The first signs are small patches of greyish-white powder, usually near the top of the young growing shoots and on the succulent young leaves. If not checked, these patches spread rapidly to cover the entire plant. In severe epidemics it will also extend to the more mature leaves and flower buds. The young leaves curl, distort and fail to develop, thus preventing the plant from functioning satisfactorily. Attacks of mildew on otherwise healthy plants weaken their resistance to other diseases; black spot, in particular, flourishes when mildew has been allowed

Powdery mildew

Mildew on a branch

to take hold. Well-nourished plants, while not rendered immune, will suffer less than undernourished ones. Equally, the 'prevention is better than cure' rule applies to chemical control of the disease. A number of contact fungicides are available, but in order to be effective they should contain a wetting or spreading agent to enable sufficient chemical to adhere to the leaves. Systemic fungicides are the best method of combating mildew. Known susceptible cultivars should be sprayed well in advance of the appearance of the disease. Mildew is very persistent and has a very rapid life cycle, enabling spores to develop resistance to specific chemicals very quickly. For this reason, if the effectiveness of spraying starts to wear off, change to something else for a while. The over-use of nitrogenous fertilizers is often the cause of mildew, especially when mid-summer application leads to excessive growth in the autumn. Mildew may also follow summer drought, so try to keep the roses well-watered during such weather.

DOWNY MILDEW

This form of mildew affects roses grown under glass, especially those grown in pots. It takes the form of dull brownish or sometimes bluish patches on the surface of mature leaves, which can also spread to the stems. Infected leaves become limp and fall. Severe attacks may cause the death of whole plants. The disease is usually brought on by extremes of day and night temperatures, especially when linked to bad ventilation in greenhouses and conservatories. Some control can be achieved by the use of similar fungicides to those used against powdery mildew and black spot. The disease seldom attacks outdoor roses.

RUST

Of all rose diseases, a bad infestation of rust can be the most devastating. If conditions are right – it enjoys moist warm weather – susceptible cultivars will deteriorate rapidly and die. Signs of infection are often not noticed until the disease is established but if spotted early enough it can be controlled. Small orange pustules attach themselves to the undersides of leaves and multiply rapidly until they have spread all over the plant including, on occasions, the stems and thorns. As the spores age, they turn to dark brown and eventually to black, killing the leaf in the process. In some extra-susceptible cultivars where the stem has also been affected, the lifeless, brown leaves hang on to the plant as it dies.

Rust on leaves in summer

In others, they fall to the ground where the spores overwinter in readiness for the following season.

At the first sign of the disease, all infected foliage should be removed and burned. Chemical control is difficult because spray has to be directed upwards on to the undersides of the leaves. The same fungicides as used for black spot have some preventative qualities but, if an attack is diagnosed at an advanced stage, oxycarboxin, a chemical available under several trade names, is quite effective. Cultivars most prone to this disease tend to act as hosts, thus causing the less susceptible ones to become infected. If rust is found to occur repeatedly on the same plants it is best to remove and burn them. 'Conrad Ferdinand Meyer' and 'Sarah Van Fleet', both Hybrid Rugosas, are particular culprits and should be kept out of gardens where rust has proved a problem.

STEM CANKER

This is not a serious problem on good, well-nourished bushes. It is more frequently seen on older plants which have been allowed to develop lots of old wood, much of which has outlived its usefulness. It also appears on very old climbers, where constant pruning over the years has permitted the disease to enter the plant through exposed tissue. The disease takes the form of large, irregular-shaped lesions, usually parched brown, sunken near the edges and swollen in the centre. Sometimes the bark is slightly lifted at the edge and rather gnarled in appearance. If infection occurs on expendable branches, these should be removed and burned; but older plants frequently develop the disease in awkward places. Careful removal of the lesions with a sharp knife and painting the wound with grafting wax or a similar substance will sometimes succeed. Such surgery is only worth trying if the bush or climber has great sentimental value. The best course is to destroy the old badly infected plant and replace it with another.

MINERAL DEFICIENCIES

Iron deficiency is probably the most common nutritional ailment of roses; this manifests itself in a yellowing of the leaves, especially younger leaves either on the margins, or along the veins, or both. The leaves eventually turn completely yellow and drop off. Since the deficiency commonly occurs in calcareous soils, an application of sequestered iron to the soil in early spring should correct it. In the longer term, it is worth applying potash to the soil to help release locked-up iron.

The other common deficiency is that of magnesium, which, in the case of roses, is probably a major requirement for successful performance. Symptoms of deficiency are not easily recognizable, but the leaves, especially the older ones, show chlorosis and are sometimes badly developed, especially at their apex. Epsom salts, applied to the soil once or twice a season in liquid form, will help rectify this. Where symptoms are markedly obvious, it can be applied as a foliar feed.

MOSAIC VIRUS

My experience of viruses inasmuch as they infect roses in Britain is limited to observing, from time to time, obvious symptoms of mosaic in one or two cultivars. However, if the virus is present in other cultivars, and this could well be so, it does not manifest itself in our climate to anywhere near the same extent as it does in the warmer parts of the world, where it can be quite a serious problem in outdoor-grown roses of all types but especially in some of the older cultivars. Accepting my limited knowledge, therefore, and believing that the problem of mosaic virus should be more clearly understood, I am delighted to include the following essay by Malcolm Manners of the Citrus Institute, Florida Southern College, who is not only an authority on this subject but also a devotee of the old garden roses.

Rose Mosaic Virus Disease

By Malcolm M. Manners

The subject of rose mosaic disease has received considerable attention in the popular rose press over the past few years. Unfortunately, much of the information presented has not been based on demonstrable fact, and some is patently false.

There are many virus diseases of roses, including rose wilt, rose rosette, and rose spring dwarf, but this discussion will be concerned only with rose mosaic disease, which is by far the most commonly encountered viral disease of roses. Rose mosaic is actually a group of diseases having similar leaf symptoms, caused by at least three different viruses. These viruses normally attack fruit trees in the rose family (Rosaceae), such as peach, cherry and apple, and in these trees the disease spreads from tree to tree in the orchard by natural means. In roses, however, the disease apparently is *not* contagious and will not infect healthy bushes adjacent to an infected bush.* Rather, the disease is spread in the nursery, when uninfected roses are grafted or budded on to an infected understock. In areas of the world where understocks are traditionally grown from seed (e.g. the UK and much of Europe), mosaic is not a great problem, since the virus is not transmitted by seed propagation. In areas where understock plants are grown from cuttings (as in the USA), the disease will be present in the newly propagated plants, if the original stock plants were infected. American rose cultivars are therefore very often infected. Once a scion variety is infected, merely budding it to virus-free understock will not cure it; all such newly propagated plants will also be infected.

Symptoms of rose mosaic consist of wavy yellow to white lines on the leaves, arranged symmetrically around the veins, or sometimes irregular yellow to white patches on the leaves. Usually the first growth flush of the spring will show the most obvious symptoms. Most bushes show no obvious symptoms at all, most of the time. Sometimes a plant will remain symptomless for years, and then suddenly show strong symptoms, evidently in response to some aspect of the weather as the leaves developed. This phenomenon has promoted the (false) notion that bushes were 'catching' the disease in the garden, when in reality they were infected all along, and now finally showed some symptoms.

Rose mosaic would be of no great concern if these fleeting leaf symptoms were the only effect of the disease. But tests done on greenhouse roses in Holland, and on outdoor-grown roses in England, California, and more recently Florida (in our

* Arabis mosaic virus, the least common form of mosaic in roses, is spread by a nematode through the soil, but the probability of a rose garden being infected with that rare form of mosaic and the correct nematode, simultaneously, is small. M.M.

gardens), have shown that an infected plant will produce fewer flowers, poorer quality flowers and shorter stems and show reduced overall growth of the bush, reduced winter hardiness, and a number of other undesirable characteristics. These bushes may be of entirely acceptable quality, but probably could be better if they weren't infected. From the nurseryman's point of view, an uninfected bush would also be superior, in that he could produce plants of higher calibre and more vigorous growth, allowing him to sell a higher quality plant, perhaps in somewhat less time.

Once a plant is infected, there is nothing the gardener can do to cure it. Plants can be cured by holding them at precisely 38°C (100°F) for four or more weeks, after which buds are cut and budded to virus-free understocks. Most of the new plants will be free of the disease. But this procedure requires special facilities to keep the plant at the proper temperature without killing it, and only a few institutions actually use the procedure. In the USA, the University of California (at Davis), Florida Southern College (Lakeland, Florida), and Bear Creek Nurseries (who own Jackson & Perkins Roses and Armstrong Roses) are currently doing rose heat-therapy. If there are such programmes in other countries, I am unaware of them.*

Since rose mosaic is not contagious, nor is it deadly or otherwise devastating, there is no great reason to destroy a bush in the garden simply because it shows symptoms. Still, one probably could achieve better vigour and productivity with an uninfected plant of the same variety, so it is worth trying to find mosaic-free plants, when shopping for roses.

Malformation of Flowers

PROLIFERATION

Some of the more double-flowered old-fashioned roses will occasionally sprout a malformed bud from their centre. This is known as proliferation, and is a most unpleasant sight. The phenomenon usually occurs in the early flowers, and in the case of the repeat-flowering shrubs, seldom reappears on autumn flowers. Close inspection of the

Proliferation

misshapen flowers reveals that for some reason, probably genetic, the reproductive organs, in particular the pistils, have become fused, and instead of developing normally have changed into another complete flower bud, which grows out of the centre of the bloom. Close examination of this secondary bud shows that it appears to be complete in every way; sometimes it is even carried on a stalk and protrudes as much as half an inch (1.5 cm). I have occasionally seen this in less obvious form in the very first blooms of some modern large-flowered roses, but this is rare.

Although some authorities consider it to be a virus, so far as I know this has not been proved. I know of no other scientific explanation, but since its incidence does not seem to be related to the soil in which a cultivar is grown, at least out of doors, nor to any noticeable geographical location, we must assume it to be a form of genetic mutation, inherent in particular cultivars and pepetuated by careless selection of propagation material. I believe that the severity of the malformation is in some ways influenced either by temperature or sunlight or both. Flowers appear to be more severely affected following a dull, cold spring, and bushes growing in partial shade are invariably worse than those in the open. I have noticed, too, that the problem is less severe on plants growing under glass. I find it interesting that 'Mme Isaac Pereire' is more prone to this problem than her sport 'Mme Ernst Calvat'. The same applies to 'Souvenir de la Malmaison', which sometimes suffers, and her sport 'Souvenir de St Anne's', which does not. Apart from those already mentioned, some of the other more double Bourbons are also badly affected, as are one or two Damasks, some of the Centifolias and a few Mosses. The occasional Hybrid Perpetual – closely related to the Bourbons – is also troubled from time to time; likewise the Chinas 'Bloomfield Abundance'

---

* The facility for heat treatment described by Malcolm Manners is available at a number of both educational and private establishments in the UK, but not specifically for roses. – P.B.

and, to a lesser extent, 'Cécile Brünner'. Little can be done by way of prevention or cure beyond the removal of affected blooms as they appear.

BALLING OF FLOWERS

Some old-fashioned roses, in common with some modern roses, do not like wet weather in summer. This is particularly true of the many-petalled, fully double cultivars with tightly folded flowers. They can usually endure it when open, but if prolonged rain occurs during the late bud stage, their outer petals will rot and congeal, thus preventing the flower from opening. Balling can become worse if strong sunshine follows rain, causing the petals to become encased in a crisp cocoon of decay, from which there is no escape. The whole flower then rots and falls off or, worse still, remains on the plant in a ruined, unsightly mess. There is not much to be done about this beyond cursing the weather, although in smaller gardens, where an individual rose is suffering, the outer petals can be teased carefully from the bud with thumb and forefinger before the rot has gone too deep, thus allowing the flower to unfurl without hindrance. Cultivars particularly prone to this are the Bourbons 'Souvenir de la Malmaison' and 'Boule de Neige',

Above, a balled flower, and
below, a balled flower after being teased open

and the Hybrid Perpetuals 'Baronne Prévost', 'Georg Arends' and 'Frau Karl Druschki'. Some of the Centifolias and Mosses are also prone.

OTHER AILMENTS

Other minor ailments can, from time to time, trouble roses. The most common of these stem from our own careless use of chemicals, particularly herbicides. Great care must be taken with these, especially the hormone variety. By far the most common diagnosis I make is that of spray damage. Always use a separate sprayer for weed-killers. No matter how carefully you think you have washed herbicide from a machine, there could be just enough left inside to kill or disfigure your plants.

Commercial Production

Although no one is certain of the exact figure, between eighteen and twenty-five million rose bushes are produced annually in Great Britain – up to one bush for every three people in the population. Do a similar sum for the rest of the rose-loving world and the answer is – a very large number.

I decided to include a brief word about commercial production after a rather unpleasant experience with a customer who could not understand why it should take us two years to propagate a rare rose for her. Like all businesses, rose nurseries have to run at a profit so methods have changed somewhat since the beginning of this century, but the basic principles have remained unchanged since it was first discovered that two plants could be united by budding. In very recent times, in fact in the last ten years, other methods of production have been tried – micropropagation, for example, though it is by no means certain that the technique will ever become widespread, nor indeed whether all types of roses can be grown by this means. I shall confine my thoughts to a general outline of conventional practice; micropropagation is discussed on page 454.

Commercial rose growers need to own, or have access to, at least four times more land than is needed to grow a single crop. This is because rotation is important and also because roses take two full growing seasons to become saleable, so there will always be two crops of different ages growing at the same time. And, just as in the garden, roses never like growing on land that has previously grown them without, at least, two years' rest in between.

Growers these days are well mechanized, for good land-implements are important. Land is prepared by ploughing and surface cultivation well in advance; rootstocks are ordered from specialist growers many months beforehand, too. Stocks arrive in November and are kept, either heeled-in or in a cold store, until land and weather are suitable for planting. In Britain, this is usually in February or March. Stocks are planted by a tractor-drawn machine with four operators feeding them in. The rows are usually from 30 to 36″ (75–90 cm) wide, with 6″ (15 cm) between the plants in each row. At these planting distances, the density is roughly 25,000 plants per acre. On a good day, a crew can plant about an acre. When planting is finished, the sprayer moves in and sprays the soil with a pre-emergence herbicide. Fertilizers will have been applied well beforehand.

By mid-June the stocks are ready for budding (see page 449). Apart from lifting, this is the most expensive and time-consuming of all the tasks relating to the production of roses. Budding is a skill, the basics of which are not too difficult to learn providing the pupil is reasonably dextrous. Speed is acquired through practice and experience. It is very much a job for the young, for, although it is not physically demanding, it is not easy to work all day with the body bent double. The real secret of good budding is the speed at which it is carried out; the faster the budder works the more likely the buds are to 'take'. Budders usually work in pairs followed by a 'patcher' who places a small latex patch over the wound where the bud has been inserted. A good team of three will put on as many as 6,000–7,000 buds in a day. Budders are serviced by another team whose job is to cut the budwood from the correct cultivars and dethorn them for ease of handling. Weather permitting, budding is usually finished by the end of July. It is never done in the rain. After July the buds will still 'take' but the percentage that live declines as the days get shorter. In peak season budders hope to get at least 90 per cent to take; 100 per cent is not uncommon on some cultivars. Anything less than 85 per cent on modern cultivars is considered poor, although with old-fashioned roses such a take would be considered good. Throughout the summer the stocks are kept clear of pests and diseases by regular spraying.

After budding, the next stage in the process is 'heading back', as it is known in Norfolk; in other parts of Britain it is called variously 'cutting down', 'heading off' or 'topping'. This takes place in the winter months, usually January or February depending on the weather, and involves the removal of all the top growth from the stock by cutting it off just above the point where the bud was inserted. Secateurs or long-handled pruners are used, though some large nurseries speed up the process with pneumatically operated secateurs. In early spring a balanced fertilizer is applied, together with further applications of pre-emergence herbicide. By May, the buds will have grown to about 3 or 4″ (7.5–10 cm). At this stage, some growers cut the young shoots back to just 1″ (2.5 cm) to encourage several shoots to grow from the union. By early June, the young maiden plants are about 6″ (15 cm) high and it is then that nurserymen pray for calm weather, for the plants are now very vulnerable and easily blown off at the union by wind; invariably there are a few windy days and losses can be heavy. By early July, the roses are in flower and in turn become the source of budding eyes for the next year's crop, and so on. As they grow, a careful watch is kept for suckers which appear from below the bud. These are removed as soon as they are spotted. A regular spraying programme is carried out against aphids, black spot, mildew and rust.

By October, the young plants will have ripened and lifting starts. This is usually done by a special tractor-drawn lifting plough which undercuts the plants, enabling them to be pulled easily from the ground with a gloved hand. On large, wholesale nurseries part of the crop is lifted and placed in cold stores where the roses come to no harm. On retail nurseries some growers do likewise; others simply lift the roses as they are needed for orders. Grading is important and by the time the roses have become saleable about 75 per cent of most cultivars will be first quality; the remainder will have been lost through failure to take, by wind damage or inadequate size. It is impossible to forecast the demand for each cultivar two years ahead of sales, so few retail growers ever sell completely out of all cultivars, although, of course, this is their aim. Roses, like most long-term crops, are both capital- and labour-intensive, and any form of bad husbandry can have dire consequences. Good training and skilled workers are therefore essential.

Breeding New Cultivars

Plant breeding and hybridizing is a subject in itself and an elementary knowledge of botany is probably necessary for it to be fully understood.

Of all facets of roses and rose growing, it is probably fair to assume – judging by the questions I am asked – that breeding new cultivars holds the most mystery. Many people appear to confuse this process with that of vegetative propagation, which I have already discussed. The breeding of roses is achieved by manual, sexual fertilization and is concerned only with the flowers of the two roses which are being crossed, and the resulting seeds.

Propagation, on the other hand, is achieved by inducing parts of plants to produce roots, as in cuttings; or to join with other plants, as in grafting or budding, thus increasing their numbers by non-sexual means; it therefore concerns only the shoots and roots of plants, not the flowers.

Beauty, fortunately, is in the eye of the beholder, so no one will ever know if the perfect rose is produced; perhaps, if we judge on flowers alone, all roses are perfect; hybridizers, however, seek much more than perfection in flower. They nowadays look for health, vigour, attractive foliage, scent, resistance to weather, and an agreeable habit of growth.

The first step for a hybridizer is to select potential parent roses with care. This choice will depend upon the type of rose he wishes to breed. A professional will give first consideration to parents likely to satisfy public demand. The present vogue for so-called ground-cover roses is the hybridizer's reaction to the modern preference for labour-saving, cost-effective plants. In Victorian times, fashion demanded large, shapely flowers for the show bench, and in the Edwardian era, ramblers and climbers for arches and pergolas. This is not to say, of course, that hybridizers merely follow fashion; they sometimes create it, as, for example, the brightly coloured Floribunda roses of the 1950s and 1960s, and the Miniature roses of the 1970s.

The selected breeding stock will either be planted in cold greenhouses or grown in pots. Hybridizing begins as soon as the roses start to flower in late spring or early summer. The first stage is to remove all petals from the selected seed parent. This must be done just before the petals unfold, thus ensuring no previous cross-fertilization. The next stage is to render the seed parent totally female by removing the stamens very carefully, usually with small scissors or tweezers. The stamens can be kept in small containers for use later as a male parent. Removal of stamens is a delicate operation, and any damage caused to the young seed pod will quickly result in the failure of the cross. The prepared potential mother is then left for about 24 hours, during which time the stigma will be seen to have become 'receptive' by deepening in colour and becoming slightly sticky. It is then ready for fertilization. Ripe pollen (visible as fine powder on the anthers) is then selected from a pre-chosen, compatible cultivar, and dusted on to the receptive female with a fine, soft brush. It should then be labelled and recorded. If pollen is plentiful, a further application the next day may benefit germination. Particular care must be taken with pollen to ensure that it

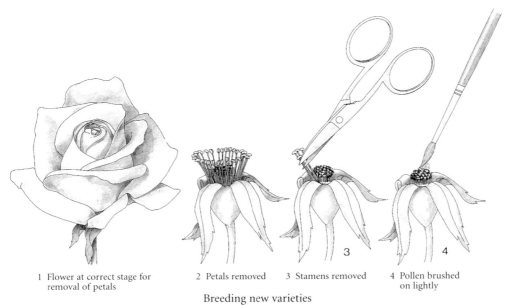

1 Flower at correct stage for removal of petals 2 Petals removed 3 Stamens removed 4 Pollen brushed on lightly

Breeding new varieties

does not become mixed; and any brushes used should be reserved for each individual batch of pollen and cleaned thoroughly after use. When pollen of selected parents is plentiful, commercial hybridizers often dust it straight on to the stigma from a fully open rose.

After about two weeks, a successful mating will manifest itself in a healthy green hip which will eventually ripen to rich red or orange. If the cross has failed, the pod and stalk will start to wither and eventually turn brown or, in some cases, just drop off. Sometimes, fertile hips which have gone through the ripe stage become brown and rotten, but these are still good and will contain seeds.

The pods should be taken from the plants in late autumn and stored in readiness for sowing in early spring.

When the seedlings come into flower, any that are worth keeping should be either potted on, for another year's growth and testing, or budded in the nursery. If many eventually useless seedlings are kept, it can become a very expensive waste of time; so for commercial purposes only about one in fifty seedlings is taken to a second year of testing. After that time any seedlings with potential can be propagated in larger numbers for further trial. This is never more than one in every 500 or so, and by the third year of trial this could well be reduced to one in 5,000. Consequently, unless hybridizing is done on a very large scale, the chances of breeding a top-selling rose are very remote.

World Climatic Map

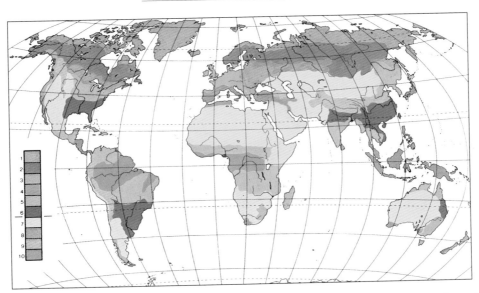

The following are brief notes on the main climatic regions of the world where roses can be grown. Temperature ranges are only an average and from time to time can be far exceeded. Wild, species roses are found widely across Central Asia, but for the main in less arid and less mountainous parts. Areas of desert, Arctic waste, high mountains and humid jungle – numbers 7, 8, 9 and 10 respectively on the map colour key – are not conducive to growing roses.

1 Temperature range –3°C (26°F) (winter) to 22°C (72°F) (summer)

Most roses require winter protection, except for *pimpinellifolia* hybrids, *kordesii* hybrids and the very hardy species. Most other types will grow well in summer, but the less hardy ramblers and climbers seldom reach their full potential.

2 Temperature range –25°C (–13°F) (winter) to 16°C (61°F) (summer)

Roses will require winter protection. Avoid all Teas, Chinas, Noisettes and less hardy Hybrid Teas and Floribundas.

3 Temperature range 0°C (32°F) (winter) to 23°C (73°F) (summer)

All roses enjoy such conditions, though Teas, Noisettes, Chinas and some less hardy Hybrid Teas and Floribundas may suffer some frost damage in more severe winters.

4 Temperature range 10°C (50°F) (winter) to 23°C (73°F) (summer)

All roses will flourish in such conditions, except for some hybrid Rugosas, Centifolias, Gallicas and hybrid Pimpinellifolias which will not enjoy the heat of summer and may struggle, especially in areas of low rainfall.

5 Temperature range 10°C (50°F) (winter) to more than 30°C (86°F) (summer)

Almost all roses will grow reasonably well where rainfall is sufficient. In these conditions hybrid Rugosas, Pimpinellifolias and *kordesii* hybrids will suffer in the heat of the summer, as will some Hybrid Perpetuals, Bourbons and older types such as Centifolias and Gallicas.

6 Temperature range 5°C (41°F) (winter) to 25°C (77°F) (summer)

Most roses will grow well, especially Teas, Chinas and Noisettes. Rugosa and Pimpinellifolia hybrids will dislike the heat of summer, as will older roses such as Centifolias, Damasks and Gallicas.

Height and Colour Charts
An Introduction and User's Guide

With so many cultivars to choose from, designing a completely new rose garden or even just selecting a few cultivars for strategic positioning amongst other plants in the garden can be a daunting task, no matter how knowledgeable the gardener.

While other variables such as fragrance, flowering seasons, resistance to disease, autumn colour and availability inevitably come into play, linking colour and ultimate stature is the most important consideration when landscaping with roses. These charts are therefore an attempt to bring together these two criteria and will, I hope, make selection a little easier. Readers should, however, bear in mind that many arbitrary factors prevail and that by their nature such charts can only be a rough guide or, more accurately, a starting point to selection.

HEIGHTS

In all cases heights given are approximate and indicate the probable ultimate size of a species or cultivar if grown in good, normal soil, in temperate climates and assuming that pruning, feeding and health care are practised along the lines explained in the Cultivation section of this book (page 437).

The height differential bands were selected after much careful thought but I am well aware that in some particularly agreeable climates the Teas, Noisettes and Chinas, for example, are very capable of considerably exceeding the heights given.

COLOURS

While it is simple to differentiate between soft yellow and deep yellow or scarlet and crimson, there are many shades in between where the difference is not so clearly defined. The pinks, for example, are particularly difficult. When does a blush become a soft pink, or a bright pink a salmon, or a deep pink a carmine or cerise? The orange cultivars are not so much difficult as impossible, for many roses of these shades possess just those subtle variations of colour that transpose them from yellowy-orange to reddish-orange or vice versa. In each case the decision to allocate a rose to this rather than that colour band has been a matter of personal opinion based on the predominant colour of the rose at the point when the flower is fully open.

Other more tangible factors also affect colour – climate, soils, aspects and even air pollution are just four examples. Readers are therefore well advised, if colour is a critical factor in any design, not to rely too heavily on these charts but to seek out examples of particular roses in their own districts before making their choice.

IMPERIAL/METRIC CONVERSION TABLE				
20 feet and over	=	6 m ⟶		
15 to 20 feet	=	4.5	to 6	m
10 to 15 feet	=	3	to 4.5	m
7 to 10 feet	=	2	to 3	m
4 to 7 feet	=	1.2	to 2	m
3 to 4 feet	=	90	to 120	cm
2 to 3 feet	=	60	to 90	cm
1 to 2 feet	=	30	to 60	cm
less than 1 foot	=	⟶	30	cm

Climbers, Ramblers and Scramblers

WHITE AND SOFT CREAMY SHADES

BLUSH

SOFT PINK

20 FEET AND OVER'

'Bennett's Seedling'
'Bobbie James'
'Dundee Rambler'
'La Mortola'
R. arvensis
R. banksiae alba plena
R. banksiae normalis
R. brunonii
R. cymosa
R. foetida
R. gentiliana
R. helenae
R. longicuspis
R. moschata floribunda
R. moschata grandiflora
R. mulliganii
R. phoenicia
R. rubus
'Rambling Rector'
'Seagull'
'Sir Cedric Morris'
'Wedding Day'

15 TO 20 FEET

'Astra Desmond'
'City of York'
'Cooper's Burmese'
'Félicité Perpétue'
'Frau Karl Druschki'
'Iceberg'
'Janet B. Wood'
'Mme Plantier'
R. anemoneflora
R. × fortuniana
R. laevigata
R. multiflora
R. multiflora wilsonii
R. sempervirens
'Silver Moon'
'The Garland'

10 TO 15 FEET

'Aimée Vibert'
'Autumnalis'
'Devoniensis'
'Ilse Krohn Superior'
'Lamarque'
'Long John Silver'
'Louise d'Arzens'
'Mrs Herbert Stevens'
'Niphetos'
'Purity'
R. luciae
R. sinowilsonii
R. soulieana
'Sanders White'
'Snowdrift'
'Spectabilis'
'Thalia'
'Toby Tristram'
'Wickwar'

UP TO 10 FEET

'Blanc Pur'
'Paul's Perpetual White'
'Princess of Nassau'
R. bracteata
R. moschata
'Sombreuil'
'White Cockade'

20 FEET AND OVER

'Brenda Colvin'
'Cécile Brünner'
'Dr W. Van Fleet'
'Ethel'

15 TO 20 FEET

'Belle Vichysoise'
'Champneys' Pink Cluster'
'Francis E. Lester'
'Ophelia'
'Princesse Louise'
R. multiflora carnea
R. multiflora cathayensis
'Venusta Pendula'

10 TO 15 FEET

'Adélaide d'Orléans'
'Awakening'
'Blush Rambler'
'Flora'
'Lady Emily Peel'
'Mme Alfred Carrière'
'Mme d'Arblay'
'New Dawn'
'Souvenir de la Malmaison'
'Wickmoss'

UP TO 10 FEET

'Eden Rose '88'
'Swan Lake'

20 FEET AND OVER

'Paul's Himalayan Musk'
'Ruga'
'Splendens'

15 TO 20 FEET

'Baltimore Belle'
'Breeze Hill'
'Captain Christy'
'Evangeline'
'Lady Waterlow'
'May Queen'
'Mme Butterfly'
'Tea Rambler'

10 TO 15 FEET

'Alida Lovett'
'Apple Blossom'
'Belle Portugaise'
'Blairii No. 2'
'Blush Boursault'
'Cupid'
'Debutante'
'Gerbe Rose'
'Mary Wallace'
'Paul Lédé'
'Sourire d'Orchidée'

UP TO 10 FEET

'Agatha Christie'
'Anemone Rose'
'Colcestria'
'Cupid'
'Kathleen Harrop'
'L'Abundance'
'Martha'
'Mme Abel Chatenay'
'Tausendschön'

Climbers, Ramblers and Scramblers

BRIGHT PINK AND SALMON

DEEP PINK

CERISE

OVER 20 FEET

None

15 TO 20 FEET

'Albertine'
'Blessings'
'Chaplin's Pink'
'Chaplin's Pink Companion'
'Constance Spry'
'Coral Creeper'
'Eden Rose'
'Euphrosine'
'François Juranville'
'Home Sweet Home'
'Kew Rambler'
'Köln am Rhein'
'Lady Sylvia'
'Laura Louise'
'Mme Caroline Testout'
'Mme Édouard Herriot'
'Mme Grégoire Staechelin'
'Picture'
'Queen Elizabeth'
'Queen of the Prairies'
'Shot Silk'
'Vicomtesse Pierre du Fou'

10 TO 15 FEET

'America'
'Auguste Gervais'
'Auguste Roussel'
'Bantry Bay'
'Blairii No. 1'
'Château de La Juvenie'
'City Girl'
'Coral Dawn'
'Dorothy Perkins'
'Fashion'
'Galway Bay'
'Handel'
'Intervilles'
'John Grooms'
'Lauré Davoust'
'Lavinia'
'Leaping Salmon'
'Léontine Gervais'
'Mary Wallace'
'Minnehaha'
'Mme Alice Garnier'
'Mme de Sancy de Parabére'
'Paul Transon'
'Pinkie'
'Souvenir de Mme Léonie
    Viennot'

UP TO 10 FEET

'Aloha'
'Antique'
'Clair Matin'
'Columbia Climber'
'Lorraine Lee'
'Mrs F. W. Flight'
'Norwich Salmon'
'Rosy Mantle'
'Sénateur Amic'
'Zéphirine Drouhin'

20 FEET AND OVER

'Sénateur La Follette'

15 TO 20 FEET

'American Pillar'

10 TO 15 FEET

'Jean Lafitte'
'Leuchtstern'
'Morlettii'
'Morning Jewel'
'Pink Perpétue'
'Pompon de Paris'
R. × l'heritierana
R. multiflora platyphylla

UP TO 10 FEET

'Étude'
'Karlsruhe'
'Malaga'
'Mme Driout'
'Ramona'
'Rhonda'
'Ritter von Barmstede'
'Summer Wine'
'Wind Chimes'

20 FEET AND OVER'

None

15 TO 20 FEET

'Cerise Bouquet'
'General MacArthur'

10 TO 15 FEET

'Parade'
'Reine Marie Henriette'

UP TO 10 FEET

'Captain Hayward'
'Norwich Pink'
'Sophie's Perpetual'

VERMILION AND ORANGE

20 FEET AND OVER

None

15 TO 20 FEET

None

10 TO 15 FEET

'Autumn Sunlight'
'Della Balfour'
'Korona'

UP TO 10 FEET

'Dixieland Linda'
'Pinata'
'Warm Welcome'

SCARLET

20 FEET AND OVER

None

15 TO 20 FEET

None

10 TO 15 FEET

'Allen Chandler'
'Altissimo'
'Danse de Feu'
'Danse des Sylphes'
'Deschamps'
'Fragrant Cloud'
'Raymond Chenault'
'Soldier Boy'
'Sparkling Scarlet'

UP TO 10 FEET

'Blaze'
'Grand Hotel'
'Paul's Scarlet'
'Richmond'

CRIMSON AND DEEP RED

20 FEET AND OVER

None

15 TO 20 FEET

'Château de Clos Vougeot' 429
'Crimson Conquest' 429
'Crimson Glory' 421
'Ena Harkness' 430
'Josephine Bruce' 431
'Tempo' 786

10 TO 15 FEET

'Ards Rover'
'Chevy Chase'
'Cramoisi Supérieur'
'Crimson Rambler'
'Crimson Showers'
'Dr Huey'
'Étoile de Hollande'
'Excelsa'
'Guinée'
'Hiawatha'
'Parkdirektor Riggers'
'Reine Olga de Wurtemberg'
'Roundelay'
'Souvenir de Claudius
    Denoyel'

UP TO 10 FEET

'Cadenza'
'Don Juan'
'Dortmund'
'Dublin Bay'
'Fountain'
'Fugue'
'Hamburger Phoenix'
'Noella Nabonnand'
'Souvenir du Docteur
    Jamain'
'Surpassing Beauty'
'Sympathie'

PURPLE-RED

20 FEET AND OVER

None

15 TO 20 FEET

None

10 TO 15 FEET

'Erinnerung an Brod'
'Russelliana'

UP TO 10 FEET

'Amadis'
'Souvenir d'Alphonse
    Lavallée'

Climbers, Ramblers and Scramblers

PURPLE TO VIOLET LAVENDER AND LILAC	CREAM TO CREAMY YELLOW	SOFT YELLOW PRIMROSE	BRIGHT YELLOW (LEMON)

PURPLE TO VIOLET LAVENDER AND LILAC

20 FEET AND OVER

None

15 TO 20 FEET

None

10 TO 15 FEET

'Améthyste'
'Bleu Magenta'
'De la Grifferaie'
'Violette'

UP TO 10 FEET

None

20 FEET AND OVER'

None

15 TO 20 FEET

'Princesse Marie'
R. moschata nastarana
'Rose Marie Viaud'

10 TO 15 FEET

'Ash Wednesday'
'Veilchenblau'

UP TO 10 FEET

'Blush Noisette'
'Narrow Water'

CREAM TO CREAMY YELLOW

20 FEET AND OVER

R. gigantea

15 TO 20 FEET

'Albéric Barbier'
'Fräulein Octavia Hesse'
'Gardenia'
'Lykkefund'
'Mrs Aaron Ward'

10 TO 15 FEET

'Belle Lyonnaise'
'Jersey Beauty'
'Louise d'Arzens'
'Madeleine Selzer'
'Primevère'

UP TO 10 FEET

'Trier'

SOFT YELLOW PRIMROSE

20 FEET AND OVER

'Mermaid'
'Paul's Lemon Pillar'
R. banksiae lutea
R. banksiae lutescens

15 TO 20 FEET

'Emily Gray'
'Maréchal Niel'

10 TO 15 FEET

'Casino'
'Golden Dawn'

UP TO 10 FEET

'Aglaia'
'Céline Forestier'
'Goldfinch'
'Solfaterre'

BRIGHT YELLOW (LEMON)

20 FEET AND OVER

'Easlea's Golden Rambler'
'Lawrence Johnston'

15 TO 20 FEET

'Aviateur Blériot'
'Spek's Yellow'

10 TO 15 FEET

'Allgold'
'Arthur Bell'
'Christine'
'Golden Glow'
'Golden Showers'
'Leverkusen'
'Leys Perpetual'

UP TO 10 FEET

'Night Light'
'Royal Gold'
'Star of Persia'

ORANGE YELLOW	APRICOT AND FLAME	PEACHY BUFF AND COPPER	YELLOW AND RED BICOLOUR

ORANGE YELLOW

20 FEET AND OVER

None

15 TO 20 FEET

'Bettina'
'Grandmère Jenny'

10 TO 15 FEET

'Alchymist'
'Alister Stella Gray'
'Bouquet d'Or'
'Butterscotch'
'Claire Jacquier'
'Cloth of Gold'
'Crépuscule'
'Dreaming Spires'
'Lady Hillingdon'
'Maigold'
'Rêve d'Or'
'Whisky Mac'

UP TO 10 FEET

'Ghislaine de Féligonde'
'Laura Ford'
'Mme Jules Gravereaux'
'Norwich Gold'

APRICOT AND FLAME

20 FEET AND OVER

None

15 TO 20 FEET

'Mrs Sam McGredy'

10 TO 15 FEET

'Breath of Life'
'Mme Bérard'
'Mme Henri Guillot'

UP TO 10 FEET

None

PEACHY BUFF AND COPPER

20 FEET AND OVER

'Desprez à Fleurs Jaunes'
'Treasure Trove'

15 TO 20 FEET

None

10 TO 15 FEET

'Compassion'
'Duchesse d'Auerstädt'
'Gloire de Dijon'
'Highfield'
'Schoolgirl'
'William Allen Richardson'

UP TO 10 FEET

'Adam'
'Meg'

YELLOW AND RED BICOLOUR

20 FEET AND OVER

None

15 TO 20 FEET

'Masquerade'
'René André'

10 TO 15 FEET

'Alexander Girault'
'Mrs G. A. van Rossem'
'Phyllis Bide'
'Sutter's Gold'
'Talisman'

UP TO 10 FEET

'Irish Fireflame'
'Joseph's Coat'
'Réveil Dijonnais'

Old Roses, Modern Shrub Roses etc., and Procumbents

Spreading cultivars indicated by (G)

WHITE TO CREAMY-WHITE   BLUSH

OVER 7 FEET

'Frühlingsanfang'
'Frühlingsschnee'
'Heather Muir'
'Mme Legras de St Germain'
'Mme Plantier'
'Pleine de Grâce'
R. beggeriana
R. dupontii
R. henryi
R. murielae
R. roxburghii normalis
R. rugosa alba
R. sericea
R. sericea chrysocarpa
R. sericea pteracantha
R. sericea pteracantha
    atrosanguinea

4 TO 7 FEET

'Blanc Double de Coubert'
'Blanche de Belgique'
'Boule de Neige'
'Frau Karl Druschki'
'Gloire Lyonnaise'
'Hawkeye Belle'
'Jeanne d'Arc'
'Karl Förster'
'Marguerite Guillard'
'Marie Bugnet'
'Maxima'
'Mme Georges Bruant'
'Mme Hardy'
'Mme Joseph Schwartz'
'Morning Blush'
'Mrs Foley Hobbs'
'Nyveldt's White'
'Pax'
'Prosperity'
R. alba
R. coriifolia froebelii
R. fedtschenkoana
R. maximowicziana
R. × micrugosa alba
R. pimpinellifolia 'Altaica'
R. wardii
'Schneelicht'
'Schneezwerg'
'Shailer's White Moss'
'Sir Thomas Lipton'
'Snowdon'
'White Blush'

2 TO 4 FEET

'À Feuilles de Chanvre'
'Anna-Maria de Montravel'
'Blanc de Vibert'
'Blanche Moreau'
'Botzaris'
'Double White'
'Glamis Castle'
'Horstmann's Rosenresli'
'Irene of Denmark'
'Mabel Morrison'
'Margaret Merril'
'Mary Manners'
'Merveille de Lyon'
'Paulii' (G)
'Pinta'
'Pompon Blanc Parfait'
'Pompon Panachée'
'Quatre Saisons Blanc
    Mousseux'
R. carolina alba
R. × involuta
R. pyrifera
R. × sabinii
'Reine Blanche'
'Sir Frederick Ashton'
'Snowflake'
'Swany' (G)
'The Bride'
'The Nun'
'White Bath'
'White Grootendorst'
'White Max Graf' (G)
'White Provence'
'White Spray'
'White Wings'

UNDER 2 FEET

'Alba Meidiland' (G)
'Francine Austin' (G)
'Katharina Zeimet'
'Kent' (G)
'Partridge' (G)
'Pour Toi'
'Repens Meidiland' (G)
'Rose de Meaux White'
'Snowball'
'Temple Bells' (G)
'White Meidiland' (G)
'White Pet'
'Yvonne Rabier'

OVER 7 FEET

'Blush Hip'
R. corymbifera
R. × polliniana
R. stylosa
R. webbiana

4 TO 7 FEET

'Anna Pavlova'
'Blanchefleur'
'Bloomfield Abundance'
'City of London'
'Claire Rose'
'Coquette des Blanches'
'Dentelle de Malines'
'Emanuel'
'English Elegance'
'Heinrich Münch'
'Homère'
'Hume's Blush'
'James Bourgault'
'Janet's Pride'
'Lucetta'
'Lyda Rose'
'Maiden's Blush, Great'
'Manning's Blush'
'Marchioness of
    Londonderry'
'Marie-Jeanne'
'Mrs Paul'
'Paul's Early Blush'
'Penelope'
R. × collina
R. multiflora watsoniana
R. × reversa
'Royal Blush'
'Shropshire Lass'
'Souvenir de Philémon
    Cochet'
'Stanwell Perpetual'
'The Prioress'
'Village Maid' (Striped)

2 TO 4 FEET

'Alfred de Dalmas'
'Belle Story'
'Butterfly Wings'
'Cécile Brünner'
'Country Living'
'Daphne'
'Double Pink'
'Dove'
'Giuletta'
'Hebe's Lip'
'Juno'
'Leda'
'Maiden's Blush, Small'
'Many Happy Returns'
'Mme Bravy'
'Mme de Tartas'
'Mme Pierre Oger'
'Mme Zöetmans'
'Pearl Drift'
R. koreana
R. macrantha
R. pulverulenta
'Rival de Paestum'
'Sally Holmes'
'Scintillation'
'Sharifa Asma'
'Sidonie'
'Souvenir de la Malmaison'
'Souvenir de St Anne's'
'Triomphe de Laffay'
'William R. Smith'
'Yolande d'Aragon'

UNDER 2 FEET

'Avon'
'Clotilde Soupert'
'Grouse' (G)
'Lady Plymouth'
'Mignonette'

SOFT TO MID-PINK

BRIGHT PINK

OVER 7 FEET

'Carmenetta'
'Catherine Seyton'
'Edith Bellenden'
'Frühlingsduft'
'Frühlingszauber'
'Gros Choux d'Hollande'
'Marguerite Hilling'
R. agrestis
R. caudata
R. davidii
R. gymnocarpa
R. inodora
R. roxburghii
R. setipoda
R. tomentosa

4 TO 7 FEET

'À longues pédoncules'
'Antonia d'Ormois'
'Archiduchesse Elizabeth
  d'Autriche'
'August Seebauer'
'Catherine de Würtemberg'
'Celestial'
'Celsiana'
'Charles Lawson'
'Chloris'
'Comtesse de Murinais'
'Coralie'
'Country Music'
'Coupe d'Hébé'
'Cymbeline'
'Dainty Maid'
'Dapple Dawn'
'Duchesse de Brabant'
'Fantin-Latour'
'Fritz Nobis'
'Gloire de Guilan'
'Grüss an Aachen'
'Honorine de Brabant'
  (Striped)
'Ipsilanté'
'Kazanlik'
'La Noblesse'
'La Ville de Bruxelles'
'Maman Cochet'
'Martin Frobisher'
'Mary Hayley Bell'
'Mateo's Silk Butterflies'
'Mme Ernst Calvat'
'Prairie Princess'
R. × dumalis
R. eglanteria
R. glauca
R. hemsleyana
R. macrantha
R. majalis

4 TO 7 FEET contd

R. majalis plena
R. marretii
R. × micrugosa
R. multibracteata
R. nanothamnus
R. roxburghii plena
'Reine des Centfeuilles'
'Schoener's Nutkana'
'Sparrieshoop'
'York and Lancaster'
  (Striped)

2 TO 4 FEET

'Admired Miranda'
'Agathe Incarnata'
'Amelia'
'Anna Olivier'
'Ballerina'
'Baronne Henriette de Snoy'
'Beauty of Rosemawr'
'Belle Isis'
'Bibi Maizoon'
'Brother Cadfael'
'Camellia Rose'
'Catherine Mermet'
'Clio'
'Cottage Rose'
'Dainty Bess'
'Double Delight'
'Duchesse d'Angoulême'
'Duchesse de Montebello'
'Ellen Willmott'
'Enfant de France'
'Falkland'
'Félicité Parmentier'
'Fimbriata'
'Fru Dagmar Hartopp'
'Gloire de France'
'Gloire des Mousseux'
'Her Majesty'
'Ispahan'
'Kathryn Morley'
'Lady Curzon'
'Lady Mary Fitzwilliam'
'Le Vésuve'
'L'Ouche'
'Mme Antoine Mari'
'Mme Dubost'
'Mme Louis Lévêque'
'Mrs B. R. Cant'
'Omar Khayyam'
'Potter & Moore'
'Princesse Adélaide'
'Quatre Saisons'
R. carolina
R. carolina plena

2 TO 4 FEET contd

R. davurica
R. melina
R. mohavensis
R. mollis
R. pisocarpa
R. prattii
R. richardii
R. serafinii
R. sicula
R. suffulta
'René d'Anjou'
'Rose d'Hivers'
'Rosy Cushion' (G)
'Rubens'
'Scepter'd Isle'
'Spencer'
'The Miller'
'Tricolore de Flandre'
  (Striped)

UNDER 2 FEET

'Dresden Doll'
'Fairy Changeling' (G)
'Fairyland' (G)
'Northamptonshire' (G)
'Nozomi' (G)
'Pink Drift' (G)
'Pink Wave' (G)
'Queen Mother'
R. orientalis
'Regensberg'
'Rosy Carpet' (G)

OVER 7 FEET

'Complicata'
'Conrad Ferdinand Meyer'
'Fred Streeter'
'Frühlingsmorgen'
'Jeanne de Montfort'
'Kathleen'
R. bella
R. sweginzowii macrocarpa
'Sealing Wax'

4 TO 7 FEET

'Adam Messerich'
'Armada'
'Arrillaga'
'Bellard'
'Belle Amour'
'Comtesse Vandal'
'Daisy Hill'
'Dame Edith Helen'
'Duchesse de Verneuil'
'Felicia'
'Fred Loads'
'Georg Arends'
'Gloire d'un Enfant
  d'Hiram'
'Glory of Edzell'
'Harry Maasz'
'Julia Mannering'
'Kathleen Ferrier'
'Léon Lecomte'
'Märchenland'
'Marie de Blois'
'Mme Lauriol de Barny'
'Old Blush'
'Papillon'
'Poulsen's Park Rose'
'Queen Elizabeth'
R. acicularis
R. × hibernica
R. jundzillii
R. woodsii fendleri
'Rachel Bowes Lyon'
'Rose d'Amour'
'Vanity'
'Vick's Caprice'
'Victor Verdier'

2 TO 4 FEET

'Angelina'
'Baroness Rothschild'
'Blessings'
'Blush Damask'
'Bonica '82'
'Célina'
'Charles Rennie Mackintosh'
'Chaucer'

Old Roses, Modern Shrub Roses etc., and Procumbents

BRIGHT PINK contd

DEEP PINK

2 TO 4 FEET contd

'Corylus'
'Duke of York'
'Félicité Bohain'
'Ferdy' (G)
'Flamingo Meidiland' (G)
'Gabriel Noyelle'
'Général Kléber'
'Heinrich Schultheis'
'Henri Foucquier'
'Hermosa'
'Hero'
'Hilda Murrell'
'Irène Watts'
'James Mitchell'
'John Hopper'
'La France'
'Mary Rose'
'Mme Berkeley'
'Mme Laurette Messimy'
'Mme Lombard'
'Mrs Campbell Hall'
'Mrs William Paul'
'Nathalie Nypels'
'Nigel Hawthorne'
'Papa Hémeray'
'Paulii Rosea'
'Petite de Hollande'
'Pink Grootendorst'
'Pink La Sevillana'
'Pink Leda'
'Pink Parfait'
'Pink Prosperity'
'Queen Mab'
R. ultramontana
R. woodsii
'Raubritter'
'Robert Léopold'
'Rose d'Orsay'
'Sarah Van Fleet'
'Shot Silk'
'Simon Robinson' (G)
'Smarty' (G)
'Spong'
'St Nicholas'
'The Countryman'
'Triomphe de Luxembourg'
'Violinista Costa'
'Zoé'

UNDER 2 FEET

'Cameo'
'Crested Jewel'
'Dick Koster'
'Euphrates'
'Fairy Moss'

UNDER 2 FEET contd

'Magic Carpet'
'Margo Koster'
'Marie Louise'
'Pheasant' (G)
'Pink Bells' (G)
'Pinkie'
'Rose de Meaux'
'Rutland' (G)
'Summer Sunrise'
'Summer Sunset'
'Surrey' (G)

OVER 7 FEET

'Amy Robsart'
'Applejack'
'Eos'
'Flora McIvor'
'Greenmantle'
'Master Hugh'
'Mechtilde von Neuerburg'
R. holodonta
R. × kamtchatica
R. moyesii 'Pink Form'
R. rugosa
R. villosa
'William Baffin'
'Wintoniensis'

4 TO 7 FEET

'Agatha'
'Andrewsii'
'Angélique Quetier'
'Baronne Prévost'
'Belinda'
'Belle Poitevine'
'Belle sans Flatterie'
'Boule de Nanteuil'
'Bourbon Queen'
'Bullata'
'Calocarpa'
'Champion of the World'
'Chapeau de Napoléon'
'Comtesse Cécile de
  Chabrillant'
'Cornelia'
'Doncasterii'
'Duc de Guiche'
'Duchesse de Rohan'
'Elmshorn'
'Empress Josephine'
'Enchantress'
'Erfurt'
'George Will'
'Goethe'
'Hans Mackart'
'Hon. Lady Lindsay'
'Königin von Dänemark'
'La Plus Belle des Ponctuées'
'Mme Gabriel Luizet'
'Mme Isaac Pereire'
'Mme Scipion Cochet'
'Mrs Doreen Pike'
'Nymphenburg'
'Oeillet Parfait' (Striped)
'Paul Ricault'
'Paul Verdier'
'Prairie Breeze'
'Prairie Flower'
'Prolifera de Redouté'
R. acicularis nipponensis

4 TO 7 FEET contd

R. blanda
R. centifolia
R. × coryana
R. corymbulosa
R. forrestiana
R. pendulina
R. setigera
R. sherardii
R. villosa duplex
R. virginiana
R. × waitziana
R. willmottiae
R. yainacensis
'Rose Bradwardine'
'Rose des Peintres'
'Sadler's Wells'
'Scabrosa'
'The Alexander Rose'
'The Reeve'
'Thérèse Bugnet'
'Will Alderman'
'William Grant'
'Wretham Rose'

2 TO 4 FEET

'Anna de Diesbach'
'Autumn Bouquet'
'Biddulph Grange'
'Candy Rose' (G)
'Canterbury'
'Charmain'
'Common Moss'
'Comte de Chambord'
'Cramoisi Picoté'
'Delambre'
'Delicata'
'Dr Grill'
'Financial Times Centenary'
'Gertrude Jekyll'
'Heritage'
'Hunslett Moss'
'Jacques Cartier' (syn.
  'Marquise Boccella' USA)
'Jean Rosenkrantz'
'La Reine'
'La Reine Victoria'
'Lewison Gower'
'Louise Odier'
'Magna Charta'
'Mirifica'
'Mme Bérard'
'Mme Knorr'
'Mme Wagram'
'Mozart'
'Mrs John Laing'
'Nestor'
'Ombrée Parfaite'

SCARLET TO
BRIGHT RED

CRIMSON TO
DEEP RED

2 TO 4 FEET contd

'Paul Neyron'
'Petite Orléanaise'
'Picasso'
'Prairie Lass'
'Président de Sèze'
'Pretty Jessica'
'Queen of Bedders'
R. foliolosa
R. gallica
R. × kochiana
R. nitida
R. palustris
R. sertata
R. stellata
'Radio Times'
'Rembrandt'
'Reynolds Hole'
'Salet'
'Sir Walter Raleigh'
'Soupert et Notting'
'Souvenir de Pierre Vibert'
'Striped Moss'
'The Doctor'
'Trevor Griffiths'
'Ulrich Brunner Fils'
'Velutinaeflora'
'Warwick Castle'
'Wife of Bath'

UNDER 2 FEET

'Berkshire'
'Chatsworth'
'Essex' (G)
'Flower Carpet'
'Hampshire' (G)
'Jean Mermoz'
'Laura Ashley' (G)
'Max Graf'
'Pink Chimo' (G)
'Pink Meidiland'
'Rouletii'
'Wiltshire'

OVER 7 FEET

'Anne of Geierstein'
'Copenhagen'
'Geranium'
'Highdownensis'
'Kiese'
'Scharlachglut'

4 TO 7 FEET

'Berlin'
'Bonn'
'Dorothy Wheatcroft'
'Général Jacqueminot'
'Henry Kelsey'
'Kassel'
'La Belle Distinguée'
'Mons. Tillier'
'Morning Mist'
'Papa Gontier'
'Red Coat'
'Robusta' (Rugosa)
'Summer Blush'
'Summer Wind'
'Will Scarlet'

2 TO 4 FEET

'Dr Jackson'
'Eugène E. Marlitt'
'Freckles'
'Jiminy Cricket'
'La Sevillana'
'Ohio'
R. arkansana
'Red Blanket' (G)
'Red Max Graf' (G)
'Red Trail' (G)
'Robin Hood'
'Scarlet Meidiland' (G)
'Single Cherry'

UNDER 2 FEET

'Eyeopener'
'Gloria Mundi'
'Golden Salmon Supérieur'
'Hampshire' (G)

OVER 7 FEET

'Arthur Hillier'
'Baron de Wassenaer'
'Dortmund'
'Eddie's Crimson'
'Eddie's Jewel'
'Hillieri'
'Meg Merrilies'
R. moyesii
'Till Uhlenspiegel'

4 TO 7 FEET

'Alexandre Laquement'
'Assemblage des Beautés'
'Baron de Bonstetten'
'Baron Girod de l'Ain'
    (Striped)
'Capitaine Basroger'
'Commandant Beaurepaire'
    (Striped)'
'Conditorum'
'Crimson Blush'
'Culverbrae'
'Cuthbert Grant'
'Ferdinand Pichard'
    (Striped)
'Fountain'
'Frensham'
'Gipsy Boy'
'Grüss an Teplitz'
'Henri Martin'
'Henry Nevard'
'Herbstfeuer'
'Hugh Dickson'
'Hunter'
'James Mason'
'John Franklin'
'Jules Margottin'
'Le Havre'
'Michel Bonnet'
'Mme Victor Verdier'
'Néron'
'Nur Mahal'
'Parkjuwel'
'Parkzierde'
'Prestige'
R. amblyotis
R. rugosa rubra
R. rugosa typica
'Robusta' (Bourbon)
'Wilhelm'
'Xavier Olibo'

2 TO 4 FEET

'Alfred Colomb'
'Carmen'
'Champlain'
'Chrysler Imperial'
'Cramoisi Supérieur'

2 TO 4 FEET contd

'Crimson Globe'
'Crimson Glory'
'D'Aguesseau'
'Dark Lady'
'Dusky Maiden'
'Ena Harkness'
'Étoile de Hollande'
'Fabvier'
'Fiona'
'Fisher Holmes'
'Fisherman's Friend'
'F. J. Grootendorst'
'Grootendorst Supreme'
'Horace Vernet'
'Laneii'
'L. D. Braithwaite'
'Little Gem'
'Louis Philippe'
'Malcolm Sargent'
'Marchioness of Salisbury'
'Mme Louis Laperrière'
'Mrs Anthony Waterer'
'Nanette'
'Ohl'
'Papa Meilland'
'Pierre Notting'
'Prince Charles'
'Robert le Diable'
'Rose à Parfum de l'Hay'
'Rosemary Rose'
'Roundelay'
'Ruskin'
'Saint Prist de Breuze'
'Sir Edward Elgar'
'Sir Joseph Paxton'
'Slater's Crimson China'
'The Squire'
'Tradescant'
'Tuscany'
'Tuscany Superb'
'Uncle Walter'
'Victor Hugo'
'Wenlock'

UNDER 2 FEET

'American Beauty'
'Charles Gater'
'Charles Lefèbvre'
'Chilterns'
'Countess of Oxford'
'Fairy Damsel' (G)
'Freiherr von Marschall'
'Little Buccaroo'
'Miss Edith Cavell'
'Peon'
'Suma' (G)

Old Roses, Modern Shrub Roses etc., and Procumbents

PURPLE-REDS, PURPLES, VIOLETS AND LAVENDER SHADES		CREAMY-YELLOW TO SOFT CLEAR YELLOW	BRIGHT YELLOW AND ORANGE TO YELLOW SHADES

PURPLE-REDS, PURPLES, VIOLETS AND LAVENDER SHADES

OVER 7 FEET

R. californica
R. californica plena
R. latibracteata
'Tour de Malakoff'
'William Lobb'

4 TO 7 FEET

'Ambroise Paré'
'Beau Narcisse'
'Bérénice'
'Capitaine John Ingram'
'Catinat'
'Chianti'
'Daphné'
'De la Maître d'École'
'Duc de Fitzjames'
'Duchesse de Buccleugh'
'Eugène Fürst'
'Eugénie Guinoisseau'
'Great Western'
'Hansa'
'Hippolyte'
'Jens Munk'
'La Belle Sultane'
'Lavender Lassie'
'Magnifica'
'Moja Hammarberg'
'Orphéline de Juillet'
R. elegantula-persetosa
R. nutkana
'Roseraie de l'Hay'
'Ruth'
'The Bishop'
'Variegata di Bologna'
    (Striped)

2 TO 4 FEET

'Alain Blanchard'
'Arthur de Sansal'
'Belle de Crécy'
'Black Prince'
'Cardinal de Richelieu'
'Cardinal Hume'
'Charles de Mills'
'Cosimo Ridolfi'
'Crown Prince'
'Deuil de Paul Fontaine'
'Ferdinand de Lesseps'
'Georges Vibert' (Striped)
'Gloire de Ducher'
'Indigo'
'James Veitch'
'Jean Bodin'
'Louis XIV'
'Magenta'
'Marcel Bourgouin'
'Maréchal Davoust'
'Mary Queen of Scots'
'Mme de la Roche-Lambert'
'Mrs Colville'
'Nuits de Young'
'Othello'
'Panachée de Lyon'
'Pélisson'
'Pergolèse'
'Pompon de Bourgogne'
'Prince Camille de Rohan'
'Prospero'
'Reine des Violettes'
'Roger Lambelin' (Striped)
'Rose de Rescht'
'Rose du Roi'
'Rose du Roi à Fleurs
    Pourpres'
'Sissinghurst Castle'
'The Prince'
'William Shakespeare'
'William III'
'Wise Portia'
'Yesterday'

UNDER 2 FEET

'Baby Faurax'
'Lilac Charm'

CREAMY-YELLOW TO SOFT CLEAR YELLOW

OVER 7 FEET

'Albert Edwards'
'Cantabrigiensis'
'Headleyensis'
'Nevada'
R. hugonis

4 TO 7 FEET

'Amazone'
'Bishop Darlington'
'Bloomfield Dainty'
'Callisto'
'Candeur Lyonnaise'
'Clytemnestra'
'Danäe'
'Daybreak'
'English Garden'
'Golden Moss'
'Jacqueline du Pré'
'Lemon Blush'
'Moonlight'
'Peace'
R. pimpinellifolia hispida
R. primula
R. × pteragonis
'Red Wing'
'Thisbe'

2 TO 4 FEET

'Aurora'
'Dunwich Rose'
'Fair Bianca'
'Kaiserin Auguste Viktoria'
'Kronprinzessin Viktoria'
'Mme de Watteville'
'Mrs Dudley Cross'
R. pimpinellifolia
'Sea Foam' (G)
'Swan'
'Symphony'
'The Pilgrim'
'Winchester Cathedral'
'Windrush'
'Yellow Button'
'Yellow Dagmar Hastrup'

UNDER 2 FEET

'Broadlands'
'Happenstance'
'Norfolk' (G)
'Pearl Meidiland' (G)
R. pimpinellifolia 'Nana'
'Tall Story' (G)

BRIGHT YELLOW AND ORANGE TO YELLOW SHADES

OVER 7 FEET

'Canary Bird'
'Earldomensis'
'Frühlingsgold'
'Frühlingstag'
'Goldbusch'
'Hidcote Gold'
'Jayne Austin'
R. foetida
R. xanthina

4 TO 7 FEET

'Agnes'
'Chinatown'
'Francesca'
'Golden Chersonese'
'Golden Wings'
× *Hulthemosa hardii*
'Lady Sonia'
'Mountbatten'
R. foetida persiana
R. × harisonii
R. × hemisphaerica
'Yellow Charles Austin'

VERMILIONS, APRICOTS AND FLAMES

PEACHY BUFF AND COPPER

YELLOW-RED BICOLOURS AND MULTI-COLOURS

2 TO 4 FEET

'Allgold'
'Angèle Pernet'
'Double Yellow Scotch'
'Fortune's Double Yellow'
'Golden Melody'
'Graham Thomas'
'Isabella Sprunt'
'Joanna Hill'
'Just Joey'
'Lady Hillingdon'
'Lichtkönigin Lucia'
'Mlle Franziska Krüger'
'Mrs Oakley Fisher'
'Norwich Castle'
'Ormiston Roy'
'Parks' Yellow'
'Pat Austin'
'Perle des Jardins'
'Queen Nefertiti'
R. ecae
R. pimpinellifolia lutea
'Safrano'
'Soleil d'Or'
'Wild Flower'

UNDER 2 FEET

'Étoile de Lyon'
'Gwent'
'Harvest Fayre'
Hulthemia persica
'Norwich Union'

OVER 7 FEET

None

4 TO 7 FEET

'Abraham Darby'
'Alexander'
'Alexander Hill Gray'
'Autumn Sunset'
'Charles Austin'
'Grandmaster'
'Heidelberg'
'Helen Traubel'
'Lafter'
'Leander'
'L'Oréal Trophy'
'Perdita'

2 TO 4 FEET

'Ambridge Rose'
'Ellen'
'Evelyn'
'Lady Roberts'
'Lilian Austin'
'Sweet Juliet'

UNDER 2 FEET

None

OVER 7 FEET

'Dr Eckener'
'Lady Penzance'
'Lord Penzance'
'Vanguard'

4 TO 7 FEET

'Buff Beauty'
'Carefree Beauty' (G)
'Cressida'
'Mutabilis'

2 TO 4 FEET

'Arethusa'
'Autumn Delight'
'Bredon'
'Chanelle'
'Dean Hole'
'Diamond Jubilee'
'Général Galliéni'
'Jean Ducher'
'Marie Van Houtte'
'Michèle Meilland'
'Peach Blossom'
'Perle d'Or'
'Souvenir d'Elise Vardon'
'The Yeoman'
'Troilus'

UNDER 2 FEET

'Baby Darling'
'Sussex' (G)
'Sweet Dream'

OVER 7 FEET

R. foetida bicolor

4 TO 7 FEET

'Cocktail'
'Frank Naylor'
'Grüss an Coburg'
'Joseph's Coat'
'Pike's Peak'
'Xerxes'

2 TO 4 FEET

'Clementina Carbonieri'
'Comtesse du Cayla'
'Général Schablikine'
'Juliet'
'Léonie Lamesch'
'Masquerade'
'Radway Sunrise'
'Rosette Delizy'

UNDER 2 FEET

'Cambridgeshire'
'Little Flirt'
'Tigris'

APPENDIX C
Rose Societies of the World

Rose lovers in many countries can join societies and associations specifically set up to promote and encourage the growing and enjoyment of roses. Most, if not all, of these organizations have display gardens to show large collections of roses at their best and trial grounds to test new cultivars. They also issue periodicals, some annually, others quarterly. Almost all organize rose shows at least twice a year and arrange conferences or conventions where rosarians can keep abreast of developments and exchange views on all aspects of the subject.

There are no boundaries or frontiers in the rose world and most of the national societies are affiliated to the World Federation of Rose Societies. This organization operates internationally and among other liaison work arranges conventions in various countries every three years. The last four were held in Canada, Australia, Northern Ireland and New Zealand. The Benelux countries will be hosts in 1997.

ARGENTINA
THE ROSE SOCIETY OF ARGENTINA
Solis, 1348 Hurlingham, Buenos Aires

AUSTRALIA
THE NATIONAL ROSE SOCIETY OF AUSTRALIA
271 Belmore Road, North Balwyn, Victoria 3104

AUSTRALIAN STATE SOCIETIES
NEW SOUTH WALES
279 North Rocks Road, North Rocks, New South Wales 2151
QUEENSLAND
Box 1866, GPO Brisbane, Queensland 4001
SOUTH AUSTRALIA
18 Windybanks Road, Happy Valley, South Australia 5159
TASMANIA
263 Main Road, Austins Ferry, Tasmania 7011
VICTORIA
40 Williams Road, Blackburn, Victoria 3130
WESTERN AUSTRALIA
105 Hemsmans Street, South Perth, Western Australia 6151

AUSTRIA
OSTERREICH GEPRUFTE ROSE
Baden bei Wien, Vienna

BELGIUM
LA SOCIÉTÉ ROYALE NATIONALE DES AMIS DE LA ROSE
Vrijheidslaan 28, B-9000 Ghent

BERMUDA
THE BERMUDA ROSE SOCIETY
Box PG162, Paget 6

CANADA
THE CANADIAN ROSE SOCIETY
686 Pharmacy Avenue, Scarborough, Ontario M1L 3H8

CHINA
THE BEIJING ROSE SOCIETY
97 Mu-nan Road, Tianjin, People's Republic of China

CZECHOSLOVAKIA
ROSA KLUB PRAHA
Hradec Kralove

DENMARK
THE VALBY PARK ROSE GARDEN
Copenhagen

EIRE
THE CLONTARF HORTICULTURAL SOCIETY
20 Chapel Street, Dublin 1

FRANCE
LA SOCIÉTÉ FRANÇAISE DES ROSES
Parc de la Tête d'Or, 69459 Lyon

GERMANY
VEREIN DEUTSCHER ROSENFREUNDE
Mainaustrasse 198A, 775A Konstanz

GHANA
Miss Adjei, P.O.B. 180, Achimota

HOLLAND
NEDERLANDSE ROSENVERENIGING
Mildestraat 47, 2596 SW, S'Gravenhage

INDIA
THE ROSE SOCIETY OF INDIA
1–267 Defence Colony, New Delhi 17

ISRAEL
THE ISRAEL ROSE SOCIETY
Ganot-Hadar, PO Netanya

ITALY
ASSOCIAZIONE ITALIANA DELLA ROSA
Villa Reale, 20052 Monza, Milano

JAPAN
THE JAPANESE ROSE SOCIETY
4–12–6 Todoroki Setabaya-ku, Tokyo

NEW ZEALAND
THE NATIONAL ROSE SOCIETY
PO Box 66, Bunnythorpe
HERITAGE ROSES NEW ZEALAND
91 Richmond Hill Road, Christchurch 8

NORTHERN IRELAND
THE ROSE SOCIETY OF NORTHERN IRELAND
36A Myrtlefield Park, Belfast

NORWAY
THE NORWEGIAN ROSE SOCIETY
c/o Hageselskatet, PB 9008 Vaterland, N-0134, Oslo

POLAND
Browieskiego 19m7, Warsaw 86

SOUTH AFRICA
THE ROSE OF SOUTH AFRICA
PO Box 65217, Bensmore, Transvaal 2010

SPAIN
Apatado, 29 San Pedro de Alcantara, Malaga

SWEDEN
THE NATIONAL HORTICULTURAL COLLEGE
Norrköping

SWITZERLAND
GESELLSCHAFT SCHWEITZERISCHER ROSENFREUNDE
Haus Engelfried, 8158 Regensberg

UNITED KINGDOM
THE ROYAL NATIONAL ROSE SOCIETY
Chiswell Green, St Albans, Hertfordshire AL2 2NR

UNITED STATES OF AMERICA
THE AMERICAN ROSE SOCIETY
PO Box 30,000, Shreveport, Louisiana 71130
HERITAGE ROSE FOUNDATION
1512 Gorman Street, Raleigh, North Carolina 27606

URUGUAY
THE ROSE ASSOCIATION OF URUGUAY
Blanes Viale 6151, Montevideo

Rose Gardens of the World

In addition to the gardens of the various rose societies around the world, many parks, private gardens and commercial nurseries have displays and collections of roses which can be visited by the public either throughout the year or in the flowering season. The following are the most important and well known. Most include both older historical roses and modern cultivars.

AUSTRALIA
CANBERRA, The Rose Gardens
NEW SOUTH WALES, The Botanic Gardens, Rumsey Nurseries, Swane's Nurseries, all in Sydney
SOUTH AUSTRALIA, The 'Botanic' Gardens, Adelaide; The Ruston Rose Gardens, Renmark; Carrick Hill Gardens, Springfield; The Duncan's Rose Garden, Watervale; The Ross Rose Gardens and Nursery, Willunga
VICTORIA, The Benalla Rose Gardens, Benalla; The Rose Gardens, Melbourne
WESTERN AUSTRALIA, The Peace Memorial Gardens, Nedlands

AUSTRIA
BADEN, Osterreichisches Rosarium
LINZ, The Rose Garden
VIENNA, Donau Park; Baden bei Wien

BELGIUM
HAINAULT, Rosarium du Roeulx
GENK, Genk Rozentium, Koningin Astridpark
HEERS, Château de Hex
MELLE, Rosarium de Rijksstation
STEENWEG, International Rozentium

BERMUDA
Camden House; many other small but interesting collections, especially in private gardens occasionally open to the public

CANADA
BRITISH COLUMBIA, Buchart Gardens, Vancouver; Minter Gardens, Rosedale; University of British Columbia, Vancouver
MONTREAL, The Floralies Rose Garden
NIAGARA, The Canadian Horticultural Society Rose Garden
ONTARIO, Hortico Inc. (Nursery), Waterdown; The Ontario Royal Botanic Gardens, Hamilton; Pickering Nurseries Inc., Pickering
OTTAWA, The Dominion Arboretum and Botanic Gardens

CZECHOSLOVAKIA
PRAGUE, Rosarium Academy of Science
ZVOLEN, Rosarium Forestry School; Rosarium Hlavne

DENMARK
COPENHAGEN, The Valby Park Rose Garden

EIRE
DUBLIN, The Parks Department, St Anne's

FRANCE
ALSACE, Roseraie de Saverne
GRASSE, L'Oustaou deï Baïléa
LYONS, La Bonne Maison; Roseraie de Berty, Largentière, south of Lyons; Roseraie du Parc de la Tête d'Or
ORLEANS, Roseraie du Parc Floral de la Source
PARIS, Château de la Malmaison; Roseraie de l'Hay-les-Roses; Roseraie du Parc de Bagatelle
PITHIVIERS, André Eve
POITIERS, Roseraie de Poitiers Parc Floral
VERNON, Monet's Garden, Giverny

FINLAND
HELSINKI, University Rose Gardens

GERMANY
BADEN-BADEN, Gönner Park, Kurgarten, Lichtentaler Allee
DORTMUND, Deutsches Rosarium, Westfalenpark
FRANKFURT AM MAIN, Palmengarten
HAMBURG, Planten und Blumen
KARLSRUHE, Rosengarten
LAUSITZ, The Forest Rose Garden
MAINAU, Rosengarten, Insel Mainau, Lake Konstanz
SAARBRUCKEN, Rosengarten
SANGERHAUSEN, The Rosarium
TAUGAU, The Rose Gardens
UETERSEN, Rosarium
ZWEIBRUCKEN, Rosengarten

HOLLAND
AMSTERDAM, Amstelpark Rosarium
THE HAGUE, Westbroekpark Rosarium

INDIA
LUCKNOW, Friends Rosery
NEW DELHI, The Rose Society of India Gardens
PUNJAB, The Zakir Rose Gardens, Chandigarh

ISRAEL
JERUSALEM, The Wohl Rose Park

ITALY
FLORENCE, the rose garden of Maria Giulia Cimarelli
ROME, Municipal Rose Gardens; Cabriglea D'Arezzo – private collection of Professor Fineschi (by appointment only)
La Landriana, near Rome
GENOA, Municipal Rose Gardens; La Mortola (a Mediterranean garden on the border with France)
LATINA, Ninfa Gardens
SIENA, Villa Cetinale
VALLERANELLO, near Rome, the rose garden of Maresa del Bufalo

JAPAN
CHOFU, The Botanic Gardens
TOKYO, Yatsu-Yuen Rose Gardens

NEW ZEALAND
AUCKLAND, The Parnell Rose Gardens including the Nancy Steen Gardens; Bell's Roses
CHRISTCHURCH, Mona Vale Rose Gardens and Botanic Gardens
HASTINGS, Frimley Rose Gardens
INVERCARGILL, The City Gardens
MOTUEKA, Tasman Bay Roses
NAPIER, The Kennedy Park Rose Gardens
OPOTIKI, The Rose Gardens
PALMERSTON NORTH, The Rose Trial Gardens
ROTORUA, The Murray Linton Rose Gardens

TAUPO, The Rose Gardens
TE AWAMUTU, The Rose Gardens
TIMARU, Trevor Griffiths Roses
WAIKATO, The Rose Gardens
WELLINGTON, The Lady Norwood
Rose Gardens

NORWAY

VOLLEBEKK, Agricultural College

PAKISTAN

QUETTA, Department of Agriculture,
Baluchistan

SOUTH AFRICA

SWELLENDAM, Western Cape Province
JOHANNESBURG, The Botanical
Gardens

SPAIN

MADRID, Parque de Oeste

SWEDEN

NORRKOPING, Horticultural College
GOTEBORG, a recently planted rose
garden

SWITZERLAND

GENEVA, Parc de la Grange
ST GALL, Rapperswill Gardens
SCHAFFHAUSEN, Neuhausen am
Rheinfall Gardens

UNITED KINGDOM

ENGLAND
BERKSHIRE, Saville Gardens, Windsor
BUCKINGHAMSHIRE, Cliveden
(National Trust), Maidenhead;
Hambledon Manor, Marlow
CAMBRIDGESHIRE, Abbots Ripton
Hall, near Cambridge; Anglesey Abbey
Gardens, Lode; The Botanic Gardens,
Cambridge; Childerley Hall, near
Cambridge; The Manor, Hemingford
Grey, near Cambridge
CHESHIRE, C. & K. Jones (Nursery),
Chester; Fryer's Nurseries, Knutsford
CLEVELAND, Borough Park, Redcar
DEVON, Castle Drogo, Drewsteignton;
Rosemore Gardens, Torrington (Royal
Horticultural Society Gardens)
GLOUCESTERSHIRE, Hidcote Manor
(National Trust), Chipping Camden;
Kiftsgate Court, Chipping Camden
HAMPSHIRE, The Sir Harold Hillier
Gardens and Arboretum, Ampfield,
Romsey; Mottisfont Abbey (National
Trust Historic Collection), Romsey
HERTFORDSHIRE, Harkness Rose
Gardens, Hitchin; Hatfield House,
Hatfield; The Gardens of the Royal
National Rose Society, Bone Hill,
St Albans

KENT, Leeds Castle, near Canterbury;
Goodnestone Park, Deal; Sissinghurst
Castle, Maidstone
LEICESTERSHIRE, Gandy's Roses
(Nursery), Lutterworth; Rearsby Roses
(Nursery), Rearsby
LONDON, The Queen Mary Rose
Gardens, Regent's Park; Kew Gardens,
Richmond, Surrey
NORFOLK, Elsing Hall, near Dereham;
Heigham Park Rose Gardens, Norwich;
LeGrice Roses (Nursery and Display
Gardens), North Walsham;
Mannington Hall Rose Gardens,
Saxthorpe; Peter Beales Roses (Nursery
and Display Gardens), Attleborough;
Wretham Lodge, near Thetford
NORTHUMBERLAND, Eglingham Hall,
near Alnwick
NOTTINGHAMSHIRE, Rosemary Roses
(Nursery), The Arboretum
(Rose Gardens), Wheatcroft Roses
(Nursery), all near Nottingham
OXFORDSHIRE, Broughton Castle, near
Banbury; Haseley Court, near Thame;
Mattock's (Nursery), Nuneham
Courtney; Botanic Gardens, Oxford
SOMERSET, Scotts (Nursery), Merriott;
'Time Trail of Roses', near Bath; Vivary
Park Rose Gardens, Taunton
STAFFORDSHIRE, David Austin Roses
(Nursery and Display Gardens),
Albrighton
SUFFOLK, Helmingham Hall,
near Ipswich; Notcutts' Nurseries,
Woodbridge
SURREY, The Gardens of the Royal
Horticultural Society, Wisley,
near Woking
SUSSEX, Charleston Manor, West Dean;
Nyman's Gardens (National Trust),
Handcross; Pashley Manor, near
Ticehurst
WARWICKSHIRE, Warwick Castle
Gardens, Warwick
WILTSHIRE, Corsley Mill,
Chapmanslade; Sheldon Manor,
Chippenham
YORKSHIRE, Castle Howard Gardens,
York; Harlow Carr Gardens
(the Gardens of the Northern
Horticultural Society), Harrogate
NORTHERN IRELAND, Dickson Roses
(Nursery), Newtownards; Lady Dixon
Park, Belfast; Rowallane Garden,
County Down

SCOTLAND, Brodick Castle, Isle of
Arran; City of Roses, Aberdeen; Cocker
Roses (Nursery and Display Gardens),
Aberdeen; Crathes Castle Gardens,
Banchory, Grampian; Malleny House,
Balerno, near Edinburgh; The Botanic
Gardens, Edinburgh; Mellerstain,
Gordon, Berwickshire; Tyninghame,
near Dunbar
WALES, Bodnant Gardens, Gwynedd;
Queen Park Gardens, Colwyn Bay;
Roath Park Gardens, Cardiff

UNITED STATES OF AMERICA

CALIFORNIA, Amesti Road, Corralitos,
Santa Cruz (the garden of Kleine
Lettunich); The Rose Gardens,
Berkeley; The Rose Acres Nursery,
Diamond Springs; Descanso Gardens,
La Canada; The Exposition Park Rose
Gardens, Los Angeles; The Municipal
Rose Garden, Oakland; The
Tournament House and Wrigley
Gardens, Pasadena; Liggett's Rose
Nursery, The Municipal Rose Garden,
San José; The Huntington Botanical
Gardens, San Marino; Mills Avenue,
San Mateo (the garden of Barbara
Worl); Armstrong's Roses (Nursery),
Somis; Sonoma Mountain, Santa Rosa
(the garden of Michael Bates); Moore's
Miniature Roses (Nursery), Visalia; The
Pageant of Roses Garden, Whittier
COLORADO, Longmont Memorial Rose
Garden, Longmont
CONNECTICUT, The Elizabeth Park
Rose Gardens, Hartford; Norwich
Memorial Rose Gardens, Norwich
DISTRICT OF COLUMBIA, United States
Botanic Garden, Washington DC;
Dumbarton Oaks, Washington DC
FLORIDA, Giles Rose Nursery,
Okeechobee
GEORGIA, Rose Test Garden,
Thomasville
ILLINOIS, Chicago Botanic Gardens;
Washington Park Rose Gardens,
Springfield
INDIANA, The Lakeside Rose Garden,
Fort Wayne; Krider Nurseries Inc.,
Middlebury; Richmond Rose Gardens,
Richmond
IOWA, Vander Veer Park Rose Gardens,
Davenport; Greenwood Park Rose
Gardens, Des Moines
KANSAS, The Rose and Trial Garden,
Topeka
KENTUCKY, The Memorial Rose
Garden, Louisville

LOUISIANA, Hodges Gardens, Many; The American Rose Center, Shreveport (headquarters of the American Rose Society)

MAINE, The Rose Circle, Portland

MARYLAND, Rosehill Farm Nursery, Galena

MASSACHUSETTS, The James P. Kelleher Rose Gardens, Boston; The Arnold Arboretum, Jamaica Plain; Nor-East Miniatures (Nursery), Rowley

MICHIGAN, The Frances Park Memorial Rose Garden, Lansing

MINNESOTA, The Lyndale Park Rose Gardens, Minneapolis

MISSOURI, The Capana Park Rose Display Gardens, Cape Girardeau; The Municipal Rose Gardens, Kansas City; The Missouri Botanic Gardens, St Louis

NEBRASKA, The Memorial Park Rose Gardens, Omaha

NEVADA, Municipal Rose Gardens, Reno

NEW HAMPSHIRE, Fuller Gardens Rose Gardens, North Hampton; Lowe's Rose Gardens, Nashua

NEW JERSEY, The Rudolf van der Goot Rose Gardens, Colonial Park Arboretum, East Millstone; The Jack D. Lissemore Rose Gardens, Tenafly

NEW YORK, The Cranford Rose Garden, Brooklyn Botanic Gardens; Kelly Bros. Nurseries, Dansville; The Queens Botanic Gardens, Flushing; Madoo, Sagaponack, Long Island; The New York Botanical Gardens; The Maplewood Park Rose Gardens, Rochester; Central Park Rose Garden; The Peggy Rockefeller Rose Garden, The Bronx

NORTH CAROLINA, Raleigh Municipal Rose Gardens

OHIO, The Park of Roses, Columbus; The Michael H. Hovath Garden of Legend and Romance, Wooster

OKLAHOMA, The Municipal Rose Garden, Tulsa; Charles E. Sparks Rose Garden, Oklahoma City

OREGON, Heirloom Old Garden Roses (Nursery), St Paul; Oregon Miniature Roses (Nursery), Beaustrom; Jackson & Perkins (Nursery), Medford; The International Rose Test Garden, Portland; Owen Memorial Rose Garden, Eugene

PENNSYLVANIA, The Rose Gardens, Hershey; The Gardens, Kennett Square, Longwood; The Marion W. Reamus Rose Garden (in the Arboretum), Philadelphia; Robert Pyle Memorial Gardens, West Grove

SOUTH CAROLINA, Wayside Gardens (Nursery), Hodges; Edisto Gardens, Orangeburg

TENNESSEE, The Municipal Rose Gardens, Memphis

TEXAS, The Municipal Rose Garden, Tyler; Antique Rose Emporium (Nursery), Brenham; Fort Worth Botanic Gardens; Samuell-Grand Municipal Rose Garden, Dallas; Houston Municipal Rose Garden

UTAH, The Municipal Rose Gardens, Salt Lake City

VIRGINIA, Bon Air Memorial Rose Garden, Arlington; The Botanic Garden Rose Garden, Norfolk

WASHINGTON, The Manito Gardens, Spokane; Woodland Park Rose Gardens, Seattle

WEST VIRGINIA, The Ritter Park Gardens, Huntington

WISCONSIN, The Boerner Botanical Gardens, Hales Corner

APPENDIX E
Rose Producers and Suppliers of the World

Those marked * specialize in old roses.

AUSTRALIA
Rainbow Roses, Ferntree Gulley, Victoria 3156
Reliable Roses, Silvan, Victoria 3795
*Ross Roses, Willunga, South Australia 5172
Swane's Nursery, Dural, New South Wales 2158
Treloar Roses, Pty Ltd, Portland, Victoria 3305
*Walter Duncan Roses, Watervale, South Australia

BELGIUM
Pepinières Louis Lens, Mechelbaan 147 B2860, Onze-Lieve-Vrouw-Waver

BERMUDA
Aberfeldy Nurseries, Box 237, Warwick WK BX

CANADA
Aubin Nurseries Ltd, Carman, Manitoba R0G 090
Carl Pallek & Son, Virgil, Ontario L0S 1T0
Hortico Inc., Waterdown, Ontario L0R 2H0
Morden Nurseries, Manitoba R0G 1J0
*Pickering Nurseries Inc., Pickering, Ontario L1V 1A6
Walter le Mire Roses, Oldcastle, Ontario N0R 1L0

DENMARK
*Lykkes Rosen, Soby, Horslet
Poulsen Roses, Hillderodvej

FRANCE
Bernard Boureau, Grisy, Suyisnes
George Delbard, Paris Cedex
La Vallée Blonde, L'Hotellère, Lisieux
*Les Roses anciennes de André Eve, Morailles, 45300 Pithiviers-le-Vieil
Meilland Richardier, Tassu-la-Demi-Lune, Cedex
Meilland et Cie, 06601 Antibes
Pépinières Jean Rey, 83250 La Londe, Var
*Roseraie de Berty, 07110 Largentière, Ardèche
Roseraie Laperrière, La Verpillière, Cedex
Roseraies Gaujard, Feyzm Isère

GERMANY
W. Kordes' Söhne, D-25365 Klein Offenseth-Sparrieshoop
Ingwer J. Jensen GmbH, Am Schlosspark 2b, D-24960 Glucksberg
Rosen von Schultheis, Rosenhof, D-6350 Bad Nauheim-Steinfurth
Tantau Roses, Uetersen, Hamburg

HOLLAND
J. D. Maarse & Zonen, Aalsmeer
Buisman, Heerde
De Ruiter, Hazers Woode
*Rosenkwekerij de Wilde, Bussum

INDIA
Friends Rosery, Mahamaga, Lucknow
K. S. Gopalas Wamiengar Son, Chamarajpet, Bangalore

ISRAEL
Ruben Fischel, Schadmot, Drona

ITALY
Barni Nursery, Pistoria 4
Maria Giulia Cimarelli, Florence
Mini Arboretum Guido Piacenza, Pollone, Biella
Centro Botanico, Via Dell'Orso, Milan

JAPAN
Hirakata Nurseries, Hirakata-shi, Osaka
Itami Rose Nursery Ltd, Itami-shi, Hyogo-Ken
Kersei Rose Nurseries, Yachiyo-shi, Tokyo
Komaba Rose Nursery, Meguroko, Tokyo
Kowa Creative Art Co., Tokyo

NEW ZEALAND
Avenue Roses, Levin
Egmont Roses, New Plymouth
Frank Mason & Sons Ltd, Fielding
Roselyn Nurseries, Whenuapai, Auckland
*Tasman Bay Roses, Motueka, near Nelson
*Trevor Griffiths Nurseries, Timaru

SOUTH AFRICA
Ludwigs Roses, Pretoria

SWITZERLAND
Roseraies Hauser Vaumarcus, Neuchâtel
Richard Huber AG, 5605 Dottikon AG

UNITED KINGDOM
*David Austin Roses, Albrighton, Wolverhampton WV7 3HB
*Peter Beales Roses, Attleborough, Norfolk NR17 1AY
Bentley's Roses, Loughborough, Leicestershire
Cants Roses, Colchester, Essex CO4 5EB
James Cocker & Sons, Whitemyres, Aberdeen AB9 2XH
Dickson Nurseries Ltd, Newtownards, Northern Ireland BT23 4SS
Fryer's Nurseries Ltd, Knutsford, Cheshire WA16 0SX
Gandy's Roses, Lutterworth, Leicestershire LE17 6HZ
Hillier's Nurseries Ltd, Ampfield, Romsey, Hampshire SO51 9PA
R. Harkness and Co., Hitchin, Hertfordshire SG4 0JT
C. & K. Jones, Tarvin, Cheshire CH3 8JF
Bill LeGrice Roses, North Walsham, Norfolk NR28 0DR
John Mattock Ltd, Nuneham Courtney, Oxfordshire OX44 9PY
Rearsby Roses Ltd, Rearsby, Leicestershire LE7 8YP
*Cottage Roses, Stafford
Wheatcroft Ltd, Edwalton, Nottingham NG12 4DE
Warley Rose Gardens, Brentwood, Essex CM13 3JH
*Trevor White, Norwich, Norfolk NR10 4AB

USA
*The Antique Rose Emporium, Brenham, Texas 77833
Armstrong's Roses, Somis, California 93066
Carroll Gardens, Westminster, Maryland 21157
Conrad-Pyle Co., West Grove, Pennsylvania 19390–0904
Donovan's Roses, Shreveport, Louisiana 71133–7800
Farmer Seed and Nursery Co., Fairbault, Minnesota 55021
Forestfarm, Williams, Oregon 97544
Fred Edmunds Inc., Wilsonville, Oregon 97070
Gloria Dee Nursery, High Falls, New York 12440
Hastings, Atlanta, Georgia 30302– 4274
*Heirloom Old Garden Roses, St Paul, Oregon
*Heritage Rose Gardens, Branscomb, California 95417

High Country Rosarium, Denver, Colorado 80218
*Historical Roses Inc., Painsville, Ohio 44077
Interstate Nursery, Hamburg, Iowa 51640–0208
Jackson & Perkins, Medford, Oregon 9751
Justice Miniature Roses, Wilsonville, Oregon 97070
Kelly Brothers Nurseries Inc., Dansville, Kentucky 14437
Lamb Nurseries, Spokane, Washington 99202
Liggett's Rose Nursery, San José, California 95125
*Limberlost Roses, Van Nuys, California 91406
*Lowe's Own Root Roses, Nashua, New Hampshire 03062
McDaniel's Miniature Roses, Lemon Grove, California 92045
Mellinger's, North Lima, Ohio 44452–9731

Miller Nurseries, Cananadaigua, New York 14424
Nor-East Miniature Roses, Rowley, Massachusetts 10969
North Creek Farm, Sebasco Estates, Maine 04565
Richard Owen Nurseries, Bloomington, Illinois
Ros-Equus, Branscomb, California 95417
The Rose Ranch, Salinas, California 93912
Roseway Nurseries Inc., Woodland, Washington WA 98674
Sequoia Nurseries, Visalia, California 93277
Stocking Rose Nurseries, San José, California 95133
P. O. Tate Nursery, Tyler, Texas 75708
Thomasville Nurseries, Thomasville, Georgia 31799
Vintage Gardens, Sebastopol, California 95472

Glossary

Throughout this book, rightly or wrongly, I have used the minimum of technical and botanical terms; however, in the interest of accuracy it has been impossible to avoid them altogether.

Anther	That part of the male part of the flower which bears the pollen
Axil	Where a leaf joins the stalk
Bract	A reduced leaf-like structure usually on a flower stalk
Calyx	The leaf-like, outer protective part of a flower
Cambium layer	The growth cells between the bark and the woody part of a stem
Clone	An identical offspring produced vegetatively
Corymb	A group of flowers held on stems of differing lengths
Glabrous	Lacking hairs or glands
Glaucous	Bluish-greyish colour
Hispid	With bristly hairs or thin spines
Inflorescence	Group of flowers forming a cluster on one stem
Lanceolate	(Of leaves.) Long and pointed, but wider towards the base
Lateral	A side branch growing from a main shoot or cane
Node	The point on a stem where a leaf and/or bud can be found
Ovate	(Of leaves.) Oval shaped, usually with the broadest part of the leaf towards the apex
Panicle	Branched inflorescence
Pedicel	The stalk of a flower (also peduncle)
Petiole	The stalk of a leaf
Pinnate	Having leaflets on each side of the axis or midrib
Pistil	The female part of a flower
Procumbent	Naturally growing along the ground
Pubescent	With fine hairs
Receptacle	The part of the flower which holds the seed and later becomes the hip
Recurrent	Flowers produced in succession throughout a flowering season
Reflexed	With petals which curl back as flowers open
Remontant	Of continuous or repeat-flowering habit
Scion	The part of a plant which is grafted on to another
Sepal	The green, individual leaf-like part of the calyx
Spine	A long, thin, sharp thorn
Stamens	The male part of the flower
Stigma	The female part of the flower which receives the pollen on fertilization
Stipule	The small, variously shaped wings at the base of a leaf stalk
Stock	A plant on to which another is grafted
Sucker	A shoot which develops from the root of the stock on a grafted plant
Truss	A group or cluster of flowers forming one head
Umbel	A flat-topped inflorescence
Vegetative propagation	Reproduction other than by seeds, viz. by cuttings, grafting, budding etc.

Further Reading

The following are some recommended books on roses and their cultivation still in print and available from most good bookshops, their authors or libraries; many of them were referred to in the compilation of this book.

Allison, S., *Climbing and Rambling Roses*, Moa Beckett, New Zealand, 1993

Austin, D., *English Roses*, Conran Octopus, London, 1993

Austin, D., *The Heritage of Roses*, Antique Collectors' Club, London, 1986, and Antique Collectors' Club, Ithaca, NY, 1988

Beales, A., *Old Fashioned Roses*, Cassell, London, 1990, and Globe Pequot Press, Chester, CT, 1990

Beales, P., *Classic Roses*, Collins Harvill, London, and Henry Holt & Co., New York, 1985

Beales, P., *Roses*, Harvill, London, 1992

Beales, P., *Twentieth-Century Roses*, Collins Harvill, London, and Harper & Row, New York, 1988

Beales, P., *Visions of Roses*, Little Brown, London, and Bulfinch, New York, 1996

De Raedt, E., *Rozen*, Roularta Books, Belgium, 1995

Dickersen, B. C., *The Old Rose Adviser*, Timber Press, Portland, OR, 1992

Dobson, B., and Schneider, P., *Hard to Find Roses and Where to Find Them*, Combined Rose List (published annually), PO Box 677, Mantua, OH 44255 USA

Druit, L., and Shoup, M., *Landscaping with Antique Roses*, The Taunton Press, USA, 1992

D'Ursal, N., *Roses des Jardins de Hex*, Lannoo, Belgium, 1995

Fagan, G., *Roses of the Cape of Good Hope*, private publication. Limited edition, 1988

Fearnley-Whittingstall, J., *Rose Gardens*, Chatto & Windus, London, 1989

Find That Rose (published annually), British Rose Growers' Association, Colchester

Fisher, J., *The Companion to Roses*, Viking, London, 1986

Garnett, T. R., *Man of Roses*, Kangaroo Press, Australia, 1990

Gault, S. M., and Singe, P. M., *The Dictionary of Roses in Colour*, Michael Joseph and Ebury Press, London, 1970

Gibson, M., *Growing Roses*, Croom Helm, London, 1985, and Timber Press, Portland, OR, 1984

Gibson, M., *The Rose Gardens of England*, HarperCollins, London, 1988, and Globe Pequot Press, Chester, CT, 1988

Griffiths, T., *My World of Old Roses* (Volumes I and II), Whitcoulls, Christchurch, 1983 and 1986

Griffiths, T., *The Best of Modern Roses*, Pacific, Auckland, NZ, 1987

Griffiths, T., *A Celebration of Roses*, Viking Pacific, Christchurch, NZ, 1988

Haglund, G., *Rosen Blommornas Drotting*, Haglund, Göteborg, 1986

Harkness, J., *Roses*, J. M. Dent & Sons, London, 1978

Harkness, J., *The Makers of Heavenly Roses*, Souvenir Press, London, 1985

Harkness, P., *Modern Roses*, Century Hutchinson, London, 1987, and in the USA as *Modern Garden Roses*, Globe Pequot Press, Chester, CT, 1988

Hessayon, D. C., *The New Rose Expert*, PBI Publications, London, 1996

Hessayon, D., *The Rose Expert*, PBI Publications, London, 1981

Krüssman, G., *Roses*, Batsford, London, 1982, and Timber Press, Portland, OR, 1981

LeGrice, E. B., *Rose Growing Complete* (revised edition), Faber & Faber, London, 1976

Le Rougetel, H., *A Heritage of Roses*, Unwin Hyman, London, 1989, and Stemmer House, Owings Mills, MD, 1988

Le Rougetel, H., *A Little Book of Roses*, Appletree, London, 1994

McCann, S., *Miniature Roses for Home and Garden*, David & Charles, London, 1985

Modern Roses 8: The International Checklist of Roses (ed. C. E. Meikle), McFarland, Harrisburg, 1980

Modern Roses 9: The International Checklist of Roses (ed. P. A. Haring), The American Rose Society, Shreveport, 1986

Modern Roses 10: The International Checklist of Roses, The American Rose Society, Shreveport, 1993

Money, K., *The Bedside Book of Old-Fashioned Roses*, Degamo, London, 1986

Nottle, T., *Growing Old-Fashioned Roses in Australia and New Zealand*, Kangaroo Press, Kenthurst, 1983

Phillips, R., and Rix, M., *Roses*, Pan Books, London, 1988, and Random House, New York, 1988

Pratt, N., *Old Garden Roses in Summer*, General Printing Services, New Zealand, 1993

Rose, G., King, P., and Squire, D., *The Love of Roses*, Quiller Press, London, 1990

Ross, D., *Rose Growing for Pleasure*, Lothian, Adelaide, 1985

Ross, D., *A Manual of Roses*, private publication, 1989

Ross, D., *Guide to Rose Growing*, Lothian, Australia, 1990
Scanniello, S., *Easy Care Roses*, Brooklyn Botanic, New York, 1995
Scanniello, S., *A Year of Roses*, Henry Holt, New York, 1996
Scanniello, S., and Bayard, T., *Climbing Roses*, Prentice Hall, New York, 1992
Scanniello, S., and Bayard, T., *Roses of America*, Henry Holt & Co., New York, 1990
Swain, V., *The Australian Rose Book*, Angus & Robertson, Sydney, 1983
Swim, H. C., *Roses from Dreams to Reality*, Stump, USA, 1988
Taylor, Lee B., *Old Fashioned Roses*, David Bateman, New Zealand, 1993
Taylor, Lee B., *Growing Old Fashioned Roses*, David Bateman, New Zealand, 1996
Testu, C., *Les Roses Anciennes*, Flammarion, Paris, 1984
Thomas, A. S., *Growing Roses in Australia*, Nelson, Sydney, 1983
Thomas, C., *In Search of Lost Roses*, Summit, New York, 1989
Thomas, G. S., *An English Rose Garden*, Michael Joseph, London, 1991, and published in the USA as *The Art of Gardening with Roses*, Henry Holt & Co., New York, 1991
Thomas, G. S., *Climbing Roses Old and New*, J. M. Dent & Sons, London, 1979
Thomas, G. S., *Shrub Roses of Today*, J. M. Dent & Sons, London, 1974
Thomas, G. S., *The Graham Stuart Thomas Rose Book*, John Murray, London, 1994
Thomas, G. S., *The Old Shrub Roses*, J. M. Dent & Sons, London, 1978
Verrier, S., *Rosa Gallica*, Capability's Books, USA, 1996
Walpole, J., *Roses in a Suffolk Garden*, Images, Woolpit, Suffolk, 1990
Warner, C., *Climbing Roses*, Century Hutchinson, London, 1987

GENERAL

Some general botanical or horticultural books containing valuable information on the genus *Rosa*.

Bean, W. J., *Trees and Shrubs Hardy in the British Isles* (8th edition revised), John Murray, London, 1980
Hillier's *Manual of Trees and Shrubs* (4th edition), Hillier, Winchester, 1974
Keble Martin, W., *The Concise British Flora*, Ebury Press and Michael Joseph, London, 1965
RHS Dictionary of Gardening, Royal Horticultural Society, Wisley, 1956
RHS Garden Encyclopaedia of Plants and Flowers, Royal Horticultural Society, Wisley, 1989

FURTHER READING FOR THE CONNOISSEUR

Some books on roses for the connoisseur – most are available from second-hand booksellers or from specialist gardening libraries.

Anderson, F. J., *An Illustrated Treasury of Redouté Roses*, Crown, New York, 1979
Beales, P., and Money, K., *Early Victorian Roses*, Jarrolds, Norwich, 1978
Beales, P., and Money, K., *Edwardian Roses*, Jarrolds, Norwich, 1980
Beales, P., and Money, K., *Georgian and Regency Roses*, Jarrolds, Norwich, 1978
Beales, P., and Money, K., *Late Victorian Roses*, Jarrolds, Norwich, 1980
Blunt, W., and Russell, J., *Old Garden Roses. Part II*, George Rainbird, London, 1957
Buist, Robert, *The Rose Manual*, New York, 1844. Facsimile reprint, Coleman, New York, 1978
Bunyard, E. A., *Old Garden Roses*, Collingridge, London, 1936. Facsimile reprint, Coleman, New York, 1978
Curtis, Henry, *Beauties of the Rose*. Facsimile edition, Sweetbrier Press, New York, 1981
Dodds, F. W., *Practical Rose Growing in All Forms*, publisher not known, *c.* 1908
Fitch, C. M., *The Complete Book of Miniature Roses*, Hawthorn, London, 1977
Foster, M. A., *The Book of the Rose*, Macmillan, London, 1864
Genders, R., *The Rose: A Complete Handbook*, Robert Hale, London, 1965
Gibson, M., *Shrub Roses for Every Garden*, William Collins, London, 1973
Gibson, M., *The Book of the Rose*, Macdonald General Books, London, 1980
Goor, A., *The History of the Rose in Holy Lands throughout the Ages*, Agricultural Publications Division, State of Israel, 1969. English edition, 1981
Gore, C. F., *The Book of Roses or The Rose Fancier's Manual*, 1838. Facsimile reprint, Heyden, London, 1978, and Coleman, New York, 1978
Hellyer, A. G. L., *Simple Rose Growing*, W. H. & L. Collingridge, London, *c.* 1930
Henslow, T. G. W., *The Rose Encyclopaedia*, C. Arthur Pearson, London, *c.* 1922

Hole, S. Reynolds, *A Book about Roses*, William Blackwood, London, 1869

Jäger, August, *Rosenlexicon* (republished from the 1936 edition), Zentralartigariat, Leipzig, 1960

Jekyll, G. and Mawley, E., R*oses for English Gardens*, Country Life, London, 1902, and Ayar Company Publishers, Salem, 1984

Keays, Ethelyn E., *Old Roses*, New York 1935. Facsimile reprint, Coleman, New York, 1978

Kingsley, R. G., *Roses and Rose Growing*, Whittaker & Co., New York, 1908

Kordes, W., *Roses*, Studio Vista, London, 1964

Macself, A. J., *The Rose Grower's Treasury*, Collingridge, London, 1934

Mansfield, T. C., *Roses in Colour and Cultivation*, William Collins, London, 1947

Mayhew, A., and Pollard, M., *The Rose, Myth, Folklore and Legend*, New English Library, London, 1979

McFarland, J. H., *The Rose in America*, Macmillan, New York, 1923

McFarland, J. H., *Roses of the World in Colour*, Cassell & Co., London, 1936

Park, B., *Collins Guide to Roses*, Collins, London, 1965

Parkman, Francis, *The Book of Roses*, J. E. Tilton & Co., Boston, 1866

Parsons, S. B., *Parsons on the Rose*, Orange Judd Co., New York, 1888

Paul, W., *A Shilling Book of Roses*, Simpkin, Marshall, Hamilton, Kent & Co., London, *c.* 1880

Paul, *W., The Rose Garden* (10th edition), Simpkin, Marshall, Hamilton, Kent & Co., London, 1903. Facsimile reprint of the 1848 edition, Coleman, New York, 1978

Poulsen, S., *Poulsen on the Rose*, MacGibbon & Kee, London, 1955

Redouté, P. J., *Roses, Books One and Two* (facsimile reprint), Ariel Press, London, 1954 and 1956

Ridge, A., *For the Love of a Rose*, Faber & Faber, London, 1965

Rigg, C. H., *Roses of Quality*, Ernest Benn Ltd, London, 1933

Rivers, T., *The Rose Amateur's Guide*, Longman Green, London, 1837

Rose Annuals, The National Rose Society, St Albans, from 1911 onwards

Rose Annuals, American Rose Society, Shreveport, 1917 and others

Ross, D., *Shrub Roses in Australia*, Deane Ross, Adelaide, 1981

Rossi, B. V., *Modern Roses in Australia*, Mitchell & Casey, Sydney, 1930

Royal Horticultural Society Journals, numerous and various back issues

Sanders, T. W., *Roses and Their Cultivation*, W. H. & L. Collingridge, London, 1938

Shepherd, R., *History of the Rose*, Macmillan, New York, 1954. Facsimile reprint, Coleman, New York, 1978

Sitwell, S., and Russell, J., *Old Garden Roses, Part I*, George Rainbird, London, 1955

Steen, N., *The Charm of Old Roses*, Herbert Jenkins, Wellington, NZ, 1966

'*The Rose*' magazine, various issues 1950s and 1960s

Thomas, H. H., *The Rose Book*, Cassell, London, 1913

Weathers, J., *Beautiful Roses*, Simpkin, Marshall, Hamilton, Kent & Co., London, 1903

Wright, W. P., *Roses and Rose Gardens*, Headley, London, 1911

INFORMATIVE ROSE CATALOGUES, ESPECIALLY CLASSIC ROSES

David Austin, Bowling Green Lane, Albrighton, Wolverhampton WV7 3HB, England

Antique Rose Emporium, Brenham, Texas 77833, USA

Peter Beales, London Road, Attleborough, Norfolk NB17 1AY, England

André Eve, Morailles, 45300 Pithiviers-le-Vieil, France

Heirloom Roses, St Paul, Oregon, USA

Roseraie de Berty, 07110 Largentière, France

Ross Roses, Willunga, Adelaide, South Australia 5172, Australia

Tasman Bay Roses, Motueka, Nelson, New Zealand

Trevor Griffiths, Timaru, New Zealand

General Index

Albas (forms and hybrids), 185–8
  history of, 10–11
Allen, E. F., 'A Simplified Rose Classification', 93n.
Allison, Sally and Bey, 17
American Rose Society, 94, 97; Rose classes, 98
Annals of Horticulture, The, 1844/5, 9n.; 1846, 16n.
Aphids, 456
Austin, David, 39, 94, 410
Austin, Robert, 22
Austrian Briars *see* Pimpinellifoliae; R. pimpinellifolia
Ayrshires (forms and hybrids), 241–2
  history of, 27–9

Balling of flowers *see* Malformation of flowers
Banksianae, 108–10
Barbier, 30, 45
Barton, Marjorie, 76
Bennett, Charles, 34
Bennett, Henry, 33–4
Bentall, J. A., 25
Bermuda Rose Society, 19–20, 391
Bermuda Roses *see* Mystery roses of Bermuda
Bide, 46
Black spot, 458–9
Bourbons, 363–70
  history of, 14–15
Boursaults (forms and hybrids), 211–13
Bracteatae, 114–16
Breeding new cultivars, 465–7
British Association Representing Breeders (BARB), 93n., 97–9
  Rose classes, 98
British National Rose Society, 33
British Rose Growers' Association, 94, 437
British Standards Institute, 437
Brownell, 30
Budding, 449–52, 464
Burdett, Ruth, 34
Burnet roses *see* Pimpinellifoliae; R. pimpinellifolia

Cabbage roses *see* Centifolias
Cane borers, 458
Caninae, 183–98
Canker *see* Stem canker
Cant, B. R., 46
Capsid bugs, 456
Carolinae, 199–202
Cassiorhodon, 203–39
Caterpillars, 456

Centifolias (forms and hybrids), 149–55
  history of, 6–7
Champneys, John, 15, 44
Château de Malmaison, 30–1
Chinas (forms and hybrids), 353–62
  history of, 11–12
Chinensis, 351–436
Choosing and buying roses, 437–9
Classification of genus *Rosa,* 93
Classification systems, 97–100
Climatic map, 467
Climbers, history of, 44–5
  for poorer soils, 52
  as standards, 83–4
  see also Modern Climbers; Old climbing roses
Climbing Bourbons, 371–2
Climbing Floribundas, 315–16
Climbing Hybrid Teas, 428–36
Climbing Roses Old and New (Thomas, 1979), 45
Cluster-flowered Roses *see* Floribundas
Commercial production of roses, 463–4
Compact Floribundas *see* Miniatures and Patios
Companion plants for old and shrub roses, 85–92:
  annuals and biennials, 89
  bulbs, corms, etc., 88–9
  climbers, 88
  fruit and vegetables, 90–1
  herbs, 89–90
  perennials, 86, 88
  shrubs, 86, 88
  trees, 87, 88
  wild flowers, 91
Crown gall, 459
Cuckoo spit, 457
'Cutting down' *see* 'Heading back'
Cuttings, roses from, 452–4

Damasks (forms and hybrids), 169–74
  history of, 8
De Vink, 42
Dead-heading, 446–7
Deer, 457
Dickson & Brown of Perth, 22
Dickson, Patrick, 35
Dickson's, 35
Diseases, 456, 458–60
Division, 455
Dog Rose *see* Caninae
Downy mildew, 460
Dwarf Polyanthas, 36

East India Company, 11, 18
English roses *see* New English Roses

Eurosa (*Rosa* subgenus), 93, 108–436
Evergreens *see* Sempervirens roses

Fane de Salis, Mr Peter A., 9n., 16n.
Farrer, 51
Fertilizers, 440
Festing, Sally, 12n.
Floribundas, 305–14
  history of, 36–7
Flower arranging, old roses for, 75–6
Foliage, ornamental, 79–80
Fortune, Robert, 18
Froghoppers, 457

Gallicanae, 135–82
Gallicas (forms and hybrids), 137–48
  history of, 8–9
Geschwind, Rudolf, 31
Grafting, 448–9
Grandiflora, 37, 41–2, 65
Grant, William, 31, 223
  'Rustling Roses', 31–2
Griffiths, Trevor, 15, 94, 112
Ground-cover Roses *see* Procumbent Shrub Roses
Guillot, Jean-Baptiste, 33

Harkness, Jack, 94, 99, 'Heading back', 464
'Heading off' *see* 'Heading back'
Hedges, 64–6
Heeling-in, 439–40
Heritage Roses Australia, 32
Hesperhodos (*Rosa* subgenus), 93, 104–5
Hips, roses grown for their, 78–9
Hulthemia (*Rosa* subgenus), 93, 101–3
Hulthemia persica (forms and hybrids), 101, 102
× *Hulthemosa* (forms and hybrids), 101, 102
Hurst, Dr C. V., 7, 7n.
Hybrid Chinas, 353n.
Hybridizing, 465
Hybrid Musks, 255–61
  history of, 25
Hybrid Perpetuals, 394–409
  history of, 20–2
Hybrid Teas, 420–7
  history of, 33–5

Jackson & Perkins, 30
Japanese beetles, 458
Jekyll, Gertrude, 28, 45, 49, 70
Josephine, Empress, 13, 30–1

Kennedy, 31
Kordes, Wilhelm, 24
Kordesii *see* R. kordesii

Laevigatae, 111–13
Lambert, Peter, 25
Large-flowered Climbers *see* Climbing Hybrid Teas
Large-flowered Roses *see* Hybrid Teas
Layering, 454
Leaf-rolling sawfly, 457
Lee & Kennedy, 22
Lee, 24
LeGrice, Edward Burton, 14, 25
Lelieur, Comte, 12
Le Rougetel, Hazel, 12
Lindsey, 42
Lowe, Malcolm (Mike), 440, 452, 458
  'Three Persistent North American Pests', 458

MacGregor IV, John C., 12n.
Malformation of flowers, 462–3
Malmaison, Château de, rose garden, 30
Manda, 45
Manners, Malcolm, 461
  'Rose Mosaic Virus Disease', 461–2
Manure, 440
McGredy, Samuel, 35
McGredy's, 35
McQueen, Janet, 29
Meier, Margaret, 34
Mercer, Bill, 20, 391
Mercer, Lorna, 20, 20n., 391
  'Mystery Roses in Bermuda', 391
Micropropagation, 454
Midge, 458
Mildew *see* Downy mildew; Powdery mildew
Mineral deficiencies, 461
Miniatures and Patios, 317–20
  history of, 41–4, 57
Modern Climbers, 273–86
  as hedges, 64–6
  as standards, 84
  history of, 44–8
  use of, 70–1
Modern Roses 10 (American Rose Society), 94, 97
Modern Shrubs, 287–301
  history of, 38–9
  in a mixed shrubbery, 74–5
Money, Keith, 34
Mosaic virus, 461–2
Mosses (forms and hybrids), 156–68
  history of, 7
Mulching, 440
Multiflora Ramblers, 263–71
  history of, 27
Murrell, Hilda, 47
Musks (forms and hybrids), 249–52

Mystery roses of Bermuda, 391–3
  history of, 19–20

New English Roses, 39, 410–19
Noisettes, 373–8
  history of, 15–17, 18
North American pests, 458
North American planting and pruning seasons, 444

Old climbing roses
  for hedges, 64–6
  for pergolas, trellis, pillars and arches, 67–71
  for trees, 72–4
  for walls, fencing panels and northerly aspects, 71–2
Old procumbent and semi-procumbent roses, 88–9
Old roses
  for an established garden, 52–4
  for autumn colour, 79–80
  for flower arranging, 75–6
  for fragrance, 81–2
  for hedges, 80–81
  for mixed shrubberies, 55–6
  for parks and municipal planting, 58–9
  for pots and tubs, 66–7
  for woodland, wild gardens and partial shade, 60–1
  with water features, 61–2
Old shrub roses under glass, 77–8

Parks, John, 18
Patio roses see Miniatures and Patios
Paul, William, 7, 15, 16, 27, 34, 46, 47, 83
Pegging down, 22, 84–5
Pemberton, Joseph, 25, 38, 46
Penzance Briars, 24, 38
  history of, 24
  see also Shrub roses
Pernet–Ducher, Joseph, 34
Pernetianas, 35
Pests, 456–8
Pimpinellifoliae (Scotch Roses), 117–34
  history of, 22–4
Planting, 439–42
  bush, shrub and old-fashioned roses, 441
  climbing roses, 442
  containerized roses, 441–2
  heeling-in, 439–40
  in North America, 444
  into pots, 442
  soils and soil preparation, 440
  specific replant disease, 441
  specimen roses in lawns, 442
  standard roses, 425
  winter protection, 440
Platyrhodon (Rosa subgenus), 93, 106–7

Polyanthas, 302–4
  history of, 36–7
Polypompons, history of, 36
Portlands (forms and hybrids), 175–9
  history of, 12–14
Poulsen roses, 37
Powdery mildew, 459
Procumbent Shrub Roses, 321–33
  history of, 39–40
  use of, 75
Proliferation see Malformation of flowers
Propagation, 448–56
Provence roses see Centifolias
Pruning, 443–7
  climbing roses and ramblers, 444–6
  dead-heading, 446–7
  in North America, 444
  modern roses, 447
  neglected roses, 447
  once-flowering roses, 443–4
  repeat-flowering shrubs, 444
  weeping standards, 446

R. agrestis, 185
R. arvensis see Ayrshires
R. banksiae (forms and hybrids), 109–10
R. biebersteinii, 188
R. bracteata (and hybrid), 115–16
R. britzensis, 188
R. brunonii (and hybrid), 243–4
R. canina (and hybrid), 189–90
R. carolina (forms and hybrids), 200–1
R. centifolia see Centifolias
R. chinensis see Chinas
R. damascena see Damasks
R. ecae (forms and hybrids), 119
R. filipes (forms and hybrids), 245–6
R. foetida (forms and hybrids), 120–2
R. gallica see Gallicas
R. gigantea (and hybrids), 352
R. glauca (forms and hybrids), 196–8
R. helenae (and hybrid), 247–8
R. hugonis (forms and hybrids), 123
R. kordesii (form and hybrids), 207–10
R. laevigata (forms and hybrids), 112–13
R. macrantha (forms and hybrids), 181–2
R. macrophylla (forms and hybrids), 214–16
R. moschata see Musks
R. moyesii (forms and hybrids), 217–20
R. multibracteata (forms and hybrid), 221
R. multiflora (forms and hybrids), 253–4

R. nutkana (forms and hybrids), 222–3
R. pimpinellifolia (Scotch Roses) (forms and hybrids), 124–30
R. roxburghii (forms), 107
R. rubrifolia see R. glauca
R. rugosa see Rugosas
R. sempervirens (forms and hybrids), 334–5
R. sericea (forms and hybrids), 131–2
R. setigera (and hybrids), 336–7
R. sinowilsonii (and hybrid), 338
R. soulieana (and hybrids), 339–40
R. stellata (forms), 105
R. virginiana (forms and hybrids), 202
R. wichuraiana (and hybrids), 341–50; see also Wichuraianas
R. xanthina (forms and hybrid), 133
Rabbits, 457
Ramblers, history of, 45–6
Red spider, 457
Redouté, Pierre Joseph, 30
Réunion rose, 15
Rivers, 7, 16n., 34
Rootstocks see Understocks
Rose Garden, The (Paul, 10th edn, 1903), 7
Rose mosaic virus, 461–2
Roses for English Gardens (Jekyll and Mawley, 1902), 28, 70
Rose sickness see Specific replant disease
Roses of America (Scanniello and Bayard, 1990), 24
Roses of Provins see Gallicas
Ross, Deane, 34
Rotation, 441, 463
Roulet, 42
Royal National Rose Society, 33, 93n., 94, 98, 125
Rugosas (forms and hybrids), 224–39
Russell, James, 12
Rust, 460
Rustling, 31–2
Ruston, David, 47

Scent, older roses and their, 81–2
Schmidt, 46
Schmitt, 46
Schoener, George, 148, 223
Scotch Roses see Pimpinellifoliae; R. pimpinellifolia
Scramblers, history of, 46–8
Seasons in rose cycle, in northern and southern hemispheres, 96

Seasons, planting and pruning, in North America, 444
Seed, roses from, 455–6
Sempervirens roses (the Evergreens), history of, 29, 47
  see also R. sempervirens
Shepherd, Roy, 24
Shoup, Mike and Jean, 452
Shrub roses, 38–9, 52–64
  for an established garden, 52–4
  for poorer soils, 52
  as standards, 84
Simplicifoliae, 101–3
Soils and soil preparation, 440
  roses for poorer soils, 51–2
Species roses, history of, 1–8
Specific replant disease 441
Standard roses, 83–4
  for an established garden, 52–3
  planting and staking, 442
  pruning and training, 446
Steen, Nancy, 15, 32
Stem canker, 460
Suckers, 438–9
Sweet, Robert, 42
Sweet Briars (forms and hybrids), 191–5
  history of, 24
Synstylae, 240–350

Teas, 379–90
  history of, 17–19
Temperature ranges, 467
Thomas, Graham Stuart, 7n., 45, 49, 94, 341n.
Thory, Claude Antoine, 30
Thrips, 457
'Topping' see 'Heading back'
Turbat, 46

Understocks, 27, 438–9, 464

Van Fleet, Walter, 45
Virus, Rose mosaic, 461–2

Walsh, 46
Water features, 61–2
Weed control, 447–8
White roses see Albas
Wichuraianas, 28, 45
  history of, 30
Wild roses, distribution of, 2–6
  American, 3
  European, 2–3
  Middle Eastern, 5–6
  Oriental and Asian, 4–5
Winter protection, 440
World Federation of Rose Societies, 97–9
  rose classes, 98
Wyatt, Arthur, 366n.

Index of Roses

Page numbers in *italics* refer to illustrations. References in the *Colour and Height Charts*, pages 469–83, are not included.

Abbotswood, 63, 189
Abraham Darby, 411, *411*
Abunancia *see* Mary Hayley Bell
Adam, 379, *380*
Adam Messerich, 363, *363*
Adélaïde d'Orléans, 29, *29*, 334
Adèle Pradel *see* Mme Bravy
Admired Miranda, 411
À Feuilles de Chanvre, 185
Agatha, *136*, 137
Agatha Christie, 273
Agathe Incarnata, 137
Aglaia, 25, 46, 263
Agnes, 65, 225, *226*
Agrippina *see* Cramoisi Supérieur
Aimée Vibert, 17, 72, 373, *374*
Alain Blanchard, 90, 138, *139*
Alba Maxima *see* Maxima
Alba Meidiland, 322
Alba Semi-plena *see* Semi-plena
Alba Suavolens *see* Semi-plena
Albéric Barbier, 5, 30, 45, 69, 72, 84, 341, *342*
Albert Edwards, 126
Albertine, 5, 30, 45, 69, 80, 84, 341
Alchymist, 273, *274*
Alexander, 287, *287*
Alexander Girault, 341
Alexander Hill Gray, 379
Alexandre Laquement, 138
Alfred Colomb, 394, *395*
Alfred de Dalmas, 56, 66, 156, *157*
Alida Lovett, 342, *342*
Alister Stella Gray, 17, 69, 373, *374*
Allen Chandler, 428, *428*
Allgold, 305
Allgold Climbing, 315, *315*
Aloha, 71, 273, *274*
À longues pédoncules, 156
Alpine Rose *see* R. pendulina
Altissimo, *272*, 273
Amadis, 212, *213*
Amanda *see* Red Ace
Amazone, 379
Amber Queen, 305, *306*
Ambridge Rose, 411
Ambroise Paré, 138
Amelia, 185
America, 273
American Beauty, 394
American Pillar, 342
Améthyste, 342

Amruda *see* Red Ace
Amy Robsart, 191
Anaïs Ségalas, 138, *139*
Andersonii, 189, *190*
André *see* Calocarpa
Andrewsii, 126
Anemone Rose, 112, *112*
Angèle Pernet, 420
Angelina, 287, *288*
Angélique Quetier, 156
Angelita *see* Snowball
Anna de Diesbach, 394
Anna Olivier, 20, 379, *380*
Anna Pavlova, 81, 420, *420*
Anna Zinkeisen, 287, *287*
Anneliese Rothenberger *see* Miss Harp
Anne-Maria de Montravel, 302
Anne of Geierstein, 64, 191, *192*
Antike '89 *see* Antique
Antique, 275
Antoine Ducher, 35
Antoine Rivoire, 35, 78
Antonia d'Ormois, 138
Apothecary's Rose *see* R. gallica officinalis
Apple Blossom, 263
Apple Rose *see* R. villosa
Applejack, 288
Archduke Charles, 19, 353
Archiduc Charles *see* Archduke Charles
Archiduc Joseph, 78, 379, *380*
Archiduchesse Elizabeth d'Autriche, 394
Ardoisée de Lyon, 394
Ards Rover, 394
Arethusa, 20, 354, *354*
Armada, 288
Armosa *see* Hermosa
Arrillaga, 395
Arthur Bell Climbing, 6, 315
Arthur de Sansal, 175, *175*
Arthur Hillier, 214
Aschermittwoch *see* Ash Wednesday
Ash Wednesday, 275, *275*
Aspen *see* Gwent
Assemblage des Beautés, 139, *139*
Asso di Cuori *see* Ace of Hearts
Astra Desmond, *262*, 263
August Seebauer, 305, *306*
Auguste Gervais, 342
Auguste Roussel, 214, *215*
Aurora, 255
Austrian Briar *see* R. foetida
Austrian Copper *see* R. foetida bicolor
Austrian Yellow *see* R. foetida
Autumnalis, 249
Autumn Bouquet, 288

Autumn Damask *see* Quatre Saisons
Autumn Delight, 255, *255*
Autumn Fire *see* Herbstfeuer
Autumn Sunlight, 275
Autumn Sunset, 288, *288*
Aviateur Blériot, 5, 343
Avon, 322
Awakening, 343, *343*
Ayrshire Queen, 241
Ayrshire Splendens *see* Splendens

Baby Carnaval *see* Baby Masquerade
Baby Darling, 317
Baby Faurax, 302
Baby Masquerade, 317, *317*
Baby Mermaid *see* Happenstance
Ballerina, 25, 56, 66, *66*, 67, 84, 255
Baltimore Belle, 336, *337*
Bantry Bay, 30, 71, 275, *275*
Baron de Bonstetten, 395
Baron de Wassenaer, 156
Baroness Rothschild, 22, 56, 395, *395*
Baron Girod de l'Ain, 395
Baronne Adolphe de Rothschild *see* Baroness Rothschild
Baronne Henriette de Snoy, 380, *380*
Baronne Prévost, *21*, 22, 56, 395, *396*
Bassimo *see* Suffolk
Beau Narcisse, 139
Beauty of Glazenwood *see* Fortune's Double Yellow
Beauty of Rosemawr, 354, *354*
Beauty of the Prairies *see* Queen of the Prairies
Belinda, *255*, 256
Bellard, 139
Belle Amour, 63, 169, *170*
Belle de Crécy, 82, 139
Belle des Jardins *see* Village Maid
Belle Isis, 139
Belle Lyonnaise, 380
Belle of Portugal *see* Belle Portugaise
Belle Poitevine, 65, 226, *226*
Belle Portugaise, 352
Bellert *see* Bellard
Belle sans Flatterie, 139
Belle Story, 411
Belle Vichysoise, 373
Belvedere *see* Ethel; Princesse de Marie
Bengal Rose *see* R. chinensis
Bennett's Seedling, 241
Bérénice, 140
Berkshire, 322

Berlin, 288
Bettina Climbing, 428
Betty Uprichard, 35
Bibi Maizoon, 411
Biddulph Grange, 288
Bishop Darlington, 256, *256*
Black Jack *see* Tour de Malakoff
Black Prince, 396
Blackberry Rose *see* R. rubus
Blairii No. 1, 371
Blairii No. 2, 371, *371*
Blanc de Vibert, 175
Blanc Double de Coubert, 5, 65, 226, *227*
Blanche de Belgique, 185
Blanchefleur, 149
Blanche Moreau, 157, *157*
Blanche Superbe *see* Blanche de Belgique
Blanc Pur, 373
Blaze, 343
Blessings, 421
Blessings Climbing, 428
Bleu Magenta, 263, *264*
Bloomfield Abundance, 354
Bloomfield Dainty, 256, *256*
Blue Rose *see* Veilchenblau
Blush Boursault, 212
Blush Damask, 169, *169*
Blush Hip, 186
Blush Maman Cochet *see* William R. Smith
Blush Noisette, 16, *16*, 17, 373
Blush Rambler, 46, 68, 263, *264*
Bobbie James, 47, 74, 265, *265*
Bon Silène, 380
Bonica '82, *83*, 288, *289*
Bonn, 289
Bonnie Prince Charlie's Rose *see* Maxima
Botzaris, 169, *170*
Boule de Nanteuil, 140
Boule de Neige, 363
Bouquet de la Mariée *see* Aimée Vibert
Bouquet d'Or, 17, 78, 374, *374*
Bourbon Queen, 15, 64, 364
Bourbon Rose *see* R. × borboniana
Breath of Life, 275, *276*
Bredon, 411
Breeze Hill, 343, *343*
Brenda Colvin, 246
Brennus, 355, *355*
Briarcliffe, 78
Brightside Cream, 20, 392, *392*
Broadlands, 322
Brother Cadfael, 411
Buffalo Bill *see* Regensberg
Buff Beauty, 25, 65, 66, 84, 256, *256*
Bullata, 149

Burgundian Rose see Pompon de Bourgogne
Burnet Double White see Double White
Burnet Rose see R. pimpinellifolia
Burning Sky see Paradise
Burr Rose see R. roxburghii
Butterfly Wings, 289
Butterscotch, 275

Cabbage Rose see R. centifolia
Cadenza, 70, 343, 344
Callisto, 256
Calocarpa, 227
Calypso see Blush Boursault
Camaieux, 140, 140
Cambridgeshire, 322
Camellia Rose, 355
Cameo, 302, 303
Canary Bird, 55, 84, 133, 133
Candeur Lyonnaise, 396
Candy Rose, 322
Canina Abbotswood see Abbotswood
Cantab, 222
Cantabrigiensis, 117, 122, 123
Canterbury, 289
Capitaine Basroger, 157, 157
Capitaine John Ingram, 157
Captain Christy Climbing, 70, 428, 429
Captain Hayward, 34
Captain Hayward Climbing, 396
Cardinal de Richelieu, 140, 140
Cardinal Hume, 289, 290
Carefree Beauty, 322
Carmen, 227
Carmenetta, 196
Carnation, 392
Casino, 275, 276
Caterpillar see Pink Drift
Catherine de Würtemberg, 158
Catherine Guillot see Michel Bonnet
Catherine Mermet, 78, 381
Catherine Seyton, 192
Catinat, 140
Cécile Brünner, 52, 67, 355, 355
Cécile Brünner Climbing, 54, 356
Cécile Brünner White, 356
Celeste see Celestial
Celestial, 56, 61, 80, 81, 82, 186
Célina, 158, 158
Céline Forestier, 17, 69, 374, 374
Celsiana, 56, 170
Centenaire de Lourdes, 305, 307
Centfeuilles des Peintres see Rose des Peintres
Cerise Bouquet, 63, 63, 221, 221
Champion of the World, 396
Champlain, 207
Champneys' Pink Cluster, 16, 16, 16n., 374
Chanelle, 305, 306

Chapeau de Napoléon, 90, 158, 158
Chaplin's Pink, 69, 74, 343
Chaplin's Pink Climber see Chaplin's Pink
Chaplin's Pink Companion, 344
Charles Austin, 411
Charles de Mills, 82, 140, 141
Charles Dingee see William R. Smith
Charles Gater, 396
Charles Lawson, 364
Charles Lefèbvre, 396, 396
Charles Rennie Mackintosh, 411
Charmain, 412
Château de Clos Vougeot Climbing, 429
Château de La Juvenie, 276
Chatsworth, 322
Chaucer, 412
Cherokee Rose see R. laevigata
Cheshire Rose see Maxima
Chestnut Rose see R. roxburghii
Chevy Chase, 339, 339
Chianti, 39, 39, 181
Chilterns, 322
China Rose see R. chinensis
Chinatown, 36, 37, 306
Chloris, 186
Christine Climbing, 429
Chromatella see Cloth of Gold
Chrysler Imperial, 421
Cinderella, 42, 318
Cinnamon Rose see R. majalis
City Girl, 276
City of London, 290
City of York, 276, 277
Clair Matin, 277
Claire Jacquier, 374
Claire Rose, 412
Clementina Carbonieri, 381, 381
Clementine see Janet's Pride
Clifton Moss see White Bath
Clio, 396
Cloth of Gold, 78, 375
Clotilde Soupert, 302
Clytemnestra, 257
Cocktail, 290, 290
Colcestria, 277
Columbia Climber, 429, 429
Commandant Beaurepaire, 66, 364
Common Monthly see Old Blush
Common Moss, 8, 159
Communis see Common Moss
Compassion, 277, 277
Complicata, 61, 73, 141
Comte de Chambord, 13, 14, 66, 67, 90, 175, 176
Comtesse Cécile de Chabrillant, 396
Comtesse d'Oxford see Countess of Oxford
Comtesse de Labarthe see Duchesse de Brabant

Comtesse de Murinais, 158
Comtesse de Turin see Mme Wagram
Comtesse du Cayla, 356, 356
Comtesse Ouwaroff see Duchesse de Brabant
Comtesse Vandal, 421
Comtesse Vandal Climbing, 429
Conditorum, 141
Conrad Ferdinand Meyer, 82, 227, 227
Constance Spry, 39, 277, 277
Cooper's Burmese, 113, 113
Copenhagen, 56, 290
Coquette des Blanches, 364
Coral Creeper, 277
Coral Dawn, 30, 278
Coralie, 170
Cornelia, 25, 66, 257, 257
Coryana see R. × coryana
Corylus, 56, 80, 227, 228
Cosimo Ridolfi, 141
Cottage Rose, 412
Countess of Oxford, 397
Country Dancer, 290
Country Living, 412
Country Music, 290
Coupe d'Hébé, 364
Cramoisi Picoté, 141
Cramoisi Supérieur, 12, 19, 58, 356, 357
Cramoisi Supérieur Climbing, 356
Crépuscule, 375, 375
Cressida, 412
Crested Jewel, 158
Crested Moss see Chapeau de Napoléon
Crimson Blush, 188
Crimson Boursault see Amadis
Crimson Conquest, 70, 72, 429
Crimson Globe, 159
Crimson Glory, 421
Crimson Glory Climbing, 429
Crimson Rambler, 46, 265
Crimson Showers, 344
Cristata see Chapeau de Napoléon
Crown Prince, 397
Cuisse de Nymphe see Maiden's Blush, Great
Cuisse de Nymphe Émue, 10, 186
Culverbrae, 227
Cupid, 429, 430
Cuthbert Grant, 290, 291
Cymbeline, 290

D'Aguesseau, 141, 141
Daily Mail Rose Climbing see Mme Édouard Herriot Climbing
Dainty Bess, 421, 421
Dainty Maid, 306
Daisy Hill, 75, 181
Dame Edith Helen, 35, 421, 421
Danaë, 25, 26, 257
Danse de Feu, 278

Danse des Sylphes, 278, 278
Daphne (Hybrid Musk), 257
Daphné (Gallica), 141
Dapple Dawn, 291
Dark Lady, 412
Daybreak, 257
Dean Hole, 381
De la Grifferaie, 27, 27, 265
De la Maître d'École, 141, 141
Delambre, 176
Delge see Centenaire de Lourdes
Delicata, 227
Della Balfour, 278
Dembrowski, 397
Dentelle de Malines, 291
Deschamps, 375, 375
Desprez à Fleurs Jaunes, 70, 375, 375
Deuil de Paul Fontaine, 159, 159
Devoniensis, 78, 381
Diamond Jubilee, 422, 422
Dianthiflora see Fimbriata
Dick Koster, 303
Direktor Benschop see City of York
Dixieland Linda, 278, 278
Dog Rose see R. canina
Doncasterii, 214, 215
Don Juan, 278
Dorothy Perkins, 37, 84, 344, 344
Dorothy Wheatcroft, 291
Dortmund, 207, 208
Double Delight, 422
Double French Rose see R. gallica officinalis
Double Marbled Pink, 125
Double Pennsylvanian Rose see R. carolina plena
Double Pink, 125
Double White, 64, 90, 125, 125
Double Yellow Forms, 125
Doubloons, 336
Dove, 412
Dr Andry, 397, 397
Dreaming Spires, 278
Dr Eckener, 227, 229
Dresden Doll, 159
Dr Grill, 78, 381, 381
Dr Huey, 344
Dr Jackson, 291
Dr W. Van Fleet, 30, 45, 344
Dublin Bay, 71, 279, 279
Duc d'Angoulême see Duchesse d'Angoulême
Duc de Fitzjames, 142, 142
Duc de Guiche, 142, 142
Duc de Rohan see Duchesse de Rohan
Duchesse d'Angoulême, 142, 143
Duchesse d'Auerstädt, 78, 376, 376
Duchesse de Brabant, 381
Duchesse de Buccleugh, 143
Duchesse de Montebello, 143, 143

Duchesse de Rohan, 149
Duchesse de Verneuil, 159
Duchesse d'Istrie *see* William Lobb
Duchess of Portland, 12, 66, 176, *177*
Duftzauber '84 *see* Royal William
Duke of Edinburgh, 397, *397*
Duke of Wellington, 397
Duke of York, 357
Dundee Rambler, 241
Dunwich Rose, 75, *75*, 117, 126
Dupontii *see* R. *dupontii*
Dupuy Jamain, 22, 397, *397*
Dusky Maiden, 307, *308*
Düsterlohe, 242

Earldomensis, 123
Easlea's Golden Rambler, 344, *345*
Éclair, 398
Eddie's Crimson, 218
Eddie's Jewel, 56, *78*, 79, *217*, 218
Eden Rose Climbing, 430
Eden Rose '88, 279, *279*
Edith Bellenden, 192
Eglantine Rose *see* R. *eglanteria*
Elegance, 345
Elisa Boelle, 398
Elizabeth of Glamis, 307
Ellen, 412
Ellen Poulsen, 37
Ellen Willmott, 422
Elmshorn, 56, 291, *291*
Else Poulsen, 37
Emanuel, 412
Emily Gray, 5, 69, 72, 84, 345, *345*
Empereur du Maroc, 398
Emperor of Morocco *see* Empereur du Maroc
Empress Josephine, *30*, 56, 82, 90, 137, 143
Ena Harkness, 422
Ena Harkness Climbing, 430
Enchantress, 381
Enfant de France, 398, *398*
Engineer's Rose *see* Crimson Rambler
English Elegance, 412
English Garden, 413, *413*
Eos, 218, *218*
Erfurt, 56, 291, *292*
Erinnerung an Brod, 336
Escapade, 307, *308*
Essex, 323
Étendard, *279*, 280
Ethel, 346
Étoile de Hollande, 422
Étoile de Hollande Climbing, 70, 82, 430, *430*
Étoile de Lyon, 382
Étude, 280
Eugène E. Marlitt, 365
Eugène Fürst, 398
Eugénie Guinoisseau, 159, *160*
Euphrates, 102, *102*

Euphrosine, 265
Eva, 257
Evangeline, 346
Evelyn, 413
Everest, 398
Eyeopener, 323
Excelsa, 30, 69, *83*, 84, 346, *347*
Exception *see* Märchenland

Fabvier, 357
Fair Bianca, 413
Fairy Changeling, 323
Fairy Damsel, 323, *323*
Fairyland, 323, *323*
Fairy Lights *see* Avon
Fairy Moss, 160
Fairy Rose *see* Minima
Falkland, 126
Fantin-Latour, *51*, 82, 150, *150*
Fashion Climbing, 315
Fée des Neiges *see* Iceberg
Felicia, 66, 84, 257, *257*
Félicité Bohain, 160
Félicité Perpétue, 29, *29*, 69, 72, 84, 334
Félicité Parmentier, 66, 186, *186*
Fellemberg, 357, *357*
Ferdinand de Lesseps, 398
Ferdinand Pichard, 398, *399*
Ferdy, 323
Field Rose *see* R. *arvensis*
Fiery Sunsation *see* Chilterns
Fimbriata, 229, *229*
Financial Times Centenary, 413
Fiona, 56, 323
Fisher and Holmes *see* Fisher Holmes
Fisher Holmes, 399
Fisherman's Friend, 413, *413*
F. J. Grootendorst, 229, *229*
Flamingo Meidiland, 324
Flora, 334
Flora McIvor, 192
Flower Carpet, 324
Fortuné Besson *see* Georg Arends
Fortune's Double Yellow, 18, 382, *382*
For You *see* Pour Toi
Fountain, 291, *292*
Fragrant Cloud Climbing, 430
Francesca, 25, 258, *258*
Francine Austin, 324
Francis Dubreuil, 382, *382*
Francis E. Lester, 265, *266*
François Juranville, 69, 84, *86*, 346
Frank Naylor, 291
Frau Dagmar Hartopp *see* Fru Dagmar Hartopp
Frau Karl Druschki, 22, 85, 399
Frau Karl Druschki Climbing, 22, 399
Fräulein Octavia Hesse, 346
Freckles, 292
Fred Loads, 292, *293*
Fred Streeter, 219
Freiherr von Marschall, 382

French Rose *see* R. *gallica*
Frensham, 308
Fresia *see* Korresia
Friesia *see* Korresia
Fritz Nobis, 56, 292
Fru Dagmar Hartopp, 5, 63, 75, 229, *229*
Fru Dagmar Hastrup *see* Fru Dagmar Hartopp
Frühlingsanfang, 126, *126*
Frühlingsduft, 126
Frühlingsgold, 24, 55, 127, *127*
Frühlingsmorgen, 24, 127
Frühlingsschnee, 63, 127, *127*
Frühlingstag, 127
Frühlingszauber, 127
Fugue, 280
Fulgens, *364*, 365

Gabriel Noyelle, 160
Galway Bay, 280
Gardenia, 346, *348*
Général Galliéni, 382
General Jack *see* Général Jacqueminot
Général Jacqueminot, 399
Général Kléber, 82, 160, *160*
General MacArthur Climbing, 430
Général Schablikine, 78, 382, *383*
Georg Arends, 56, 399, *399*
George IV *see* Rivers George IV
George Will, 229
Georges Vibert, 143
Geranium, 79, *218*, 219
Gerbe Rose, 346
Gertrude Jekyll, 413, *413*
Ghislaine de Féligonde, 46, 266, *266*
Gioia *see* Peace
Gipsy Boy, 56, 365, *365*
Giuletta, 365
Glamis Castle, 413
Gloire de Bruxelles, 399
Gloire de Chédane-Guinoisseau, 399
Gloire de Dijon, 44, *45*, 82, 382, *383*
Gloire de Ducher, 399, *400*
Gloire de France, 143
Gloire de Guilan, 171, *171*
Gloire de l'Exposition *see* Gloire de Bruxelles
Gloire de Paris *see* Anna de Diesbach
Gloire des Mousseux, 82, 160, *161*
Gloire des Rosomanes, 358
Gloire d'un Enfant d'Hiram, 400
Gloire Lyonnaise, 400, *400*
Gloria Dei *see* Peace
Gloria Mundi, 42, 303, *303*
Glory of Edzell, 127
Goethe, 160
Goldbusch, 192, *193*
Golden Chersonese, *118*, 119
Golden Dawn Climbing, 430

Golden Glow, 84, 346
Golden Melody, 422, *422*
Golden Moss, 161
Golden Rambler *see* Alister Stella Gray
Golden Rose of China *see* R. *hugonis*
Golden Salmon Superior, 303
Golden Sceptre *see* Spek's Yellow Climbing
Golden Showers, 280, *280*
Golden Wings, 24, 56, 128
Goldfinch, 266, *266*
Gold Magic Carpet *see* Gwent
Gold of Ophir *see* Fortune's Double Yellow
Grace Darling, 423
Graham Thomas, 56, 414, *414*
Grand Duc Héritier de Luxembourg *see* Mlle Franziska Krüger
Grand Hotel, 280
Grandmaster, 293
Grandmère Jenny Climbing, 431
Grandpa Dickson, 35, 422
Great Double White *see* Maxima
Great Western, 365
Green Rose *see* Viridiflora
Greenmantle, 61, 192
Grootendorsts *see* Pink Grootendorst, Red Grootendorst, White Grootendorst
Grootendorst Supreme, 230
Gros Choux d'Hollande, 365
Grouse, 324, *324*
Grüss an Aachen, 56, 67, 308, *309*
Grüss an Coburg, 383
Grüss an Teplitz, 31, 358
Guinée, 82, 431, *431*
Gwent, 324

Hamburger Phoenix, 56, 207, *208*
Hampshire, 324
Handel, 71, 281, *281*
Hansa, 230, *230*
Hans Mackart, 401
Happenstance, 115
Harison's Yellow *see* R. *harisonii*
Harry Maasz, 75, 181
Harvest Fayre, 318, *318*
Hawkeye Belle, 293
Headleyensis, 123
Heather Muir, 132, *132*
Hebe's Lip, 171
Heidekönigin *see* Pheasant
Heidelberg, 293
Heinrich Münch, 401
Heinrich Schultheis, 401, *401*
Helen Knight, *118*, 119
Helen Traubel, 423, *423*
Helmut Schmidt *see* Simba
Henri Foucquier, 143, *143*
Henri Martin, 161, *161*

Henry Kelsey, 207, *208*
Henry Nevard, 401
Herbstfeuer, 61, 65, 192, *193*
Heritage, 414, *414*
Her Majesty, 401
Hermosa, 358, *358*
Hero, 414
Hertfordshire, 324
Hiawatha, 46, 266, *266*
Hidcote Gold, 132, *132*
Hidcote Yellow *see* Lawrence Johnston
Highdownensis, 79, 219, *219*
Highfield, 281
Hilda Murrell, 414
Hillieri, 219, *219*
Hippolyte, *134,* 143
Holy Rose *see R. richardii*
Home Sweet Home Climbing, 431
Homère, 20, 383, *383*
Hon. Lady Lindsay, 293
Honorine de Brabant, 56, 365
Horace Vernet, 401
Horatio Nelson, 293, *293*
Horstmann's Rosenresli, 308, *309*
Hudson Bay Rose *see R. blanda*
Hugh Dickson, 35, *35,* 82, 85, 401
Hulthemia persica, 102
x *Hulthemosa hardii,* 102
Hume's Blush Tea-scented China, 17, *17,* 384
Humpty Dumpty, 42
Hunslett Moss, 161
Hunter, *230,* 231

Iceberg, 50, 308
Iceberg Climbing, 316, *316*
Ilse Krohn Superior, 281
Immensee *see* Grouse
Incarnata *see* Maiden's Blush, Great
Incense Rose *see R. primula*
Indigo, 176
Intervilles, 281, *281*
Ipsilanté, 144, *144*
Irene Churruca *see* Golden Melody
Irene of Denmark, 308
Irene von Dänemark *see* Irene of Denmark
Irène Watts, 308, *310*
Irish Beauty *see* Elizabeth of Glamis
Irish Elegance, 35
Irish Fireflame Climbing, 431
Irish Gold *see* Grandpa Dickson
Isabella Sprunt, 384
Iskra *see* Sparkling Scarlet
Ispahan, 56, 171, *171*

Jack Rose *see* Général Jacqueminot
Jacobite Rose *see* Maxima
Jacqueline du Pré, 294, *294*

Jacques Cartier, 14, 66, 67, *176,* 177
James Bourgault, 401, *402*
James Mason, 13, 144, *144*
James Mitchell, 162
James Veitch, 162, *162*
Janet B. Wood, 29, 242
Janet's Pride, 192
Japonica *see* Mousseux du Japon
Jaune Desprez *see* Desprez à Fleurs Jaunes
Jayne Austin, 294
Jean Bodin, 162
Jean Ducher, 384
Jeanette Heller *see* William R. Smith
Jean Lafitte, 337
Jean Mermoz, 303
Jean Rosenkrantz, 401
Jeanne d'Arc, 186
Jeanne de Montfort, 162, *162*
Jenny Duval, 144
Jens Munk, 231, *231*
Jersey Beauty, 346
Jiminy Cricket, 310, *310*
Joanna Hill, 423
John Cabot, 56, 208, *209*
John Franklin, 294
John Grooms, 281, *282*
John Hopper, 402, *402*
Josephine Bruce Climbing, 431
Joseph's Coat, 294
Jules Margottin, 402
Julia Mannering, 193
Juliet, 402
Juno, 150, *151*
Just Joey, 423

Kaiserin Auguste Viktoria, 402
Karen Poulsen, 37
Karl Förster, 61, 128, *128*
Karlsruhe, 209, *209*
Kassel, 295, *295*
Katharina Zeimet, 303
Kathleen, 258, *258*
Kathleen Ferrier, 56, 295, *295*
Kathleen Harrop, 371, *372*
Kathryn Morley, 414
Kazanlik, 82, 135, 172, *172*
Kent, 324
Kew Rambler, 74, 339, *339*
Kiese, 190, *190*
Kiftsgate, 47, 61, 62, 74, *245,* 246
Kiki Rose *see* Pink Drift
Kirsten Poulsen, 37
Köln am Rhein, 281
Königin von Dänemark, 66, 82, 186, *186*
Korona Climbing, 316
Korresia, 310
Kronprinzessin Viktoria, 365

La Belle Distinguée, 193, *193*
La Belle Marseillaise *see* Fellemberg
La Belle Sultane, 145, *145*
Labrador Rose *see R. blanda*

L'Abundance, 376
Lady Banks Rose *see R. banksiae lutea*
Lady Curzon, 63, 75, 231
Lady Emily Peel, 376
Lady Hillingdon, 32, 78, 384, *384*
Lady Hillingdon Climbing, 384
Lady Mary Fitzwilliam, *33,* 34, 423
Lady Penzance, 61, 193, *194*
Lady Plymouth, 385
Lady Roberts, 385
Lady Sonia, 295
Lady Sylvia Climbing, 431, *431*
Lady Waterlow, 70, 431
La Follette *see* Sénateur La Follette
La France, 33, *33,* 34, 423
La Mortola, *73,* 74, 80, 243, *244*
Laneii, 162, *162*
Lane's Moss *see* Laneii
La Noblesse, 150, *151*
La Petite Duchesse *see* La Belle Distinguée
La Plus Belle des Ponctuées, 145
La Reine, 402
La Reine Victoria, *frontispiece,* 15, 365, *366*
La Rosière *see* Prince Camille de Rohan
La Royale *see* Maiden's Blush, Great
La Rubanée *see* Village Maid
La Séduisante *see* Maiden's Blush, Great
La Sevillana, 56, 295
Laura Ashley, 326
Laura Ford, 281
Laura Louise, 209, *209*
Lauré Davoust, 267
Lavender Lassie, 258, *259*
La Ville de Bruxelles, 172
Lavinia, 282
La Virginale *see* Maiden's Blush, Great
Lawinia *see* Lavinia
Lawrence Johnston, 121
Laxa *see R. coriifolia froebelii*
L. D. Braithwaite, 414
Leander, 414
Leaping Salmon, 282
Leda, 172, *172,* 379n.
Lee's Crimson Perpetual *see* Rose du Roi
Le Havre, 402
Lemon Blush, 188
Lens Pink *see* Dentelle de Malines
Léonie Lamesch, 310
Léon Lecomte, 172
Léontine Gervais, 346
Le Rêve, 121, *121*
Lettuce-leaved Rose *see* Bullata

Leuchtstern, 267
Leverkusen, 52, 71, 210, *210*
Le Vésuve, 358
Lewison Gower, 366
Leys Perpetual, 376
Lichtkönigin Lucia, 295, *296*
Lilac Charm, 310, *311*
Lilian Austin, 414
Little Buckaroo, 318
Little Flirt, 3, 318, *318*
Little Gem, 163, *163*
Little White Pet *see* White Pet
Long John Silver, 337, *337*
Lord Penzance, 193
L'Oréal Trophy, 296
Lorraine Lee, 352
L'Ouche, 358
Louis Gimard, 163
Louis Philippe, 359
Louis XIV, 359, *359*
Louise d'Arzens, 377
Louise Odier, 15, 66, 82, *82,* 366, *366*
Lucetta, 415
Lucy Ashton, 194
Lutea *see R. pimpinellifolia lutea*
Lyda Rose, 296
Lykkefund, 247

Mabel Morrison, 402, *403*
Macartney Rose *see R. bracteata*
Macrantha Raubritter *see* Raubritter
Madeleine Selzer, 3, 267, *267*
Magenta, 296, *296*
Magic Carpet, 326
Magna Charta, 402, *403*
Magnifica, 64, 194, *195*
Magnolia Rose *see* Devoniensis
Maiden's Blush, Great, 10, *10, 54,* 56, 61, 80, 82, 187
Maiden's Blush, Small, 187
Maigold, 52, 71, 128, *128*
Maitland White, 392
Maître d'École *see* De la Maître d'École
Major *see* Rose des Peintres
Malaga, 282, *282*
Malandrone *see* Don Juan
Malcolm Sargent, 296
Malmaison Rouge *see* Lewison Gower
Maltese Rose *see* Cécile Brünner
Malton *see* Fulgens
Maman Cochet, 20, 385, *387*
Manettii, 377
Manning's Blush, 24, 194, *195*
Many Happy Returns, 296, *296*
Ma Ponctuée, 163
Marbrée, 56, 177
Marcel Bourgouin, 145, *145*
Märchenland, 296
Marchioness of Londonderry, 403
Marchioness of Salisbury, 423

Maréchal Davoust, 163, *164*
Maréchal Niel, *frontispiece*, 78, 377, *378*
Margaret McGredy, 35
Margaret Merril, 311, *311*
Margo Koster, 303
Marguerite Guillard, 403, *404*
Marguerite Hilling, 65, 219, *220*
Marie Bugnet, 231
Marie de Blois, 163
Marie-Jeanne, 311
Marie Lambert *see* Snowflake
Marie Louise, 172
Marie van Houtte, 385
Marjorie Fair, 84, 297
Marjorie W. Lester *see* Lauré Davoust
Marquise Boccella *see* Jacques Cartier
Martha, 372
Martin Frobisher, 231, *231*
Mary Hayley Bell, 297
Mary Manners, 231
Mary Queen of Scots, 128, *128*
Mary Rose, 56, 415, *415*
Mary Wallace, 348
Masquerade, 311
Masquerade Climbing, 316
Master Hugh, *78*, 79, 215, *215*
Mateo's Silk Butterflies, 359
Maurice Bernadin *see* Ferdinand de Lesseps
Max Graf, 5, 75, 231
Maxima, 10, 56, 64, *184*, 187
May Queen, 45, 348
McGredy's Yellow, 35, *36*
Meadow Rose *see* R. *blanda*
Mechtilde von Neuerburg, 194
Meg, 432, *433*
Meg Merrilies, 24, 61, 64, 194, *195*
Mélanie Lemaire *see* Hermosa
Mermaid, 47, *47*, 72, 115, *116*
Merveille de Lyon, 403
Mevrouw Nathalie Nypels *see* Nathalie Nypels
Michel Bonnet, 366
Michèle Meilland, 423
Micrugosa *see* R. × *micrugosa*
Mignon *see* Cécile Brünner
Mignonette, 303
Mildred Scheel *see* Deep Secret
Minima, 42, 359
Minnehaha, 84, 348, *348*
Mirato *see* Chatsworth
Mirifica, 105, *105*
Miss Atwood, 20, 392, *392*
Miss Edith Cavell, 304, *304*
Miss Lawrance's Rose *see* Minima
Miss Lowe's Rose *see* Sanguinea
Mlle Franziska Krüger, 385, *386*
Mme A. Meilland *see* Peace
Mme Abel Chatenay, 35, *35*, 432
Mme Alfred Carrière, 17, 52, 70, 72, 377, *377*
Mme Alice Garnier, 348
Mme Antoine Mari, 385

Mme Bérard, 385
Mme Berkeley, 385
Mme Bravy, 78, 385
Mme Bruel, 403
Mme Butterfly Climbing, 432
Mme Caroline Testout, 34, 35
Mme Caroline Testout Climbing, 34, 82, 432, *432*
Mme d'Arblay, 46, 267
Mme de la Roche-Lambert, 163, *164*
Mme de Sancy de Parabère, 212, *212*
Mme de Sertot *see* Mme Bravy
Mme de Tartas, 20, 386
Mme de Watteville, 386
Mme Driout, 377
Mme Dubost, 367
Mme Édouard Herriot Climbing, 432
Mme Ernst Calvat, 367
Mme Eugène Marlitt *see* Eugène E. Marlitt
Mme Ferdinand Jamin *see* American Beauty
Mme François Bruel *see* Mme Bruel
Mme Gabriel Luizet, 404
Mme Georges Bruant, 232, *232*
Mme Grégoire Staechelin, *frontispiece*, 70, 72, 79, 432, *433*
Mme Hardy, *8*, 50, 56, 82, 173, *173*
Mme Hébert *see* Président de Sèze
Mme Henri Guillot Climbing, 432
Mme Isaac Pereire, 15, 56, 82, 367, *367*
Mme Joseph Schwartz, 386
Mme Jules Gravereaux, *385*, 386
Mme Knorr, 177
Mme Laurette Messimy, 359, *359*
Mme Lauriol de Barny, 367
Mme Legras de St Germain, 187, *187*
Mme Lombard, 386
Mme Louis Laperrière, 424, *424*
Mme Louis Lévêque, 164, *164*
Mme Neumann *see* Hermosa
Mme Norbert Levavasseur, 37
Mme Pierre Oger, 15, 367, *367*
Mme Plantier, 187, *187*
Mme Scipion Cochet, 404
Mme Victor Verdier, 404
Mme Wagram, 386, *386*
Mme Zöetmans, 173
Mogador *see* Rose du Roi à Fleurs Pourpres
Moje Hammarberg, 232
Monique, 424
Mons. Paul Lédé *see* Paul Lédé Climbing
Mons. Tillier, 78, 386
Monsieur Pélisson *see* Pélisson
Monthly Rose *see* Old Blush

Moonlight, 25, 258, *259*
Morlettii, 80, 212, *212*
Morning Blush, 188
Morning Jewel, 282
Morning Mist, 187
Mountbatten, 297, *297*
Mousseline *see* Alfred de Dalmas
Mousseux du Japon, *164*, 165
Moussu du Japon *see* Mousseux du Japon
Mozart, 259
Mr Bluebird, 318, *319*
Mrs Aaron Ward Climbing, 433
Mrs Anthony Waterer, 232
Mrs B. R. Cant, 387
Mrs Campbell Hall, 387
Mrs Colville, *128*, 129
Mrs de Graw *see* Champion of the World
Mrs Doreen Pike, 232
Mrs Dudley Cross, 387
Mrs Foley Hobbs, 387
Mrs F. W. Flight, 267, *267*
Mrs G. A. van Rossem Climbing, 433
Mrs Harkness *see* Paul's Early Blush
Mrs Henry Morse, 35
Mrs Herbert Stevens Climbing, 35, 82, 434
Mrs John Laing, 34, 404, *404*
Mrs Jones *see* Centenaire de Lourdes
Mrs Oakley Fisher, 424, *424*
Mrs Paul, 367, *367*
Mrs Sam McGredy, 424
Mrs Sam McGredy Climbing, 70, 434
Mrs William Paul, 165, *165*
Mrs W. J. Grant, 35
Musk Rose *see* R. *moschata*
Mutabilis, 359, *360*
My Choice, 6
Myrrh-scented Rose *see* Splendens

Nanette, 145
Narrow Water, 250, *250*
Nathalie Nypels, 312, *312*
Néron, 145
Nestor, 145
Nevada, 55, 65, 219, *220*
New Dawn, 5, 30, 44, 45, 69, 71, 348, *349*
New Dawn Rouge *see* Étendard
Nigel Hawthorne, 103
Night Light, 283
Niphetos, *77*, 78, 387
Nivea *see* Aimée Vibert
Noella Nabonnand Climbing, 387
Noisette, 16
Norfolk, *325*, 326
Northamptonshire, 326
Norwich Castle, 312, *312*
Norwich Gold, 283
Norwich Pink, 283

Norwich Salmon, 283
Norwich Union, 312
Nova Zembla, 232, *232*
Nozomi, 84, 326, *326*
Nuits de Young, 165, *165*
Nur Mahal, 259, *259*
Nymphenburg, 56, 297, *297*
Nyveldt's White, 232, *232*

Odorata *see* Hume's Blush Tea-scented China
Oeillet Flamand, 145
Oeillet Parfait, 146
Ohio, 340
Ohl, 146, *146*
Old Black *see* Nuits de Young
Old Blush, *10*, 11, 12, 14, 15, 44, 360
Old Crimson China *see* Slater's Crimson China
Old Pink Moss *see* Common Moss
Old Spanish Rose *see* Russelliana
Old Velvet Moss *see* William Lobb
Old Velvet Rose *see* Tuscany
Old Yellow Scotch, 125, *125*
Omar Khayyam, 173, *173*
Ombrée Parfaite, 146
Ophelia, 424, *424*
Ophelia Climbing, 434
Orangefield Rose *see* Janet B. Wood
Orange Meillandina *see* Orange Sunblaze
Orange Sunblaze, 318
Orléans Rose, 37
Ormiston Roy, 129
Orpheline de Juillet, 146, *146*
Othello, *415*, 416

Pacific, 392
Painted Damask *see* Leda
Palissade Rose *see* Pheasant
Pallida *see* Old Blush
Panachée de Lyon, 177
Papa Gontier, 387, *387*
Papa Hémeray, 360
Papa Meilland, 425
Papillon, 360, *360*
Para Ti *see* Pour Toi
Parade, 283, *283*
Parfum de l'Hay *see* Rose à Parfum de l'Hay
Parkdirektor Riggers, 52, 71, 210, *210*
Parkjewel *see* Parkjuwel
Parkjuwel, 297
Parks' Yellow Tea-scented China, 18, *18*, 387
Parkzierde, 367, *368*
Parson's Pink *see* Old Blush
Partridge, 326
Parvifolia *see* Pompon de Bourgogne
Pat Austin, 416
Paulii, 75, 203, 326
Paulii Rosea, 75, 203, 326

Paul Lédé Climbing, 434, *434*
Paul Neyron, 22, 56, 404, *404*
Paul Ricault, 405
Paul's Early Blush, 405
Paul's Himalayan Musk, 52, 251
Paul's Lemon Pillar, 70, 434, *434*
Paul's Perpetual White, 251, *251*
Paul's Scarlet, 72, 267, *268*
Paul's Single White *see* Paul's Perpetual White
Paul Transon, 348
Paul Verdier, 367
Pax, 25, 65, 259
Peace, 35, 425, *425*
Peach Blossom, 297
Pearl Drift, 327, *327*
Pearl Meidiland, 327
Pélisson, 166
Penelope, 25, 259, *260*
Peon, 42, 319
Perdita, 416
Pergolèse, 177
Perla de Montserrat, 319
Perle des Jardins, 9, 388, *388*
Perle d'Or, 56, 67, *360*, 361
Persian Musk Rose *see R. moschata nastarana*
Persian Yellow *see R. foetida persiana*
Petite de Hollande, 151, *152*
Petite Junon de Hollande *see* Petite de Hollande
Petite Lisette, 151, *151*
Petite Orléanaise, 153
Pfander, 190
Pfander's Canina *see* Pfander
Pheasant, 327
Phoebe's Frilled Pink *see* Fimbriata
Phyllis Bide, 46, 267
Picasso, 313
Piccadilly, 35
Picture, 35
Picture Climbing, 434
Pierre de Ronsard *see* Eden Rose '88
Pierre Notting, 405
Pike's Peak, 298
Pinata, 283
Pink Bells, 327, *328*
Pink Chimo, 327
Pink Drift, 327
Pink Form *see R. moyesii* 'Pink Form'
Pink Grootendorst, 66, 233, *233*
Pinkie, 304
Pinkie Climbing, 283
Pink La Sevillana, 298
Pink Leda, 173
Pink Meidiland, 328
Pink Parfait, 313, *313*
Pink Perpétue, 30, 71, 283, *284*
Pink Prosperity, 259
Pink Sensation *see* Berkshire
Pink Wave, 328
Pinta, 425, *425*
Pleine de Grâce, 298

Plentiful, 313, *313*
Pomifera Duplex, 63
Pompon Blanc Parfait, 188
Pompon de Bourgogne, 153
Pompon de Paris Climbing, 361
Pompon des Dames *see* Petite de Hollande
Pompon Panachée, 146
Portland Rose *see* Duchess of Portland
Portland Trailblazer *see* Big Chief
Potter & Moore, 416
Poulsen's Yellow, 37
Poulsen's Park Rose, 298
Pour Toi, 319
Prairie Belle *see* Queen of the Prairies
Prairie Breeze, 298
Prairie Flower, 298
Prairie Lass, 298
Prairie Princess, 298
Prairie Rose *see R. setigera*
Président de Sèze, 144–5, 146
President William Smith *see* William R. Smith
Prestige, 298
Pretty Jessica, 416
Primevère, 349
Primrose *see* Primevère
Prince Camille de Rohan, 405, *405*
Prince Charles, 56, 368, *368*
Princesse Adélaïde, 166
Princesse de Lamballe, 188
Princesse de Nassau *see* Princess of Nassau
Princesse Louise, 334
Princesse Marie, 335, *335*
Princess of Nassau, 251, *251*
Probuzini *see* Awakening
Prolifera de Redouté, 153
Prosperity, 25, 66, 260, *260*
Prospero, 416
Provence Rose *see R. centifolia*
Pumila, 361
Purity, 349

Quatre Saisons, 8, 12, 14, 135, 173, *173*
Quatre Saisons Blanc Mousseux, 174
Queen Elizabeth, 313
Queen Elizabeth Climbing, 316
Queen Elizabeth Rose *see* Queen Elizabeth
Queen Mab, 361
Queen Mother (Procumbent), 328
Queen Mother (Floribunda) *see* August Seebauer
Queen Nefertiti, 416
Queen of Beauty and Fragrance *see* Souvenir de la Malmaison
Queen of Bedders, 368
Queen of Bourbons *see* Bourbon Queen

Queen of Denmark *see* Königin von Dänemark
Queen of the Belgians, 242, *242*
Queen of the Prairies, 337
Queen of the Violets *see* Reine des Violettes

R. acicularis, 203, 204
R. acicularis nipponensis, 203, 204, *204*
R. agrestis, 183, 185
R. alba, 10, 11, 183, 185
R. alba cimbaefolia see À Feuilles de Chanvre
R. alba 'Maxima' *see* Maxima
R. alba nivea see Semi-plena
R. alba suaveolens see Semi-plena
R. alpina see R. pendulina
R. altaica, 79, 80
R. amblyotis, 203, 204
R. anemoneflora, 240, 241
R. × anemonoides see Anemone Rose
R. arkansana, 203, 204
R. arvensis, 2, 3, 5, 27, 47, 61, 240, 241, *242*
R. banksiae, 4, 80, 241
R. banksiae alba plena, 108, 109, *109*
R. banksiae banksiae see R. banksiae alba plena
R. banksiae lutea, 78, 108, 109, *109*
R. banksiae lutescens, 108, 109, *110*
R. banksiae normalis, 108, 110
R. banksiopsis, 203, 204
R. beggeriana, 203, 204
R. bella, 203, 204
R. berberifolia see Hulthemia persica
R. biebersteinii, 183, 188, *188*
R. blanda, 3, 203, 204, *205*
R. × borboniana, 351, 363
R. bracteata, 4, *4*, 114, 115
R. britzensis, 183, 188
R. brunonii, 5, 61, 80, 240, 243, *243*
R. burgundica see Pompon de Bourgogne
R. californica, 203, 205
R. californica plena, 61, 203, 205, *205*
R. × calocarpa see Calocarpa
R. canina, 1, 2, *2*, 7, 10, 183, 189, *189*
R. canina inermis, 189
R. canina 'Pfander' *see* Pfander
R. cannobina see À Feuilles de Chanvre
R. × cantabrigiensis see Cantabrigiensis
R. carolina, 3, 199, 200
R. carolina alba, 199, 200
R. carolina plena, 199, 200
R. caudata, 203, 205
R. centifolia, 6, *6*, 7, 82, 135, 149

R. centifolia alba see White Provence
R. centifolia bullata see Bullata
R. centifolia 'Major' *see* Rose des Peintres
R. centifolia muscosa, 135, 156
R. centifolia 'Parvifolia', 66, 90
R. centifolia variegata see Village Maid
R. chinensis, 4, 11, 12, 15, 17, 36, 42, 44, 351, 353
R. chinensis minima see Minima
R. chinensis spontanea, 353
R. cinnamomea see R. majalis
R. cinnamomea plena see R. majalis plena
R. × collina, 183, 190
R. cooperi see Cooper's Burmese
R. coriifolia froebelii, 203, 205, 448
R. × coryana, 61, 203, 205
R. corymbifera, 183, 190
R. corymbulosa, 203, 205
R. cymosa, 108, 110
R. damascena, 6, 7, 10, 135
R. damascena bifera see Quatre Saisons
R. damascena trigintipetala see Kazanlik
R. damascena versicolor see York and Lancaster
R. davidii, 79, 203, 206
R. davurica, 203, 206
R. doncasterii see Doncasterii
R. × dumalis, 183, 190
R. dumetorum laxa see R. coriifolia froebelii
R. dunwichensis see Dunwich Rose
R. dupontii, 61, 64, 240, 243, *243*
R. earldomensis see Earldomensis
R. ecae, 117, 119, *119*
R. eglanteria, 2, *2*, 24, 52, 61, 82, 183, 191, *191*
R. elegantula-persetosa, 63, 80, 203, 206
R. fargesii, 203, 220
R. farreri persetosa see R. elegantula-persetosa
R. fedtschenkoana, 80, 203, 206, *206*
R. filipes, 5, 47, 240, 245
R. filipes 'Kiftsgate' *see* Kiftsgate
R. foetida, 5, *6*, 6, 24, 117, 120, *120*
R. foetida bicolor, 5, 117, 120, *120*
R. foetida persiana, 5, *5*, 35, 117, 120
R. foliolosa, 3, 199, *200*, 201
R. forrestiana, 203, 206
R. × fortuniana, 108, 110, *110*
R. × francofurtana see Empress Josephine

R. × francofurtana agatha see
   Agatha
R. gallica, 3, 7, 9n., 10, 135, 137
R. gallica officinalis, 8, 9, 12,
   13, 66, 90, 137, 138
R. gallica versicolor, 8, 9, 66,
   90, 137
R. gallica violacea see La Belle
   Sultane
R. gentiliana, 47, 61, 240, 246
   246
R. gigantea, 3, 17, 44, 45, 351,
   352
R. glauca, 64, 80, 183, 196, 196
R. glutinosa see R. pulverulenta
R. gracilis see R. × involuta
R. graveolens see R. inodora
R. gymnocarpa, 3, 61, 203, 206
R. × hardii see × Hulthemosa
   hardii
R. × harisonii, 23, 24, 125
R. headleyensis see
   Headleyensis
R. helenae, 47, 61, 62, 74, 240,
   247, 247
R. hemisphaerica, 5, 117, 122,
   122
R. hemsleyana, 203, 206
R. henryi, 240, 247
R. × hibernica, 64, 117, 129, 130
R. holodonta, 203, 220
R. horrida see R. biebersteinii
R. hugonis, 117, 122, 123
R. indica see R. chinensis
R. indica odorata see Hume's
   Blush
R. inermis morlettii see
   Morlettii
R. inodora, 183, 196
R. × involuta, 117, 123
R. jundzillii, 183, 197
R. × kamtchatica, 203, 206
R. × kochiana, 80, 80, 199, 201,
   201
R. kordesii, 203, 207, 207
R. koreana, 117, 123
R. laevigata, 3, 4, 111–12, 112
R. latibracteata, 203, 210
R. × l'heritierana, 203, 211, 211
R. longicuspis, 240, 247
R. luciae, 30, 45, 240, 247, 341n.
R. lutea see R. foetida
R. lutea punicea see R. foetida
   bicolor
R. macounii see R. woodsii
R. macrantha, 61, 135, 180, 181
R. macrophylla, 203, 214, 214
R. macrophylla rubricaulis see
   Rubricaulis
R. majalis, 203, 215
R. majalis plena, 215
R. marginata see R. jundzillii
R. × mariae-graebnerae, 199,
   201
R. marretii, 203, 215
R. maximowicziana, 203, 216
R. melina, 203, 216, 216
R. micrantha, 183, 197
R. microcarpa see R. cymosa

R. microphylla see R. roxburghii
R. × micrugosa, 80, 203, 216
R. × micrugosa alba, 203, 216,
   216
R. mohavensis, 203, 216
R. mollis, 183, 197
R. moschata, 3, 7, 15, 25, 36,
   44, 47, 240, 249, 250
R. moschata 'Autumnalis' see
   Autumnalis
R. moschata floribunda, 249
R. moschata grandiflora, 249
R. moschata nastarana, 240,
   249, 250
R. moschata nepalensis see
   R. brunonii
R. moyesii, 5, 5, 55, 61, 203, 217
R. moyesii 'Geranium' see
   Geranium
R. moyesii 'Pink Form', 217
R. mulliganii, 50, 61, 74, 240,
   252, 252
R. multibracteata, 203, 221
R. multiflora, 3, 4, 25, 27, 27,
   36, 44, 45, 46, 47, 240, 253
R. multiflora carnea, 240, 253
R. multiflora cathayensis, 240,
   253
R. multiflora grevillei see
   R. multiflora platyphylla
R. multiflora platyphylla, 240,
   253, 254
R. multiflora watsoniana, 240,
   254
R. multiflora wilsonii, 240, 254
R. murielae, 203, 221
R. myriadenia see R. yainacensis
R. nankiniensis see R. chinensis
R. nanothamnus, 203, 221
R. nitida, 3, 80, 199, 201, 201
R. noisettiana manettii see
   Manettii
R. nutkana, 61, 203, 222, 222
R. obtusifolia see R. inodora
R. × odorata see Hume's Blush
   Tea-scented China
R. × odorata ochroleuca see
   Parks' Yellow Tea-scented
   China
R. omeiensis see R. sericea
R. omissa see R. sherardii
R. orientalis, 183, 197
R. palustris, 3, 199, 201
R. paulii see Paulii
R. paulii rosea see Paulii Rosea
R. pendulina, 203, 223, 223
R. pendulina plena see
   Morlettii
R. persica see Hulthemia
   persica
R. phoenicia, 6, 7, 240, 333
R. pimpinellifolia, 2, 3, 24, 52,
   58, 80, 117, 124
R. pimpinellifolia 'Altaica', 23,
   124
R. pimpinellifolia andrewsii see
   Andrewsii
R. pimpinellifolia hispida, 124
R. pimpinellifolia lutea, 124

R. pimpinellifolia 'Nana', 124
R. pisocarpa, 203, 223
R. × polliniana, 240, 333
R. polyantha grandiflora see
   R. gentiliana
R. pomifera see R. villosa
R. pomifera duplex see
   R. villosa duplex
R. portlandica see Duchess of
   Portland
R. prattii, 203, 223
R. primula, 82, 117, 130
R. pruhoniciana hillieri see
   Hillieri
R. × pteragonis, 117, 130
R. pteragonis cantabrigiensis
   see Cantabrigiensis
R. pulverulenta, 183, 197
R. pyrifera, 203, 223
R. × reversa, 117, 130
R. richardii, 135, 182, 182
R. rouletii see Rouletii
R. roxburghii, 106, 107
R. roxburghii normalis, 106, 107
R. roxburghii plena, 106, 107,
   107
R. roxburghii roxburghii see R.
   roxburghii plena
R. rubella see R. × involuta
R. rubiginosa see R. eglanteria
R. rubra see R. gallica
R. rubrifolia see R. glauca
R. rubus, 240, 333
R. × ruga see Ruga
R. rugosa, 5, 52, 59, 203, 224,
   224
R. rugosa alba, 65, 79, 80, 203,
   225, 225
R. rugosa atropurpurea see
   R. rugosa rubra
R. rugosa repens alba see Paulii
R. rugosa rubra, 203, 225
R. rugosa rugosa see R. rugosa
   typica
R. rugosa typica, 203, 225
R. × sabinii, 117, 130
R. sancta see R. richardii
R. semperflorens see Slater's
   Crimson China
R. sempervirens, 29, 47, 240, 334
R. serafinii, 183, 197
R. sericea, 1, 117, 131
R. sericea chrysocarpa, 131
R. sericea pteracantha, 80, 131,
   131
R. sericea pteracantha
   atrosanguinea, 131
R. sertata, 203, 237
R. setigera, 240, 336, 336
R. setipoda, 203, 237, 237
R. sherardii, 183, 197
R. sicula, 183, 198
R. sinica see R. chinensis
R. sinowilsonii, 240, 338
R. sorbiflora see R. cymosa
R. soulieana, 240, 339, 339
R. spaldingii, 203, 237, 237
R. spinosissima see
   R. pimpinellifolia

R. spinosissima 'Altaica' see R.
   pimpinellifolia 'Altaica'
R. spinosissima nana see
   R. pimpinellifolia 'Nana'
R. stellata, 104–5
R. stellata 'Mirifica' see Mirifica
R. stylosa, 183, 198
R. suffulta, 203, 237, 237
R. sweginzowii macrocarpa,
   79, 79, 203, 238, 238
R. tomentosa, 183, 198
R. triphylla see R. anemoneflora
R. turkistanica see Mutabilis
R. ultramontana, 203, 238
R. ventenatiana see R. ×
   kamtchatica
R. villosa, 2, 79, 183, 198, 198
R. villosa duplex, 183, 198, 198
R. virginiana, xii, 3, 58, 61, 65,
   80, 199, 202, 202
R. virginiana alba see R.
   carolina alba
R. virginiana plena see Rose
   d'Amour
R. viridiflora see Viridiflora
R. × waitziana, 183, 198
R. wardii, 203, 238
R. webbiana, 203, 238, 238
R. wichuraiana, 4, 30, 41, 44, 45,
   58, 61, 63, 75, 100, 240, 341
R. willmottiae, 63, 203, 239, 239
R. wilsonii see R. × involuta
R. woodsii, 203, 239
R. woodsii fendleri, 58, 59, 61,
   203, 238, 239
R. xanthina, 117, 133
R. xanthina lindleyii, 133, 133
R. xanthina spontanea see
   Canary Bird
R. yainacensis, 203, 239
Rachel Bowes Lyon, 298
Radio Times, 416
Radway Sunrise, 298
Ragged Robin see Gloire des
   Rosomanes
Rambling Rector, 46, 46, 51,
   72, 72, 74, 268, 268
Ramira see Agatha Christie
Ramona, 113, 113
Raubritter, 75, 75, 181, 182
Raymond Chenault, 210
Red Ace, 319
Red Bells, 328
Red Blanket, 328, 329
Red Cherokee see Ramona
Red Coat, 299
Red Damask see R. gallica
   officinalis
Red Dorothy Perkins see
   Excelsa
Red Druschki see Ruhm von
   Steinfurth
Red Grootendoorst, 66
Red Max Graf, 328, 329
Red Moss see Henri Martin
Red New Dawn see Étendard
Red Riding Hood, 37
Red Robin see Gloire des
   Rosomanes

Red Rose of Lancaster *see R. gallica officinalis*
Red Star, 37
Red Trail, 329
Red Wing, 132
Regensberg, 319
Reine Blanche (Moss), 166
Reine Blanche (Damask) *see* Hebe's Lip
Reine des Centfeuilles, 153
Reine des Français *see* La Reine
Reine des Iles Bourbon *see* Bourbon Queen
Reine des Neiges *see* Frau Karl Druschki
Reine des Violettes, *21*, 22, 56, 82, 405
Reine Marguerite *see* Tricolore
Reine Marie Henriette, 434
Reine Olga de Wurtemberg, 377
Rembrandt, 178
René André, 350
René d'Anjou, 166
Repens Meidiland, 329
Rêve d'Or, 25, 378, *378*
Réveil Dijonnais, 435, *435*
Reverend H. d'Ombrain, 368
Reynolds Hole, 405
Rhonda, 283
Richmond, 37
Richmond Climbing, 435
Ritter von Barmstede, 3, 284
Rival de Paestum, 388
Rivers George IV, 368
Robert le Diable, 153, *153*
Robert Léopold, 166, *166*
Robin Hood, 260, *260*
Robin Redbreast, 319, *320*
Robusta (Bourbon), 368
Robusta (Rugosa), 233
Roger Lambelin, 405, *406*
Roi des Pourpres *see* Rose du Roi à Fleurs Pourpres
Rosa Mundi *see R. gallica versicolor*
Rosarium *see* Uetersen
Rose à Parfum de l'Hay, 82, 233, *233*
Rose Bradwardine, 194
Rose d'Amour, 202, *202*
Rose de l'Isle *see* Blush Boursault
Rose de Meaux, 66, 67, 90, 153, *153*
Rose de Meaux White, 153
Rose de Rescht, 66, 178, *178*
Rose des Maures *see* Sissinghurst Castle
Rose des Peintres, 154
Rose d'Hivers, 174
Rose d'Isfahan *see* Ispahan
Rose d'Orsay, 202
Rose du Maître d'École *see* De la Maître d'École
Rosé du Matin *see* Chloris
Rose du Roi, 12–13, 178, *178*
Rose du Roi à Fleurs Pourpres, 178, *179*

Rose du Saint Sacrement *see R. majalis plena*
Rose Édouard, 15, 368
Rose Edward, 15; *and see* Rose Édouard
Rose Lelieur, 12
Rose Marie Viaud, 234, 268
Rose of Provins *see R. gallica officinalis*
Rosée du Matin *see* Chloris
Rosemary Rose, *313*, 314
Roseraie de l'Hay, 5, 65, *65*, 66, 79, 80, *80*, 82, 233, *234*
Rosette Delizy, 388, *388*
Rosier de Philippe Noisette *see* Noisette
Rosy Carpet, 329
Rosy Cushion, 329
Rosy La Sevillana *see* Pink La Sevillana
Rosy Mantle, 30, 284, *285*
Rote Max Graf *see* Red Max Graf
Rouge Éblouissante *see* Assemblage des Beautés
Rouletii, 42, *43*, 319
Roundelay (Modern Shrub), 299, *299*
Roundelay (Climbing Hybrid Tea), 435
Royal Blush, 188
Royal Gold, 284, *285*
Royal William, 425
Rubens, 388
Rubricaulis, 215
Rubrotincta *see* Hebe's Lip
Ruga, 242
Ruhm von Steinfurth, 406
Ruskin, 233, *235*
Russell's Cottage Rose *see* Russelliana
Russelliana, 268
Rustica '91 *see* Yellow Dagmar Hastrup
Rusticana *see* Poppy Flash
Ruth, 146
Rutland, 329

Sacramento Rose *see* Mirifica
Sadler's Wells, 261, *262*
Safrano, 19, 388, *388*
Saint Prist de Breuze, 361
Salet, 166, *166*
Sally Holmes, 299, *299*
Sanders White, 30, 84, 350, *350*
Sanders White Rambler *see* Sanders White
Sanguinea, 19, 361, *361*
San Rafael Rose *see* Fortune's Double Yellow
Sarah Van Fleet, 233, *234*
Scabrosa, 65, 79, *79*, 235, *235*
Scarlet Fire *see* Scharlachglut
Scarlet Grevillei *see* Russelliana
Scarlet Meidiland, 330
Scarlet Sweetbriar *see* La Belle Distinguée
Scepter'd Isle, 416

Scharlachglut, 13, 56, 61, *74*, 79, 147, *147*
Schloss Heidegg *see* Pink Meidiland
Schneelicht, 235, *236*
Schneewittchen *see* Iceberg; Iceberg Climbing
Schneezwerg, 235, *236*
Schoener's Nutkana, 223
Schoolgirl, 284, *285*
Scintillation, 181
Scotch Briar *see R. pimpinellifolia*
Scotch Double Pink *see* Double Pink
Scotch Double White *see* Double White
Scotch Rose *see R. pimpinellifolia*
Sea Foam, 330
Seagull, 47, *68*, 74, 269
Sealing Wax, 220
Semi-plena, 61, 64, 188
Semperflorens *see* Slater's Crimson China
Sénateur Amic, 352, *352*
Sénateur La Follette, 352
Seven Sisters Rose *see R. multiflora platyphylla*
Shafter *see* Dr Huey
Shailer's White Moss, 166
Sharifa Asma, 416
Shell *see* Duchesse de Brabant
Shot Silk, 35, 426
Shot Silk Climbing, 435
Shropshire Lass, 299
Sidonie, 406
Silver Jubilee, *425*, 426
Silver Moon, 113, *113*
Simon Robinson, 330, *330*
Single Cherry, 129, *129*
Sir Cedric Morris, 196, *197*
Sir Edward Elgar, 417
Sir Frederick Ashton, 426, *426*
Sir Joseph Paxton, 368
Sir Thomas Lipton, 235
Sir Walter Raleigh, 416, 417
Sissinghurst Castle, *147*, 148
Skyrocket *see* Wilhelm
Slater's Crimson China, 11, *11*, 12, 19, 361
Smarty, 330
Smith's Parish, 20, 392, *393*
Smooth Rose *see R. blanda*
Snowball, 320
Snow Carpet, 330
Snowdon, 235
Snowdrift, 350
Snow Dwarf *see* Schneezwerg
Snowflake, 388
Snow Queen *see* Frau Karl Druschki
Soldier Boy, 284
Soleil d'Or, 35, 426
Solfatare *see* Solfaterre
Solfaterre, 389
Sombreuil Climbing, 78, 82, 389, *389*
Sommermärchen *see* Berkshire

Sonnenkind *see* Perestroika
Sonnenschirm *see* Broadlands
Sophie's Perpetual, 362, *362*
Soupert et Notting, 167
Sourire d'Orchidée, 285, *285*
Souvenir d'Alphonse Lavallée, 406, *406*
Souvenir de Brod *see* Erinnerung an Brod
Souvenir de Claudius Denoyel, 435
Souvenir de Jeanne Balandreau, 407
Souvenir de la Malmaison, *14*, 15, 78, 82, 369, *369*
Souvenir de la Malmaison Climbing, 82, 372
Souvenir de la Princesse de Lamballe *see* Bourbon Queen
Souvenir d'Elise Vardon, 389
Souvenir de Mme Auguste Charles, *369*, 370
Souvenir de Mme Léonie Viennot Climbing, 389
Souvenir de Philémon Cochet, 235
Souvenir de Pierre Vibert, 167
Souvenir de St Anne's, 370, *370*
Souvenir du Docteur Jamain, 82, *82*, 407, *407*
Souvenir d'un Ami, 389
Spanish Beauty *see* Mme Grégoire Staechelin
Sparkling Scarlet, 285
Sparrieshoop, 299
Spectabilis, 335
Spectacular *see* Danse de Feu
Spek's Yellow Climbing, 435
Spencer, 407, *407*
Spice, 392
Splendens, 28, *28*, 242
Spong, 154, *154*
Spray Cécile Brünner *see* Bloomfield Abundance
Stanwell Perpetual, 24, 129, *129*
Star of Persia, 121
Star of Waltham, 407
St Davids, 20
St Mark's Rose *see* Rose d'Amour
St Nicholas, 174, *174*
Striped Moss, 167, *167*
Suffolk, 330, *330*
Sulphur Rose *see R. hemisphaerica*
Suma, 330
Summer Blush, 188
Summer Sunrise, 330, *331*
Summer Sunset, *331*, 332
Summer Wind (Modern Shrub), 299
Summerwind (Procumbent Shrub) *see* Surrey
Summer Wine, 286
Suncover *see* Gwent
Sunnyside *see* Avon
Sunsprite *see* Korresia
Surpasse Tout, *147*, 148

Surpassing Beauty, 82, 407
Surrey, 332, *332*
Sussex, 332
Sutter's Gold, 427
Sutter's Gold Climbing, 435
Swamp Rose *see R. palustris*
Swan, 417
Swan Lake, 71, 286, *286*
Swany, 332, *333*
Sweet Briar *see R. eglanteria*
Sweet Dream, 320
Sweetheart Rose *see* Cécile Brünner
Sweet Juliet, 417, *417*
Sympathie, 286
Symphony, 417, *417*

Talisman Climbing, 436
Tall Story, 332
Tanbakede *see* Baby Masquerade
Tausendschön, 269
Tea Rambler, 46, *46*, 269
Temple Bells, 332
Tempo, 286
Thalia, 46, 269, *269*
The Alexander Rose, 188
The Bishop,155
The Bride, 78, 389, *390*
The Countryman, 417
The Doctor, 427
The Fairy, 25, *26*, 56, 67, 84, 304
The Garland, 47, 252, *252*
Thelma, 350
The Miller, 417
The Nun, 417
The Pilgrim, 418
The President *see* Adam
The Prince, 418
The Prioress, 418
The Reeve, 418
Thérèse Bugnet, 235, *236*
The Squire, 418
The Yeoman, 418
Thisbe, 261
Thoresbyana *see* Bennett's Seedling
Thousand Beauties *see* Tausendschön
Threepenny Bit Rose *see R. elegantula-persetosa*
Tigris, 103

Till Uhlenspiegel, 299
Tipo Ideale *see* Mutabilis
Tipsy Imperial Concubine, 12, 390, *390*
Toby Tristram 269, *270*
Tom Thumb *see* Peon
Topaz Jewel *see* Yellow Dagmar Hastrup
Tour de Malakoff, 155
Tradescant, 418
Trevor Griffiths, 418
Treasure Trove, 246, *246*
Tricolore, 148
Tricolore de Flandre, 148, *148*
Trier, 25, 269
Trigintipetala *see* Kazanlik
Trinity, 20, 393
Triomphe de Laffay, 362
Triomphe de Luxembourg, 390, *390*
Troilus, 418
Turner's Crimson *see* Crimson Rambler
Tuscany, 148
Tuscany Superb, 90, 148
Twenty-Fifth, *40*, 320

Uetersen, 300, *300*
Ulrich Brunner *see* Ulrich Brunner Fils
Ulrich Brunner Fils, 22, 407
Uncle Walter, 300, *300*
Unique Blanche *see* White Provence

Vanguard, 236
Vanity, 25, 261, *261*
Variegata di Bologna, 370
Veilchenblau, 46, 69, 84, 270, *271*
Velutinaeflora, 148
Venusta Pendula, 242
Vick's Caprice, 407, *408*
Vicomtesse Pierre du Fou, 436, *436*
Victor Hugo, 409
Victor Verdier, 409
Vierge de Cléry *see* White Provence
Village Maid, 83, *154*, 155
Vincent Godsiff, 393
Violette, 270, *270*

Violinista Costa, *426*, 427
Viridiflora, 362, *362*
Vivid, 370

Warm Welcome, 286
Warwick Castle, *418*, 419
Warwickshire, 332
Wedding Day, 74, 338, *338*
Weisse Immensee *see* Partridge
Weisse Max Graf *see* White Max Graf
Wendy *see* Pour Toi
Wenlock, 419
Westerland, 56
Whisky Mac Climbing, 436
White American Beauty *see* Frau Karl Druschki
White Baby Rambler *see* Katharina Zeimet
White Bath, 167, *167*
White Bells, 332
White Blush, 188
White Cockade, 30, 286, *286*
White Cover *see* Kent
White Flight *see* Astra Desmond
White Grootendorst, 66, 236
White Hermosa *see* Snowflake
White Maman Cochet, 20
White Max Graf, 332
White Meidiland, 332
White Moss *see* White Bath
White Pet, 66, 67, 84, 314, *314*
White Provence, 135, *154*, 155
White Rambler *see* Thalia
White Rose of York *see* Maxima; *and R. alba*
White Spray, 301, *301*
White Wings, 427, *427*
Whitsuntide Rose *see R. majalis plena*
Wickmoss, 350
Wickwar, 340, *340*
Wife of Bath, 419
Wild Flower, 301
Wilhelm, 261
Will Alderman, 236
William Allen Richardson, 18, 78, *378*, 378
William and Mary, 301, *301*
William Baffin, 56, *57*, 210
William Grant, 148
William Lobb, 167, *168*

William R. Smith, 390, *390*
Williams' Double Yellow, 125
William Shakespeare, 419, *419*
William III, 129
Will Scarlet, 261, *261*
Wiltshire, 333
Winchester Cathedral, 419
Wind Chimes, 270
Windermere, 350, *350*
Windrush, 301
Wintoniensis, 220
Wise Portia, 419
Wolly Dodd's Rose *see R. villosa duplex*
Woolverstone Church Rose *see* Surpassing Beauty
Wretham Rose, 155, *155*

Xavier Olibo, *408*, 409
Xerxes, 103

Yellow Banksia *see R. banksiae lutea*
Yellow Button, 419
Yellow Cécile Brünner *see* Perle d'Or
Yellow Charles Austin, 419
Yellow Cochet *see* Alexander Hill Gray
Yellow Dagmar Hastrup, 236, *236*
Yellow Doll, 320
Yellow Maman Cochet *see* Alexander Hill Gray
Yellow Rambler *see* Aglaia
Yellow Rose of Texas *see R. × harisonii*
Yellow Tausendschön *see* Madeleine Selzer
Yesterday, 84, 301, *301*
Yolande d'Aragon, 409, *409*
York and Lancaster, 174
Young Mistress *see* Regensberg
Yvonne Rabier, 67, 84, 314

Zenith *see* Uetersen
Zenobia, 167
Zéphirine Drouhin, 15, 44, 70, 82, 372, *372*
Zigeunerknabe *see* Gipsy Boy
Zoé, 168
Zwergkönig *see* Dwarfking